THE TWILIGHT OF THE TSARS

THE TWILIGHT

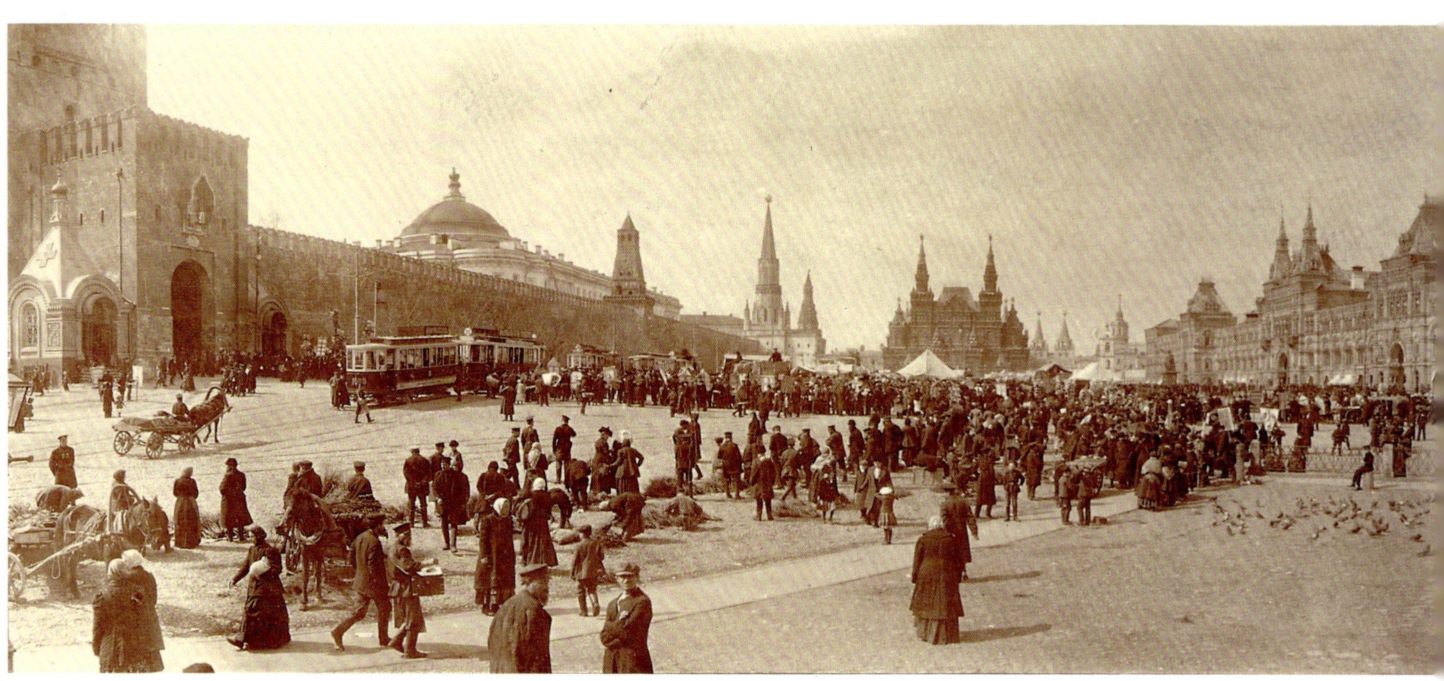

OF THE TSARS

RUSSIAN ART AT THE TURN OF THE CENTURY

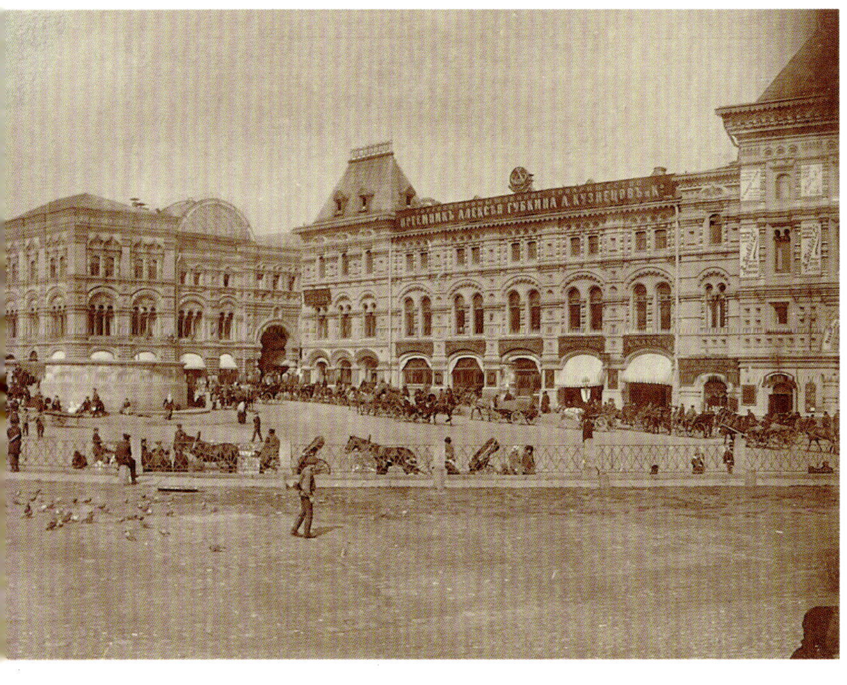

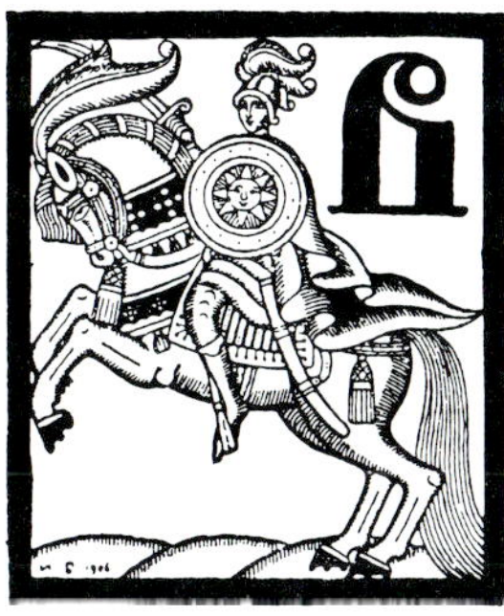

HAYWARD GALLERY, LONDON
7 MARCH – 19 MAY 1991

ORGANISED BY THE
SOUTH BANK CENTRE, LONDON
AND THE
ALL-UNION ARTISTIC
PRODUCTION ASSOCIATION,
MOSCOW

SOUTH BANK CENTRE

CONTENTS

FOREWORD
AND ACKNOWLEDGEMENTS

The title of our exhibition is intended to attract anyone interested in the life and culture of one of the great nations. Its content represents a remarkably full survey of the artistic movement known as Symbolism which flourished in Russia at the turn of the century and of the style in architecture and the decorative arts which we call *Art Nouveau* or "Arts and Crafts" but for which the Russian term is *Style Moderne*. Both were international movements in the arts which developed specific national characteristics in different countries. We have included early photographs, which bring the period to life, and also an account of Russian cinema before 1917, a subject which is little known here.

Our project, which is part of a Russian festival at the South Bank Centre, was initiated at the Soviet Ministry of Culture in discussions with Lidiya Zalyotova and Natal'ya Myshkova under the guidance of the Minister. However, the work of coordinating arrangements for the exhibition and its catalogue in the U.S.S.R. has been carried out by the All-Union Artistic Production Association, to whose Vice-Director Valentin Rivkind we are very grateful. It is he and his staff, especially Elena Karavaeva and Zelfira Tregulova of the Exhibitions Department, who have dealt with the considerable administrative detail. Elena Karavaeva has been in effect commissioner for the exhibition, and we are greatly indebted to her for her tireless work and for the resolve she has demonstrated throughout. Communications between us have been facilitated as ever by our colleagues in the British Council, especially Penny Steer. Welcome support from Visiting Arts has enabled the Russian curators to visit London to work on the exhibition.

The exhibition is drawn from the collections of six major institutions in the U.S.S.R.: the State Tretyakov Gallery, the State Historical Museum, the State Lenin Library and the State Shchusev Museum of Architecture in Moscow as well as from the State Russian Museum in Leningrad and the State Museum of Art in Saratov. All have lent so substantially that each group of material might have formed an exhibition in its own right. To be able to show all these treasures under one roof makes this exhibition a major occasion. We should like to express our gratitude to the Directors, Deputy Directors and Curators of each participating museum: to Lidiya Iovleva, Alla Gusarova, Roksana Rassudina, Evgeniya Plotnikova, Yuliya Zabrodina, Ol'ga Zabitskaya and Ekaterina Selezneva of the Tretyakov Gallery; Evgeniya Petrova, Marina Shumova, Anna Kiseleva, Galina Krechina, Tat'yana Korol', Tat'yana Sventorzhetskaya and Elena Karpova of the Russian Museum; Tamara Igumnova, Nina Asharina, Ol'ga Strugova, Galina Smorodinova, Tat'yana Saburova, Tat'yana Aleshina, Ol'ga Gordeeva, Tat'yana Dul'kina, Inna Sergeenko, Marianna Bobchikova and Natal'ya Sharikova of the Historical Museum; Tat'yana Kondakova, Svetlana Artamonova and Elena Denisenko of the Lenin Library; Vladimir Rezvin, Igor' Kazus', Lyudmila Saigina and Tat'yana Nikitina of the Shchusev Museum. In the United Kingdom we are grateful for small but important groups of loans from the Ashmolean Museum in Oxford, the British Library and the Victoria & Albert Museum in London.

Advisers on this project in Moscow have been Professor Dmitry Sarab'yanov and Dr Tat'yana Minkina. The South Bank Centre's adviser has been David Elliott, Director of the Museum of Modern Art in Oxford. During early discussions it was he who saw the importance of the subject of our exhibition and, in no small measure, it is his determination which has seen it through. Ian Christie of the British Film Institute has devised the programmes of early Russian cinema which are featured in the exhibition and for which we are grateful to the British Film Institute. Another adviser has been the architectural historian Catherine Cooke, whose knowledge has been invaluable. Our thanks are also due to Julian Graffy of the University of London's School of Slavonic and East European Studies for his contribution on Symbolist literature, to Julia Engelhardt for her chronology of historical and cultural events, and to Barbara Dombrowski for researching the photographs by Netta Peacock. Our thanks also to the Technology Faculty of the Open University and to Cyril Hughes for making the model of Shekhtel's Russian pavilion in Glasgow. We are also grateful for advice from Dr Christine Thomas of the British Library, Richard Davies of the Russian Archive at the University of Leeds, and Mark Haworth-Booth of the Victoria & Albert Museum; and to Monica Mackay and Sarah Giles for interpreting and other help. Margaret Macrae Duff's love of Russia has been an inspiration.

Once again we are grateful to Michael Raeburn for carrying out the considerable task of editing this catalogue and overseeing its production. Both he and the designer David Warner have produced a sizeable and complex publication in a short period of time. The same is true, of course, of our printers Balding and Mansell, and indeed of the translators, particularly Roderick Riesco who undertook the bulk of the work, but also Chris Barnard and Armorer Wason of Polyglossia, and Christina Raeburn, who in addition helped with compiling the artists' biographies.

We would also like to thank the photographers Vladimir Babailov, Leonid Gavrilov, Boris Groshnikov and Feliks Solov'ev, who provided a wealth of material. We would have liked to have had more more space for the fine architectural photographs of Igor' Palmin – once tracked down in Moscow, his small flat proved to be an Aladdin's Cave of photographs of buildings of this and later periods.

JOANNA DREW
Director, Hayward and Regional Exhibitions

ANDREW DEMPSEY
Assistant Director, Hayward Gallery

THE SOUTH BANK'S RUSSIAN FESTIVAL

The Twilight of the Tsars presents a picture of Russia during the reign of the last Tsar, a world which was changed dramatically by the First World War and the Russian Revolution. It includes architecture, painting, sculpture, photography and the decorative and graphic arts, as well as early Russian cinema. This is the first Russian turn-of-the-century exhibition to take place on this scale in the West. It forms, with the literature programme *The Revolution of the Word* and the concert series *Russian Spring*, the South Bank Centre's festival inspired by the spirit of Russia and the imagination of its artists, writers and composers.

At the South Bank Centre we have the exciting possibility of being able to mount interdisciplinary festivals such as this, enabling the public to draw parallels and enjoy contrasts between creators working in different art forms. Our celebration of Russia forms part of a series which has featured France and, more recently, post-war Modernism, and which will in the future include a Czech festival, a survey of the twentieth century, *Towards the Millennium*, and a project examining improvisation.

Though Russia's art of the last hundred years has enjoyed wide appreciation throughout the world, much significant work dating from the early years of the century and the Revolutionary period has been obscured. It is particularly exciting that this Hayward exhibition will include unfamiliar artists such as the painters Mikhail Vrubel', Viktor Borisov-Musatov and Pavel Kuznetsov, the sculptors Anna Golubkina and Sergei Konenkov and the architect Fedor Shekhtel',

whilst *Russian Spring* will be bringing little-known composers of the period such as Aleksandr Mosolov, Sergei Protopopov and, above all, Nikolai Roslavets to the attention of concert audiences. It is indeed incredible that Roslavets, a pioneer like his contemporary Arnold Schoenberg of twelve-tone music, should have had to wait until now to be revealed. The festival will present a number of premières as well as the first British performance of Roslavets' Violin Concerto, which as recently as the Centre Pompidou's *Paris-Moscow* festival in 1979 could be given only in piano reduction.

The Revolution of the Word presents all the major pre- and post-Revolutionary literary movements in readings and discussions, featuring celebrated figures such as Mayakovsky, Akhmatova and Mandel'shtam as well as introducing lesser known writers of the period. The continuing effervescence of Russia's response to revolution and turbulence will be present both in an exhibition of contemporary printmaking and in performances of works by living composers of the post-war and younger generation.

We hope our festival will give a fuller picture than has been possible in the past of the remarkable response of Russia's artists to the profound changes which characterise the recent history of their country.

NICHOLAS SNOWMAN
General Director (Arts)
South Bank Centre

PREFACE

The turn of the twentieth century was a time of unusual movement in all forms of the arts in Russia. Great poets, musicians, performing artists and painters strode forward, as aestheticism and the cult of beauty reigned supreme. Not surprisingly, this period came to be known as the "Silver Age", just as the time of Pushkin was known as the "Golden Age". During the nineteenth century Russian art had devoted itself to external ideas – drawn from the heart of the social struggle and from philosophical and religious debates – more often than it had served itself. At times it had penetrated remarkably deeply into the very essence of human existence, but this was principally in literature, which had managed to withstand the uninspired positivism that had sought to define both the social mentality and the objective reality of the individual. This progress in literature did not, however, solve the problem of the intrinsic value of artistic endeavour. The idea of the complete independence of art, its self-sufficiency, captured the imagination at the turn of the century.

The founders of the struggle for purity in art were the Symbolist poets and artists of the *Mir Iskusstva (World of Art)* group. At times internal disputes arose between the champions of the new movement. While Valery Bryusov was an advocate of absolute artistic autonomy, Aleksandr Blok maintained that Russian culture was young and synthetic, and that art and other areas of intellectual and spiritual human activity (in particular philosophy and religion) could therefore not manage without each other. But these and similar internal arguments did not weaken the general impulse towards new principles of artistic thought, which developed into both theory and creative practice.

This exhibition was conceived to put on view works of Russian art and design that express these ideas and lie within the framework of Symbolism and the *Style Moderne*, the Russian version of *Art Nouveau*. It is difficult entirely to separate these two phenomena from each other; they are closely linked though not identical. Symbolism and *Style Moderne* are two sides of the same coin. Unlike poetry, where Symbolism created a certain formal unity which one can designate a style, in painting and sculpture it did not become a style but was embodied within *Moderne* stylistic forms. Symbolism was a way of perceiving the world, but it also defined a number of theoretical positions; for the artist it was also a particular way not just of feeling but of being. It was broader than a style or artistic direction. Something similar can be said about *Style Moderne*, which became almost a way of life, since it encroached so closely upon everyday things.

In nearly all the countries where *Art Nouveau* styles took hold, with a local name in each place, they did not originate in architecture, painting or sculpture, but in applied and graphic arts. Everyday articles predominate in this exhibition, drawn not just from the estates of aristocrats and rich enlightened merchants, but from an extensive consumer culture: posters advertising a great variety of goods – from macaroni, beer and cigarettes to travel, books and journals – labels on scent bottles, sweet-wrappers, restaurant menus and theatre programmes. Beside them are the most delicate vessels of silver, valuable cigarette-cases, elegant jewellery and inlaid furniture. The *Style Moderne* pervaded all of this, from the aristocratic boudoir to shops selling beer and tobacco. Surely no previous style had so broad a range.

Perhaps the greatest achievements of the style were in architecture, where the name of Fedor Shekhtel' stands out. In his hands the private residence becomes the ideal environment for a man to live in, where everything serves his interests, creating an aesthetic comfort and making it possible to mythologise everyday life. The complex stylistic unity had many components – the construction itself, its natural surroundings, the ornamental design, stucco moulding of various kinds, stained-glass windows, majolica friezes, painted panels and much else. The *Moderne* private house is like a living organism, with its external composition reflecting the internal space that flows freely from one room into another. These elements of the new style were also incorporated into other types of building – shops, banks, offices, hotels, financial institutions and restaurants. Here there were rivals to the *Style Moderne*. Several architects sought to revive classical forms, while others favoured the forms of ancient Russian architecture. Of course, neither style was simply mechanically borrowed. Each lent itself to stylisation and was transformed under *Moderne* influence, to form a kind of alliance of opposites.

A similar blend of styles is found in easel painting, graphic art and sculpture, where the combination of Impressionism and *Moderne* formed a specifically Russian style that superseded the Critical Realism of the "Wanderers". With the painters of the *Mir Iskusstva* group, this became tinged with romanticism, as they looked back to different historical epochs and artistic styles. They seemed to go from eclecticism to modernism, appealing to cultural memory, at times creating courtly genres in the spirit of Rococo or modest scenes of everyday Biedermeier domesticity, at times turning to antiquity, at times inspired by the style of ancient Rus', at times evoking the Russian eighteenth century or Versailles. However, this abundance of sources did not inhibit the development of many general features that linked all the painters, particularly their romantic irony and the primacy of the graphic principle in their elegant stylisations. Their dreams of a bygone beauty, embodied in delicate linear form, staved off the chaos of the present. It did not inspire hope of changes in real life but opened up the way to comprehending a different reality, another existence.

It was this different reality that was sought by the Symbolist painters, particularly the members of the *Golubaya Roza (Blue Rose)* group, although they did not develop their own theory, drawing rather on that of the poets. However, the poets had absorbed the practical experience of the painters, particularly that of Mikhail Vrubel', whom they considered their forerunner. His greatness as a painter permeated their work, and they saw his life's work as an embodiment of the act of creativity, his images as proof of the inexhaustibility of the symbol. According to the Symbolists, the poet has a theurgic role; the creator is clairvoyant, able to penetrate through the surface of phenomena and to reach their deeper meaning.

The Symbolist painters knew this. It was not just that they were in harmony with the poets or that Symbolist ideas – already interpreted in music and the theatre – were in the air. Painters like Viktor Borisov-Musatov and Pavel Kuznetsov had startling insight, and Russian painting, now that it had overcome the earlier passion for Realism, had found that measure of freedom which allowed the artists to devote themselves to the quest for beauty that hides in the ineffable and is communicated in the plastic metaphor of balance and composition.

As Russian Symbolist art asserted itself and developed, conscious and often unconscious parallels occurred with artists from Western European schools; such parallels can be drawn between the French Nabis and Borisov-Musatov and several of the *Golubaya Roza* artists, or between Pavel Kuznetsov and Gauguin, Petrov-Vodkin and Hodler. We should not be surprised by these parallels; Russian artists travelled to Paris and Munich and studied in private studios there, while French, English and German artists took part in exhibitions in Moscow and St Petersburg.

This exhibition offers just a small quantity of all that is rich in Russian artistic culture at the turn of the century, but it lets us imagine how this culture lived in the expectation of a new order and the changes it brought.

DMITRY SARAB'YANOV

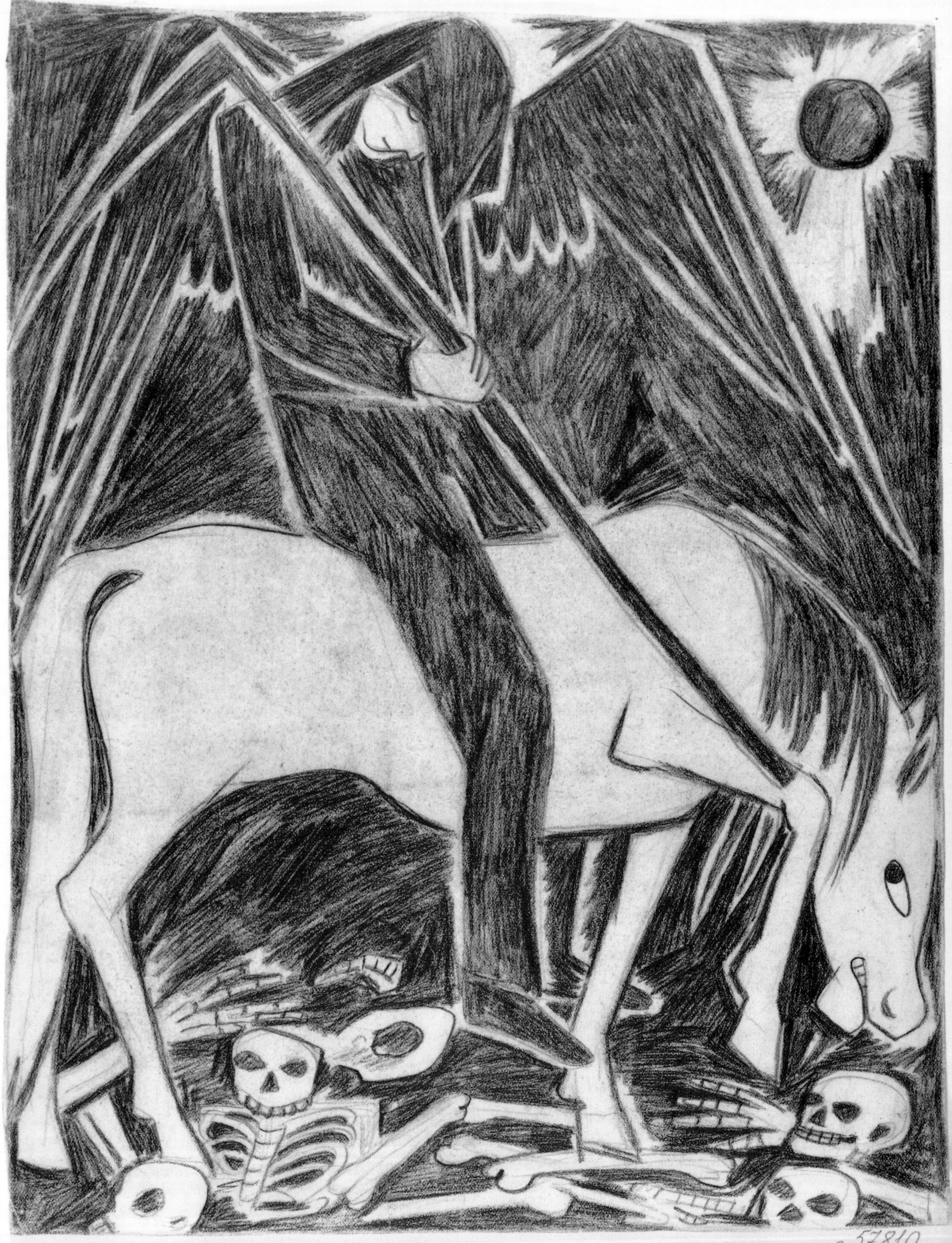

1

RUINED PALACES

DAVID ELLIOTT

"We are the witnesses of a great historical moment of reckoning which will end in a new, unknown culture . . . And henceforth with neither fear nor disbelief, I raise my glass to the ruined walls of the beautiful palaces as I do to the behests of the new aesthetics. And all that I, an incorrigible sensualist, can wish for is that the impending struggle will not abuse the aesthetics of life and that death will be as beautiful and as radiant as the Resurrection."[1]

Sergei Diaghilev gave this fulsome toast in Moscow in 1905 against a background of strikes, demonstrations and brutal repression by the government. He was speaking at a banquet given in his honour at the newly opened Hotel Metropol to mark a large exhibition of historical Russian portraiture which he had organised in St Petersburg. Four years previously Andrei Bely had communicated the same sense of impending crisis in a more stark form: "European culture has uttered its word . . . and this word has arisen like an ominous symbol . . . And this symbol was a dancing skeleton . . ."[2]

Such sentiments highlight the prophetic deathwish which characterises Russian culture at the turn of the century; animated by incessant premonitions of apocalypse, the arts presided over the twilight of the old world and began, tentatively, to confront the dawn of the new.

Russia was not to be alone in seeing its Empire fall as the effects of the Great War redrew the map of Europe. Yet the Russian above all other empires had corroded from within and, for better or worse, had taken responsibility for its own destiny after the Revolution of October 1917.

The rigid structure which had characterised society under the Tsars had fallen apart, and the landowning rural families and bureaucracy, which had previously administered the country, found themselves bereft of serfs, cash and land. New social categories – masters and servants of industry – were forged while both the Tsarist court and the intelligentsia, powerless in the face of such intractable change, sought escape in fantasy, or in the febrile hyperactivity of messianic prediction.

Many artists, writers, poets, architects and musicians had sought to create a world of dreams. The elegant visions of palaces, castles, marquises and *fêtes champêtres* – echoes of an earlier age which populate the paintings of Viktor Borisov-Musatov, Aleksandr Benois, Ivan Bilibin and Konstantin Somov – had started to crumble. In 1908 Benois prophesied an end to such artificiality: ". . . the era of marquises is over . . . It is painful for me, the passionate champion of this affected art, to reflect on this, but I realise that the corpse can be galvanised no more; we are in need of a new life."[3]

For Aleksandr Blok the "new life" was what was going on around him; society and art were in transformation; the abortive Revolution of 1905 could be seen in a metaphysical dimension as it had taken place "not only in the here and now but also in other universes. . . . The events at which we stood witness occurred within our own souls . . . and Russia finds itself to be our own soul. . . ."[4] In other contexts Blok could be more direct: "Like painting, music, prose and poetry – philosophy, religion and even politics are indivisible. They all come together to form the powerful current which upholds the nation's culture."[5]

Regarded in this way, Russia itself had become a gigantic Wagnerian *Gesamtkunstwerk* – a total work of art in which culture was both artifice and an expression of a higher destiny. Seemingly irreconcilable artistic tendencies: Historicism, Neo-nationalism, *Style Moderne*, Decadence, Paganism or Symbolism, as well as all the different disciplines of the arts, could be united within the same "powerful current".[6]

ART AND POLITICS Political events had strengthened the feeling of impending apocalypse. Tsar Nikolai II had proved to be no less reactionary than Aleksandr III, his predecessor, and the optimism of the liberal dawn of the 1860s was now in complete eclipse. This, combined with the effects of the disastrously managed war with Japan (1904–05), fanned social discontent, which broke out in the series of strikes and uprisings throughout Russian cities that sparked off the Revolution of 1905. The brutal suppression of a demonstration in front of the Winter Palace in St Petersburg led to international outcry. The Tsar had to make concessions, and, for a limited period, censorship was lifted and a measure of constitutional government was granted. Artists and writers welcomed this, and many within the Diaghilev circle contributed drawings to the satirical, anti-Tsarist magazines which blossomed during the brief thaw. Such social upheavals, however, with their accompanying backlash could only confirm already present feelings of unease. Many believed that the problems the country was experiencing were due to a

spiritual arhythmia: natural cycles had been broken and chaos had ensued.

Russia has been stereotyped at this time as a backward, virtually medieval country cut off from the rest of Europe. Such a view masks the vast and rapid changes which were underway. A massive growth of population in the years between 1860 and 1913 had far outstripped that of other European countries – surpassing even that of the U.S.A., which had been attracting floods of emigrants from the Old World, many of them persecuted Jews from Russia.[7] But the movement was not all in one direction; migration was also taking place within Russia itself – from the countryside to the towns and from the West to the East.[8] Mortality was high in the countryside, but far more so in the insanitary and overcrowded workers' barracks which had become a depressing feature of city life.

The population growth had been partially stimulated by the liberal reforms of the 1860s. Serfdom, one of the most visible expressions of Russia's backwardness, had been abolished in 1861 by Aleksandr II. He had also made a number of educational, legal and administrative reforms; however, after a series of attempts on his life, progress had become increasingly sclerotic. Ironically, on the morning of his death (13 March 1881), from a bomb thrown by a young Polish student, he had given his assent to limited constitutional reform; this had been immediately cancelled by Aleksandr III, his successor.

If the former serfs now had a kind of freedom, the landowners were under increasing duress. The plays of Chekhov chronicle, not without humour, the social and intellectual paralysis of these people. It was a new world and they struggled to find a place in it. Many of the sons

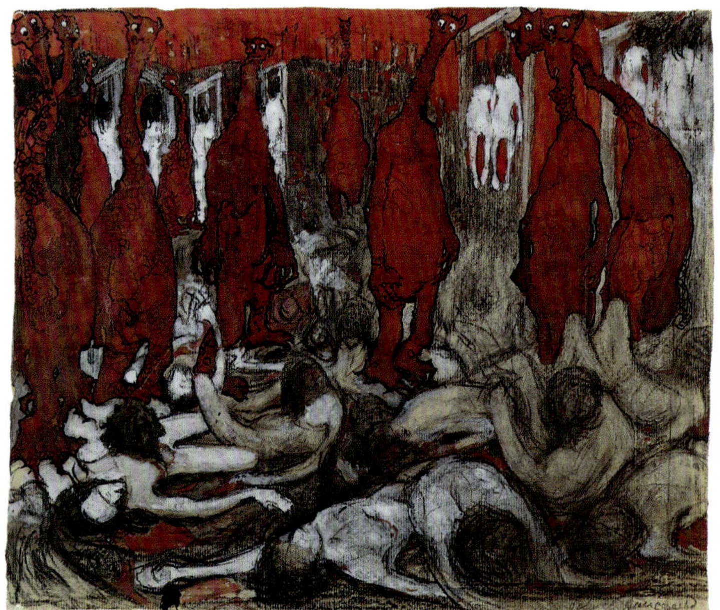

PREVIOUS PAGE: **Natal'ya Goncharova**
136. *The Pale Horse*
1914
Drawing for the album *War 1914: Mystical Images of War*
Lead pencil on paper, 31.8 × 24.3
State Russian Museum

RIGHT: **Boris Anisfel'd**
13. *Monsters Striding over Corpses*
1905
Cover design for *Zhupel (Bugbear)*
Mixed.media on paper, 30.2 × 34.8
State Russian Museum

and daughters of this generation settled in the cities and became the writers, poets and artists of the first decade of this century.

The frenetic search for social and cultural identity which characterised these years created a climate which nurtured a younger generation of artists who, immediately before and after the Revolutions of 1917, created new forms of art which owed a vast, and often concealed, debt to the ideas of their predecessors.

THE MERCHANTS' PALACES Although the Industrial Revolution arrived late in Russia, it came with a vengeance. Fortunes were made in the textile, chemical and mining industries as well as in the building of railways, the means of communication and transport which held the new economy together. The wealth from these enterprises created a new class of people – known as "merchants" – who became a major source of patronage for the new art. Pavel Tretyakov, who gave his name, collection and a building to the City of Moscow for a permanent Museum of Russian art, derived his wealth from textile manufacture. Savva Mamontov, patron, collector, singer, sculptor, founder of the artists' colony of Abramtsevo and backer of a private opera company in Moscow, made his wealth in the first railway boom of the 1860s; he lost it thirty years later when a new company he had floated went bankrupt. Nikolai Ryabushinsky, patron, collector, editor and publisher of *Zolotoe Runo* (*The Golden Fleece*), a sumptuously produced and illustrated Symbolist art journal, arguably, was on safer ground than Mamontov as he was the scion of one of Moscow's most established banking families.[9]

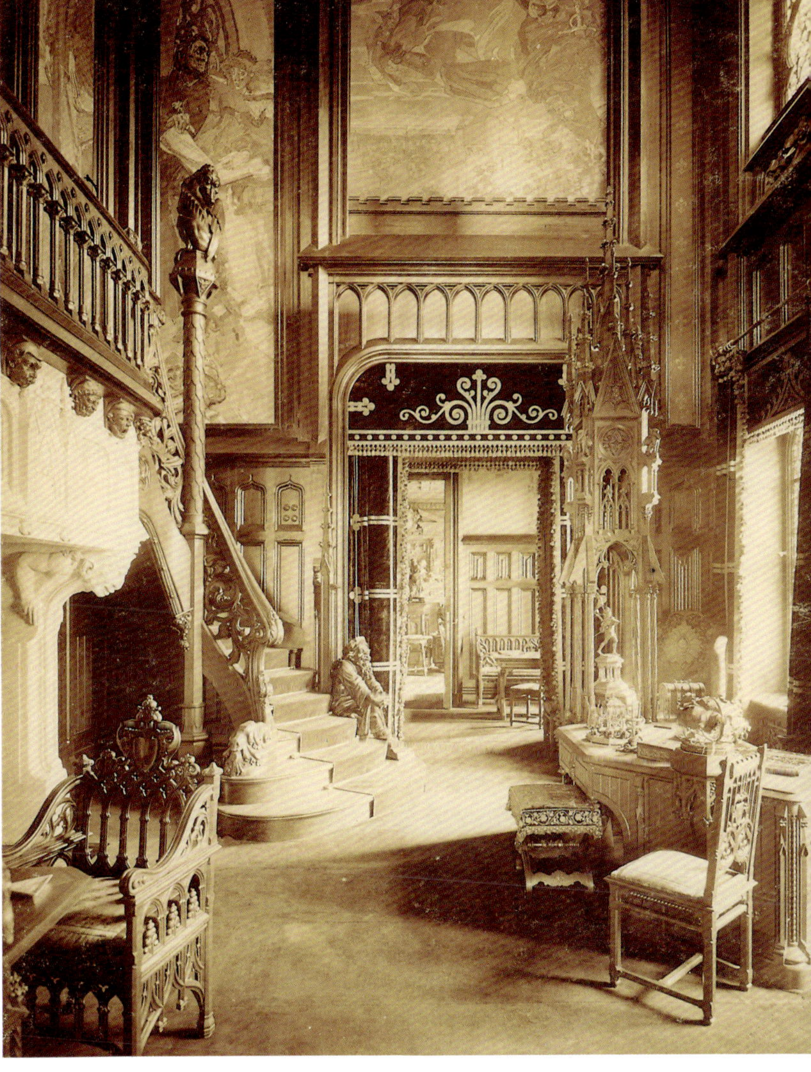

ABOVE: **Fedor Shekhtel'**
336. Mansion of A. V. Morozov, Moscow: Gothic Study. The painted panels are by Mikhail Vrubel'.
1895
Photo (1890s)
A. V. Shchusev State Museum of Architecture

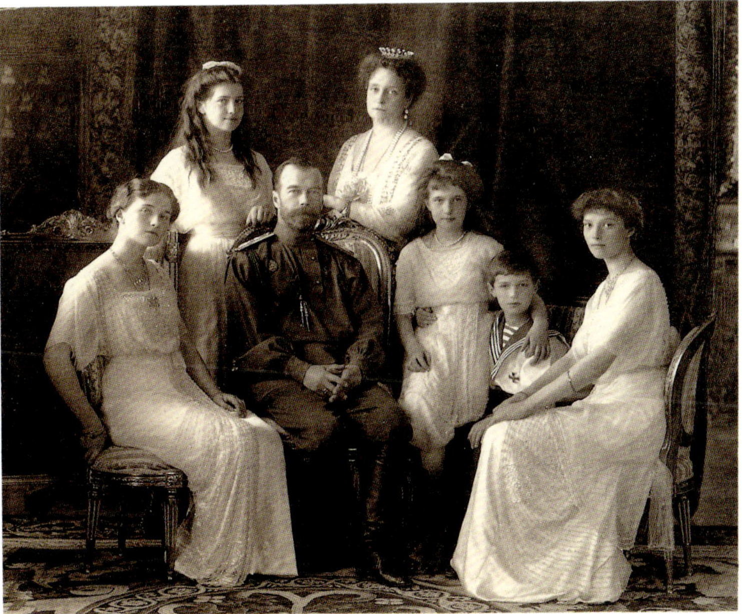

LEFT: 585. Tsar Nikolai II with his family: the Tsaritsa Aleksandra Fedorovna (who married Nikolai in 1894) and their children, Tsarevich Aleksei (b.1904), Grand Duchesses Ol'ga (b.1895), Tat'yana (b.1897), Mariya (b.1899) and Anastasiya (b.1901).
Photo (1910s) by Boissonas & Eggler photo studio.
State Historical Museum

All these people not only collected art but also commissioned architecture, applied arts and design in the latest styles. Both Tretyakov and Mamontov favoured the Neo-Russian fantasies of artist-architect Viktor Vasnetsov, while Ryabushinsky preferred the more westernised *Style Moderne* palaces and villas designed by Fedor Shekhtel'. But as the work in this exhibition so clearly shows, Shekhtel', true to the principles of synthesis, could work in many different styles. Vasnetsov was his acknowledged master, as is clear in the drawings for the Russian pavilions at the International Exhibition in Glasgow (1901), or in his related designs for Moscow's Yaroslavl' Railway Station made in the following year. But at the same time, working on private commissions, Shekhtel' could don the mantle of a Guimard or Horta by making his own organic inventions of Parisian or Belgian *Art Nouveau*. The 1890s had seen him working in a mixture of Neo-Gothic and Scottish baronial styles in the house he designed for Aleksei Morozov. After 1907 he worked in a more austere, Classical style for banks, insurance companies, newspaper offices and cinemas – buildings which were symbols of the new kind of country Russia had become.

A NATIONAL ART At the moment that Russia had started to modernise there arose, as if by some unconscious process of compensation, an intense interest in folk art and tradition. The Pan-Slav impulse, which extended as far east as the Urals and as far south as the Balkans, was to search for a common identity which would consolidate the historic destiny of the Slavic peoples. There were also less sinister reasons for taking an interest in folk art: increased mobility put old traditions at risk (this was as true in the Bohemian, Hungarian or English countryside as it was in Russia). Secondly, the encouragement of the production of folk art was a form of job creation in areas where work was scarce and old skills were falling fallow as they were rendered obsolete by mass production.

Savva and Elizaveta Mamontov at Abramtsevo and Princess Mariya Tenisheva at Talashkino established museums of folk art, artists' colonies and workshops. By doing this they created a climate in which traditional motifs and skills were preserved so that they could be used to sustain the art of the present. Through the pursuit of such traditions Russia began to discover herself. Present-day travellers see the degenerate progeny of such initiatives in the homogeneous and mechanical folk art which graces every Russian souvenir and hard currency shop.

The Mamontovs moved to Abramtsevo, a country estate about thirty miles from Moscow, in 1870. Many of their artist friends came to stay, and paintings of this period by Il'ya Repin, Viktor Vasnetsov, Valentin Serov, Vasily Polenov and Mikhail Nesterov often depict the house and its surrounding landscape. Vasnetsov had been working on designs for large wall paintings for the Cathedral of St Vladimir in Kiev and was also completing a number of large romantic history paintings which depicted the *Bogatyri*, the knights who are celebrated in the heroic lays of medieval Russia. Nesterov, on the other hand, focused on the mystical heritage of ancient Russia in his depictions of visions of piety and miraculous events. In 1881, at the instigation of Elizaveta Mamontova, Vasnetsov designed a small church for the estate, which was modelled on the ecclesiastical orders of medieval Novgorod; he also decorated the interior, Polenov designed the iconostasis and both Repin and Mamontova contributed icons.

The interest in craft work that this aroused in the group led to the foundation of a Folk Art Museum on the estate. Elena Polenova, Polenov's sister, worked with Mamontova in building up the collection as well as in gathering together and illustrating a range of old Russian fairy tales. The artefacts which had been brought together in this way provided the design ideas for the furniture workshop which was then set up on the estate. Neo-Russian style furniture of a rather eclectic nature became the fashion, and in 1888 a special Abramtsevo shop was set up in Moscow. The following year, encouraged by the success of this, Mamontov set a ceramics workshop on the estate. Vrubel', Golovin and Mamontov himself made a number of striking sculptures here, but architectural work was also produced: stoves, fireplaces, outside tiling such as that used on the Hotel Metropol – even garden benches. In 1896 the Abramtsevo ceramics workshop moved to premises in Moscow.

Princess Tenisheva was also a collector and patron of the arts but, unlike Mamontov, came from a titled family. For ten years from 1894 she funded an Art Foundation School in St Petersburg known as the Tenisheva Academy; for a shorter time a filial institution was also opened in Smolensk near her country estate at Talashkino.

She had moved there in 1893 and had quickly resolved to make it the rival of Abramtsevo. Actors, writers, poets and painters were invited to stay. Workshops for woodcarving, furniture making, ceramics, theatre, embroidery and balalaika making and playing were all set up. At the same time she assembled a collection of folk art and donated this to the Museum in Smolensk. Sergei Malyutin, a painter, ran the furniture and woodcarving shops and designed much of the furniture; Vrubel' worked on ceramics. Embroidery using only vegetable dyes was put out to the peasant women of the locality. In 1896 building work was started on a church on the estate according to Tenisheva's own designs. In 1904 the workshops were given a commercial outlet in a specially designed shop called *The Source*, which was modelled on Samuel Bing's *Art Nouveau* emporium in Paris. It was a financial disaster. Disillusioned by this, as well as by the social disturbances of 1905, she left Russia to live in Paris. When she returned in 1908 the workshops were not reopened, athough the interior decoration of the church she had built was eventually completed by Nikolai Roerich and the firm of Fabergé.

During 1900 *le Style Russe* had been one of the great international successes of the *Exposition Universelle* in Paris. The Russian pavilions by Konstantin Korovin and Aleksandr Golovin attracted much attention, Valentin Serov won a gold medal for his paintings, and the goods and decorations from Abramtsevo were highly esteemed. The image of historic Russia was also kept alive in the finely worked costumes of Boyars and Boyarinas of the early sixteenth century worn by the Court and nobility at the formal and costume balls in St Petersburg.

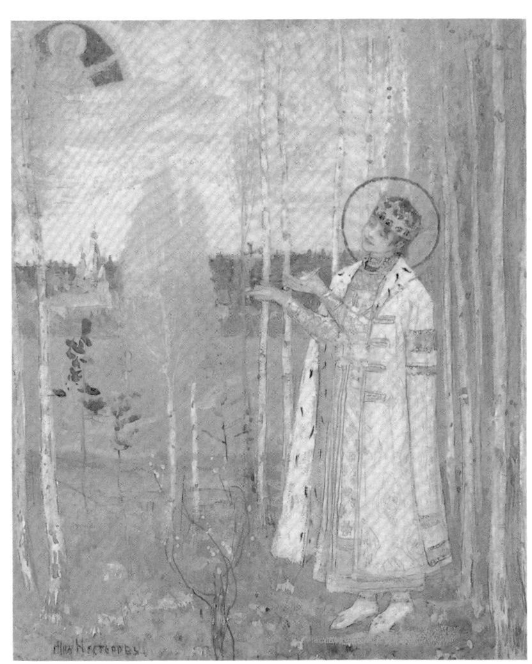

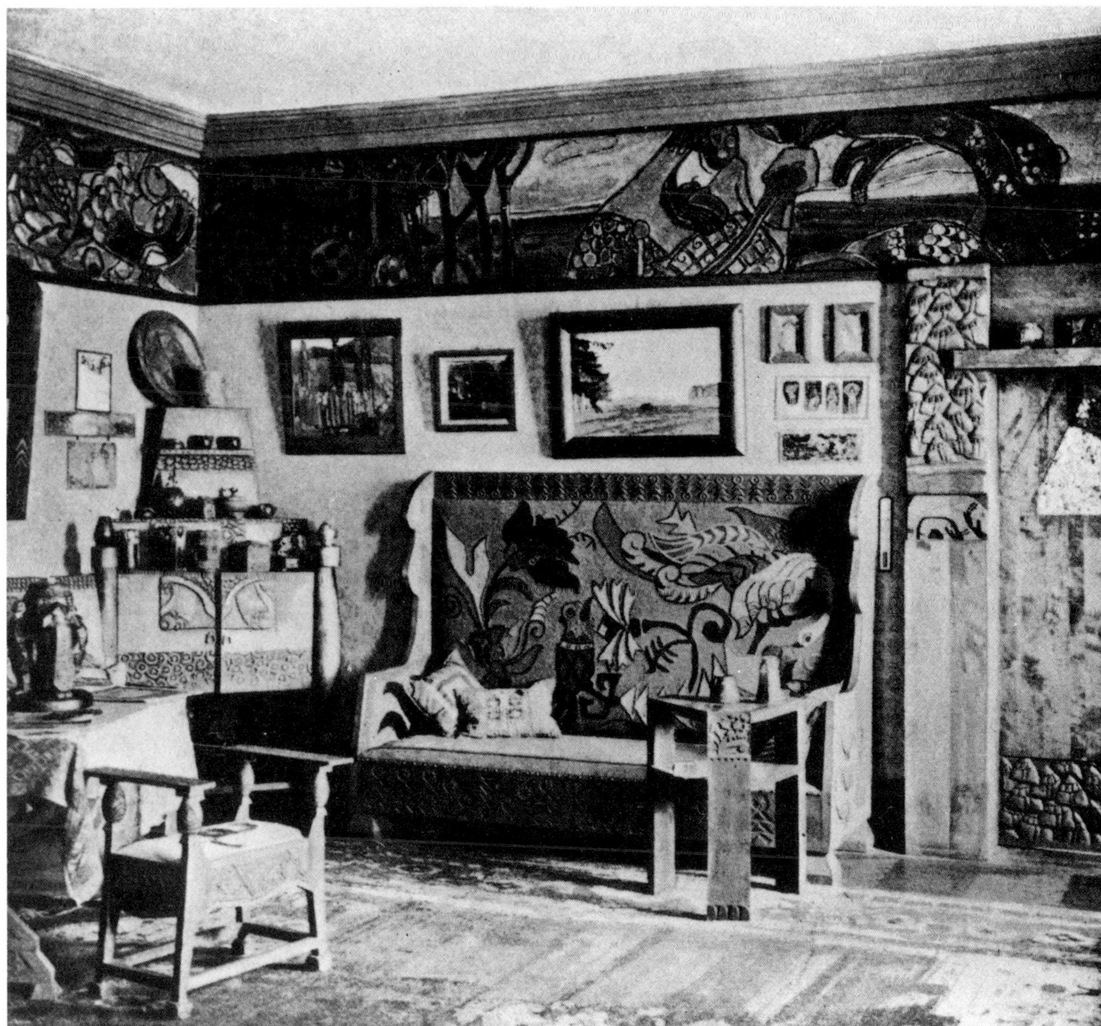

ABOVE: **Mikhail Nesterov**
246. *The Murdered Tsarevich Dmitry*
1899
Mixed media on paper, 32.5 × 26
State Tretyakov Gallery

RIGHT: **Aleksei Zinov'ev**
Interior of the house at Talashkino with furniture and decoration from the workshops
1903–05

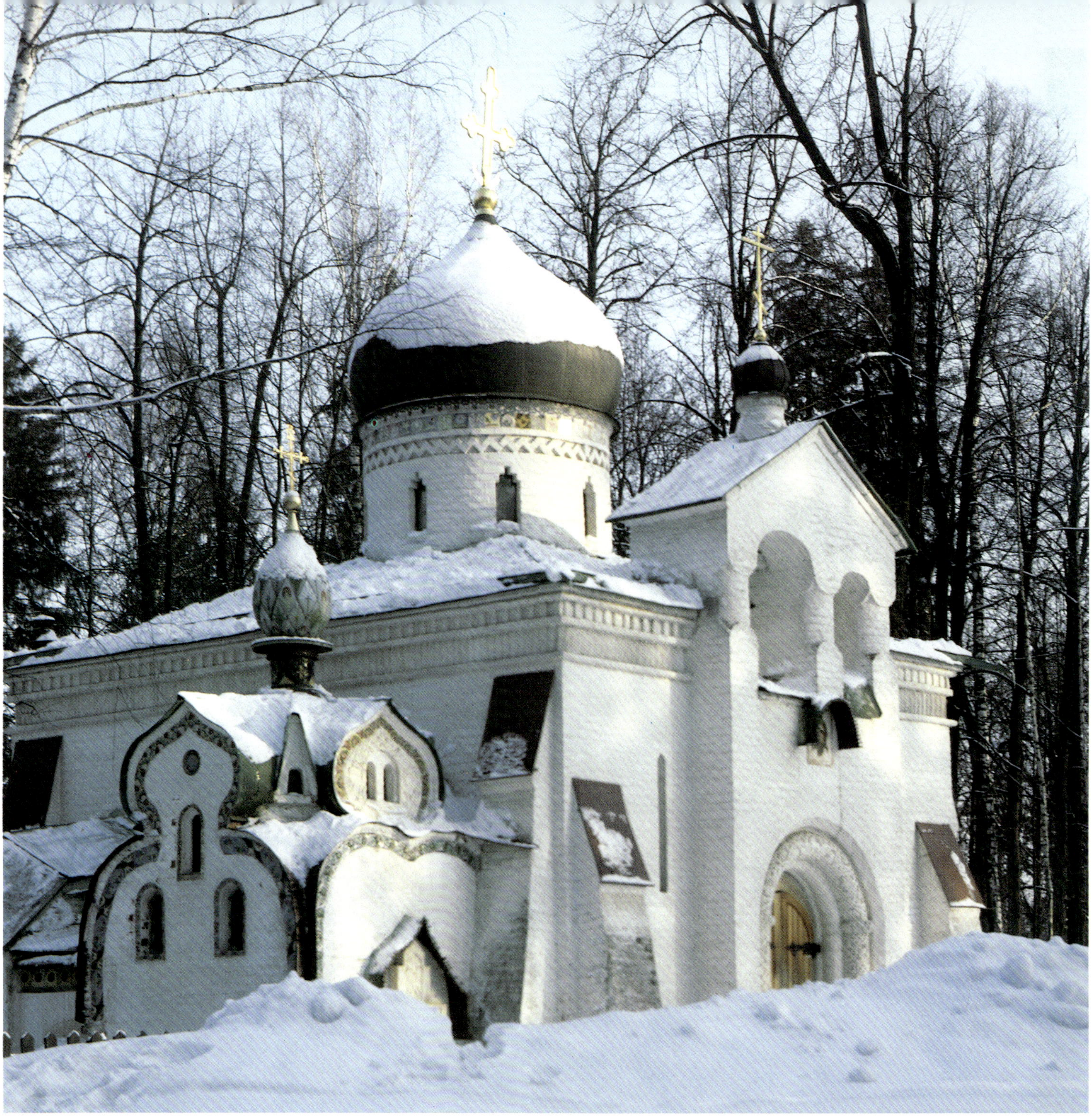

Above: **Viktor Vasnetsov and
Vasily Polenov**
Abramtsevo church
1880–82

Right: **Vasily Polenov, Apollinary
Vasnetsov, Viktor Vasnetsov, Ilya Repin,
Elizaveta Mamontova**
Iconostasis of Abramtsevo church
1882

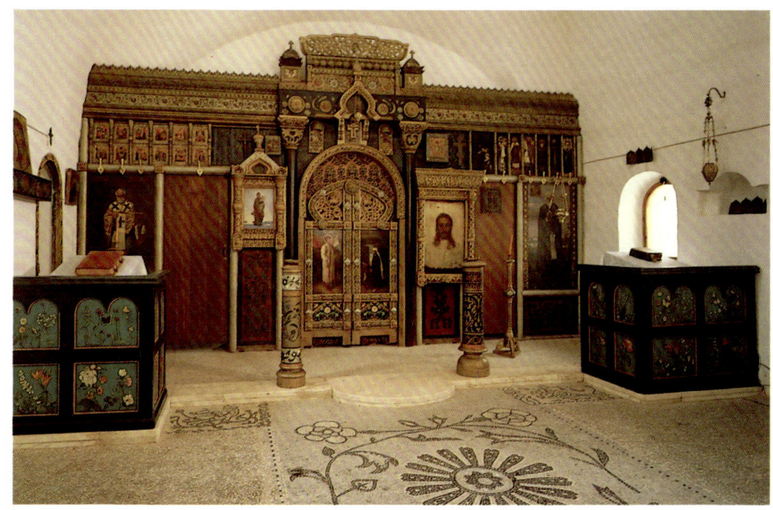

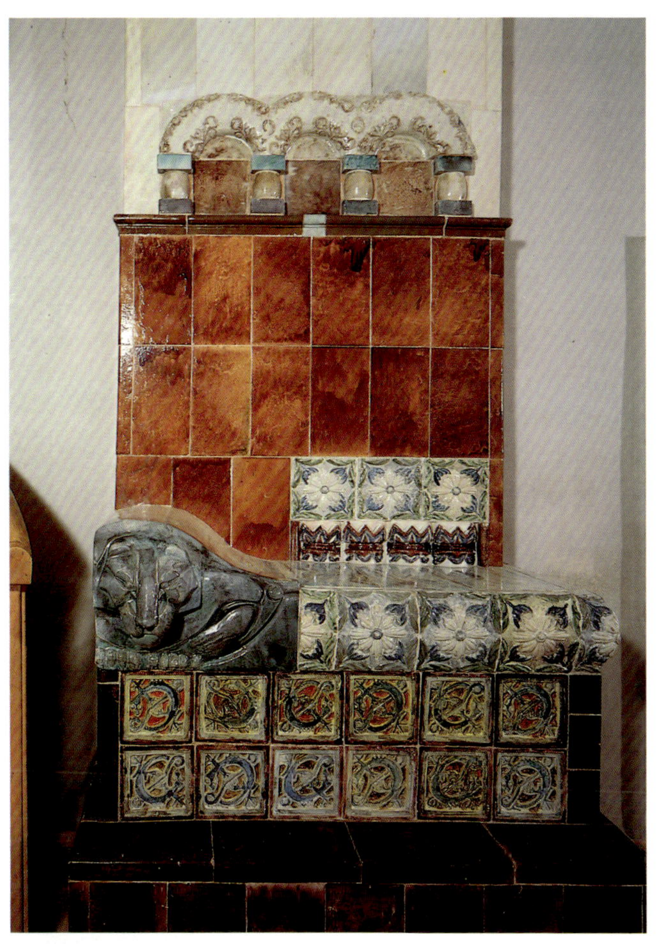

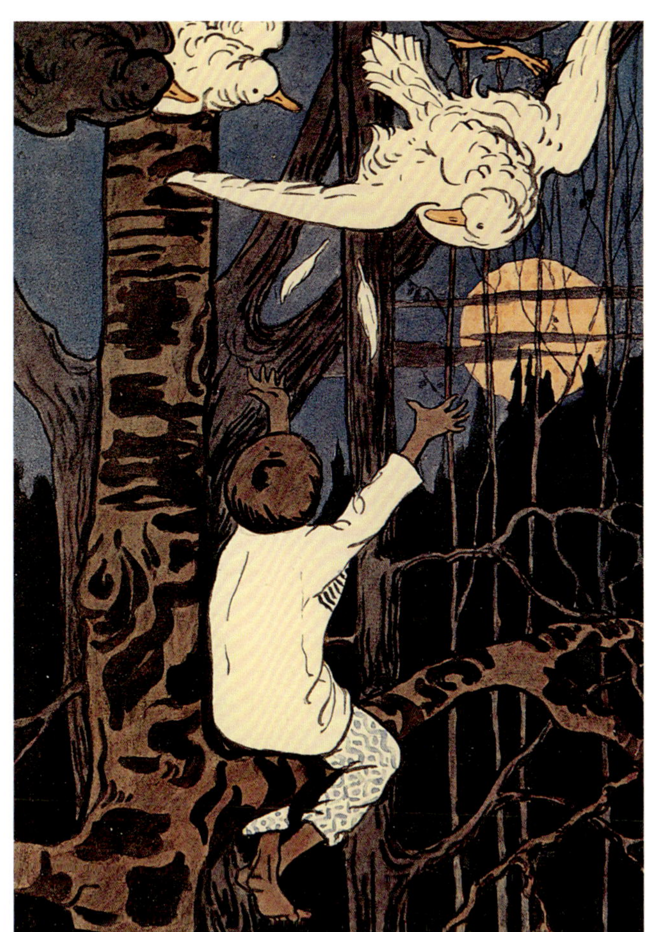

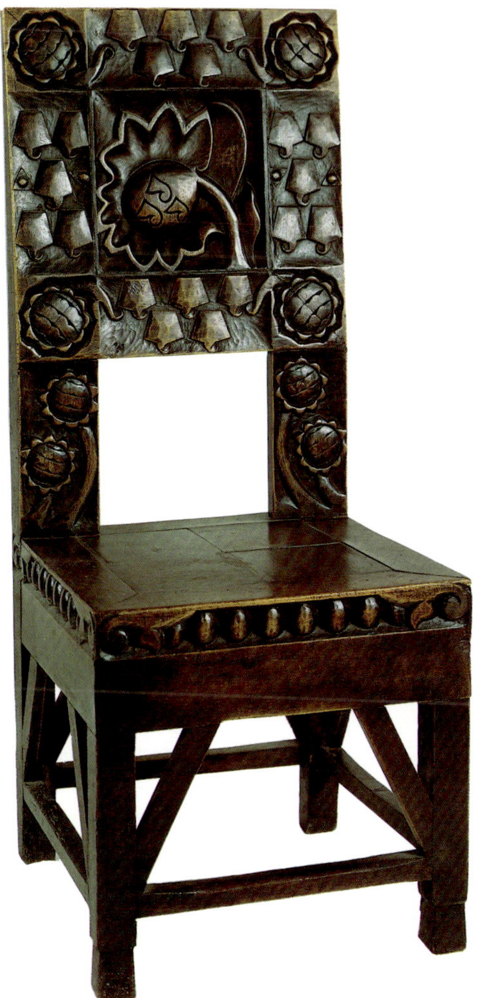

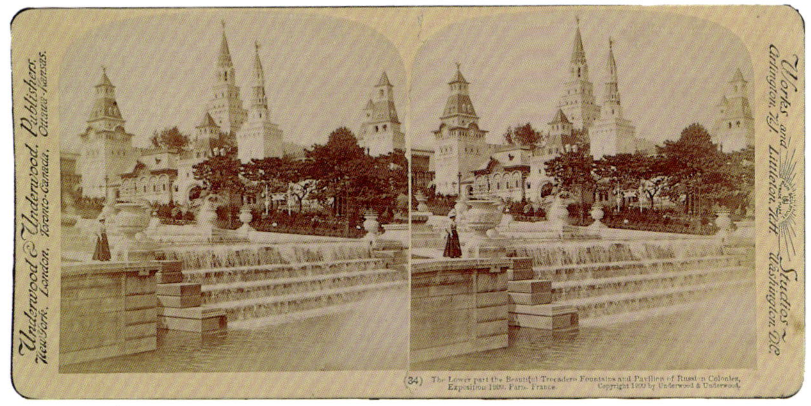

TOP LEFT: **Mikhail Vrubel'**
Majolica stove-seat at Abramtsevo
1890
It incorporates the lion mask also used on
the gates of Savva Mamontov's house in
Moscow (see p.198)

LEFT: **Sergei Malyutin**
221. Chair
Talashkino, 1900s
Carved oak, 110 × 43 × 43
State Historical Museum

TOP: **Elena Polenova**
284. Illustration for *Russian Folk Tales
and Stories*, Moscow, 1906
State Lenin Library

ABOVE: **Konstantin Korovin and
Aleksandr Golovin**
181. Russian Pavilion at the Paris
Exposition Universelle
1900
Stereoscopic photo (1900)
A. V. Shchusev State Museum of
Architecture

WINDOWS ON THE WEST Although in 1900 Moscow and St Petersburg were hardly on speaking terms and had quite separate cultural traditions, their links with the rest of Europe were much stronger than is often appreciated. As the century progressed, communications between the two cities improved. News travelled quickly, and if developments elsewhere were disregarded it was out of volition rather than ignorance. Censorship and the activities of the Okhrana meant that the Russian intelligentsia had to travel.[10] Lenin's sojourn in London – living in Soho and working in the Library of the British Museum – is well known, but many Russians visited Britain: it may seem incongruous, but Turgenev conceived an important part of his novel *Fathers and Sons* while staying at Ventnor on the Isle of Wight, a popular spot with Russian emigrés as well as (separately) with Dickens and Swinburne; Herzen, who wanted some quiet, headed for Bournemouth.

Sergei Diaghilev, exhibition organiser, editor of *Mir Iskusstva* (*The World of Art*) and future impresario of the *Ballets Russes*, visited London in 1898, stopping at Dieppe to meet his hero, the artist Aubrey Beardsley. A few months later, he went to Paris to see Oscar Wilde, whose works were also adulated by young artists and writers in Russia.[11] Diaghilev published Beardsley's drawings in *Mir Iskusstva*, and his style was developed and embellished by a number of its associates, particu-

larly by Nikolai Feofilaktov, Georgy Narbut and Sergei Chekhonin. The experiments of Beardsley were also of interest to an even younger generation – future members of the post-revolutionary avant-garde – who were influenced by his work as students. This is attested by the earliest drawings of Aleksandr Rodchenko made at the art school in Kazan; at the same time he was reading Wilde's play *The Duchess of Padua*, and in 1914 he was to make a series of set and costume designs for a production of this, which was never realised.[12]

British art, architecture and literature were well-known and respected in Russia. The works of Rossetti, Burne Jones, William Morris, Ruskin, Whistler, Mackintosh, Brangwyn, Conder and Sargent as well as the productions of the Arts and Crafts movement were highly thought of and influential. There were also a large number of British trading companies operating in Russia. One of the most visible was the vast Gothic pile of the Muir and Mirrielees Department Store designed by Roman Klein between 1907 and 1908 (now TsGUM). Situated in Moscow's Teatralnaya Square at the side of the Bolshoi it faces the Hotel Metropol (1898–1903), one of the masterworks of William Walcot, a British architect who commissioned Vrubel' and Golovin to design the mosaics and reliefs on its ornate façades. In spite of these affinities, however, London failed to attract many young Russian artists as students; Paris, Munich

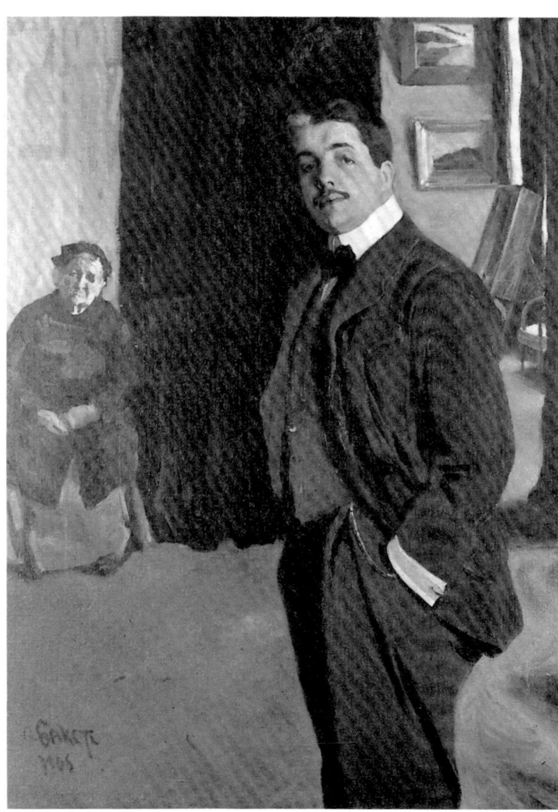

LEFT: **Lev Bakst**
Portrait of Sergei Diaghilev with his Nanny
1906
Oil on canvas, 161 × 116
State Russian Museum

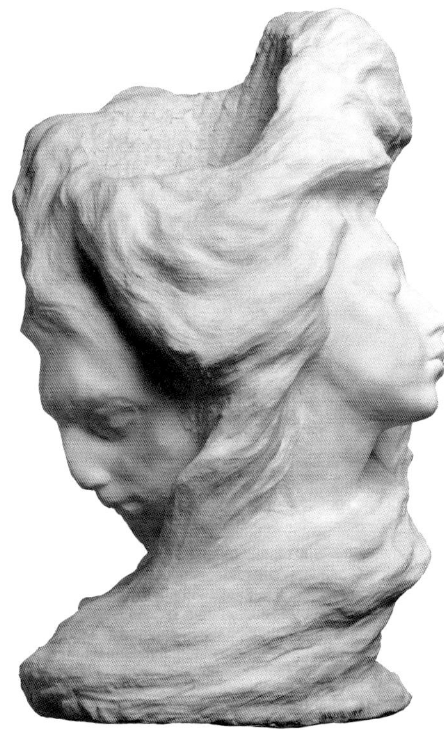

BELOW: **Anna Golubkina**
130. Vase: *Mist*
1899
Marble, 52.5 × 32.5 × 31
State Tretyakov Gallery

and Vienna were the arbiters of artistic taste and their bohemian quarters provided a more convivial environment.

Russian art students gravitated towards these centres as many established painters made their livings there by giving tuition. Paris was the most popular: Viktor Borisov-Musatov studied at Cormon's studio from 1895 and was impressed by the large decorative paintings of Puvis de Chavannes. This encounter was of vital importance to the work he made on return to Saratov in 1898; he had grasped the possibility of making allusion rather than representation the basis of his work. Sculptors Anna Golubkina and Nikolai Andreev studied with Rodin, although they were both able to transcend his strong formative influence in their later work; Lev Bakst had been studying with Gérôme and Julian while familiarising himself with the erotic art of Félicien Rops; but the majority of the Russian artists who made the pilgrimage to Paris in the 1890s attended the large *Académies* of Julian, Cormon or Colarossi.

Few of these students appear to have taken an interest in the work of the French avant-garde, neither was there yet great enthusiasm for this work among critics or collectors in Russia itself.[13] Pleinairism had entered Russian painting in the work of Vasily Polenov, a painter associated with the earlier Realist generation. This, with the influence of Impressionism, was subse-

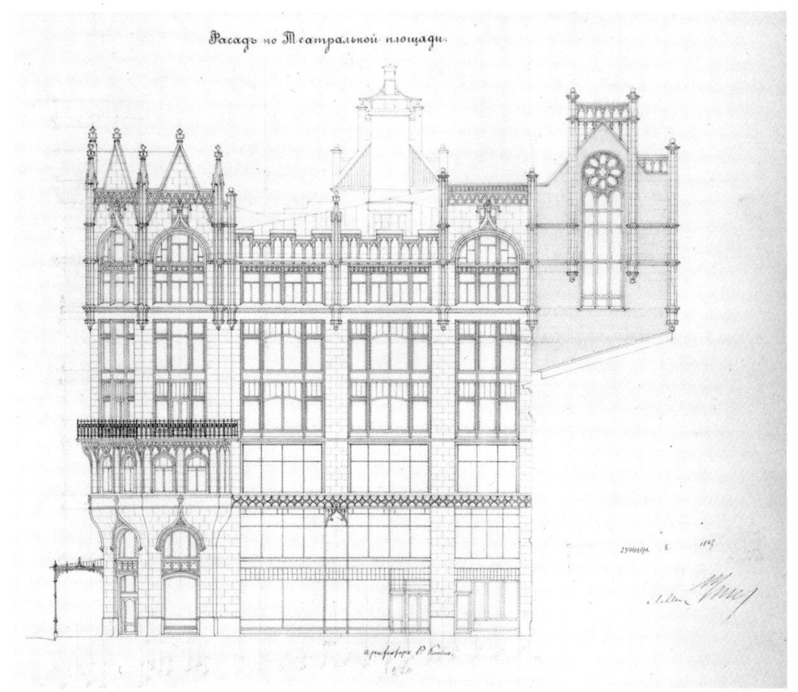

BELOW LEFT: **Viktor Borisov-Musatov**
67. *Meeting by the Column*
1901–03
Watercolour, pen and Indian ink on paper, 17.8 × 12.2
State Russian Museum

ABOVE: **Roman Klein**
166. Muir and Mirrielees Department Store, Moscow: elevation on Teatralnaya Square
1907–08
Indian ink and pencil on paper, 65.5 × 60.1
A. V. Shchusev State Museum of Architecture

quently continued in the work of Konstantin Korovin, Valentin Serov, Leonid Pasternak and later, in the early 1900s, by such artists as Kazimir Malevich, Alexei Jawlensky, Mikhail Larionov and Vasily Denisov. By 1908, however, the newest French painting could be seen in Russia. Moscow merchants Savva Morozov and Sergei Shchukin competed with each other to build up the better collection of avant-garde art. To rooms full of masterpieces by Van Gogh, Gauguin, Monet and Derain the latest works by Picasso and Matisse were soon added. The collections were thrown open to the public at the weekends, and young Moscow artists had an unparalleled opportunity to appreciate the latest developments in French painting.

Artists such as Kandinsky, Jawlensky, Maryana Verefkina, Igor' Grabar', Mtislav Dobuzhinsky and Kuzma Petrov-Vodkin went to Munich to study, where the "Rembrandtism" of Franz von Lenbach, the erotic symbolism of the *wunderkind* Franz von Stuck and the relaxed atmosphere of Anton Ažbè's atelier attracted many foreign students. Ažbè, in particular, seems to have been important to those artists who were later to constitute the *Blaue Reiter* in that he encouraged students to find their own style of work and to use bright unmixed colour directly from palette to canvas; he also took them on painting excursions in the countryside by bicycle.[14]

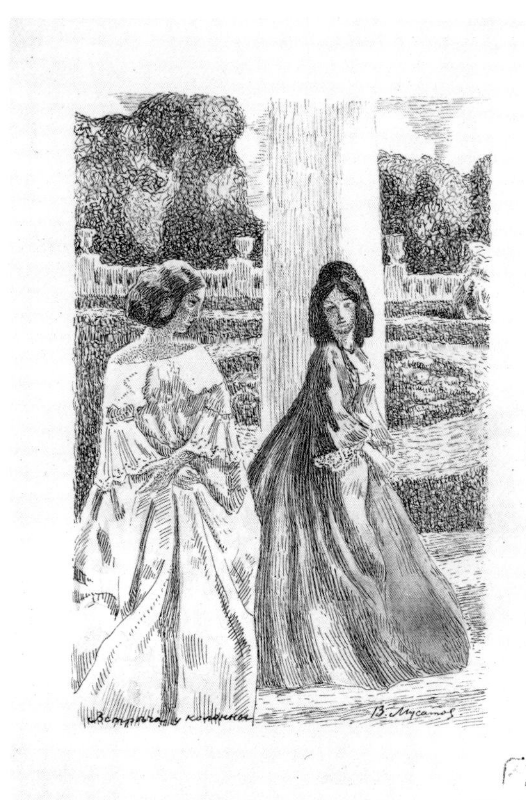

AN AZURE BREEZE If, paradoxically, the historicist National Style can be seen as one of the sources of modern art in Russia, further impetus came from *Mir Iskusstva*. Under the direction of Sergei Diaghilev the "World of Art" exhibition society and journal provided a forum for new ways of thinking about culture and forged a link between the "European" predilections of St Petersburg and the more "Russian" inclinations of the Moscow art world. *Mir Iskusstva*, jointly funded at its inception by Savva Mamontov and Princess Tenisheva and later privately by the Tsar, gave Russia its first opportunity of seeing a multifaceted reflection of its own art. New developments from abroad were also published, particularly in the field of Arts and Crafts. Its production, in *mis-en-page* and printing, found its only rival in *Ver Sacrum*, the journal of the Viennese Secession. Following the model of *Le Japon Artistique*, which had been first published in Paris in 1888, vignettes, drawings and titles interpenetrated the text. Illustrations – blocks, colour lithographs and photogravures – were of the highest quality. The new standard of presentation for a periodical set by *Mir Iskusstva* was matched in 1906 by Ryabushinsky's *Zolotoe Runo* (*The Golden Fleece*), produced in Moscow, and later, in 1909, by Sergei Makovsky's *Apollon*, which was produced on a more modest scale in St Petersburg.[15]

Although consciously primitivist in their form, the innovatory artists' books published by the Russian Futurists between 1912 and 1916 are an important further development in the culture of the book as a work of art and would have been inconceivable without the inventions of their predecessors.

Diaghilev also organised a number of exhibitions under the banner of *Mir Iskusstva*, the first of which, showing Russian and international work, was unexpectedly visited by the Tsar, who made purchases of items from the Tiffany and Abramtsevo workshops. At the exhibition the following year, only of Russian work, the Tsar again made similar purchases. Although the Imperial taste is most closely linked with the house of Fabergé, the Tsarina was the sister of Ernst Ludwig, Grand Duke of Darmstadt-Hesse, one of the leading patrons of German *Jugendstil*. In 1899 he had commissioned from a number of young artists and architects plans for the building of a *Jugendstil* artists' colony on the Mathildenhöhe in Darmstadt; the ambitious scale of this project was unequalled. *Mir Iskusstva* published a feature on the colony at the time of its opening in 1901.

The *Mir Iskusstva* exhibition of the same year signalled a split between the St Petersburg and the Moscow artists: the Muscovites rejected the Petersburg hanging jury and wished to assert the artistic primacy of colour and painting over line. The Moscow group, headed by Vrubel' and Serov, called itself *The 36* and began to exhibit under that name – even including a number of the Petersburg artists! In 1903 this group became transformed into the *Union of Russian Artists* in a move which broke the artistic hegemony of St Petersburg and disrupted the cycle of *Mir Iskusstva* exhibitions. These lapsed until 1906, although Lanceray, Benois and Bakst worked with Diaghilev on the elaborate installation of the vast *Exhibition of Historic Russian Portraits* held in the Tauride Palace in 1905. This was a new kind of exhibition, which depended on design and

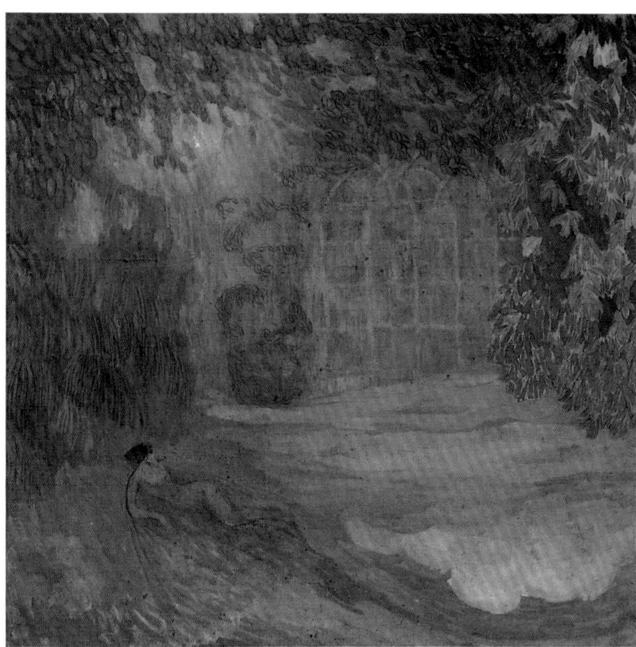

RIGHT: **Petr Savvich Utkin**
437. *Sleep*
1905
Tempera on canvas, 68 × 69
State Russian Museum

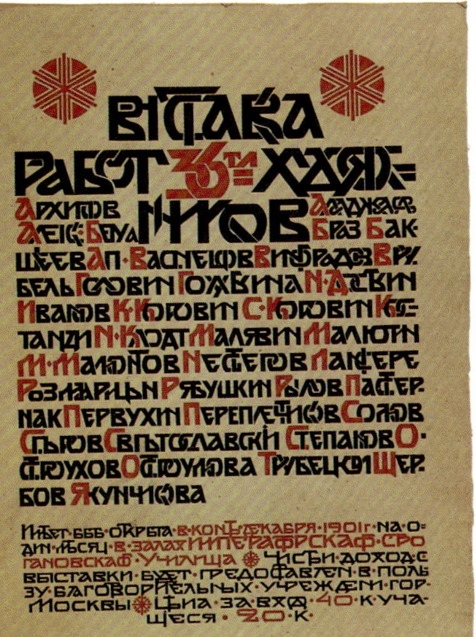

ABOVE: **Mikhail Vrubel'**
469. *Exhibition of the Work of 36 Artists*
Moscow, 1901
Lithographic poster, 61 × 47
State Lenin Library

RIGHT: **Nikolai Milioti**
226. *Round Dance*
N.d.
Oil on cardboard, 71 × 75.5
State Russian Museum

BELOW: **Pavel Kuznetsov**
197. *Oriental Scene*
1912–13
Oil on canvas, 78 × 87.5
State Russian Museum

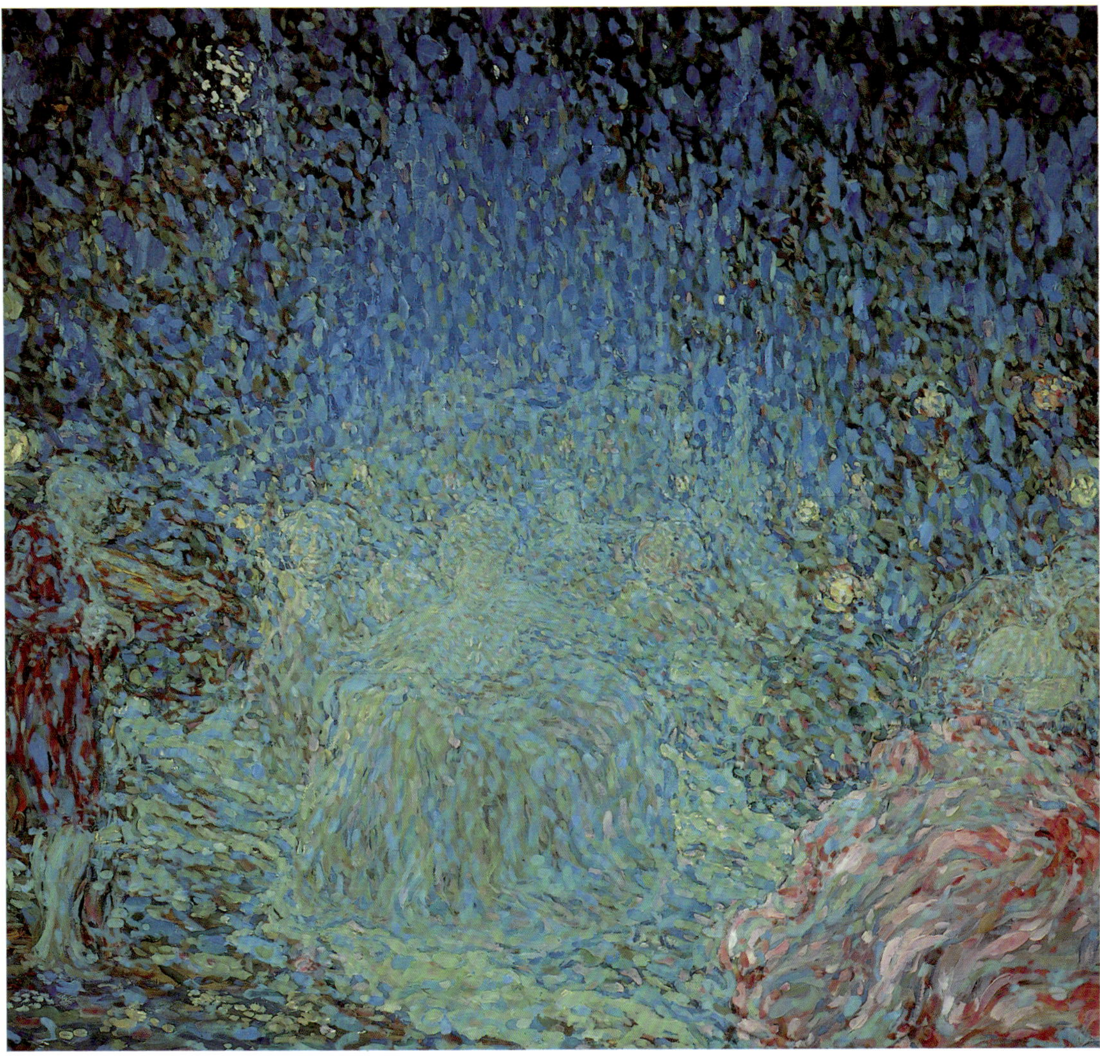

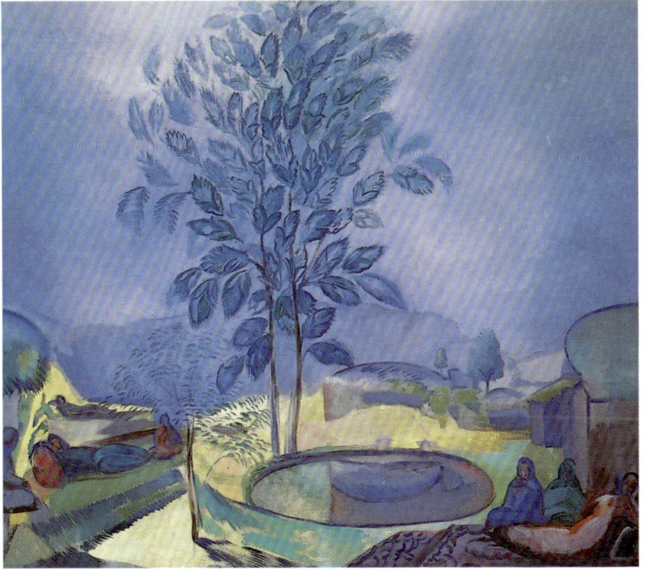

subtle manipulation of the environment, as well as scholarship, to make its impact with the public.

The last *Mir Iskusstva* exhibition looked to the future. Starting with a posthumous retrospective of the work of Borisov-Musatov and a substantial display of paintings by Vrubel', critical attention was focused on the group of young provincial artists, admirers of Borisov-Musatov, who were to exhibit together as *Golubaya Roza (The Blue Rose)*: Pavel Kuznetsov, Nikolai and Vasily Milioti, Sergei Sudeikin, Nikolai Sapunov, Petr Utkin and later Martiros Sar'yan. The idea of a *Blue Rose* was as elusive as that of the *Golden Fleece*; the two were well matched, for this journal was their champion. Compared with what had been seen before, these paintings, described by one critic as "dreams in azure" and "mystical flowers", had no real subject other than mood or ambiance.[16] In the purity of their intention and the immediacy of their impact they seemed to aspire to the condition of music.

ART, POETRY AND MUSIC The earliest performances of Wagner's *Ring* in Russia had taken place at the Mariinsky Theatre in St Petersburg early in 1889; Rimsky Korsakov and Glazunov studiously attended rehearsals by the German guest company with the admitted objective of industrial espionage: "Wagner's method of orchestration struck Glazunov and me and thenceforth Wagner's devices gradually began to form a part of our orchestral tricks of the trade. The first application of Wagner's orchestral methods . . . was made in my orchestration of the Polish Dance from *Boris Godunov*."[17]

Sitting in the audience was a group of college boys – Aleksandr Benois, Konstantin Somov and Dmitri Filoso-fov – who, almost a decade later, were to become the nucleus of *Mir Iskusstva*. Wagner had become a passion in St Petersburg, and new productions in Bayreuth were regularly reviewed in the group's journal, as well as in *Zolotoe Runo*.[18] In 1902, working with architect and painter Konstantin Korovin, Benois, already a painter, critic and art historian, designed the sets for a Russian

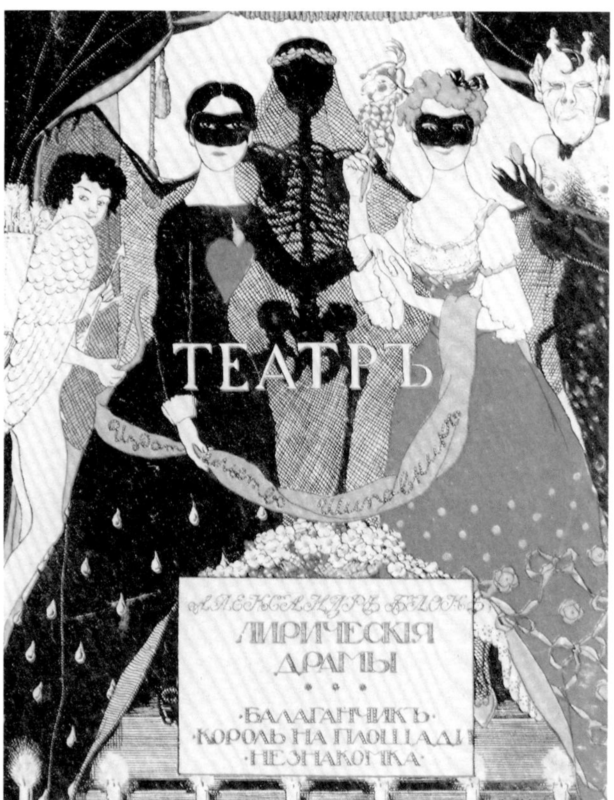

Konstantin Somov
401. Cover for Aleksandr Blok's *Lyric Dramas*,
St Petersburg, 1908
State Lenin Library

production of *The Twilight of the Gods*, also at the Mariinsky Theatre.

Wagner was the high priest of new music and, in the rarefied atmosphere of the 1890s, music seemed to be the most pure of art forms from which all others flowed. The writings of Schopenhauer, translated into Russian at this time, described music as the route to a higher level of consciousness. The Russian mystic philosopher Vladimir Solov'ev regarded poetry as a kind of divine music: "the incantatory magic of rhythmic speech which mediates between man and the world of divine things."[19] Of course, there was also the decisive influence of the French Symbolist poets Mallarmé, Rimbaud and Verlaine whose work had been translated at the beginning of the 1890s by the twenty-one-year-old Valery Bryusov and included in a series of slim volumes entitled *The Russian Symbolists*.[20] For Bryusov, as for Mallarmé, "the object of Symbolism is to hypnotise the reader with a series of juxtaposed images, to invoke in him a certain mood."[21] Bryusov's friend, Konstantin Bal'mont, had similar ideas and was renowned for the musicality of his verse, which often elevated the search for rhythmical effect above that for meaning; significantly, Andrei Bely called a number of his early writings *Symphonies*.[22]

More obsessed by twilight than dawn, Bely, Blok and Bryusov were typical of their age, yet their views on art were far from identical. Bryusov, following the models of Algernon Swinburne and Oscar Wilde, believed that art was an end in itself; Bely adhered to the idea of the symbol as an expression of a higher state of being and experimented in putting together streams of ideas and sentences which anticipated the work of Velimir Khlebnikov and James Joyce. Bitterly ironical, Blok thought that Symbolism had come to an end and symbolised little more than its own demise; as a result he began to parody what he felt was the naivety of his earlier work. Blok's play *The Fairground Booth* subverted the conventions of the *commedia dell'arte* which had become a cliché of the Petersburg "World of Art"; Vsevolod Meyerhold's production ended with the inversion of a circus joke: Harlequin jumped through a window, but the stage scenery had been drawn on paper and he left a large hole; in performing this trick Harlequin had ruptured the illusion of the play itself and with it his continuing existence.[23]

The musicality of poetry was part of a general tendency in the arts towards synaesthesia, a cross-referencing of the senses not unlike the *correspondances* of Baudelaire. In response, music became more like poetry, art or literature. Rakhmaninov's tone poem *The Isle of the Dead* (op.29) of 1909 "describes" a painting by the Swiss artist Arnold Böcklin, which through its mass reproduction as a popular print had become an icon of

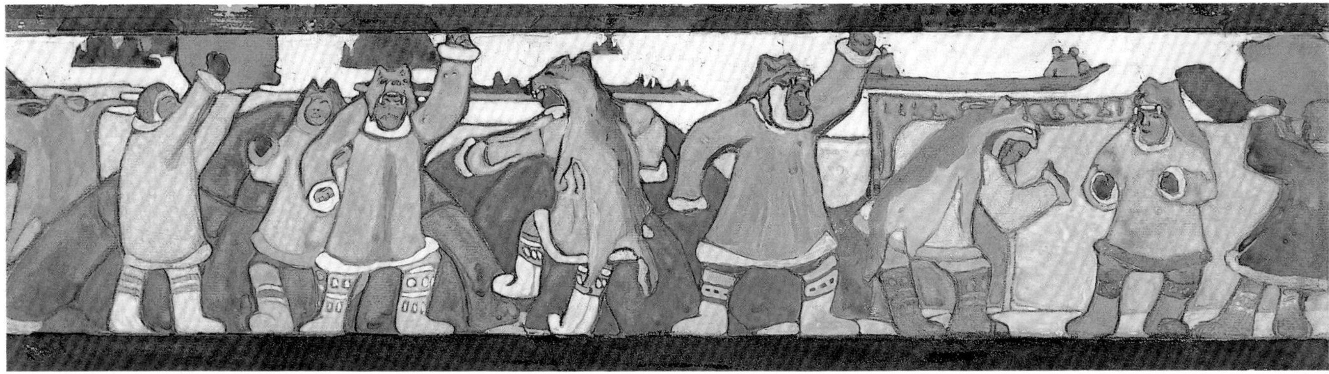

Symbolism.[24] The steady rhythm of Charon's oars, the death-like chant and suggestion of *Dies Irae*, which, at the climax, are set against a melody which Rakhmaninov described as a "life theme", evoke a rite of passage which is rooted in myth and poetry. One of the last pieces which Rakhmaninov composed before emigrating to America were the *Six Songs* (op.38) of 1916, which gave settings to verses by contemporary Russian poets.[25]

Aleksandr Skryabin planned but never completed a Nietzschean "philosophical opera" and then, fired by the teachings of Mme Blavatsky, completed in 1907 *Le Poème d'Extase* (op.54), an initial step in his programme to unite all the arts.[26] At its performance in Moscow the young Boris Pasternak, whose father, Leonid, was a close friend of the composer, described his impressions: "The music was let loose. Multicoloured, shattering to infinite fragments, multiplying like lightning. . . . Then suddenly rising to a roar of unprecedented unity as a whirlwind raged in the bass, it would break off, die away entirely, and flatten out along the footlights. This was man's first settlement in those worlds discovered by Richard Wagner for fictitious beings and mastodons. And on this land was erected a quite unfictitious lyrical dwelling house, equal in substance to the entire universe that had been ground up to make its bricks . . ."[27] Skryabin believed, as did the Russian painter Vasily Kandinsky who was working in Munich at the same time, that sounds could invoke colours. He wrote music with a colour score and designed a "colour organ" to accompany the orchestra. Such experiments are the forerunners of the multi-media light shows of the 1960s.

Often based on Russian folk tales and with the multi-media panache of the Wagnerian *Gesamtkunstwerk*, Diaghilev's *Ballets Russes* took Europe by storm. From the first season in 1909, new music, opulent sets and costumes designed by leading artists and a new style of choreography using the most talented dancers created a world of dream-like artifice. Based in Paris, but using Russian artists, the production of *The Firebird*, first performed in 1910, established Stravinsky's reputation

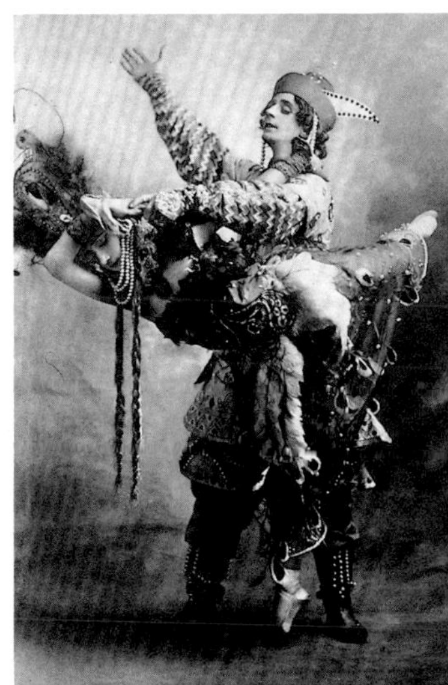

ABOVE: **Nikolai Roerich**
290. *Stone Age Dance in the North*
1904
Design for a pottery frieze
Gouache on paper, 13.4 × 60.8
State Tretyakov Gallery

LEFT: Mikhail Fokine and Tamara Karsavina wearing Bakst's costumes in Stravinsky's *Firebird*, based on the Russian folk tale. It was choreographed by Fokine and given in the second season of Diaghilev's *Ballets Russes* in Paris (1910)

as a composer; Fokine's choreography, with Tamara Karsavina in the lead role, was set against exotic sets and costumes designed by Aleksandr Golovin and Lev Bakst.

In the following year Stravinsky completed *Petrushka*, a pathetic, Hoffmannesque story of a Russian puppet; Vaslav Nijinsky played the lead, with Karsavina as the ballerina with whom he fell in love. However, most momentous of all the *Ballets Russes* productions in these years was Stravinsky's *The Rite of Spring* with choreography by Nijinsky and sets and costumes by Nikolai Roerich. First performed in Paris in 1913, this thirty-four minute work eschewed the luxuriant exoticism of earlier ballets in favour of a raw, rhythmic and anti-melodic primitivism. The audience did not see or hear what they expected and were in uproar; the evening was a *succès de scandale*. As Stravinsky later recalled: "We were excited, angry, disgusted . . . and happy. . . . Diaghilev's only comment was: 'Exactly what I wanted.'. . ."[28] With unerring instinct, Diaghilev had shown that he could survive the night.

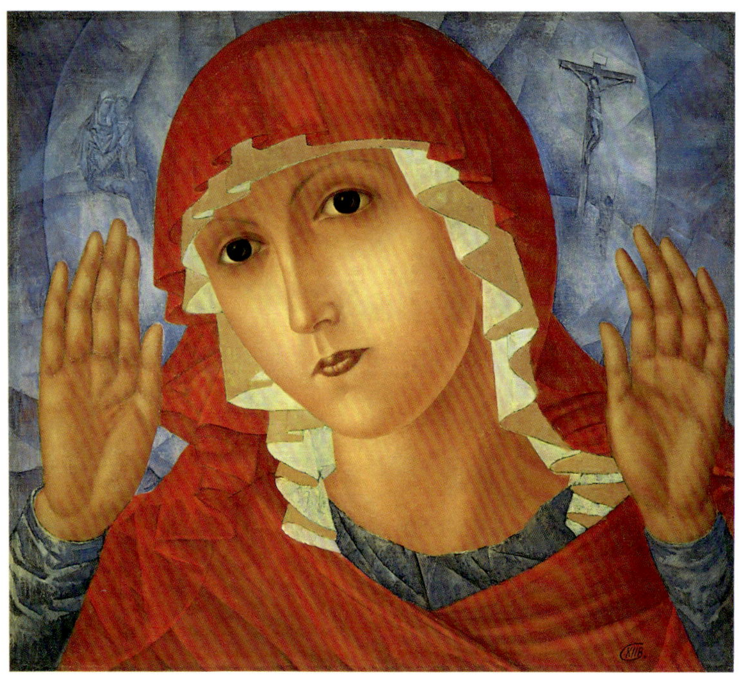

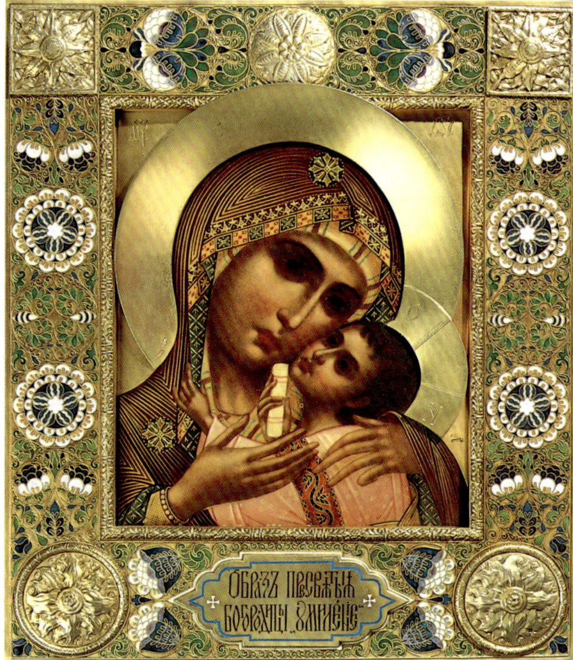

THE ARTIST AS PROPHET Even today writers and artists have a prophetic status in Russian culture which many British people find difficult to understand. The two artistic giants who dominated the latter part of the nineteenth century were Lev Tolstoy and Fedor Dostoevsky, described respectively by a contemporary critic as "a seer of the flesh" and a "seer of the soul".[29] Dostoevsky was particularly important for the 1890s because of his withdrawal from the world and his search for spiritual values. He, too, became a cult figure and Vladimir Solov'ev, a writer and philosopher who as a young man had known him (he was the model for Alesha Karamazov), did much to establish this. Solov'ev's importance as a philosopher lies in his unified approach towards the spiritual and the prosaic. Unity could be found only in God the Creator. To find a way forward the Church would have to break out of its chauvinism to unite in a world theocracy.

The Russian Orthodox Church had been undergoing a revival and was associated with the Pan-Slavist ambitions of the Tsarist empire; there was a strong revival in Church architecture and interest in liturgy. Solov'ev sought to take the energy and spirituality of the Orthodox Church and make it universal. For many this was anathema: under the banner of Christ and the Tsar the Black Hundreds persecuted and slaughtered in the Jewish settlements; superstition and faith-healing became a mania through all levels of society, and the search for prophets at any price opened the Tsarist Court to the malevolent influence of Grigory Rasputin.

Artists and writers, also, sought a messianic role but with more beneficent results. Taking up Solov'ev's ideas about the divinity of female beauty and the applicability of the Book of Revelations to the present, Symbolists became high priests of a new synthetic religion: Art. In the mediation between the world and a higher reality, St Petersburg writers such as Dmitry Merezhkovsky, Andrei Bely, Aleksandr Blok and Vyacheslav Ivanov played a central role. Ivanov took Solov'ev's ideas of a universal religion and gave them substance: all previous beliefs, pagan and Christian, could be subsumed within a single image of the world.

Such a perspective on the great and vanished civilisations undoubtedly added to the hubris of the present, yet a new system of belief based on a synthesis of the religions and images of former cultures did seem to offer the possibility of redemption.

The visionary paintings of Mikhail Vrubel', one of the fathers of the Symbolist movement, illustrate this synthetic approach. Like Viktor Vasnetsov, his earliest work was in the decoration of churches, and many of his later easel paintings have the same tesselated surfaces that can be found on the Byzantine mosaics which he worked alongside at this time. Although the figure of the Demon which became a central motif in his work is derived from a poem written some fifty years earlier by Lermontov, the sense of pathos and conflict encapsulates the mood of the 1890s. In this context Vrubel's many images of the Demon should be regarded alongside the wistful *Prophet* (p.30) as well as his large paintings of the Greek god Pan and the ancient god-like heroes of Slavic history. Sergei Konenkov also depicted Slavic deities in

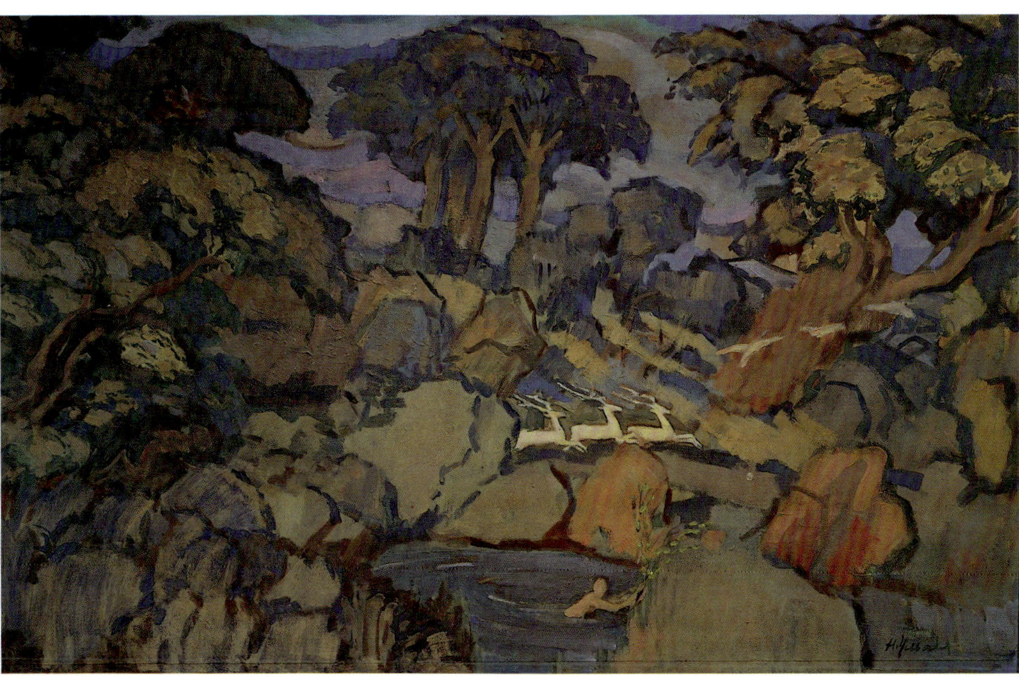

OPPOSITE LEFT: **Kuz'ma Petrov-Vodkin**
269. *The Virgin of Tenderness Moving Evil Hearts*
1914–15
Oil on canvas, 100.2 × 100
State Russian Museum

OPPOSITE RIGHT: **P. I. Olovyanishnikov & Sons**
257. Icon of the *Virgin of Tenderness* in silver frame
Moscow, 1908–17
Icon: Oil on wood; frame (by Olovyanishnikov Co.): silver gilt and enamel, 27 × 31
State Historical Museum

RIGHT: **Nikolai Ul'yanov**
435. *The Invasion of Pan*
c. 1914–15
Illustration for Ovid's *Metamorphoses*
Tempera on cardboard, 64 × 100
Saratov Museum of Fine Art

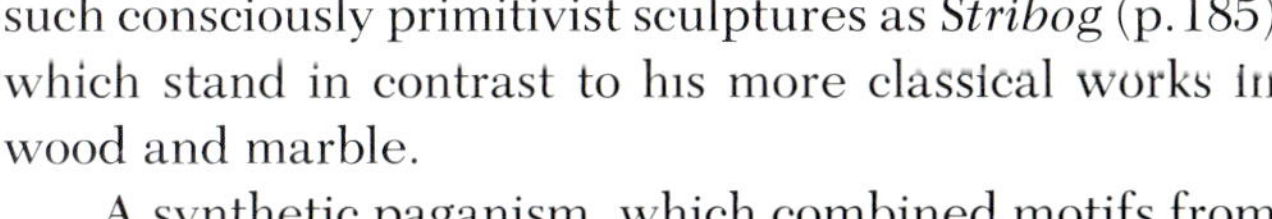

such consciously primitivist sculptures as *Stribog* (p.185) which stand in contrast to his more classical works in wood and marble.

A synthetic paganism, which combined motifs from Russian, Chinese, Persian and Greek mythology, became the hallmark of many of the illustrators who were associated with *Mir Iskusstva*. Lev Bakst, who provided many vignettes and illustrations for the journal and who was later an artist-designer for the *Ballets Russes*, also had a strong visual interest in the pagan past – in his case in the art of Greece and Rome. Dionysian and erotic motifs recur frequently in his work, often with humorous intent. His large painting *Terror Antiquus* (1908, State Russian Museum, Leningrad), however, strikes a less frivolous note by depicting, in a style worthy of John Martin, the last moments of the ancient civilisation of Atlantis.

Working in Munich, Vasily Kandinsky also pursued a path which sought transcendence through disintegration, although in a less literal way. *Twilight*, a painting of 1901 (Städtische Galerie im Lenbachhaus, Munich), depicts a horse and rider in a landscape, a motif which, transformed in many ways, was to recur even in his abstract paintings after 1911. On occasion, as in the woodcut for *Poems without Words* (p.146), printed in Moscow in 1903, the image of the rider suggests a medieval or Russian folktale, at other times it is the icon of St George battling against the dragon – a motif which synthesised memories of Russia with the Bavarian folk art which he was then collecting.

During the first decade of this century Kandinsky was refining his ideas about the transcendental qualities of art and by doing so was searching for a universality of form which could be divorced from the literal or literary depiction of person, setting or object. A leading member of the Munich *Blaue Reiter* group (as we have already seen, blue was the colour of both twilight and spirituality), and with Franz Marc the editor of its Almanac (1912), Kandinsky had kept in close contact with his Russian colleagues. In the Almanac Futurist David Burlyuk wrote on the "Savages" of Russia, Nikolai Kul'bin on Free Music and Leonid Sabaneev contributed a piece on Skryabin's *Prometheus*; these appeared alongside articles on different aspects of the arts by leading French and German avant-garde artists and critics.

At this time the Theosophical beliefs of Rudolph Steiner and Mme Blavatsky, which stated that people and objects had a spiritual force-field which could be perceived by the sensitive as a multi-coloured aura, had become important not only for Kandinsky but also for Skryabin, Andrei Bely and the Lithuanian Symbolist artist-composer, Mikalojus Čiurlionis. This provided a framework within which they could experiment with the correspondences of sense data in a more abstract form. Kandinsky's book *Concerning the Spiritual in Art*, published in 1911, provided valuable and timely guidance for artists and critics on the way in which they might be able to transcend the literalism of the Symbol to pass through into a world of authentic emotion and beautiful form. Working in St Petersburg, Pavel Filonov, a close associate of Nikolai Kul'bin, was also influenced by this approach.

At the same time, in Moscow the young provincial artists, Kazimir Malevich and Ivan Klyun were experimenting with different styles of art in an attempt to capture the spiritual reality that lay behind surface appearance. The 1907 exhibition of *The Blue Rose* organised by Ryabushinsky was a revelation to them, and for the next three years they experimented with the language of Symbolism alongside other approaches. The colours Malevich used are hot rather than cool and reflect the palette of Gauguin and the Nabis, whose work he would have seen in the Morozov and Shchukin collections. Much of the imagery has a religious or autobiographical subject. By 1911, however, he had begun to look in other directions: to the monumentalism of late Cézanne, to the naive painting of countryside shop signs and to the primitivism of Picasso. The forms of Symbolism constituted only a brief interlude for both Malevich and Klyun, but the rhetoric and search for transcendance continued. In 1915, when he had completed a series of absurdist Cubo-Futurist abstractions and was preparing paintings with the flat colour planes of Suprematism, Malevich wrote: "I imagine a world of inexhaustible, unseen forms. From that which I do not see – an endless world arises. . . . The mystery remains an open reality and each reality is endlessly multifaceted and polyhedral. . . . The artist uncovers the world and shows it to man . . .".[30]

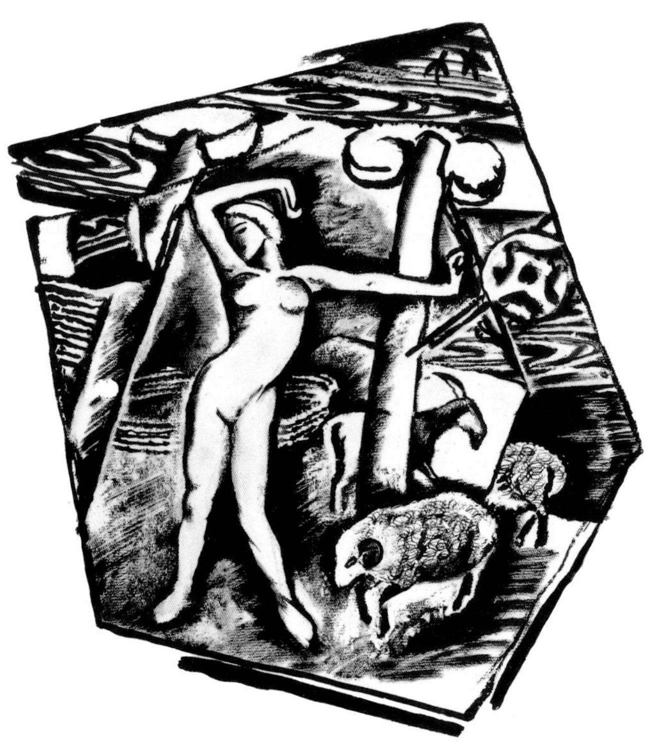

THE WIND FROM THE EAST When Malevich exhibited his historic painting of a black square in 1915 at the 0.10 exhibition in Petrograd it was a tabula rasa in European art. Nothing like it had been seen before. A younger generation of artists saw in this a new beginning, others thought it was the end of art.

This younger, more aggressive generation had progressed to this point by throwing over the traces of Western civilisation to embrace the vital energy of the primitive.

The previous Symbolist generation had been keenly aware of the duality between East and West in Russian culture. In Andrei Bely's novel *The Silver Dove* (1909) the remorseless yet seductive threat of the old pagan religions of Asiatic Russia is the central motif. In *Petersburg* (1915) he set the superficiality of western civilisation against the intransigent and destructive force of "eastern" Anarchism. In his poem *The Coming of the Huns* (1903) Valery Bryusov also entertained the same self-destructive fantasies. He longed for a modern day Mongolian invasion which would clear out dead culture and make way for the new. Such sentiments became increasingly popular: Sergei Prokofiev's *The Scythian Suite* (op.20) of 1915 was the younger composer's response to Stravinsky's *The Rite of Spring* (1913), and Aleksandr Blok's immediately post-revolutionary contribution to this genre, *The Scythians* (1918), celebrates the vigorous primitivism of a newly founded state.

BELOW: **Kazimir Malevich**
Shroud of Christ
1908
Gouache on cardboard,
23.3 × 37.4
State Tretyakov Gallery

ABOVE RIGHT: **Lev Bruni**
79. *Nude*
1915
Drawing from the series
Reminiscences of the Khevsurs
Indian ink, pen, brush and white
on paper, 36.3 × 29.9
State Russian Museum

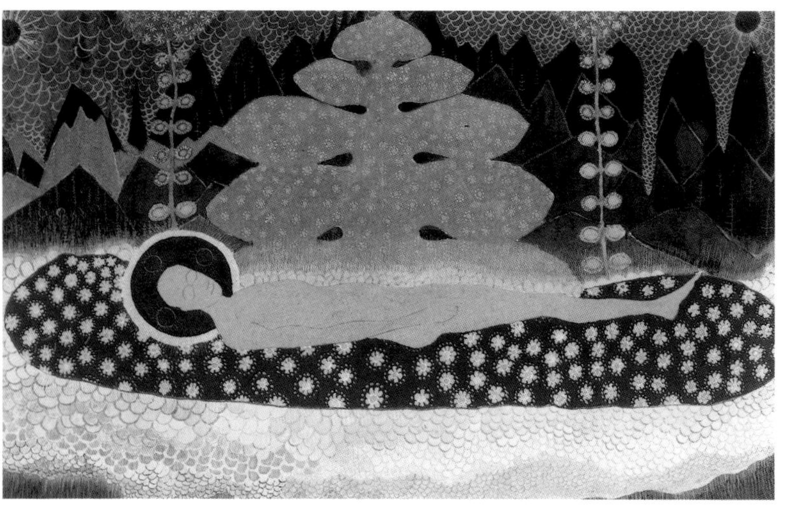

By 1909 Pavel Kuznetsov and other members of *The Blue Rose* had begun to travel to Asiatic Russia and to introduce a new range of eastern motifs into their work. For many years Kuznetsov painted the pastoral innocence of the nomadic peoples of Kirghizia; Martyros Sar'yan depicted scenes from Armenia, the country of his origin.

In 1910 a younger group of artists and poets, many of them students, which included David Burlyuk, Vasily Kamensky, Vladimir Mayakovsky and Aleksei Kruchyenich called themselves *Hyleans*, the Greek name for the old Scythian region in which the country estate of Burlyuk's parents was situated. Deliberately confrontational, consciously primitivist yet confidently aware of the regenerative power of art, this group put its energies into the demolition of bourgeois vulgarity and established standards. In Moscow they became closely associated with Mikhail Larionov and Natal'ya Goncharova, who in 1912 had shown their calculatedly primitive paintings in an exhibition provocatively entitled *The Donkey's Tail*.

In 1913 in the preface to the catalogue of an exhibition of her increasingly abstract work, Natal'ya Goncharova wrote of her admiration for the art, culture and energy of the East: "Now I shake the dust from my feet and leave the West, considering its vulgarising significance trivial and insignificant – my path is towards the source of all the arts, the East."[31]

For Aleksandr Blok the rebirth was predicated by the destruction of the Old World:

> Your gloss faced Europe through the unending
>   plain
> We'll live within our forest spaces
> Our tangled deeps, and turn on you again,
> Swooping, our Asiatic faces.[32]

The parallel with the fall of the Roman Empire did not go unheeded; a new era was about to be born. When the barbarians stood at the Caesar's gate, the age of palaces had come to an end.

NOTES

1 Cited in J. Bowlt, *The Silver Age: Russian Art of the Early Twentieth Century and the "World of Art" Group*, Newtonville, 1982, p.169.
2 A. Bely, *The Dramatic Symphony* (trans. A. and R. Keys), Edinburgh, 1986, p.92.
3 M. Etkind, *A. Benois*, Leningrad and Moscow, 1965, p.88.
4 A. Blok, *Sobr. Sotch.*, vol.6, Moscow and Leningrad, 1960–63, pp.175–6.
5 Blok, *ibid.*
6 The Russian term *Moderne* approximates to what we would describe as *Art Nouveau*. Its application and meaning is, however, broader as it can include Classical and Gothic references. The term *Decadence* was often interchangeable with that of *Symbolism*, although now distinction is often made between the work of the Decadents: Valery Bryusov (1873–1924), Konstantin Bal'mont (1867–1942), Fedor Sologub (1863–1927) et al., who felt that there was no higher reality than art, and the Symbolists: Andrei Bely (1880–1934), Aleksandr Blok (1880–1921), Vyacheslav Ivanov (1866–1949), Dmitry Merezhkovsky (1865–1941) et al., who believed in its transcendent power.
7 P. Gatrell, *The Tsarist Economy 1850–1917*, London, 1986, pp.48–61. During the same period population in the U.K. increased by 16 million and in the U.S.A. by approx. 60 million.
8 *Ibid.*, pp.61–69. In the same fifty years the urban population of Russia almost quadrupled. Voluntary resettlement in Siberia and Asiatic Russia was greatly stimulated by the completion of the Trans-Siberian Railway in 1904 and by the ending of the war with Japan in 1905.
9 B.W. Kean, *All the Empty Palaces*, London, 1983, gives much useful information on the art-collecting merchants of Moscow. Even Ryabushinsky was eventually driven to bankruptcy by the high production costs of *Zolotoe Runo*. From 1908 it was published in a smaller format, but this failed to make the necessary saving.
10 The Okhrana was the Tsarist Secret Police.
11 R. Buckle, *Diaghilev*, London, 1979, pp.37–8.
12 Aleksandr Rodchenko (1891–1956), one of the leading Moscow Constructivists after the Revolution and a member of the LEF group during the 1920s.
13 The first *Mir Iskusstva* exhibition Diaghilev organised in St Petersburg in 1899 showed work from over nine countries. The French painters displayed included Carrière, Degas, Monet, Moreau and Puvis de Chavannes.
14 P. Weiss, *Kandinsky in Munich*, Princeton, 1979, pp.15–17.
15 The journal *Mir Iskusstva* was published from 1899 to 1904; *Zolotoe Runo* appeared from 1906 to 1909; *Apollon* appeared from 1909 to 1917.
16 Nikolai Tarovaty, *Zolotoe Runo*, 1906 no.3, p.124. Cited in Bowlt, *op. cit.*, p.106.
17 Rimsky-Korsakov, *My Musical Life*, London, 1989 ed., p.298.
18 R. Buckle, *op. cit.*, pp.11–13.
19 Arthur Schopenhauer (1788–1860), German philosopher who inadvertently influenced Wagner's aesthetics; his seminal work *Die Welt als Wille und Vorstellung (The World as Will and Representation)* was published in Russia in 1896.
20 V. Bryusov, *Russkie Symvolisty*, Moscow, 1894.
21 G. Struve, *The Cultural Renaissance*, in T.G. Stavrou (ed.), *Russia under the Last Tsar*, Minneapolis, n.d., p.188.
22 See Bely, *op. cit.*, p.18.
23 First directed by Vsevolod Meyerhold at the Komissarzhevsky Theatre, St Petersburg, 1906; designed by Nikolai Sapunov.
24 This kind of cross-fertilisation between the arts also took other forms; for example, Andrei Bely wrote poems inspired by paintings by Borisov-Musatov and Somov.
25 Bely, Blok, Bryusov, Bal'mont and Fedor Sologub.
26 Elena Petrovna Blavatsky (1831–91), co-founder in 1875 of the Theosophical Society, published the key work of the movement, *The Secret Doctrine*, in 1889.
27 B. Pasternak, "Safe Conduct", in C. Barnes (ed.) *The Voice of Prose*, vol.1., Edinburgh, 1986, p.25.
28 I. Stravinsky, *Conversations*, London, 1959, pp.46–7.
29 D. Merezhkovsky, *L. Tolstoy i Dostoevsky*, St Petersburg, 1901.
30 K. Malevich, "The Artist", in *The Artist, Infinity, Suprematism: Unpublished Writings 1913–33*, [ed. T. Andersen], vol.IV, Copenhagen, 1978, p.9.
31 Cited in J. Bowlt, *Russian Art of the Avant Garde: Theory and Criticism*, London, 1988, p.55.
32 A. Blok, *The Scythians* (1918), trans. J. Lindsay, London, 1982.

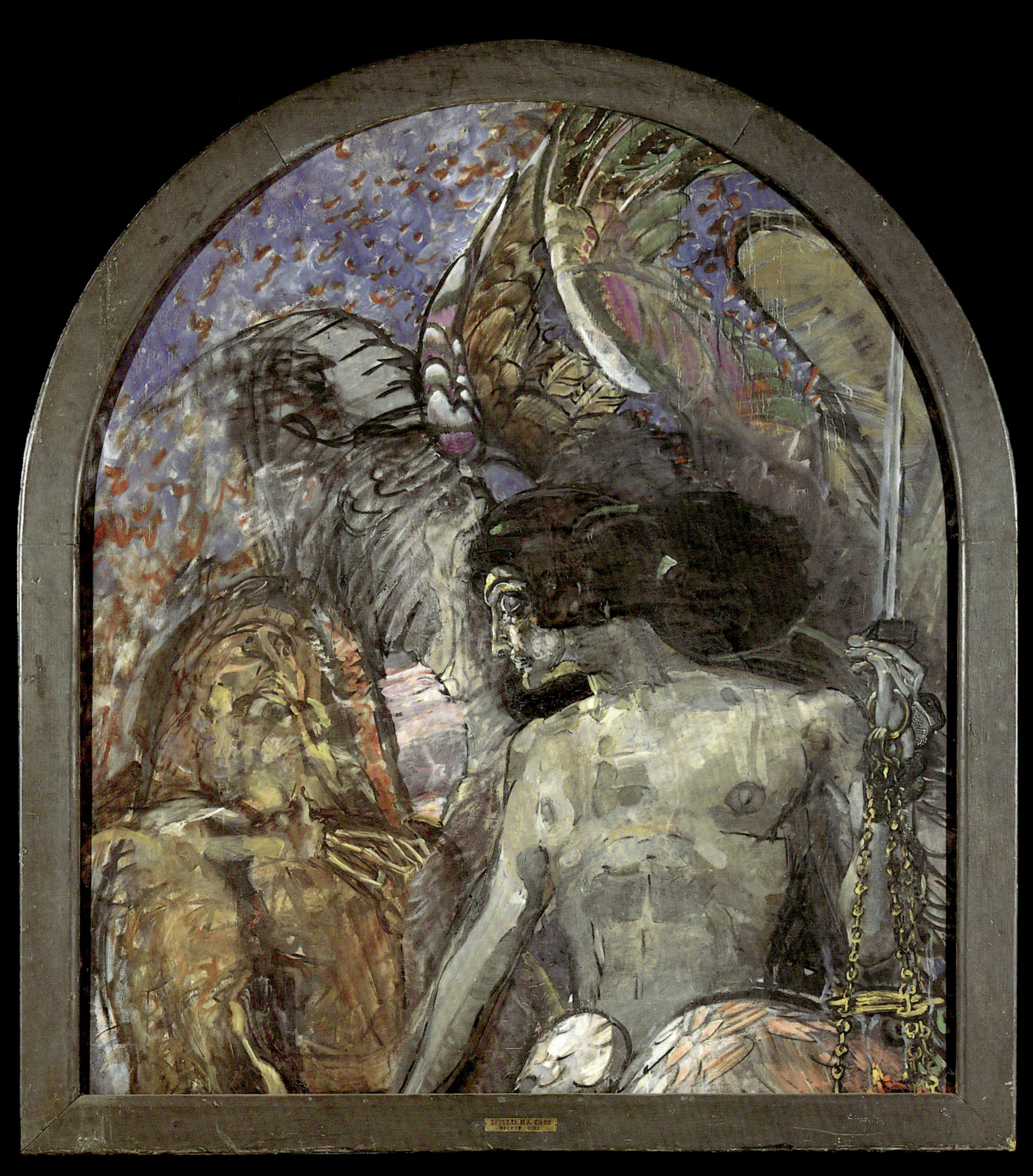

2

THE RUSSIAN *STYLE MODERNE*
Art and Design at the Turn of the Century

TAT'YANA MINKINA

For Russian history and culture, the period from the nineteenth to the early twentieth century was a time of creative discoveries and bitter disenchantments, brilliant insights and colossal Utopian fantasies: an era which came into its own through the assassination of Tsar Pavel in 1801 and ended with the death of a Russian monarch and his family in 1918. The social and political conflicts in nineteenth century Russia, which grew with the approach of the twentieth century, gave rise to myths and dreams which were fully reflected in the magic mirror of Russian art.

As early as the 1830s Aleksandr Ivanov (1806–58) attempted to show a way out of the political crisis of Russia under Nikolai I in his epic painting *The Appearance of Christ before the People*. The path he advocated was that of individual moral self-improvement; but the artist himself was the first to be affected by disenchantment with this Utopian vision: he refused to complete the picture.

After the abolition of serfdom in 1861 there were renewed Utopian hopes for the future of Russia, expressed in the work of the *Peredvizhniki (Wanderers)*, who ardently believed in the possibility of developing the country by educating the broad masses of the people and giving them access to the ideals of a just society. The artists put this into practice by making long journeys around the far-flung corners of "remote" Russia, taking their works with them and arranging exhibitions of them wherever they went. But this unique artistic experiment, a new way of trying to reach the grass-roots, led once again to disenchantment, which provoked a crisis throughout the movement. The illusory nature of the ideals of the *Peredvizhniki* was pointed out early on in the critical works of the Russian satirist Mikhail Saltykov-Shchedrin, who several times described the sceptical and guarded way in which the provincial public greeted the propagandists of the new social art.

Then, at the turn of the century, a renewal of optimism gave rise to the most fantastic artistic Utopia, which found its embodiment in the refined forms of Russian *Style Moderne*. This was part of the new artistic movement which spread almost simultaneously through the countries of Europe in the mid-1890s. In Germany and Austria it was called *Jugendstil*, in France and Belgium *Art Nouveau*, and in Spain *Modernismo*. The development of this common European artistic process did not exclude Russia, where the newborn style was christened *Moderne*, a name which carried a presentiment of renewal. The appearance of Russian *Style Moderne* at this particular time signified much more than a simple change of artistic direction. In fact, Russia was now included on equal terms in the general European process of cultural evolution for the first time in all the decades of development of the art of the new period.

Despite the efforts of Peter the Great in the early eighteenth century to break down the barriers between East and West, Russia had stubbornly gone its own way in its artistic culture, sometimes proudly claiming its historical and national exclusiveness, sometimes aware that it was simply playing the part of a provincial European school. This gave to the Russian fine arts and architecture their extreme lack of uniformity and caused the alternation of long periods of stagnation, which delayed the development of artistic styles (e.g. Realism), with sudden advances, which produced results whose innovative qualities were unexpected (such as the Russian avant-garde).

One further characteristic feature of the evolution of Russian culture is the mismatch between the rhythms of development of artistic styles in Russia and in Western Europe. The rather weak expressiveness of the Russian Romantic tradition, which was conceived in the 1810s and was fully developed by the start of the 1820s, the extremely lengthy development of academic and Realist styles, and the very late appearance of individual elements of the Impressionist vision (in the late 1880s), all indicated the distinctiveness of Russia in the system of European culture. The uniqueness of the Russian

situation was also intensified by its relatively closed nature, reflected in the rather limited participation by Russian artists in general European exhibitions in the second half of the nineteenth century and in the way in which their work, particularly that of the *Peredvizhniki*, concentrated on the solution of acute national problems.

THE FORMATION OF *STYLE MODERNE* In the 1890s the situation in Russian art changed radically. Having made the leap from Critical Realism to *Style Moderne*, the local variant of *Art Nouveau*, Russia became part of the general European artistic culture without losing its national uniqueness. Despite the popularity of Morris and Puvis de Chavannes, Klimt and Redon, Stuck and Beardsley in Russia at this time and the way in which they unquestionably made their contribution to the development of Russian culture, and despite the clearly Western orientation of the St Petersburg group of Russian artists and architects, *Style Moderne* was a Russian phenomenon, an integral part of the whole previous course of development. Its roots reached deep down into the native soil, and its flowering is to be seen in all the art of the period.

One of the basic characteristics of *Style Moderne* was the fact that it appeared quite unexpectedly in Russia, without any transitional links with the Realist era. Indeed Realism and *Style Moderne* are based on diametrically opposite principles of perception of the world and means of expressing it in works of art. Whereas the Realist method was developed on the principle of direct reflection of reality, *Style Moderne* was based on a powerful system of aesthetic transformation of a real situation, whose initial impulse was often difficult to detect in the finished work.

This abyss which separated Realism from *Style Moderne* in the Russian situation appears even more significant when it is remembered that the Russian version of Realism bore a heavy burden of powerful social and political criticism. It was often felt that the work of art should contain almost documentary reportage of places and events, and this imposed upon it a corresponding artistic form. It was a system where the accuracy of specific details was prized, rather than general aesthetic principles. In European art, by contrast, the approach to *Art Nouveau* was by way of Impressionism, which lent an aspect of conditionality to artistic form and affirmed the primacy of the individual vision of the real world, and Post-Impressionism, which finally removed the boundary between the real and the imaginary.

The abruptness of the jump made by Russian culture from Realism to *Style Moderne* enables us to date the creation of this style quite precisely to the first half of the

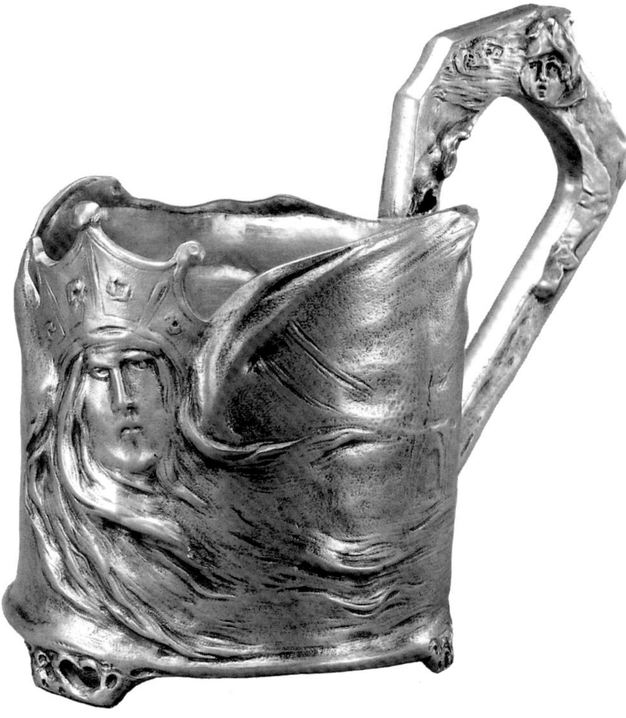

PREVIOUS PAGE: **Mikhail Vrubel'**
465. *The Prophet*
1898
Oil on canvas, 145 × 131
State Tretyakov Gallery

ABOVE: **Anonymous silversmith**
576. Tea-glass holder
Moscow, 1899–1908
Silver, 10.2 × 13.5 × 7
State Historical Museum

1890s. In European art it is extremely difficult to do this, since the boundary between Post-Impressionism and *Art Nouveau* is sometimes hard to detect. The date of the end of Russian *Style Moderne* can also be determined precisely as the middle 1900s, in other words the period of the birth of avant-garde art.

Moreover, the evolution of European styles which prefigured *Art Nouveau* took place through two separate generations of artists. In Russia, on the other hand, owing to the compressed development of artistic processes, the transition from realism to *Style Moderne* was registered in the creative biography of individual artists. Thus, Serov, Somov, Malyavin and many others began their work in the context of Realism, very rapidly passed through the mastery of individual elements of impressionistic art, and found themselves in the embrace of *Style Moderne*. There were other possible approaches to the new style – directly from Critical Realism (Vasnetsov) or from the academic tradition (Vrubel'). The absence of a single stylistic pre-*Moderne* stage of development in Russian art gave rise to the variety of points of departure from which the Russian artists finally came to the new style. This phenomenon was one of the basic features of the formation of *Style Moderne* and the source of its multifariousness and the variety of tendencies found within it.

Style Moderne was not only dependent on various stylistic sources, but also developed in parallel with other movements (Impressionism, Realism). This situation enabled the artist to move freely beyond the confines of the new style, renewing his Impressionist or Realist studies, and then, after overcoming any inner contradictions, to return again to *Moderne*, or, as happened frequently, simply to unite elements of various styles within a single work. Works by Serov, Bilibin, Roerich, Polenova, and Golubkina are particularly significant in this context.

Below left: **Elena Samokish-Sudovskaya**
300. Poster for the journal *Niva* for 1899
St Petersburg, 1898
Lithographic poster, 103 × 70
State Lenin Library

Below: **Vasily Milioti**
228. *Kiss*
1906
Drawing for *Vesy*, 1906 no.9
Mixed media on paper, 32.5 × 24.3
State Tretyakov Gallery

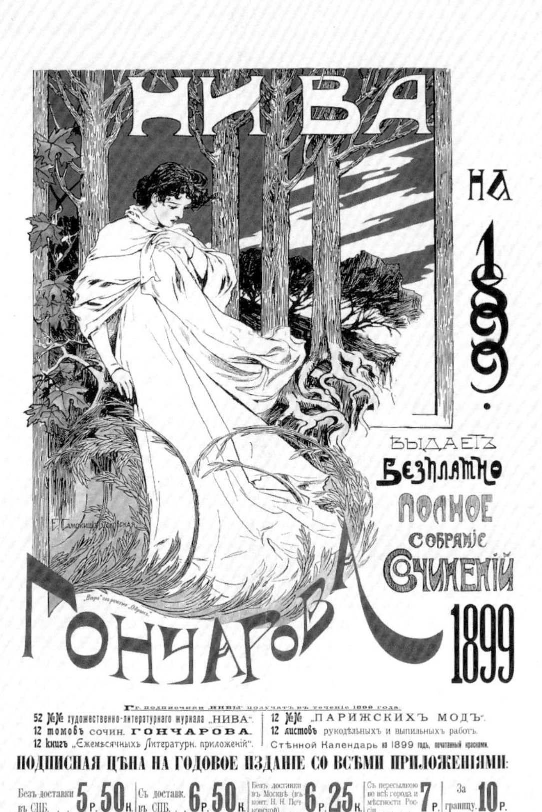

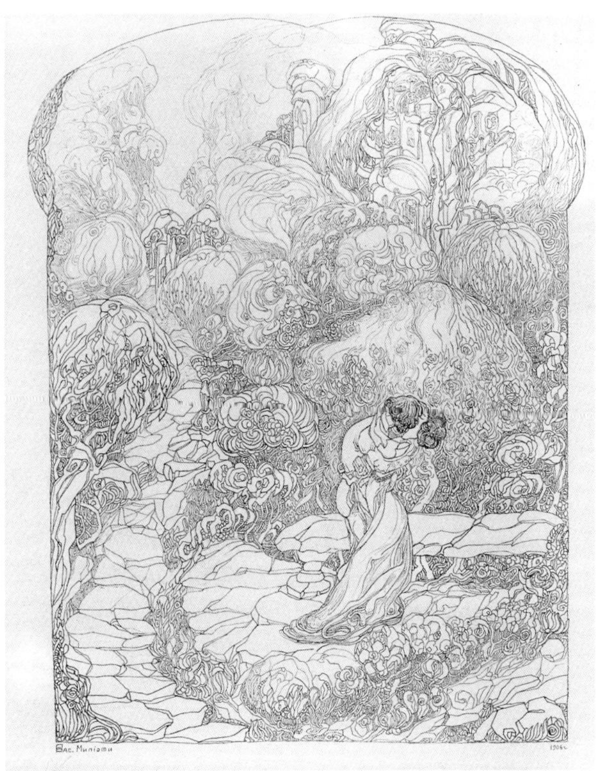

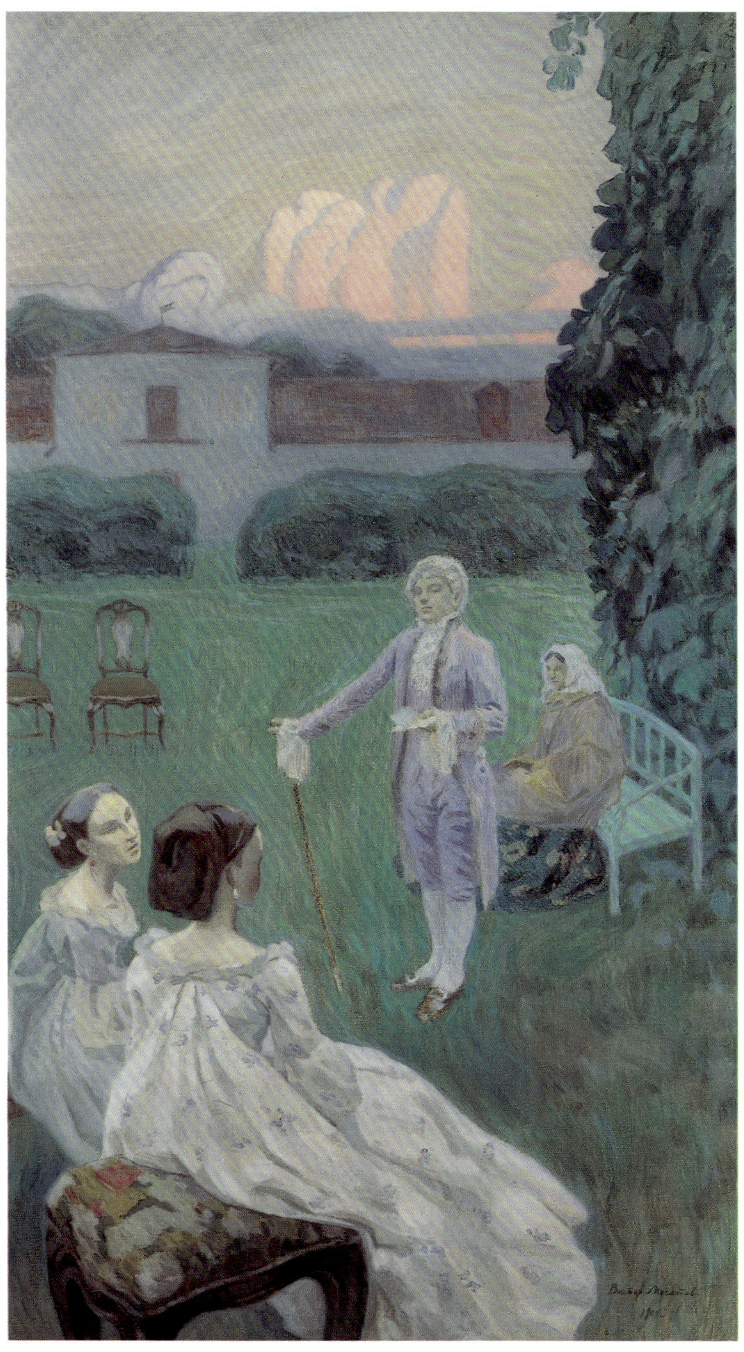

properties of different materials, was embodied in all forms of art, from the architecture of a private house to a music cover or a refined piece of jewellery.

As with any major style of a period with pretensions to universality, the central problem of *Style Moderne* was that of the synthesis of various art forms. The foundation of the new synthesis was architecture, which combined the work of the architect, the sculptor and the decorative artist, and showed its embodiment in the new type of aesthetically designed environment. The most significant works in this context are the Moscow private houses by Shekhtel'.

The striving for synthesis in *Style Moderne* was also manifested in other ways, for example in the artist's desire to go beyond the confines of narrowly professional work and try his hand in other areas of creation, like the Renaissance masters whose universality intrigued the artists of this period. This is what lies behind Vrubel''s experiments in majolica sculpture and fireplace design at the Abramtsevo estate, and his decoration of balalaikas and combs at the country house of Princess Tenisheva at Talashkino.

The idea of synthesis also eroded the traditional boundaries between art forms. Easel painting took on the qualities of decorative panels, the painterly quality of sculptural forms was striking, and architecture developed similarities to natural organisms. Moreover, the synthesising principle even penetrated into the artistic essence of the works, opening up new possibilities in techniques which had apparently been familiar for many years. For example, in the hands of Borisov-Musatov, oil paint could suddenly take on either the nervous fragility of pastel or the tangible texture of Gobelin tapestry. In the sculptures of Konenkov and Golubkina, wood unexpectedly became plastic and flowing, marble became fragile and brittle, and metal viscous and sluggish.

THE SEARCH FOR ARTISTIC SYNTHESIS Despite the clearly expressed pluralism in Russian artistic life at the turn of the century, *Style Moderne* developed as a unified style, including practically all forms of art within its gravitational field. This was particularly remarkable in the context of Russia, since from the beginning of the nineteenth century there had been an active process of erosion of any unified style. For the first time since the period of Classicism, *Style Moderne* retrieved a common basis for all forms of art. The new artistic language based on the interpenetration of soft forms, frequently of organic appearance, on the extreme expressiveness of lines resembling spiders' webs, and on the paradoxical play of the textural

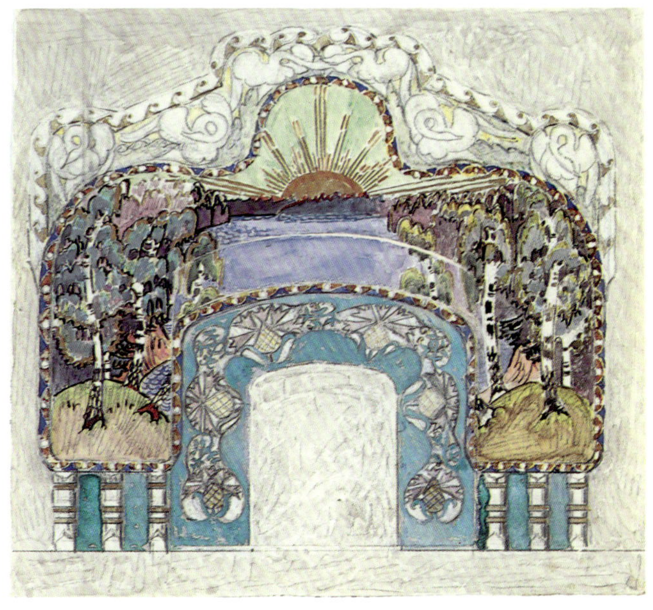

The search for a synthesis not only spread to related creative fields, but also led to the building of bridges between apparently widely different art forms. For example, Blok actively "decorated" his poetic images of this period, using colour characteristics, Skryabin attempted to unite music and colour in his light-and-music installation, and the artists of the *Golubaya Roza (The Blue Rose)* group approached the same synthesis from the opposite direction, constructing the colour ranges of their works according to the laws of musical harmony. It was also no accident that *Style Moderne* in Russia gave a new inspiration to the evolution of such inherently synthetic art forms as theatrical performance and book design, which had previously been virtually overlooked in the general development of art.

OPPOSITE LEFT: **Viktor Borisov-Musatov**
63. *Harmony*
1900
Tempera on canvas, 162 × 90.5
State Tretyakov Gallery

OPPOSITE BELOW: **Mikhail Vrubel'**
468. Design for a fireplace
1899–1900
Mixed media on paper, 27 × 28.2
State Tretyakov Gallery

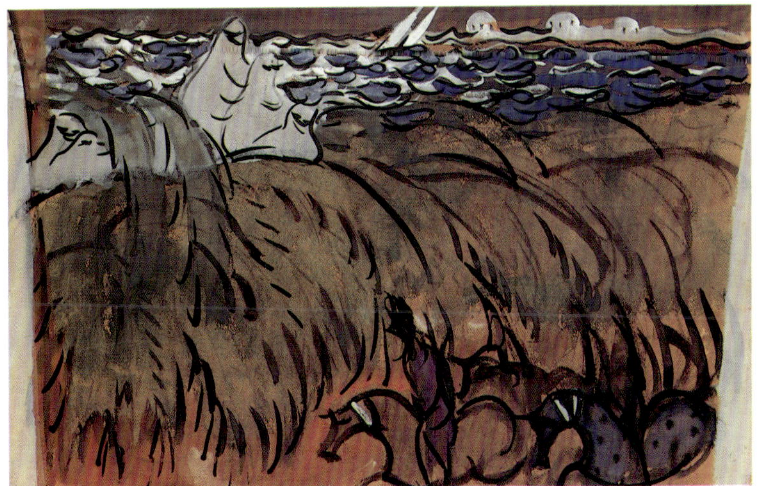

ABOVE: **Anna Golubkina**
134. *"Oh, yes! . . ."*
1913
Tinted wood bust, 47 × 35 × 30
State Tretyakov Gallery

LEFT: **Valentin Serov**
315. *Departure for the Hunt*
1910
Design for a detail of the curtain for the ballet *Sheherazade*, to music by Rimsky-Korsakov
Gouache on paper, 38.5 × 57.5
State Tretyakov Gallery

Another important task for the new style was to search for ways of uniting life and art. This was also responsible for the great interest shown by architects and artists in the smallest details, whether of domestic interiors, issues of magazines, or cycles of paintings. Particularly significant in this respect were the exhibition designs of the *Mir Iskusstva* (*World of Art*) group, where everything was subordinated to the idea of universal beauty, beginning with the posters, which were designed with particular care, and ending with the provision of lighting and music in the gallery, selected in accordance with the works to be exhibited. Moreover, it was no accident that *Style Moderne* gave the impetus to the creation of industrial art as an art form, requiring the articles produced by industry to carry beauty into every home in objects of daily use.

The refined sensation of beauty characteristic of the new style was associated with another, purely Russian, situation. The Utopian urge to fight against ugliness in the world with the aid of art in all its manifestations was particularly symptomatic of Russia, and not only because of the special social role which art was always striving to play in Russian society. In their relation to their art as a method if not of eliminating social antagonism then at least of creating a harmonious living environment, the *Moderne* artists and architects continued the tradition of Russian social art of the previous century.

ST PETERSBURG AND MOSCOW In the process of development of the *Style Moderne* there was a gradual separation of the main artistic centres, each of which had its own clearly expressed aspect both in architecture and in the visual arts. The leading centre was undoubtedly St Petersburg. The characteristics of Petersburg *Moderne* in all its manifestations were conditioned by two factors. The first of these was the life-style of the northern capital, in which the Tsar's court played a most important part. It was the presence of this eminent client that determined the appearance here of the famous workshops of Carl Fabergé, each of whose objects was an extraordinary fusion of the artistic fantasy of the master and the rarest materials – precious metals, decorative enamels, and precious many-coloured stones.

Furthermore, the function of St Petersburg as the capital city also determined the predominance of building types such as apartment houses, banks and company offices in its architecture at this time. The appearance of Petersburg *Moderne* was characterised by its severity, logicality and highly selective use of decorative details. The restrained style of these buildings recalls the architectural work of Scandinavian *Art Nouveau*, spiritually close to the *Style Moderne* of Russia, the Palmyra of the North.

Petersburg *Moderne* was also characterised by its artists' active links with Western Europe, which had

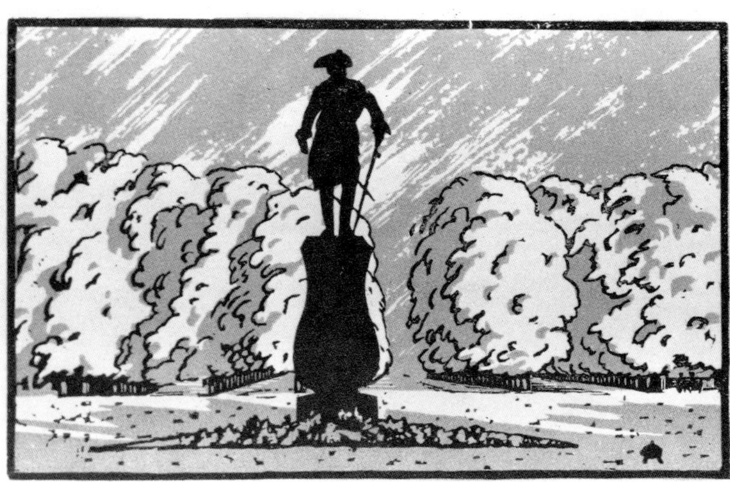

ABOVE: **Anna Ostroumova-Lebedeva**
263. *Monument to Pavel I*
Illustration from *Pavlovsk Landscapes*, 1923
Woodcut, 18.5 × 14
State Lenin Library

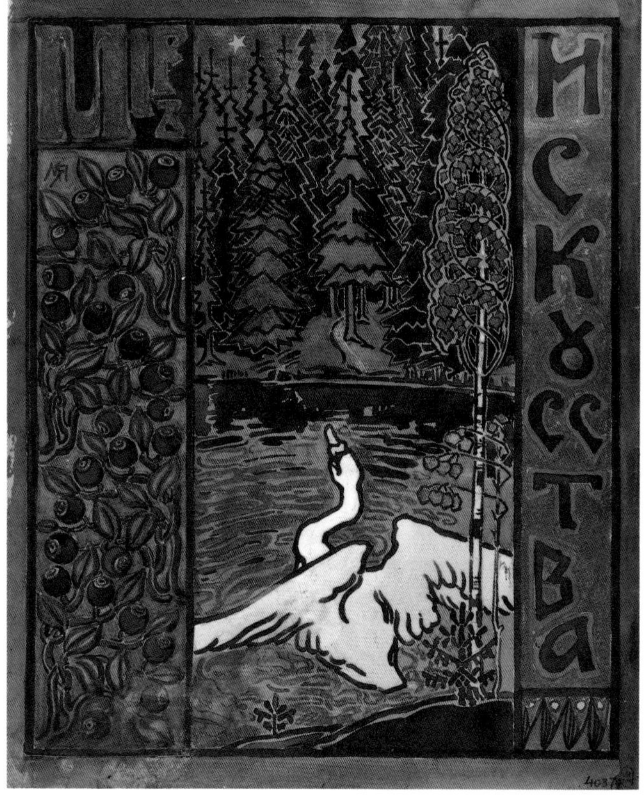

RIGHT: **Mariya Yakunchikova-Weber**
479. Cover design for
Mir Iskusstva
1899
Mixed media on paper,
34.4 × 27.8
State Russian Museum

always been close ever since the time of the foundation of the city. These contacts took various forms, but it was the *Mir Iskusstva* group that made the greatest use of them in its activities. These included the organisation of exhibitions of Western artists in St Petersburg and the use of Western culture as a subject for stylistic treatment in the group's works (e.g., Benois's *Versailles* cycle). The distinctive Europeanism of the *Mir Iskusstva* artists was also revealed in their deep reverence for the authority of Peter the Great, considered as one of the active Westernisers in Russian history. In addition to its clearly expressed Westernism, St Petersburg *Moderne* painting is also characterised by its associations with literature.

At the opposite pole to St Petersburg was the other centre of Russian *Style Moderne*, Slavophile Moscow. The retrospective thinking that underlies the style and its artistic procedures led the Moscow artists to turn to the study of medieval Russian tradition, and this also formed the basis of the so-called National or Neo-Russian style, one of the branches of *Moderne*. The old tradition was used in a variety of ways. Sometimes there was a direct adoption of the style of ancient models (as in the buildings on the Abramtsevo estate), sometimes there was a revival of individual motifs (as in the jewellery workshop of Ovchinnikov). More often the medieval Russian aesthetic penetrated into the very being of Moscow *Moderne*, now embodied in the

decorative multi-coloured majolica on the walls of Moscow private houses, now flaring up violently with a primordial Russian spontaneity of colour in the painted fantasies of Malyavin.

It was this Moscow soil that saw the flowering of the art of Viktor Vasnetsov, one of the founders of the National style, who worked with equal success in easel painting (themes from Russian folklore), monumental art (the wall-paintings for the Cathedral of St Vladimir in Kiev), for the theatre (scenery designs for Rimsky-Korsakov's opera *The Snow-Maiden*) and architecture (the design of the façade for the old building of the

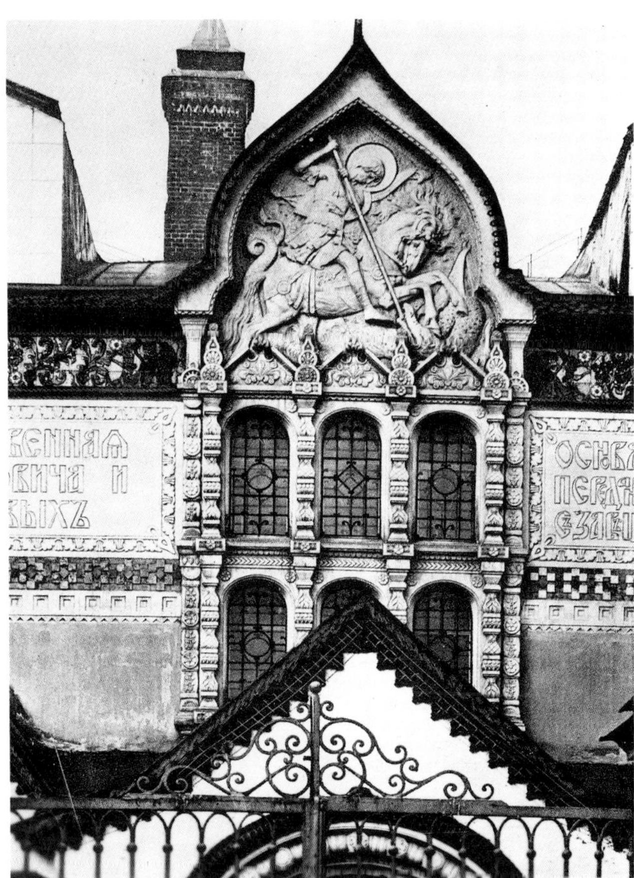

ABOVE: **Viktor Vasnetsov**
Detail of façade of the Tretyakov
Gallery, Moscow
1900–05

LEFT: **Ivan Bilibin**
52. Poster design: *Historical
Exhibition of Works of Art in the
Rooms of the Museum of Baron
Stieglitz*
1904
Mixed media on paper, 63.6 × 46
State Russian Museum

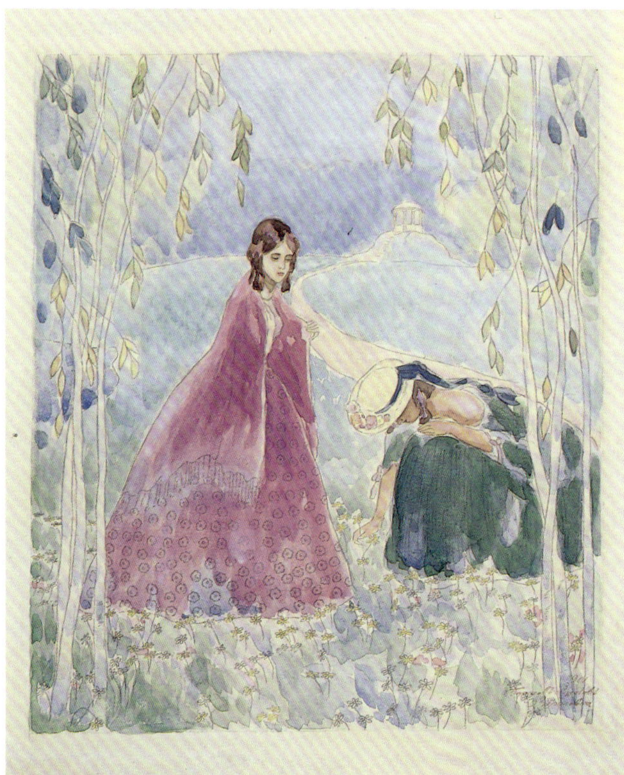

ABOVE: **Viktor Borisov-Musatov**
65. *Zubrilovka*
1901
Mixed media on cardboard,
46.2 × 36.9
State Tretyakov Gallery

BELOW RIGHT: **Vasily Milioti**
227. *Morning*
1905
Mixed media on plywood,
21.8 × 22.2
State Russian Museum

inferior to that of the capital only in its external glitter and luxury. One of its centres was Saratov, the home of Borisov-Musatov, Utkin, Milioti, Sapunov and Sudeikin, a city which saw the growth of Russian Symbolist painting, characterised by an extraordinary musicality of colour structure and delicacy of artistic images, and a city which gave the impetus to the creation of the Russian artistic association with the highest degree of refinement in its paintings, known as *Golubaya Roza (The Blue Rose)*.

PATRONS AND PROMOTERS OF THE NEW ART Fortunately, the period of the creation and development of *Style Moderne* in Russia coincided with the heyday of patronage. Whereas in the 1860s and 1870s Pavel Tretyakov was almost alone in his desire actively to support the Russian Realists, there were now more than enough patrons eager to take the artists of the new style under their protection. In St Petersburg the patrons of the new style were usually members of the hereditary aristocracy, but in Moscow they came from the developing class of the commercial and industrial bourgeoisie. They invested large amounts of money in young artists and in schemes which promised no commercial gain. Examples of this type of support for *Style Moderne* were Princess Mariya Tenisheva's subsidies for the publication of the *Mir Iskusstva* magazine in St Petersburg, Nikolai Ryabushinsky's publication of the magazine *Zolotoe Runo (The Golden Fleece)* in Moscow, Prince Sergei Shcherbatov's organisation of contemporary art exhibitions, Savva Mamontov's creation of a Neo-Russian centre at his Abramtsevo estate near

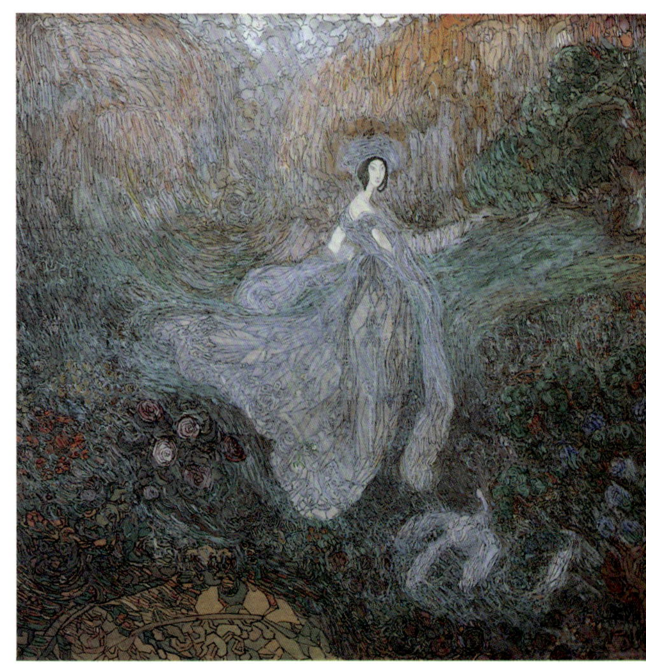

Tretyakov Gallery in Moscow). He also became one of the initiators of the study of folk art, which together with the mastery of the medieval Russian tradition became a characteristic of Moscow *Moderne*. At the Mamontov estate at Abramtsevo Vasnetsov participated in the opening of pottery and joinery workshops, whose main purpose was to revive the traditional crafts of Russia – an enterprise that was not purely ethnographic in nature, but was closely associated with the *Style Moderne*.

The study of the traditions of folk art, with its inherently conventional artistic language, also played its part in the establishment of new methods of painting, thus greatly facilitating the transition of artists such as Bilibin, Polenov and Vasnetsov from the naturalistic vision of Realism to the metaphorical language of *Style Moderne*.

In addition to the two rival capitals, *Style Moderne* had a third base, located in the vast expanse of the Russian provinces. Their artistic life at this time was marked by a particularly high level of activity and was

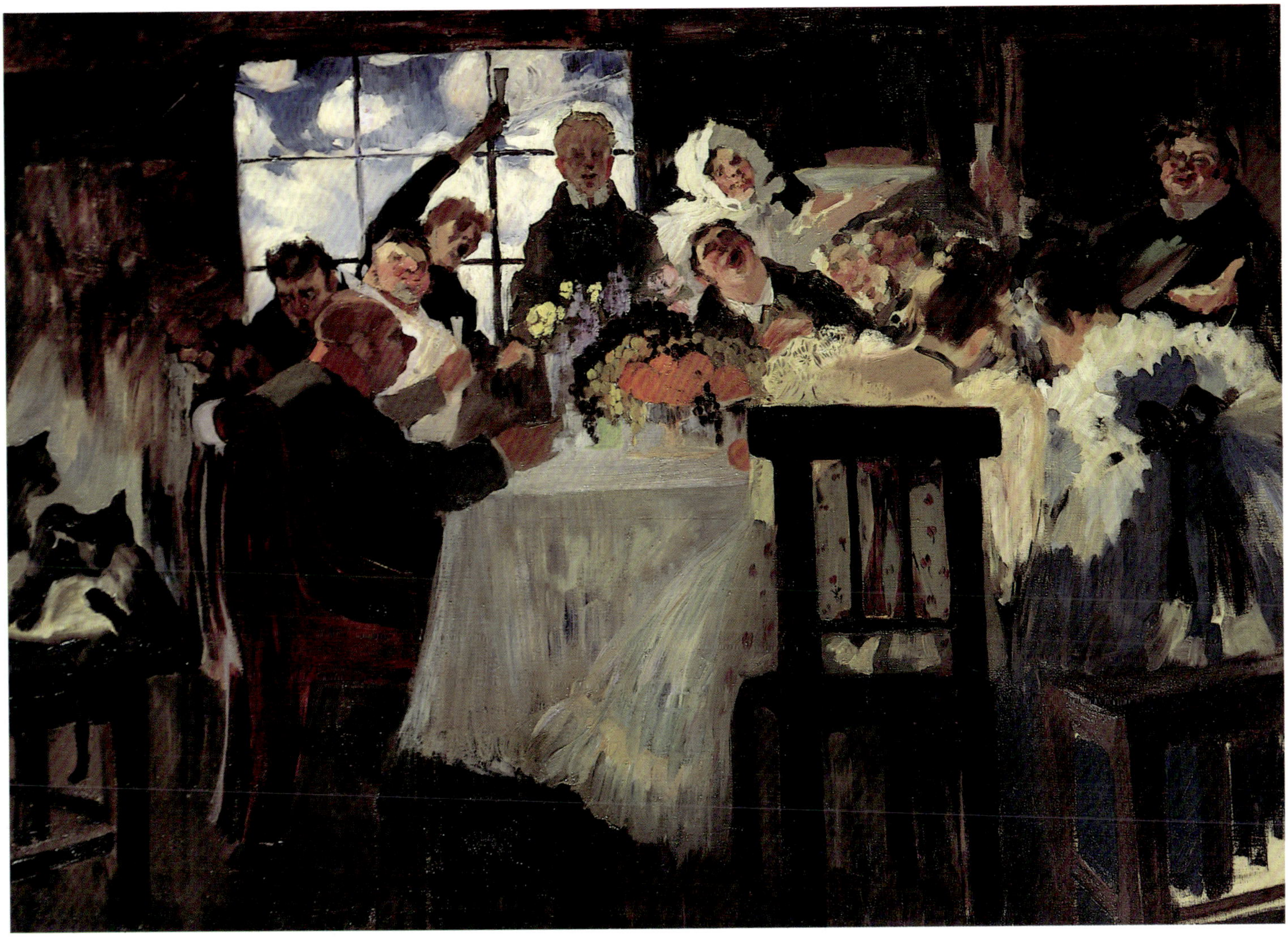

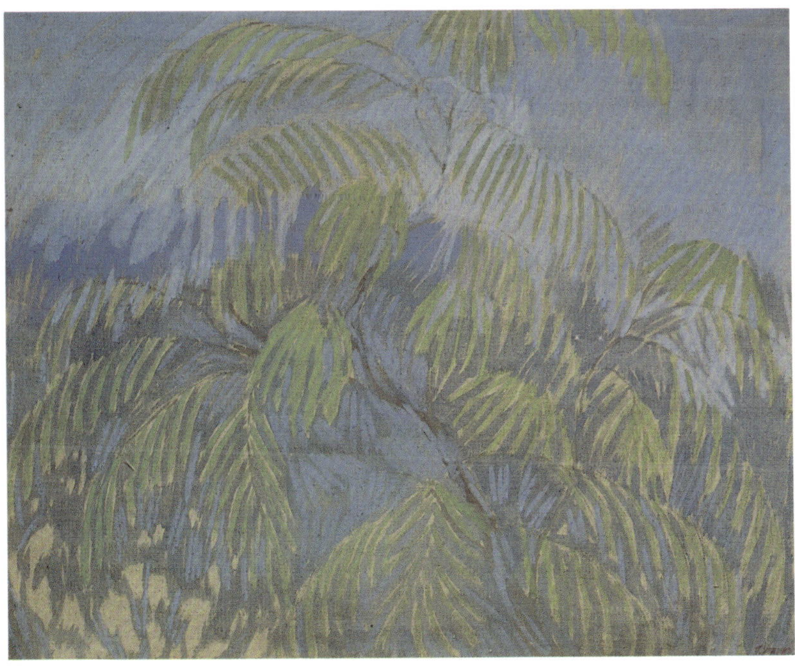

ABOVE: **Nikolai Sapunov**
305. *Mystic Tea-drinking*
1912
Oil on canvas, 93.5 × 128
State Tretyakov Gallery

LEFT: **Petr Utkin**
439. *Mimosa*
N d.
Oil on canvas, 45 × 63
State Saratov Art Museum

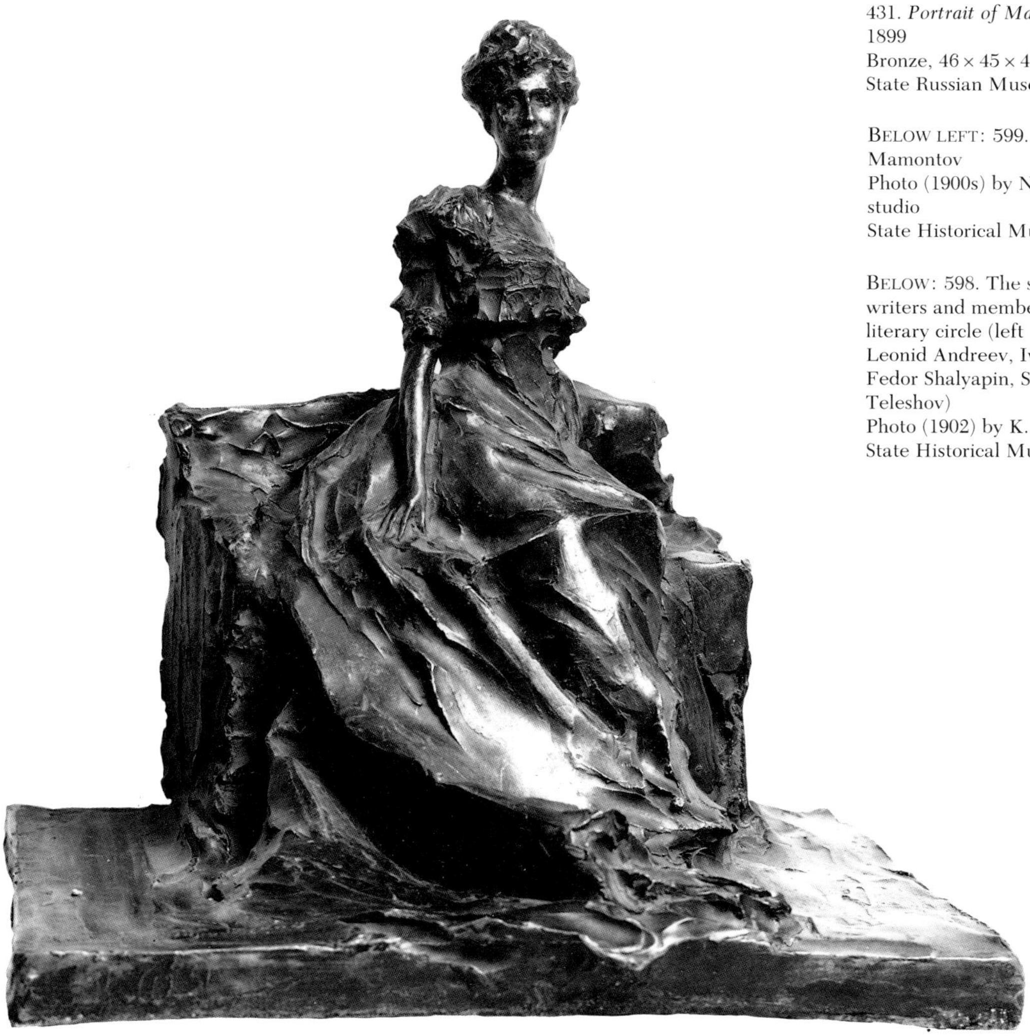

LEFT: **Pavel Trubetskoi**
431. *Portrait of Mariya Tenisheva*
1899
Bronze, 46 × 45 × 44
State Russian Museum

BELOW LEFT: 599. Portrait of Savva
Mamontov
Photo (1900s) by N. Krotkov, "Paola" photo
studio
State Historical Museum

BELOW: 598. The singer Fedor Shalyapin with
writers and members of the "Wednesday"
literary circle (left to right: Maxim Gorky,
Leonid Andreev, Ivan Bunin, Evgeny Chirikov,
Fedor Shalyapin, Stepan Skitalets, Nikolai
Teleshov)
Photo (1902) by K. Fischer Photo Studio
State Historical Museum

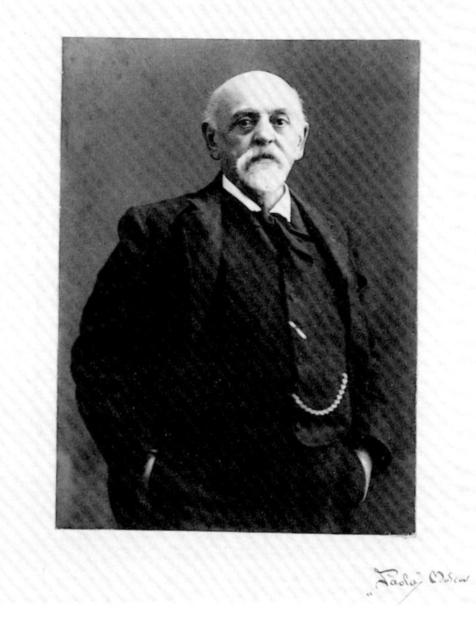

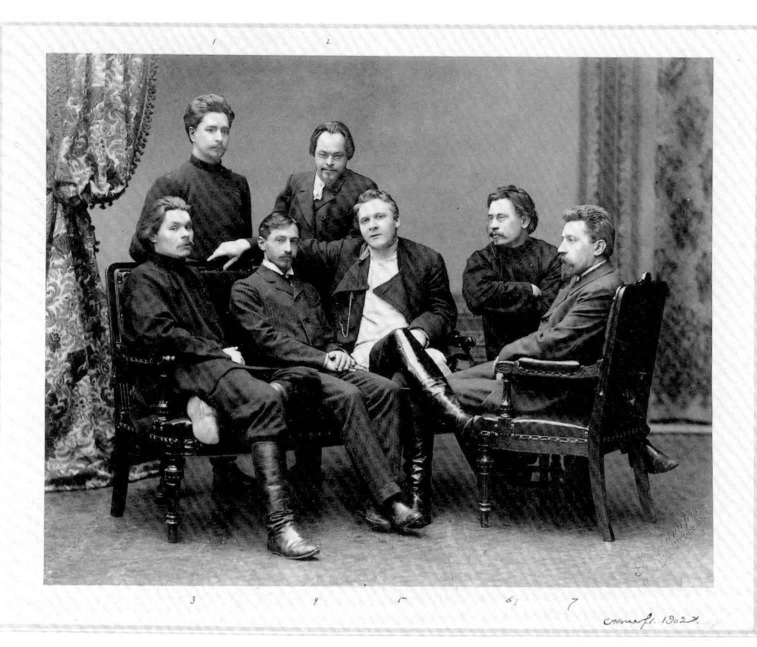

Moscow and his funding of the construction of a pavilion at the Nizhny Novgorod exhibition of 1896 to show the rejected works of Vrubel'. This active support for contemporary culture was a distinctively Russian phenomenon. As a rule, the idea of selfless service to art overcame any purely mercantile interest. Moreover, in addition to patrons, the new style in Russia rapidly attracted talented critics and theoreticians of art such as Aleksandr Benois, Stepan Yaremich, N. Vrangel' and Igor' Grabar'.

The main conduit for the aesthetics of the new style in Russia was the magazine *Mir Iskusstva* (1899–1904). On one hand, it may be placed in the category of similar European publications of the time, such as *La Revue Blanche* in France, *The Studio* in England, *Dekorative Kunst* in Germany, *Kunst* in Denmark; on the other, it had its own purely Russian characteristics. Thus, throughout the period of its publication, *Mir Iskusstva* was distinguished by an unusually high level of artistic design. In addition to the colour illustrations, the publishers normally included facsimile reproductions of the works of contemporary artists. The use of such expensive technology in a periodical publication was a very rare occurrence, but there were explanations for this. First, the founders of the magazine, having set themselves the basic objective of seeking artistic beauty in all its manifestations, strove to turn the publication itself into a work of graphic art. Then, this task was linked with the secondary function of the magazine, namely to educate the artistic taste of the Russian public. In taking on this social and educational role, the publishers of the magazine continued the work of their predecessors among the activists of Critical Realism. The only difference lay in the fact that the dissemination of the truth about life was replaced by passionate propaganda in favour of a heightened beauty.

The *Style Moderne* period in Russia also found its own leader. This was Sergei Diaghilev, the organiser of many exhibitions of the new European and Russian art, manager of *Mir Iskusstva*, a talented critic and historian of Russian culture, and the creator of the famous *Ballets Russes*, which in the spirit of the new style combined the talents of such artists as Benois, Dobuzhinsky and Bakst, the musical gifts of Stravinsky and the virtuoso dancing of Fokine, Nijinsky and Karsavina. Diaghilev realised his lifelong dream of bringing the strength and originality of Russian art to the whole world. It was Diaghilev's programme for a triumphal progress of Russian culture through the Western countries that gave *Style Moderne* a breadth and scale not found in any of the European schools.

The *Moderne* period left its mark not only in architecture and the fine arts, theatre and literature,

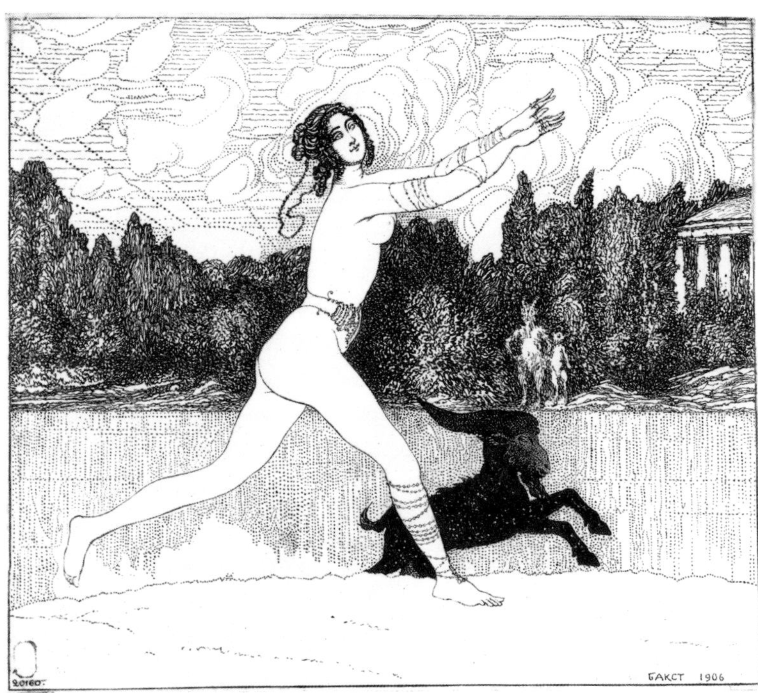

Lev Bakst
32. Antique Vision
1906
Drawing to illustrate A. K. Kondratsev's
Satyress in *Zolotoe Runo*, 1906 no.4
Pen and Indian ink on paper, 16.1 × 17.9
State Russian Museum

music and poetry. Photographs, covered with the patina of antiquity, also remain. It is these that have brought to us the human faces of this period, now seen as resurrected mirages rather than documents of the last century. Here are the outwardly untroubled faces of the Imperial family; here are the singers, writers and artists whose work was bringing Russian culture to Europe and beyond; and here are the Russian people still living in a world that had vanished from the West centuries earlier. All these widely differing characters were united by a single historical fate. Theirs was the lot of living on the boundary of two eras. Nineteenth-century Russia had ceased to exist, and twentieth-century Russia stood on the threshold of its great moral ordeal.

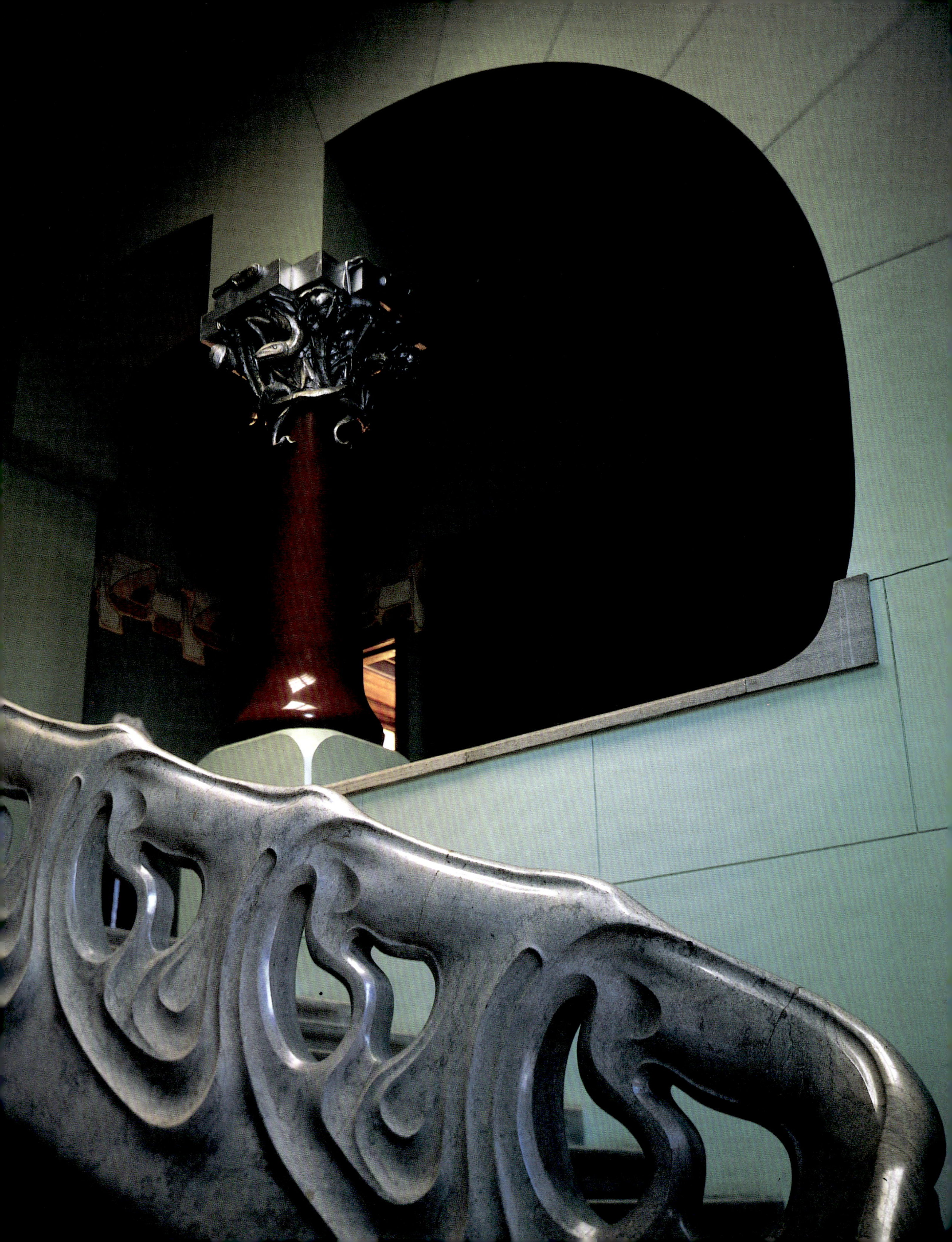

3

FEDOR SHEKHTEL':

Architect to Moscow's "Forgotten Class"

CATHERINE COOKE

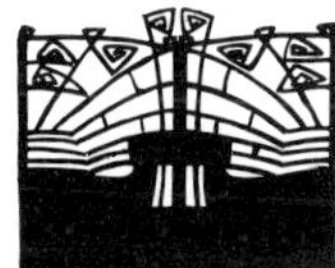

"We knew Fedor Shekhtel' for at least thirty-five years. Son of a cook from Saratov, he came to Moscow in 1875 and enrolled at the College of Painting, Sculpture and Architecture where he became the close friend of my painter brother Nikolai. After his death he transferred his friendship to my other brother, Anton Chekhov, and always considered him his closest friend.

"Shekhtel' often came round to our house during 1877 whilst he was still a young student on the architecture course. We were especially poor at that time, and it only needed my mother to complain at her lack of firewood, for him and his friend Khelius to arrive with a pair of sturdy logs for her tucked under their arms, stealthily removed from another household's log-pile somewhere along the way. Very inventive and ingenious, and endowed by nature with a wonderfully sociable and amiable character, Shekhtel' quickly outpaced his contemporaries. . . . After his design for [public entertainments] at Aleksandr III's Coronation in 1883 his fame grew with every day. [For Moscow's popular theatres] Shekhtel' created dizzying spectacles such as no theatre had known before him . . . astonishing the public with all possible scenic tricks and stunts. . . . In later times he was well known as an architect."[1]

Architecture in turn-of-the century Russia was a rich mix. Many elements can be recognised as parallels with contemporary European work or derivatives of it, but underlying the serious work is a purely Russian situation and set of intentions within which it has to be judged. Fedor Shekhtel's work in particular needs to be seen in this context, for he, more perhaps than any other architect of the period, was attempting a new synthesis of the European with the specifically Russian, for clients of an entirely new type.

Since the mid-nineteenth century architecture in Russia had been a field of vigorous debate. Like the other arts, it had been a medium through which sentiments of political allegiance or aspiration were made, both by officialdom and by those to whom that same officialdom denied the right of direct political debate. The nature of the national heritage, the relevant political message of its elements, the appropriate manner in which such cultural archeology or epistemology might be transmitted or reworked for a new age, were all themes for lively discussion, and contributors ranged from literary figures like Nikolai Gogol' in the 1830s to the French architectural theorist Viollet-le-Duc in the 1870s. Inseparable from these themes was the issue of the appropriate response to the new building materials and technologies of iron, steel, concrete and plate glass.

Though paralleled in Europe, these debates in Russia had a specific sharpness and urgency which derived from the strained and constrained cultural situation. Having been bypassed by the Renaissance and held in tight thrall by a strictly anti-positivist Orthodox church, philosophical enquiry and intellectual speculation were still seen by the Russian establishment essentially as deviant activities. Their exponents had to grasp at nuggets of Western contact and stimulus where they could find them. Closed borders, suspicion of

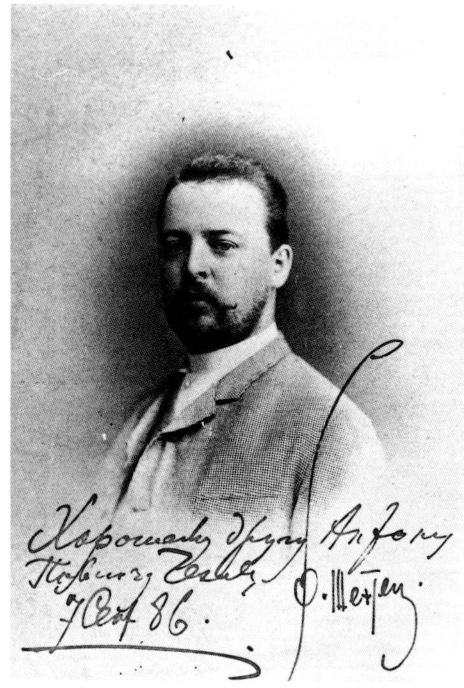

PREVIOUS PAGE: **Fedor Shekhtel'**
Mansion of S. P. Ryabushinsky,
Moscow
Upper part of the main staircase
1900–03

ABOVE: Fedor Shekhtel', 1886.
Photo dedicated to his "great
friend Anton Pavlovich Chekhov".

foreigners, powerful censorship and secret police were
no invention of the twentieth century in Russia, and as
the West advanced through the Industrial Revolution,
distance exacerbated the isolation caused by increasing
technical and cultural backwardness.

Only in the mid-nineteenth century, almost a
century after Europe, did Russia experience the beginnings of modern industrial development. Without bene-
fit of the deep roots in medieval craft- and guild-based
entrepreneurial or financial culture from which capita-
lism grew in Europe, industry created economic and
geographical islands of modernity amidst a sea of feudal
social relationships and commensurately low levels of
urbanisation and literacy. Only in 1861 did the Act of
Emancipation open a door for serfs to obtain freedom
from their masters. The effect of this on development
was not only to launch a new reserve of energetic, self-
improving talent into the market place, but to raise
morale and stimulate forward-looking investment
amongst the liberal intelligentsia and growing middle
classes. As a result, by the turn of the century Russia was
at the beginning of an economic boom, which in the
decade before the First World War gave her the highest
growth rate of any "developed" country in the world.

New fortunes had been made, and millionaire
dynasties already achieved their second or third generation, out of businesses started from nothing by serfs
who had bought their freedom earlier in the century. But
all this was taking place within the unyielding skin of a
body politic ossified in its bureaucratic routines and its
rigid system of social ranks. What remained of land-
based aristocratic fortunes was generally supporting
empty pretensions. New money on a new scale had been
made in the traditional industries of the industrial
revolution everywhere: in railways, banking, engineering, textiles, oil and other forms of mining. It was made
by people with no place in that court-centred social
hierarchy, and more threatening still to the establishment, by people indifferent or actively hostile to it.

From this unpreparedness of Russia's cultural and
intellectual fabric derived two characteristics which run
through the whole of progressive, experimental culture
at the turn of the century, and are typically integral to the
new architecture. The first is a deep uncertainty – to
some exhilarating, to others threatening – as to where
this extraordinary speed of growth and unstable power-
relations can be leading. The second is an extreme
eclecticism in pursuit of elements for building a way
forward. The former is to be expected, and from a
Western viewpoint is intellectually easy enough to
understand. The latter is much more difficult genuinely
to comprehend. Indeed from a Western point of view it
perhaps represents the main impediment to projecting
oneself into the thinking which runs through all branches
of Russian cultural experiment and political programme-
making at this vigorously exploratory time.

Whether in the artistic tastes of the *Mir Iskusstva*
movement, the philosophical systems of the Symbolists
and their mentor Vladimir Solov'ev, in the political
programmes of the new industrial magnates, or in
debates on the role of this new force called "technology"
in the moral and aesthetic structures of the future,
Russians drew ideas from their own and Western
cultures without that constraint of history which sancti-
fies certain ideas or elements of a formal language as
"belonging" to, or inalienable from, a given system of
thought. We see them assembling synthetic systems of
forms and meanings out of elements which elsewhere
are regarded as belonging to wholly separate traditions.
The signs in these languages may sometimes be familiar,
but the semantics are new and locally quite specific, for
their audiences had only scanty knowledge of the origins
of elements which spoke of "abroad", to which we bring
a disproportionate knowledge. Conversely, there are
powerful indigenous references entirely obvious to the
Russian eye which the untutored Westerner misses or
misreads.

Throughout Europe of course, the "new art" of this period was precisely characterised by a local specificity, and a local political or cultural significance, which makes it entirely correct to maintain the many names under which it went, as *Art Nouveau*, *Jugendstil*, *Stile Liberty*, *Modernisme*, *Secession*, National Romanticism and so on. Everywhere it was characteristically an architecture of freethinking, iconoclastic protest and, whether explicitly or not, of a Nietzschean re-embracing of deeply suppressed latent energies in man and nature. In Russia, more perhaps than anywhere, however, the nature of this architecture as the postulation of an alternative, anti-establishment set of morals and values has been submerged, even forgotten (though it has taken long enough, it must be said, for its nature to be recognised with any seriousness or positive scholarship elsewhere). The wideranging free-style variant which developed in Russia was called the *Moderne*. In Moscow particularly, where the new money gathered away from its former oppressors in the capital, the *Moderne* was simultaneously the first and last flowering of a new cultural idea and social class; they had hardly settled into their new mansions and citadels of business before the 1917 Revolution nationalised their assets and left them living in one room amongst their former servants. In the few emigré memoirs of those who fled just in time, they sadly but accurately called themselves "the forgotten class".

ARCHITECTURAL PRINCIPLES OF THE *MODERNE* The *Moderne* had strong indigenous roots in Russian nineteenth-century theory. Ideas (which also emerged in Ruskin, Viollet-le-Duc or Otto Wagner) about the primacy of structure and function in generating a form, and the subordinate role of "art" in giving it "aesthetic refinement" were the basis of theory taught by the St Petersburg Professor Apollinari Krasovsky at the Institute of Civil Engineers' school back in the 1850s. His book *Grazhdanskaya Arkhitektura* (*Civil Architecture*) of 1851 had laid the basis for this Rationalist approach through the whole later nineteenth century. During the next decade, a particular emphasis on the necessity for a modern architecture to be based on "free analysis and our own experience" rather than *a priori* canons,[2] was established as the basis of a particularly Moscow tradition by Mikhail Bykovsky. He restructured the Moscow architecture school around his violently anti-Classical programme, laying new foundations in the teaching of free spatial composition and stylistic independence, and a new attitude in the profession.

Bykovsky's tradition of an architecture rooted in function and convenience laid firm foundations for the free planning and asymmetrical compositions of the Moscow *Moderne*. Indeed the *Moderne* can be seen as

its first flowering. For the first time in a country where urban building had for centuries been regulated by officially authorised standard plans and elevations, massive one-off buildings of a socially new type were required for highly individual clients. But what the Symbolist generation added to the nineteenth-century Rationalist view of architecture was a richer definition of the nature of "function".

The Russian *Moderne* movement generated few theoretical statements. An important rarity therefore was the short book published in 1905 by the St Petersburg architect and teacher Vladimir Apyshkov, *The Rational in the Latest Architecture*. Apyshkov traced the genealogy of the new direction back to Ruskin, Morris and Voysey, and through its Germanic links related it to new work in the "modern" spirit in Austria, France, Belgium and Finland, with scholarly quotation of Krasovsky, Otto Wagner and the contemporary journals. Coming to Russia, he did not hesitate to point out that "many architects' attempts at the *Moderne* deserve little attention, since they contain nothing beyond a blind imitation of the external forms of Western European works." By 1905 the boom in commercial development, middle-class apartment housing and European-style "villas" in both Moscow and St Petersburg offered a ready market for fashionable decorative detailing copied from pattern books, which increased the value of speculative boxes of increasing height. It is to this work that Apyshkov was referring as he continued ruefully, "These designers of the new style have probably never suspected that the new direction is absolutely not a matter of new forms, but of fresh and healthy ideas, from which forms flow as a result."[3]

These "fresh and healthy ideas" had of course to be "reworked in accordance with the spirit of Russia and her general set up of life".[4] In the new "modernist" formulation of Rationalism the building must not merely satisfy practical requirements elegantly. It must also satisfy "the *dukhovnye* requirements" – the requirements of the spirit. It was the function of aesthetic refinement "to produce an artistic expression of the inner purpose of the object". Thus the "radical basis of the new architecture" had become a dual one. It involved "the satisfaction of the material requirements of a civilised human being, and the aspiration to a beauty which will serve as the artistic expression of the idea of the thing being created."[5] "Originality", or literally "the possession of a life of its own" (*samobytnost'*), derived from the design's resolution of these two.

Writing in 1905, after some concessions to democracy had been made by Nikolai II in the formation of a partially representative Parliament, the *Duma*, Apyshkov used the opportunity of a certain political liberation to identify the allegiances of this new architecture with a new outspokenness.

"If we discard certain products of modernism which are too subjectively pursuing only originality for its own sake, and see these as a kind of local sickness within the movement, the latest architecture as a totality, in all its aspirations and its best products, has to be seen by us as a great movement of liberation from outdated and constraining traditions. No single individual to whom art is dear is in a position to resist this movement, whose strength derives not from the subjective views of individual people but from a profound and solid link with our culture, with our technology, and with the best democratic aspirations of our age."[6]

At that date it was not yet so clear that precisely these links would lead to a greater flowering of the *Moderne* in Moscow than in St Petersburg. The modern demand for hygiene which Apyshkov stresses, and the use of glazed facing tiles pioneered to that end in Vienna, were certainly demonstrated at their purest in the elegant little hospital by Roman Mel'tser which he cited as an example of the new style in St Petersburg. In work by his second St Petersburg example, Fedor Lidval', and later by others, there were literary and romantic uses of natural materials like granite, carved as birds and animals, or ruggedly expressive of primal nature, as in Helsinki work of the Finns Sonck and Saarinen which certainly influenced this style, known to Soviet historians as the "Northern" or "Petersburg" *Moderne*.

Of the trio whom Apyshkov names from Moscow, the work of Lev Kekushev and William Walcot (Val'kot) likewise often offered this surface engagement for the mind and senses as well as the free planning and volumetric composition that was such a radical innovation to the city of standard classical boxes. But the truly new synthesis at a deeper level came from Fedor Shekhtel'. He was the most intimately involved with Symbolist artists of the period; he was the closest friend since their student days of Anton Chekhov and himself a prolifically successful theatrical designer before devoting all his energies to architecture. His conceptions of how a building might actually express the type of intention outlined by Apyshkov can be seen as an architectural interpretation of the aesthetic principles developed in those circles. It would do so by integrating all means available to architecture and to its sister arts of painting and sculpture "to put the viewer into that *mood* [Shekhtel''s own italics] which suits the building's purpose". At one level, the aim of this synthesis was the very characteristic Symbolist intention "to beautify our existence, to give delight to our eyes", but underlying this was something more rigorous: literally "to raise the muscle-tone [*povysit' tonus*] of our life".[7]

SHEKHTEL':
THE FIRST
WORKS

When Mikhail Chekhov described Shekhtel' as "the son of a cook" he was referring to his mother. After the death of her husband, an engineer of German Catholic origins in her own family town of Saratov, this woman from a cultured and active provincial family came to Moscow to be domestic manager to the household of close family friends, Pavel and Vera Tretyakov. A little less rich and less *nouveaux* than some of the merchant millionaire class, the Tretyakovs were pioneer collectors of painting from the anti-academic Russian tradition. The Tretyakov Gallery, for which they commissioned a new building in 1901 from the artist Viktor Vasnetsov, was only one of their many contributions to developing a sense of Russian identity in the culture of the city. One of the many equally rich industrialists with whom the Tretyakovs were related by marriage was the railway millionaire Savva Mamontov. When the Shekhtel's arrived in Moscow in 1875, he and his wife had just established an arts and crafts colony on their country estate of Abramtsevo, north of Moscow, on the inspiration of William Morris, to revive actual techniques of peasant crafts as well as researching their aesthetics, and to feed them back into the material culture of contemporary Russia.

For a sixteen-year-old boy of brilliant artistic talent himself, bursting with energy, the opportunities that

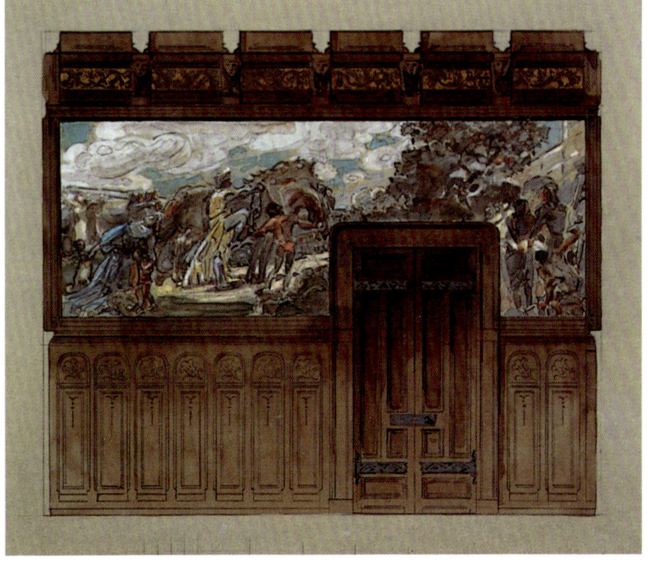

Mikhail Vrubel'
464. *The Departing Knight*
1897
Design for *Midday*, central panel
of the triptych *Times of the Day*

in the mansion of Z. G. Morozova
in Moscow
Mixed media on paper,
28.8 × 32.7
State Tretyakov Gallery

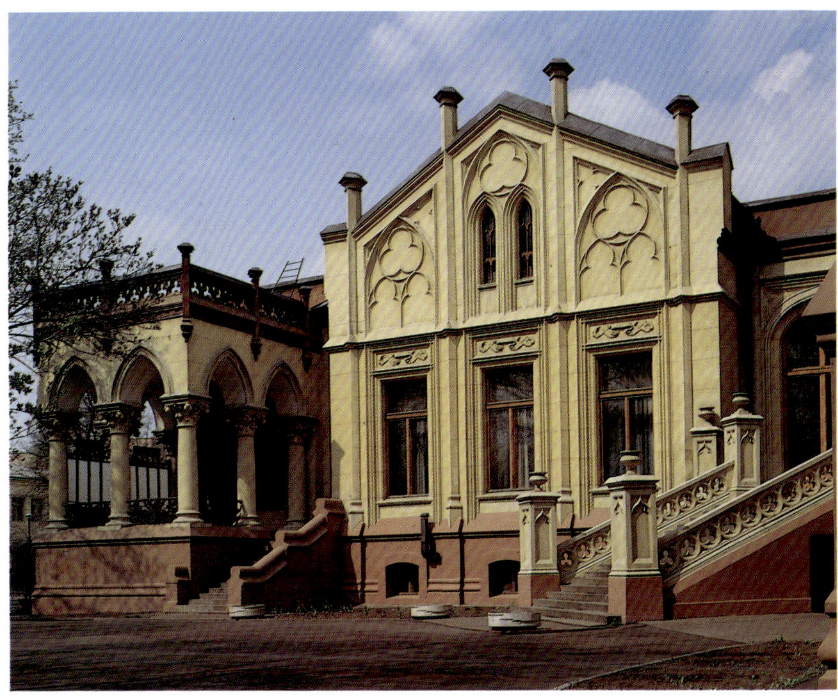

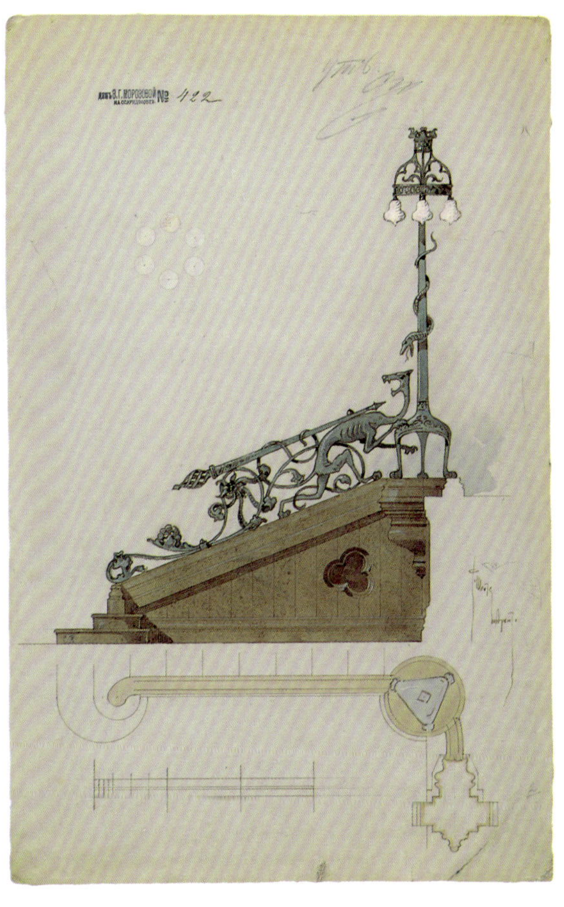

Fedor Shekhtel'
Mansion of Z. G. Morozova
1893–96

ABOVE: Courtyard façade

RIGHT: 326. Design for
balustrade of stair from lobby into
entrance hall (as executed)
Mixed media on coloured
cardboard, 46.3 × 29
A. V. Shchusev State Museum of
Architecture

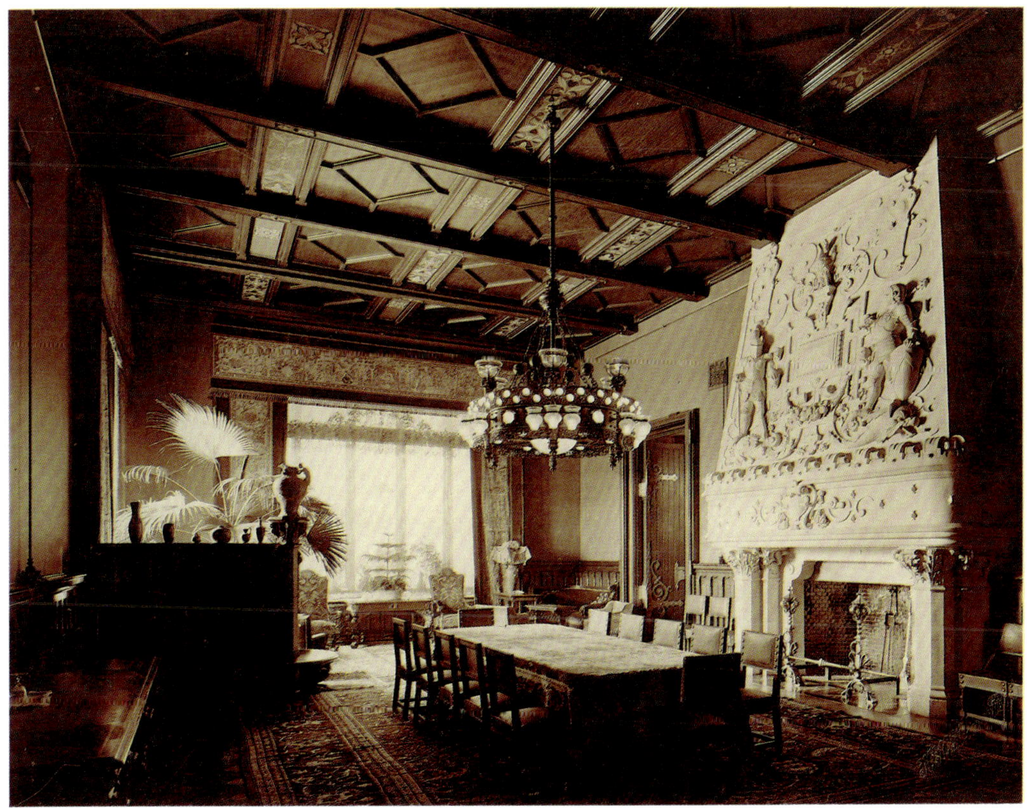

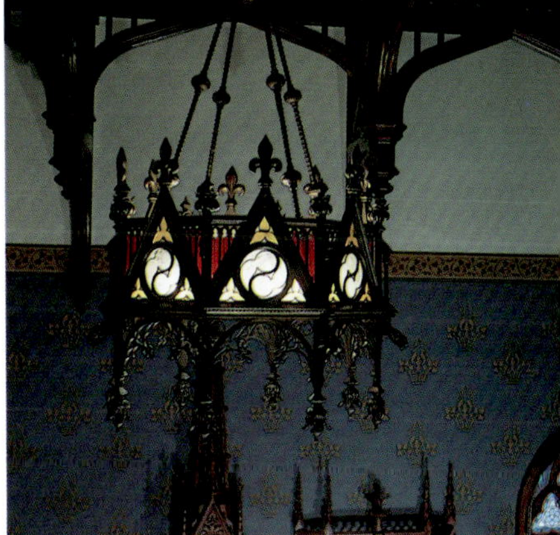

ABOVE: Bronze and stained glass
lamp

LEFT: 334. Dining-room
Photo (1890s)
A. V. Shchusev State Museum of
Architecture

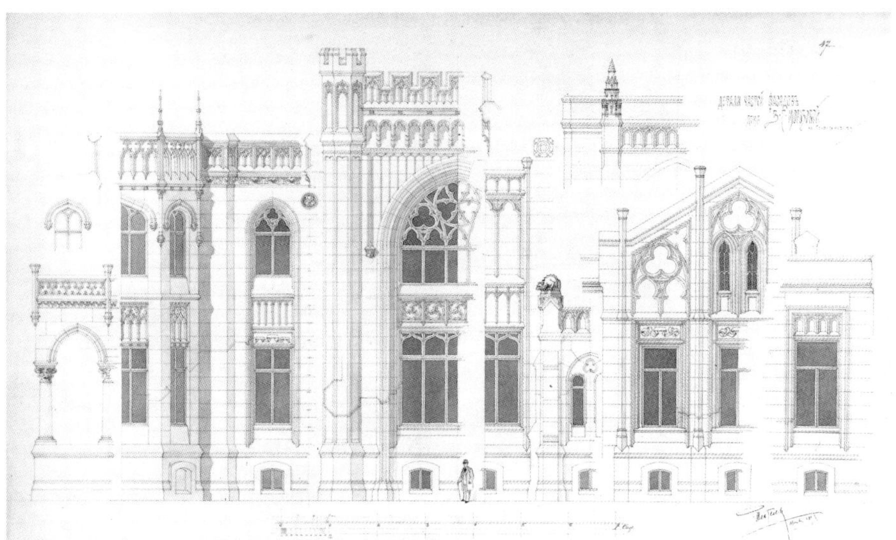

Fedor Shekhtel'
322. Mansion of Z. G. Morozova
Details of elevations
1893
Inks and watercolour on paper, 59.7 × 96.2
A. V. Shchusev State Museum of Architecture

were presented by the real world at this level were plainly greater than those of even the lively Moscow Architecture School. He left it after one year for apprenticeship with another relative by marriage of the Tretyakovs, the architect Aleksandr Kaminsky. This equally cultured and historically knowledgable man, steeped in the thinking of the Moscow profession as reoriented in the previous decade by Bykovsky, was simultaneously Shekhtel''s academic and professional mentor. The career in theatrical design recalled by Mikhail Chekhov ran in parallel with yet another in graphics, where Shekhtel' made an equally brilliant impact under pseudonyms.

By the early 1880s he was already building vast country estates for branches of other industrialist dynasties such as the Von Dervizes and the Morozovs. Stylistically they were freely eclectic, in the Muscovite taste of the time, but in detail and in overall volumetric organisation highly inventive. The turning-point of his career was a central Moscow mansion for the current head of the great Morozov dynasty, Savva Timofeevich Morozov, designed in 1893 and completed in 1898.

The Morozov empire was founded by a serf who bought his freedom early in the century, making his fortune by that commonest route out of serfdom, ribbons and textiles. Typically for the second and third generations of this millionaire class, Savva Morozov was a highly complex personality. As well as directing the vast industrial and financial empire, he was passionate about chemistry, fascinated by Rutherford's experiments and electric lighting techniques, especially in the theatre. A practising member of the Old Believer sect of Orthodoxy and a sternly disciplinarian employer of thousands, he also secretly funded Lenin's revolutionary newspaper *Iskra*, and on occasion later hid revolutionaries from the

police in his Shekhtel' house. So anti-autocratic was he that when Moscow's Governor-General Grand Duke Sergei Aleksandrovich asked to be shown around this new landmark, Morozov refused to be present in person to be patronised by a close relative of the Tsar.

Suitably enough, the house was built and owned in the name of his wife Zinaida, for it was her pretentious tastes, as a *nouvelle riche* peasant girl from his works, which formed what Apyshkov would have called "the idea of the thing being created". Maxim Gorky, whom Morozov also supported, described her as a lady conducting lengthy correspondence with her friends about the significance of her dreams, on deep blue paper, and wrought "with a tension she doesn't always manage to hide" as she "played the role of elegant lady".[8] Before settling on this particular Gothic style, seen then as combining the flexibility of medieval building traditions with the cultural and political liberties of England, Shekhtel' had offered other variants, including a more elaborate Perpendicular and another in "François I Renaissance".

Underneath all that, however, he produced a house which thoroughly exemplified the criterion Apyshkov would later describe as "satisfying the material requirements of a civilised human being". The functionality of the plan was one of its most truly original features in the context of traditionally organised Russian domestic architecture at that date: a family wing provided appropriately for the different tastes and needs of Morozov, his wife and the nursery, while the reception rooms of the other wing provided for formality and entertainment. The free planning responded carefully to the site orientation, and orientation was then used as the basis of its spatial theatricality, dramatically manipulating the varieties of north and south daylight. The relationships to street and garden are as unlike those of the normal Classical box of that time as is the picturesque overall massing, which refers not only to European models but to the functional free planning of indigenous timber palaces in Russia before Peter the Great's Westernisation.

Equally traditional to Russia in Shekhtel''s mind, and one of the lessons he attributed to Viktor Vasnetsov, was the incorporation of painting and sculpture into architecture, which he saw as the means for creating "mood". For this house he commissioned mural paintings of *Morning, Midday* and *Evening*, and stained glass and sculpture on chivalric medieval themes, from the young painter protégé of Savva Mamontov, Mikhail Vrubel'. This was one of Vrubel''s earliest architectural commissions, and several more followed from Shekhtel' himself. This work had a reciprocal effect, in leading Vrubel' ever further from easel painting towards a view of his work as inherently part of the equipment for aesthetically "tuning up", giving "muscle-tone" to architectural spaces. He came to detest the thought of his paintings entering museums. "'A museum is a morgue,' he once told Viktor Zamirailo. He said that he wanted his things to be fitted into a wall in a home, to be fused with it as if painting and wall were one." [9] Vrubel''s inspiration here also derived from mural painting in Russian churches, where he had early experience and acknowledged (as Shekhtel' did) "a powerful influence from Vasnetsov. . . . We are in debt to him for a great deal." [10]

When the drawings for this house were exhibited at the Second Congress of Russian Architects in Petersburg in 1895, with other Moscow work by Kekushev and Ivanov-Shits, they attracted much attention for their verve and originality, but were still seen as an exercise in the historicist Eclecticism of the late nineteenth century. Only later was the house seen, as now, to be the seminal work of a new direction, both for the architect and as a house-type for this new class of client.

By the end of the decade Shekhtel''s business premises for these leading industrialists had reached a similar stage of development. After doing a house for the head of the Kuznetsov glass and porcelain empire, he designed their central Moscow headquarters and showrooms on a prominent corner site in 1898. Here too eclectic detailing still covered a pioneering frame and bold fenestration. Like the Morozov house, this was a dramatic statement for its date, but Shekhtel''s architectural language was rapidly moving towards greater purity.

The influences in this process were probably two. The first was his own awareness of developments abroad. The young architect Il'ya Bondarenko, who worked in his office at this time, recorded that Shekhtel'

"went abroad every year, read a great deal, spoke languages, and worked persistently", as well as running an exceptionally civilised office in which "a hot luncheon was formally served by a footman." "The very comfortable drawing tables were to Shekhtel's own design" and "every detail of the projects was designed down to the smallest fitting". "He had a very good library from which he drew motifs for his architecture. This library was an important stimulus to us all in our work and we used it constantly." [11] It seems reasonable to assume that the latest foreign architectural books and journals joined this library regularly, and Brussels and Paris would surely have been on Shekhtel''s itinerary abroad, as well as Germany and Vienna. His young assistant Ivan Fomin had spent about a year in Paris during 1898–99, and the *Exposition Universelle* of 1900 gave many in their circle the excuse to return there. From about 1899, in jobs like the Arshinov Company building of that year, or the house conversion for the vodka magnate Smirnov (1901), elements of recognisably European inspiration start appearing in Shekhtel''s work in characteristically empirical syntheses with more traditional ones.

The second purifying influence on Shekhtel''s style seems to have been Viktor Vasnetsov, to whom Shekhtel' later referred as "my teacher". [12] This elderly painter was a key member of the Abramtsevo circle, which was another integral part of Shekhtel''s own life. Though

Fedor Shekhtel'
Balcony on house of P. P. Smirnov, Moscow
1901

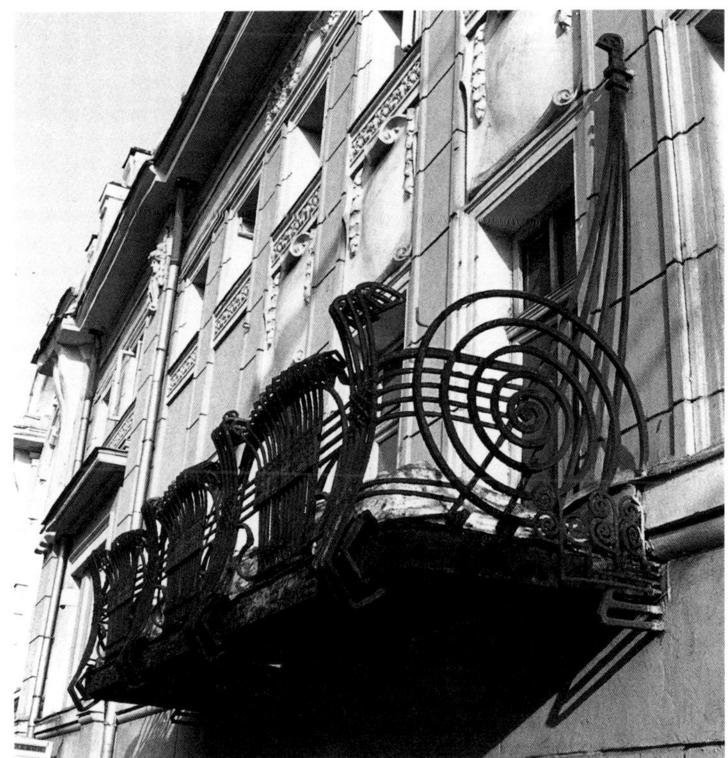

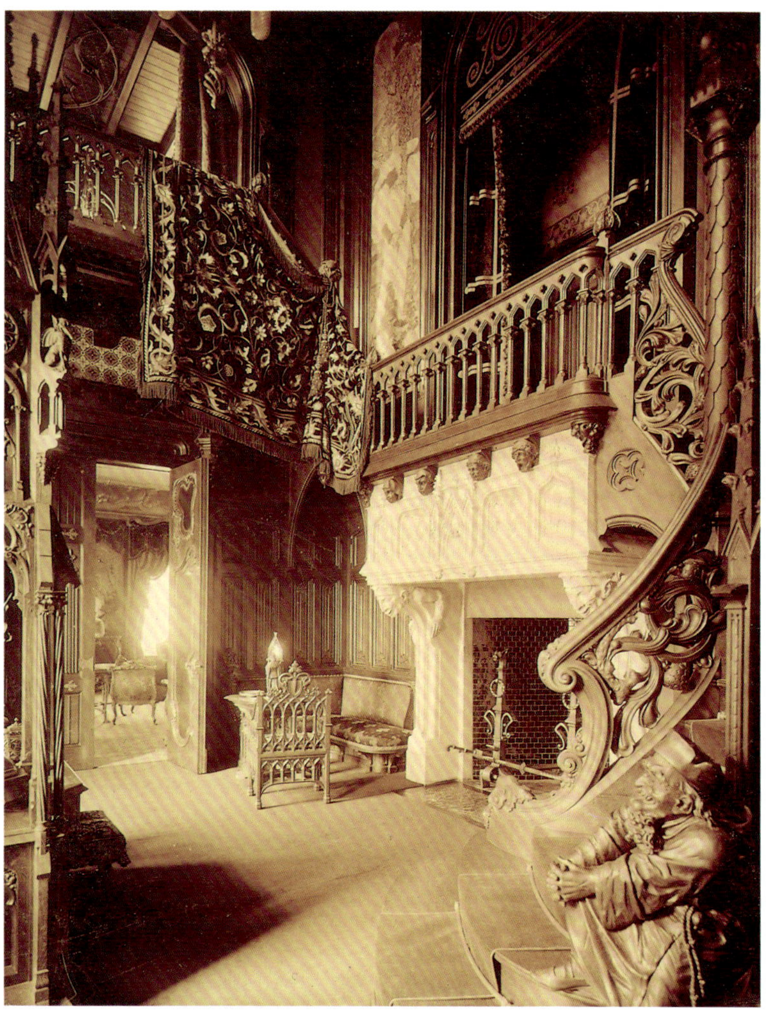

Fedor Shekhtel'
337. Mansion of A. V. Morozov
Gothic Study
Photo (1890s)
A. V. Shchusev State Museum of
Architecture

Shekhtel' himself plainly preferred the pace of the city to rural seclusion and handicrafts, his commissions to the Abramtsevo habitué Vrubel' were the start of a constant involvement by these various artists with their diverse métiers in his own building projects.

Vasnetsov's little white chapel at Abramtsevo, done with Vasily Polenov in 1881 (p.18), had been a pioneering demonstration of the constructive nature of old Russian masonry architecture, in particular here the traditions of Novgorod, when the Russian Revivalists were in general focused entirely on the traditions and decorations of timber building. In his own studio-house in central Moscow of 1892 Vasnetsov brought these two together. Stripped of all decoration, the design was a dramatic demonstration in its time, akin to that of Philip Webb, say, in the Red House for Morris, of how constructive honesty and the functional assembly of volumes could produce a modern house within the native historical tradition and hope thereby to transmit its cultural and spiritual values.

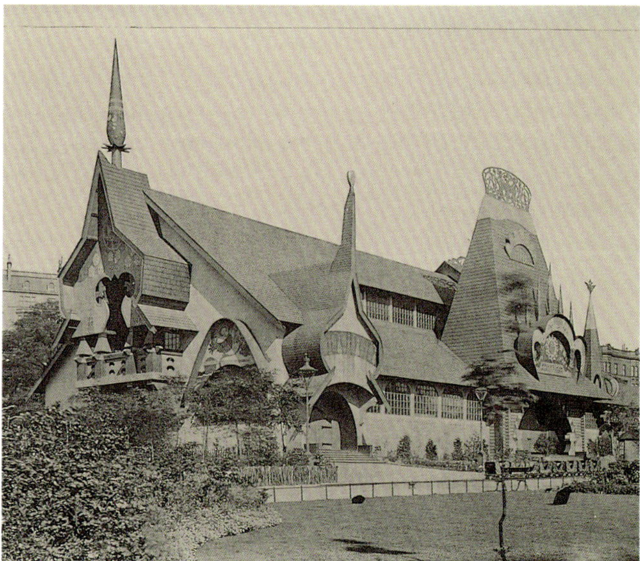

RUSSO-BRITISH EXHIBITIONS The first two years of the century were a time of growing internal unrest in Russia, but Shekhtel' was at the height of his powers and inventiveness, with a vast amount of prestigious work on his drawing-board. By December 1902 his two masterpieces of the *Moderne* mansion were completed, and he had won acclaim for his performance on Russia's behalf on the international stage. Although he had spent only one year at architecture school and had acquired only the minimum certification of "the right to execute buildings in accordance with civil regulations" when he built Morozov's house, he was now given the title of Academician of Architecture by the august Imperial sanctum in St Petersburg, whose line of thought he so totally rejected. Strangely enough, but appropriately here, it was largely a work executed in Britain which brought him this official recognition.

Big trade fairs were a regular feature of Russia's growing but still traditionally organised internal commerce, and like many architects Shekhtel' had contributed pavilions for them. For the 1900 *Exposition Universelle* in Paris, he did the pavilion of the vast Kharitonenko Sugar Company, for whose director he had already created some Gothic domestic interiors back in the 1880s (Kharitonenko's house is now the British Embassy). For the Glasgow International Exhibition of 1901, held in Kelvingrove Park, the Russian Government decided to spend more than ever before on such an international advertisement for their export trade, and the group of four separate pavilions was commissioned from Shekhtel'.

Erected in a cluster that became known as "the Russian street", the form of each pavilion derived from a traditional building type associated with its display

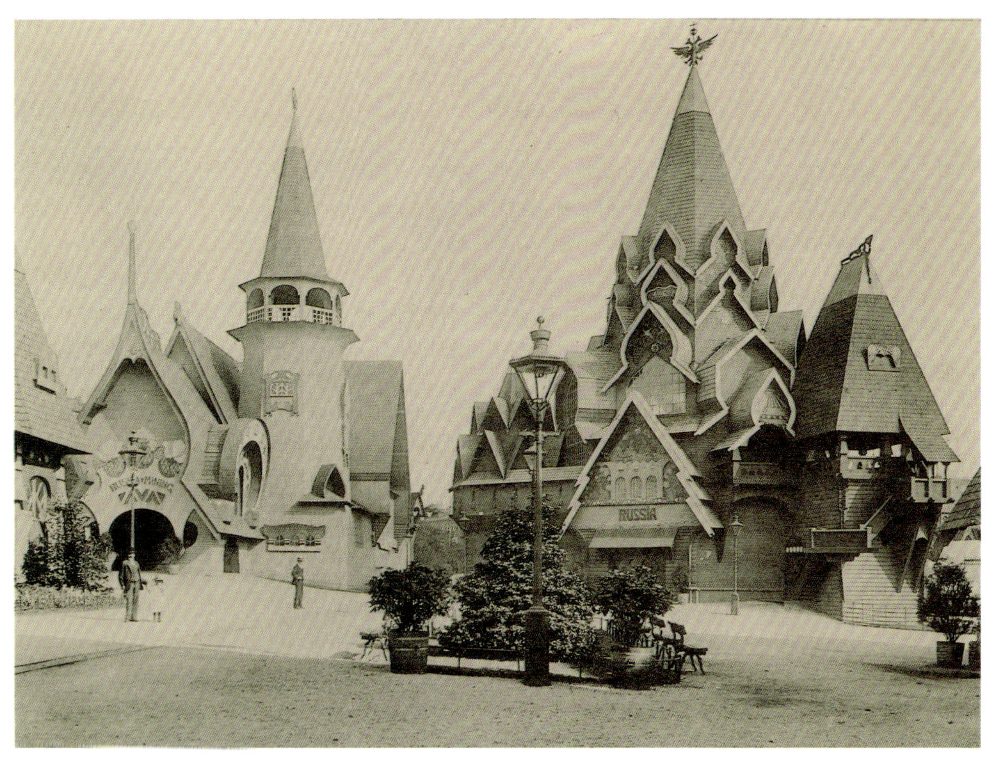

Fedor Shekhtel'
Russian Pavilions at the Glasgow International
Exhibition
1901

OPPOSITE: 351. Agriculture Pavilion
Phototype from photograph, 20 × 30
A. V. Shchusev State Museum of Architecture

RIGHT: 350. Mining and Central Pavilions
Phototype from photograph, 20 × 30
A. V. Shchusev State Museum of Architecture

BELOW LEFT: 343. Central Pavilion: details of
elevation, section and plan and of finials
1901
Mixed media on coloured paper, 71 × 103.5
A. V. Shchusev State Museum of Architecture

BELOW RIGHT: 342. Central Pavilion: plan and
section with constructional details
1901
Pencil on coloured paper, 106.5 × 70
A. V. Shchusev State Museum of Architecture

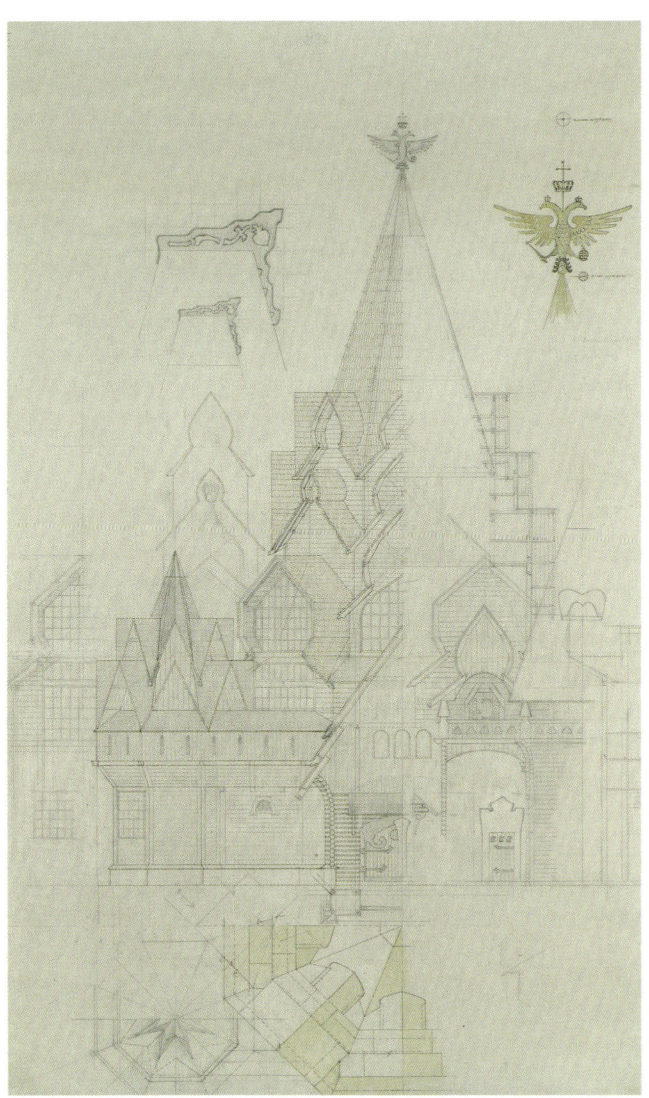

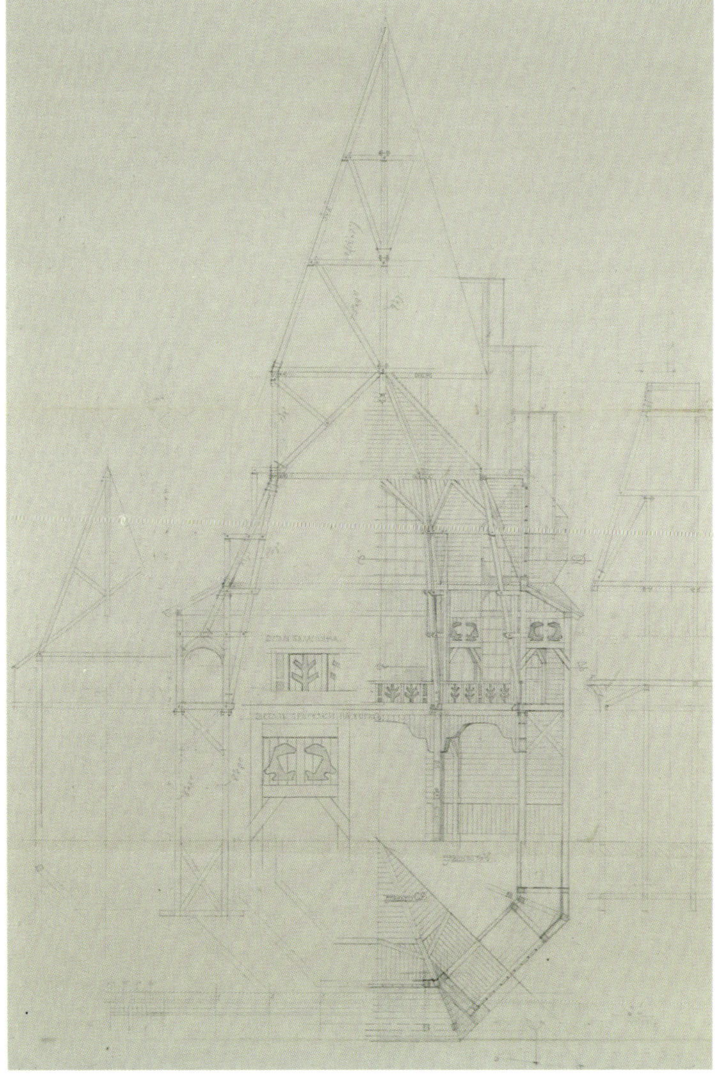

function. Thus a North Russian timber church provided the model for the Central ceremonial pavilion, whence the others would be blessed at the opening; this displayed carpets and precious stones. A long low barn was the starting point for the Agricultural Products pavilion, and a more cubic shed for displaying the wares of Russia's Forestry Industry. Shekhtel' himself recognised this Glasgow project as seminal in his development, calling it "my motto" (*moi deviz*),[13] and he recorded part of the ceremonial pavilion as the image on his personal bookplate (p.170). The buildings were constructed on site by Russian carpenters, coloured in bright colour-washes, and students from the Stroganov Design School came over to execute the richly polychromatic decorative panels of stylised fruit, plant and animal forms in the manner established by Elena Polenova at Abramtsevo. Art critics up from London for journals like *The Studio* and *The Architectural Review* varied in their reactions from the polite to the horrified, but the popular press in Glasgow was captivated. The Russian authorities considered them brilliantly successful as the vehicle for their export campaign.

To Shekhtel' their significance certainly lay in the new synthesis he had found between the structural forms and aesthetic traditions of Russian building and the line, surface and tensely exaggerated hyper-real proportions characteristic of the International "new

Fedor Shekhtel'
349. Cover of album *The Buildings of Russian Section of International Exhibition in Glasgow. Archit: F. Schechtel in Moscow*, Moscow, 1901
A. V. Shchusev State Museum of Architecture

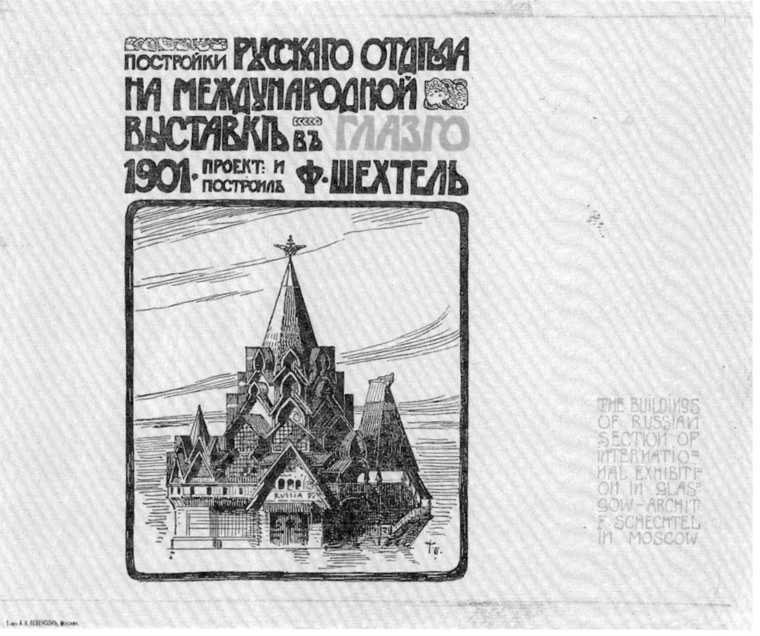

art". His reuse of these Glasgow forms for the reconstruction of an existing building of masonry, Mamontov's Northern (now Yaroslavl') Railway Station in Moscow, the next year had more to do with theatre – even with advertising – than with architecture. But the ceramic work by Abramtsevo artists and the paintings by Konstantin Korovin made it another integrated example of the creation of "mood" – this time as an unforgettable "gateway to the North" for customers of a commercial railway.

An interesting question hangs over Shekhtel''s participation in Glasgow. Did he meet Charles Rennie Mackintosh on any of his visits? No records on either side have yet emerged to indicate that he did. However, in December of the next year, 1902, an exhibition opened in Moscow entitled *Architecture and Design of the New Style*, organised from Shekhtel''s office, which included a room of Mackintosh furniture. The Russian press reported that the Mackintoshes were "too fearful of the Russian winter"[14] to visit Moscow in person, but Joseph Maria Olbrich came from Darmstadt to install the display of his work in person.

The main organiser was Ivan Fomin, a thirty-year-old in Shekhtel''s office of comparable energy and talent to himself. Fomin was currently principal designer on a conversion job to create a purpose-built home for Stanislavsky's Moscow Arts Theatre company, whose geometrical entrance foyer and cool décor contain some of the most Mackintosh-like work to come from Shekhtel''s office. The company was still enjoying the acclaim brought by their production of Anton Chekhov's *The Seagull*, which had flopped in St Petersburg, and Savva Morozov was funding the project to produce a theatre of the highest convenience and the least visual distraction to theatrical communication. Chekhov's *Seagull* became its trademark, and is still used today in the form designed by Shekhtel'.

The Russian contributors to the *New Style* exhibition included Shekhtel' himself, with architectural drawings, furniture and light fittings from his most recent domestic project, the Derozhinskaya house. Fomin showed extensively, in furniture installations, ceramic stoves and individual fittings that fluently brought together elements of leading European work and of Moscow and Abramtsevo circles around him. Much of the furniture by Walcot and others was specially made, as part of their sponsorship, by the workshops of the Muir and Mirrielees Department Store, and Walcot's coloured elevational drawing of the Hotel Metropol attracted much attention. Indeed this may have been a presentation drawing done specially for this exhibition. Other contributors in the eighteen rooms included Korovin, the Abramtsevo workshops, students of the Stroganov

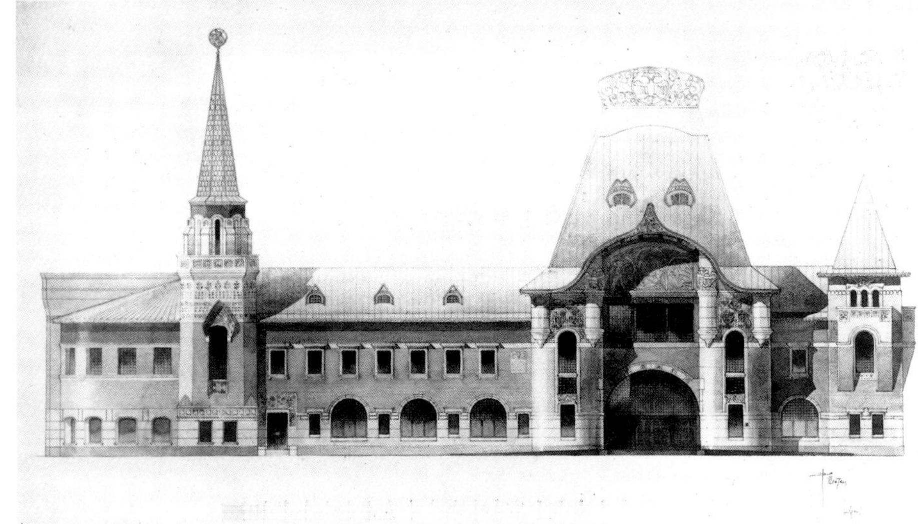

Fedor Shekhtel'
Yaroslavl' Station, Moscow
1902–03

LEFT: 354. Elevation
Photograph (1900s) of architect's
drawing
A. V. Shchusev State Museum of
Architecture

BELOW: Entrance hall

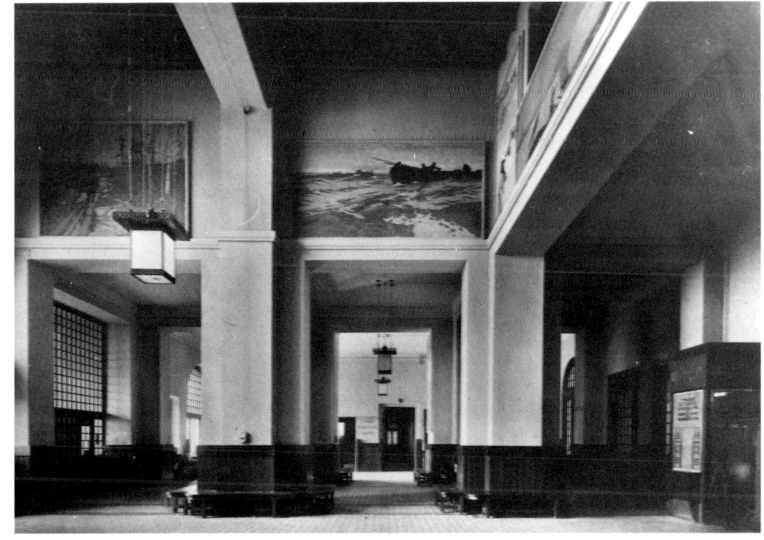

Design School, even Vrubel', with a carpet design, as well as numerous lesser known Russians and some minor foreigners. In total the catalogue listed names and addresses of 34 designers and 28 manufacturers, which indicates the show's underlying intention. Russian and foreign works were integrated into single displays, but the aim was not to demonstrate that the Russians were up with the international masters. The aim was a local propagandist one, of showing Moscow's middle-class consumers that there could be "a 'Russian style' which is appropriate to the requirements of modern life and contemporary technology".[15] High attendances indicated that the synthesis they were seeking was well calculated.

Critics' reactions to the European work are interesting for reflecting a sense of its deficiency. Cognoscenti like Diaghilev, who came from St Petersburg to report it for *Mir Iskusstva*, reacted with predictable recognition and receptiveness. To the unprepared Russian eye, however, it was as alien as the "barbaric" Shekhtel' pavilions had been in Britain.[16] The critic in one influential architecture and design magazine typically found Olbrich's dining room "flabby . . . as if for a special race of small, affectionate and spineless human beings." Margaret Mackintosh's drawings were "a page from a sexual psycho-pathology". He "could not understand for whom the white drawing room by Charles and Margaret Mackintosh was created. It reminds one of an operating theatre, or a Moscow hairdressers. Staying in it was very boring and wearisome: everyone fled from it, from those dreadful straight lines, the lifelessness. . . . But I do not believe it is created without a precise symbolism: the white colour presumably speaks of desires that are out of control."[17] The energetic young Fomin and his friends,

at least, had a different view of women from those described by this critic as "cut off from the Earth and its delights . . . whom Mrs Mackintosh celebrates." An advertisement in the exhibition catalogue announced "Building Courses for Women" being run by Fomin from Shekhtel''s office. The other teachers were engineers in seven different specialist fields, a Doctor of Natural Sciences, and one fellow architect, William Walcot.[18]

BELOW: **William Walcot (Val'kot)**
472. Drawing for main elevation of the Hotel
Metropol, Moscow (as executed)
1902
Indian ink and watercolour on paper,
56 × 135.5
A. V. Shchusev State Museum of Architecture

OPPOSITE: **Fedor Shekhtel'**
Yaroslavl' Station, Moscow
1902–03

ABOVE: Detail of façade

BELOW: 356. General view of station
Tinted photographic postcard, 9 × 13.7
A. V. Shchusev State Museum of Architecture

**SHEKHTEL':
THE MATURE
SYNTHESIS**

Moscow had plainly found the message of Olbrich and Mackintosh alien, even disappointingly superficial. The disappointment was certainly genuine, for behind any serious artistic manifestation in Russia at that time, especially in the circles involved here, there lay deep philosophical questioning and serious attempts to formulate some interpretations relevant to their present cultural position and possible futures. This was an eclectic process, as I have observed, drawing simultaneously on everything from the latest technologies to paganism, but it was never purely sensual. Reactions to Mackintosh in particular may have been expressed with a certain hyperbole, but I think they accurately perceived a genuine difference of content from the indigenous work, in which Shekhtel' set the standards.

It was not only in social origins that his clients had no connection with the rank structure of official Russia; their spiritual roots and value systems lay precisely in that "old Russia" which urban Slavophiles of the previous century had had to re-explore like a closed continent. Many continued, like Savva Morozov, to be practising members of the strict Old Believer sect.

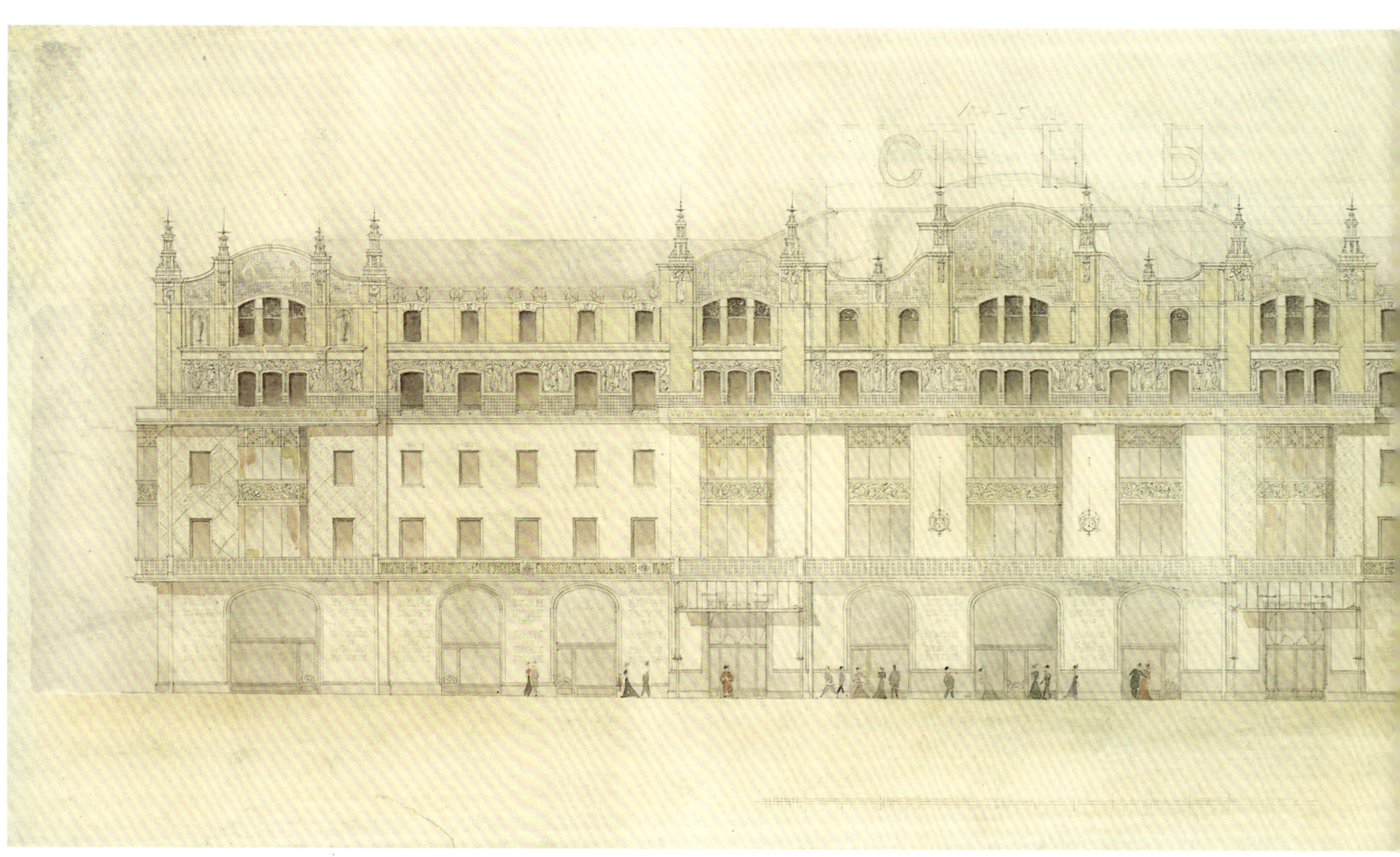

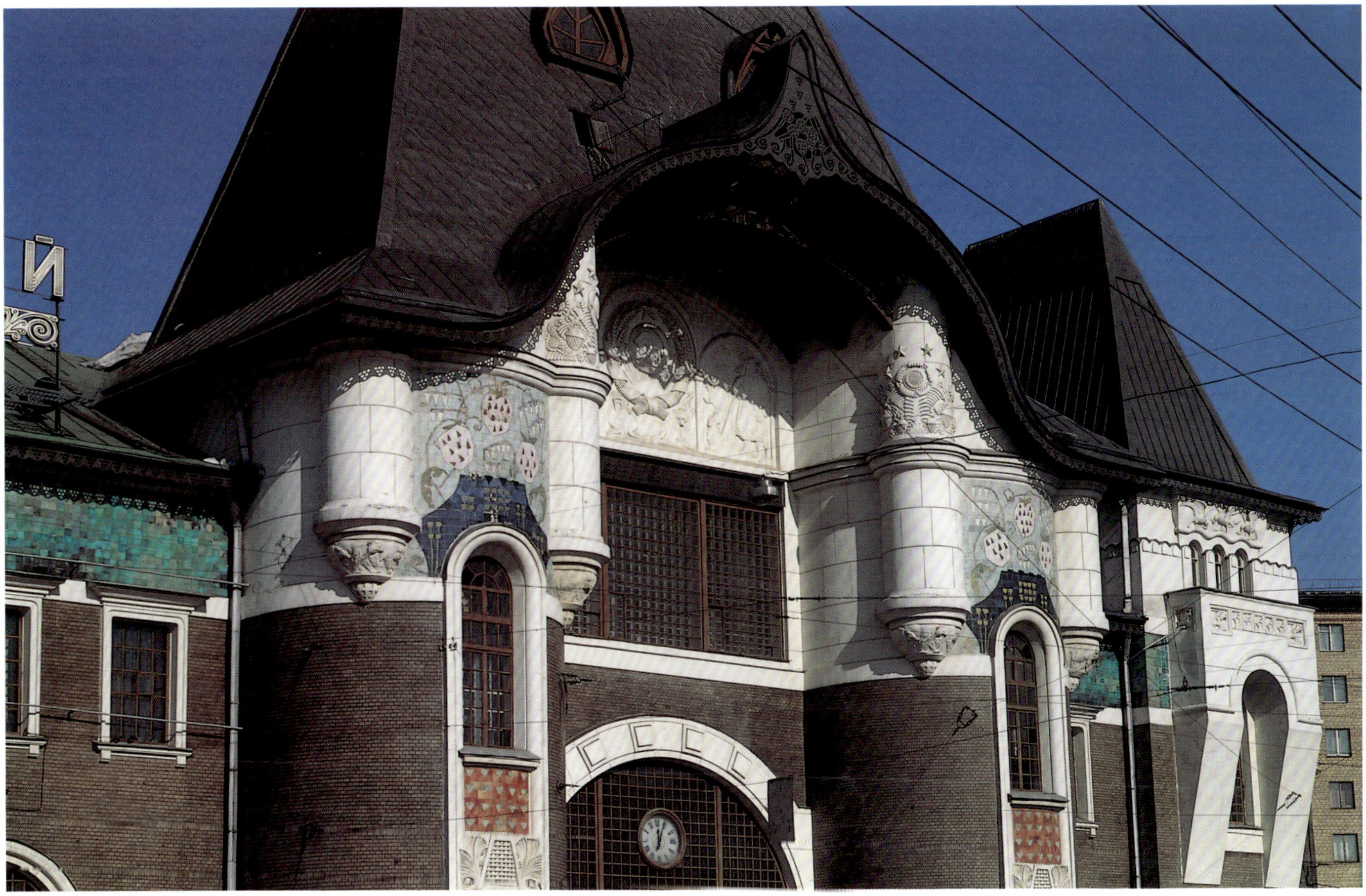

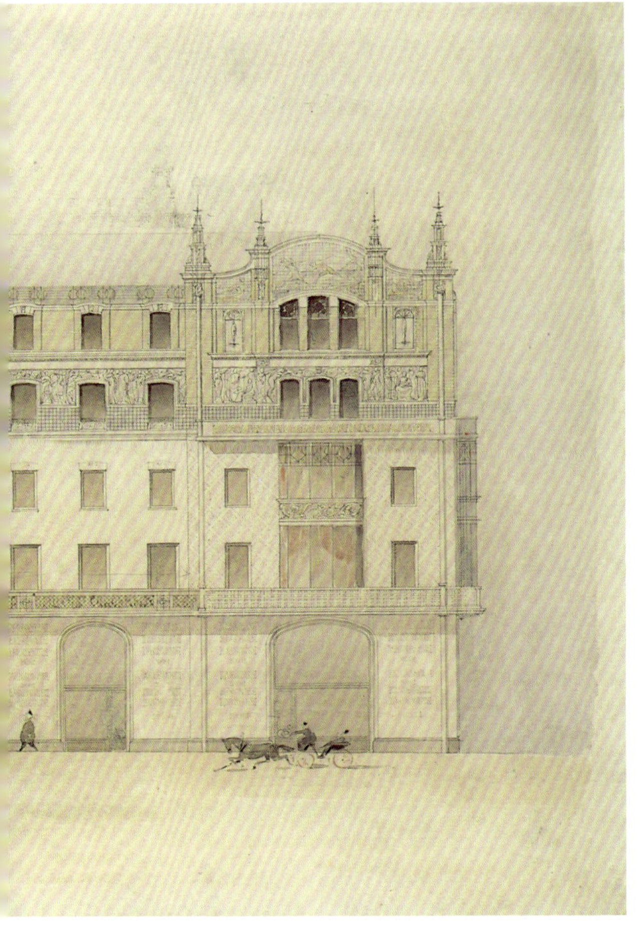

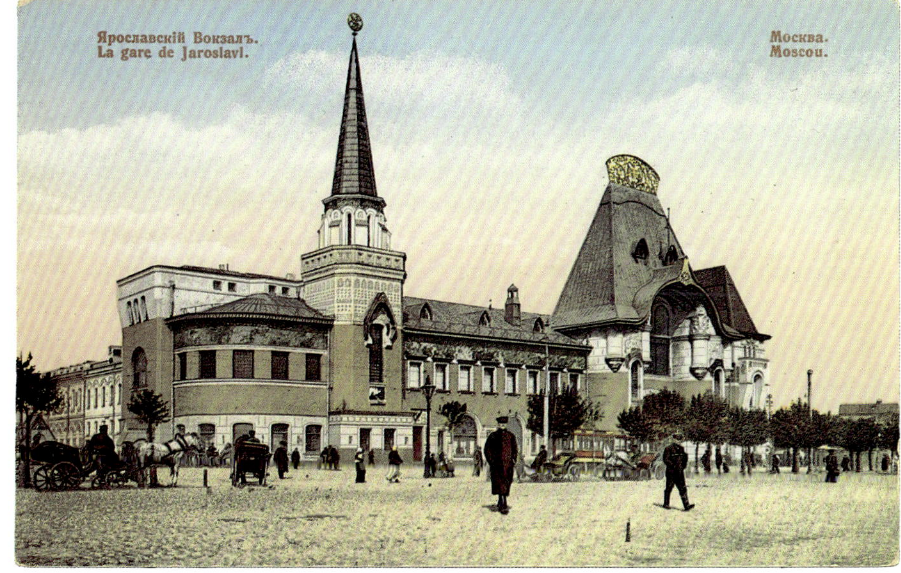

Ярославскій Вокзалъ.
La gare de Jaroslavl.
Москва.
Moscou.

Though the religious parallel is not direct, their impact on Moscow business circles can be compared to that of Quakers as founders of highly principled and socially active industrial dynasties in the early development of British industry. As a whole they represented a distinct political group with a specific model for a future Russia. It would be based on meritocratic power as created by industrial and commercial initiative, but would take its moral and social basis from the strong patriarchal values of Orthodox faith. Materially, technically and economically it would be on the level of the West, but culturally it would owe more to the spirituality and collectivist interpersonal structures of the traditional rural community of Orthodoxy, the *sobor*.

The cultural synthesis envisaged might have had a great future under such dynamic leadership had it not carried the millstone of inertia and bureaucratisation of late-Tsarist Russia around its neck. That is a question on which Shekhtel''s buildings still invite one to speculate. It was of course precisely the question which they were intended to raise, and answer affirmatively, in the minds of Russian people of the time.

Shekhtel' left almost no published statements of his approach or its origins, but certain notes indicate that he read, amongst others, Spengler, Schopenhauer and the contemporary Russian philosopher who was the main inspiration of the Symbolist movement, Vladimir Solov'ev. In this last, it seems to me, we come closest to a source and model for Shekhtel''s method, with ideas that map well onto his works and these typical aspirations of his clients. Solov'ev insisted that Eastern and Western European characteristics were necessarily interdependent and complementary in contributing to the "free unity" which can create "integral life" and a larger "integral wholeness". Of his three spheres of human activity, creativity, knowledge and social practice, the first corresponds to design. Creativity in his system of "a free and scientific theosophy" involved a fusion of technology, as the first or material level, with art, the formal level, and mysticism, as the highest and absolute level, in an undifferentiated whole.[19] The best examples of Shekhtel''s eclectic fusion of elements in this way were the two mansions he built in central Moscow between 1900 and 1902, for Stepan Ryabushinsky and Aleksandra Derozhinskaya.

In their relationship to the street and their plots, in their form and planning, these houses declare their anti-autocratic values as loudly to the Russian passer-by as Savva Morozov's did. At the same time, the coloured surfaces fit them immediately into the Russian Classical tradition, as their square-based proportions do into a still older Russian one. Their functional organisations were moulded around particular lifestyles, and they set standards of a "modern man's" environmental comfort that were reached almost nowhere else in Russia at that date. Both had systems of centralised warm-air heating circulating to all rooms, and the basement of Derozhinskaya's house in particular indicates a provision for efficient staff operations that is up to the standard of an equivalent household in Edwardian England.

Another striking feature of these houses alongside their stucco-box predecessors in Moscow – or indeed alongside the pebbledash and painted woods still characteristic of the housing by Mackintosh or Hoffmann in Europe at this date – is their powerful materiality. This is not status from paste-on conventions, as in Classicism. The rich real materials and enormous value added by craftsmanship in every detail of these houses communicate powerfully to the street the strength of their financial roots in Nature's raw materials and the wealth that comes from processing them. (The Derozhinskys were also in textiles, though not on the Morozov scale. This house was a wedding gift to Aleksandra from her father.) Such mastery of the material world was the hallmark of these industrial millionaires and the basis of their claim to offer Russia a prosperous future.

Eclectic though the means typically are, the thematic synthesis in each of these two Shekhtel' houses was addressed to evoking a "mood" of duality and profundity, as well as a heightened, almost theatrical statement of the nature of the client. The house for Stepan Ryabushinsky is not flashy by its size. The Ryabushinskys were by now relatively "old money", and, with one playboy exception, they were highly serious, both intellectually and in their contribution to debate on current political options. Stepan's brother Pavel ran the family newspaper *Utro Rossii* (*Morning of Russia*) as mouthpiece for the views and programme of the industrial class described earlier to which they belonged.

By the standards of Edwardian England this was a modest family house. Its organisation echoes that same model, with a conventional distribution of activities between ground and first floors. The owner's icon collection, one of the finest and most discriminating in Russia, was housed upstairs amongst the private rooms, though the external gilding of windows in the mosaic frieze of lilies may be a reference to them. A single – if extraordinary – staircase links the two floors, with a service stair at the back. Shekhtel''s theme here, more pagan than Christian, is of nature's primal energy arising from below the sea. Internally, the atmosphere as a whole combines studiousness with a sense of enormous reserves of primal energy. Outside, there can be few more lyrical architectural sights than this house on a sunny spring day, with its strong square proportions and

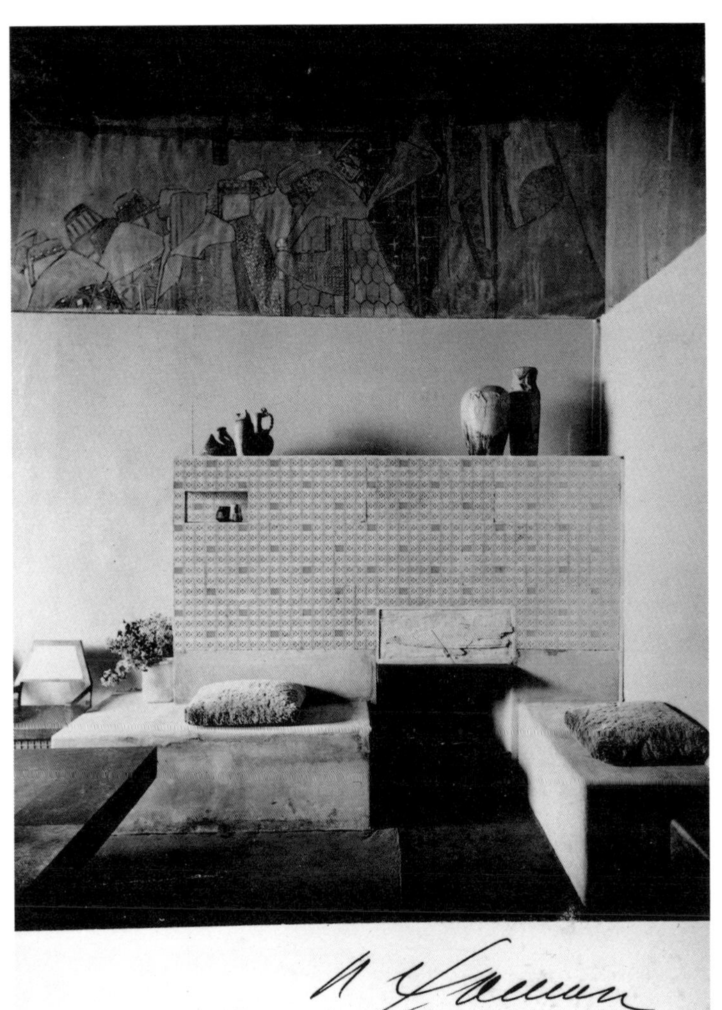

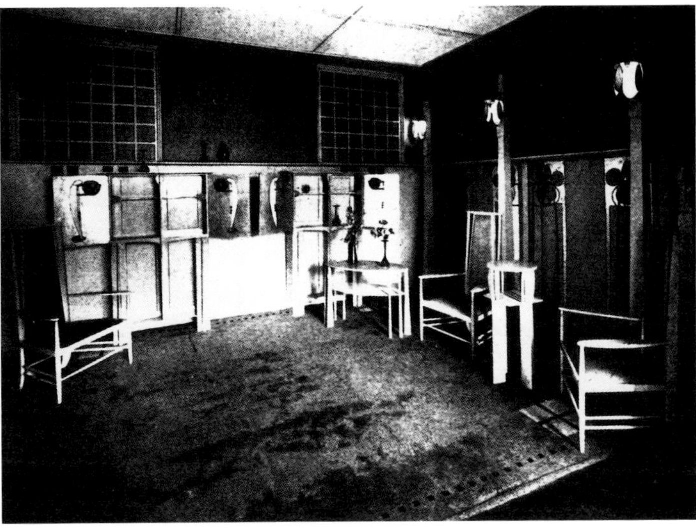

LEFT: **Ivan Fomin**
118. Maple Dining-room at
the "New Style" Exhibition in
Moscow: corner with stove
1902
A. V. Shchusev State Museum
of Architecture

ABOVE: Mackintosh Room in
the "New Style" Exhibition in
Moscow, 1902
Illustration from *Mir
Iskusstva*, 1903 no.3

BELOW: **Fedor Shekhtel'**
Design for elevation of the
Moscow Arts Theatre (not
executed)
1903

Fedor Shekhtel'
Seagull motif for the Moscow
Arts Theatre

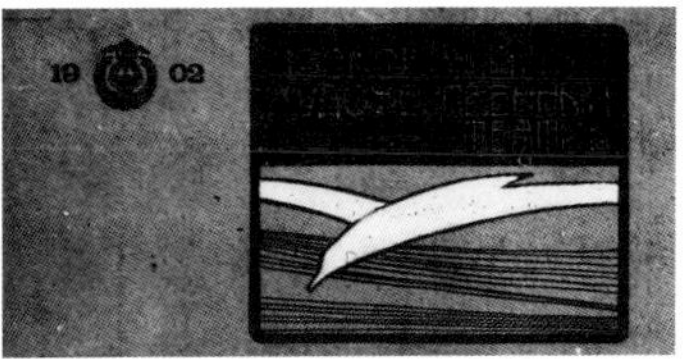

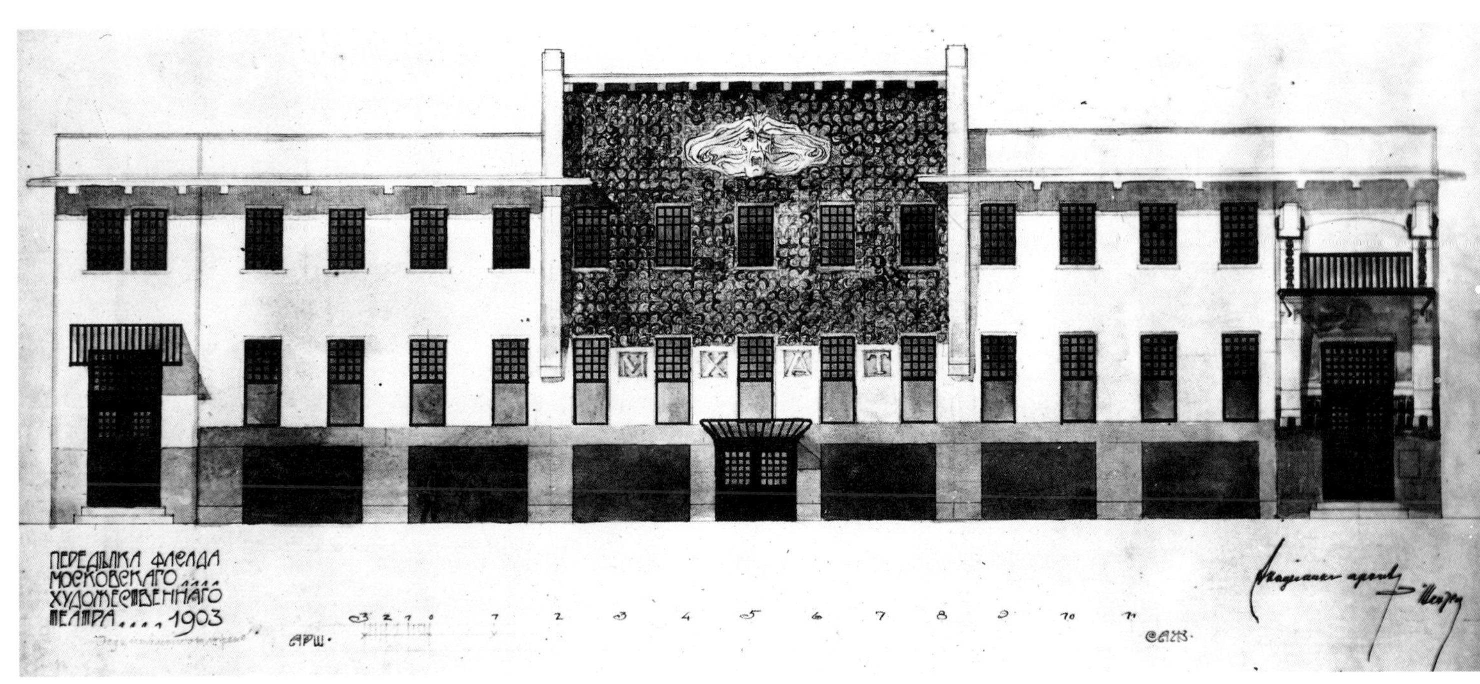

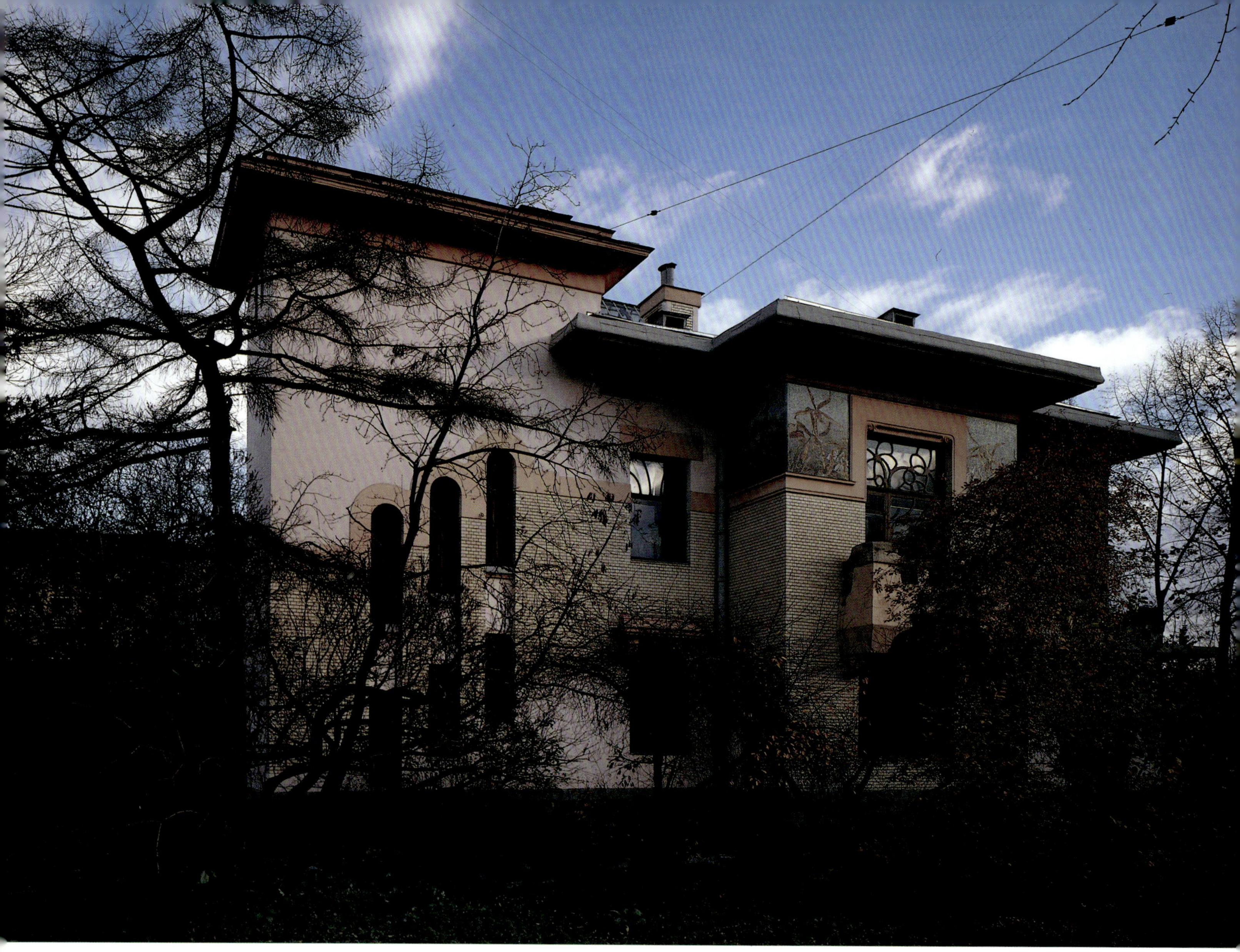

Fedor Shekhtel'
Mansion of S. P. Ryabushinsky
1900–03

ABOVE: View from the garden

RIGHT: Porch on street façade

OPPOSITE TOP: 374 (details).
Designs for wall treatment in
dining-room
Mixed media on paper
A. V. Shchusev State Museum of
Architecture

OPPOSITE BELOW: 371. View from
the street
Photo (1900s)
A. V. Shchusev State Museum of
Architecture

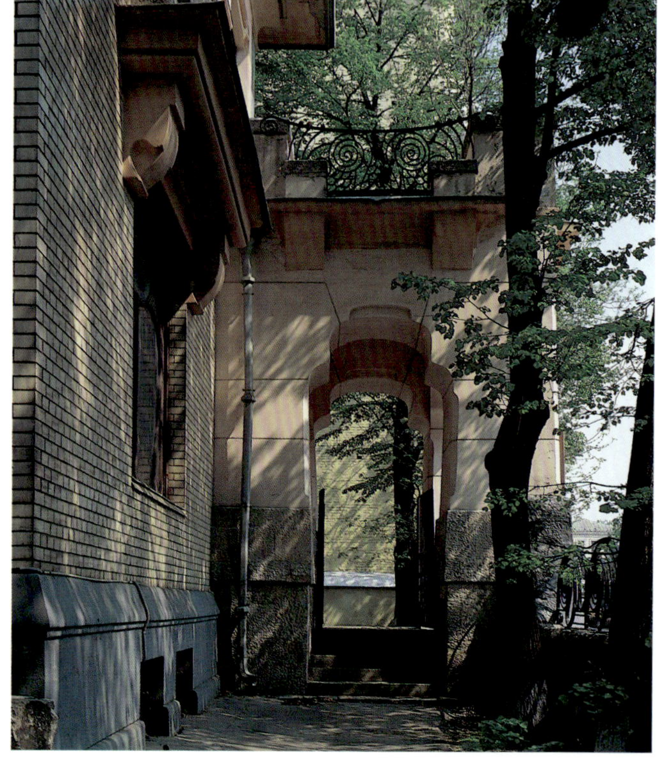

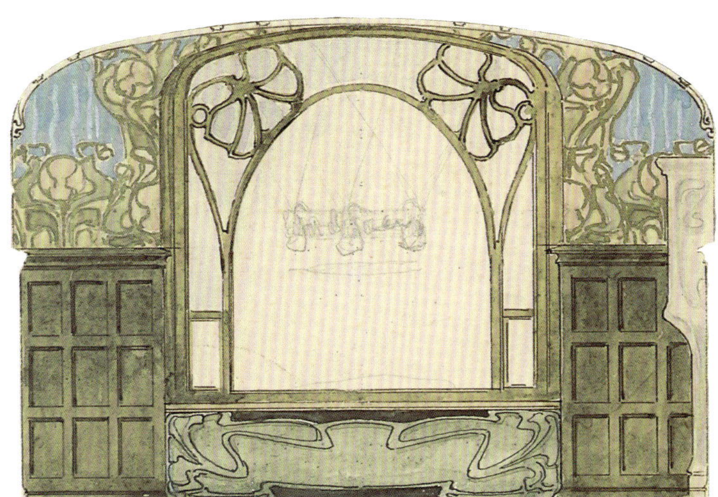 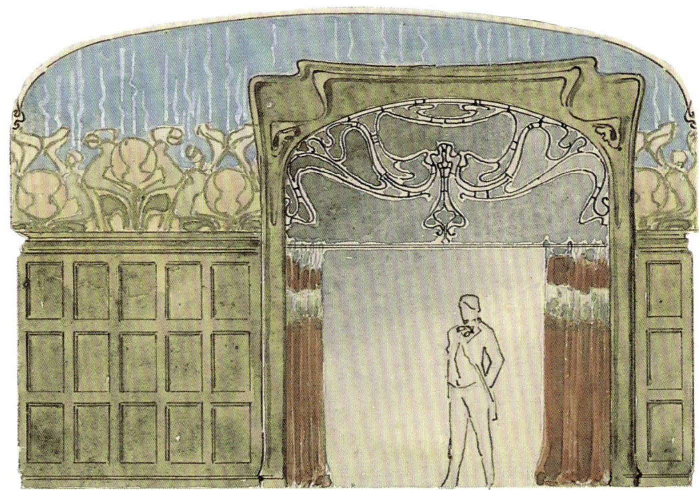

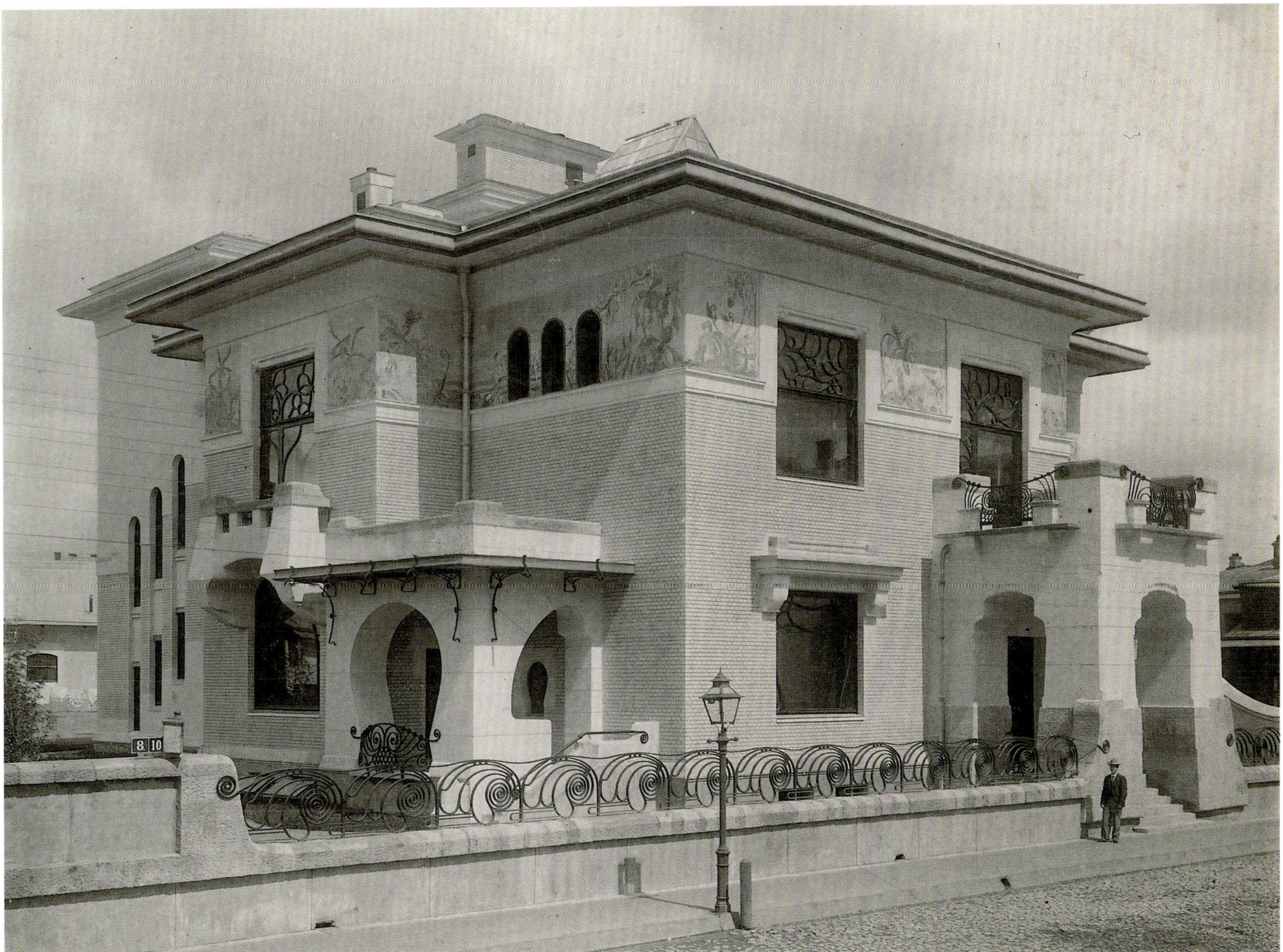

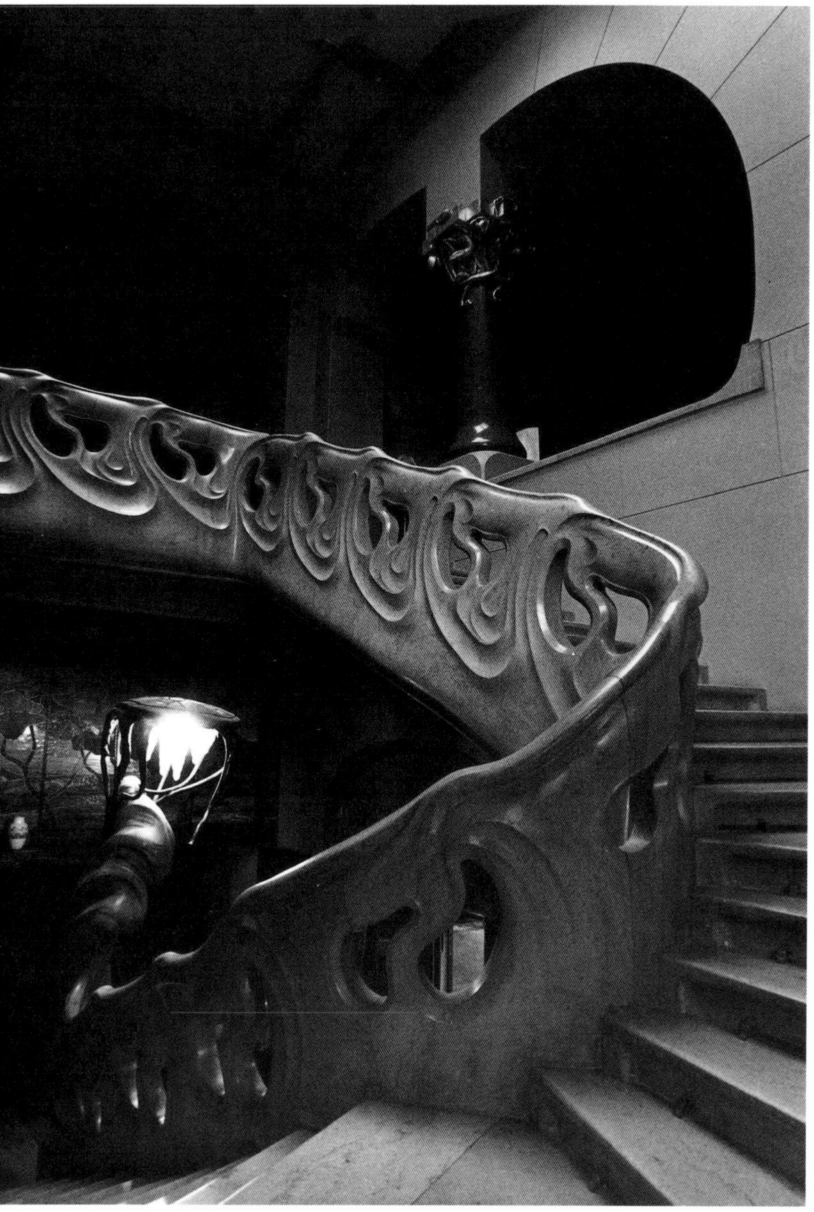

Fedor Shekhtel'
Mansion of S. P. Ryabushinsky
Main staircase
1900–03

its strong curves, its gold touches amid floral mosaic behind the flowering fruit-trees of its open garden; or rising from a sparkling, reflective layer of snow. In its sureness of plain surface and line, and in the handling of natural materials, it is a jewel on the level of the Fabergé work by the best Finnish masters like Henrik Wigström or the peasant Russian Mikhail Perchin.

Even without the unsettling *tendresse* of the paintings by Borisov-Musatov which Shekhtel' intended for it, his house for Aleksandra Derozhinskaya was manifestly a social showcase for a woman. It is strangely larger than any photograph or drawing ever conveys, and for all the masculinity of the double-height, medieval-scaled panelled hall, around which all other accommodation runs, this is a vast sugarcake palace for a little princess of

the new industrial money. From the basic organisation of the plan, it is perfectly clear which side brought the money to this marriage. Straight ahead across the great Hall, running round the whole far side of it at ground level, is a sequence of rooms which follows the sequence of Derozhinskaya's daily life, from the privacy of the bath to the great hooded couch for formal receiving which originally dominated the Hall. Behind that couch was a salon for slightly more intimate receiving, the moulded sky of its ceiling studded with small lights like stars; out of that led a morning room for her personal and domestic affairs; next came the bedroom; and in the farthest corner from the entrance, the bathroom. In relation to the placing of this great sweep, her husband's dayroom and *cabinet* were a mere appendage, leading from a secondary corner of the Hall behind the great fireplace. All first-floor accomodation is given over to children's or servants' rooms, and Derozhinsky's billiard room is in the basement.

A decorative theme runs through the whole design, from the garden railings and entrance gates to the upholstery fabrics, of shifted triangles, restless and tortured. But the geometrics of tree forms in the morning room are more relaxedly naturalistic, and the intimate space of the main bedroom has a 1930s mood of simplest Art Deco, whilst the fine marble fittings of the bathroom have all the functional simplicity and sense of "cleanliness and hygiene" associated with advanced European life as well as a pleasantly relaxed curvaciousness. In the absence of the paintings, the main representational art work is the great fireplace, probably by Anna Golubkina, where the overall theme of life as a battle to resolve opposites is expressed through appropriate classical myth. The dining room, as an alternative focus of social life, is placed adjacent to her husband's *cabinet* off the great Hall. Original photographs of it strongly evoke the dining room in Mackintosh's competition drawing for the *Haus eines Kunstfreundes* of 1901, though the furniture and surfaces here are dark. The powerful heating system makes the great Hall habitable (interestingly, it is labelled in English, "Hall", on the plans), and the new material of reinforced concrete plainly helps with the vast spans.

Here public display is "the inner purpose of the object", but even in this relatively unintellectual exercise, modern domestic comfort and the associated "cleanliness" are played against unsettling, irrational themes. It is characteristic of Shekhtel's oeuvre that each of these houses – like all his others – has its own stylistic motifs and formal themes developed out of its underlying "idea". This is very different from the relative stylistic uniformity of Shekhtel's contemporaries like Kekushev or Ivanov-Shits at any given point in

Fedor Shekhtel'
Mansion of S. P. Ryabushinsky

LEFT: Balcony outside dining-room window
1903

BELOW: Central section of façade

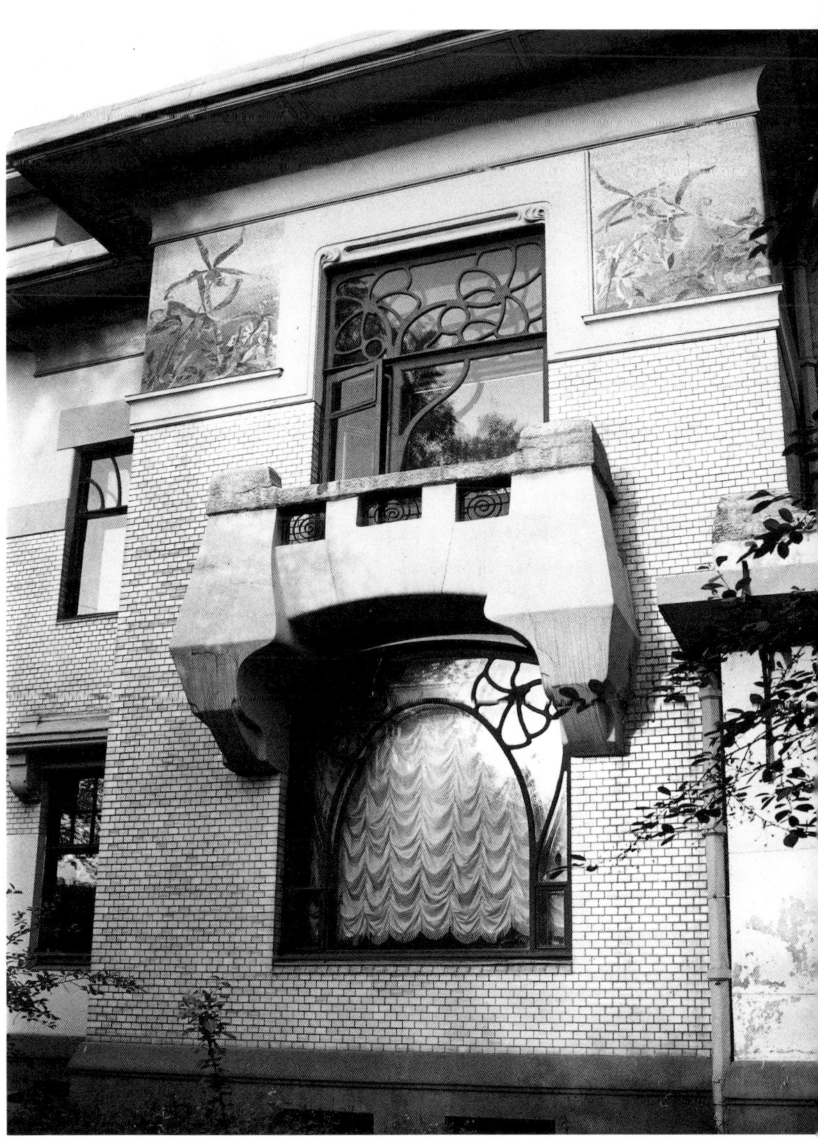

this period. The means are as eclectic as the underlying idea, and at some levels, as here in the spatial organisation and in proportions even more than in craft detailing, the medieval Russian dimension is strong. But from Shekhtel' as a pupil of Viktor Vasnetsov at Abramtsevo the interpretation of this tradition is infinitely more subtle and more genuinely architectural than in the contemporaneous products of the rival arts and crafts colony of Princess Tenisheva at Talashkino. A similar inspiration there produced little more than a folkloric decorativeness.

For Pavel Ryabushinsky's newspaper *Utro Rossii*, Shekhtel' produced editorial offices in 1907 as different from the Historicist Kuznetsov building as Derozhinskaya's house was from Morozov's: sleek to the point of streamlined, in a deep brown glazed brick with cream trim. With the newspaper's printing shop behind, this was also a factory. Perhaps that accounts for its colour, or perhaps the industrial reference is to the political lobby for which it speaks? In form it is as uncompromising as the newspaper itself, which did not hesitate to attack the Government vehemently – and in 1911 was temporarily banned for it.

Shekhtel''s most advanced and elegant commercial building followed two years later. It combined offices, showrooms and warehousing on a model dating back to the traditional Russian trading "yard". The client here was the Moscow Trading Society, a group of companies including the Buryshkins, closest allies of the Ryabushinsky's in their political campaigning. Here the concrete frame provided unbroken floor areas inside. The subtly rippling external piers were faced in off-white, matt-glazed tile. The spandrels and the top, "cornice" floor of offices were matt and cream-coloured. The plate

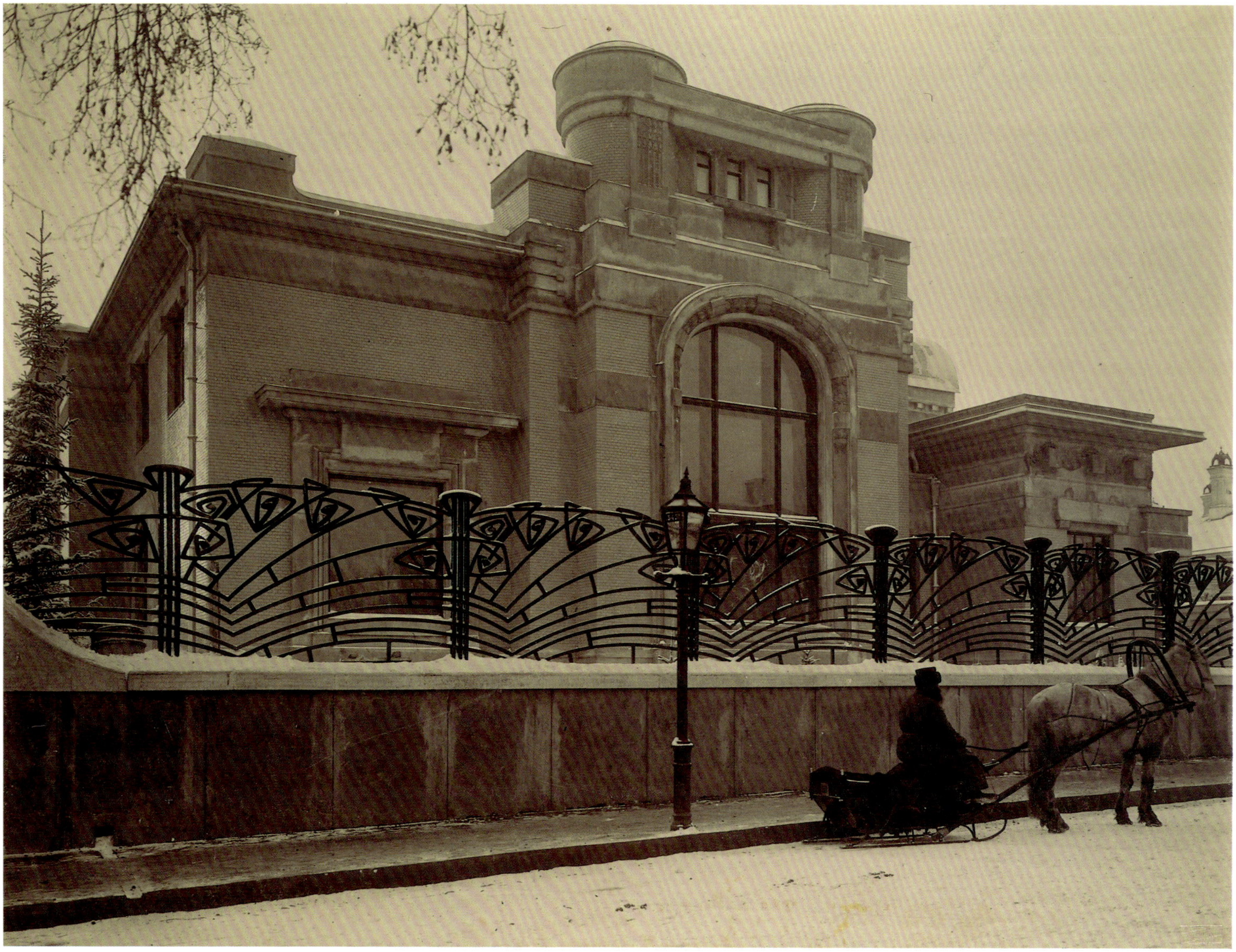

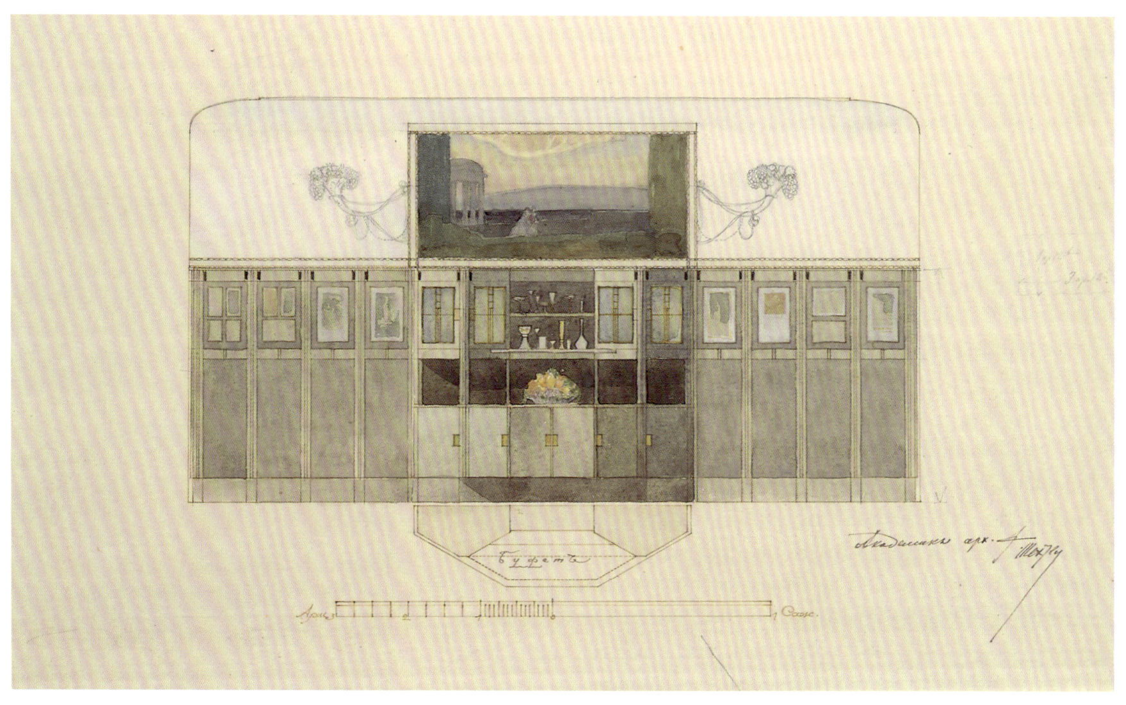

Буфетъ
Сажень.

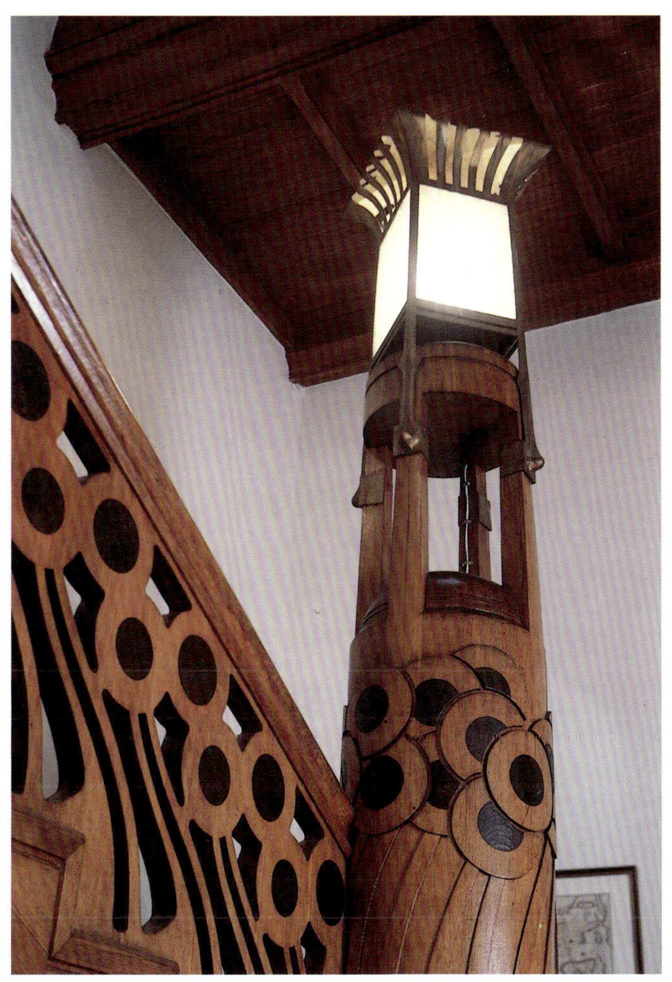

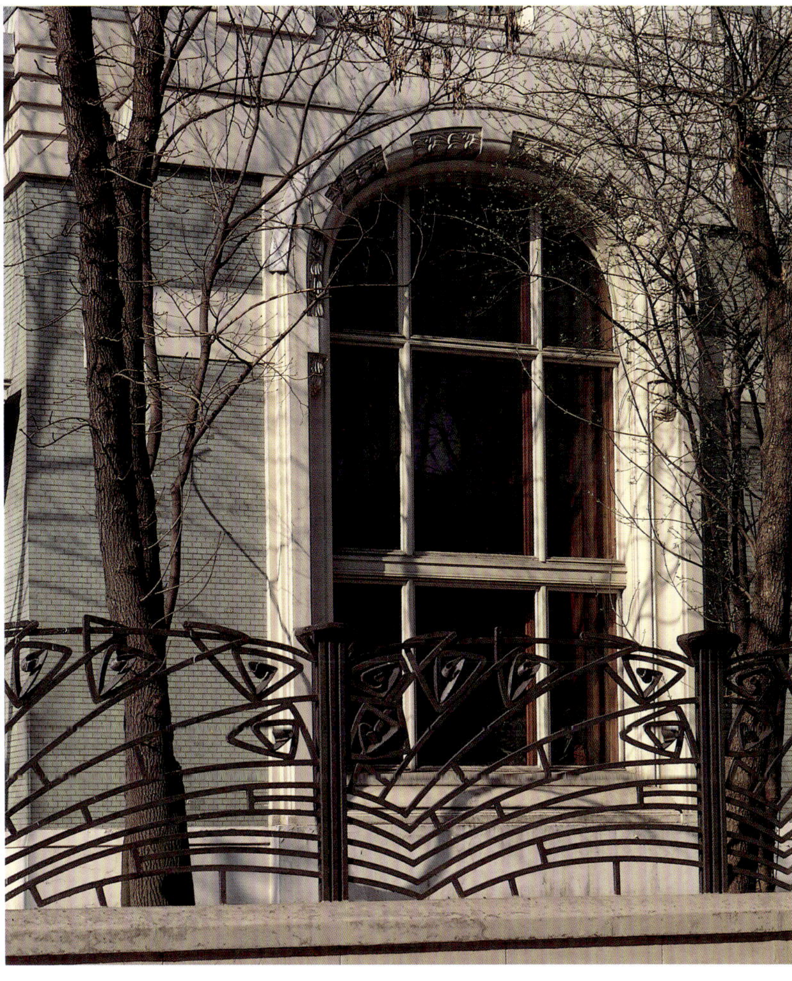

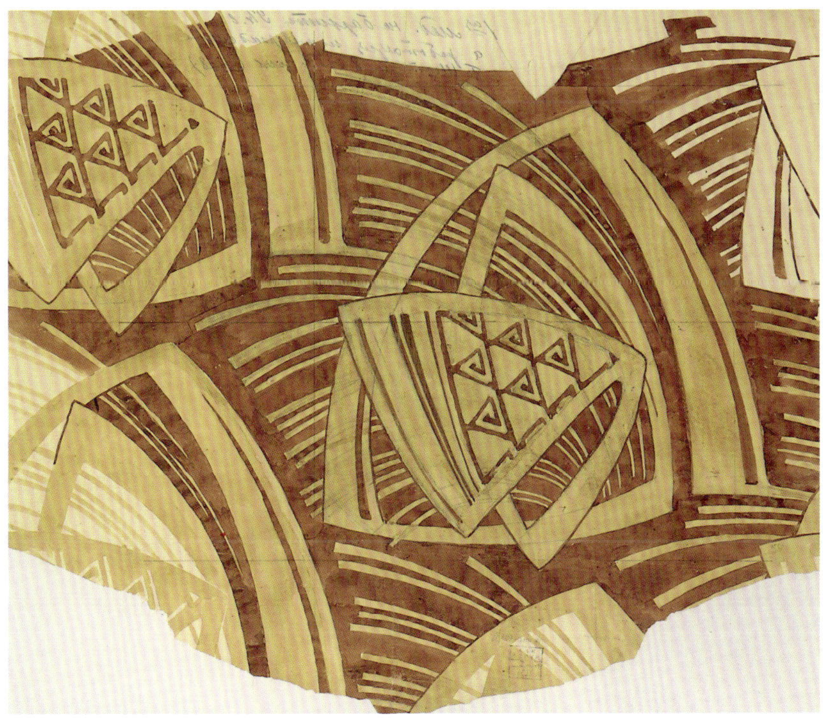

Fedor Shekhtel'
Mansion of A. I. Derozhinskaya
1901–02

OPPOSITE TOP: 359. View from
the street
Photo (1900s)
A. V. Shchusev State Museum of
Architecture

OPPOSITE BELOW: 363. Design for
end wall of dining-room with
painting by Borisov-Musatov
(version not executed)
Ink and watercolour on paper,
44.5 × 64.2
A. V. Shchusev State Museum of
Architecture

ABOVE LEFT: Lamp at foot of
staircase

ABOVE RIGHT: Central window

LEFT: 366. Design for upholstery
fabric for study
Pencil and watercolour on tracing
paper, 64 × 73.2
A. V. Shchusev State Museum of
Architecture

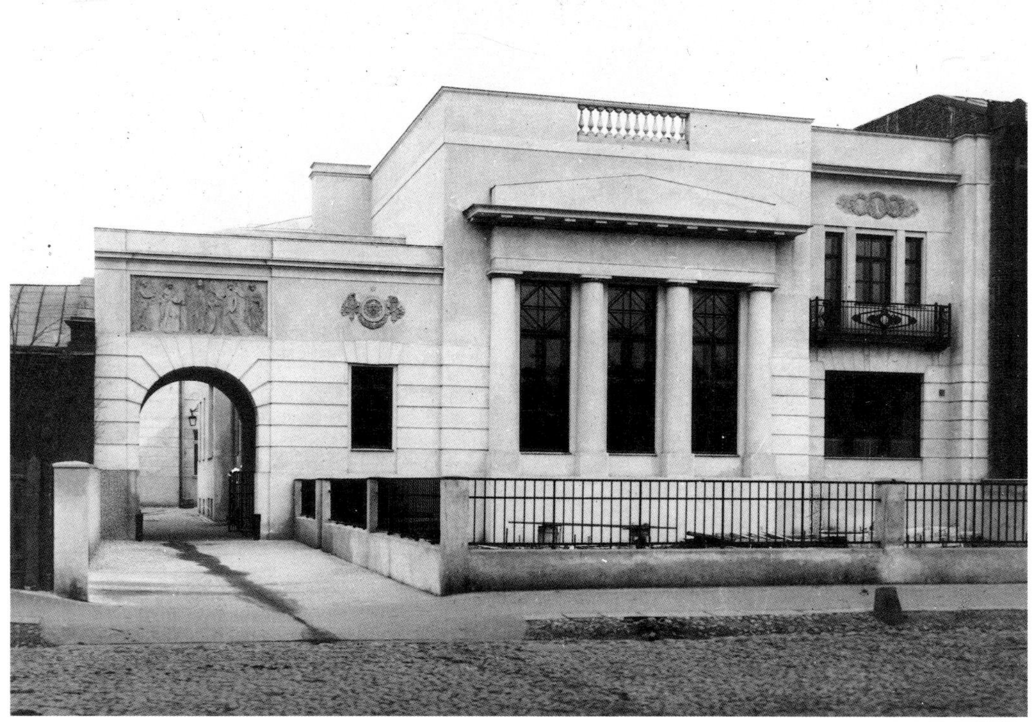

LEFT: **Fedor Shekhtel'**
The architect's house, Moscow
1909

BELOW: **Fedor Shekhtel'**
Office building for *Utro Rossii* newspaper,
Moscow
1907

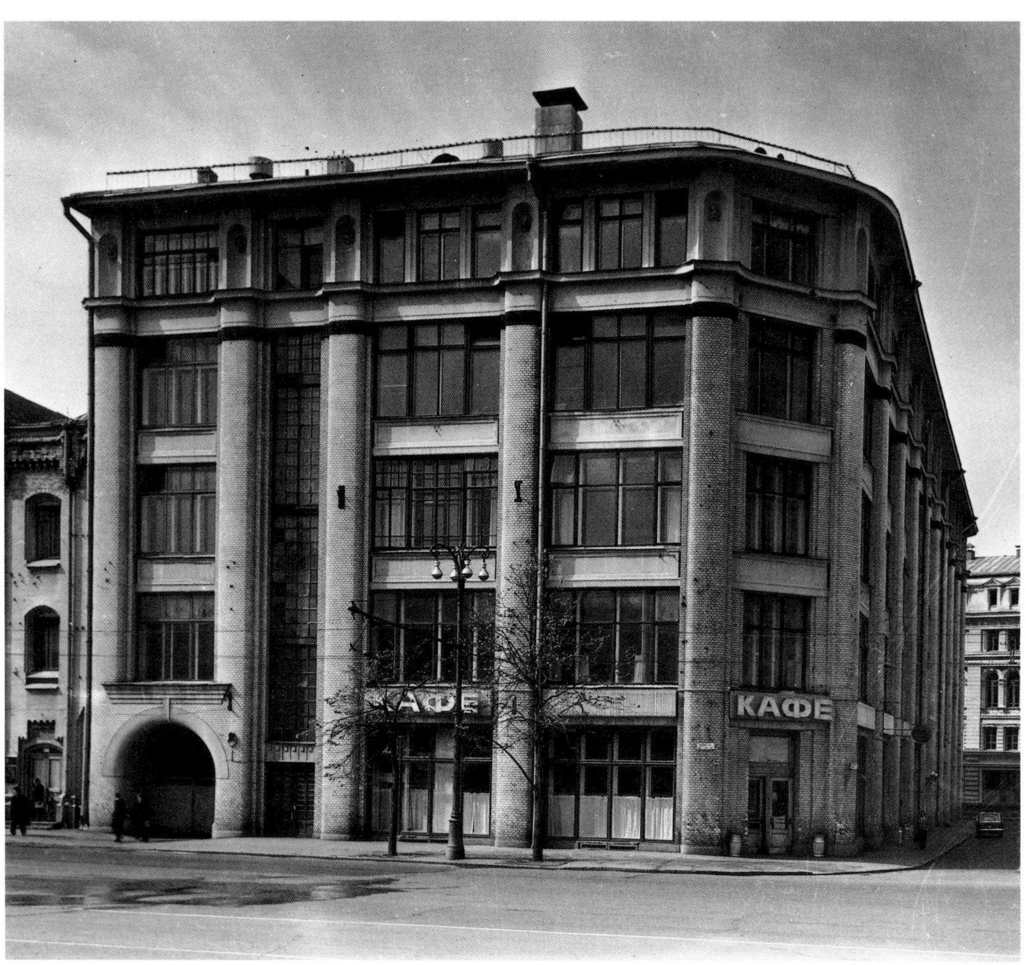

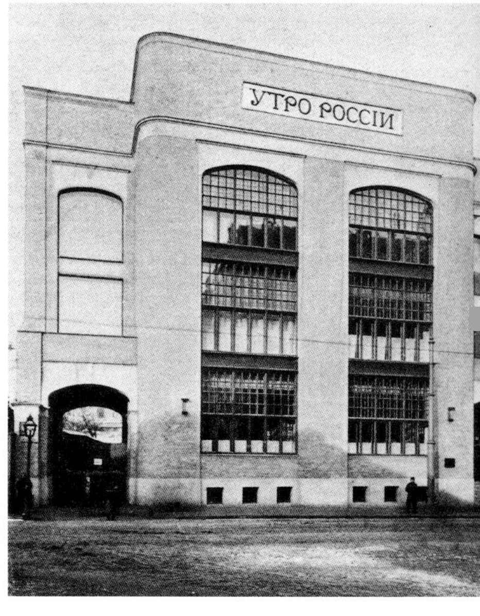

LEFT: **Fedor Shekhtel'**
Headquarters building for the Moscow
Trading Society
1909–11

glass which filled all three elevations of its prominent site. was a slightly reflective aquamarine blue. The slender window-frames were bronze. More than any other commercial building in Russia, this Shekhtel' work expressed these men's vision of commerce as a civilised, cultured, life-enhancing activity, and as something that could offer Russia a prosperous but principled way forward. As with his more hand-crafted domestic work, the extraordinary quality of the building has preserved it almost intact.

RETURN TO THE ALTERNATIVE TRADITION With the democratic optimism of 1905 dashed by increasing political ineptitude and retrenchment, the serene longterm confidence of Shekhtel''s two high-*Moderne* mansions or the commercial self-assurance of the Moscow Trading Society could not continue into further buildings of their genres. Shekhtel' was one of the first to return, in his smaller scale commissions around 1910, to a reinterpretation of that other tradition more readily understood by most of the population to be inherently Russian: to *Empire* Classicism. In this new phase, however, it incorporated the planning and compositional experience of the previous years to produce a lively free Classicism, this continuity well justifying the term *Moderne* which generally identifies it. Suitably enough, Shekhtel''s two main demonstrations of his skill in this Classical idiom were a new Moscow house and studio for himself, in 1909, and in 1910 the memorial library in Taganrog to Anton Chekhov, the closest friend of his youth, who had died six years earlier.

Very different from his earlier work though these buildings superficially appear, they continue Shekhtel''s exploration of the continuing themes of architecture in the turn-of-the-century period: how can genetically fertile stock be identified inside a cultural tradition? How much cross-fertilisation, even grafting, from the different stock of the European plant is compatible with real organic growth on the Russian root? The urgent topicality of these questions in Soviet politics and architecture today, in a period of economic stasis, makes it perhaps easier to grasp the desperate urgency which these questions assumed in the headlong rate of development Russia was experiencing at the peak of Shekhtel''s career around 1900.

NOTES

1 Mikhail P. Chekhov, *Vokrug Chekhova: Vstrechi i vpechatleniya (Around Chekhov: Encounters and Impressions)*, Moscow-Leningrad, 1933, pp.70, 247. For further detail on Shekhtel''s friendship with Chekhov, and on his life and career in general, see: C. Cooke, "Fedor Osipovich Shekhtel: An architect and his clients in turn-of-the-century Moscow", *Architectural Association Files* (London) no.5, January 1984, pp.3–31.

2 M.D. Bykovsky, Speech to the first A.G.M. of the Moscow Architectural Society, 24 November 1868, reprinted in *Ezhegodnik MAO*, no.5, 1928, p.9.

3 V.P. Apyshkov, *Ratsional'noe v noveishei arkhitekture*, St Petersburg, 1905, p.52.

4 *Ibid*, p.54.

5 *Ibid*, p.63.

6 *Ibid*, p.65.

7 F.O. Shekhtel', "Skazka o trekh sestrakh: zhivopis, skulptura i arkhitektura", lecture, 1919, in M.G. Barkhin (ed.), *Mastera sovetskoi arkhitektury ob arkhitekture*, 1975, Moscow, vol.1, pp.14–22.

8 M. Gorky, *Sobranie sochinenii v 18 tomakh*, Moscow, 1963, vol.18, pp.222–3.

9 S. Yaremich, *Mikhail Aleksandrovich Vrubel'*, Moscow, 1911, p.120.

10 *Ibid*, p.154.

11 "Vospominaniya I.E. Bondarenko o F.O. Shekhtele", in E.I. Kirichenko (ed.), *Arkhitektura SSSR*, 1984 no.5/6, pp.92–3.

12 Letter from Shekhtel' to Vasnetsov in Soviet State Archives, quoted in E.I. Kirichenko, *Fedor Shekhtel'*, Moscow, 1973, p.49.

13 Kirichenko, *Fedor Shekhtel'*, p.62.

14 Sergei Diaghilev, "Moskovskie novosti", *Mir Iskusstva*, 1903 no.3, pp.8–10.

15 M. Mikhaylov, "Ist zu wienerisch", *Iskusstvo stroitel'noe i dekorativnoe*, 1903 no.1–2, pp.12–24.

16 For a detailed account of these two exhibitions and local reactions to them, see: C. Cooke, "Shekhtel in Kelvingrove, Mackintosh in Moscow: two Russo-Scottish exhibitions at the turn of the century", *Scottish Slavonic Review* (Glasgow), no.10, Spring 1988, pp.177–205.

17 Mikhaylov, 'Ist zu wienerisch', p.18.

18 *Vystavka arkhitektury i khudozhestvennoy promyshlennosti novago stilya: katalog*, Moscow, 1903, p.3 of advertisements.

19 V.S. Solov'ev, "Philosophical principles of integral knowledge", 1877. A discussion in English may be found in Andrzej Walicki, *A History of Russian Thought*, Oxford, 1980, pp.376–8.

ВЕСЫ
1906 N5

4

SYMBOLIST LITERATURE
Symbolist writers and the Symbolist press

JULIAN GRAFFY

In 1892, six years after the publication in Paris of Jean Moréas's famous "Un manifeste littéraire", in which he suggested the term «SYMBOLISME» as "the only one capable of reasonably designating the present tendency of the creative spirit in art", the young Russian writer Dmitry Merezhkovsky published in St Petersburg a collection of poems entitled *Simvoly* (*Symbols*). At the same time Merezhkovsky (1865–1941) was engaged in writing a lengthy treatise in which he attempted to examine what he saw as the recent decline of Russian literature, consequent upon its plunge into didacticism, and the beginnings of a new tendency. This was published in 1893 and was extremely influential in setting an agenda for a new literary movement.[1]

Though Merezhkovsky's treatise can scarcely be seen as a detailed manifesto, he does insist, quoting Goethe, that all art must be symbolic, and defines the three basic elements of the new art as *"mystic content, symbols and a broadening of artistic impressionability"*.

In Moscow, meanwhile, a young university student, Valery Bryusov (1873–1924), who had also been learning about the new French writers, wrote in his diary on 4 March 1893: "Find a lodestar in the fog. And I see it: it is decadence. Yes! Whatever you may say, whether it is false or absurd, it is moving forward, developing, and the future will belong to it, especially when it finds a worthy leader. And I shall be that leader! Yes, I!" Bryusov proceeded, with his friend Aleksandr Lang, to publish in 1894–95 three small volumes under the title *Russkie Simvolisty* (*Russian Symbolists*). These collections of original poems and translations, which Bryusov described as setting "markers on an invisible path", provoked a predictably hostile reaction. The philosopher Vladimir Solov'ev (who was later to play a decisive role in forming the worldview of the younger Symbolists) was moved to opine that "It is impossible to pronounce a general assessment of Mr Valery Bryusov without knowing his age. If he is not more than 14, then he may make a decent versifier, though he may not. But if he is an adult person then, of course, all literary hopes are inappropriate." Bryusov caused particular outrage with a single-line poem in the third collection, "O, zakroi svoi blednye nogi" ("Oh cover your pale legs"). Solov'ev's sardonic reaction was as follows: "For complete clarity one should add, perhaps, 'or else you will catch cold', but even so Mr Bryusov's advice, evidently addressed to a person suffering from anaemia, is the most sensible work in all Symbolist literature, not just in Russian but in other languages too." Chekhov's reaction was similarly amused: "Don't you believe them. Their legs aren't 'pale' at all, but hairy, just like everyone else's." Nevertheless, the interest provoked by these slim collections put the young Bryusov firmly in the public eye.

Both the Symbolist writers themselves and critics writing about them show no consistency in the use of the terms "symbolism", "decadence", "modernism", "the new art". But an archetypal "decadent" writer of the 1890s is Aleksandr Dobrolyubov (1876–1944?), whose formally heterodox *Natura Naturans. Natura Naturata* (St Petersburg, 1895) is predominantly concerned with death. In 1898 Dobrolyubov withdrew from literature and took to wandering and living among sectarians in northern Russia.

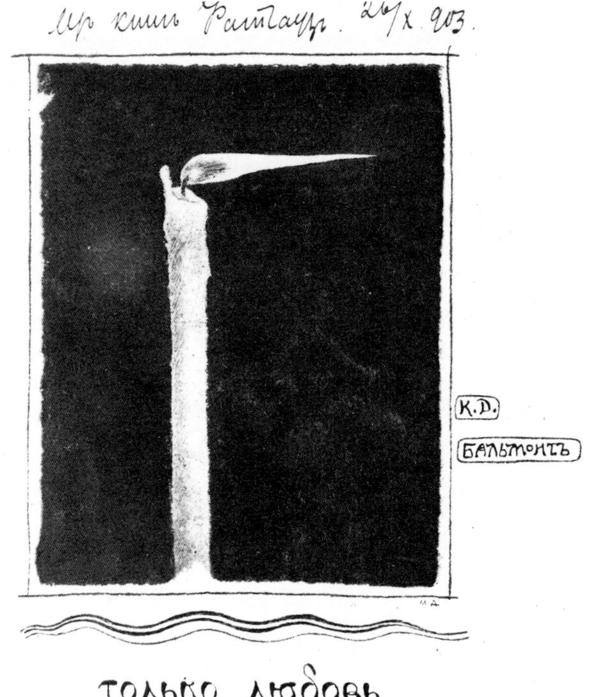

PREVIOUS PAGE:
Nikolai Feofilaktov
112. Cover from *Vesy*, 1906 no.5
State Lenin Library

ABOVE: **Modest Durnov**
102. Cover of Konstantin
Bal'mont, *Only Love*, Moscow
(Grif), 1903
State Lenin Library

By the turn of the century, the major writers of the so-called "first generation" of Russian Symbolism had established their reputations. After *Russkie Simvolisty* Bryusov had published the poetic collections *Chefs d'œuvre* (1895), *Me eum esse* (1897) and *Tertia Vigilia* (1900). The prolific poet Konstantin Bal'mont (1867–1942) had produced four collections by 1900. Merezhkovsky published the novel *Smert' bogov. Iulian Otstupnik* (*The Death of the Gods. Julian the Apostate*), the first volume of his *Christ and Antichrist* trilogy, in 1896. Zinaida Gippius (1869–1945), whom he had married in 1889, published poetry and two collections of stories. The early stories of the poet and prose writer Fedor Sologub (1863–1927) are marked by melancholy and a yearning for escape. As Sologub would later insist: "Art is a constant striving from the world of melancholy into the world of dream, it is an unquenchable thirst for exaltation, it is liberation from the fetters of the everyday. But only now, only the new art has for the first time become substantially conscious of this task." Yet the innocent protagonists of Sologub's stories, who very

frequently are children, are habitually ignored or bullied by uncomprehending adults, and the stories often end in misery or death. Sologub's first novel *Tiazhelye Sny* (*Bad Dreams*) was published in 1896.

Throughout the 1890s, the literary press, the so-called "fat journals", had maintained a general hostility to the new writers. The only regular outlet for their work had been the St Petersburg *Severnyi Vestnik* (*The Northern Messenger*), which had been bought in 1891 by the publisher Liubov' Gurevich and where the leading ideologist was Akim Volynsky. *Severnyi Vestnik* published Sologub, Merezhkovsky, Gippius and Bal'mont. Eventually Volynsky's aesthetic conservatism led to a severance of relations, and the journal closed down in 1898. Nevertheless, as Bryusov later admitted, it was *Severnyi Vestnik* which had "let the army through". The need to establish close relations with a journal that was sympathetic to the new line as a base for polemics with opponents remained pressing, and the appearance of *Mir Iskusstva* (*The World of Art*) brought this dream closer.

Mir Iskusstva was a loose grouping of artists, writers, musicians and aesthetes, many of whom had been students together in St Petersburg, which established a journal in 1898–1904 and also organised art exhibitions from 1899–1906 and 1910–24. The organiser of the group and editor of the journal was Sergei Diaghilev (1872–1929). In May 1898, when the journal was about to appear, he announced that it "must create a revolution in our artistic life, and must do the same, more or less, among the general public". Diaghilev appointed Aleksandr Benois (1870–1960) as editor of the art section, and his cousin Dmitry Filosofov (1872–1940), a close associate of Gippius and Merezhkovsky, as literary editor. As Filosofov said: "*Mir Iskusstva* never had a definite programme. . . . It was a cult of dilettantism in the good and true sense of the word." In art this dilettantism was expressed through an interest in matters as diverse as traditional Russian art and the modernism of Beardsley and Mackintosh. In literature it meant that its pages were open to Gippius and Merezhkovsky, Bal'mont, Sologub, Bryusov and later Bely, though in the final years of the journal's existence its preponderant concern with art was increasingly apparent.

THE SECOND GENERATION In the period around the turn of the century some of the Russian Symbolists became increasingly preoccupied with religious questions. In St Petersburg Merezhkovsky and Gippius instituted the "Religio-Philosophical Meetings" between leading churchmen and intellectuals, and at the end of 1902 they left *Mir Iskusstva* to found a new journal *Novyi*

Put' (*The New Path*, 1903–04), which reflected this dual concern with literature and religion. These years also saw the emergence of the so-called "second generation" of Symbolists, Vyacheslav Ivanov, Andrei Bely and Aleksandr Blok, all of them influenced by the religious philosopher Vladimir Solov'ev. Though Ivanov (1866–1949) was of an age with the older Symbolists, he had been living and studying in Europe since 1886 and re-established himself in St Petersburg only in 1905, soon becoming a leading intellectual influence within Symbolism. His first books of poetry, *Kormchie Zvezdy* (*Pilot Stars*) and *Prozrachnost'* (*Transparency*), were published in 1903 and 1904.

Andrei Bely (1880–1934) was born Boris Bugaev, the son of a Moscow professor of mathematics. As a student he became a close friend of Sergei Solov'ev, the nephew of the philosopher. His four prose *Symphonies* began to appear in 1902, and he quickly established a reputation as an original Symbolist poet and critic.

Aleksandr Blok (1880–1921) also began to read Solov'ev in 1900 and to write poetry under the influence of Solov'ev's theory of "Sophia". For Solov'ev, Sophia represented the living soul of the created world and was identified with the eternal feminine principle in the

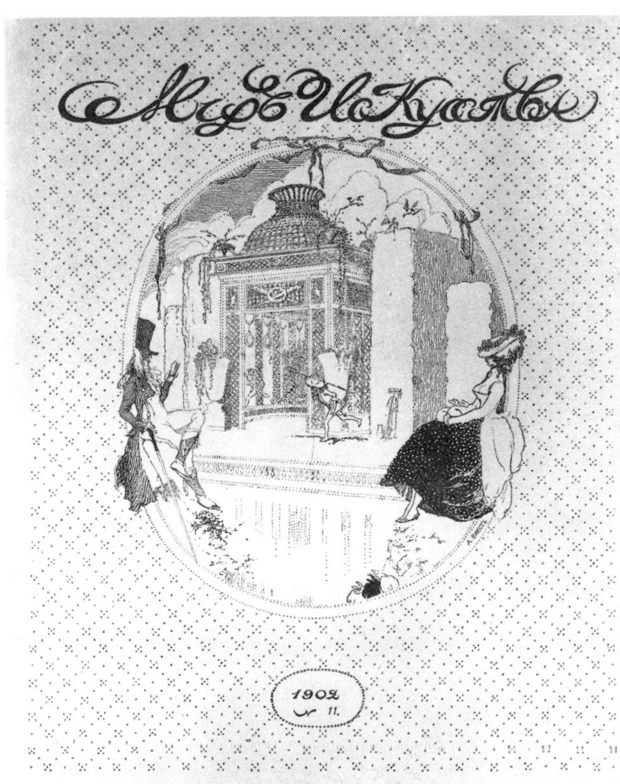

Top right: **Lev Bakst**
30. Cover of *Mir Iskusstva*,
1902 no.11
State Lenin Library

Below: **Anna Golubkina**
132. *Portrait of Andrei Bely*
1907
Bronze bust, 42 × 43 × 34
State Russian Museum

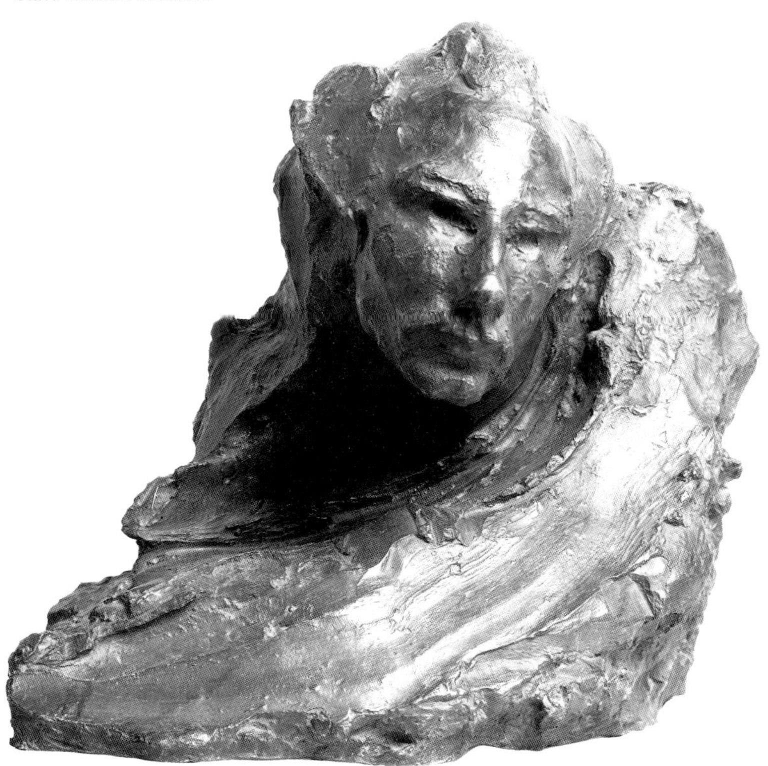

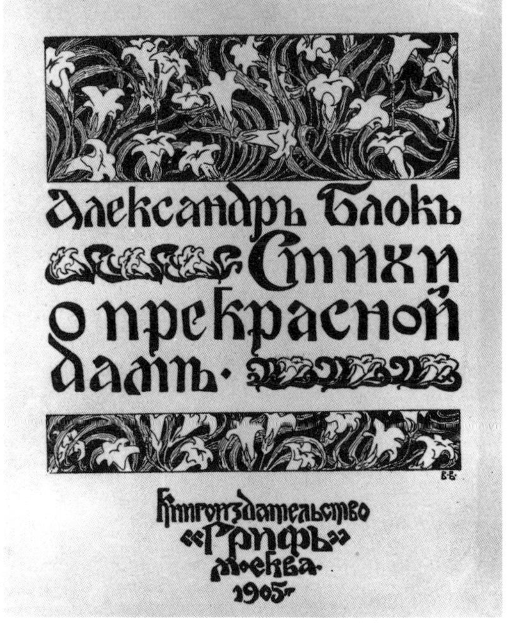

Above: **Vasily Vladimirov**
456. Cover of Aleksandr Blok,
*Verses about the Beautiful
Lady*, Moscow (Grif), [1904]
State Lenin Library

world, the natural object of aspiration of the poet who desires to penetrate the kingdom of the divine, of eternal beauty. At the beginning of 1901 Blok began to write a collection of over one hundred and fifty "Verses about the Beautiful Lady", in part inspired by Solov'ev. In these poems Blok reads the phenomena of the material world as signs of the presence of the Lady in another world of spirit. Blok made his debut as a poet in *Novyi Put'* in 1903, and the *Stikhi o Prekrasnoi Dame* (*Verses about the Beautiful Lady*) appeared as a book in 1904. By then Blok had married his childhood sweetheart, Lyubov' Dmitrievna Mendeleeva, whom he identified to a degree with the Lady, and had finally met Bely, with whom he was already engaged in an intense correspondence, and with whom he would maintain a similarly intense "inimical friendship" for several years.

The search for a journal that would be explicitly associated with the Symbolist writers came to fruition in 1904, when the *Skorpion* (*Scorpio*) publishing house in Moscow, which had been established by the industrialist and patron of the arts Sergei Polyakov (1870–1938) in 1899, launched *Vesy* (*The Scales, Libra*).[2] Though nominally edited by Polyakov, *Vesy* was in fact run by Bryusov and represents the most coherent expression of the Symbolists working together as a literary school. Its pages were closed to those who did not subscribe to its tenets, and its critical assessments consistently reflected the tastes of its leading contributors. In 1904–05 the journal was a "critico-bibliographical monthly" of (both Russian and Western) literature and art, which explicitly excluded poetry and fiction but also – and in this respect it differed radically from established Russian journals – any overt concern with politics and social issues.

The statement addressed "to readers" of the first issue asserted that the movement variously termed "Decadence", "Symbolism", "the new art" was "the furthest point reached by humanity on its path till now", and that it "concentrates all the best forces of the earth's spiritual life". In an article entitled "Kliuchi tain" ("Keys of the Mysteries"), also in the inaugural issue, Bryusov declared that Romanticism, Realism and Symbolism were three steps in the liberation of art, which was now free to pursue its higher aim, the "cognition of the world outside of rational forms, outside of thinking in terms of causality. . . . While all the crowbars of science, all the axes of social life are not in a position to break down the doors and walls that enclose us, art conceals within itself a terrible dynamite which will bring down these walls, indeed it is more than that, it is the Sesame which will make these doors melt away of their own accord." Very soon *Vesy* had become the centre of Symbolist theory, particularly in the writings of Bryusov, Bely and Ivanov.

From 1906 *Vesy* began to publish prose and poetry.

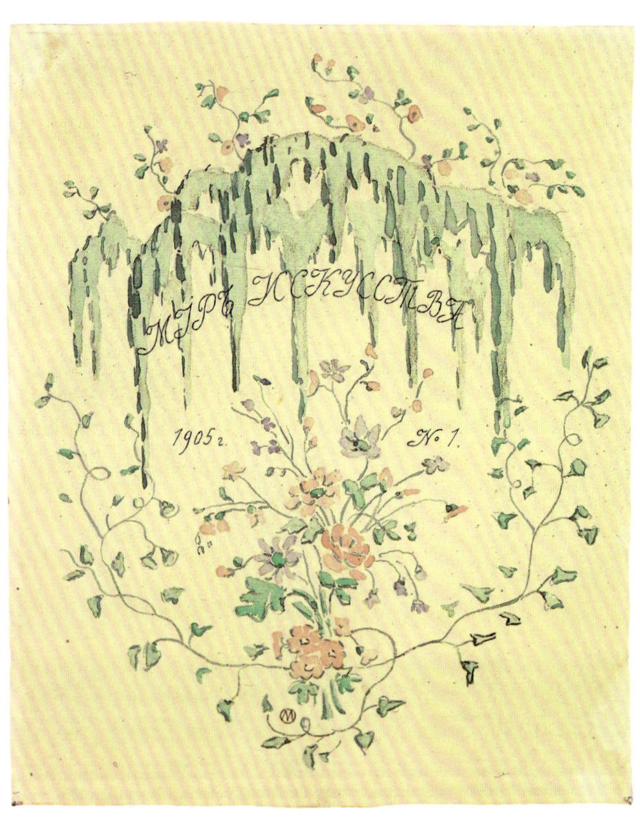

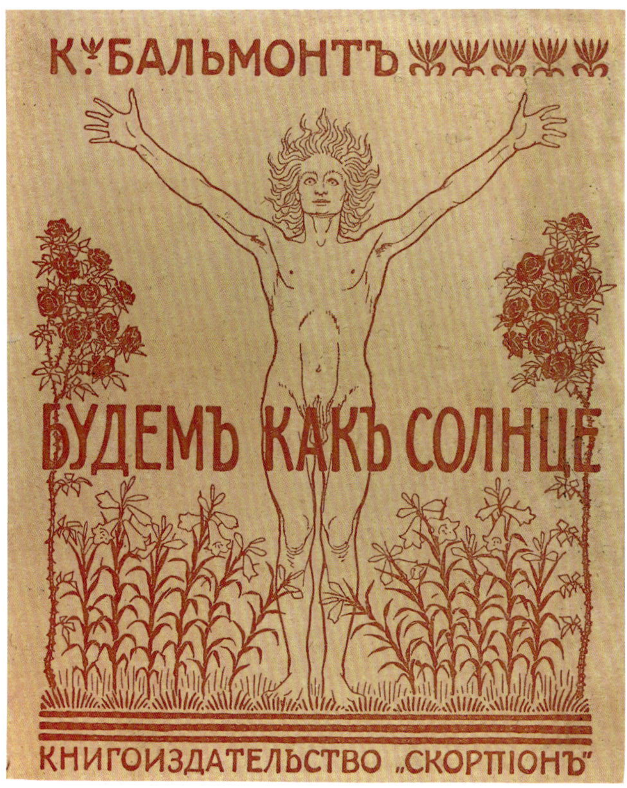

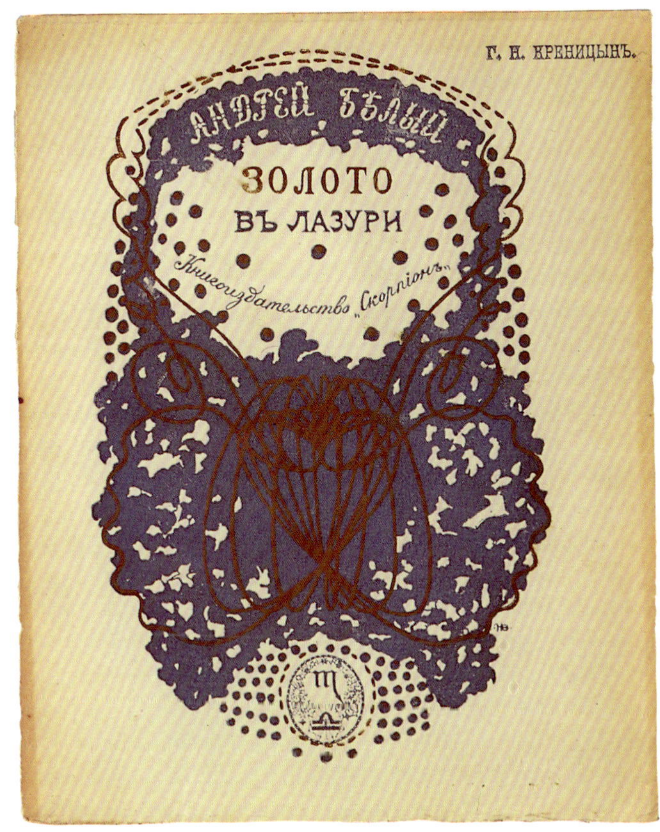

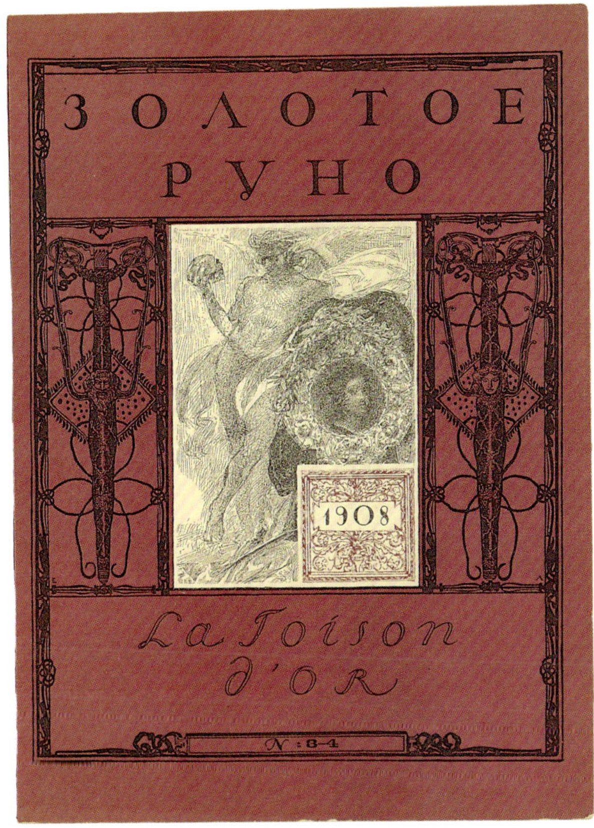

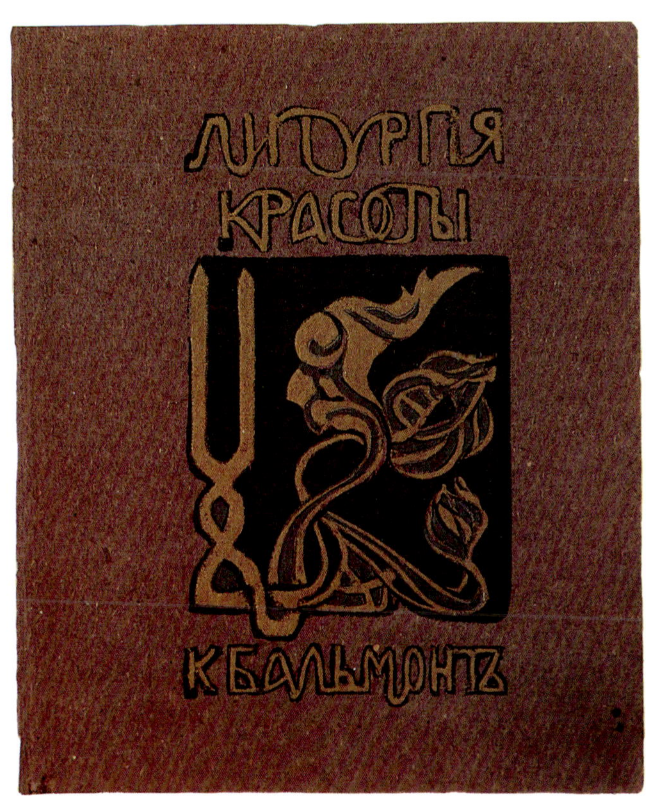

OPPOSITE LEFT: **Viktor Borisov-Musatov**
72. Cover design for *Mir Iskusstva*, 1905 no.1
1904
Mixed media on tinted paper, 33.5 × 26.6
State Tretyakov Gallery

OPPOSITE RIGHT: **Fidus (Hugo Höppener)**
114. Cover of Konstantin Bal'mont, *We Will Be
as the Sun: Book of Symbols*, Moscow
(Skorpion), 1903
State Lenin Library

TOP LEFT: **Nikolai Feofilaktov**
107. Cover from Andrei Bely, *Gold in Azure*,
Moscow (Skorpion), 1904
State Lenin Library

TOP RIGHT: **Evgeny Lanceray**
204. Cover of *Zolotoe Runo*, 1908 no.3–4
State Lenin Library

RIGHT: **Margarita Sabashnikova**
296. Cover for Konstantin Bal'mont, *Liturgy of
Beauty*, Moscow (Grif), 1905
State Lenin Library

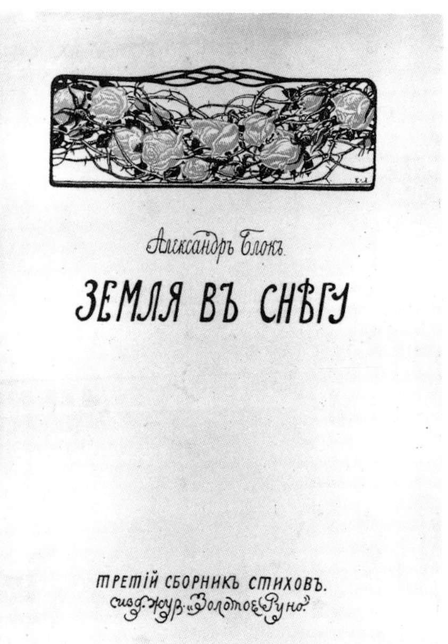

Evgeny Lanceray
203. Cover of Aleksandr Blok,
*Earth in Snow: Third
Collection of Poems*, Moscow
(Zolotoe Runo), 1908
State Lenin Library

At one time or another all the major Symbolist writers published in its pages, though the nucleus was provided by Bryusov, Bal'mont, Bely, Ivanov and Jurgis Baltrušaitis (1873–1944).

If *Vesy* provided a Moscow centre for the Symbolists, then from September 1905 the same role was played in St Petersburg by the "Tower", the flat which Vyacheslav Ivanov had taken on an upper floor of a house overlooking the Tauride Garden. This was the setting for the famous "Wednesdays", gatherings of the modernist intelligentsia to hear new poetry and prose and to engage in debate. As well as the Symbolists and their circle, including Mikhail Kuzmin (1872–1936) and Maksimilian Voloshin (1877–1932), the gatherings attracted younger writers such as Anna Akhmatova (1889–1966), Nikolai Gumilev (1886–1921), Osip Mandel'shtam (1891–1938) and Velimir Khlebnikov (1885–1922).

SYMBOLIST POLEMICS In 1906 a new Symbolist journal *Zolotoe Runo* (*La Toison d'Or, The Golden Fleece*) appeared in Moscow, published and financed by the banker Nikolai Ryabushinsky (1876–1951). Also designated a monthly journal of literature and art, and initially appearing with text in both Russian and French (the French text was dropped after June 1906), *Zolotoe Runo* was a lavish affair. In 1906 expenditure was 84,000 roubles and revenue only 12,000. The initial cover was designed by Evgeny Lanceray. The manifesto in letters of gold in Russian and French in the first issue stated that "it is impossible to live without beauty" and offered four definitions of art:

"*Art is eternal*, for it is based upon the intransient, on that which cannot be rejected.

"*Art is indivisible*, for its indivisible source is the soul.

"*Art is symbolic*, for it bears within it a symbol – the reflection of the Eternal in the temporal.

"*Art is free*, for it is created by the free creative impulse."

Zolotoe Runo was divided into four sections: art, literature, criticism and a chronicle of artistic events. In art it showed its ambition by its immediate attention to the work of Vrubel' (in the first issue) and Borisov-Musatov (in the third issue), and by the list of contributors to its art section that appeared in the second number. The literary section, in which once again Bryusov played a leading part, initially attracted contributions from all the leading Symbolists, with poetry, prose, plays and travel diaries by Bal'mont and Bryusov, Sologub, Ivanov, Bely and Blok. Its most important critic in its early stages was Bely.

During the middle of the decade, external events, particularly the inglorious Russo-Japanese war of 1904–05 and the abortive 1905 Revolution, served to bring the material world to the attention of Symbolist writers with a new urgency. In part this led to an increased interest in urban thematics in the poetry of Bryusov and Blok, and to an enthusiastic if inconsistent concern with revolutionary politics. More profoundly, it developed an interest in the Russian past and questions of national destiny.

These new concerns were reflected in an announcement in the June 1907 issue of *Zolotoe Runo* that it would now address itself especially to "examining questions of the national element in art and the 'new realism'". This stance did not suit all the Symbolists, and in the August 1907 issue of *Vesy* Merezhkovsky, Gippius, Bryusov and Bely announced that they no longer felt able to participate in *Zolotoe Runo*. The main writers for *Zolotoe Runo* now were Blok, who contributed a number of substantial surveys devoted both to literature and to the relationship of the people and the intelligentsia (a question that would remain enormously significant to him), Ivanov, Sergei Gorodetsky (1884–1967) and Georgy Chulkov (1879–1939). *Zolotoe Runo* now became closely associated with Chulkov's never adequately defined notion of "mystical anarchism", and Chulkov eventually became literary editor of the journal.

From now on, the polemic between Symbolism and its external enemies was largely supplanted by vitriolic diatribes between *Vesy* and *Zolotoe Runo*, and indeed the other Symbolist publishing outlets springing up in Moscow and St Petersburg.

The first decade of the twentieth century saw the

triumph of Symbolist aesthetics and Symbolist publishing. Bryusov and Bal'mont, Merezhkovsky and Gippius, Ivanov and Blok all consolidated their reputations in the fields of poetry, prose, drama and criticism. Sologub's *Melkii bes* (*The Petty Demon*), a disturbing novel of provincial life, appeared in March 1907. Bely's brilliant examination of the relationship between the intelligentsia and the people, based upon misapprehension on the one hand and low cunning on the other, in the novel *Serebriannyi Golub'* (*The Silver Dove*) was serialised in *Vesy* in 1909. The decade also saw the appearance of the first novels of Aleksei Remizov (1887–1957), another writer closely associated with Symbolist circles.

But, as is so often the case, triumph was closely followed by dissolution. 1909 saw the demise both of *Vesy* and of *Zolotoe Runo*, which had expended so much recent energy in trying to undermine each other. In autumn 1908 Polyakov had decided to stop his subsidy to *Vesy*, and in February 1909, after a failed attempt to take control, Bryusov withdrew, later to join the monthly *Russkaia Mysl'* (*Russian Thought*). Bal'mont also departed, in June 1909, going so far as to publish his contention that the role of *Vesy* was utterly exhausted in *Zolotoe Runo*. In a note in the final issue (1909 no. 12) readers of *Vesy* learnt that with "the victory of Symbolism" the journal was no longer necessary. (In fact the number of subscribers had fallen catastrophically from its peak of 1,691 in 1908). *Zolotoe Runo* had also been ignominiously reduced in size in 1908 and other economies were introduced. Ryabushinsky was in serious

financial trouble, and his family saw no reason to rescue his publication. It too closed with the last issue of 1909 (though this did not in fact appear until 1910). The simultaneous demise of the rivals marked a turning-point in the fortunes of the Symbolist movement in Russia, its brief period of glory being followed by its (consequent) disintegration as a coherent school.

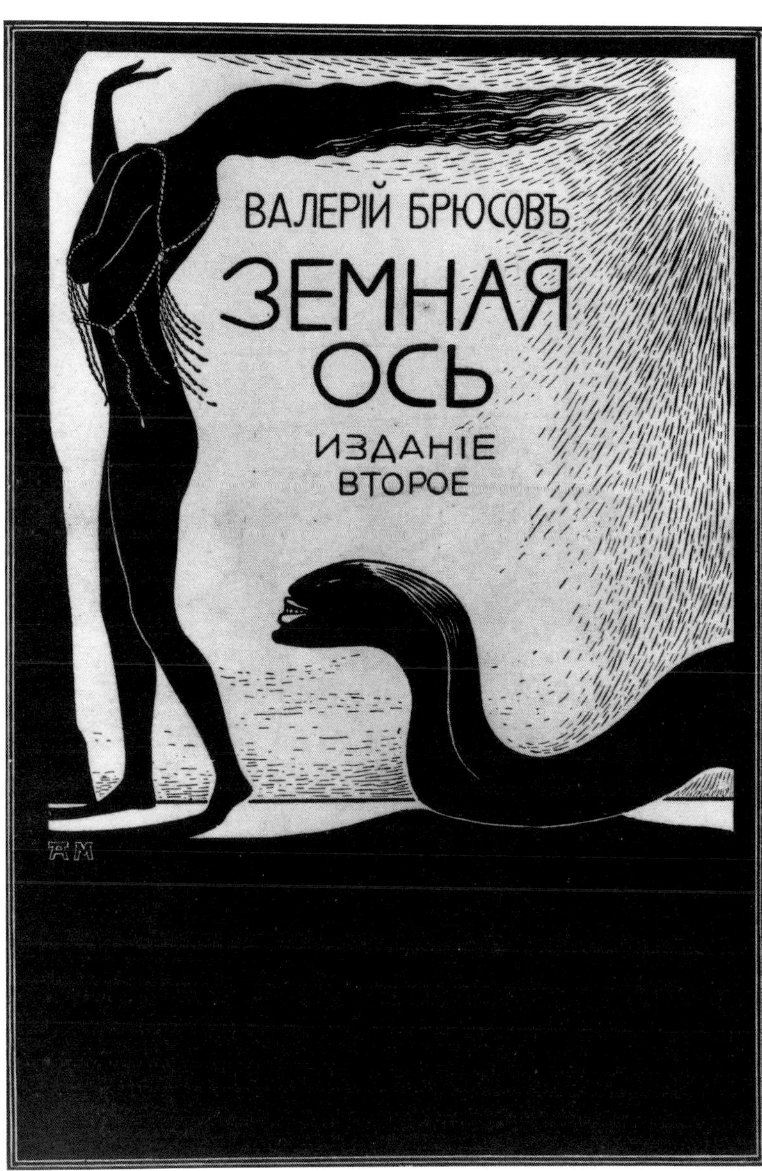

LEFT: **Vasily Milioti**
229. Vignette in first edition of Valery Bryusov, *Axis of the Equator*, Moscow (Skorpion), [1906]
State Lenin Library

ABOVE: **Alberto Martini**
224. Cover for the second revised edition of Valery Bryusov, *Axis of the Equator*, Moscow (Skorpion), 1910
State Lenin Library

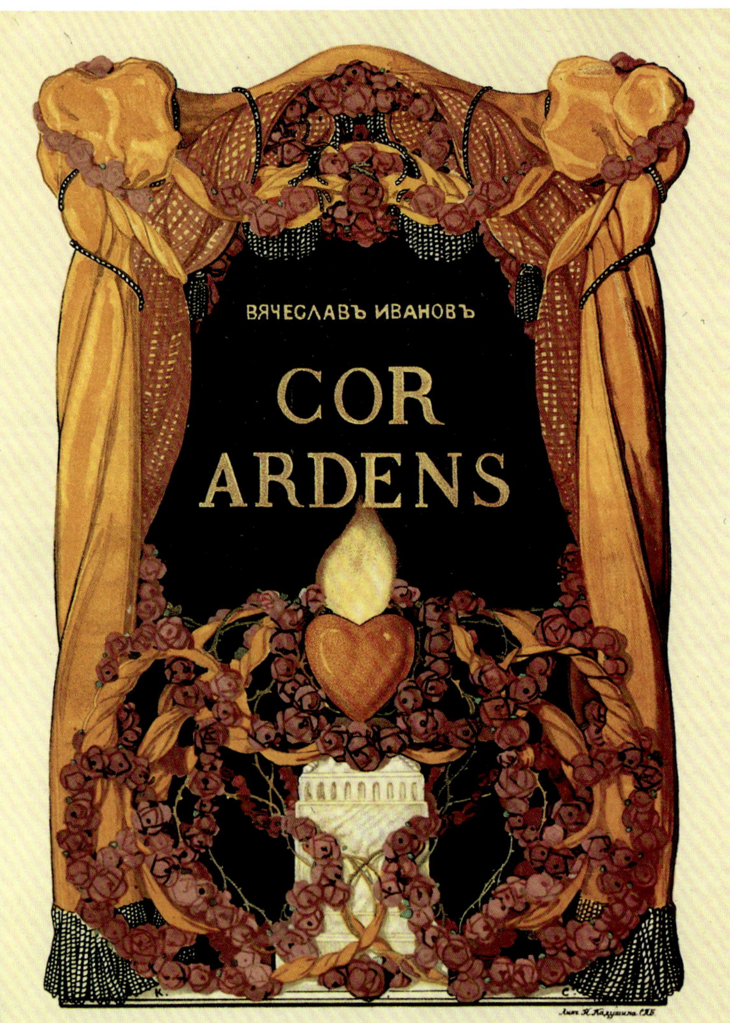

ABOVE: **Konstantin Somov**
404. Cover for Vyacheslav Ivanov,
Cor ardens, Moscow (Skorpion),
1911
State Lenin Library

RIGHT: **Yury Annenkov**
17. *Jester*
1915
Costume design for Sologub's play
Night Dances
Mixed media on paper,
29.4 × 16.4
State Russian Museum

the August 1910 issue of *Apollon*. In his article, entitled "Zavety simvolizma" ("The Precepts of Symbolism"), Ivanov insisted that "Symbolism neither wanted to be nor could be 'only art' . . .", and that "the fate of the symbolic poet depends on the linking act of his totally surrendering will and the religious system of his entire being. That is how Symbolism obligates us." Blok, in his "O sovremennom sostoianii russkogo simvolizma" ("On the present state of Russian Symbolism") echoes Ivanov: "A Symbolist from the very beginning is a *theurge*, that is a possessor of secret knowledge, behind which stands secret action . . .". These claims were acerbically denounced by Bryusov, in his article "O 'rechi rabskoi', v zashchitu poezii" ("On 'slavish speech', in defence of poetry"),[3] in which he insisted: "However trying it may be to them . . . 'Symbolism' *wanted to be*, and always *was only art. . . .* Who will prevent Vyacheslav Ivanov from announcing to us tomorrow that 'Romanticism always was and could be only a distinctive geological theory'! . . . To insist that all poets must necessarily be theurges is as crass as insisting that they must all be members of the State Duma." In an article entitled "Venok ili venets?" ("A wreath or a crown?")[4] Bely spoke out in support of Ivanov: "The *laurel wreath* that shamefully covered the *priestly crown* has been torn off by the Symbolists. . . ."

In the years that followed, Ivanov and Bely in particular would make important contributions to the

AESTHETIC THEORIES Despite the closure of their two major organs, the main practitioners of Symbolism continued to argue over its essence, and a series of articles that appeared in 1910 crystallised the differences of emphasis and interest that had long been apparent. An irony of the situation is that this fundamental clarification of positions appeared in the journal *Apollon* (*Apollo*), founded in St Petersburg in 1909 by Sergei Makovsky (1878–1962). Though Makovsky described the goals of *Apollon* as "purely aesthetic, independent of . . . ideological shades (social, ethical, religious)", it would soon carry the manifestos of the young successors (and opponents) of the Symbolists, the Acmeists, led by Nikolai Gumilev.

In March 1910 Vyacheslav Ivanov gave two speeches in defence of his understanding of Symbolism, and these were followed in April by a speech in support from Blok. These lectures were published as articles in

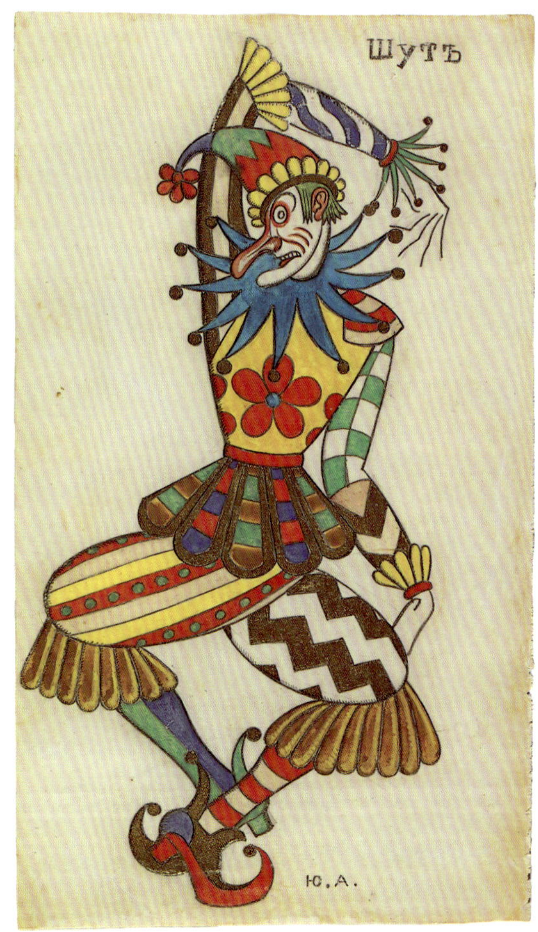

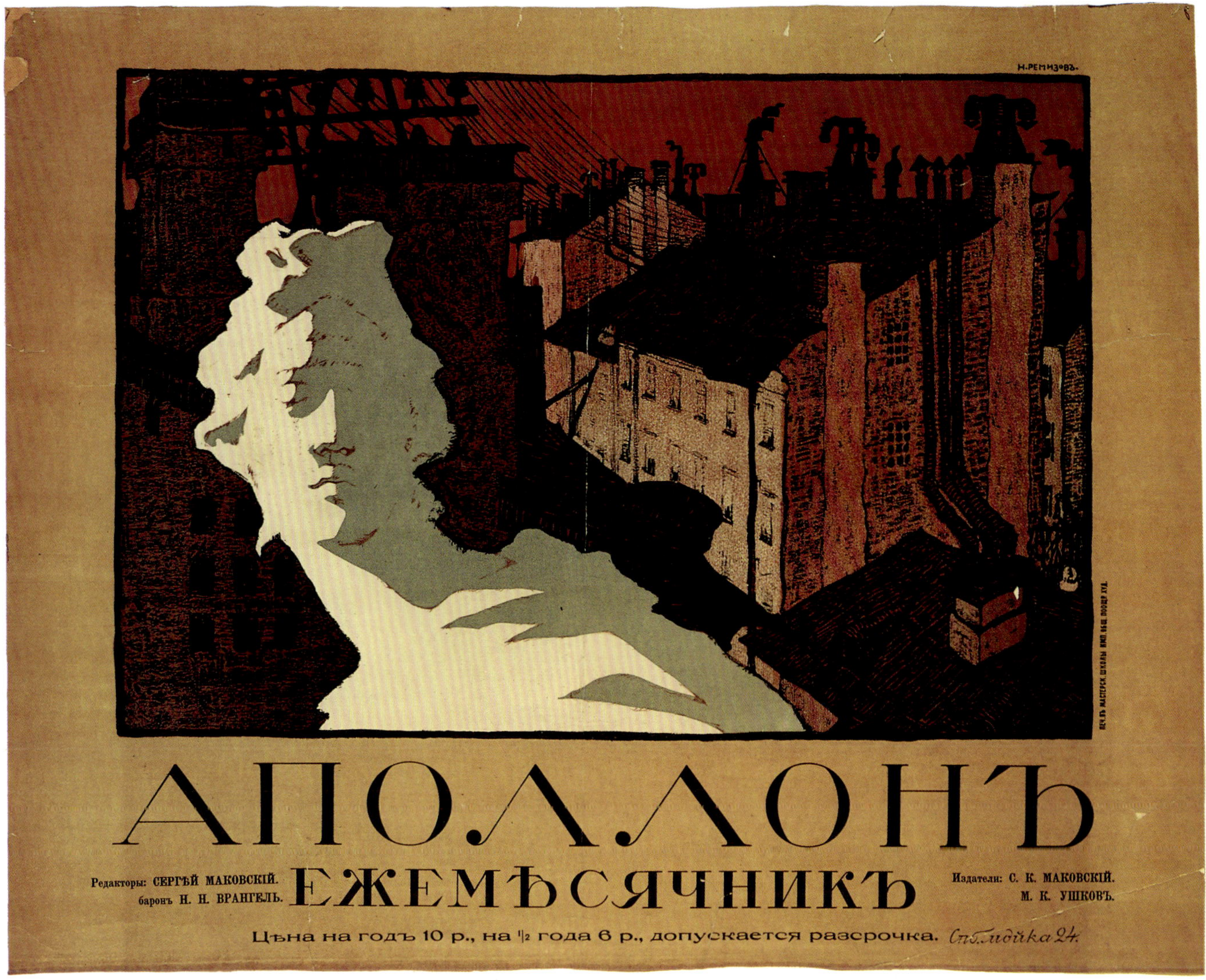

Nikolai Remizov (Re-mi)
286. *Apollon*, monthly review
St Petersburg, 1911
Lithographic poster, 58 × 69
State Lenin Library

theory of Symbolist art, but by now younger writers no longer turned automatically to the Symbolists for inspiration, associating instead with the Acmeist Poets' Workshop of Gumilev, or with the iconoclastic school of Futurists, who in their programmatic "Poshchechina obshchestvennomu vkusu" ("A slap in the Face for Public Taste") of December 1912 disdained Bal'mont's "perfumed lechery" and "the paper armour of the black frock coat of the warrior Bryusov", and unceremoniously consigned "the Bloks, Sologubs, Remizovs . . ." etc. etc. to "a dacha by the river". This did not, of course, prevent the Symbolist writers from substantial further achievement, in Blok's case the magnificent poetry of his *Third Book*, in Bely's the masterpiece of modernist prose that is *Petersburg*, which first appeared in book form in 1916.

The reactions of the Symbolist writers to the Revolution of October 1917 were predictably various. Blok, in the poetic cycle "Dvenadtsat'" ("The Twelve"), and Bely, in the long poem "Khristos Voskres" ("Christ is Risen") welcomed it, and both initially involved themselves in cultural activities for the new state. Merezhkovsky and Gippius, however, were strident in their condemnation. They emigrated soon after the revolution, as did Bal'mont, Ivanov and Remizov, all of whom were to die abroad. Sologub, after a failed attempt to emigrate, remained in Russia, but was allowed to publish no original work after 1923. Blok died, exhausted and disillusioned, in 1921. Bely, after living for a while in Berlin, returned to Russia, where he wrote several more novels and a number of important books of memoirs. And Valery Bryusov, enterprising as ever (not for nothing did Marina Tsvetaeva dub him a "hero of labour") joined the Communist party and occupied various posts in the literary division of the Commissariat of Enlightenment until his death in October 1924.

NOTES

1 *O prichinakh upadka i o novykh techeniiakh sovremennoi russkoi literatury (On the reasons for the decline and on the new currents in contemporary Russian literature)*, St Petersburg, 1893.
2 *Vesy* was named for the zodiacal sign preceding Scorpio.
3 *Apollon*, 1910 no.9.
4 *Apollon*, 1910 no.10.

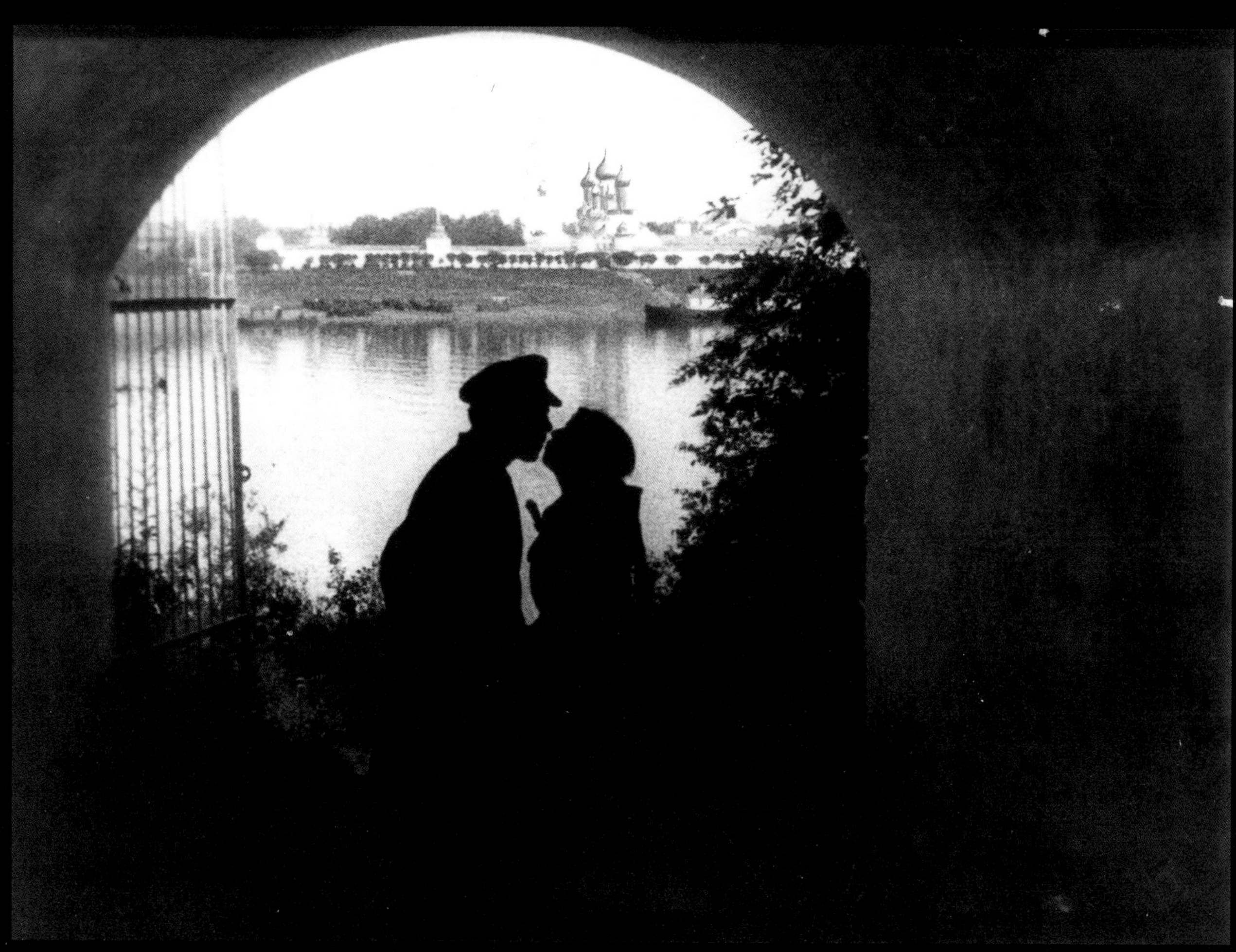

5

FROM THE KINGDOM OF SHADOWS

IAN CHRISTIE

It would be comforting to believe that pre-revolutionary Russian cinema has only become accessible due to the fissuring of Soviet dogma and censorship under *glasnost*, but in fact the possibility of exploring this rich terrain has existed at least since 1945. In that year Veniamin Vishnevsky published a pioneering filmography of some 2,000 titles, which prompted one Soviet reviewer to declare "entirely erroneous" the accepted belief that "Soviet film production started from scratch." On the contrary, "by October 1917, Russian film producers had created a definite style and artistic school which were reflected in the best pictures of that period."[1] Another forty years would pass, however, before the components and indeed the diversity of this "school" began to be analysed in detail; and only at the Pordenone Festival in October 1989 was a representative selection of the approximately 300 extant early Russian films actually screened.

Why did this discovery take so long? Chiefly, perhaps, because the director-polemicists of the young Soviet film avant-garde succeeded so well in denigrating all that had gone before (and most of what was being done elsewhere) by invoking the primacy of their "montage" technique. As variously elaborated by Vertov, Kuleshov, Eisenstein and Pudovkin, this technique soon came to be invested with a political as well as a quasi-scientific significance. What it produced had an irresistible appeal, especially for sophisticated foreigners – as the future founder of New York's Museum of Modern Art, Alfred Barr, recorded in his diary after seeing *The Mother* and *The Battleship Potemkin* in Moscow in 1927: "In the kino at least the revolution has produced great art even when more or less infected by propaganda. Here at last is a popular art; why, one wonders, does the soviet bother with painters?"[2] All the less reason for bothering with the "trash and sensationalism' (Eisenstein) of "Old Cine-Russia" (Abram Room) that the new Soviet cinema claimed to have superseded.

The polemic proved so successful that even when montage's cutting edge was blunted by the call in the 1930s for "revolutionary romanticism" and a folksy populism invaded Soviet cinema, soon to be followed by a frank appeal to patriotic sentiment as war loomed, pre-revolutionary cinema still remained in a forgotten limbo. It had to wait for the conjunction, which has taken place only within the last decade, of growing (and increasingly sanctioned) Soviet interest in the cultural dynamics of the Russian Silver Age with a worldwide trend in film scholarship that has focused fresh empirical attention on what used to be considered the "primitive" period. The result has been a new understanding of the way cinema developed in the Russia of 1907–17, which does not see this period as a mere stepping-stone to the canonic post-revolutionary epoch. We can now recognise its specific character and indeed trace its influence into the Soviet era, both in popular cinema, where a pre-revolutionary "king of the screen", Protazanov, reigned supreme at the box-office with his revolutionary melodramas and satirical comedies, and even in Eisenstein. As a shrewd contemporary wrote of the latter's *October* in 1928: "When the statues, the crystal and the porcelain begin to fill the screen persistently we are reminded not just of the symbolism of the Tsar's palace and of the autocratic Petersburg that derives from Blok and Bryusov, but also of the closely related line of Russian aestheticism that is associated with the World of Art group. Thus, beneath the Constructivist exterior of a materialistically conceived *October* there lurk the vestiges of the decadent and outdated styles of our art."[3]

As we shall see, many of the debates and attitudes that shaped Soviet cinema had at least their origins in the dynamic cinema culture of the decade *before* the Revolution.

INVENTING A HISTORY It was an auspicious coincidence that brought three of the cinema's many inventors to Russia in 1896. In fact the Lumières' *Cinématographe*, the Englishman Robert Paul's *Animatograph* and Edison's *Kinetophone* were all drawn by the promise of lavish celebrations to mark the coronation of the new tsar, Nikolai II. They were not disappointed, for this took place amid accelerating industrial and commercial development that promised a belated modernisation of the slumbering empire, and the travelling showmen found ready audiences for their novel entertainment.

As in most countries, curiosity was not confined to any single class: within weeks the imperial court had satisfied its curiosity (Nikolai was to remain an enthusiastic film fan, in spite of describing "this sideshow business" as "empty, useless and even pernicious" in the context of a police report on its growth by 1913), and soon dusty provincial towns were showing equal enthusiasm. And there is also evidence that some of the Russian intelligentsia showed an early and unusually sustained interest in the new medium.

Maxim Gorky, the future patron of Soviet "socialist realism", wrote one of the most evocative of all accounts recording the first impact of the cinematograph, which he witnessed at the 1896 Nizhny Novgorod Exhibition: "Yesterday I was in the kingdom of the shadows.

"If only you knew how strange it is to be there. There are no sounds, no colours. There, everything – earth, trees, people, water, air – is tinted in a grey monotone: in a grey sky there are grey rays of sunlight; in grey faces, grey eyes, and the leaves of trees are grey like ashes. This is not life but the shadow of life and this is not movement but the soundless shadow of movement."[4]

Gorky quickly assured his readers that he was not indulging in "symbolism" (a telling reminder of how much this had entered popular awareness), but merely describing the deep and complex impression made upon him. In a second newspaper article, he looked ahead and warned "The thirst for such strange, fantastic sensations as it gives will grow ever greater, and we will be increasingly less able to grasp the everyday impressions of ordinary life. . . . *The Salon of Death* may be brought from Paris at the end of the nineteenth century to Moscow at the beginning of the twentieth."[5]

Two months earlier, the composer Glazunov enthusiastically took an elderly friend to see the Edison demonstration in St Petersburg. The friend, a music critic, interpreted what he saw in terms strikingly different from Gorky, seeing an artistic potential that linked aspects of literature and music in true Symbolist fashion: "When a whole train flies from the distance, tearing aslant through the picture, what comes to mind in that very second is the same image in *Anna Karenina* . . .

"And then to watch the sea moving just a few feet away from our chairs – Mendelssohn's *Meeresstille*! – yet this silvery movement produces a music of its own."[6]

Soon there was clear proof that established artists were indeed drawing inspiration directly from the cinematograph. Yuri Tsivian notes that the abrupt succession of tableaux offered by early film programmes suggested to the Moscow Arts Theatre as early as 1899 a solution to the problem of staging *Boris Godunov*, with its many short scenes; and he cites the British film *That Fatal Sneeze* (Hepworth, 1907) as a probable influence on Bely's *Petersburg* (begun in 1911), suggesting the explosion motif and fragmented structure of that great modernist novel.[7] Writers as diverse as Tolstoy, Blok, Andreev and Mandelstam were equally fascinated by the medium's aesthetic challenge, and articles and even poems about the cinema began to appear regularly from around 1907. The fiction film which has traditionally been regarded as Russia's "first", Aleksandr Drankov's *Sten'ka Razin*, was launched with great publicity in 1908, accompanied by a specially-composed score from Mikhail Ippolitov-Ivanov, director of the Moscow Conservatory.

Indigenous production, it soon transpired, had in true Russian fashion "begun with the roof". Whereas film-making in most other countries started with more or less anonymous subjects, often comic or topical, the first Russian producers were seized with a patriotic and cultural ambition. Even the unscrupulous ex-newsreel-man Drankov had unsuccessfully attempted scenes from Pushkin's *Boris Godunov* before his public debut with *Sten'ka Razin*, inspired by a traditional ballad. He was soon challenged, in what would be a running competition, by Aleksandr Khanzhonkov, whose *Drama in a Gypsy Camp* (1908) echoed and improved upon Drankov's use of natural locations and popular iconography. Drankov turned next to the theatre and featured the renowned actor, Vladimir Davydov, in a truncated version of a popular comedy *Krechinsky's Wedding*; while Khanzhonkov enabled the enthusiastic Vasily

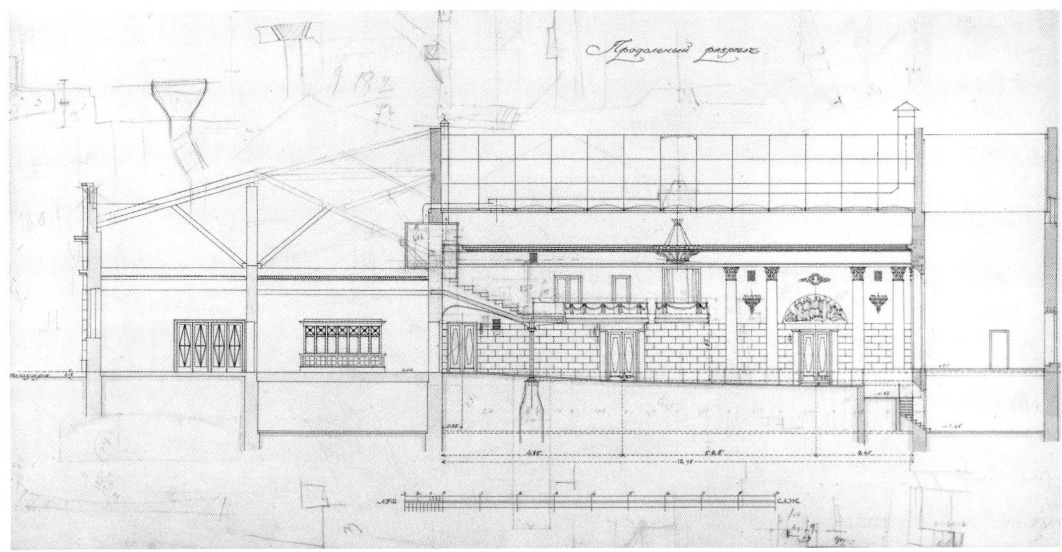

Goncharov to mount an ambitious period piece, *A Sixteenth-Century Russian Wedding* (1909), based on Konstantin Makovsky's highly ornamental paintings. Throughout 1909, Khanzhonkov pursued his cultural policy, now also aided by the actor-turned-director Petr Chardynin, with adaptations of Lermontov, Pushkin, Gogol' and even Dostoevsky's *The Idiot*.

The public response was enthusiastic and Russia's burgeoning film press gave loyal support. Pathé and Gaumont, long-established as distributors of their parent company's films, realised the potential for local production in genres which they already understood. Thus Khanzhonkov had to face competition from these two multi-nationals, initially directed by his former employee Goncharov – who made *Peter the Great* for Pathé early in 1910 and *The Life and Death of Pushkin* for Gaumont later in the same year. He fought back with Lermontov's *Vadim* and Pushkin's *Queen of Spades*, both directed by Chardynin, before the hot-tempered Goncharov returned to his first patron and inaugurated the era of "super-productions" with *The Defence of Sebastopol* (1911).

Such a compressed sketch of the highlights from this first phase of production may well suggest that it was as slavishly theatrical and traditional as later accounts claimed. And indeed one practice apparently unique to the early Russian cinema was the filming of extracts from plays, which were then projected with live actors delivering the dialogue in synchronisation. These "speaking pictures" or "film recitations" continued to be toured through the provinces by specialised troupes until 1917, and they testify to a "logocentrism" in Russian culture which Tsivian also holds responsible for the attachment to literary intertitles that resisted all experiment with completely visual films. But alongside these

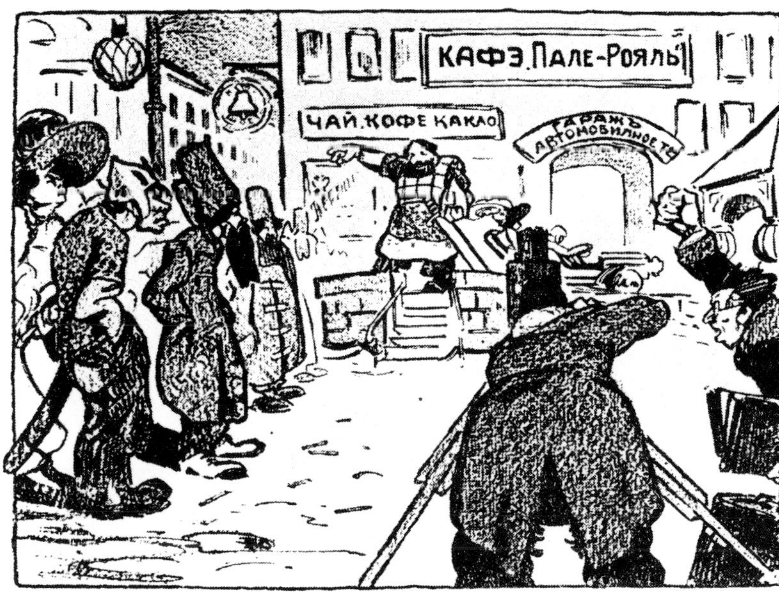

TOP: **Fedor Shekhtel'**
381. "Arts" Cinema on Arbat Square, Moscow: Longitudinal section
1912
Mixed media on paper, 38.7 × 73.5
A. V. Shchusev State Museum of Architecture

ABOVE: Caricature of early Russian filmmaking: "Old Russia is Risen"

PREVIOUS SPREAD: **Nikolai Larin**
652. *Merchant Bashkirov's Daughter:* still (cast unknown)
1913

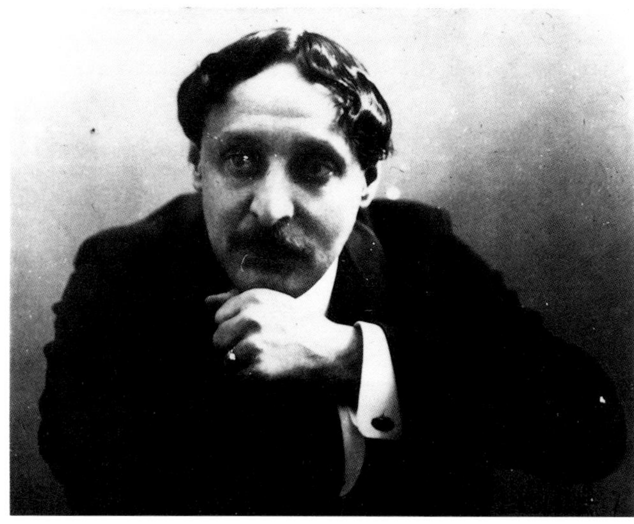

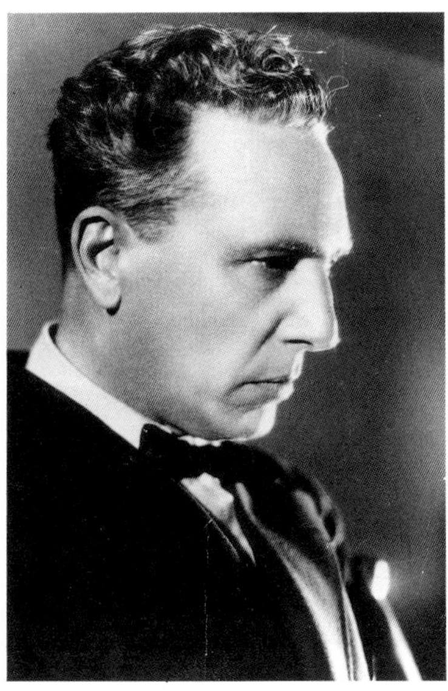

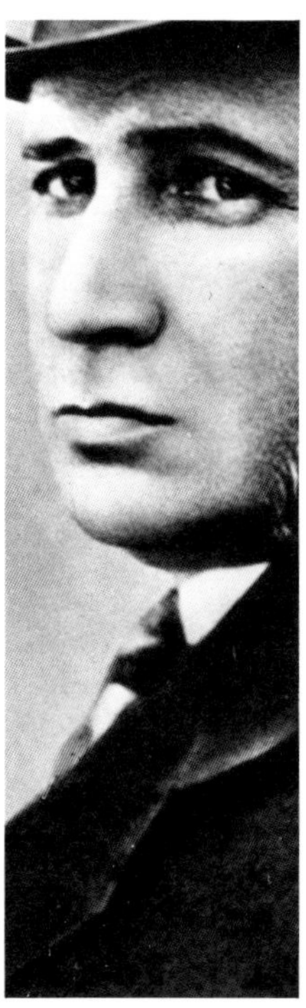

Top: Evgeny Bauer

Centre: Yakov Protozanov

Bottom: Vladimir Gardin

features the first five years also saw a striking development of *plein air* style, often used for folk subjects, which reached its summit in Goncharov's outstanding *The Brigand Brothers* (1912). There was too a notable vein of vernacular comedy (from as early as 1908 with Drankov's *The Diligent Batman*), which seems likely to be underrepresented among surviving films. Examples of the "Antoshu" and "Baldy" series from *c*.1915–16 show how licentious these could be: *Antoshu Ruined by a Corset* is more ribald, and probably also more realist, in its treatment of bourgeois marital mores than would have been allowed in most Western cinemas of the period.

Nothing, finally, in Russian culture – unless it was the inspiration of the fabulist Krylov – can explain the sudden emergence around 1910 of the animator and satirist Wladyslaw Starewicz. Drawing on his graphic skills, amateur photography and passion for entomology, Starewicz invented his own puppet world, at first peopled entirely by insects, and persuaded Khanzhonkov to back this eccentric vision. By 1912, he had moved into live-action fantasy with Gogol' and Ostrovsky adaptations, until the war gave him an opportunity to return to animation for satirical propaganda purposes.[8]

THE ELECTRIC PARADISE The year 1913 witnessed two imposing commemorative films, by the arch-rivals Khanzhonkov and Drankov, marking the tercentenary of the Romanov dynasty. Both were somewhat hampered by the strict censorship which had been reinforced on several occasions. Not only was any portrayal on screen of a tsar from Aleksandr II onwards forbidden, but since 1910 so too were stories from the Old and New Testaments, portrayals of Christ or the saints, the revolutionary events in Portugal, strikes in France and Germany, portraits of members of the disbanded Duma, foreign statesmen and officers of the Russian army. In 1913, the prohibition was extended to include films depicting hard labour, agitational activity, scenes which may arouse workers against their employers, strikes and the life of indentured peasants.

Whether such detailed restrictions indicated any special respect for the cinema's agitational power must remain open to question. But cinema-going had become a regular activity for a sizeable proportion of the urban population, despite what seemed primitive cinemas by American standards.[9] *Motion Picture World* carried a report from Moscow in April 1913 which stated that there were about 800–1,000 cinemas in the country, the largest seating only 200–300, with none having two projectors for the continuous showing of multi-reel films. The audiences, however, were judged to be "of a class far above any in the greater part of the rest of Europe."[10]

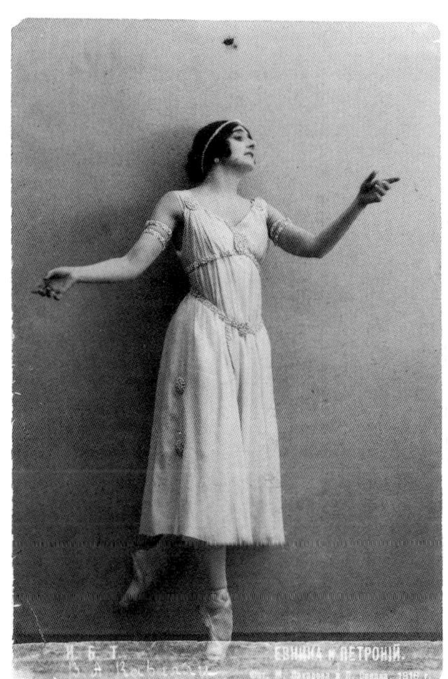

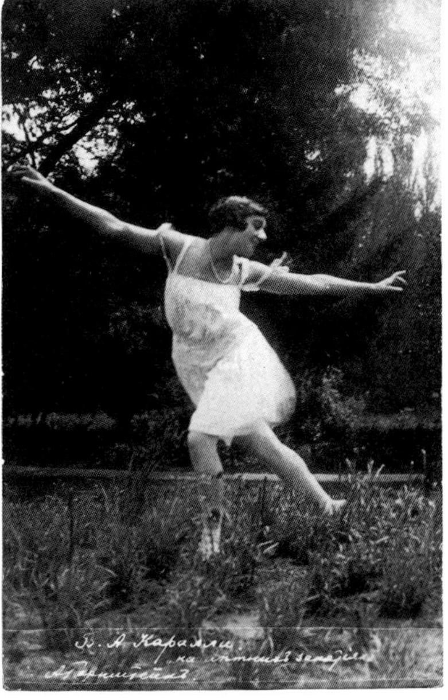

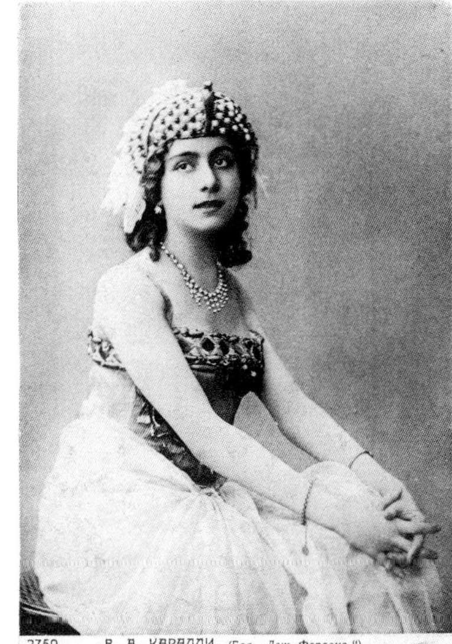

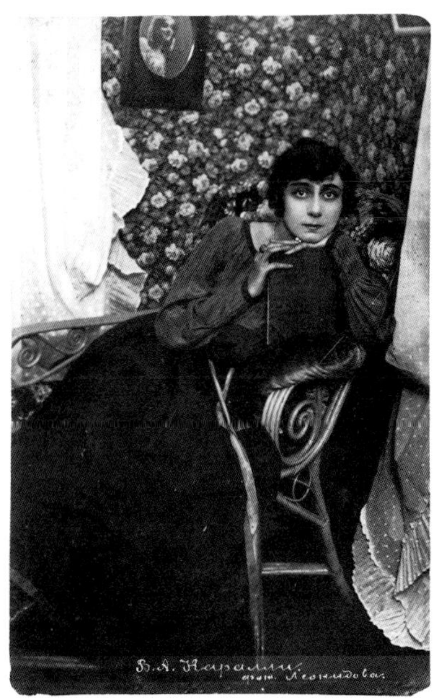

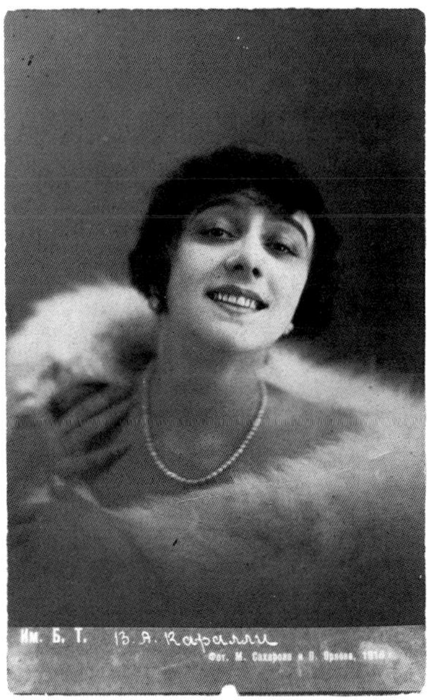

Five publicity postcards of Vera Karalli

No doubt it was this unusual enthusiasm of the upper classes and the intelligentsia that provided an audience for the intense debate about the artistic status of cinema which reached a climax in 1913. Articles by such diverse celebrities as the playwright Leonid Andreev, the theatre director Meyerhold and the young Futurist Mayakovsky all admitted that cinema had taken over a part of theatre's former role and that it was in the process of defining its own distinctive techniques and potential. If not yet truly "art", it soon might be – and all three would eventually try their hand.[11] Meanwhile, the Russian Futurists became quite possibly the first members of any artistic avant-garde to make their own film when *Drama in the Futurists' Cabaret No. 13* appeared in early 1914, reputedly a parody of the current guignol genre (possibly inspired by the decadent *Secret of House No. 5* of 1912) and starring the painters Larionov and Goncharova.

This proved to be an experiment without any immediate successors. But two months earlier, a former set designer and man-about-the-theatre, who had been art director on one of the tercentenary epics, joined Khanzhankov's company and directed his debut film.

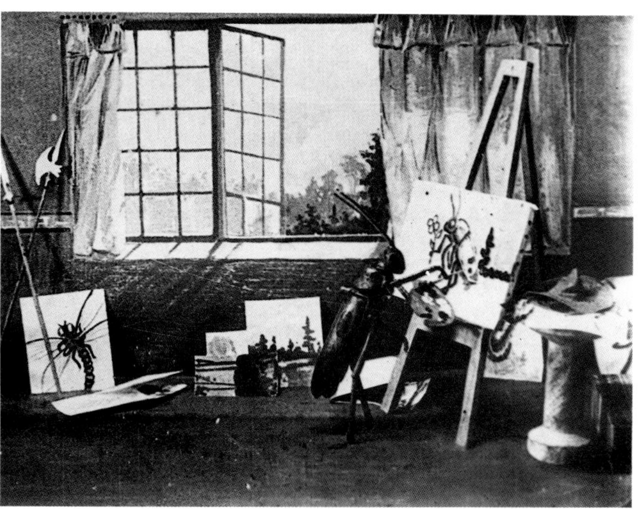

RIGHT: **Evgeny Bauer**
The Dying Swan: still with Vera Karalli
as the mute dancer Giselle
1917

This was *The Twilight of a Woman's Soul*, and its forty-eight-year-old director was Evgeni Bauer. More than anyone, he would set the tone for the remaining four years of Tsarist cinema; and in his 82 films (of which 26 survive), the ideal of combining all the elements of scenography, lighting, camera-work, acting and scripting became, for the first time in Russian cinema, a reality.[12]

Three factors contributed to Bauer's primacy. One was his background in theatre design, particularly in the *féerie* genre, and his early friendship with Fedor Shekhtel', which left its mark in the large, spare interior designs that gave his films a new sense of space. A second was the change in emotional climate, perhaps due to the war, which favoured the anguished, yet stoical, relationships and states of mind that he excelled in portraying. When later critics have spoken of the decadence and necrophilia that infected late Romanov cinema, they usually have in mind a handful of Bauer's most famous – or notorious – films, such as *Daydreams* (1915), *After Death* (1915), *The Dying Swan* (1917) and *To Happiness* (1917). And yet this atmosphere owes much to the Symbolist decade that preceded it; in many ways it could be regarded as the moment of Symbolism in Russian cinema, transposed in much the same way that German Expressionist cinema recomposed earlier motifs from literary and graphic Expressionism. The third factor essential to Bauer's achievement was the emergence of a relatively stable "star system", which indeed he helped to create by his repeated use of such players as Vera Kholodnaya, Vera Karalli, Vitol'd Polonski and Ivan Perestiani. Drawing on his experience as a portrait photographer, he was able to treat them as "models" (as his protégé Lev Kuleshov would later term the ideal film actor) and create the desired sense of inner life by cinematic means.

This, indeed, brings us to the crucial paradox of the second phase of early Russian cinema. For if the films of

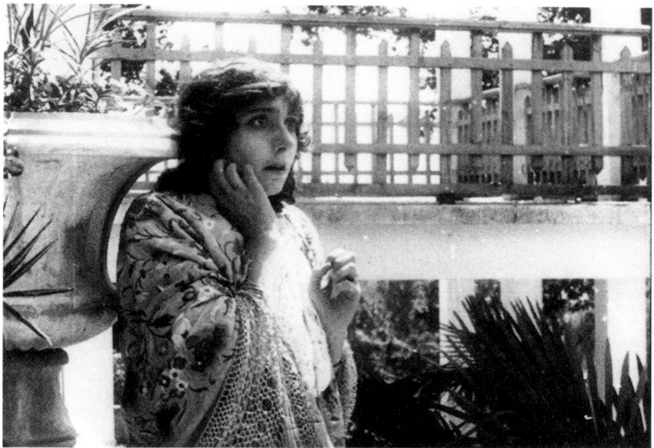

Bauer and his leading contemporaries appear to us, at first sight, "uncinematic", this is not because of a failure to grasp the requirements of cinema. It is the result of a conscious aesthetic strategy, essentially Symbolist in origin, which defines the essence of "moving pictures" as the denial of superfluous movement, identifies duration with intensity and "fullness", and seeks closure in a muted or tragic ending.

The same aesthetic of immobility can be found in much of Protazanov's pre-1918 work – together with Gardin, he and Bauer were recognised as leaders of what was irreverently known as the Russian "braking" school. But Protazanov, who began directing in 1911 and continued to 1943, also displayed a wider range, and versatility is a part of his achievement: it is difficult to imagine Bauer making the same massive adjustments to work in France, Germany and then Soviet Russia. Protazanov in fact seemed to thrive on controversy and contradiction. His impudent dramatisation of Tolstoy's last days in *The Passing of a Great Old Man* (1912) was banned amid a storm of righteous indignation, yet went on to win fame abroad. Five years later, the lifting of the Tsarist censorship after the February 1917 Revolution enabled him to film Tolstoy's *Father Sergius* before emigrating in 1918 to France with many of the leading Russian cinema personnel. In between he directed the definitive popular melodrama of ill-starred love, *The Keys to Happiness*, which enjoyed massive popularity in 1913, co-directed *War and Peace* in 1915 and made *The Queen of Spades* in a chilling new version in 1916. Interestingly, no less than three of his other films of 1917–18 are set outside Russia – the diabolic *Satan Triumphant* and *Little Ellie*, about a child-murderer, both take place in Scandinavian small towns; while *Jenny the Maid*, a class-reversal drama about an aristocrat forced to work as a chambermaid, is set in France. When Protazanov eventually sought exile in France, his first film *Une Angoissante Aventure* took the form of an acute anxiety dream set within a comedy foil – a Russian picture within a French frame and a fitting *envoi* to the lost continent of Russian cinema.

Three years earlier, in mid-1917, Lev Kuleshov was poised between two worlds when he wrote: "the artist must view cinema as the finest, most widespread and powerful of the arts, which the artist can use to realise new paths, new achievements that are impracticable in the field of pure painting, sculpture or architecture."[13] His call would fall on receptive ears in the new era of cinema's official "importance"; but his own conviction and experience, which would train the first generation of Soviet film-makers and provide the backbone of their theory, came from working as Bauer's assistant in "old Cine-Russia".

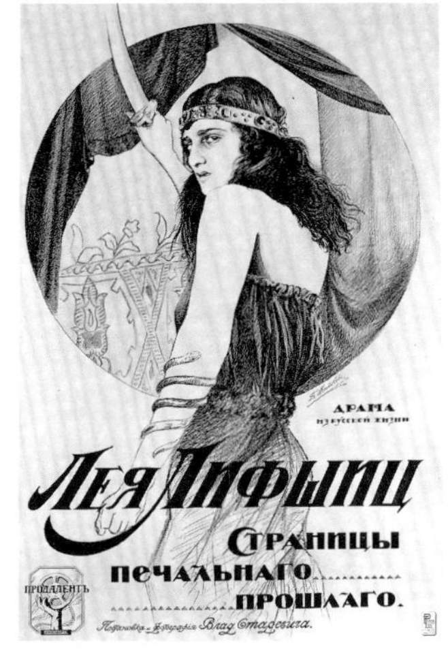

ABOVE: **P. Zhitkov**
489. Cinema poster: *Leya Lifshits: Pages of a sad past*
Moscow, n.d.
Lithographic poster, 107 × 73
State Lenin Library

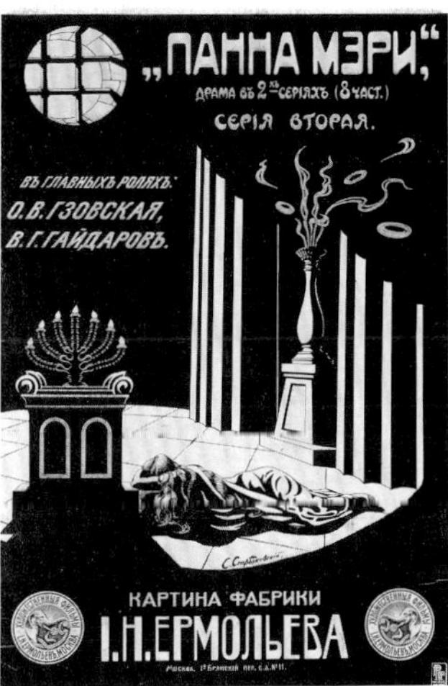

RIGHT: **S. Strenkovsky**
409. Cinema poster (for I. N. Ermol'ev's Artistic Films): *Panna Mary (Miss Mary)*
Moscow, 1910
Lithographic poster, 167 × 70
State Lenin Library

NOTES

1 Quoted in J. Leyda, *Kino: A History of the Russian and Soviet Film*, London, 1960, p.15.
2 "Russian Diary, 1927–8", *October*, 1978, no.7, p.37.
3 Adrian Piotrovsky, "*October* Must Be Re-Edited!", in *The Film Factory: Russian and Soviet Cinema in Documents 1896–1939* (eds. Richard Taylor and Ian Christie), London, 1988, p.216.
4 "The Lumière Cinematograph", *Nizhegorodskii listok* (trans. Richard Taylor) ibid., p.25.
5 Quoted in Leyda, pp.20–1.
6 Vladimir Stasov, writing in May 1896, quoted in Leyda, p.18.
7 In a lecture given at the National Film Theatre on 8 March 1990; see also, "Early Russian Cinema: Some Observations", in *Inside the Film Factory: New Approaches to Russian and Soviet Cinema*, London, 1991.
8 See *Starewicz 1882–1965* (ed. J. Pilling), Edinburgh International Film Festival, 1983.
9 M. L. Moravskaya wrote, *c.* 1915: "For those whom life has cheated/Open the electric paradise." Quoted in Leyda, p.82.
10 Leyda, p.68.
11 V. Mayakovsky, "Theatre, Cinema, Futurism"; "The Destruction of Theatre by Cinema"; "The Relationship between Contemporary Theatre and Cinema and Art"; L. Andreev, "Second Letter on Theatre"; V. Meyerhold, "On Cinema", in *The Film Factory*, pp.33–9.
12 On Bauer, see *Silent Witnesses: Russian Films 1908–1919*, ed. Y. Tsivian et al., Pordenone and London, 1989.
13 L. Kuleshov, "On the Tasks of the Artist in Cinema", in *The Film Factory*, p.43.

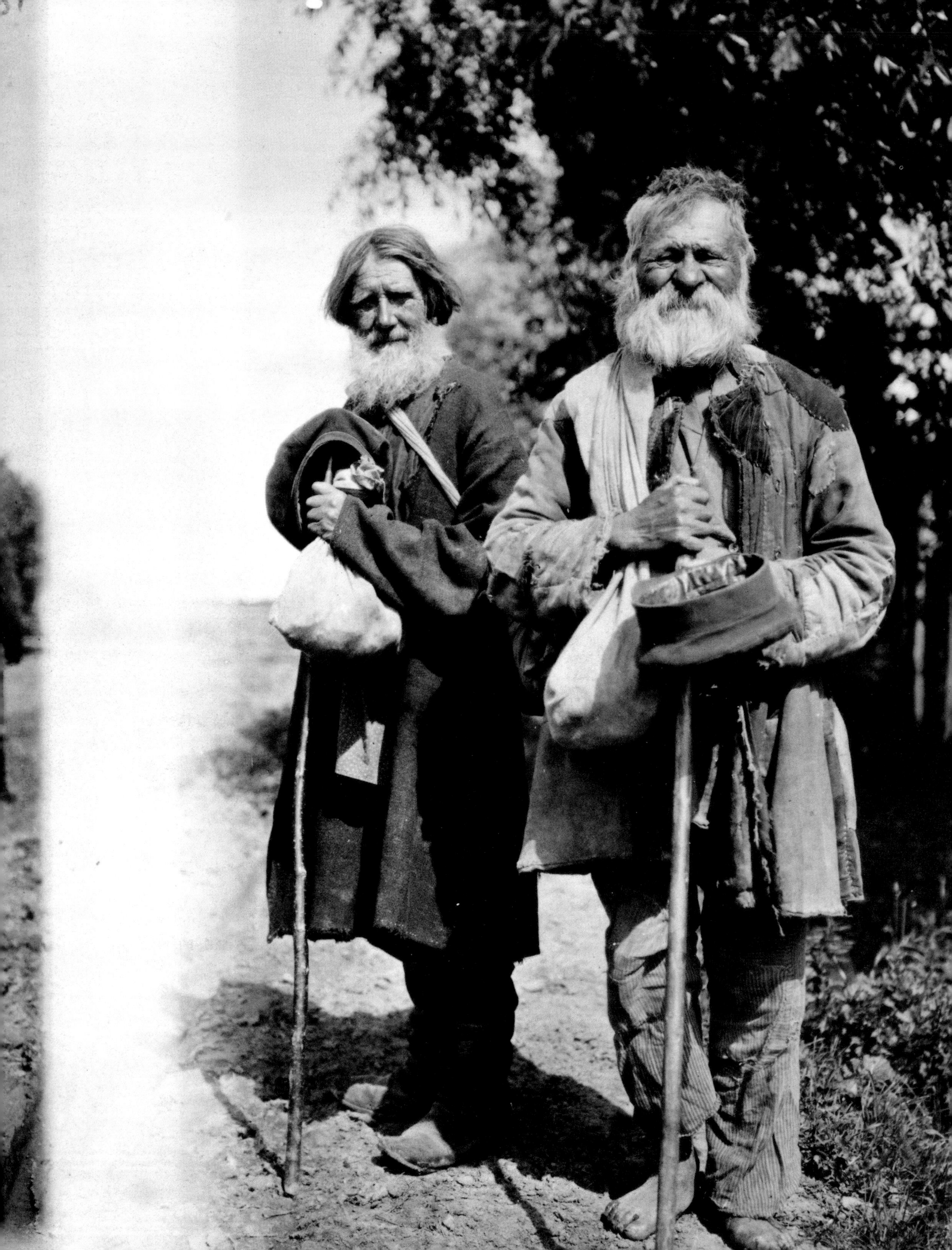

6

THE WORLD OF ART'S
ENGLISH CORRESPONDENT

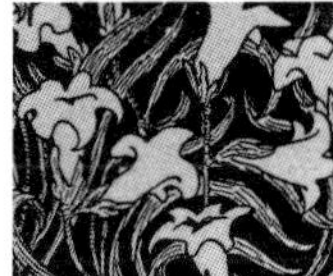

We know tantalisingly little about Netta Peacock, fourteen of whose photographs are illustrated on these pages, from a collection of some two hundred in the Victoria and Albert Museum (reproduced here by courtesy of the Trustees), but she does provide a fascinating link between Britain and the Russian crafts movement in the earliest years of the century. Peacock was co-editor of the *Russian Year-books* for 1913 and 1914 and compiled the *Russian Almanac 1919*; and she was also the author of two articles, one in *The Studio* in 1901 on "The new movement in Russian decorative art" (reprinted below), the other in *The Soul of Russia* (1916), a publication in aid of Russian refugees, on "Russian peasant industries". In the latter work she is identified as the "English correspondent" of *Mir Iskusstva (The World of Art)*. She also published a short book on Millet in 1905.

Netta Peacock is believed to be one of the six children of Dmitry Rudolf Peacock (1842–92) and his wife Tat'yana. Dmitry was the son of Charles and Concordia Peacock and was educated both in England and at the University of Moscow. He lived and made his career in Russia, being appointed vice-consul at Batoum in 1881 and consul-general at Odessa in 1891; he also published in English the original vocabularies of five west Caucasian languages: Adkhazian, Georgian, Lazian, Mingrelian and Svanetian. Netta's *Studio* article is written so knowledgeably as to suggest she knew personally the women in the Abramtsevo circle who were the chief promoters of the peasant crafts industry, and her photographs of village life reinforce the sympathy for rural Russia shown in her articles. Other photographs in the collection show her interest in people of all classes, in Moscow and St Petersburg as well as in the villages. The costumes and architecture suggest that most date from the first decade of this century, though some may have been taken in the 1890s.

The prints are of various non-standard sizes and are not high-quality final prints intended for public viewing, but rather work prints and copy prints with uneven borders and inconsistent printing.

In the context of the present exhibition, Netta Peacock's 1901 *Studio* article is of particular interest (the spelling of artists' names has been made consistent with that used elsewhere in the catalogue, and specific discussions of illustrations in the original article have been omitted).

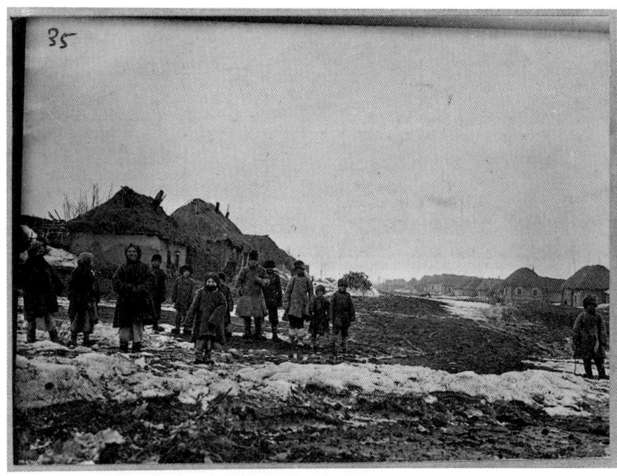

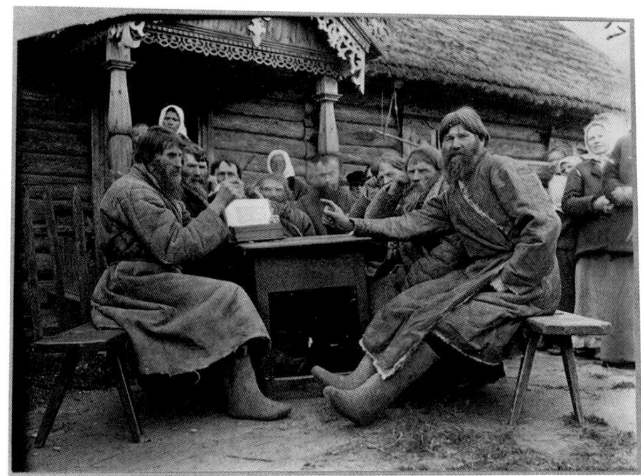

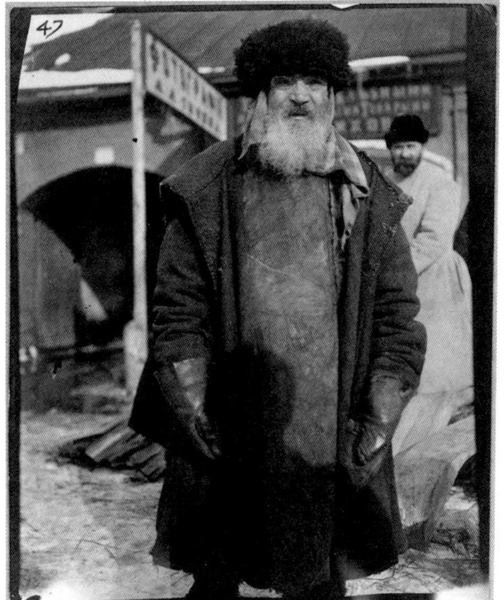

TOP LEFT: Village street

TOP RIGHT: Village elders

LEFT: Village doctor

RIGHT: Village policemen

BOTTOM LEFT: Classroom

BOTTOM RIGHT: Village school outdoors

PREVIOUS PAGE: Two pilgrims

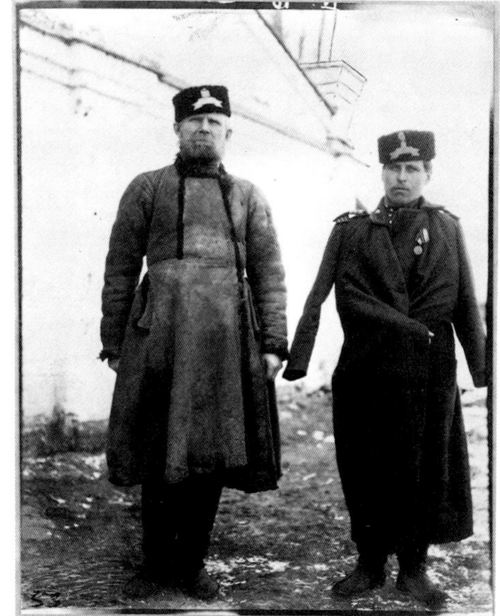

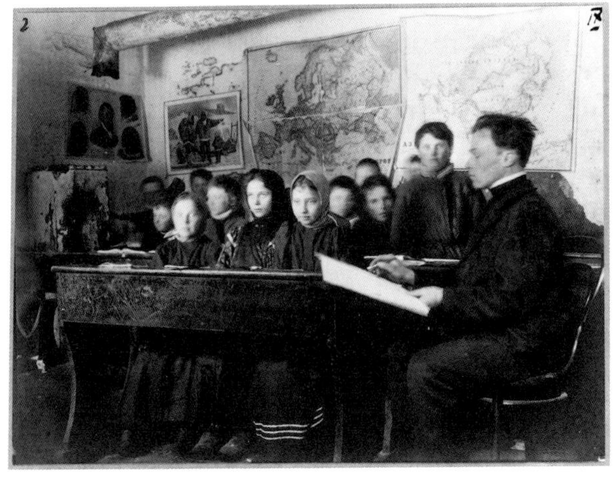

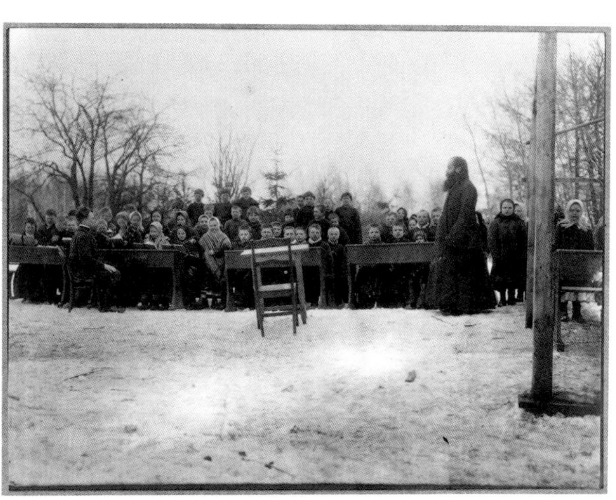

THE NEW MOVEMENT IN RUSSIAN DECORATIVE ART

NETTA PEACOCK

Until last summer, when one of the artistic successes of the Exhibition in Paris was scored by the Russian Rural Industries and – what one must call for want of a better term – the New Russian Decorative Art, the majority of Western Europeans had but little notion of the artistic genius of this people. It was a happy idea on the part of the organising committee to exhibit the two side by side, thus giving those interested the opportunity of judging for themselves how perfectly in harmony with the decorative feeling of the present the new movement is.

Elena Polenova (whose death two years ago proved so great a loss to Russian art) was the first to realise that the decorative art of a country should express popular thought in popular language, and that if not expressive of the instinctive feeling of a people it lacked distinction and was of value only as suitable design, but not otherwise. With the knowledge she possessed of the history and archaeology of her own land, she soon made herself mistress of the pecularities and characteristics of peasant production, and thoroughly imbued her own original compositions with the national stamp. She led the way, and gradually became the guiding and informing spirit of a small group of Muscovite artists who turned their attention towards decoration with such success that the movement they started is likely to grow rapidly in importance and is bound, sooner or later, to make its influence felt beyond its own country.

The future of this decoration, which appeals both to the eye and to the fancy, lies in the fact that it deals more with colour than it does with line, and, with rare exceptions, deals with simple subjects simply treated. It seeks its inspiration in the very heart of life – in nature as seen through the eyes of the peasant, who is free from all the conventionalities of civilisation, and whose eye is unspoilt by the constant contemplation of the ugliness which is so unsparingly distributed around us. The real poetry of life is the peasant's birthright – he is in ceaseless intercourse with the splendour and mystery of ever-changing nature, therefore his art is spontaneous, sane, vigorous and serene.

It may seem strange when writing of decorative art to refer to the Russian peasant; but, in order to understand the origin of this movement, it is necessary to realise the importance of the Rural Industries to lovers of all that is genuinely Russian. Through these the earliest expression of Russian art has been preserved intact. In some few villages near the large towns modifications may be observable; but in the depths of the country, as the peasant's forefather felt and expressed in by-gone days, so does he feel and express today. In other countries the rapid development of machinery and the intrusion of the railway has effectively wiped out cottage industries, except in some remote spots. In Russia the long period of intense cold which prevails all over the northern portion obliges the peasant to have some indoor occupation; instinctively, therefore, he decorates the material at hand, which he turns into the necessary utensils for daily use, disposing of these at the village fair, or, more rarely, at the nearest town. The women spin, weave, and dye their linen and woollen goods with vegetable dyes; they copy on their chemises – high-necked, long-sleeved garments – either in embroidery or drawn-thread, the designs over a hundred years old, which are regularly handed down from mother to daughter. It is generally admitted that the embroidery and drawn-thread work furnish what is most characteristic, original, and important in old Russian art; but for quaintness and exquisite appropriateness their wood objects cannot be beaten. In the shape of the various vessels, as well as in their decoration, we feel that wood is a familiar and loved possession of this people, who still remain carvers rather than carpenters, preferring their primitive tools to any modern inventions in the labour-saving direction when by chance they happen to meet with these.

With more than half of the enormous peasant population turning out domestic utensils and woven materials which are perfect treasures from the artistic point of view – though they are certainly far from "correct", or what we call "finished" – it is not surprising that the group of Muscovite artists (including such well-known names as Elena Polenova, Mariya Yakunchikova-Weber, Natal'ya Davydova, Viktor Vasnetsov, Konstantin Korovin, Aleksandr Golovin, Mikhail Vrubel', and Sergei Malyutin) should have been roused to enthusiasm and fired with the desire to strike out on new lines. Quite unconsciously, for they are no theorists, they were actuated by two motives – the one a genuine love of their popular art, and the other the fear that the building of manufactories in the large towns would gradually kill the art crafts of the villages. By the different members of this group nearly every form of decoration is expressed (I use the word decoration in its broadest sense, as opposed to applied ornament) – frescoes, furniture, pottery,

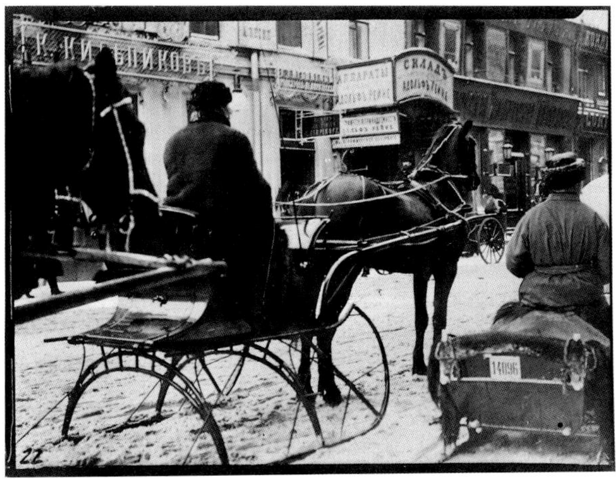

Street scene with sleigh

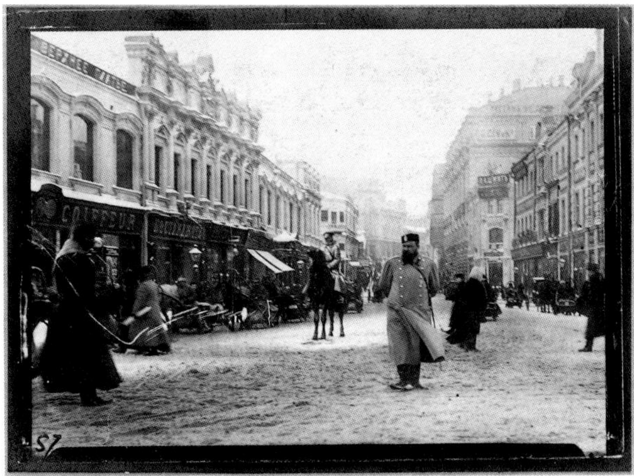

Kuznetsky Most, Moscow

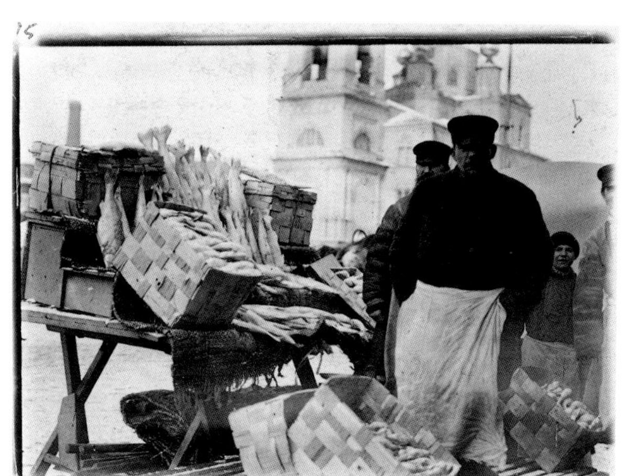

Fishmarket, Moscow

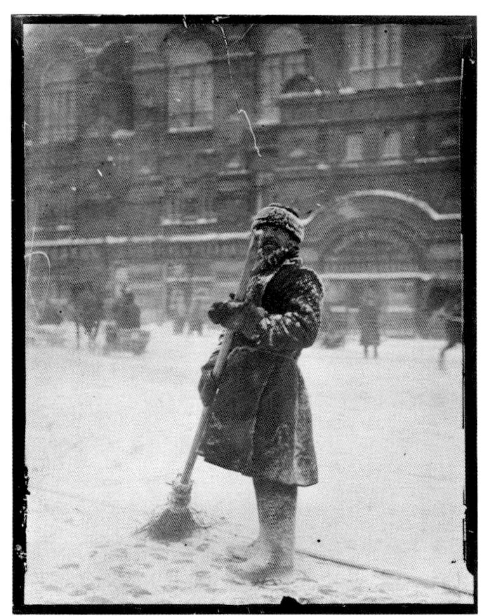

Snow sweeper, St Petersburg (?)

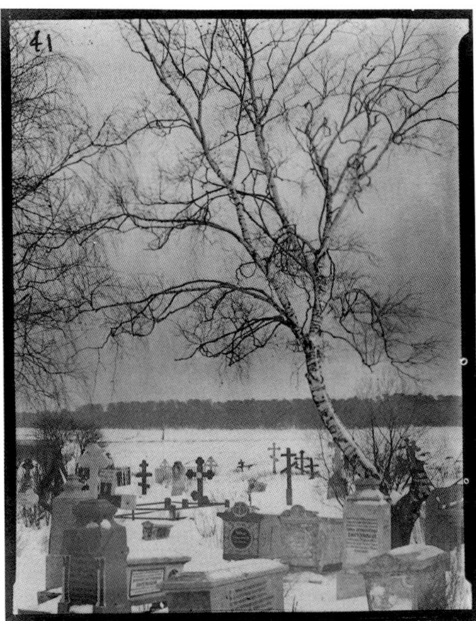

Graveyard

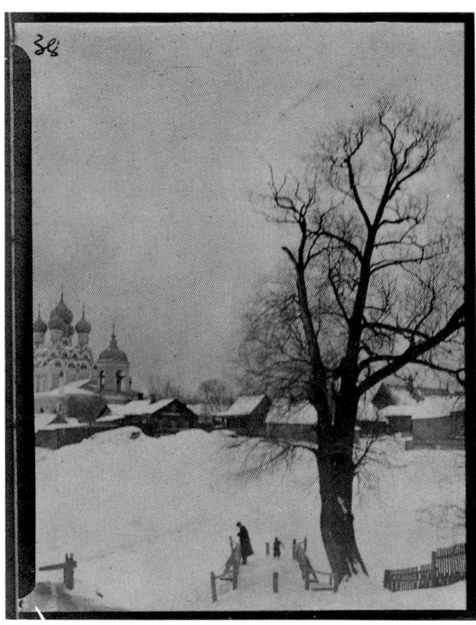

Village with church

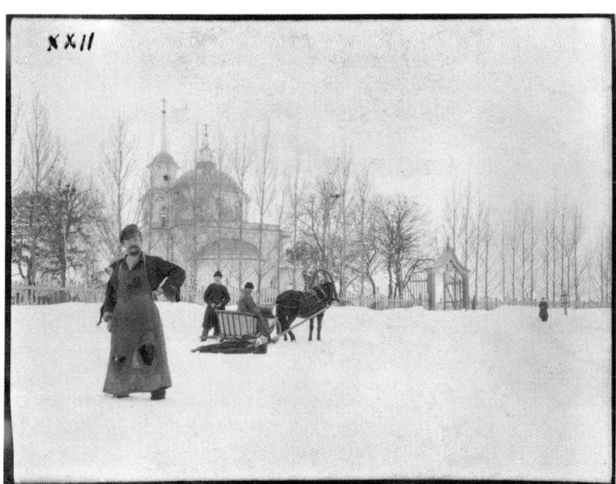

Winter scene

embroidery, enamelling, book-covers and illustrations, wall-papers, toys, etc. Naturally, the artistic expression of each individual artist is largely influenced by his temperament. Some of them have cast off all restraint and indulge in almost riotous design; others accentuate the rugged strenuous side; while the work of others, again, is remarkable for its reticence and delight of form and tone. So thoroughly have they impregnated themselves with the spirit of legend and fairy-tale as still told by the poet-peasant, so genuinely do they feel the absorbing charm of that atmosphere of old-world simplicity, with all that it contains of dreamlike and weird reality – its mingled fancy and belief – that their designs are distinctly national both in feeling and colour. This new movement is, in fact, an exaltation of the popular genius; and the designs of the artists are so perfectly executed because they answer to the inborn aesthetic sense of the village artisan.

7

CHRONOLOGY

JULIA ENGELHARDT

1861 Following Russia's defeat in the Crimean War (1853–56) Tsar Aleksandr II had resolved to abolish serfdom in Russia to forestall any movement for the liberation of the serfs. In this year reform laws provide for their emancipation. 48 million men, who with their dependents make up around four-fifths of the total population, obtain basic liberties. Village communes are to assume collective responsibility for payment of taxes and annual "redemption dues", which will ultimately give the peasants ownership of land, but in most cases the resulting financial burdens prove to be too heavy.

1864–68 Russian conquest of Turkestan, Tashkent and Samarkand.

1870 The Society for Travelling Art Exhibitions is formed; its members are known as the *Peredvizhniki (Wanderers)*. They subscribe to the ideas of Realism, Populism and national character. Over the next decades they take exhibitions to the provinces to reach a wider public with their message of social reform.

The industrialist Savva Mamontov and his wife Elizaveta acquire the estate of Abramtsevo near Moscow.

Marx's *Das Kapital* appears in Russian translation.

1873 Students form the group "Going to the People" (later known as the Populists), inspired by the veteran socialist and reformer Aleksandr Herzen. Thousands go to the countryside to preach self-help through revolution to the peasants.

1874 The Mamontovs establish an artists' colony at Abramtsevo. Over the years it attracts some of the outstanding Russian artists of the period, including Vasily and Elena Polenov, Il'ya Repin, Viktor and Apollinary Vasnetsov, Konstantin Korovin and Valentin Serov.

1875 Religious orders are abolished in Russia.

1878 The Congress of Berlin makes extensive changes to the boundaries of the Balkan nations as the European powers restrict Russia's gains in the recent war with Turkey (1877–78).

1880 Plans are made by Viktor Vasnetsov and Vasily Polenov for a little church to be built on the Abramtsevo estate, designed in the style of a medieval Novgorod

Assassination of Tsar Aleksandr II in St Petersburg

church. Many members of the Mamontov circle contribute to its decoration.

Dostoevsky's novel *The Brothers Karamazov* is published; the writer dies in January 1881.

1881 Aleksandr II approves a programme of political reform, which provides for an embryonic form of representational assembly to participate in government. On 1 March he is assassinated, and his successor, Aleksandr III, abandons the reforms. Wide-ranging emergency powers are given to the authorities.

Following the assassination of the Tsar there are many pogroms throughout southern and south-western Russia, with the connivance of the government, which hopes to divert the discontent of the peasants.

1882 Mamontov's Private Russian Opera in Moscow opens with the première of Rimsky-Korsakov's *Snegurochka (The Snow Maiden)* in a production designed by Viktor Vasnetsov. The opera house employs professional musicians and singers; it will introduce the works of Dargomyzhsky, Borodin, Musorgsky and Rimsky-Korsakov to the Russian public in productions designed by leading painters.

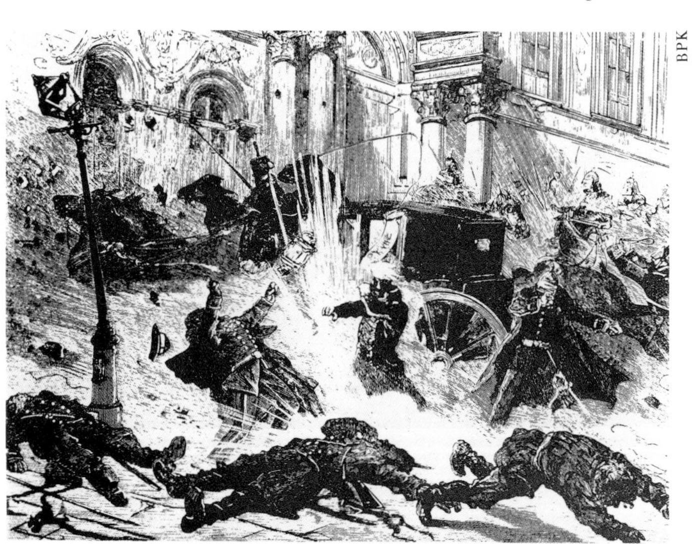

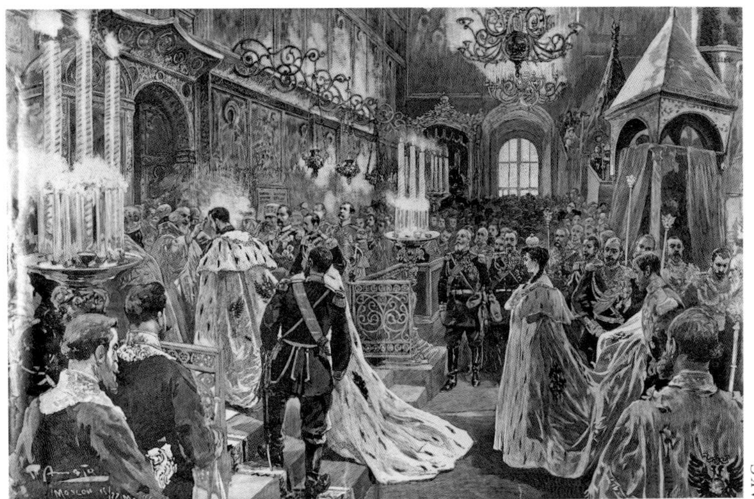

Coronation of Tsar Nikolai II in the church of the Assumption in the Moscow Kremlin

1884 Mikhail Vrubel' is commissioned to recreate twelfth-century murals in the Byzantine church of St Cyril in Kiev.

1887 Aleksandr Ul'yanov, Lenin's elder brother is executed after an attempt on the life of Aleksandr III.

1890 Vrubel' visits Abramtsevo and joins Mamontov's circle. He is active in the ceramic workshops founded the same year, making experiments in lustre glazes with the workshop's manager Petr Vaulin.

Borodin's *Knyaz' Igor'* (*Prince Igor*) – posthumously – and Tchaikovsky's *Pikovaya Dama* (*Queen of Spades*) have their first performances in St Petersburg.

1891 There is widespread famine in Russia as harvests fail in 22 provinces.

Construction of the Trans-Siberian Railway starts; it reaches Port Arthur in 1901 and is completed in 1904. Between 1890 and 1904 the length of railways in Russia virtually doubles from 30,000 km to almost 60,000 km.

The St Petersburg *Severnyi Vestnik* (*The Northern Messenger*) starts to publish work by young Symbolist writers, who will include Dmitry Merezhkovsky, Fedor Sologub, Zinaida Gippius and Konstantin Bal'mont. The journal survives until 1898.

1892 Sergei Witte is appointed finance minister. Under his direction Russia enters an era of unprecedented industrialisation. At just over 8% its annual growth rate in the 1890s is the highest in the world. Huge state support for industry is financed by indirect taxes and grain exports – leaving the peasants with insufficient food supplies – while high duties limit imports to a minimum.

A Pan-Slav conference is held in Cracow.

The Tretyakov brothers donate their art collections and the building in which they are housed to the city of Moscow. The

Tretyakov Gallery opens to the public in 1893.

Merezhkovsky's collection of poems *Simvoly* (*Symbols*) is published, followed (in 1893) by his essay "On the reasons for the decline and on the new currents in contemporary Russian literature".

1893 Princess Tenisheva acquires the estate of Talashkino, near Smolensk, and sets up an artistic colony there modelled on Abramtsevo. Visiting artists include Vrubel', Aleksandr Golovin, Nikolai Roerich and Sergei Malyutin, who at the turn of the century takes on the management of the joinery workshops and builds a church on the estate.

Vladimir Ul'yanov, later called Lenin, joins a group of Marxist intellectuals in St Petersburg.

Lev Tolstoy completes *The Kingdom of God is within You*, a full statement of his Christian anarchist beliefs.

OCTOBER: Tchaikovsky's 6th Symphony (the "Pathétique") has its first performance in St Petersburg, nine days before the composer's suicide.

1894 Following the death of Aleksandr III, Nikolai II ascends the throne.

The First Congress of Russian Artists is held in Moscow.

A more liberal art education is introduced at the Petersburg Academy, with members of the *Peredvizhniki* being admitted to the teaching staff.

Valery Bryusov publishes three collections of poems entitled *Russkie Simvolisty* (*Russian Symbolists*) (1894–5).

Viktor Borisov-Musatov goes to Paris to study at the Académie Cormon; he stays until 1898. Many young Russian painters spend a year or more of their training in Paris during the 1890s, frequenting the private academies of Cormon, Julian and

Colarossi, including Aleksandr Golovin (1889 and 1897), Lev Bakst (from 1893), Anna Golubkina (from 1895), Aleksandr Benois and his cousin Evgeny Lanceray (from 1896), Konstantin Somov (1897) and others.

1896 JANUARY: Mamontov's Private Russian Opera mounts a production of Humperdinck's *Hänsel und Gretel* designed by Vrubel'. Later in the year Fedor Shalyapin makes his Moscow début in the company's production of Glinka's *Ivan Susanin* (*A Life for the Tsar*).

MAY: Coronation of Nikolai II in St Petersburg. The ceremony is attended by three cinematographers: the brothers Lumière's *Cinématographe*, Robert Paul's *Animatograph* and Edison's *Kinetophone*. An accident during the celebrations causes great loss of life.

MAY: The All-Russian Exhibition of Industry and Art is held at Nizhny Novgorod. Korovin designs the Far North pavilion in the Neo-Russian style. Paintings by Vrubel' commissioned for the occasion are rejected, and Mamontov has a special pavilion constructed to house them.

OCTOBER: Chekhov's *The Seagull* is premièred, unsuccessfully, in St Petersburg.

NOVEMBER: The Moscow Society of Artists is formed as an exhibiting group. It continues to hold regular exhibitions until 1924.

Vasily Kandinsky and Alexei Jawlensky go to Munich, where they study at the school run by Anton Ažbè. They stay, making Germany their home until 1914. Other Russian painters who study in Munich around the turn of the century include Igor' Grabar', Iosif Braz, Mstislav Dobuzhinsky, Ivan Bilibin and Kuz'ma Petrov-Vodkin.

1897 MARCH: Sergei Diaghilev organises the exhibition *German and English*

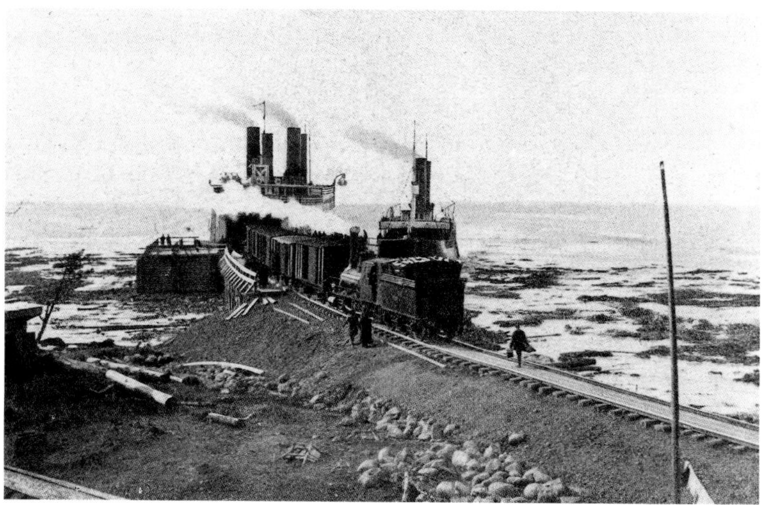

Trans-Siberian Railway: goods locomotive loaded on a steamer to cross Lake Baikal

Watercolours in St Petersburg.

Sergei Shchukin meets Paul Durand-Ruel in Paris and begins to collect contemporary French art. From 1904 his collection, housed in the Trubetskoi palace in Moscow, is made accessible to artists, and it is opened to the public in 1909.

DECEMBER: Rimsky-Korsakov's opera *Sadko* is premièred by Mamontov's Private Russian Opera with sets by Korovin, Malyutin and Vrubel'. Shalyapin plays the role of Ivan the Terrible in a revival of the same composer's *Pskovityanka (The Maid of Pskov)*, studying works in the Tretyakov Gallery to establish his characterisation.

1898　JANUARY: Diaghilev organises an *Exhibition of Russian and Finnish Painters*, which includes Isaak Levitan, Nesterov, the Vasnetsov brothers, Korovin, Serov, Vrubel', Somov and Malyutin.

MARCH: The Russian Museum of Aleksandr III opens in St Petersburg.

OCTOBER: The Moscow Arts Theatre, founded by Konstantin Stanislavsky and Vladimir Nemirovich-Danchenko, puts on its first production at the Hermitage Theatre. One of the earliest productions (in December) is Chekhov's *The Seagull*, which in Moscow is a great success.

NOVEMBER: The first number of *Mir Iskusstva (The World of Art)* appears, initially backed by Mamontov and Princess Tenisheva and produced by the group of the same name recently formed in St Petersburg under the leadership of Sergei Diaghilev, Aleksandr Benois and Dmitry Filosofov. Members include Bakst, Lanceray and Somov, and they are later joined by Ostroumova-Lebedeva, Dobuzhinsky, Golovin, Bilibin, Roerich and many others. Their interests include painting, literature, book design, music and theatre. Critical of the prevalent social and political utilitarianism in art, they believe in the renewal of man and life through art. Their magazine publishes the work of foreign avant-garde artists and writers alongside their Russian counterparts and also, under the literary editorship of Filosofov, the early work of Russian Symbolist poets such as Aleksandr Blok, Andrei Bely and Konstantin Bal'mont, as well as works by Baudelaire, Verlaine and Mallarmé.

1899　JANUARY: The first exhibition sponsored by *Mir Iskusstva* opens at the Stieglitz School in St Petersburg; it includes works by Degas, Moreau, Rivière, Whistler, Böcklin, Repin, Benois, Bakst and others, as well as crafts from the Abramtsevo colony and glass by Lalique and Tiffany. The group continues to sponsor annual exhibitions until 1906, which resume from 1910.

SEPTEMBER: Mamontov is arrested and imprisoned on charges of fraud. He is finally acquitted at his trial in June 1900, but his financial empire has collapsed.

OCTOBER: Chekhov's *Uncle Vanya* is premièred at the Moscow Arts Theatre; *The Three Sisters* follows in January 1901.

1900　APRIL: There is a large Russian section at the Paris *Exposition Universelle* with a crafts pavilion designed by Korovin and Golovin and an art section of over 400 works. *Le Style Russe* becomes fashionable in Paris.

JULY: The philosopher Vladimir Solov'ev dies. His *Three Conversations on War, Progress and the End of Human History* and *History of Antichrist* are published during the year.

Fedor Shekhtel' begins work on the Moscow mansion of S., P. Ryabushinsky and, the following year, on that of A. I. Derozhinskaya.

Lenin, who has been in detention in Siberia, goes into exile at the end of the year.

1901　APRIL: the Symbolist almanac *Severnye Tsvety (Northern Flowers)* begins publication, with contributions by Bal'mont, Bely, Blok, Bryusov etc.

Shekhtel' designs the Russian pavilions at the International Exhibition in Glasgow; built of wood, they include many features reminiscent of medieval Russian architecture.

Sergei Rakhmaninov gives the first full performance of his 2nd Piano Concerto.

DECEMBER: The Society of *The 36*, led by Vrubel' and Serov, opens its first exhibition in Moscow.

1902　MARCH: The fourth *Mir Iskusstva* exhibition opens in St Petersburg, later moving to Moscow.

APRIL: The interior minister, Sipyagin, is assassinated by a member of the Socialist Revolutionary Party.

Merezhkovsky's novel *Leonardo da Vinci* is published.

Work starts on the remodelling by Shekhtel' of the Arts Theatre and the Yaroslavl' Station in Moscow.

DECEMBER: Maxim Gorky's play *The Lower Depths* is premièred at the Moscow Arts Theatre.

DECEMBER: An exhibition of *Architecture and Design of the New Style* opens in Moscow, including work by Mackintosh and Olbrich, as well as important Russian contributions from Ivan Fomin, who is working in Shekhtel's office, Korovin, Polenova and others.

1903　JANUARY: The *Mir Iskusstva* group organises an exhibition of *Contemporary Art*, comprising *Art Nouveau* objects and interiors, in St Petersburg.

JANUARY: Première of Wagner's *Götterdämmerung* in St Petersburg in a production designed by Benois and Korovin.

EASTER: A violent three-day pogrom takes place at Kishinev.

Widespread strikes occur in the

industrial towns and ports near the Black Sea.

JULY: At its second (foundation) congress in Brussels and London the Russian Social Democratic Labour Party emerges with two opposing factions, the Bolsheviks and the Mensheviks. While the former, headed by Lenin, propagate the formation of small organisations of active revolutionaries, the latter favour a broad social democratic party.

The Symbolist journal *Novyi Put'* starts publication (until 1904).

Shekhtel' designs the Ryabushinsky Bank in Moscow.

DECEMBER: The Union of Russian Artists, successor to *The 36*, mounts its first exhibition in Moscow. These continue regularly until 1923.

1904 JANUARY: Japan attacks Russia at Port Arthur. The Russo-Japanese war, which continues into 1905, proves disastrous for Russia, with national humiliation and great loss of life.

JANUARY: The industrialist Sergei Polyakov launches the Symbolist magazine *Vesy (The Scales – Libra)* in Moscow; run by Bryusov, it focuses on Symbolist theory, then from 1900 starts introducing Russian and foreign Symbolist poets and writers. It continues publication until 1909.

JANUARY: Chekhov's *The Cherry Orchard* is premièred at the Moscow Arts Theatre. The playwright dies in July.

FEBRUARY: The New Society of Artists holds its first exhibition in St Petersburg.

MAY: The *Alaya Roza (Crimson Rose)* exhibition is organised in Saratov. Borisov-Musatov, Vrubel', Kuznetsov and a number of younger painters, later (1906) to form the *Golubaya Roza (Blue Rose)* group, participate.

JULY: the interior minister Pleve is assassinated by a Socialist Revolutionary.

The last issues of *Mir Iskusstva* are devoted to French Post-Impressionism.

1905 JANUARY: Russia is torn by civil disturbances, leading to the "1905 Revolution". A general strike in St Petersburg leads to "Bloody Sunday", in which over 1,000 peaceful demonstrators outside the Winter Palace are killed or wounded by the army.

FEBRUARY: Grand Duke Sergei, the Tsar's uncle, is assassinated by a Socialist Revolutionary.

The first ever Soviet, or elected workers' council, evolves from a strike committee in Ivanovo-Voznesensk, near Moscow.

MAY: The Russian Baltic fleet is virtually annihilated by the Japanese.

JUNE: The crew of the battleship *Potemkin* mutinies in Odessa. Street fighting follows between revolutionaries and the military, which leaves some 2,000 dead.

JUNE: The satirical magazine *Zritel' (The Spectator)* appears in the wake of the revolutionary events. Other similar magazines that appear at this period include *Adskaya Pochta (Hell's Post Office)* and *Zhupel (Bugbear)*. Their contributors include Dobuzhinsky, Chekhonin, Bilibin, Anisfel'd, Lanceray and Zamirailo.

JULY: After increasing international tension between Russia and Germany, Nikolai and his cousin Kaiser Wilhelm II meet on the Finnish island of Björkö. They sign a treaty, but this is not ratified by their governments.

AUGUST: A government decree provides for a consultative assembly to be convoked and dissolved by the Tsar; election to the assembly is to be indirect and is restricted along class and property lines.

AUGUST: Universities are granted autonomy.

"Bloody Sunday": troops fire on demonstrators outside the Winter Palace in St Petersburg

SEPTEMBER: A new wave of strikes involves many industries and areas of the country previously untouched by political unrest. The railway network throughout the country comes to a standstill. A St Petersburg Soviet is established, which, with the government virtually paralysed, effectively governs the city. Soviets are formed in many other Russian towns.

AUTUMN: The monarchist, nationalist and anti-semitic Union of the Russian People is formed. Countless pogroms take place in the south and south-west of the country, carried out by the counter-revolutionary Black Hundreds.

AUTUMN: Vyacheslav Ivanov establishes his "Wednesdays" at his house, the "Tower", in St Petersburg. These regular meetings last for several years, attracting figures such as Bryusov and Sologub and, later, younger writers including Anna Akhmatova and Osip Mandel'shtam.

OCTOBER: Viktor Borisov-Musatov dies.

OCTOBER: The Tsar's *October Manifesto* provides for fundamental civil liberties and a broadening of the August electoral law to include all classes. It also envisages a limited legislative role for the national assembly, or Duma. The Constitutional Democratic Party convenes in Moscow.

NOVEMBER: The Siberian sectarian Grigory Rasputin, who subscribes to the theory of "salvation through sin", makes his first appearance at the Tsar's court.

DECEMBER: A general strike in Moscow turns into an armed uprising lasting twelve days; it is suppressed with more than 1,000 people killed. Throughout December troops are sent on punitive expeditions all over the country.

1906 JANUARY: The Moscow Arts Theatre, which has travelled through Russia since 1900, now performs abroad for the first time, in Berlin.

JANUARY: The Symbolist magazine *Zolotoe Runo (The Golden Fleece)* starts

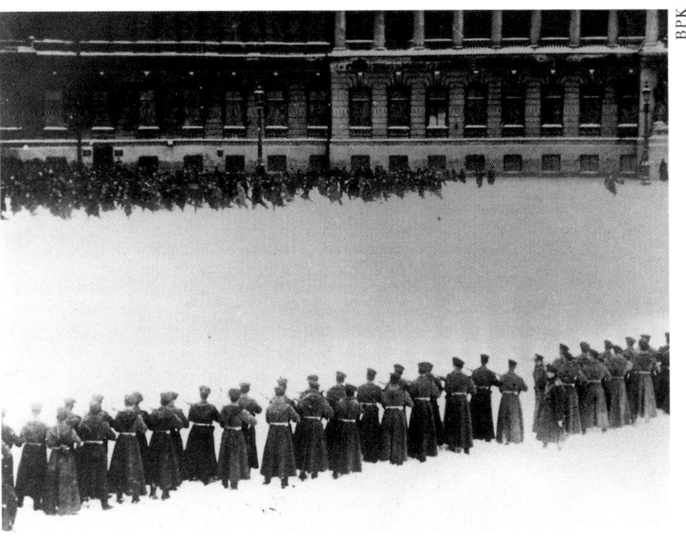

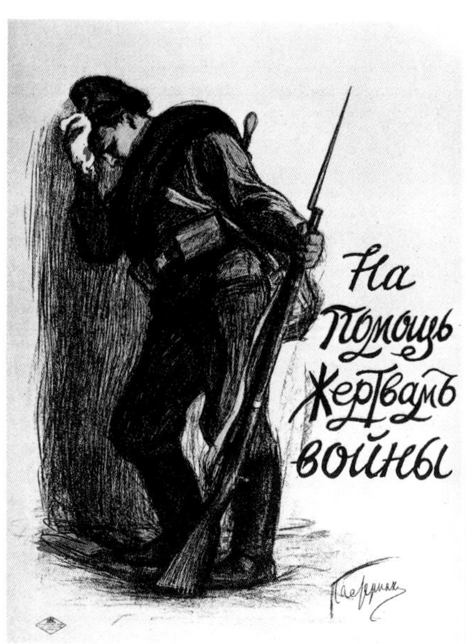

Poster, "Aid for the victims of War" (1914), by Leonid Pasternak

publication in Moscow, financed by Nikolai Ryabushinsky. It continues publication until 1909–10.

FEBRUARY: The last of the first series of *Mir Iskusstva* exhibitions is held in St Petersburg, including works by younger painters such as Kuznetsov, Jawlensky, Larionov, Goncharova, Sapunov etc., as well as a section devoted to Borisov-Musatov.

APRIL: The first Duma is inaugurated by the Tsar in the Winter Palace, but disagreements between the monarch and the assembly lead to its dissolution in July.

JULY: Petr Stolypin is appointed Chairman of the Council of Ministers.

OCTOBER: Diaghilev organises a major exhibition of Russian art in Paris within the framework of the Salon d'Automne. It includes icons, historic paintings and works by the *Mir Iskusstva* group, including the younger artists introduced at their last exhibition, but of the *Peredvizhniki* only Repin is admitted.

1907 FEBRUARY: The second Duma convenes but again proves unworkable and is dissolved in June. In November the third Duma convenes under the leadership of Stolypin. It survives until 1912.

MARCH: The Symbolist *Golubaya Roza (Blue Rose)* group, formed the previous year, organise their first exhibition in Moscow.

A young Georgian Bolshevik, later known as Stalin, masterminds a spectacular bank robbery (or "expropriation") in Tbilisi.

Lenin, who had returned from exile in 1905, leaves Russia again, living abroad until 1917.

Ivan Pavlov studies conditioned reflexes.

APRIL: Gorky's *Mat' (Mother)* is published, later seen as the literary prototype of Socialist Realism.

MAY: Diaghilev, encouraged by the success of his Salon d'Automne show the previous year, organises a concert season at the Paris Opéra of works by Russian composers.

DECEMBER: The first *Venok (Wreath)* exhibition opens in Moscow, organised by David Burlyuk and including works by Goncharova, Larionov and other young artists. Further shows are held in 1908 and 1909 in St Petersburg.

1908 APRIL: *Zolotoe Runo (The Golden Fleece)* organises the first of its "salons" in Moscow with artists of the *Golubaya Roza* group, Larionov and Goncharova and a French section including many of the Fauve paintings that had caused a scandal at the 1905 Salon d'Automne in Paris.

APRIL: The first issue of the satirical journal *Satirikon (Satyricon)* is published. It continues to appear until 1913.

Skryabin's *Poème d'extase* has its first performance.

MAY: Diaghilev takes the Imperial Theatre's production of Musorgsky's *Boris Godunov* to the Paris Opéra with Shalyapin in the title role. The sets are by Benois and Golovin, the costumes by Bilibin.

JUNE: Nikolai Rimsky-Korsakov dies.

OCTOBER: Drankov's film *Sten'ka Razin*, with accompanying score by Ippolitov-Ivanov, is released, followed in December by Khanzhonkov's *Drama in a Gypsy Camp near Moscow*.

NOVEMBER: David Burlyuk organises the *Zveno (Link)* exhibition in Kiev of works of the Russian avant-garde.

1909 JANUARY: *Zolotoe Runo* organises a second salon of French and Russian art; it includes works by Braque, Matisse, Van Dongen, Kuznetsov, Larionov, Goncharova and Petrov-Vodkin. In December their third salon is dominated by the work of Goncharova and Larionov.

MAY: Diaghilev puts on his first, enormously successful, season of Russian Ballet at the Théâtre de Châtelet in Paris. The ballets in the programme include *Le Pavillon d'Armide* with music by Cherepnin and sets by Benois, the *Polovtsian Dances* from Borodin's *Prince Igor* designed by Roerich, *Les Sylphides*, and *Cléopâtre* designed by Bakst. The *Ballets Russes* seasons are important annual events in Paris until 1914.

OCTOBER: *Zolotoi Petushok (The Golden Cockerel)*, Rimsky-Korsakov's last, satirical, opera, previously banned, has its first performance in Moscow with sets and costumes designed by Bilibin. (It is given a new production, designed by Goncharova, in Diaghilev's 1914 season.)

OCTOBER: The journal *Apollon* starts publication in St Petersburg under the editorship of Sergei Makovsky; it soon becomes the main organ of the Acmeists, including Akhmatova and Mandel'shtam. It continues publication until 1918. Both *Vesy* and *Zolotoe Runo* cease publication at the end of the year (although the final issues of *Zolotoe Runo* appear in 1910).

1910 MARCH: The newly formed *Soyuz Molodezhi (Union of Youth)* holds its first exhibition in St Petersburg. This becomes a twice yearly event until 1913. The Union also organises discussion groups.

APRIL: Mikhail Vrubel' dies after a long mental illness.

MAY: Bely publishes his novel *Serebryanyi golub' (The Silver Dove)*.

JUNE: *L'Oiseau de Feu*, with music commissioned from Stravinsky, whom Diaghilev had met the previous year, and décors by Golovin, is performed in Diaghilev's second Paris season.

Marc Chagall moves to Paris.

NOVEMBER: Lev Tolstoy dies.

DECEMBER: A new series of *Mir Iskusstva* exhibitions is instituted in St Petersburg. They continue until 1924.

DECEMBER: The first *Bubnovyi Valet (Jack of Diamonds)* exhibition opens in Moscow, including work by Kandinsky, Jawlensky, Larionov, Goncharova, the Burlyuk brothers and Kazimir Malevich. The new group, established the following year, rejects tradition – Academicians, *Peredvizhniki*, Symbolists and *Mir Iskusstva* – and fosters a new interest in folk and primitive art. Regular exhibitions are held until 1917, and foreign artists, particularly the French avant garde and German Expressionists, are invited to exhibit with them.

DECEMBER: The first issue of the journal *Zvezda (Star)* appears, edited by Lenin from abroad.

1911 MARCH: Skyrabin's *Prometheus* has its first performance in Moscow.

JUNE: Stravinsky's *Petrushka* has its first performance in Diaghilev's Paris season with sets and costumes by Benois.

Rasputin has become indispensable to the imperial family due to his ability to hypnotise the haemophiliac Tsarevich and thus stop him bleeding. Stolypin warns of his discreditable activities; Rasputin is banned from the capital.

SEPTEMBER: Stolypin is assassinated during a gala performance in Kiev of Rimsky-Korsakov's opera *Skazka o Tsare Saltane (The Tale of Tsar Saltan)*. The assassin is a police agent and Socialist Revolutionary.

AUTUMN: Goncharova and Larionov break with *Bubnovyi Valet* and form a new association, *Oslinyi Khvost (The Donkey's Tail)*. They begin their Rayonist paintings.

OCTOBER–NOVEMBER: Matisse visits Moscow and St Petersburg at the invitation of Sergei Shchukin. He is adulated by young Russian artists, including Goncharova and Larionov.

DECEMBER: Kandinsky and Franz Marc found *Der Blaue Reiter* in Munich. Kandinsky invites the Burlyuks, Goncharova, Larionov and Malevich to contribute to the second *Blaue Reiter* exhibition (February 1912).

1912 MARCH: Larionov organises the *Oslinyi Khvost* exhibition in Moscow, which includes many works by Larionov, Goncharova, Malevich and Tatlin.

APRIL: The killing of 170 striking miners at the British-owned Lena goldfields in Siberia provokes a new wave of strikes, which continues until the outbreak of war.

APRIL: The first issue of the magazine *Soyuz Molodezhi* (*Union of Youth*) appears in St Petersburg.

APRIL: The first issue of the workers' paper *Pravda* (*The Truth*) appears. Lenin establishes contact with Stalin during this year.

Goncharov's film *The Brigand Brothers* is made but not released. Protazanov's film dramatisation of Tolstoy's last days, *The Passing of a Great Old Man* is banned.

DECEMBER: The Futurist miscellany *Poshchechina obshchestvennomu vkusu* (*A Slap in the Face for Public Taste*) attacks the Symbolists.

1913 On the occasion of the tercentenary of the Romanov dynasty the Tsar grants an amnesty to many political prisoners.

An exhibition of *Ancient Russian Painting* is held in Moscow to celebrate the tercentenary. The display for the first time of icon paintings as works of art proves influential.

MARCH: Larionov organises the exhibition *Mishen'* (*Target*), which includes children's drawings and signboards alongside works by young painters, including Chagall and Pirosmanashvili. He launches his Rayonist manifesto.

MAY: Diaghilev stages Stravinsky's *Le Sacre du Printemps* in Paris in a production designed by Roerich.

AUGUST: A large individual exhibition of works by Goncharova opens in Moscow.

OCTOBER: Bely starts to publish his apocalyptic novel *Peterburg* (*Petersburg*). It appears in book form in 1916.

NOVEMBER: *The Twilight of a Woman's Soul* is released. It is the first of 82 films directed by Evgeny Bauer, a former theatrical set designer.

DECEMBER: *Soyuz Molodezhi* sponsors four performances at the Luna Park Theatre in St Petersburg of two Futurist works. The production of Mayakovsky's tragedy *Vladimir Mayakovsky* is designed by Filonov and Shkol'nik, while the opera *Pobeda nad solntsem* (*Victory over the Sun*) with music by Matyushin and texts by Khlebnikov and Kruchenykh has sets and costumes by Malevich. He later ascribes the birth of Suprematism to these designs.

1914 The first seven months of the year see almost 3,500 strikes, more than half of them politically motivated.

JULY: The Bolsheviks organise a general strike in St Petersburg early in the month. It is only ended by Russia's entry into the war. Nikolai II convokes the Duma for a single session to approve war credits; the Labour Group and Social Democrats abstain, the latter putting forward a resolution condemning the war. The Bolsheviks call on the people to fight against their own government; their leaders are subsequently deported to Siberia.

As Turkey enters the war on the Austro-German side, Russia's Baltic and Black Sea ports are effectively blockaded, while with more than 6,500,000 men under arms by the end of the year the country's agricultural and industrial production is severely affected.

The outbreak of war isolates the Russian artistic community from contacts with the west and intensifies internal developments. Kandinsky, Chagall, El Lissitzky and many others return to Russia.

St Petersburg is renamed Petrograd.

1915 FEBRUARY: The artist Ivan Puni organises *Tramway V: First Futurist Exhibition* in Petrograd; Malevich and Tatlin emerge as leaders of two rival trends – Suprematism and Constructivism.

APRIL: Aleksandr Skryabin dies.

From early May until late September, Russian troops, suffering from great shortages of arms, ammunition and supplies, are forced to retreat; more than a million men are made prisoners-of-war.

JULY: Larionov and Goncharova leave to join Diaghilev in Switzerland; they settle in Paris.

AUGUST: The Tsar assumes personal control of the Russian armies; his decision is widely attributed to the influence of the Empress and, in particular, Rasputin. Despite public outcry and the threat of resignation from eight ministers, Nikolai leaves for the front on 4 September, leaving effective power in the hands of the Empress – and Rasputin.

DECEMBER: At *0.10. The Last Futurist Painting Exhibition* Malevich shows his Suprematist paintings for the first time.

1916 MARCH: Tatlin organises the exhibition *Magazin* (*The Store*), which includes the work of Aleksandr Rodchenko.

With reduced agricultural production and the increasing use of the railways for military transport, there are severe food shortages in Russia, particularly in urban areas, by the end of the year.

DECEMBER: A court conspiracy led by Prince Feliks Yusupov arranges the murder of Rasputin.

1917 FEBRUARY: Following strike calls, large crowds take to the streets in Petrograd on the 22nd and 23rd. By 1 March the city's garrison is in mutiny. On the 27th Provisional Committees are set up by both the Duma and a Soviet of Workers' and Soldiers' Deputies. Three days later, the Duma Committee, with the Soviet's consent, forms a provisional government, promising an amnesty, basic civil liberties and immediate preparations for a constituent assembly. The German authorities allow Lenin to return to Russia from Switzerland, passing through Germany in a sealed railway carriage.

MARCH: The Tsar abdicates. He and his family are executed fifteen months later.

JUNE: The first all-Russian Congress of Soviets meets in Petrograd. The Bolsheviks are still in a minority.

JULY: The provisional government is replaced by a coalition government led by Kerensky. Lenin is forced to move to Finland after the failure of a mass uprising in Petrograd led by the Bolsheviks.

OCTOBER: Kerensky's weak government is overthrown by the Bolsheviks, and the Soviet government is established headed by the Council of Peoples' Commissars, with Lenin as Chief Commissar and Trotsky as Commissar for Foreign Affairs.

NOVEMBER: At Brest-Litovsk Lenin signs the armistice.

Design for poster encouraging voluntary Saturday labour (1920) by Aleksandr Kuprin

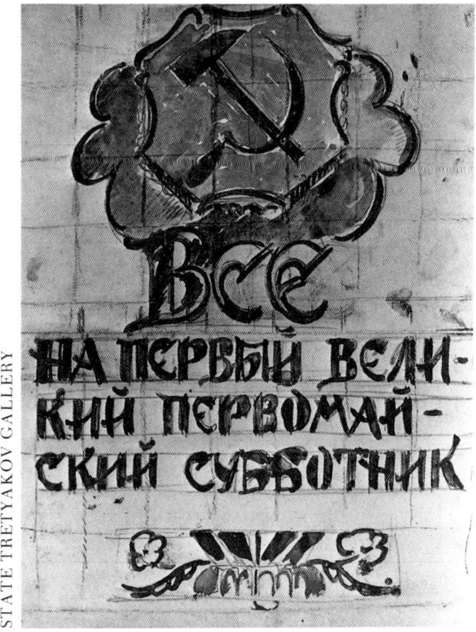

8

PAINTINGS FROM THE
TRETYAKOV GALLERY

ALLA GUSAROVA

The State Tretyakov Gallery in Moscow is rich in Russian paintings of the late nineteenth and early twentieth centuries which display those characteristics that typify the artistic explorations of *Style Moderne* and Symbolism. These first emerged in the artists associated with Savva Mamontov at Abramtsevo: Viktor Vasnetsov, Mikhail Nesterov, Konstantin Korovin and Mikhail Vrubel'.

Nesterov's *Vision of the Boy Varfolomei* (p.103) is a reminder that the work (1889–90) for which this is a sketch became a significant milestone on the road to superseding the naturalism and rationalism of the *Peredvizhniki (Wanderers)*, who greeted its religious mysticism and idealism with hostility. The subject of the painting is the intervention of Providence in the fate of a child, miraculously transforming his life. *Vision of the Boy Varfolomei* is one of the first of those paintings with which Nesterov built up his legend of Rus', the land where man and nature were united and inspired by lofty prayerful contemplation, a land of hermits, monks and wanderers. One of the heroines of Nesterov's world was the Russian woman, profound and pure, an image made manifest in the portrait he painted of his wife in 1905 (p.111).

The artists of the Abramtsevo group, while striving to penetrate into the hidden soul of nature, retained their truth to the natural world. Nesterov's declaration is characteristic: "It is as though Nature is my compass." But this natural vision was expressed still more strongly by Konstantin Korovin, one of the founders of the Neo-Russian style, a variant of *Style Moderne* based on the stylization of folk art, which was described ironically as "Mamontov-Korovinesque". Korovin was the first cover designer of *Mir Iskusstva (World of Art)*, the earliest *Moderne* magazine in Russia, but his stylistic investigations were carried out mainly in interior design, exhibition design, and also in the theatre. In painting, he was the founder of the national version of Impressionism, instilling his subjects (p.105) with a lyricism expressed in decorative form.

The artist Mariya Yakunchikova, who died young, was close to the Abramtsevo group. In her paintings she tried to express abstract and universal experiences, but used concrete images for this rather than imaginary ones. Her paintings preserve the lyrical mood of the Russian landscape, and they are coloured with nostalgia for the past (p.101), making her the precursor of the retrospective daydreaming of *Mir Iskusstva*. Sergei Diaghilev, the founder of the *Mir Iskusstva* group and promoter of its exhibitions and magazine, valued Yakunchikova highly. He invited her to participate in exhibitions, commissioned a cover for the magazine (p.36) and planned to devote a whole issue to her.

Yakunchikova and Fedor Botkin were invited by Diaghilev to join *Mir Iskusstva* when they were members of the Russian artists' colony in Paris. Botkin's decorative paintings show the influence of French *Art Nouveau* in the idealisation of the women who are his principal subject (p.109). Conversely, the influence of Munich *Jugendstil* is reflected in the work of Igor' Grabar' (p.110). However, the most characteristic exponent of the explorations of the early *Mir Iskusstva* group based in St Petersburg – which also included Aleksandr Benois, Mstislav Dobuzhinsky, Nikolai Roerich, Aleksandr Golovin and Zinaida Serebryakova – was Konstantin Somov. In 1896 he was the first to turn to painting themes from the past (p.106) and in this way determined the path that was followed by his friends, the so-called "retrospective daydreamers". The island in *Island of Love* (p.105) was a favourite motif Somov borrowed from European *Art Nouveau*, but the painting also has a lyrically grotesque quality, to which the artists of *Mir Iskusstva* were frequently drawn. The mysterious atmosphere of the enchanted island is shot through with faint notes of irony.

The designs by Benois for the ceiling decoration of the board room in Moscow's Kazan' Railway Station (p.223) are a late example of one of the most important preoccupations of the *Mir Iskusstva* group, the creation of decoration on a monumental scale. In their decorative wall-paintings the artists generally turned to Classicist or Baroque styles – the styles of old St Petersburg.

One of the few artists in the *Mir Iskusstva* group who did not return to the past was Dobuzhinsky. He turned rather to the depiction of the contemporary city in his search for its hidden soul, and in *Harbour on the Pryazhka River* (p.130), a depiction of one of the districts of St Petersburg, the landscape is fantastically transformed. Here machines have subjugated the people to become the true rulers of the city. The concept of the hostility of mechanical civilisation to mankind was frequently developed by this artist, both in his paintings and his lectures.

Of all the *Mir Iskusstva* artists represented by works from the Tretyakov Gallery, the closest to *Style Moderne* were Roerich and Golovin. Roerich, who shared the belief of his colleagues in the group that true beauty existed in the past, introduced the history of the ancient Slavs into his early canvases, while Golovin displayed his outstanding talent in a more decorative and personal variation of the style (p.116).

If Dobuzhinsky's paintings suggest an approach towards Expressionism, in Serebryakova's paintings *Style Moderne* comes close to Neo-Classicism. The image of the woman with flowing hair in her *Self-Portrait* (p.125) has none of the refinement or mystery of *Art Nouveau*, but is endowed with a noble simplicity and clarity achieved with the light colours and sharply drawn lines. A Neo-Classical clarity is also seen in the *Portrait of Anna Akhmatova* painted by the St Petersburg artist Ol'ga Della-Vos-Kardovskaya (p.125). Here it is as if the painting expressed the poet's adherence to "Acmeism", the poetic movement which strove towards a strict perfection of language.

The greatest figures in the first wave of Russian Symbolism and *Style Moderne* in painting were Mikhail Vrubel' and Viktor Borisov-Musatov. One of Vrubel''s finest works, *The Prophet* (p.30), develops the artist's favourite theme of the tragic calling of the prophet (synonymous, for Vrubel', with "poet" or "artist"), which condemned him to torment but enabled him "to fire the hearts of the people with his words". Aleksandr Pushkin's poem "The Prophet", from which this line is taken, provided the theme for Vrubel''s painting. Man's encounter with the terrible six-winged Seraph is interpreted by the artist as the tormenting and dramatic process of the birth of a new creature, and this is reflected in the movement of the bluish-violet colours and forms, from the chaos of which the figures and faces emerge. Nadezhda Zabela-Vrubel', the artist's wife and a famous singer (p.109), was the muse of Vrubel''s creation, and her figure appears in many of his fantastic, fairy-tale images. Vrubel''s successor and imitator was the remarkable artist Vladimir Denisov (p.113).

The tragic pathos of Vrubel''s art stands at the opposite pole to Borisov-Musatov's striving for harmony, a theme summed up in his early painting *Harmony* (p.34). This is still somewhat crudely executed, but it heralds the appearance of the artist's mature work, refined and decorative canvases in which he creates a strange and mysterious world populated by women in old-fashioned costume who, while not beautiful, are poetically inspired. The appearance of the Russian provinces – Borisov-Musatov was from Saratov – is combined here in a fantastical way with a certain "Elysium of the shades".

The work of Vrubel' and Borisov-Musatov inspired the artists of the second wave of Symbolism, who came together for the *Golubaya Roza (Blue Rose)* exhibitions of 1907 in Moscow and were associated with the magazines *Zolotoe Runo (Golden Fleece)* and *Vesy (Libra – The Scales):* Pavel Kuznetsov, Nikolai Krymov, Nikolai Sapunov, Sergei Sudeikin, Martiros Sar'yan, Nikolai Feofilaktov and the brothers Nikolai and Vasily Milioti. The likeness of Nikolai Milioti was recorded by Sapunov (p.120) and that of Feofilaktov by Konstantin Yuon (p.110).

The influence of Borisov-Musatov can be sensed in Kuznetsov's painting *Flowering Garden in Bakhchisaray* (p.119), which treats reality as a vague mirage. The motifs of the morning, the flowering spring garden and the fountain, which are metaphors for the awakening to life, growth and development, are characteristic of *Style Moderne* and are associated with the early Symbolist period of Kuznetsov's work. In Krymov's landscape *Approaching Spring* (p.118), the world is made immaterial and transformed into a misty haze, while the predilection of the artists of this group for subtle decorative effects, is reflected in the landscapes of Sudeikin. In Sapunov's *Mystic Tea-drinking* (p.39) a different, mysterious meaning shines through the prose of everyday life.

As their explorations in the transformation of reality developed, the *Golubaya Roza* artists began to turn to the primitive in their work: in *By the Pomegranate Tree* (p.118) Sar'yan makes use of ancient Eastern miniatures to create his magic world. It was this new style that was the cradle of the abstraction and expressionism of Vasily Kandinsky. In his *St George and the Dragon* (p.129), painted after his return to Russia in 1914, the artist went back to his early experiments, interpreting St George's fight as a Russian folk tale with a princess in a traditional headdress and a citadel with gold-topped churches and belfries.

9

PAINTINGS FROM THE RUSSIAN MUSEUM

MARINA SHUMOVA

The cultural life of St Petersburg in 1898 was marked by two events: the ceremonial opening of the Russian Museum and the first appearance of the magazine *Mir Iskusstva (World of Art)*. With this publication and the organization of an exhibition, a group of young artists, proclaiming freedom of creation and new aesthetic ideals, announced their presence. Forming the earliest of a succession of groups and unions in St Petersburg and Moscow in the 1900s and 1910s, the *Mir Iskusstva* artists were orientated towards an acceptance of Western culture and participated in the artistic discoveries and the newest tendencies of the period.

The collecting activities of the Russian Museum – the principal State museum in the capital – had at first no connection with contemporary art. Bearing the name of Aleksandr III, the museum was under the control of the Ministry of the Imperial Court, and its nature was that of an official establishment. Its collections were made up of works by well-established artists of the eighteenth and nineteenth centuries that had been transferred from the Academy of Art, the Hermitage and the palace collections of the Tsar's family. During the 1900s the museum contained only a few individual works by young artists; the large accessions of the most recent painting and graphic art were not to take place until the following decades. The most important part in the formation of the museum's collections was played by the local art-lovers: A. A. Korovin, F. F. Notgaft, M. K. Tenisheva, and, in our own times, B. N. Okunev, whose collections enriched the Russian Museum with works of the highest quality. Today the visual art of the late nineteenth and early twentieth centuries is represented in the museum in all its variety.

The works loaned to the present exhibition make it possible to compare developments in Western European and Russian art, and they include a wide variety of Russian artists who explored Symbolist imagery and were affected by the *Style Moderne*. The earliest painters come from the group which succeeded the *Peredvizhniki* (Valentin Serov, Boris Kustodiev, Filipp Malyavin), followed by the members of various groups – *Mir Iskusstva*, the Union of Russian Artists, *Golubaya Roza (The Blue Rose)* and *Soyuz Molodezhi* (the Union of Youth) – and ending with participants in the Russian avant-garde (Natal'ya Goncharova, Pavel Filonov).

The collections of the Russian Museum make it possible to see those aspects of Russian *Moderne* and Symbolism that were similar to Western tendencies, and also to discern the specifically national qualities of Russian art. Among the most important artists who determined the particular nature of Russian Symbolism, the earliest representative is Mikhail Vrubel', who, though close to European *Art Nouveau* in certain stylistic characteristics, as well as in the universality of his work – which encompasses painting, graphic art, church murals, theatre and ceramics – is entirely original in his earnest striving for profound epic images.

The artistic harmony of works such as Lev Bakst's *Supper* (p.108), Kuz'ma Petrov-Vodkin's *River Bank* (p.117), painted in Paris, and Nikolai Kalmakov's panel *Diana and Endymion* (p.131) evokes very similar associations to those called up by Western examples. However, Petrov-Vodkin's *Virgin of Tenderness Moving Evil Hearts* (p.26) makes a decisive break with this artist's earlier work. In a simple and spacious image, created in the period of the First World War and expressing its anxiety, the tradition of the medieval Russian icon is transformed. At the same time, its clearly programmatic setting is enhanced by the title Petrov-Vodkin gave to his picture, taken from the name of a canonic type of Orthodox icon.

The national version of *Style Moderne* is also demonstrated by artists who were strongly devoted to Western culture. It can be seen in the refined, backward-looking, masquerade imagery of Konstantin Somov and in the fairy-tale character-acting of Sergei Sudeikin. The works of Viktor Borisov-Musatov are distinguished by an inimitable colour harmony and an elegiac, daydream quality. More removed from the European tradition is the landscape art of Konstantin Bogaevsky, at once a Neo-Romantic and a Neo-Classicist, whose heroic images represent the landscape of the Crimean Peninsula.

The association between late Russian Symbolism and the avant-garde is embodied in Pavel Filonov (pp. 132–3), a unique collection of whose work is housed in the Russian Museum. Proclaiming a rational, "analytical" method of picture construction, and tormented by the striving to comprehend certain life forces, Filonov was a pioneer with no direct analogies in either Western or Russian art.

The works from the collections of the Russian Museum which form part of the exhibition will enable the visitor to sense the breadth of interests of the artists represented and their spiritual and mythic aspirations. Painting and drawing, theatre design, book illustration, sculpture and the design of utilitarian objects all find brilliant and masterly embodiment in their work.

10

PAINTINGS AND DRAWINGS

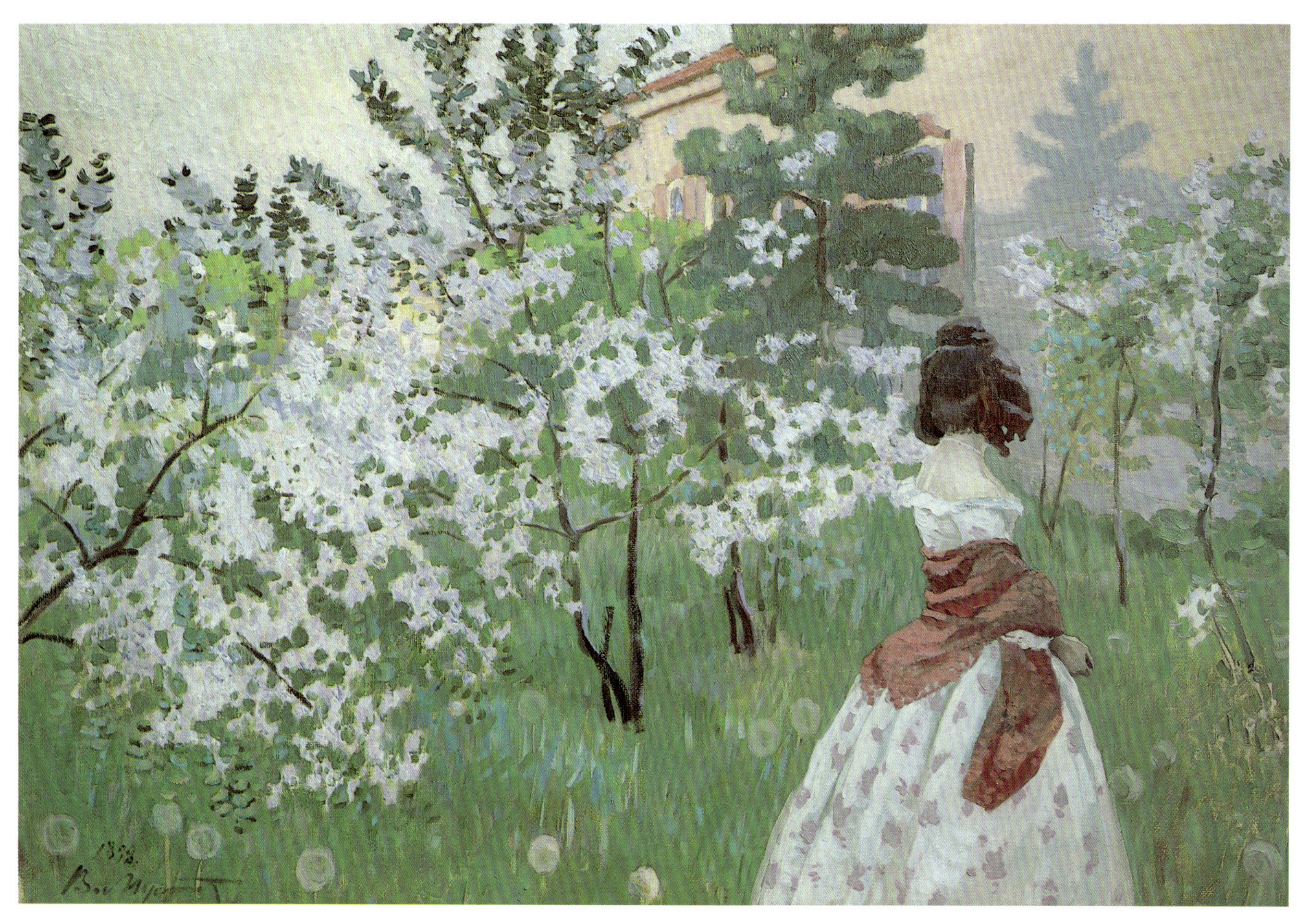

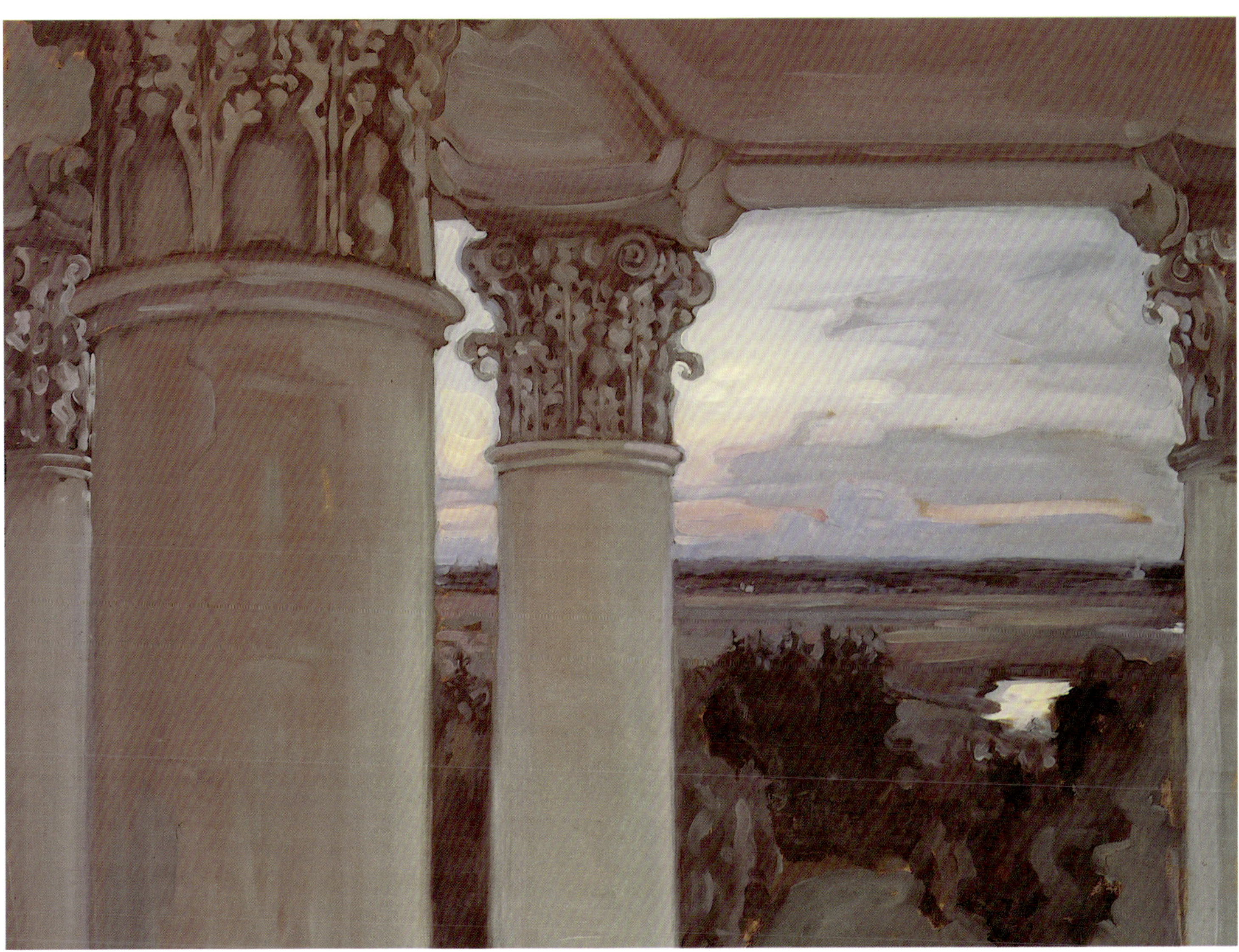

Mariya Yakunchikova-Weber
*477. From the Windows of the Old House
at Vedenskoe*
1897
Oil on canvas, 88.3 × 106.5
State Tretvakov Gallery

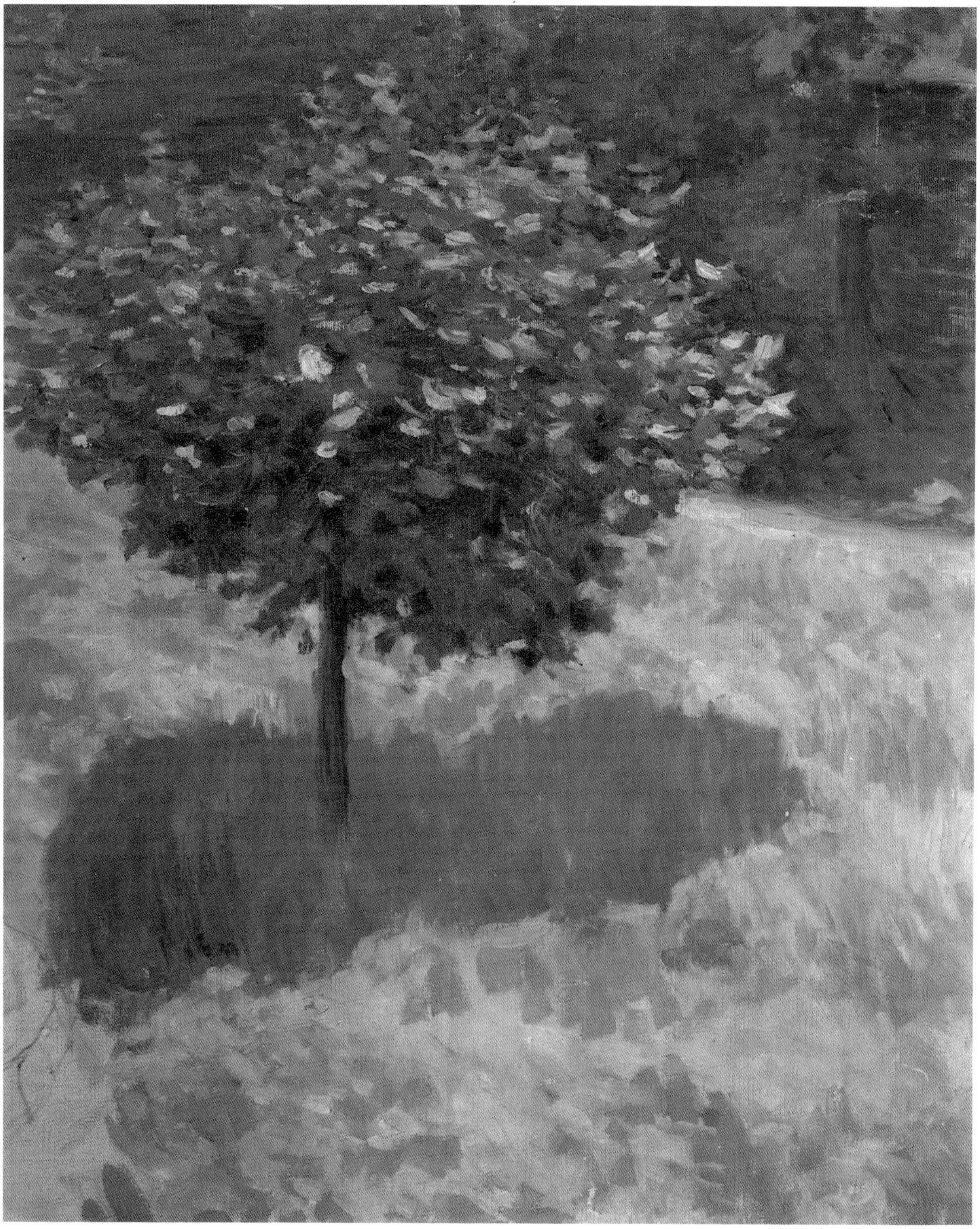

Left: **Viktor Borisov-Musatov**
62. Tree in Sunlight
1897
Oil on canvas, 63.5 × 50.6
Saratov State Art Museum

Below left:
Viktor Borisov-Musatov
66. Pond
Early 1900s
Watercolour, gouache and lead pencil
on paper, 22.5 × 22.5
State Russian Museum

Below: **Viktor Borisov-Musatov**
71. At the Summer House
1904–05
Pen and Indian ink on paper,
19.1 × 14
State Tretyakov Gallery

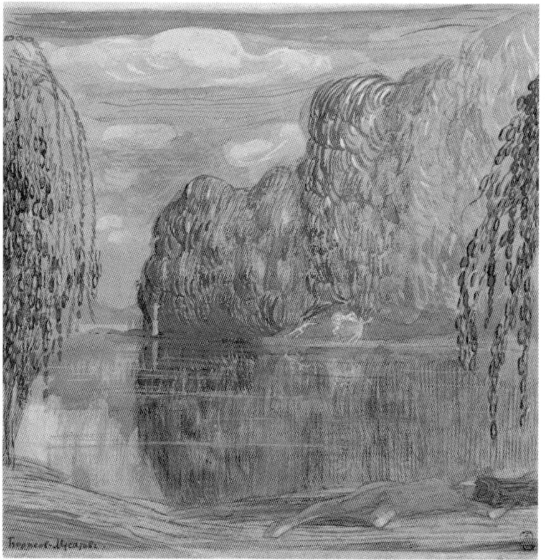

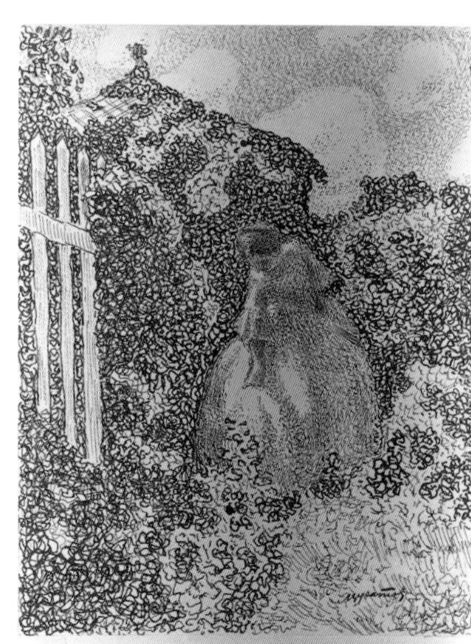

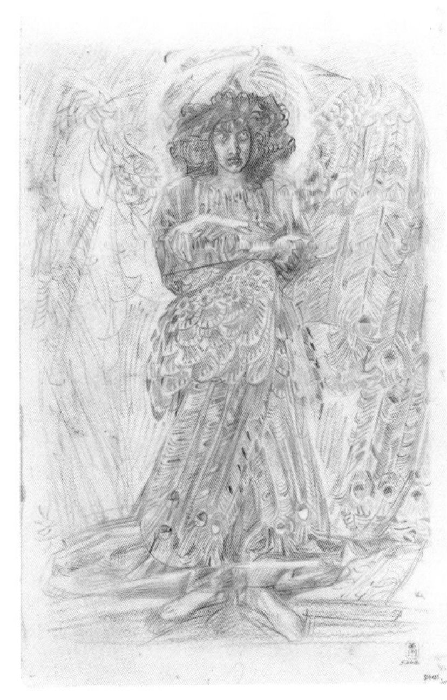

FAR RIGHT: **Pavel Zhukovsky**
490. *Woman with a Violin*
(In Memory of Böcklin)
Early 1900s
Mixed media on cardboard,
33.8 × 19.7
State Russian Museum

RIGHT: **Mikhail Vrubel'**
471. *Seraph*
1904
Lead pencil on paper, 29.1 × 18.3
State Russian Museum

BELOW: **Mikhail Nesterov**
245. *Vision of the Boy Varfolomei*
1889
Oil on canvas, 22.8 × 41.5
State Tretyakov Gallery

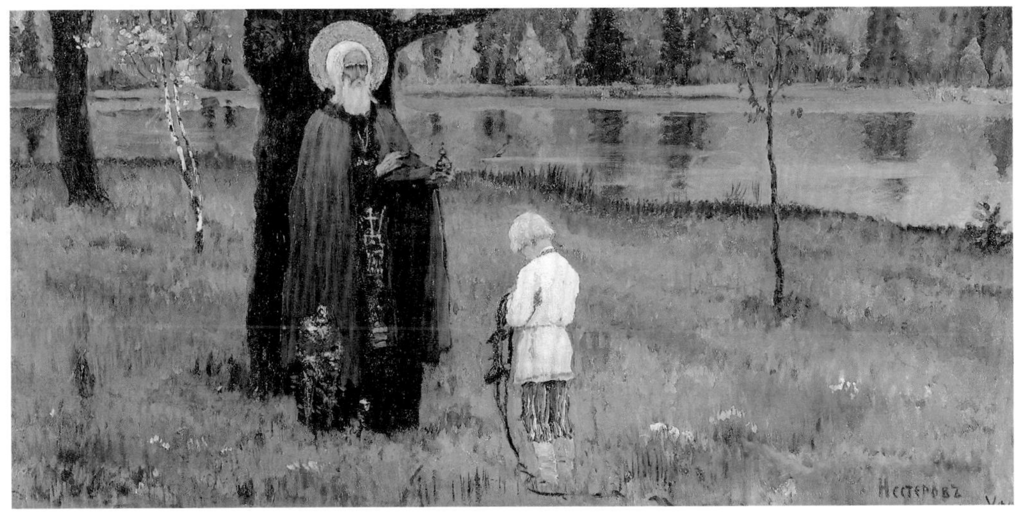

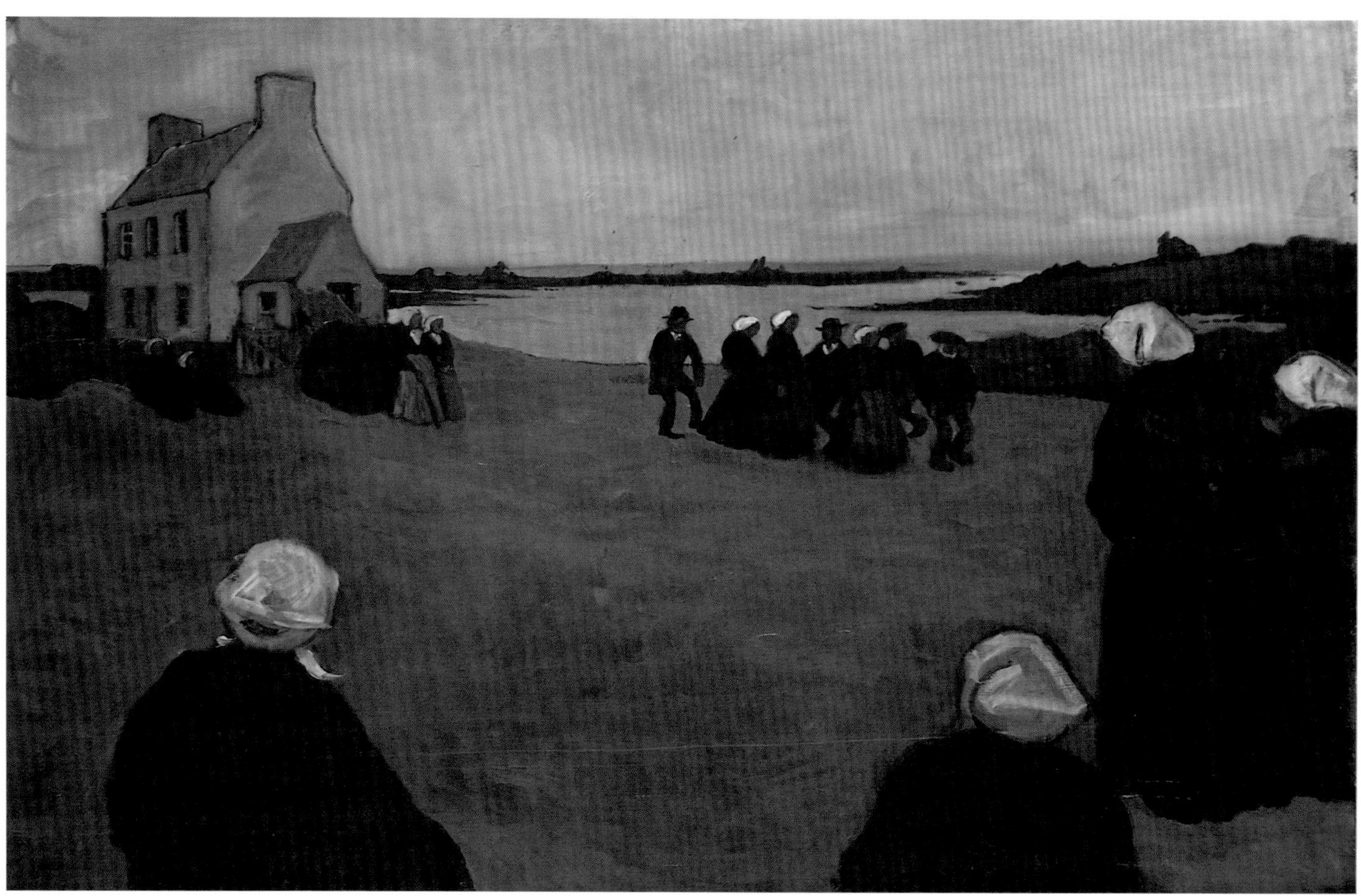

Aleksandr Benois
42. Breton Dances
Primel (Brittany), 1906
Oil on canvas, 69 × 102
State Russian Museum

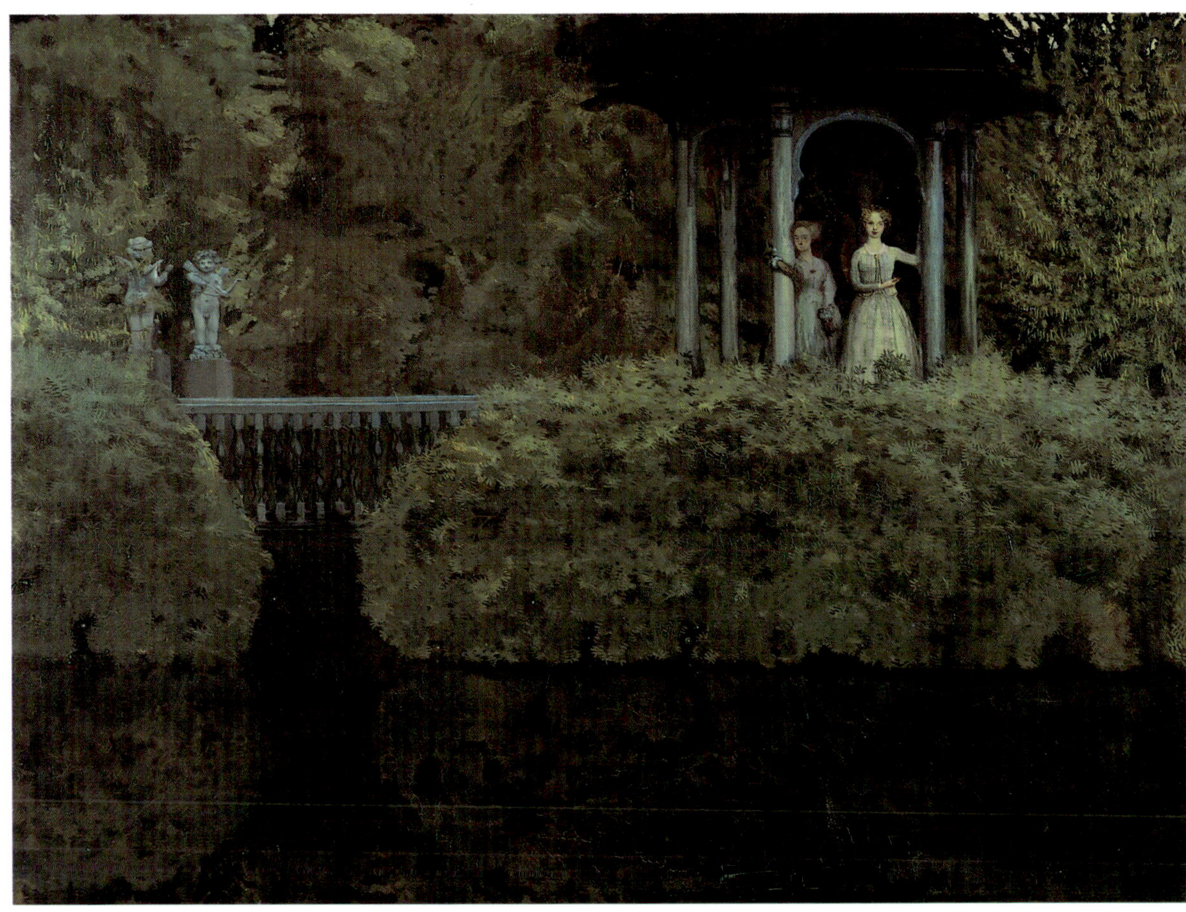

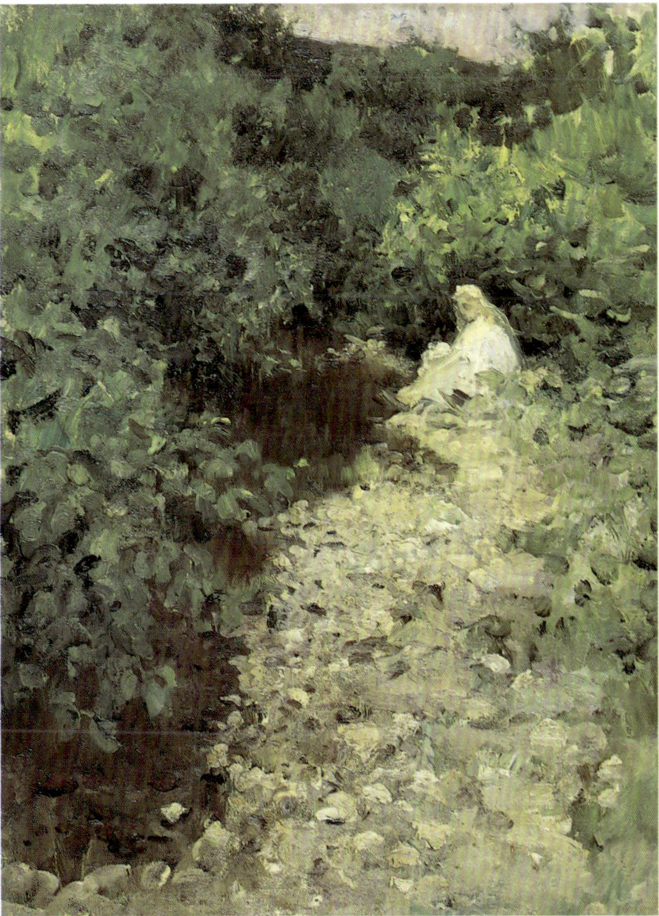

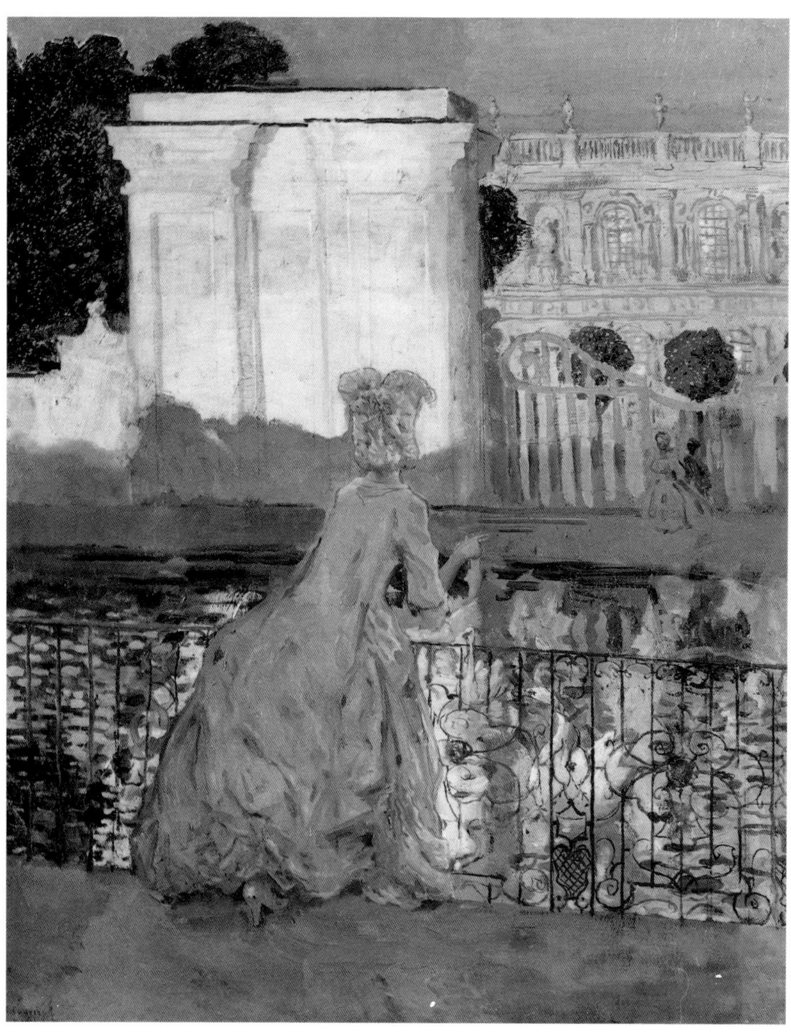

Konstantin Somov
389. *Lady by a Pond*
1896
Oil on canvas, 89 × 71
State Tretyakov Gallery

Aleksandr Benois
40. *Embankment on the Rhine at Basel
in the Rain*
1896
Gouache on cardboard, 57.5 × 47.5
Saratov State Art Museum

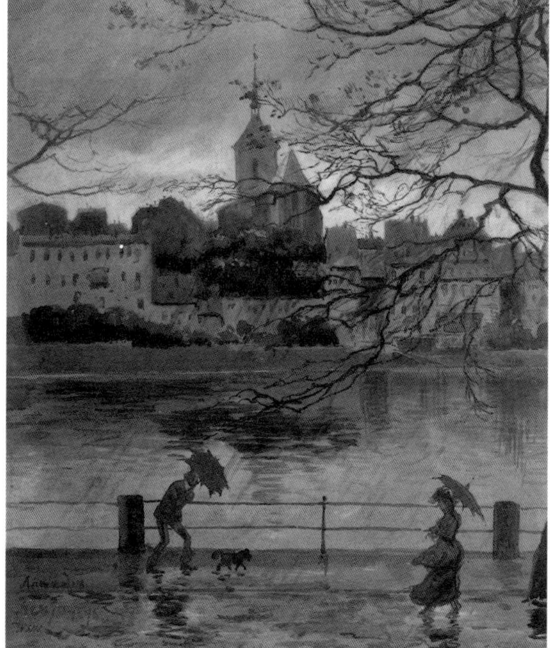

PAINTINGS AND DRAWINGS

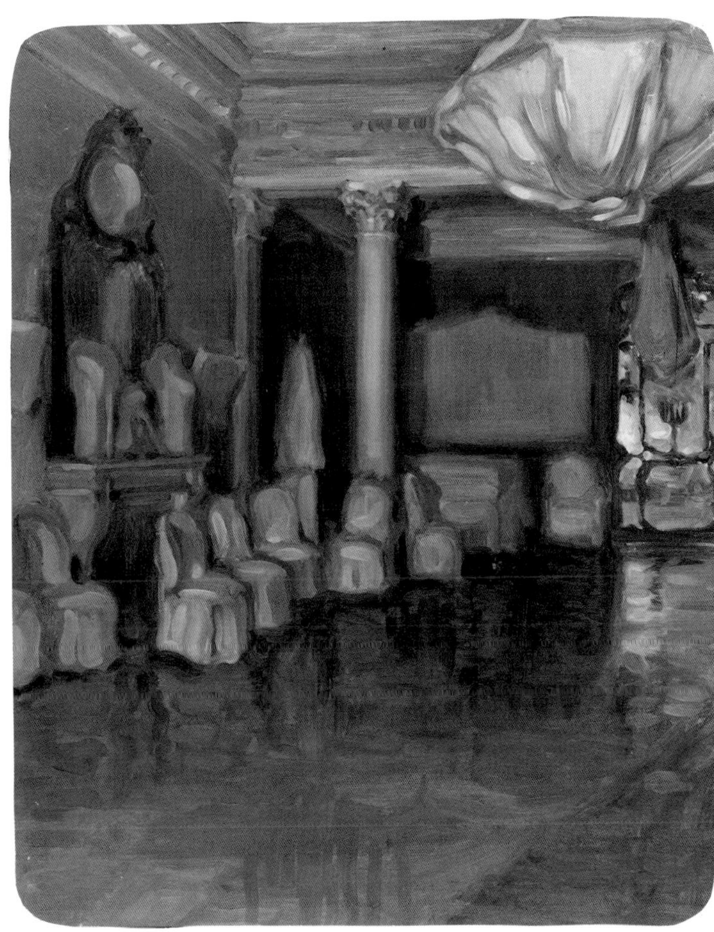

RIGHT: **Mariya Yakunchikova-Weber**
478. *Covers*
Oil on canvas, 73.5 × 56.7
State Tretyakov Gallery

BELOW: **Aleksandr Savinov**
309. *Dusk*
1902–04
Oil on canvas, 54.5 × 81
Saratov State Art Museum

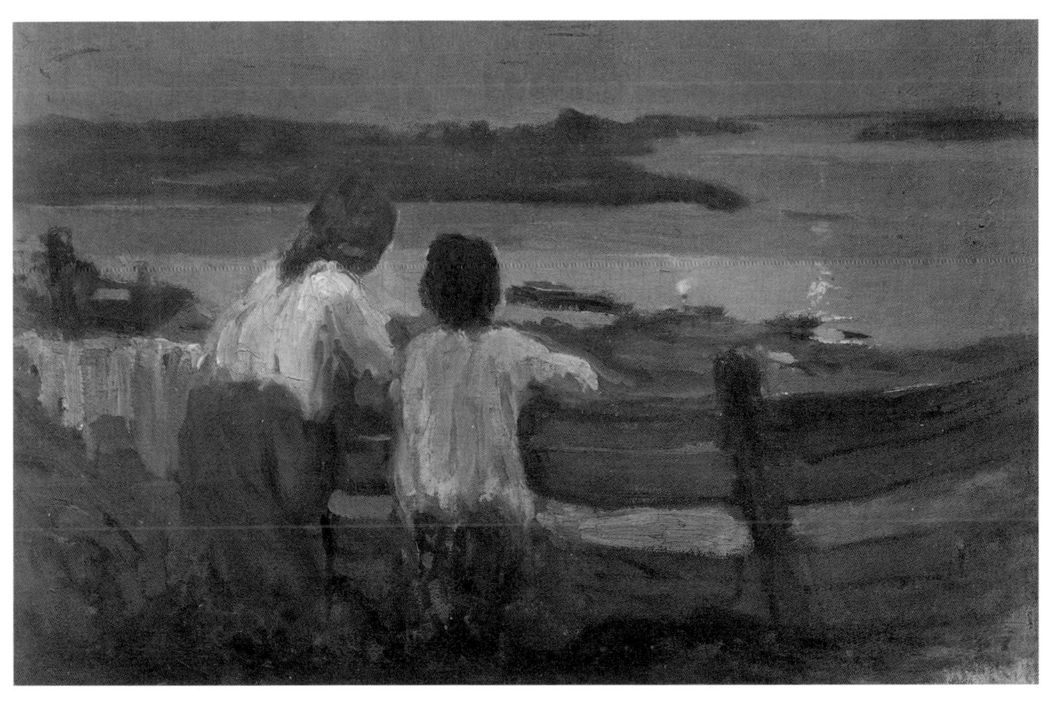

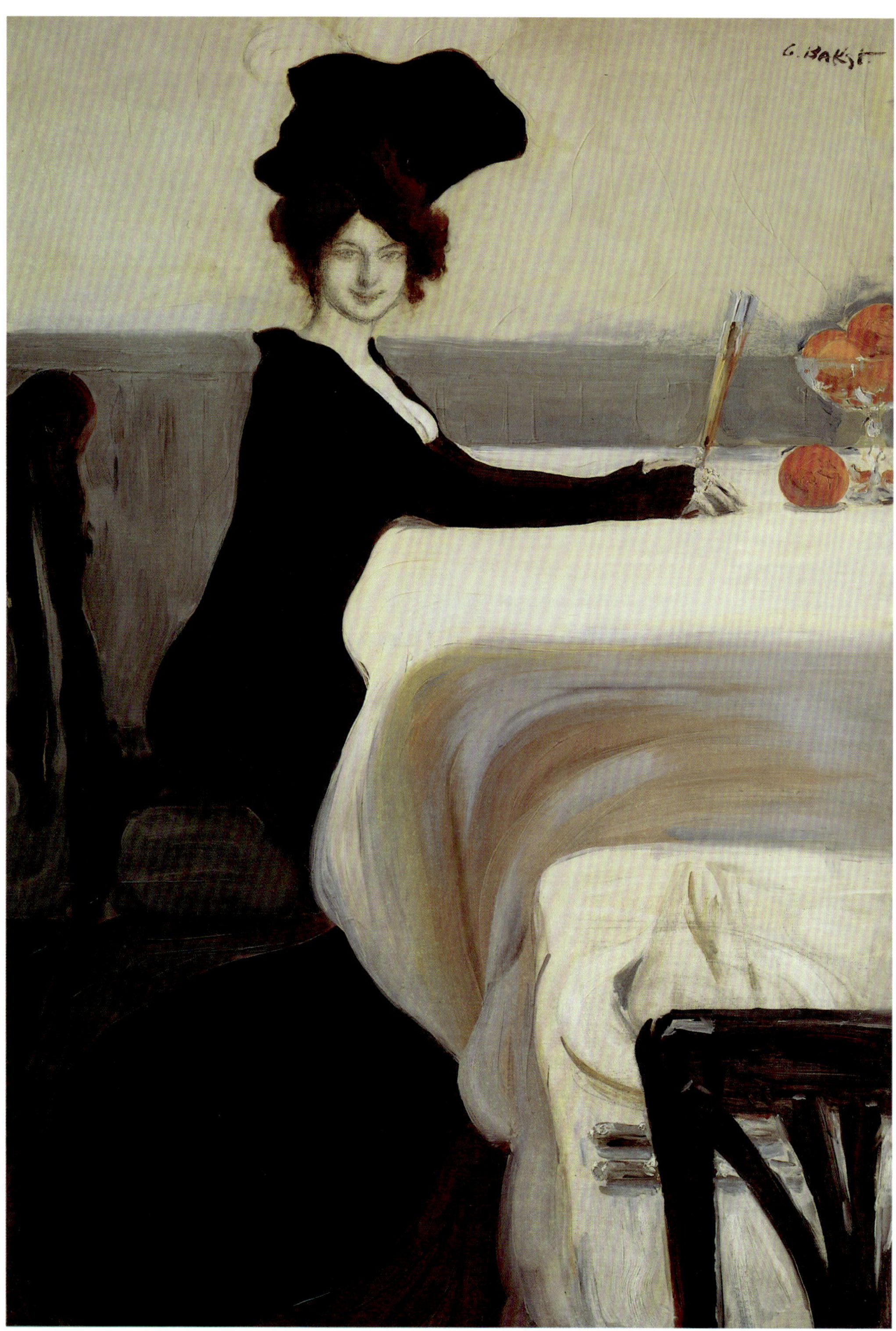

Lev Bakst
29. *Supper*
1902
Oil on canvas, 150 × 100
State Russian Museum

RIGHT: **Mikhail Vrubel'**
470. *N. I. Zabela-Vrubel' by a Piano*
Early 1900s
Oil on canvas, 189 × 60
State Tretyakov Gallery

BELOW: **Fedor Botkin**
74. *Portrait of an Unknown Woman*
1900
Oil on canvas, 91 × 63.5
State Tretyakov Gallery

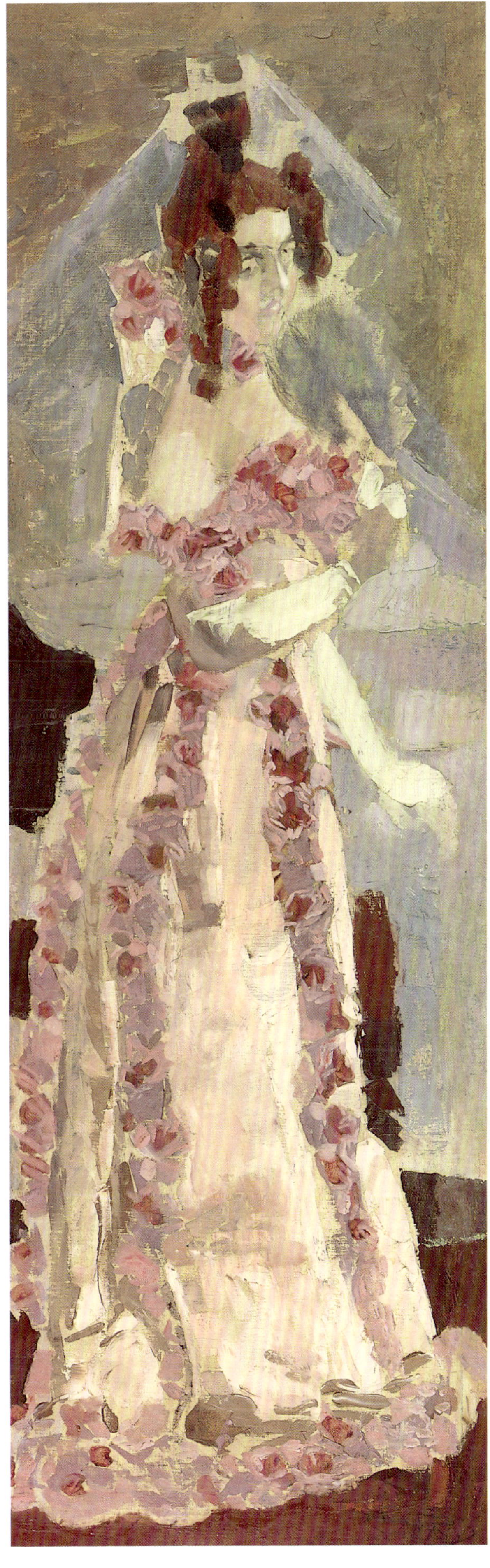

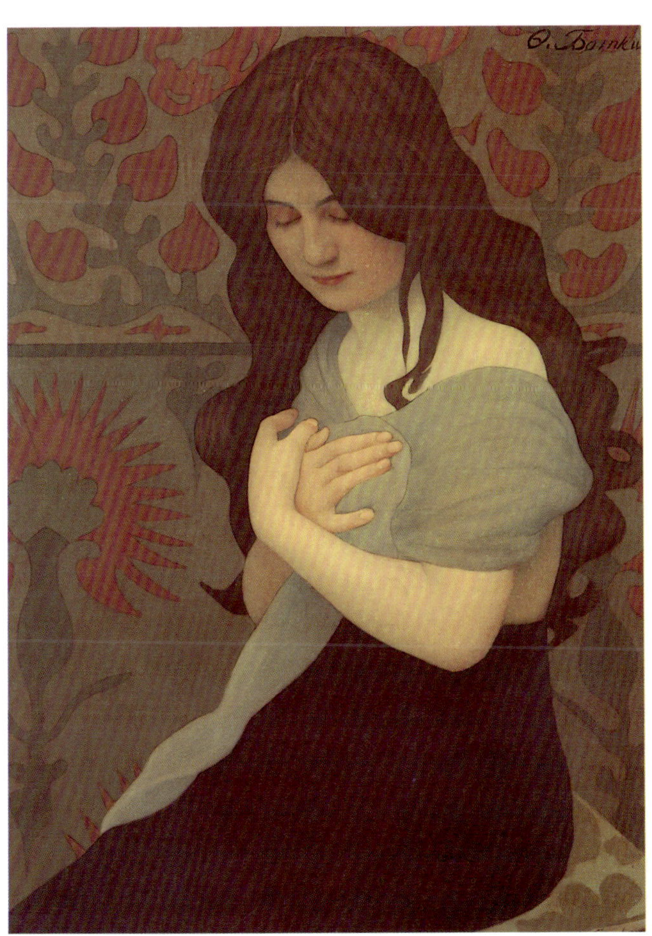

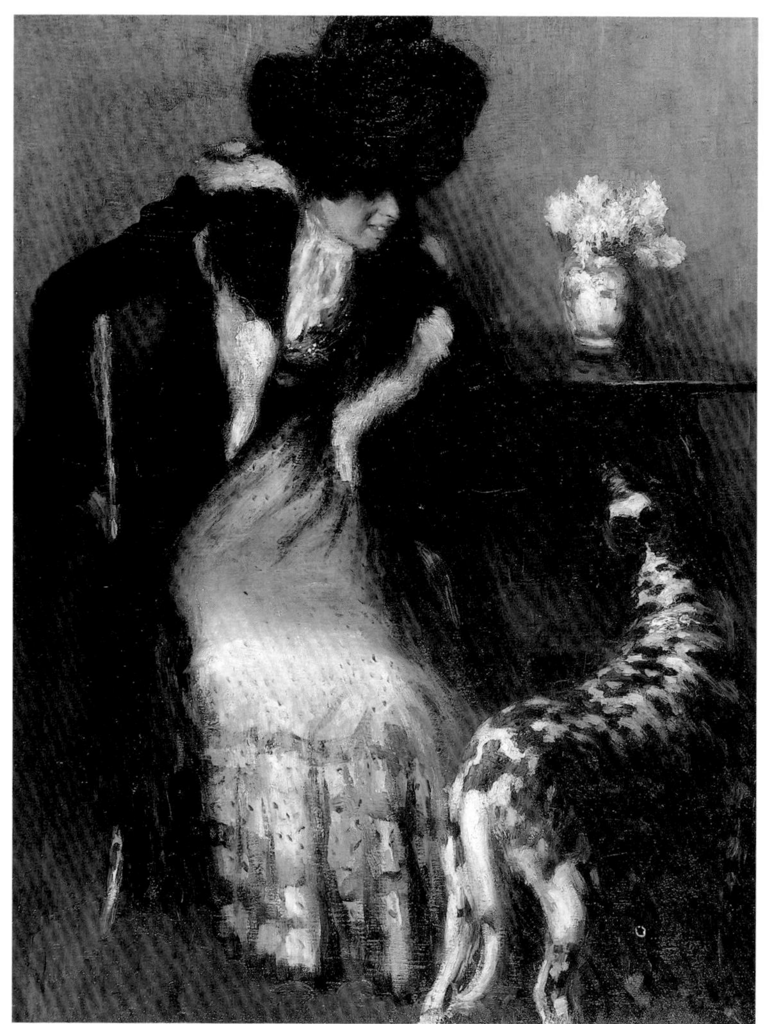

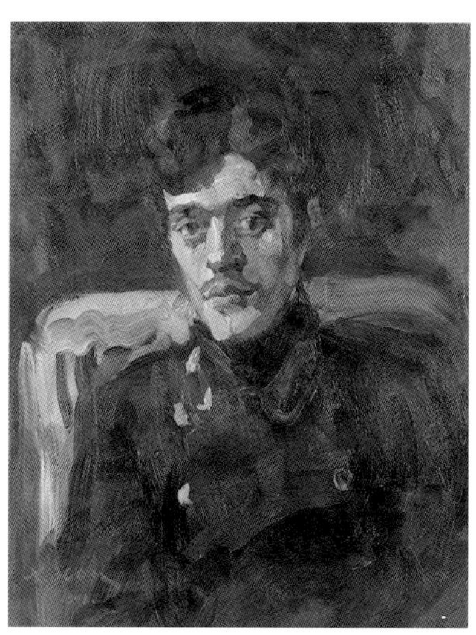

TOP LEFT: **Igor' Grabar'**
139. *Lady with a Dog*
1899
Oil on canvas, 150 × 114.5
State Tretyakov Gallery

ABOVE: **Konstantin Yuon**
481. *Portrait of the Artist Nikolai Feofilaktov*
1901
Oil on cardboard, 68.3 × 54
State Tretyakov Gallery

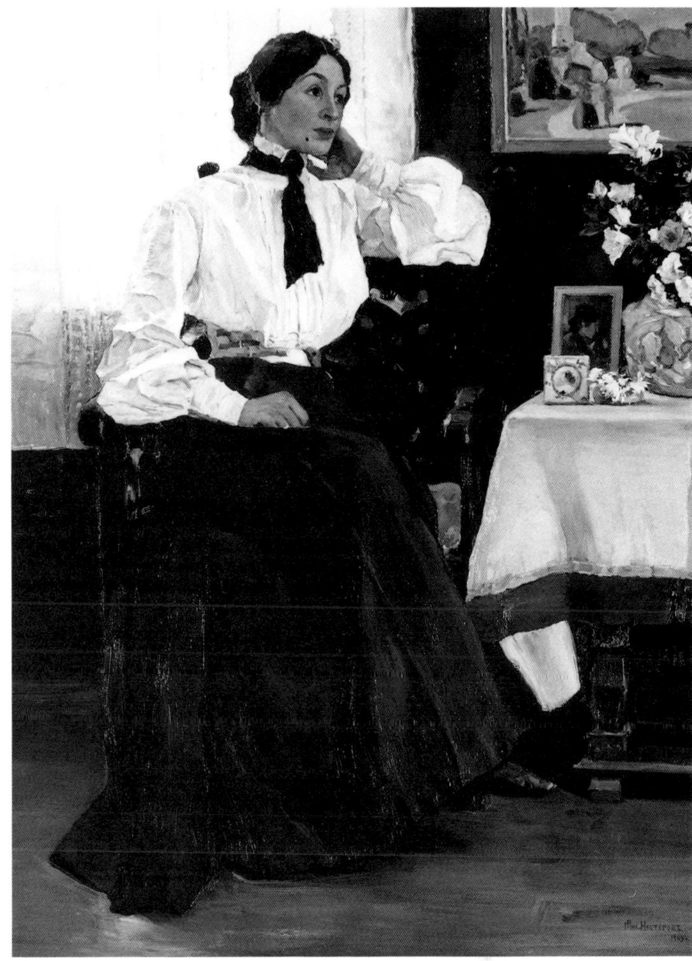

RIGHT: **Mikhail Nesterov**
247. *Portrait of Ekaterina Nesterova*
1905
Oil on canvas, 142.5 × 107.8
State Tretyakov Gallery

BELOW LEFT: **Iosif Braz**
76. *Portrait of Elena Tolstoy*
1900
Oil on canvas, 99 × 104
State Russian Museum

BELOW RIGHT:
Valentin Serov
311. *Portrait of Mara Oliv*
1895
Oil on canvas, 88 × 68.5
State Russian Museum

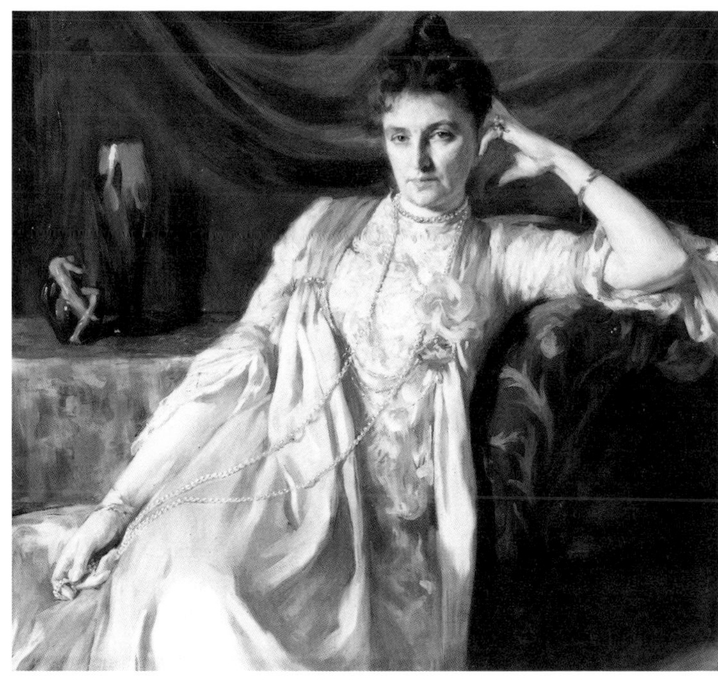

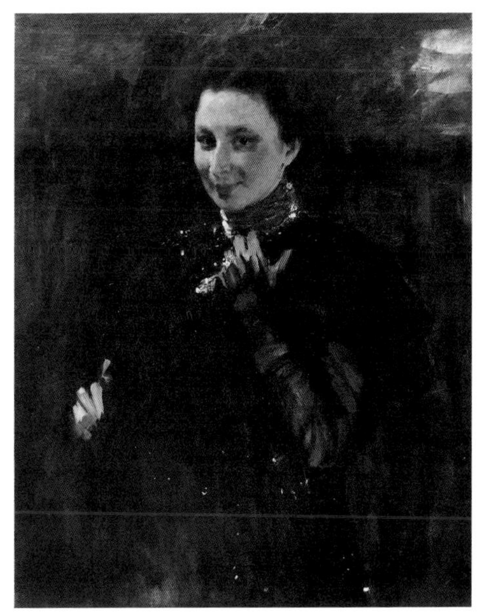

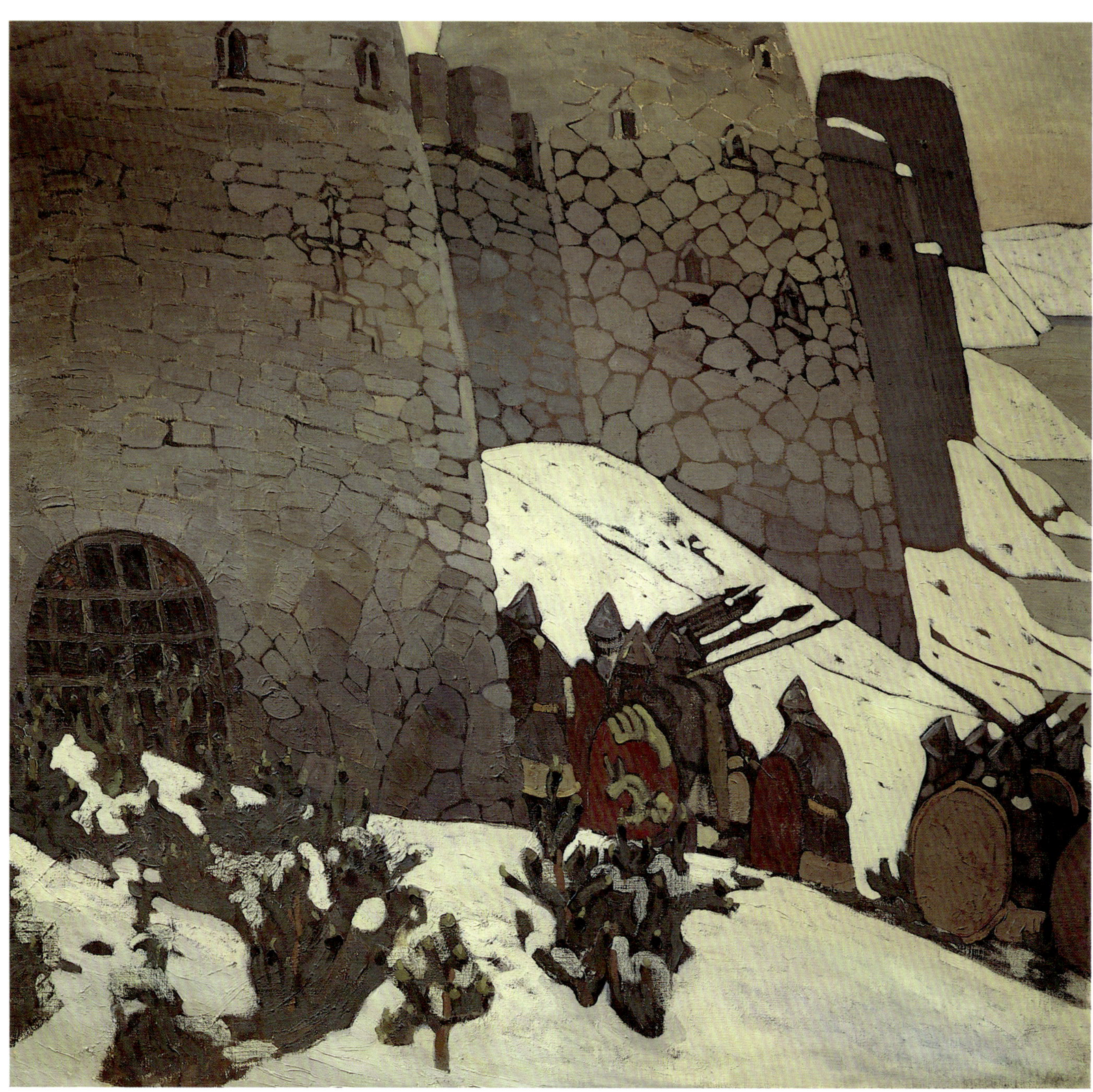

Nikolai Roerich
291. *Patrol*
1905
Oil on canvas, 148 × 148
State Russian Museum

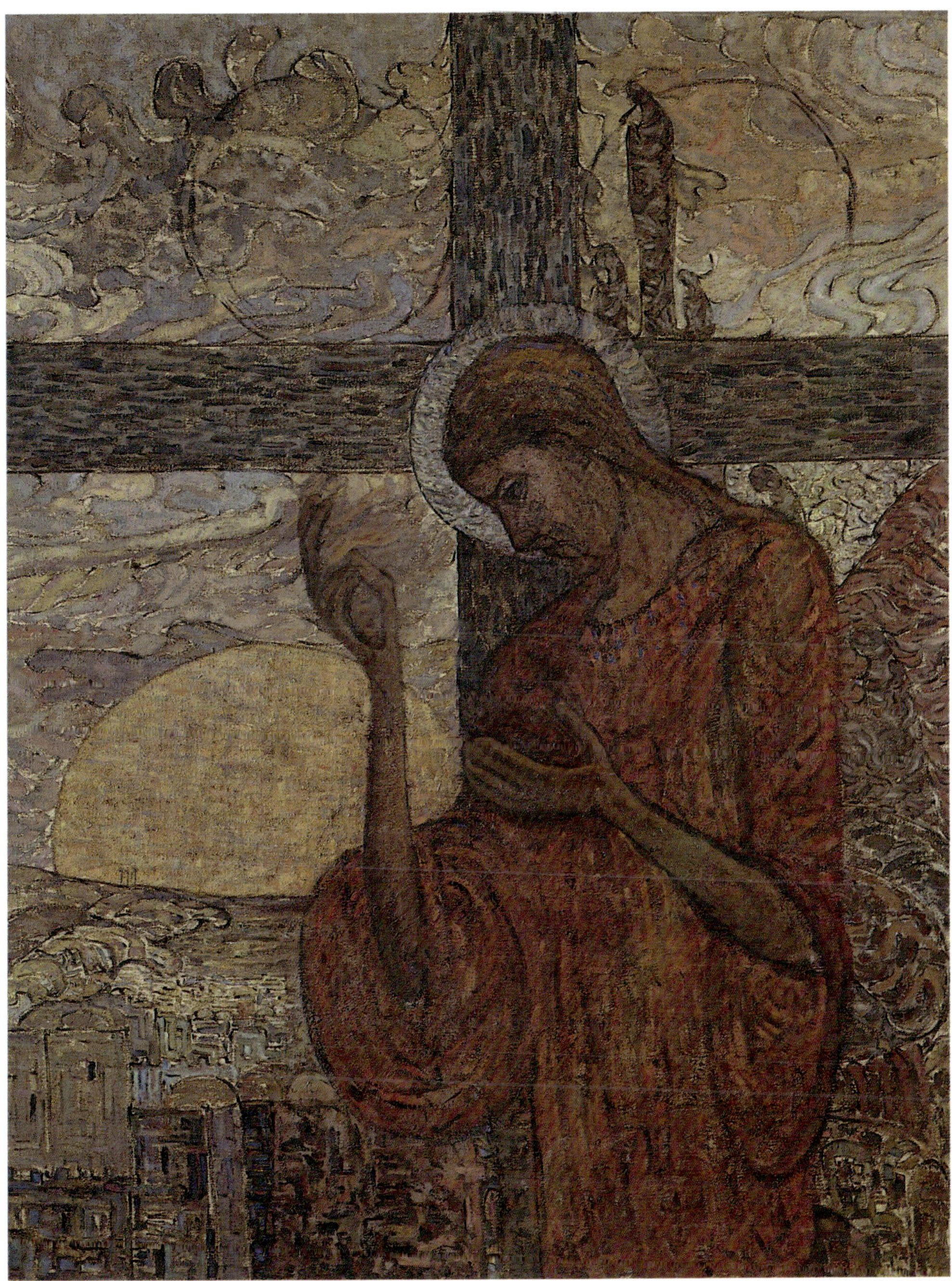

Vasily Denisov
90. *Sorrow (Giotto)*
1904
Oil on canvas, 143 × 107
State Russian Museum

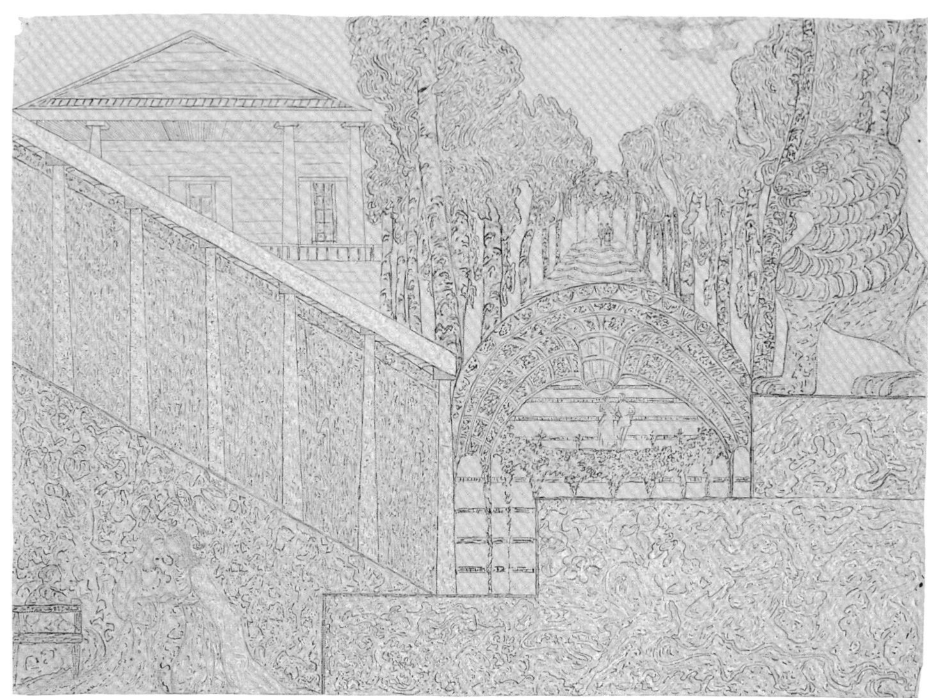

ABOVE: **Vasily Denisov**
92. *Composition*
1906
Mixed media on blue paper, 40 × 53.2
State Tretyakov Gallery

BELOW: **Konstantin Yuon**
483. *The Animal Kingdom*
1908
From the series "The Creation of the World"
Pen and Indian ink on paper, 48.8 × 65.5
State Tretyakov Gallery

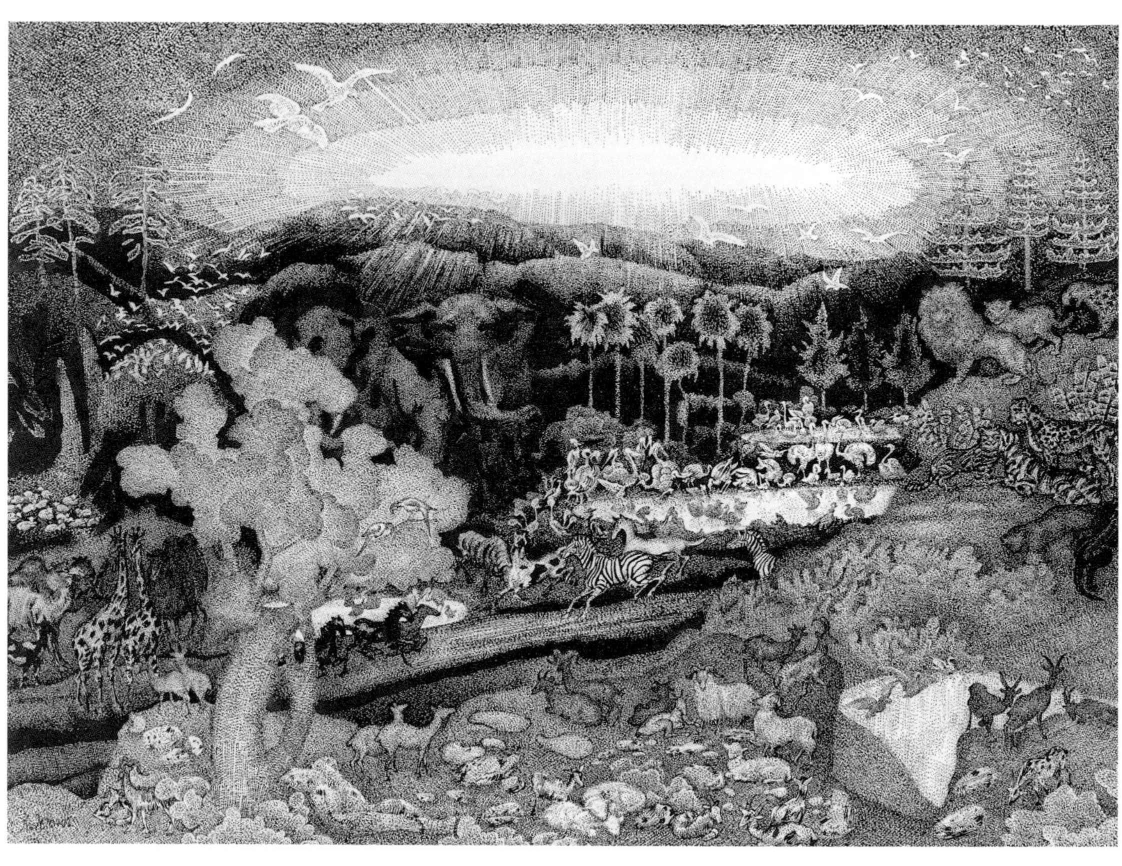

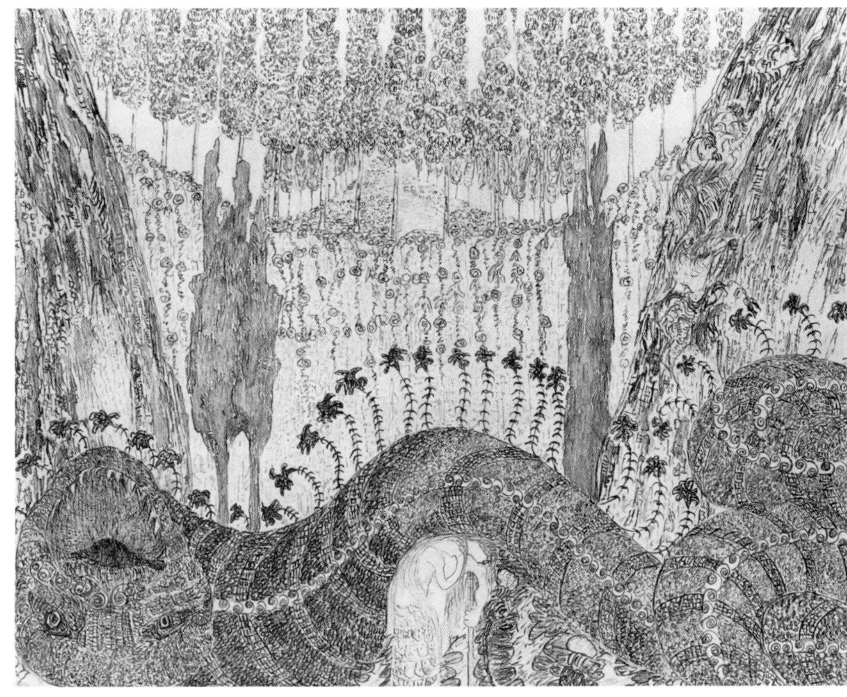

ABOVE: **Vasily Denisov**
89. *Sin*
1902
Black watercolour, black and lead pencils on
paper, 44 × 52.7
State Tretyakov Gallery

BELOW: **Konstantin Yuon**
482. *The Vegetable Kingdom*
1908
From the series "The Creation of the World"
Pen and Indian ink on paper, 50.8 × 67.8
State Tretyakov Gallery

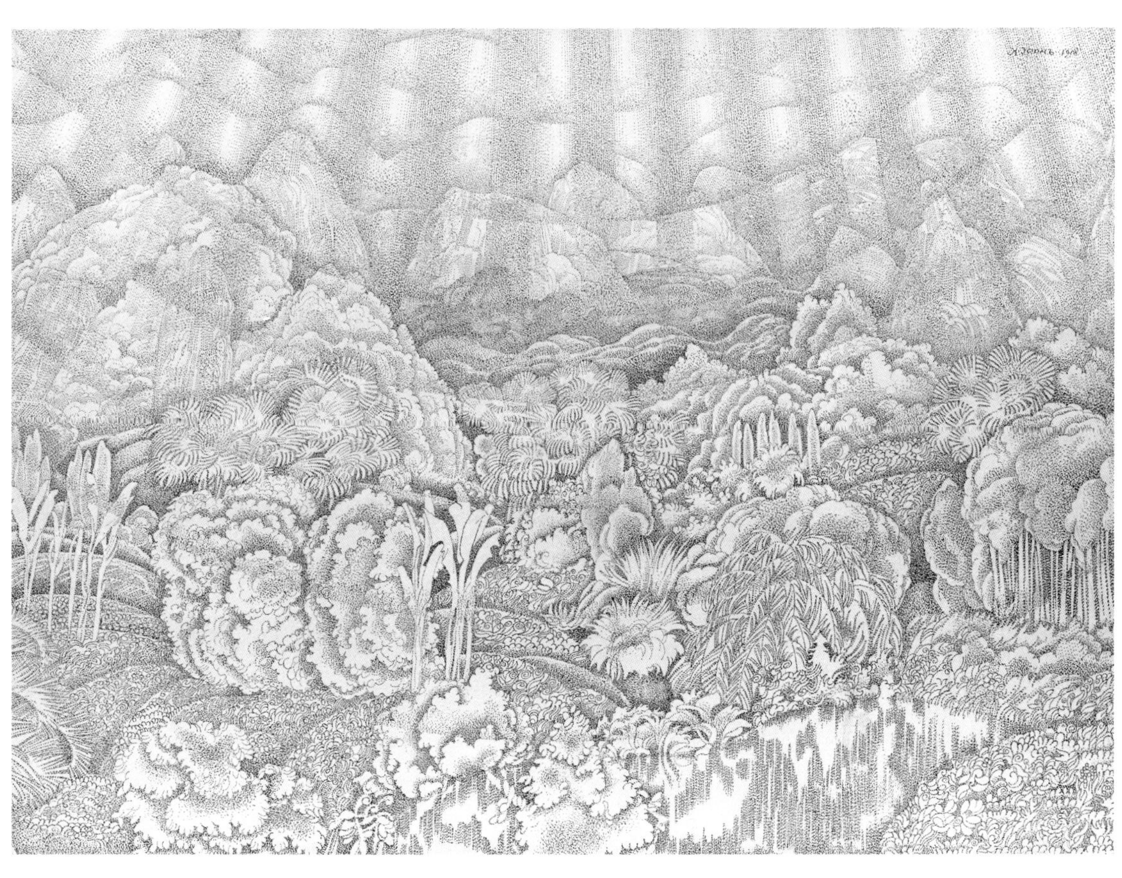

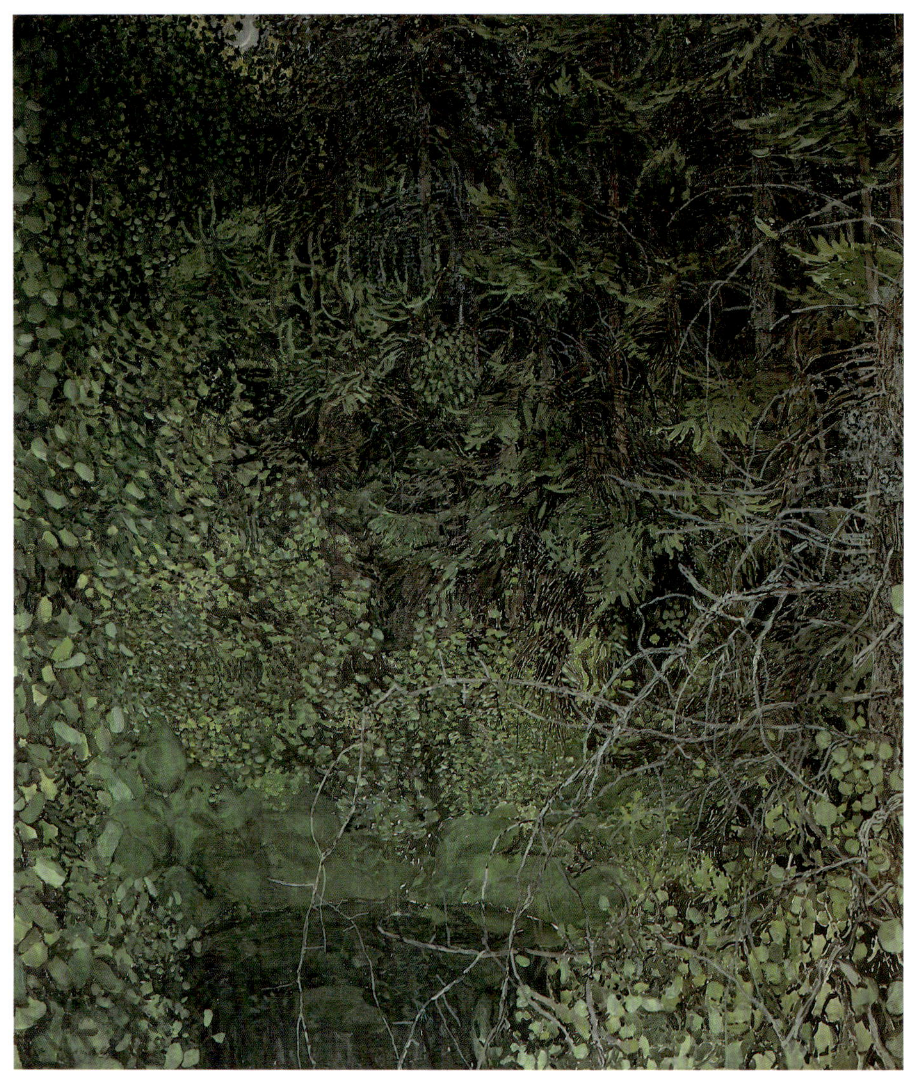

Aleksandr Golovin
124. *Pond in a Forest*
1909
Tempera on canvas, 124 × 106
State Russian Museum

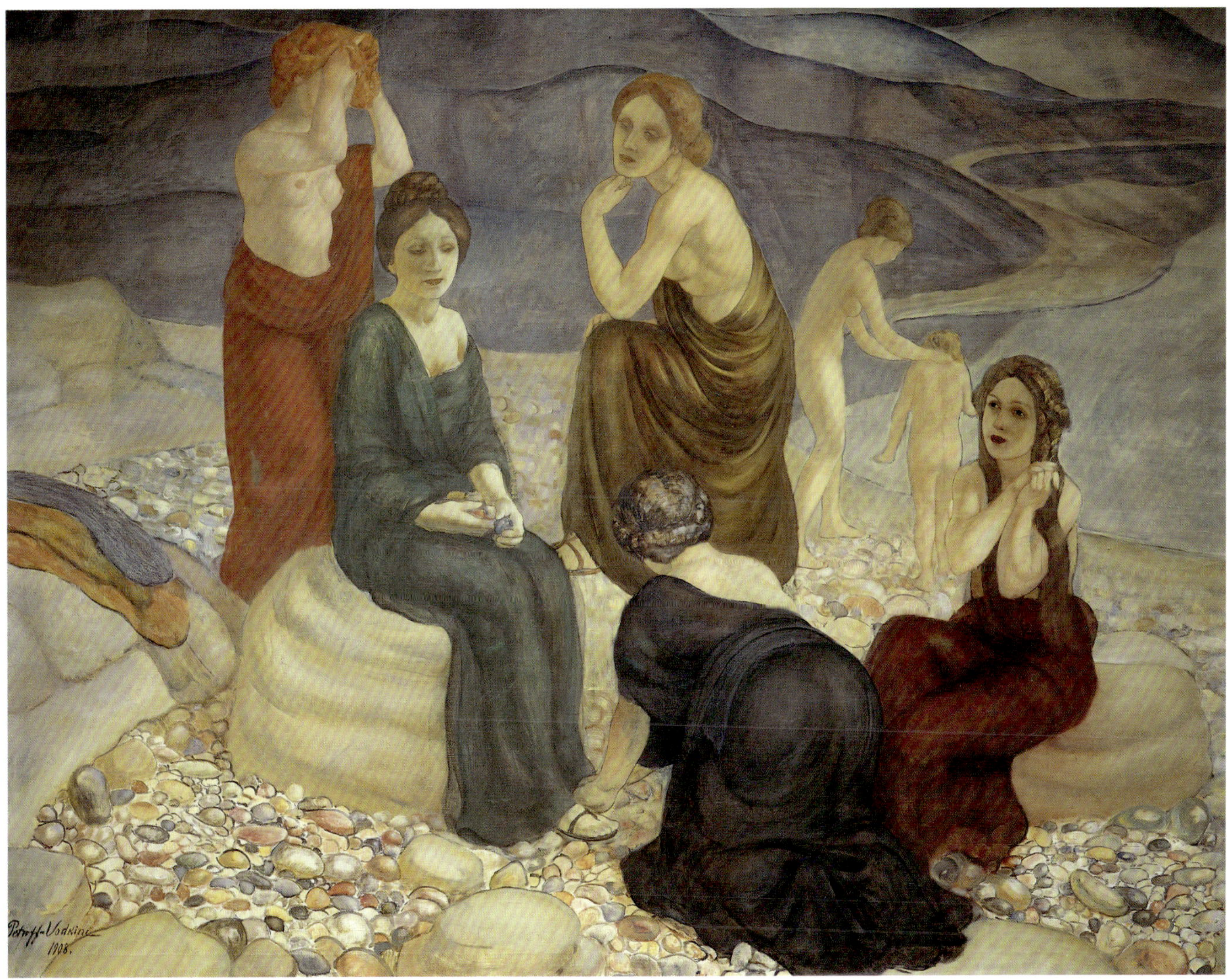

Kuz'ma Petrov-Vodkin
267. *River Bank*
Paris, 1908
Oil on canvas, 128 × 159
State Russian Museum

RIGHT: **Martiros Sar'yan**
306. *By the Pomegranate Tree*
1907
Tempera on cardboard, 34.6 × 52.5
State Tretyakov Gallery

BELOW LEFT: **Sergei Sudeikin**
413. *Russian Venus*
1907
Mixed media on cardboard, 29.4 × 37.6
State Tretyakov Gallery

BELOW RIGHT: **Petr Utkin**
438. *Peacocks in a Garden*
1905
Pen and Indian ink on brown paper, 28.1 × 23
State Russian Museum

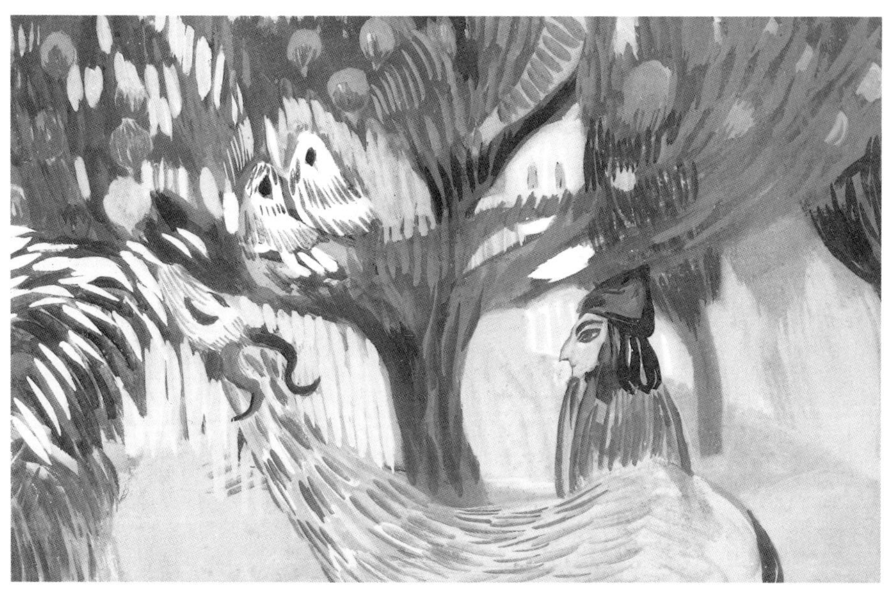

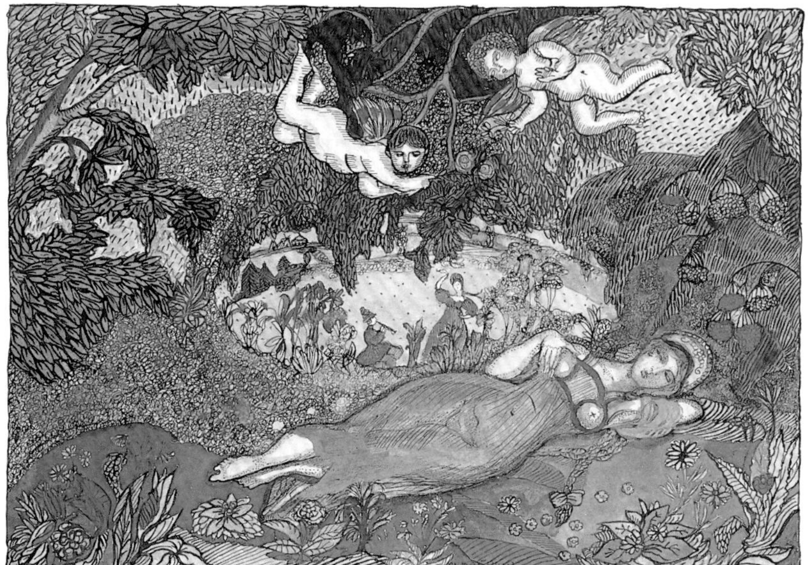

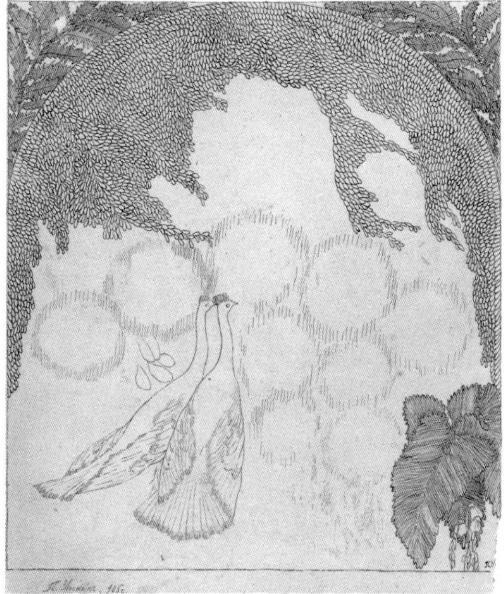

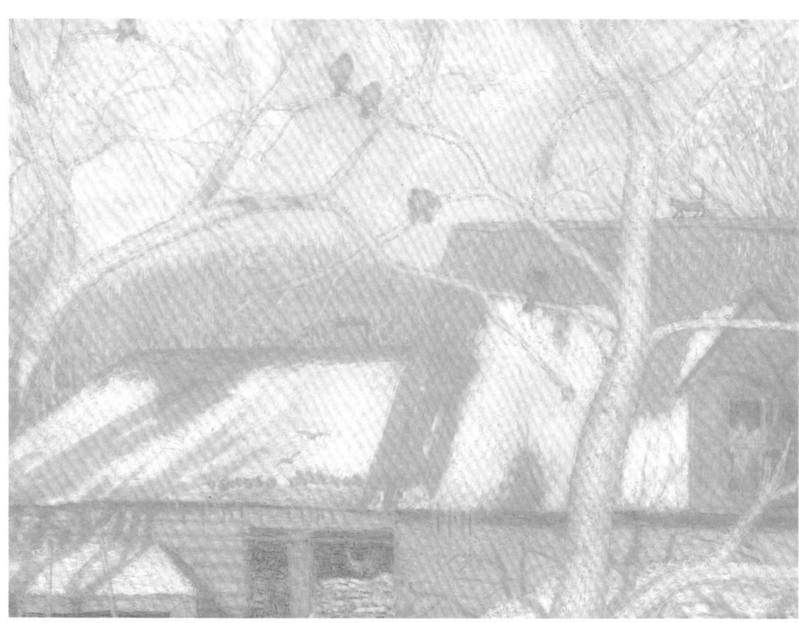

RIGHT: **Nikolai Krymov**
184. *Approaching Spring*
1907
Oil on canvas, 52 × 71
State Tretyakov Gallery

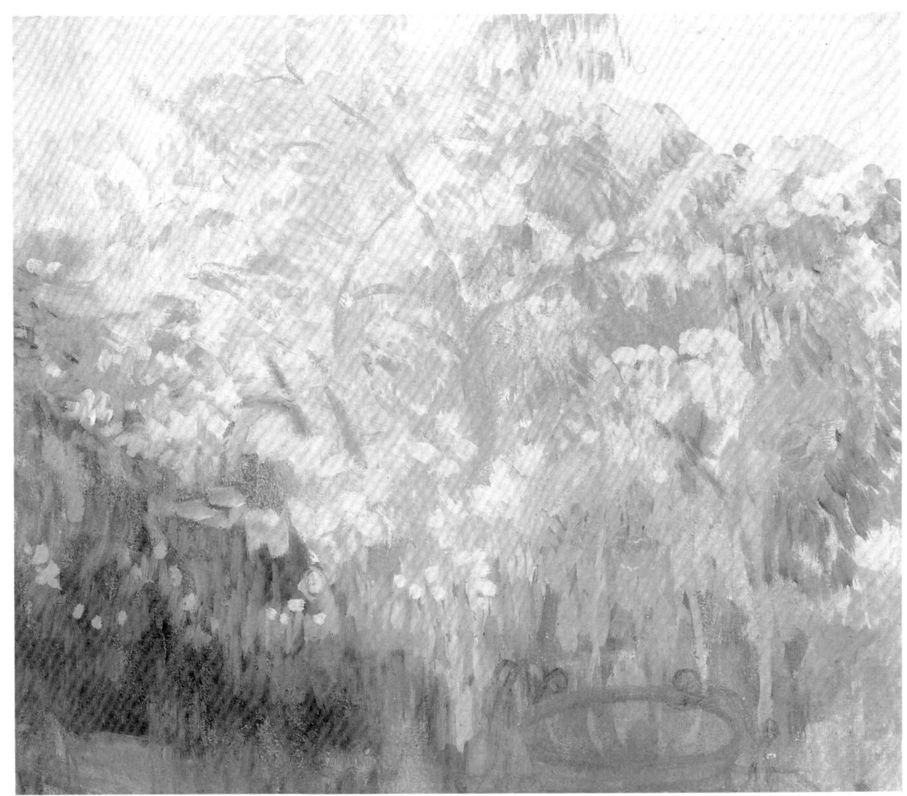

LEFT: **Pavel Kuznetov**
194. *Flowering Garden in Bakhchisaray*
1907
Tempera on canvas, 63 × 70
State Tretyakov Gallery

BELOW: **Aleksandr Gaush**
123. *Peacocks by a Fountain*
1911–15
Oil on canvas, 71.5 × 107
State Russian Museum

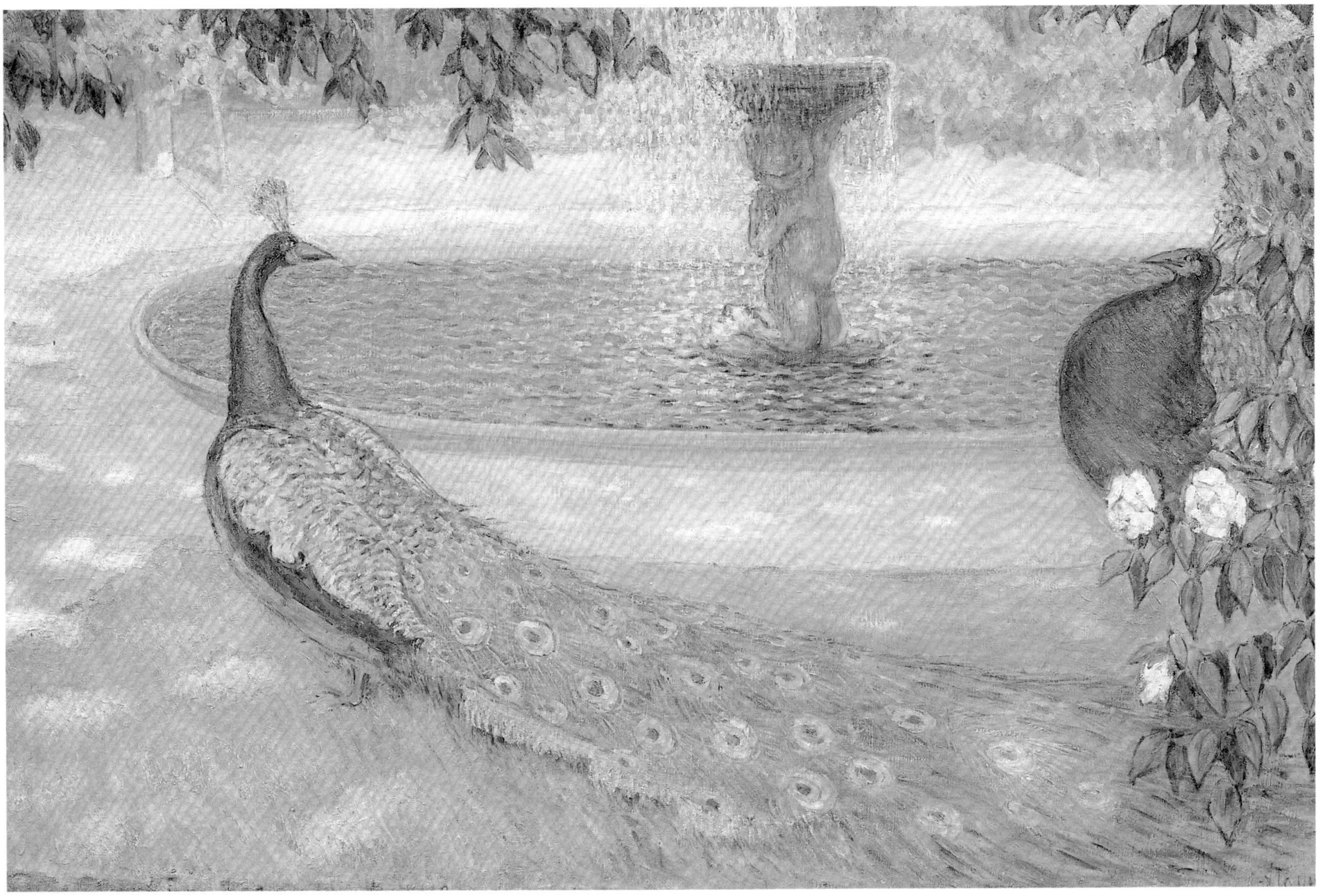

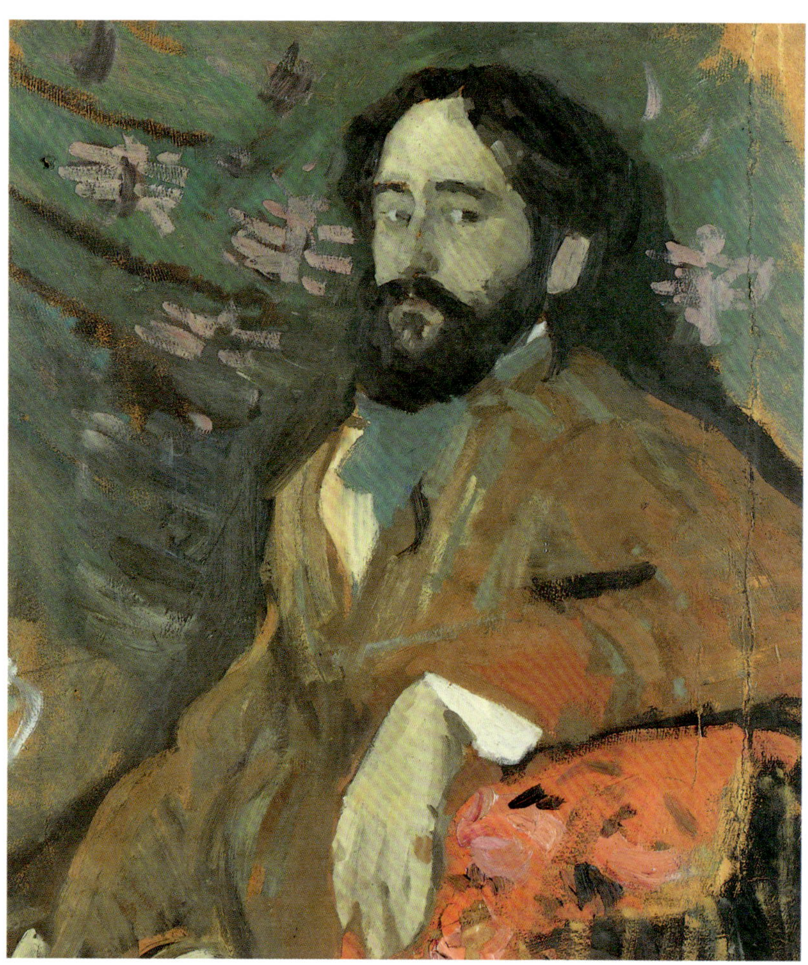

Nikolai Sapunov
304. *Portrait of the Artist Nikolai Milioti*
1908
Oil on cardboard, 77 × 66.7
State Tretyakov Gallery

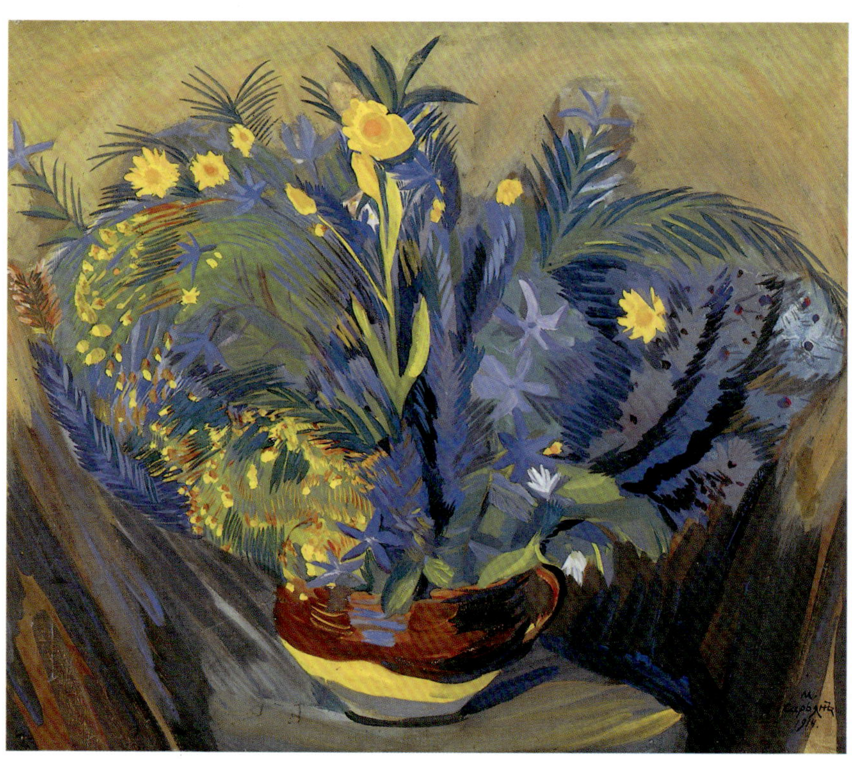

Martiros Sar'yan
307. *Flowers at Sambek*
1914
Tempera on canvas, 60 × 71
State Tretyakov Gallery

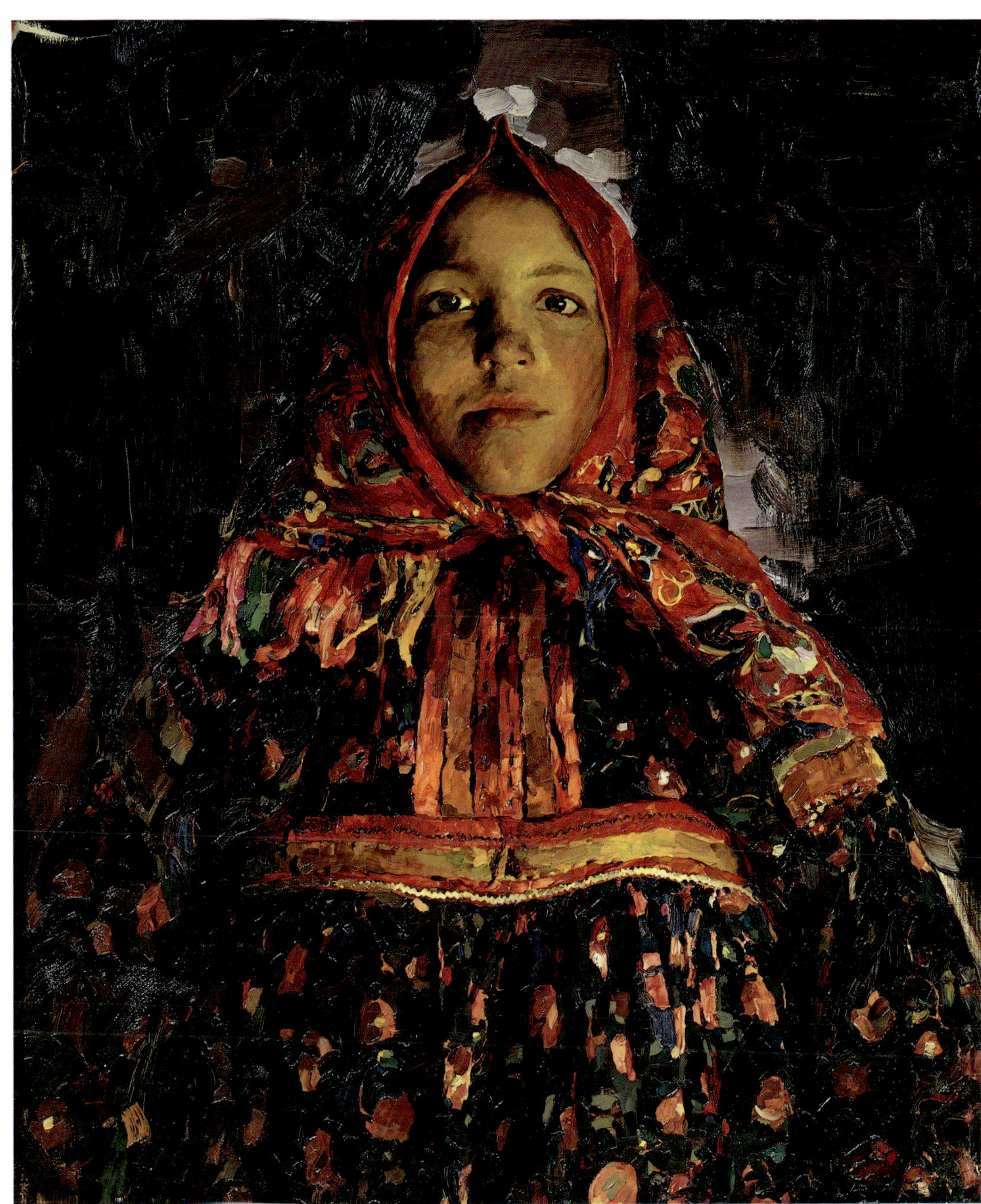

Filipp Malyavin
217. *Verka*
1913
Oil on canvas, 106 × 84
State Russian Museum

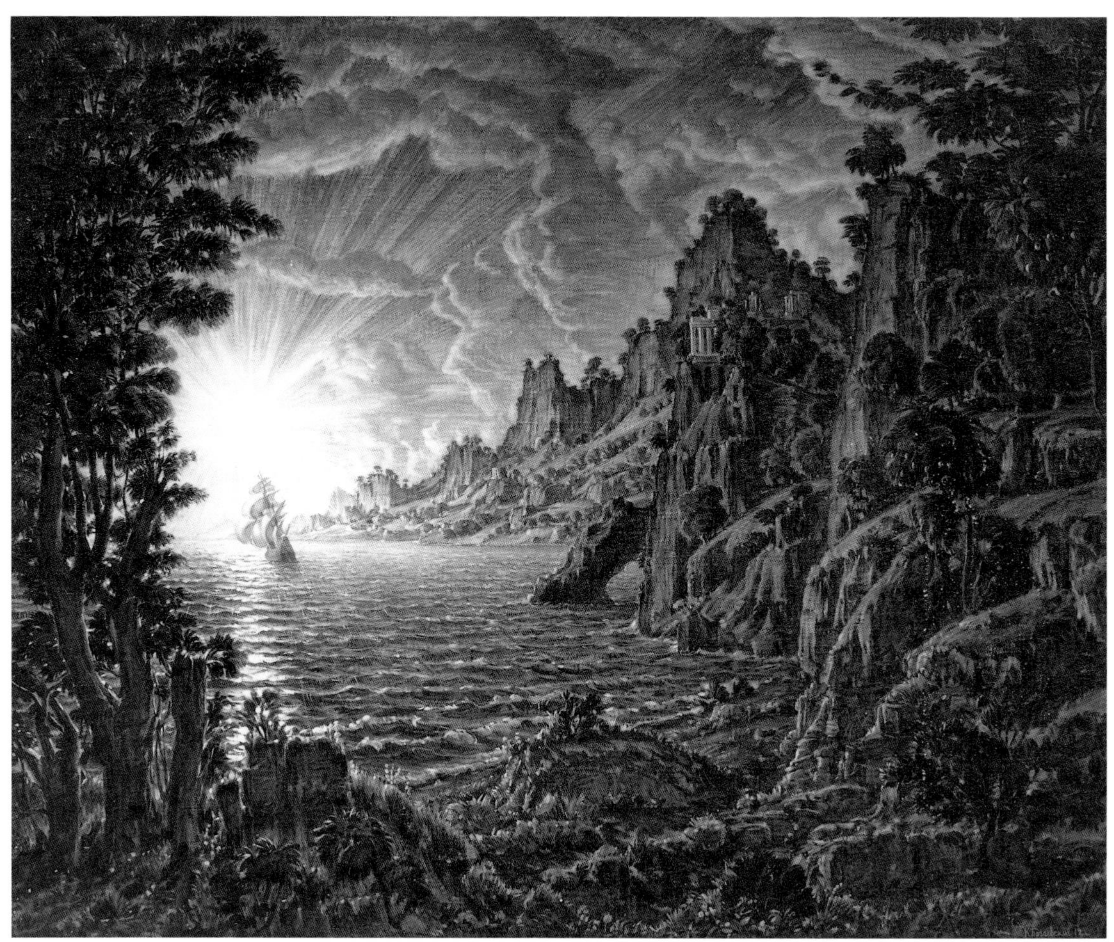

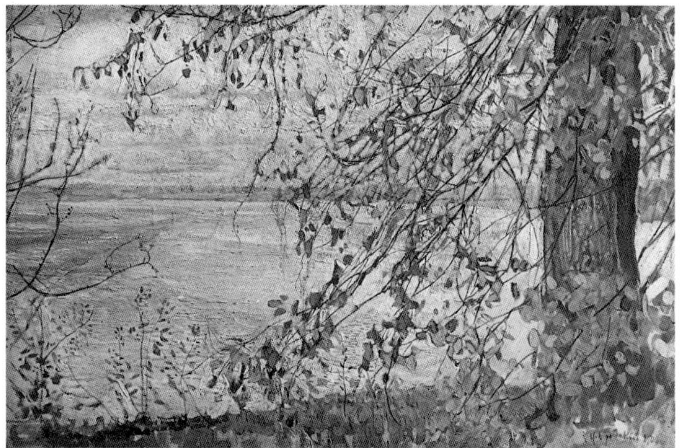

ABOVE: **Konstantin Bogaevsky**
60. *Ships: Evening Sun*
1912
Oil on canvas, 133 × 155
State Russian Museum

LEFT: **Isaak Brodsky**
77. *Grey Day*
1909
Oil on canvas, 45.5 × 69.5
State Russian Museum

RIGHT: **Sergei Sudeikin**
411. *In the Park*
1907
Oil on cardboard, 53.8 × 66.8
State Russian Museum

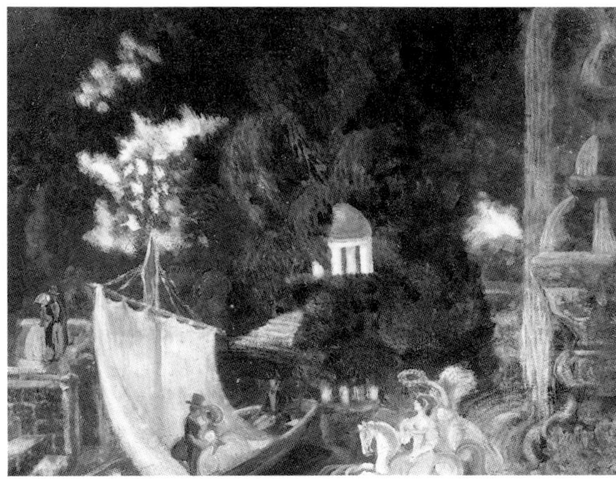

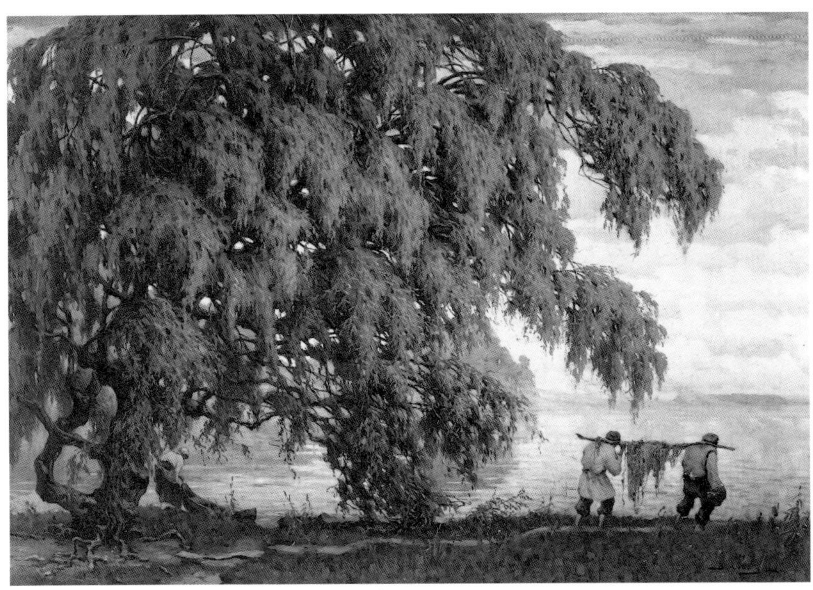

ABOVE: **Viktor Zarubin**
488. *Landscape with Fishermen*
1906
Oil on canvas, 102.3 × 142.5
State Russian Museum

RIGHT: **Konstantin Somov**
405. *In the Forest*
1914
Oil on canvas, 113 × 142
State Russian Museum

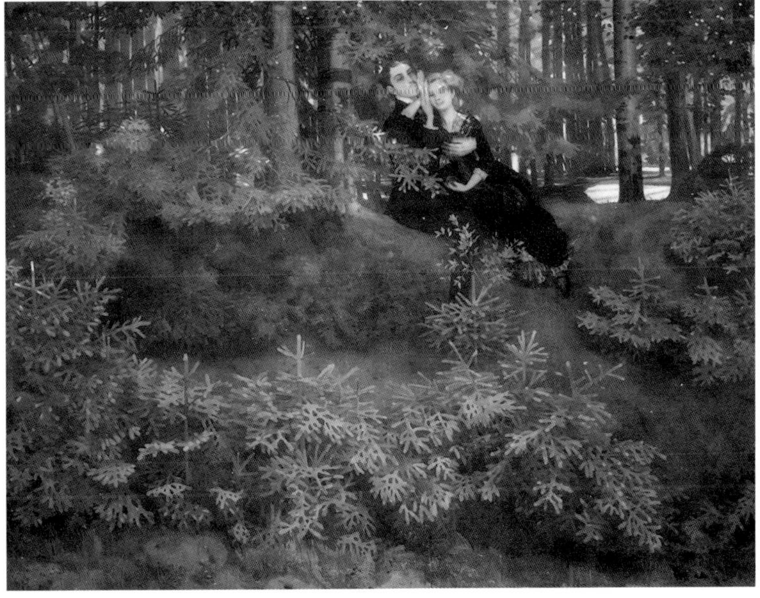

LEFT: **Anatoly Arapov**
20. *Italian Musicians*
1914
Tempera on cardboard, 58 × 65
Saratov State Art Museum

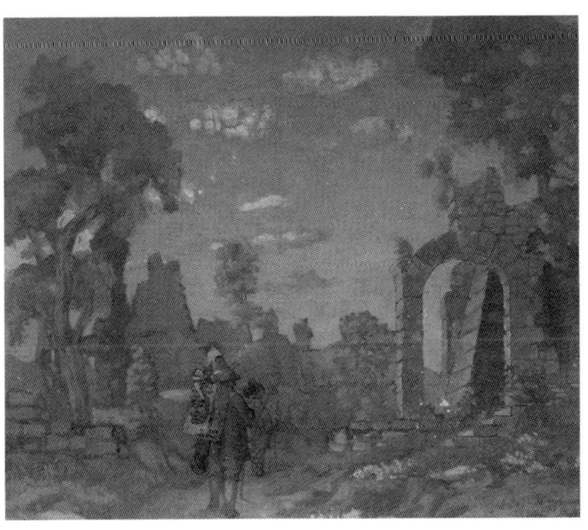

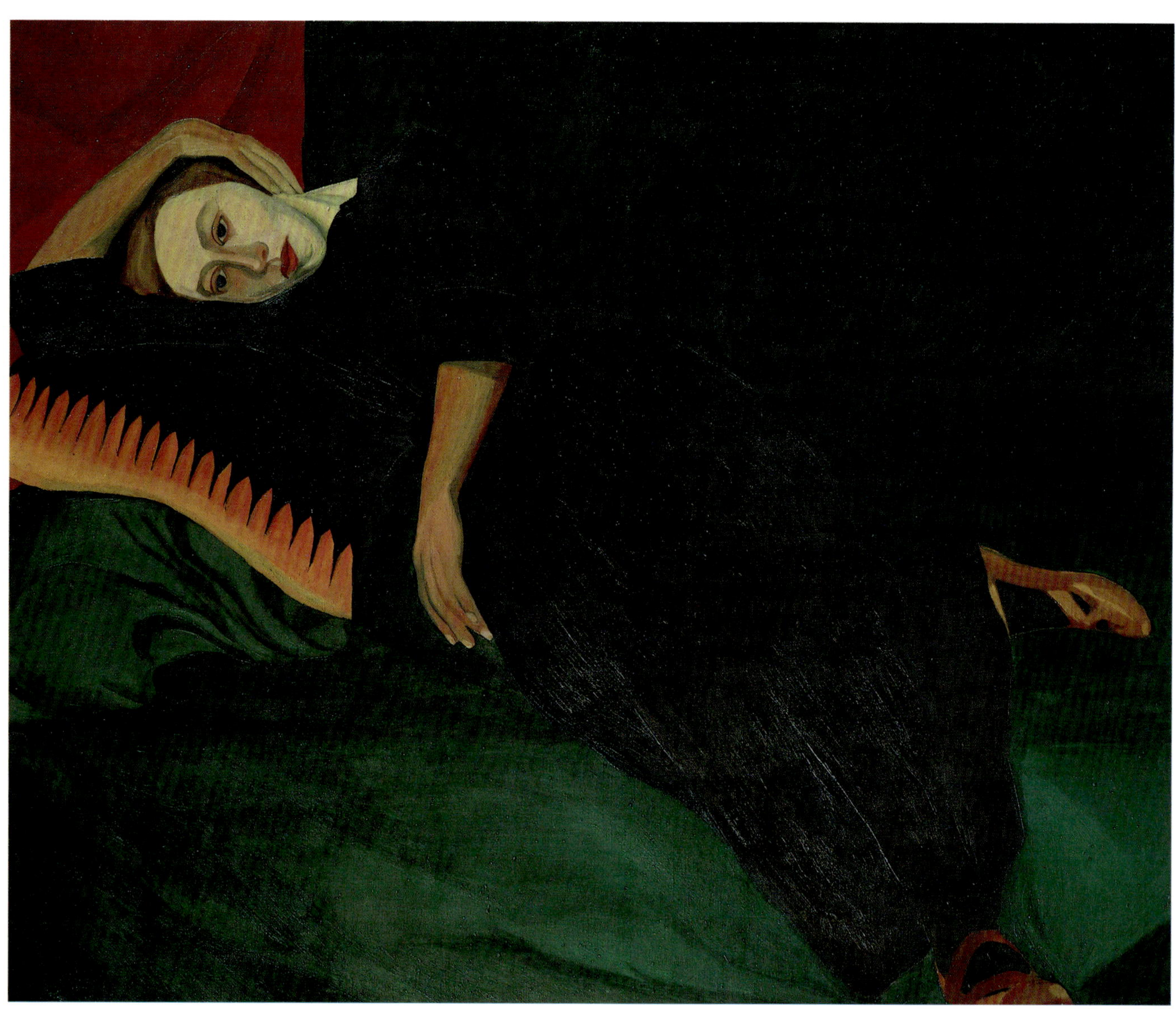

Nadezhda Lermontova
211. *On the Sofa: Self-Portrait*
1910s
Oil on canvas, 106.8 × 124.5
State Russian Museum

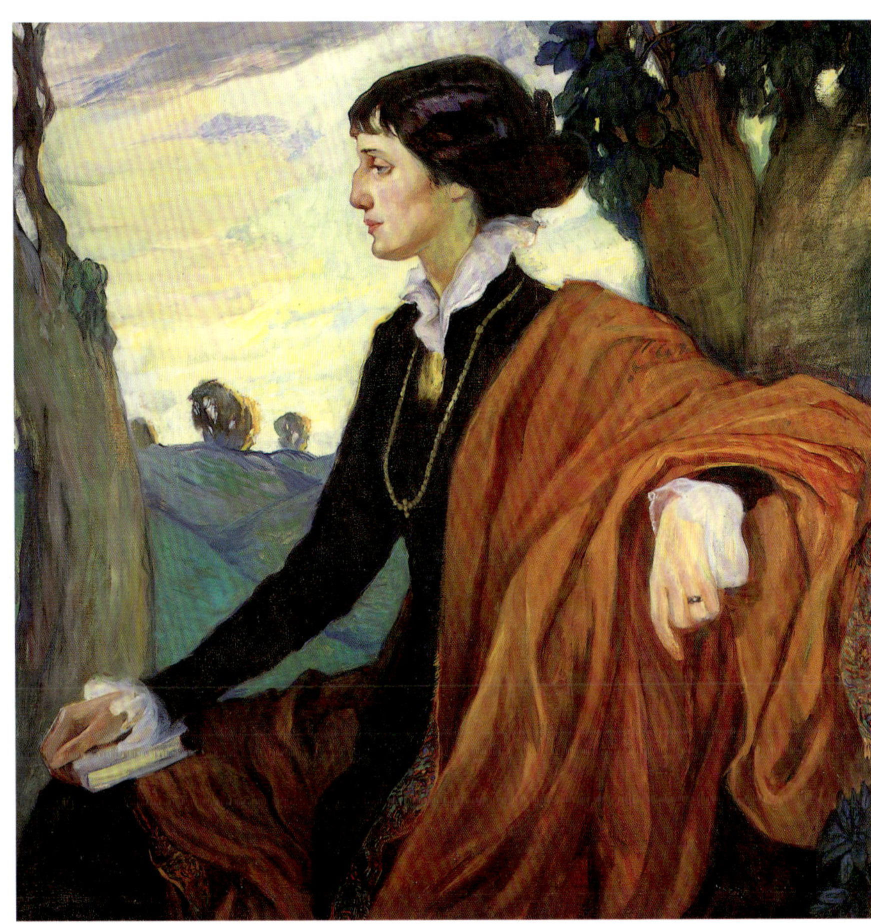

Ol'ga Della-Vos-Kardovskaya
87. *Portrait of Anna Akhmatova*
1914
Oil on canvas, 85 × 82
State Tretyakov Gallery

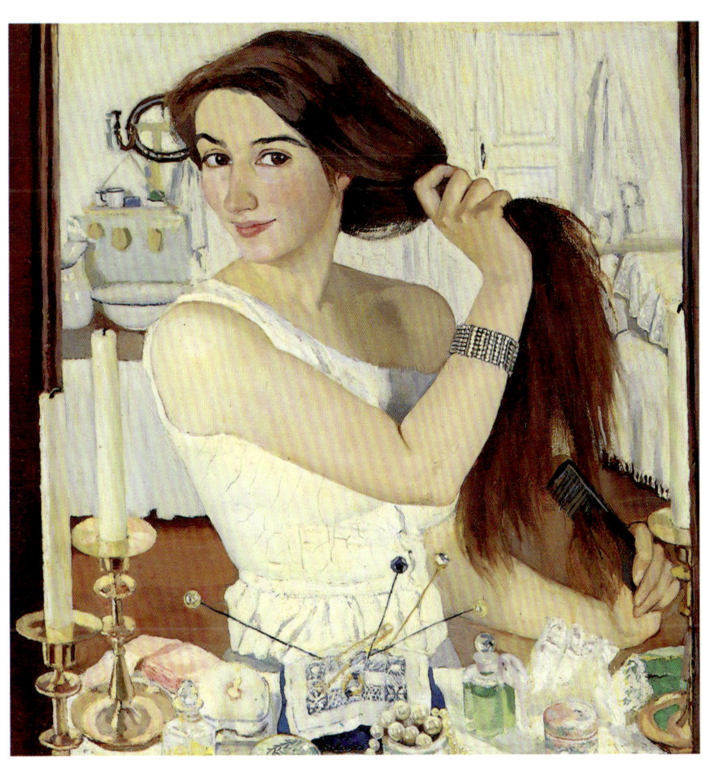

Zinaida Serebryakova
310. *At the Dressing-Table: Self-Portrait*
1909
Oil on canvas mounted on cardboard, 75 × 65
State Tretyakov Gallery

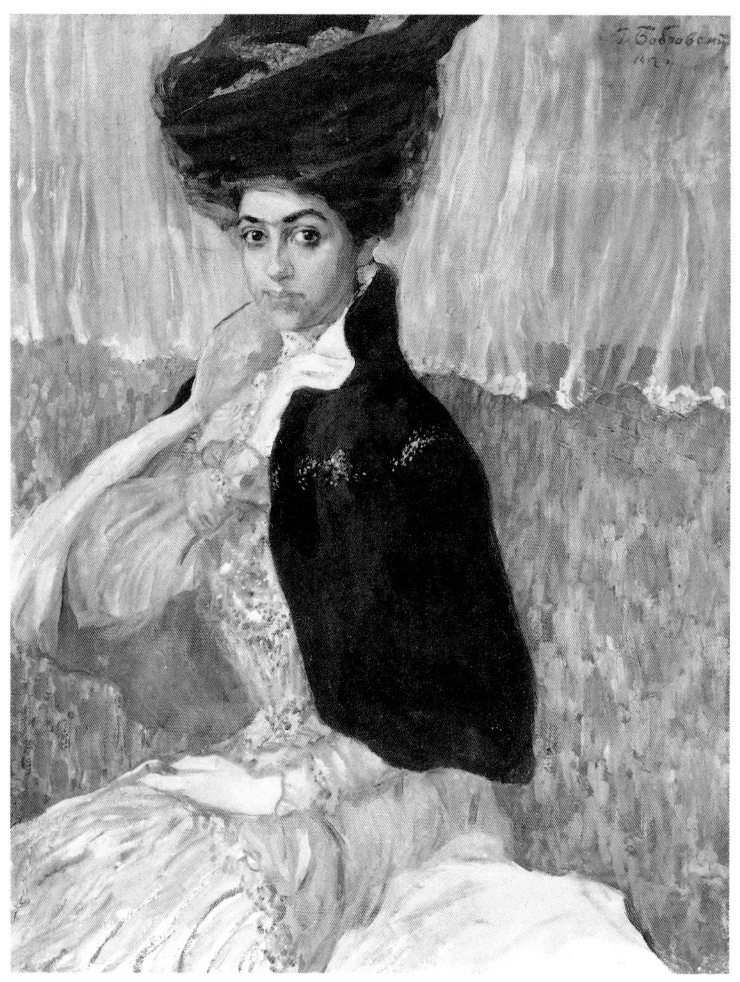

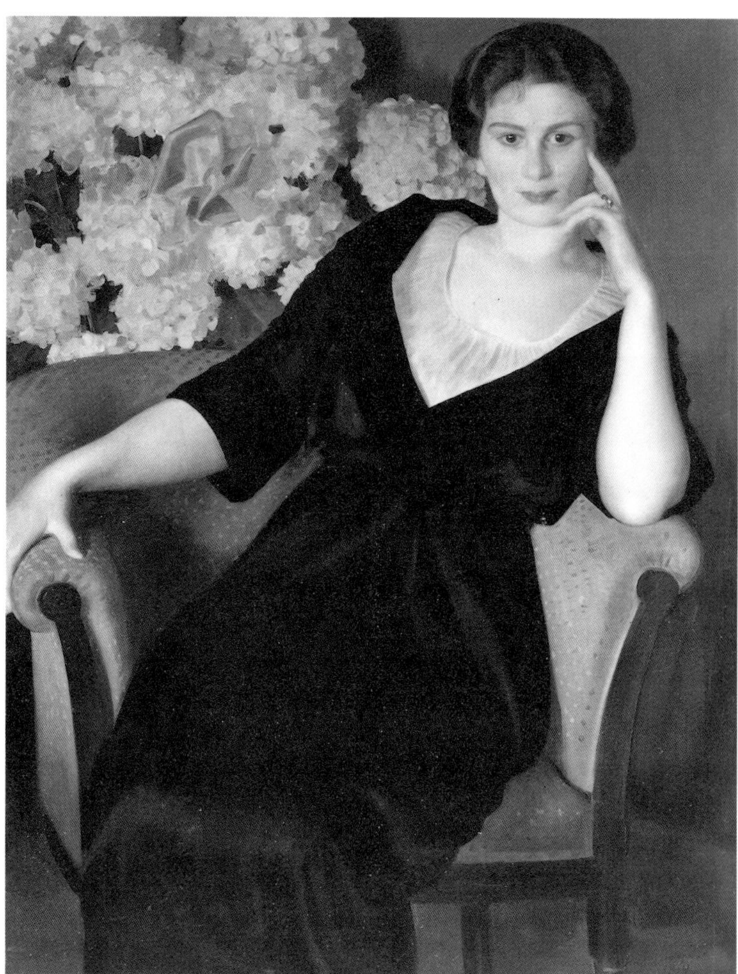

Grigory Bobrovsky
59. *Portrait of Miss Samoilova*
1912
Oil on canvas, 112 × 85
State Russian Museum

Boris Kustodiev
186. *Portrait of Renée Notgaft*
1914
Oil on canvas, 111 × 81
State Russian Museum

Opposite above: **Aleksandr Golovin**
126. *Portrait of a Woman*
1910s
Gouache and tempera on canvas, 130 × 95
State Tretyakov Gallery

Opposite below: **Filipp Malyavin**
216. *Woman with Red Umbrella*
N.d.
Oil on canvas, 58 × 75
Saratov Art Museum

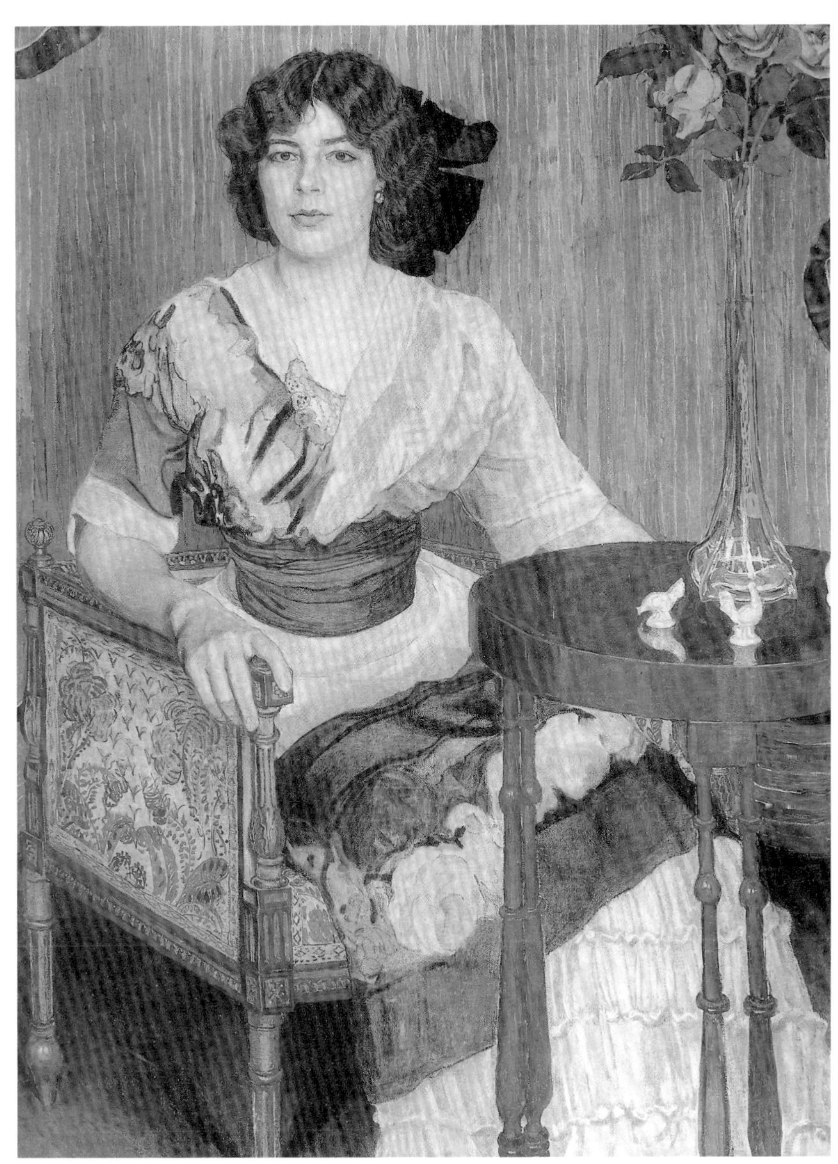

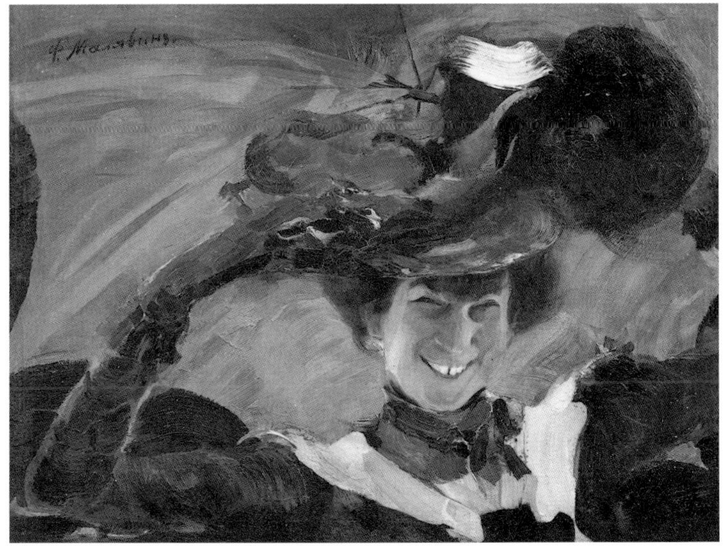

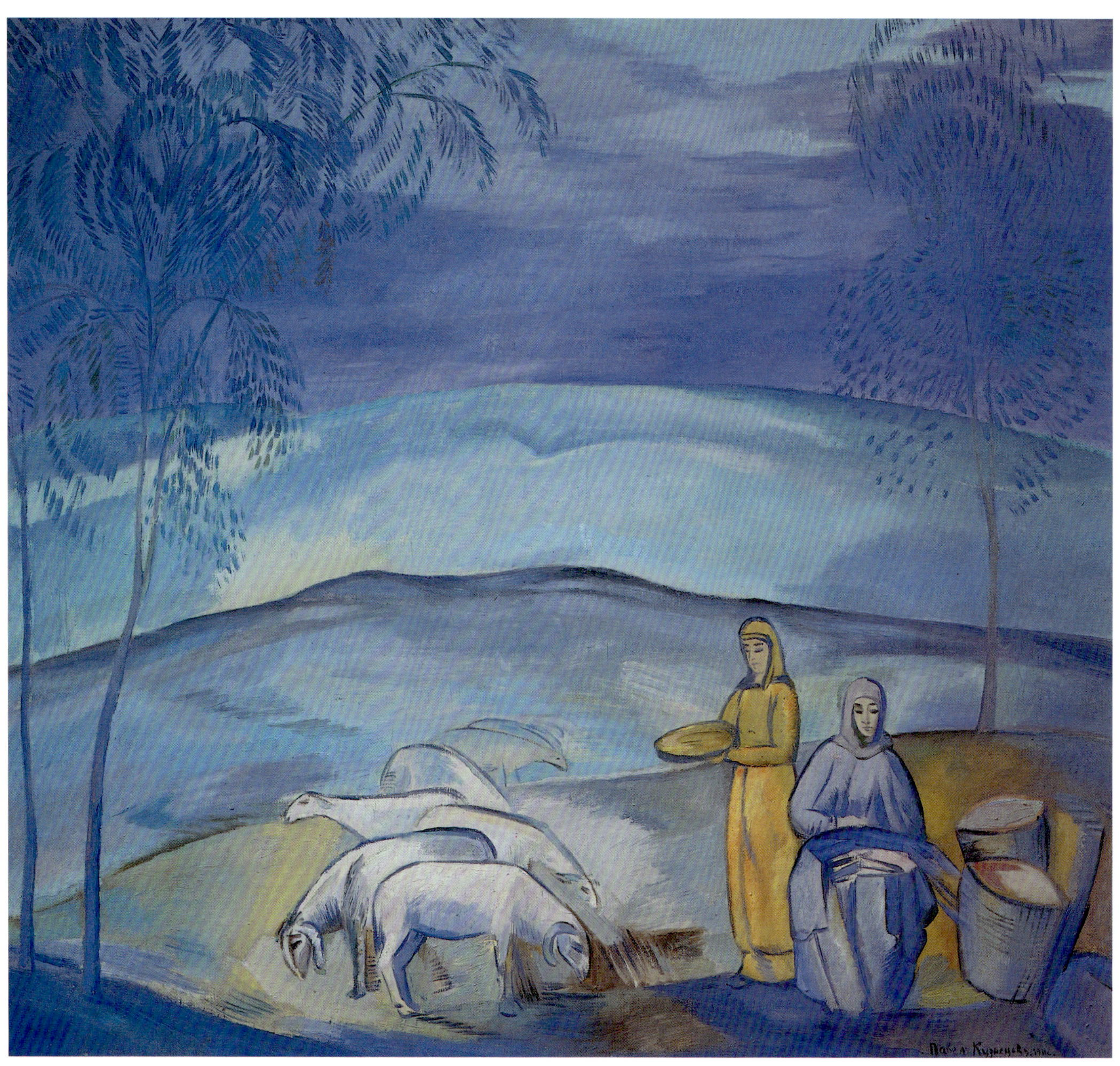

Pavel Kuznetsov
195. *On the Steppe: Mirage*
(Evening on the Steppe)
1911
Oil on canvas, 87.5 × 94
Saratov Museum of Fine Art

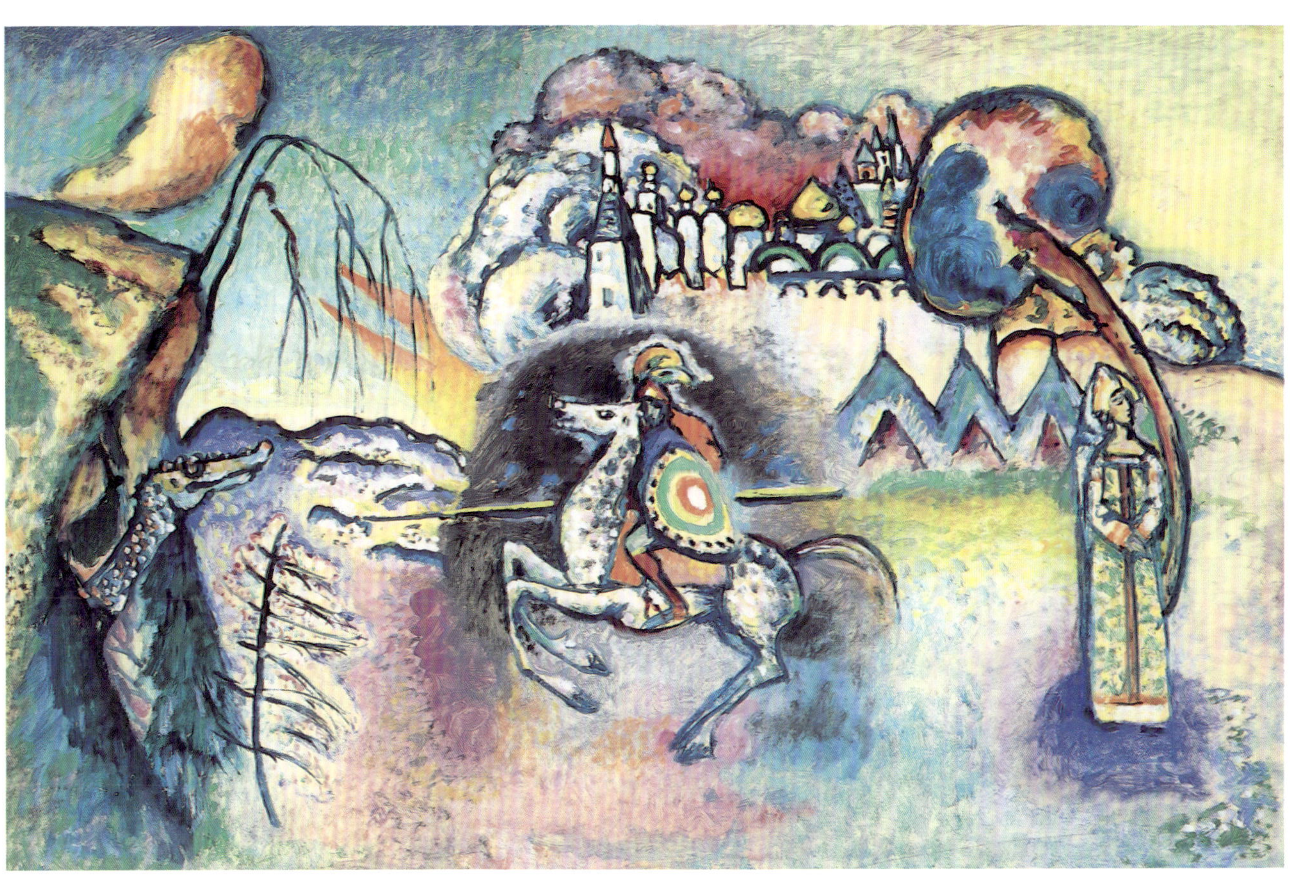

Vasily Kandinsky
164. *St George and the Dragon*
1914–15
Oil on cardboard, 61.4 × 91
State Treyakov Gallery

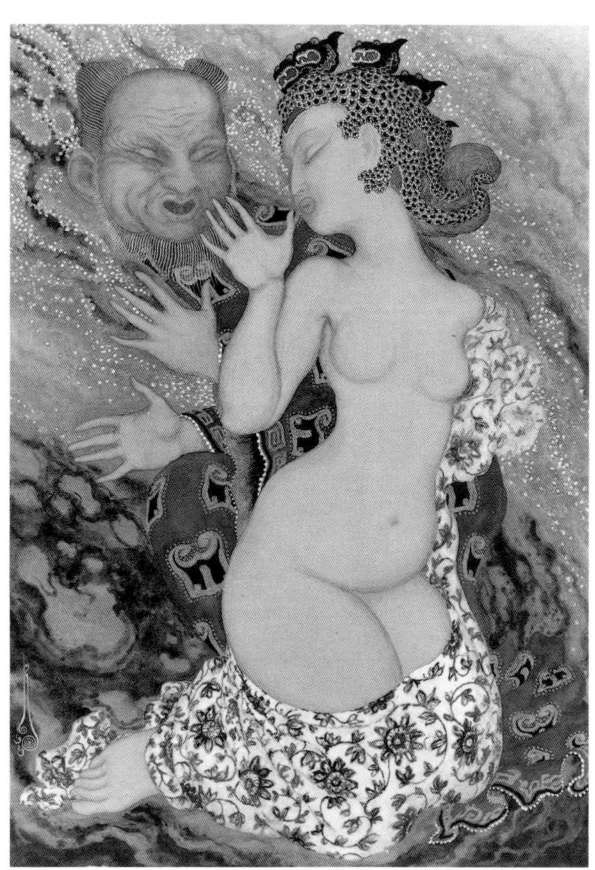

LEFT: **Nikolai Kalmakov**
160. *Chinese Woman*
1913
Mixed media on cardboard, 56 × 38.5
State Russian Museum

BELOW: **Mstislav Dobuzhinsky**
98. *Harbour on the Pryazhka River*
1914
Oil on canvas, 54.5 × 71.7
State Tretyakov Gallery

OPPOSITE PAGE

TOP: **Nikolai Kalmakov**
161. *Diana and Endymion*
1917
Oil, silver and bronze on canvas, 90 × 90
State Russian Museum

BELOW LEFT:
Nikolai Ul′yanov
433. *Venetian Shop*
1907
Watercolour and gouache on dark grey paper,
27.2 × 38.5
State Tretyakov Gallery

BELOW RIGHT:
Elizaveta Kuz′mina-Karaeva
187. *Visitation*
Not after 1917
Watercolour and wax on paper, 21.5 × 17.4
State Russian Museum

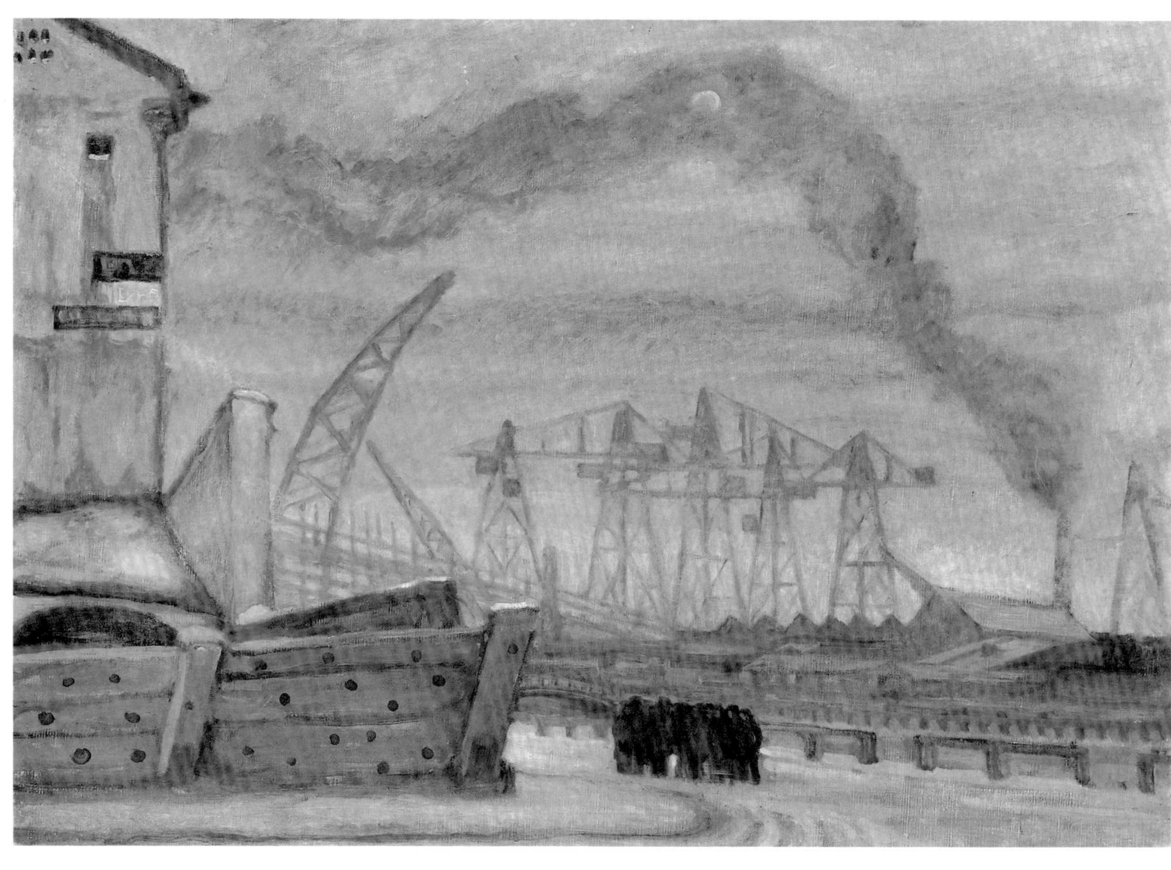

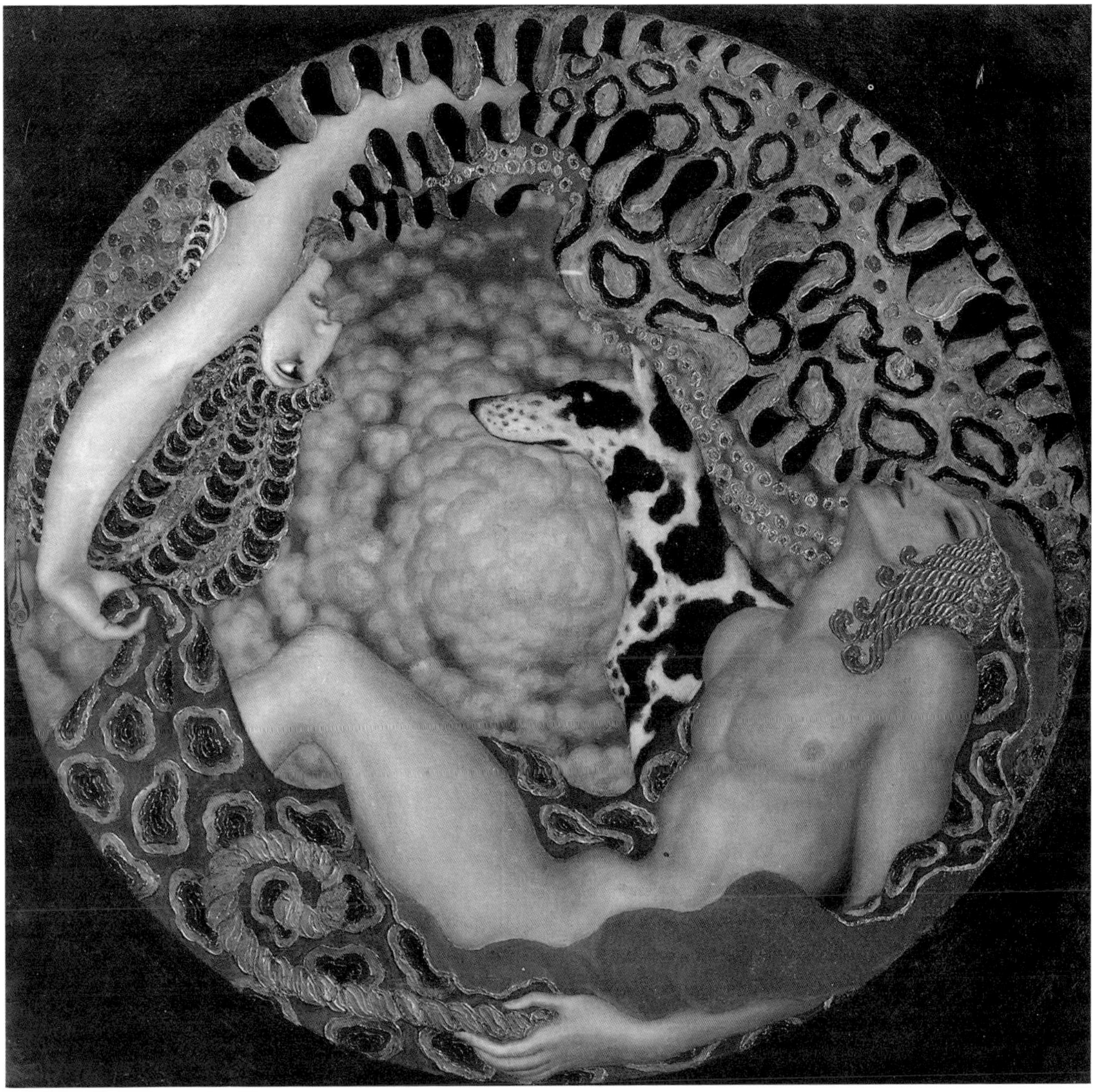

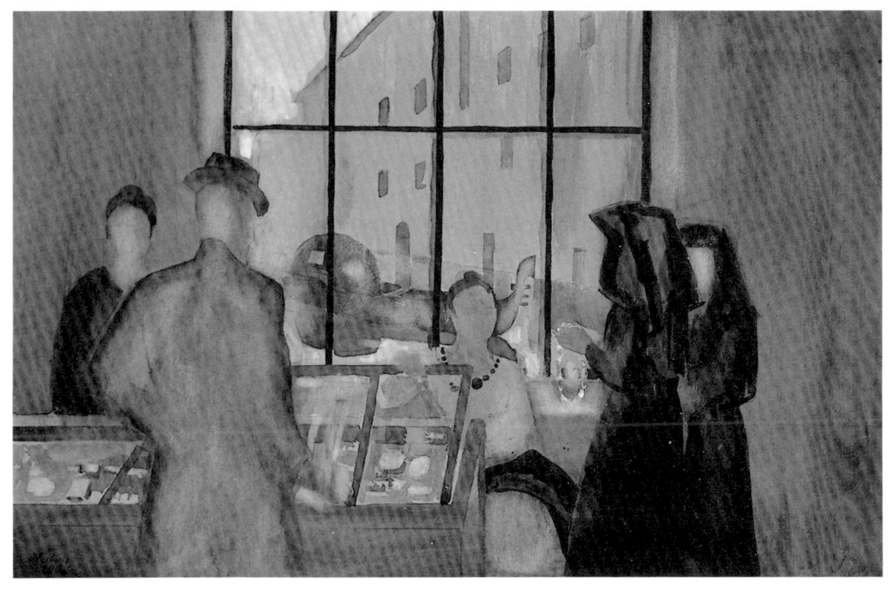

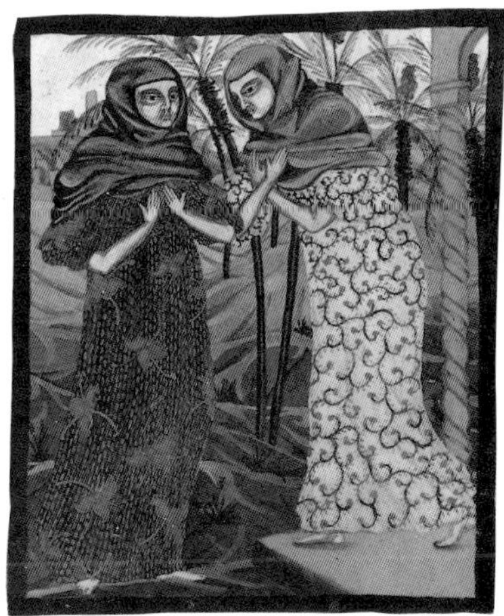

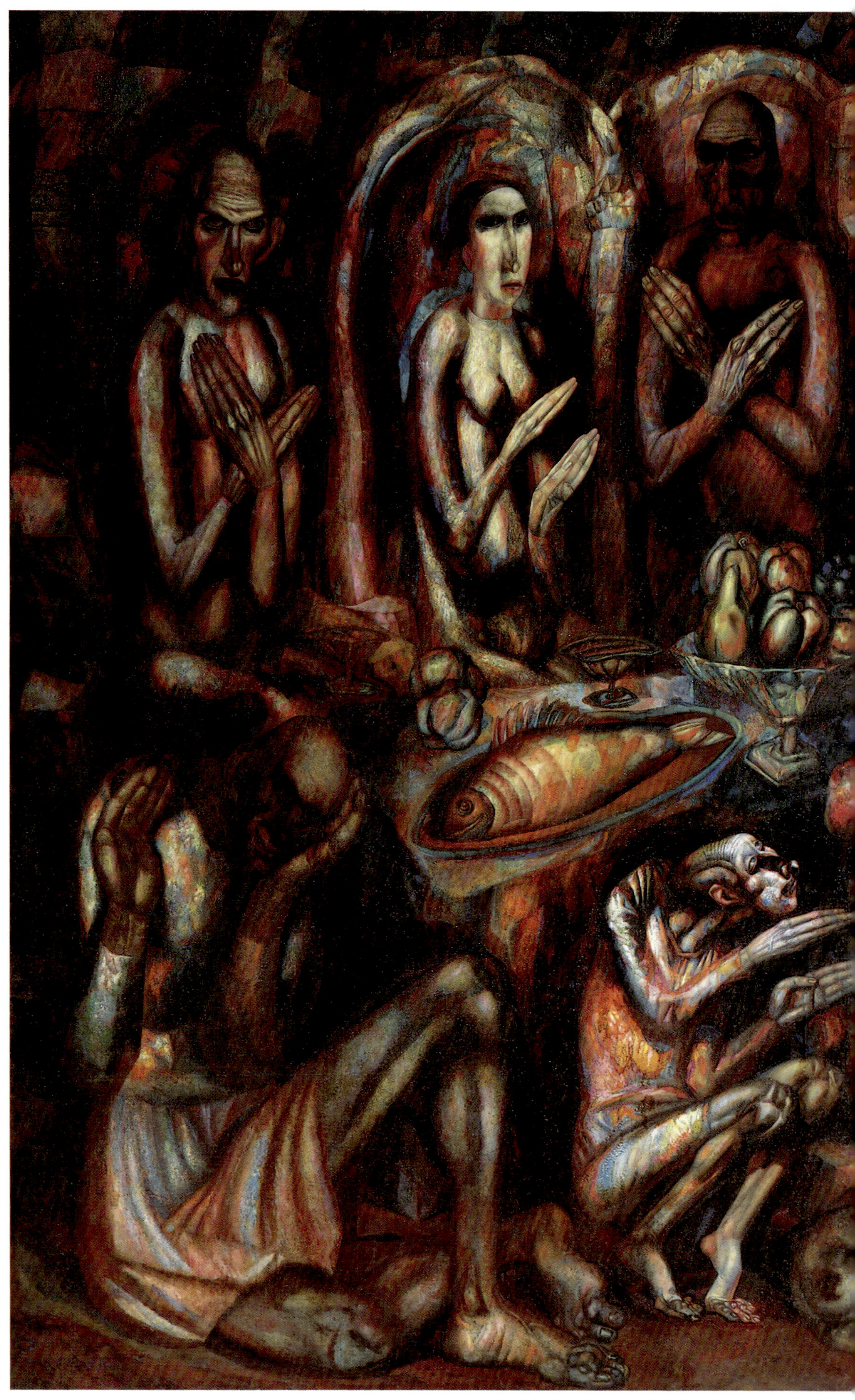

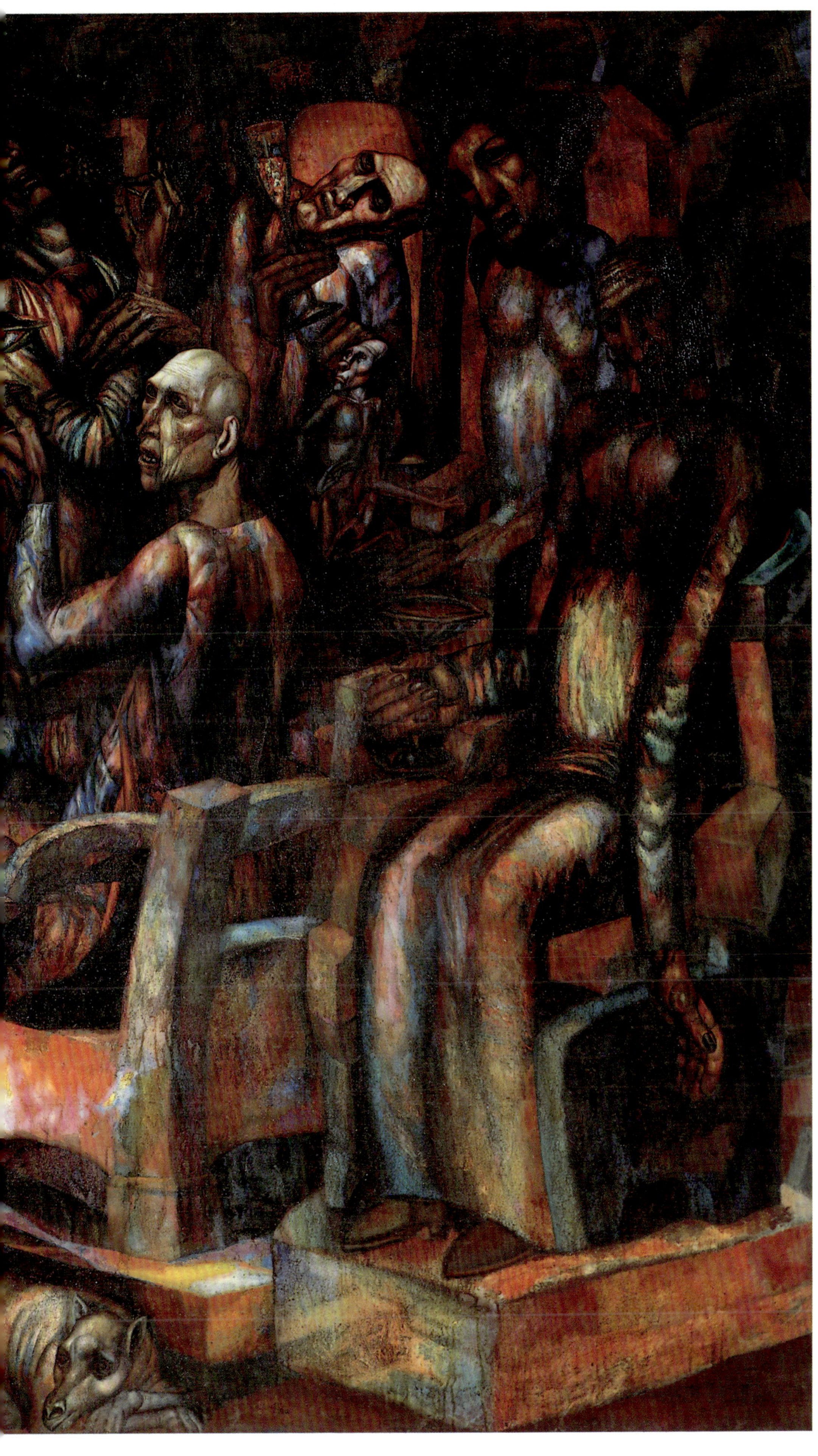

Pavel Filonov
115. *Feast of Kings*
1913
Oil on canvas, 175 × 215
State Russian Museum

11

GRAPHIC ARTS

TAT'YANA KONDAKOVA

The art of the book and poster, like the other forms of printed graphic art at the turn of the century, developed within the context of the *Style Moderne* which characterized this era. However, it was in these media, more than any other, that artists surpassed anything that had been attained by their predecessors in previous centuries and attracted an unprecedented level of interest.

The reason for this was that in printed graphic art, and especially in the art of the book, a "minor" synthesis developed within the framework of the "grand" synthesis of the various art-forms which was one of the essential features of the formation of *Style Moderne*. This period saw the achievement of the architectonic integrity of the book in all its artistic and typographic elements and in their compositional and stylistic harmonization with the nature of the text. Furthermore, the art of the *fin-de-siècle* period is characterised by the primacy of the line, which carries in itself an expressive significance, and the media of graphic art were quickest to respond to the demands of the new style.

This remarkable renaissance of the art of the book in Russia was primarily associated with the names of the artists who joined forces at the beginning of the 1890s in St Petersburg around the magazine *Mir Iskusstva (World of Art)*; they included Aleksandr Benois, Mstislav Dobuzhinsky, Evgeny Lanceray, Konstantin Somov, Lev Bakst, Ivan Bilibin and others. They made every effort to interpret the spirit and style of each literary work with individual attention, and they chose these works with great care, looking especially for imagery that conformed to the ideals of the *Style Moderne*. There is, of course, a certain common thread running through the subjects and motifs in the works of the art created under the influence of Symbolist ideas, and the *Miriskusniki* were closely associated with the design of magazines and poetry collections of the Symbolist movement, in which textual and visual aspects were closely united. But the sphere of their creative interests also included fairy tales, myths, the theatre and images of the past, for which they constructed those alternative worlds which were seen at that time as the necessary background for creation. Mythologising was accepted as one of the methods of artistic creation.

The artists of *Mir Iskusstva* felt a special affinity for book design, which corresponded to the essential nature of their visual perception, since by the nature of their talent they were primarily draughtsmen, acute and refined masters of line and of the decorative silhouette. These qualities are demonstrated in the covers for *Mir Iskusstva*, the organ of the movement, designed by Konstantin Korovin, Mariya Yakunchikova, Bakst, Lanceray and Somov, and in the work for the other new magazines which soon followed, *Vesy (Libra – The Scales)* and *Zolotoe Runo (The Golden Fleece)* in Moscow and *Apollon* in St Petersburg, by Bakst, Viktor Borisov-Musatov, Dobuzhinsky, Lanceray, Nikolai Feofilaktov and others.

The skills of the experimental artists were developed and perfected in the unique creative laboratory of the *Mir Iskusstva* magazine, whose design charts the movement from Russian *Style Moderne* to a retrospective, distinctively *Mir Iskusstva* style. The magazine opened up a whole new era in the history of the art of the book in Russia. The cult of beautiful and refined editions fostered by *Mir Iskusstva* gave rise to masterpieces such as the editions of Aleksandr Pushkin's *Bronze Horseman* and *Queen of Spades* designed and illustrated by Benois, a connoisseur of fine books, and it is clear that the artist's choice of these particular works by the great Russian poet was determined by their harmony with the ideas of the Symbolist movement. Benois intensifies the motif of the lonely and doomed individual, remote from and hostile to society, which resonates through both poems. Benois's *Bronze Horseman* and *Queen of Spades*, characterized by the total unity of design of all elements of the published work, mark the creative flowering of the graphic artists of *Mir Iskusstva*. Energetic and talented enthusiasts, who were thoroughly versed in the possibilities of graphic reproduction, they brought about a new perception of the book as a work of graphic and published art. This in turn led to a renaissance of wood engraving and lithography in a whole host of artistic editions, albums and picture postcards, which significantly influenced the aesthetic taste of the Russian public.

The best known artist of the group, Konstantin Somov, was also one of the most versatile: the fine illustrated editions of *Le Livre de la Marquise*, Aleksandr Blok's *Lyric*

Dramas (p.24) and Konstantin Bal'mont's *The Firebird* (p.148) show stylisations based on historical or folklore models, while his cover for Vyacheslav Ivanov's *Cor ardens* (p.74) and the title page of *Tsarskoe Selo* appear as still-lifes and *tableaux vivants* from the "century of powdered Marquises". The poster for the Hermitage Theatre (p.154) is an example of yet another type of design used by Somov, imitating the manner of the early nineteenth century, and the same transparent outline drawing seen in this poster, but with elements of *Style Moderne*, reappears in the postcards "Saturday" and "Sunday" from the *Days of the Week* series (p.171). Finally, Somov's talent as a portraitist is shown by his portraits of the poets Aleksandr Blok and Mikhail Kuzmin.

One genre that appealed to both younger and older generations of the *Mir Iskusstva* artists was the design and illustration of childrens' books, especially fairy tales, for, as we have seen, the world of fairy tales was particularly suited to the expressive language of artists working in the *Style Moderne*. Benois's *Picture Alphabet* (p.149) is a particularly arresting example, and the humour, the benign fantasy and the Hoffmannesque blend of reality and mystery ensured wide popularity for the book. Published in 1904, it stands, together with the earlier works of Elena Polenova and Sergei Malyutin, as one of the pioneering examples of Russian children's book illustration, a genre in which only isolated examples had appeared over the previous three centuries.

The fashion for fairy tales, taken up by Symbolism and *Style Moderne*, also found clear expression in Russia in the work of Ivan Bilibin. Pushkin's *The Tale of Tsar Saltan*, (p.149) designed by Bilibin carries the undoubted imprint of the *Style Moderne:* "an inclination towards decorativeness, the special role of the patch of colour, the revelation of the silhouette, the emphasis on the line on the paper surface, ornamentation, linear rhythm" (according to Dmitry Sarab'yanov). The fairy-tale and alphabet-book designs of the younger *Mir Iskusstva* artists Georgy Narbut and Dmitry Mitrokhin are further accomplished specimens of the style (p.152), while fairy tales and myths also provided the themes for work by Bakst (p.41) and Dobuzhinsky.

Many of the leading artists were associated with the Symbolist poets, including Bakst, who illustrated poems by Blok (p.146) and drew a portrait of Andrei Bely which was reproduced in *Zolotoe Runo*. The complex symbolism and ornamentation so characteristic of the *Style Moderne* were used by Lanceray in the covers he designed for poetry collections by Bal'mont, Blok (p.72) and Anna Akhmatova, and the younger *Mir Iskusstva* artists Sergei Sudeikin and Sergei Chekhonin also designed refined and very stylish covers for collections of poetry by N. Evreinov, Innokenty Annensky and N. Teffi (p.150).

The *Mir Iskusstva* group was a "collective of geniuses", according to P. Pertsov and A. Ostroumova, and a number of important projects were carried out as collaborative

efforts. For example, the third volume of the vast work by Nikolai Kutepov, *Tsarist and Imperial Hunting in Russia*, was created with the participation of Lanceray, Benois and Bakst, whose "fantasies" on historical themes were ideally suited to *Style Moderne* book design (pp.139, 143). The binding of the book by Nikolai Samokish was produced in the totally different, Neo-Russian style (p.244): its design has affinities with the design of N. Zvenigorodsky's fine luxury edition of *Byzantine Enamel* written by Nikodim Kondakov and designed by Ivan Ropet and Vasily Mathé (pp.141, 143, 245). As other authors have indicated, the Neo-Russian tendency developed actively in Russia within the *Style Moderne*, carrying on the traditions of national folklore.

SYMBOLISM

When considering the design of books of Russian Symbolist poetry in the early twentieth century, the major role played by the poets themselves in this process should not be overlooked; the mark of their personality was stamped on the whole structure of the published book. In planning the design of poetry collections, the artists and poets attempted to achieve a harmony between the imagery of the poetry and the graphic art, emphasizing the unconscious links between them through decoration and stylisation. The primary structural element of the Symbolists' books was rhythm, and this is echoed in the alternation of illustrations, book decorations, the printed matter and the empty spaces of the page, with great attention being paid to the design of each double-page spread. For the Symbolist poets, even the choice of typeface for the printing of their verses was important, for they saw its form as expressive of subjective stylistic associations, and they were concerned too with the symbolic associations of the colour and texture of the paper. The primary visual elements in their books were, as a rule, decorative motifs (ornaments, head-pieces and vignettes); subject illustrations interpreting the text metaphorically by allegory and symbols appear only rarely.

The poets liked to collaborate with artists with a similar world view. For example, Vasily Milioti, the designer of the first edition of Valery Bryusov's *Axis of the Equator* (p.73) was not only a Symbolist but also a theoretician of this movement in the visual arts. Another of Bryusov's collections, *Urbi et Orbi*, was designed by the poet himself. Blok and Bely entrusted the design of their collections *Verses about the Beautiful Lady* (p.69) and *Return: Third Symphony* (p.147) to the artist and dilettante Vasily Vladimirov, an associate of the "Argonauts" circle of Symbolists in Moscow, and it is an interesting fact that non-professional and semi-professional artists played an important part in the design of Symbolist books: for example, Margarita Sabashnikova for Bal'mont's *Liturgy of Beauty* (p.71) and "Fidus" for the same poet's *We Will Be as the Sun* (p.70). This particular design was well received by the public, and the contemporary review by the distinguished literary critic and historian E. Anichkov of the "Skorpion" poetry collections offers a typical reaction: "Never before has the Skorpion publishing house produced the songs and poetic duets of its poets in such elegant form. On the one hand, there is Bal'mont's *We Will Be as the Sun* in a dark pink cover designed by Fidus. Among symmetrically arranged lilies and rose bushes on tall stems, a sun-like figure, extending his arms wide and high, completely nude, with hair like a flame, sends his fiery gaze into the distance. He appears to be looking out of the book itself, underscoring with all his impetuous and sweeping movements the poet's words "I came into this world to see the sun". In contrast to this is Bryusov's *Urbi et Orbi*, a large white book, decorated with a completely simple and smooth golden lyre, the heavy rectilinear golden letters of the title contrasting with the thin strings of the lyre."

Nikolai Feofilaktov, at that time a popular artist of the movement, also worked on the design of Symbolist publications. In addition to his covers for the magazine *Vesy* (p.66), he did exceptionally fine covers and illustrations for the anthology *Northern Assyrian Flowers* (p.148) published by Skorpion, for Kuzmin's *Chimes of Love*, and for Bely's *Gold in Azure* (p.71). The historical stylisation of Aleksandr Golovin, exemplified in the cover for the collection *Notes of Dreamers* published by Alkonost, is also highly expressive.

The work of the Russian Symbolist poets, which sharply rejected the literary traditions of their predecessors and often shocked the bourgeois public, was generally printed by their own independent publishing houses. The prime example of these, Skorpion, was created in 1899 by a group of Symbolist poets in Moscow (and survived until 1916). A whole host of similar publishing houses appeared in the first quarter of the twentieth century: Grif (Griffin) (Moscow, 1903–15), Ory (St Petersburg, 1907–13), Al'tsiona (Moscow, 1910–23), Musaget (Moscow, 1909–17), Kartonnyi Domik (House of Cards) (1921–23), Alkonost (Petrograd, 1918–23) and others. Those who worked in these publishing houses were usually like-minded people – authors, artists and their associates – united by the idea of service to culture. The books they published were characterized by serious editorial preparation and a high quality of design and graphic reproduction. The imprints of these houses were designed by Yury Annenkov, Aleksandr Golovin and Modest Durnov, among others, and they are fascinating examples of the *Style Moderne*. So too are the designs executed for the collected works of Anton Chekhov, with bindings by Elena Samokish-Sudkovskaya, and V. Korolenko, designed by M. Solomonov, which represent the many mass-market editions of Russian authors designed at the beginning of the century.

At the other end of the scale were de luxe bindings designed especially for private libraries, such as the silver binding based on a drawing by Apollinary and Viktor Vasnetsov for an *Album of Russian Folktales and Legends* and the leather binding with appliqué and gold embossing made by the bookbinder R. Nilsson for an edition of Pushkin's *Evgeny Onegin*. The bibliophiles of the time are also evoked by the bookplates designed by such artists as Lev Zak, Nikolai Kalmakov, A. Malinin and Sergei Solomko (p.170). Again, the personal aesthetic taste of Russian book-collectors favoured the *Style Moderne*.

Finally, in the field of books, superb albums of lithographs and wood engravings were also produced, among the finest being *Pavlovsk Landscapes* by Anna Ostroumova-Lebedeva (p.36) and *Poems Without Words* by Vasily Kandinsky (p.146).

POSTERS AND PRINTED EPHEMERA

The Russian poster, which appeared as an original artistic phenomenon in the late nineteenth and early twentieth centuries, developed, like the book, in the new styles, both in the Western European tradition of *Art Nouveau* and in the Neo-Russian and *Moderne* styles, with which the poster form had deep and organic links. The work of the *Mir Iskusstva* artists, as well as that of other masters, had a great influence on poster design, and in the first decade of the twentieth century such outstanding artists as Vrubel', Lanceray, Bilibin, Bakst and Nikolai Remizov executed work in this medium. In this way the innovations in book design were carried through into posters, and many of exceptional artistic quality were produced. The influence was most immediate in booksellers' posters, where the characteristic trends of book design were creatively reflected in the use of many elements of graphic design: display typefaces, vignettes, head-pieces, etc., and outstanding results were attained. Artists also sought inspiration in signboards, popular prints, and newspaper graphics, and in features of Western European poster design, and Russian posters of this period for exhibitions and entertainments are characteristically highly expressive and decorative, with lively imagery and original use of graphic elements.

Russian commercial posters developed in the tradition of the shop sign. Despite their prosaic content, they publicized goods in an interesting way, and a poster could often be turned into the trade-mark of a shop or factory, becoming accepted as a sign of its reputation. Most work of this kind is anonymous.

The new styles of design at the turn of the century were applied not only to books, magazines and posters, but to many more mundane items: postcards, envelopes, theatre programmes, calendars, cigarette packets, wrappers for sweets, chocolate and soap, perfume labels, dinner-party menus, and chemists' labels. Such printed ephemera are very important for building up an image of the period. Here again, the works are generally anonymous, but they offer some splendid examples of *Moderne* and Neo-Russian styles, bearing their own characteristic witness to the tastes and interests of their time.

12

DRAWING AND DESIGN

YULIYA ZABRODINA

The drawings and watercolours shown in the exhibition have been chosen from works by artists who reflected the new trends in Russian art of the nineteenth and early twentieth centuries, and who were associated with *Style Moderne* in varying degrees. They include designs for monumental murals and objects of applied art, theatre designs, book designs, and selections from sequences produced at the easel, reflecting the universality of creative activity at the turn of the century.

At the end of the nineteenth century a new style developed in Russia against the background of Critical Realism in painting. A major part in its creation was played by the group around Savva Mamontov at Abramtsevo. Artists such as Viktor Vasnetsov and Elena Polenova devoted intense study to folk art, collecting examples they were able to find and using folk elements in their work. In Viktor Vasnetsov's sketches for the wall paintings in the Cathedral of St Vladimir in Kiev (pp.191, 192), the brilliance and decorative qualities of the colour and the complexity and richness of the ornamentation are clearly taken from the artistic vocabulary of folk art. Furthermore, they testify to the revival of interest in religious painting at the end of the nineteenth century, which was due not only to the attraction of creating monumental art, but also to the perception of the ecclesiastical image as a poetic tradition embodying the experience of history and the spiritual beauty of nature. One artist close to this perception was Mikhail Nesterov, whose work in the 1880s reflects an early Neo-Romantic national variant of *Moderne* (p.17).

The foremost among the Russian artists who recognized *Style Moderne* as a tendency in a common European culture was Mikhail Vrubel'. The complex metaphorical nature of his images, his new understanding of form, and his affirmation of the primacy of beauty permeate all his work. Vrubel', who worked in practically all art forms – painting, architecture, sculpture, graphic art – clearly recognized the specific nature of each form. His numerous panels for private houses in Moscow (pp.46, 198, 199) are brilliant embodiments of the artistic synthesis of *Style Moderne*. Playing an active part in the construction of the interior, the compositions of the paintings are woven into the overall rhythm determined by the spatial relationships. From the small sketches by Vrubel' for the Gothic study of A. V. Morozov, it is possible to appreciate not only the high degree of his mastery of watercolour, but also his subtle understanding of the specific nature of the decorative panel. The artist emphasizes the weightlessness of the forms, spreads figures over the surface, provides large expanses of colour, accenting an extended and fastidiously refined silhouette with a pen-drawn outline. He does not see his task as being the precise psychological characterization of his images, nor does he make them real beings in time. His heroes exist outside time and are caught up in the overall movement of space provided by the architecture.

The designs of Viktor Borisov-Musatov and Valentin Serov, who also worked on mural paintings, were never executed and are known only in the form of sketches. From these it is hard to assess how successfully they might have been realised on a monumental scale, but drawings and watercolours by these artists provide evidence not only of the general trends in Russian art at the turn of the century, but also of a high level of professionalism. The drawings by Serov for decorations in the Moscow house of V. V. Nosov (p.210) are filled with light and air, permeated with the sensation of the value of the paper sheet which shines through the azure flexibility of the pencil lines. In these sketches, which treat themes from Ovid's *Metamorphoses*, Serov succeeded in conveying the ceremonial majesty of antiquity in his free harmony.

A striving for a synthesis of the arts also runs through the work of artists of the next generation, who formed a group around the magazine *Mir Iskusstva*. However, they realised this not in quests for a "grand" style, but rather in minor forms, especially in the art of the book. The names of artists such as Aleksandr Benois, Lev Bakst, Mstislav Dobuzhinsky, Evgeny Lanceray, Konstantin Somov, and Georgy Narbut are associated with the heyday of book design at the beginning of the twentieth century.

Somov's cover designs (pp.24, 74, 148) are distinguished by the precision of the silhouette, the decorative use of touches of colour and a subtle understanding of the two-dimensional nature of the book page. The intricacy of the work, the accuracy and care of the drawing in his sketches for snuff-boxes (p.255) and fans, have their origins in the miniatures of the artist's beloved eighteenth century. By contrast, Dobuzhinsky, while openly admiring the refinement and harmony of urban motifs from Empire-style architecture, illustrated the gloomy streets of contemporary St Petersburg, emphasizing the phantasmagorical quality of the city's aspect.

In the theatre the masters of *Mir Iskusstva* created the concept of a stage performance as a synthetic spectacle in which the artist becomes the partner of the dramatist, composer and actor. The names of Lev Bakst, Aleksandr Benois, Nikolai Roerich, and Boris Anisfel'd are closely bound up with the successes of Sergei Diaghilev's first Russian seasons in Paris.

An inimitable originality characterized the work of the artists of the Moscow school, who imbued *Style Moderne* with a lyricism that originated with the work of Borisov-Musatov. In his watercolour *Zubrilovka* (p.38) the gentle rhythm, the smoothness of the movement and turning of his figures and the refined relationships of the pure pale tones give a sensation of musical harmony. In the drawings and watercolours of his successors, Vladimir Denisov, Nikolai Ul'yanov, Vasily Milioti, and the young Sergei Sudeikin, the emphasis on decoration, the blurring of outlines, and the complexity of composition create an impression of the instability of reality and embody the desire to seek refuge in a poetic dream-world. Konstantin Yuon's cycle *The Creation of the World* (pp.114–15), for all its refined decorativeness, embodies the weight of time as eternity and the idea of man lost in the vast universe.

Despite the great variety of artistic personalities who appeared in twentieth-century Russian art, there was a shared Utopian faith in the inherent value of art and of the free beauty of its closed world, which inspired them not only to resist external reality, but also to change it. And when this faith crumbled on contact with reality, a new art was born – the art of the Russian avant-garde.

13

GRAPHIC ART

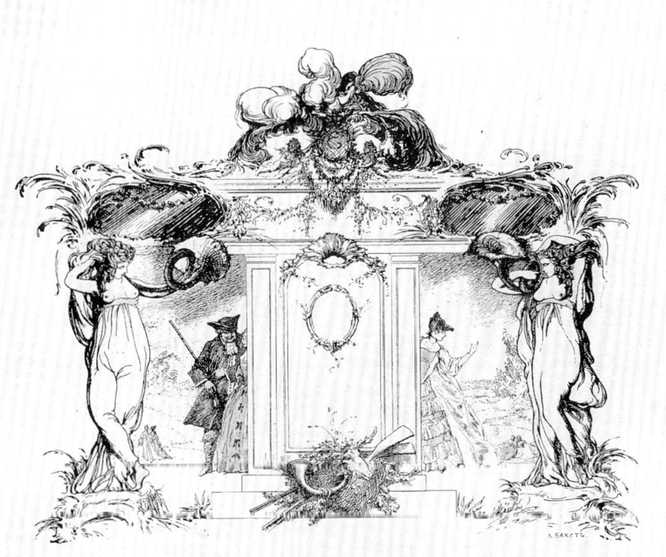

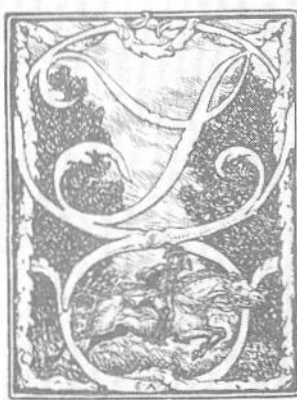

Lev Bakst
299. Chapter heading in Nikolai Kutepov,
*Tsarist and Imperial Hunting in Russia in the
late Seventeenth and Eighteenth Centuries*,
vol.3, St Petersburg, 1902
The decorative initial is by Evgeny Lanceray
State Lenin Library

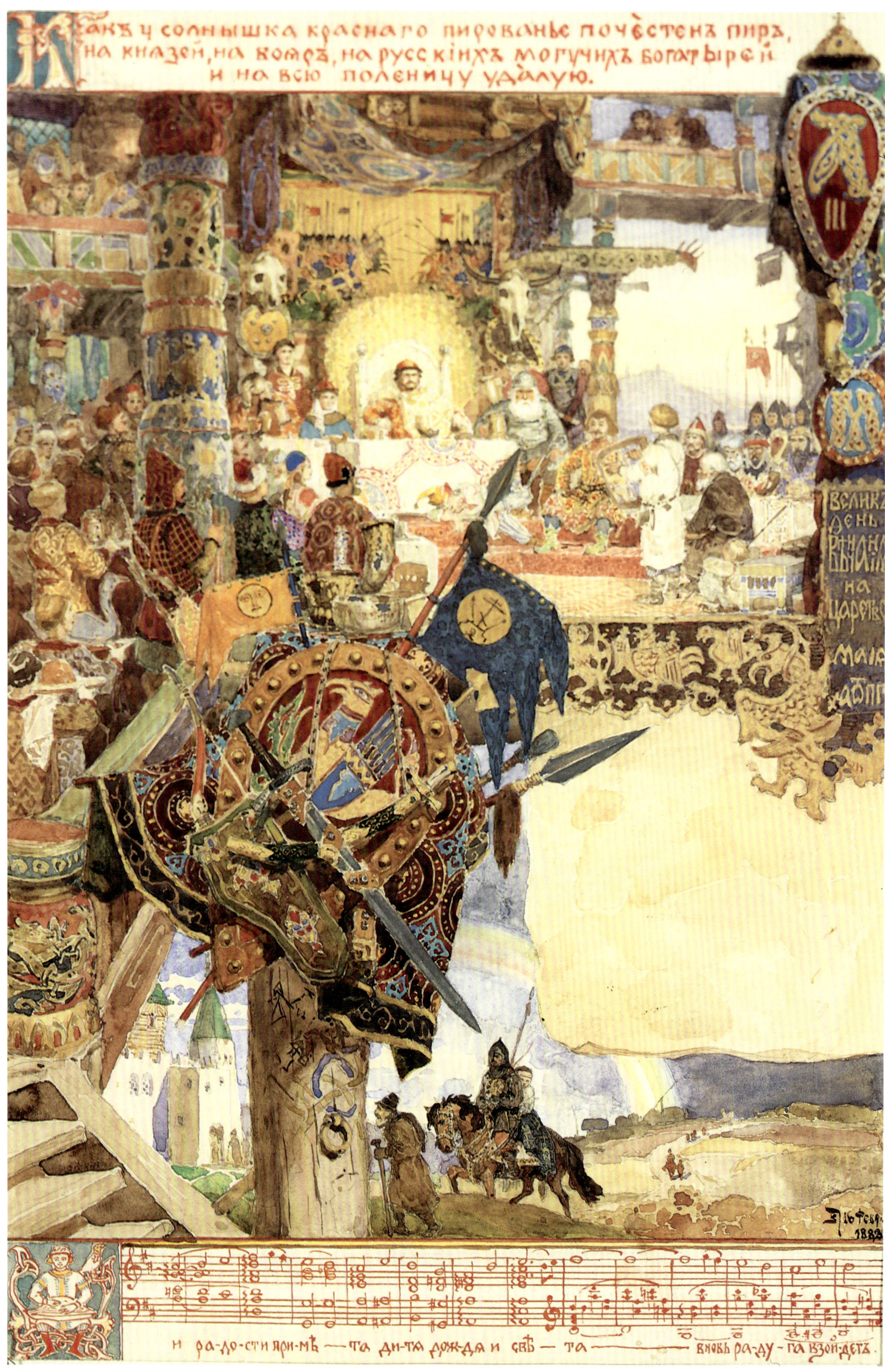
Какъ у солнышка краснаго пированье почестенъ пиръ,
на князей, на бояръ, на русскихъ могучихъ богатырей
и на всю поленицу удалую.
16 февр. 1883
и ра-до-сти при-мѣ — та ди-та рожда и свѣ — та — вновь ра-ду-га взой-детъ.

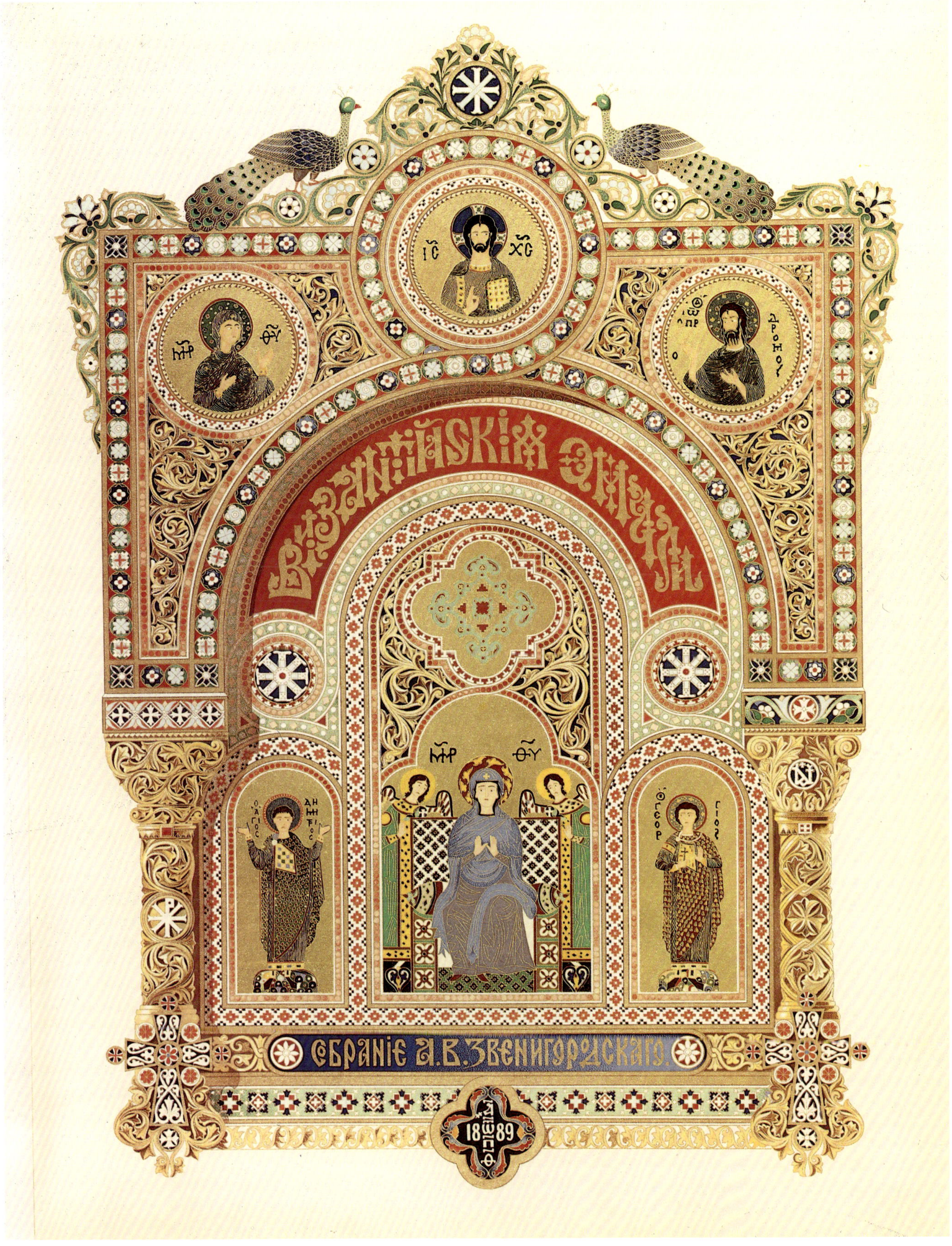

OPPOSITE: **Vasily Polenov**
274. *Feast of Vladimir at Krasnoe Solnyshko*
1883
Design for a menu for a ceremonial banquet
on the coronation day of Aleksandr III (At the

foot is a musical quotation from Glinka's
Ruslan and Lyudmila)
Watercolour and bronze powder on paper,
42.2 × 27.6
State Tretyakov Gallery

ABOVE: **Ivan Ropet**
293. Title-page of Nikodim Kondakov, *History
and Memorials of Byzantine Enamel*,
St Petersburg, 1892
State Lenin Library

TOP LEFT: **Nikolai Samokish**
299. Detail of endpapers of Nikolai
Kutepov, *Tsarist and Imperial Hunting in
Russia in the late Seventeenth and
Eighteenth Centuries*, vol.3, St Petersburg,
1902
State Lenin Library

TOP RIGHT: **Vasily Polenov**
275. *Orpheus in the Kingdom of the Dead*
1898
Design for a programme for a production
of Gluck's *Orphée* at the Private Russian
Opera
Watercolour on paper, 43.8 × 13.9
State Tretyakov Gallery

BOTTOM LEFT: **Elena Polenova**
283. Illustration for the fairy-tale *The
Firebird*
Late 1890s
Mixed media on paper, 31 × 22.2
State Russian Museum

BOTTOM RIGHT: **Elena Polenova**
281. Design for an ornament for a book
Early 1890s
Mixed media on paper, 23.8 × 11
State Tretyakov Gallery

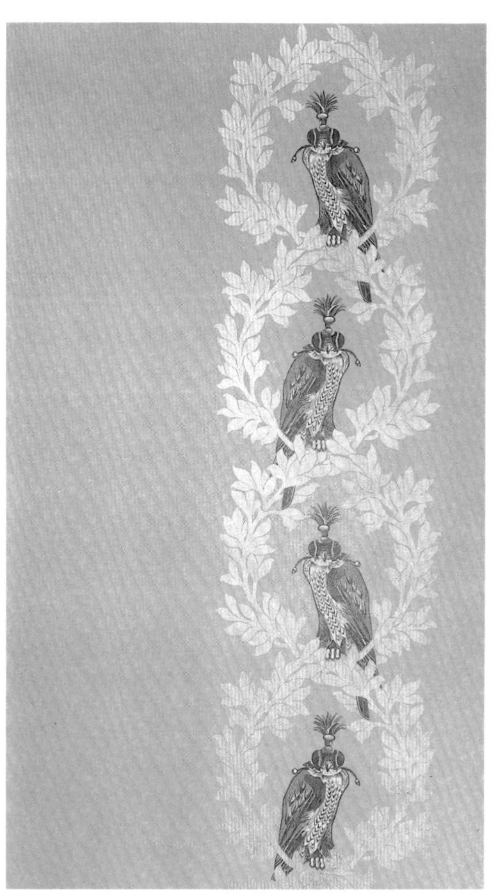

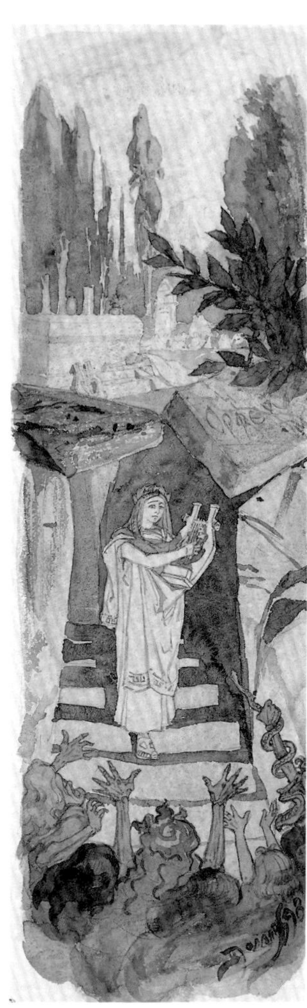

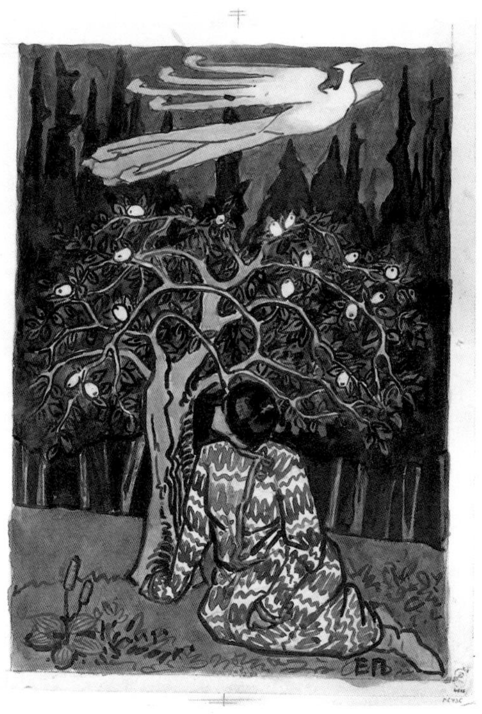

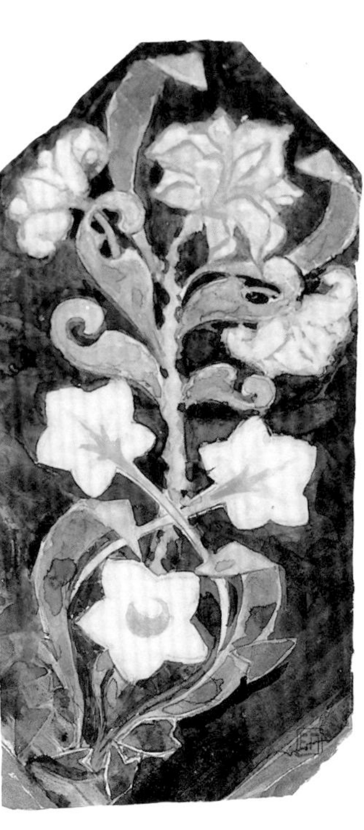

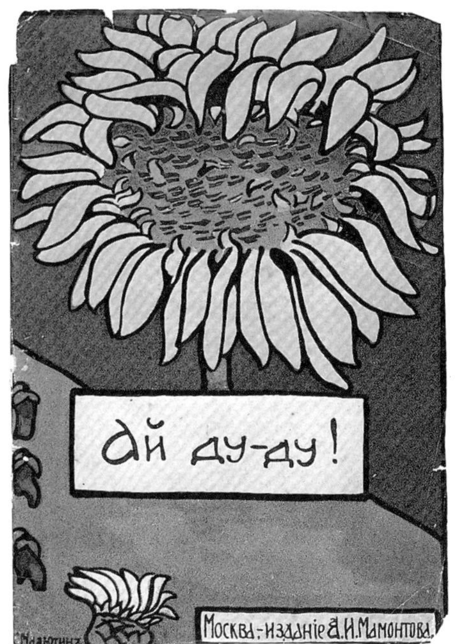

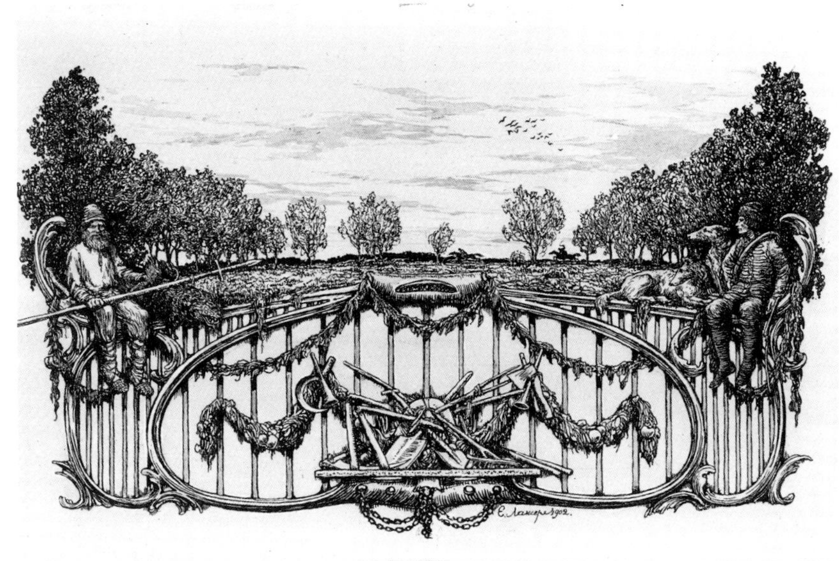

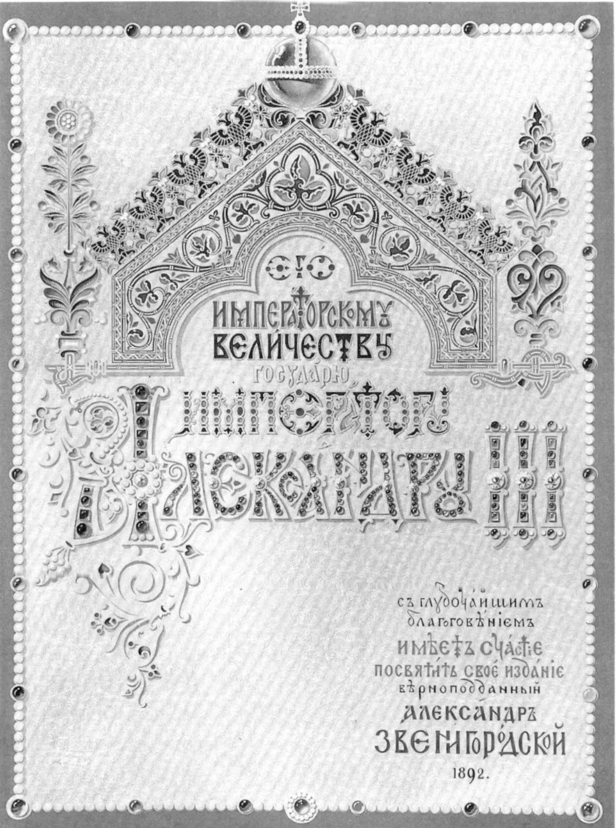

TOP LEFT: **Sergei Malyutin**
219. Cover and illustrations for *Ai, du-du!:
Russian Folk Tales, Songs, Jests and Stories*,
Moscow, 1899
State Lenin Library

TOP RIGHT: **Evgeny Lanceray**
199. *Hunting Scene*
1902
Drawing for Nikolai Kutepov, *Tsarist and
Imperial Hunting in Russia in the late
Seventeenth and Eighteenth Centuries*, vol.3,
St Petersburg, 1902
Mixed media on cardboard, 19.5 × 31
State Tretyakov Gallery

LEFT: **Ivan Ropet**
293. Dedication page to Aleksandr III, in
Nikodim Kondakov, *History and Memorials of
Byzantine Enamel*, St Petersburg, 1892
Colour lithograph with gold and silver blocking
State Lenin Library

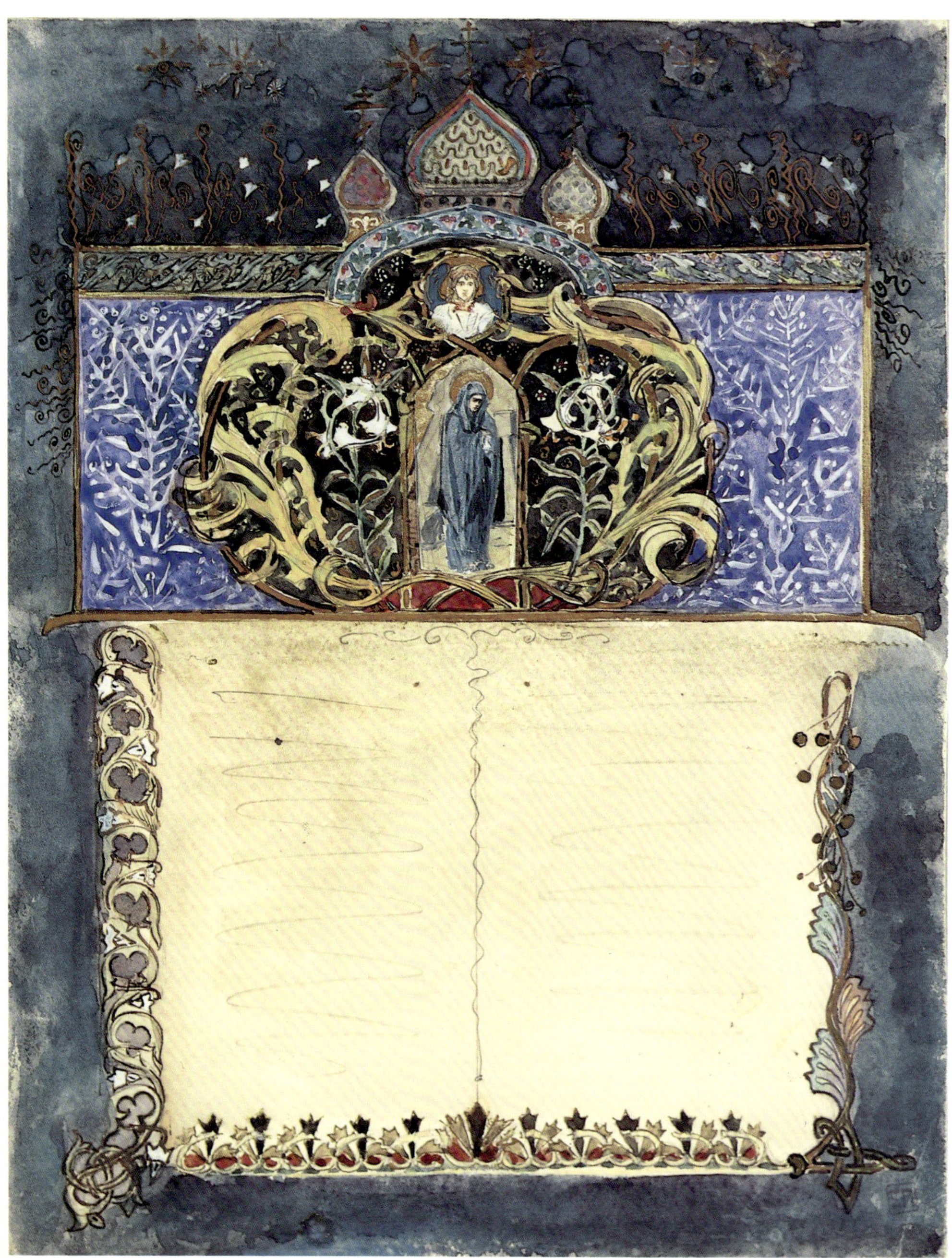

Elena Polenova
282. Frame for an address to the widow of
Emperor Aleksandr III, Mariya Fedorovna
1894
Mixed media on cardboard, 35.7 × 27
State Tretyakov Gallery

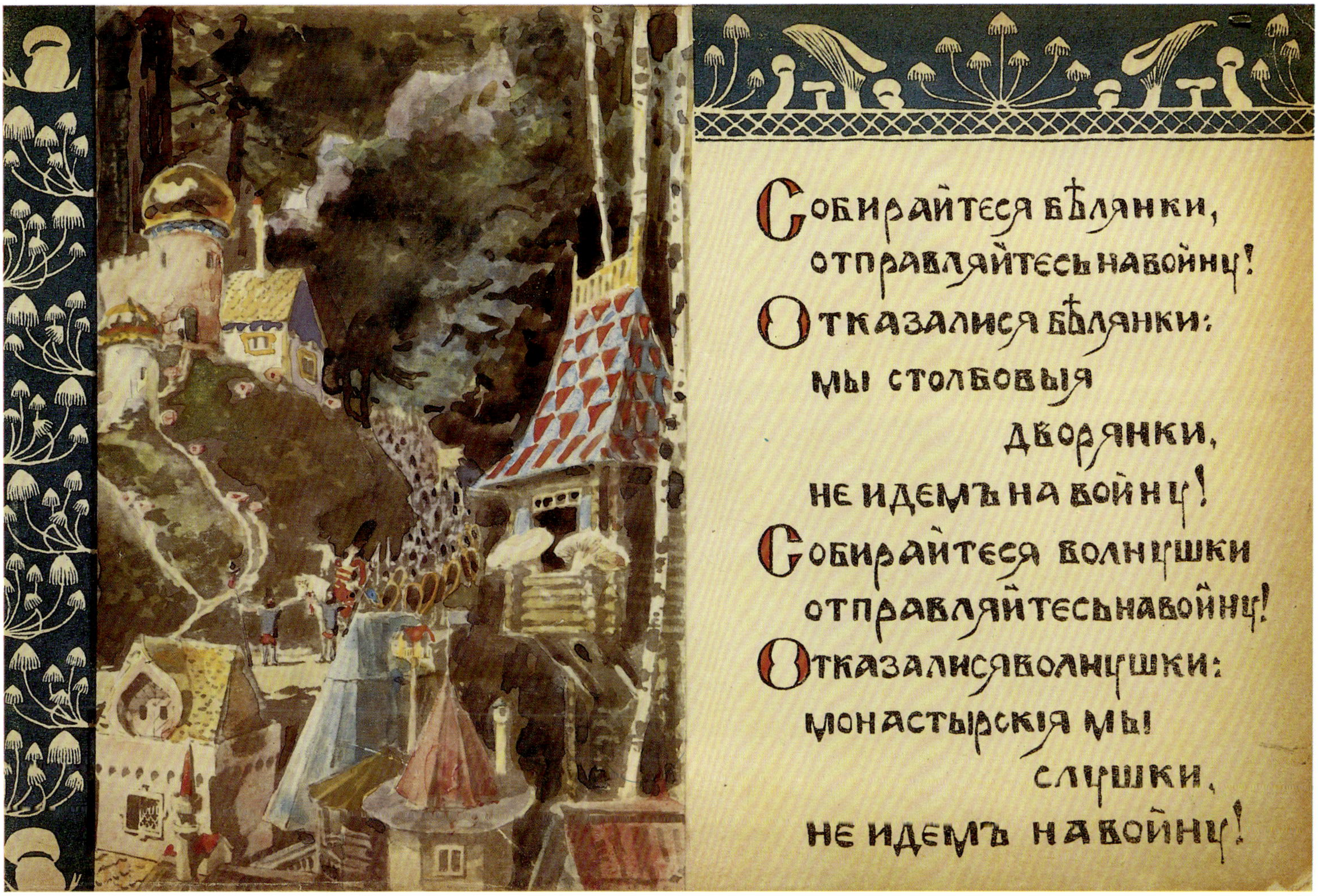

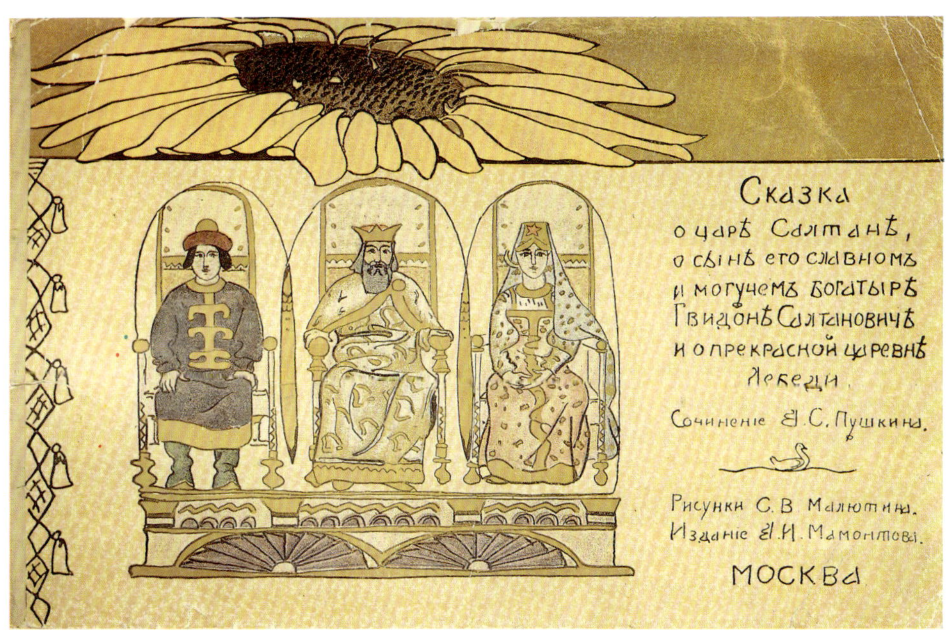

ABOVE: **Elena Polenova**
280. Illustration for *The War of the Mushrooms: Folk Tale*, Moscow, 1889
State Lenin Library

LEFT: **Sergei Malyutin**
218. Cover for Aleksandr Pushkin, *The Tale of Tsar Saltan*, Moscow, [1898]
State Lenin Library

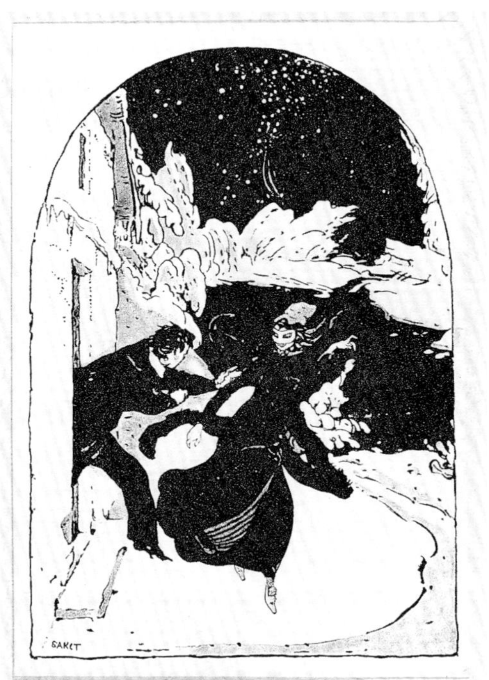

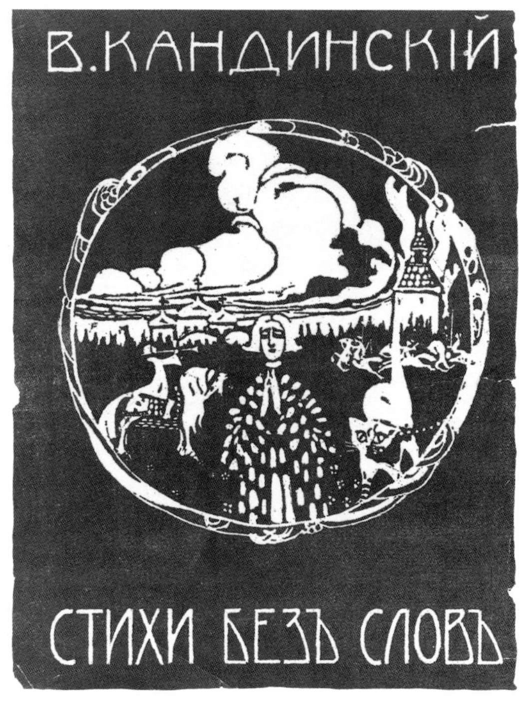

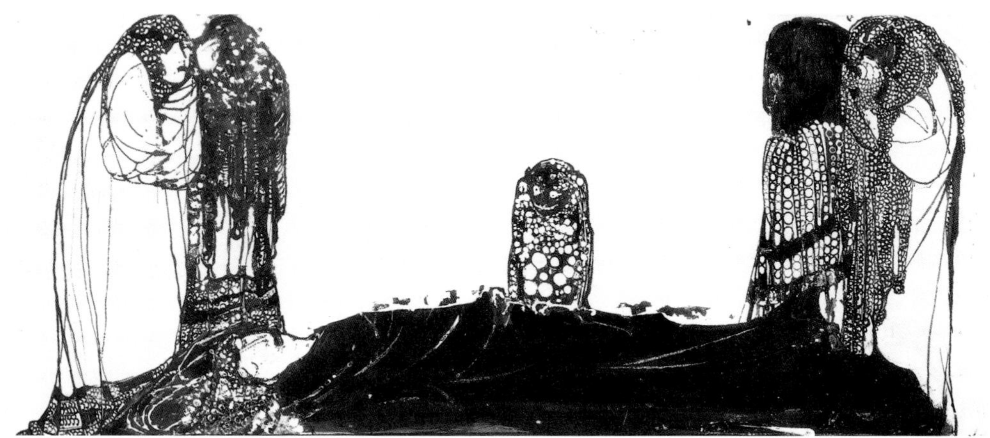

TOP LEFT: **Lev Bakst**
35. Frontispiece from Aleksandr Blok, *Snow Mask*, St Petersburg, 1907
State Lenin Library, Moscow

TOP RIGHT: **Vasily Kandinsky**
163. Cover of *Album: Poems Without Words*. Moscow (Stroganov Design School), [1903]
Woodcut, 33 × 25.5
State Lenin Library

ABOVE: **Boris Anisfel'd**
14. *Mourners*
1905
Drawing for *Zhupel (Bugbear)*
Mixed media on cardboard, 11.4 × 26.6
State Russian Museum

OPPOSITE PAGE

TOP: **Sergei Sudeikin**
412. Design for frontispiece for *Vesy*, 1907 no.3
1907
Mixed media on paper, 26 × 30.5
State Tretyakov Gallery

BOTTOM LEFT: **Vasily Vladimirov**
455. Cover of Andrei Bely, *Return: Third Symphony*, Moscow, 1905
State Lenin Library

BOTTOM RIGHT: **Mstislav Dobuzhinsky**
94. *The Devil*
1906–07
Illustration from *Zolotoe Runo*, 1907 no.1
State Lenin Library

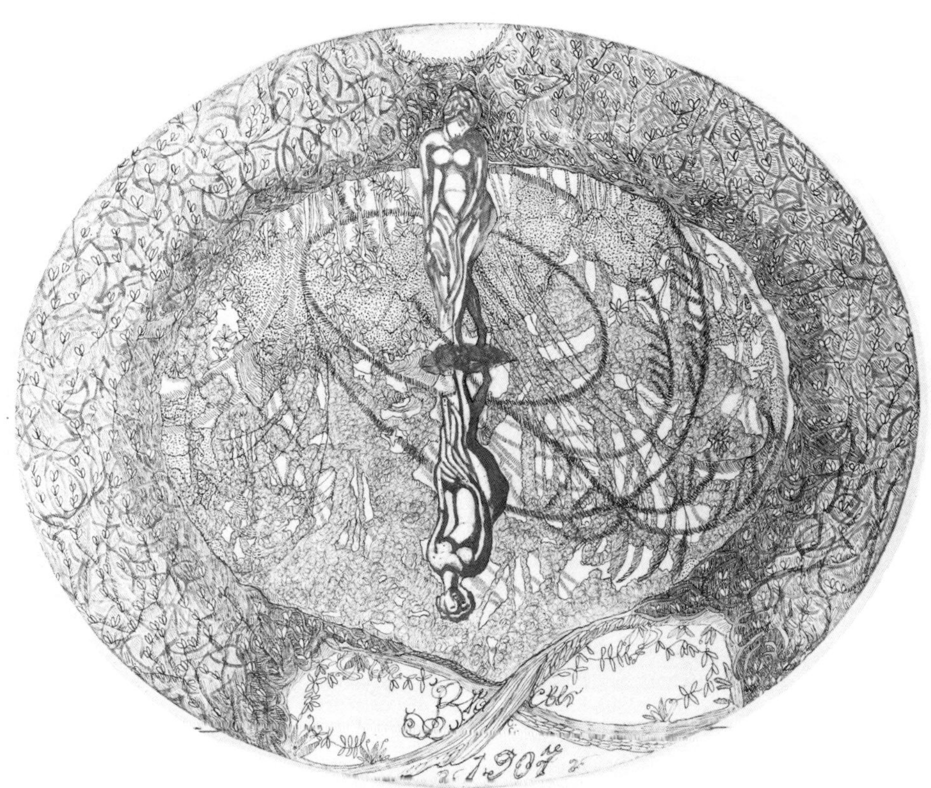

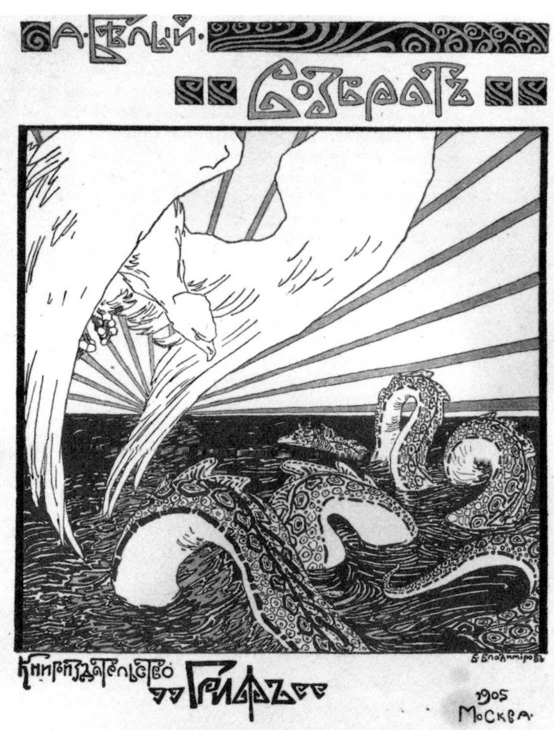

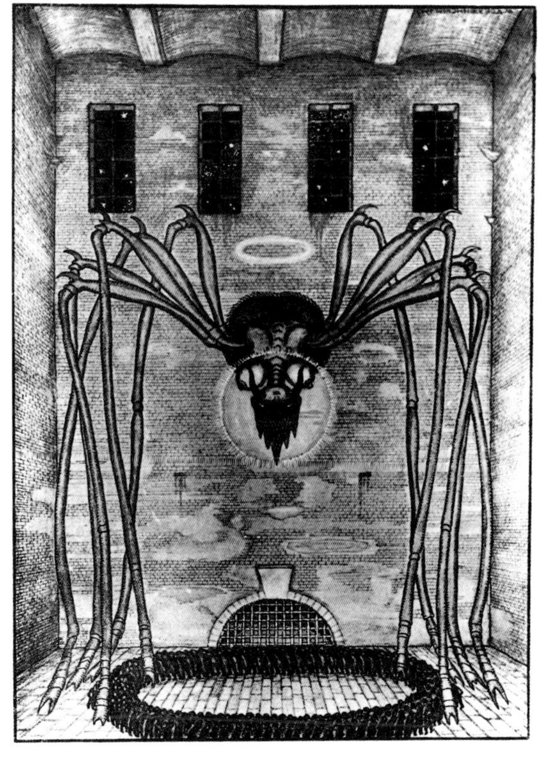

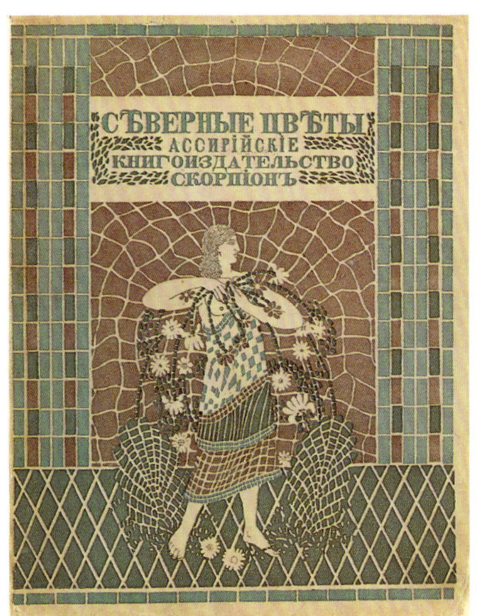

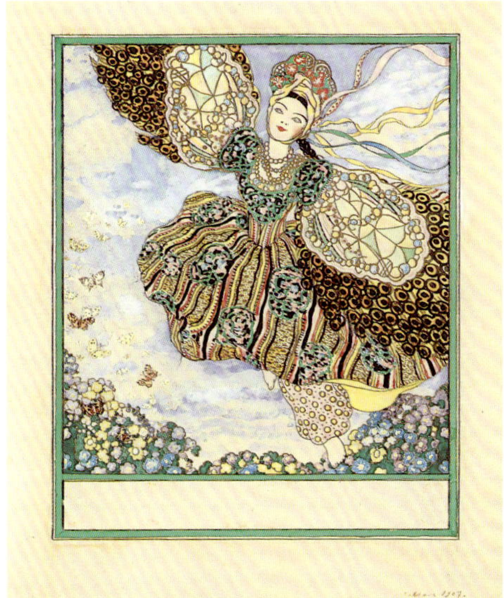

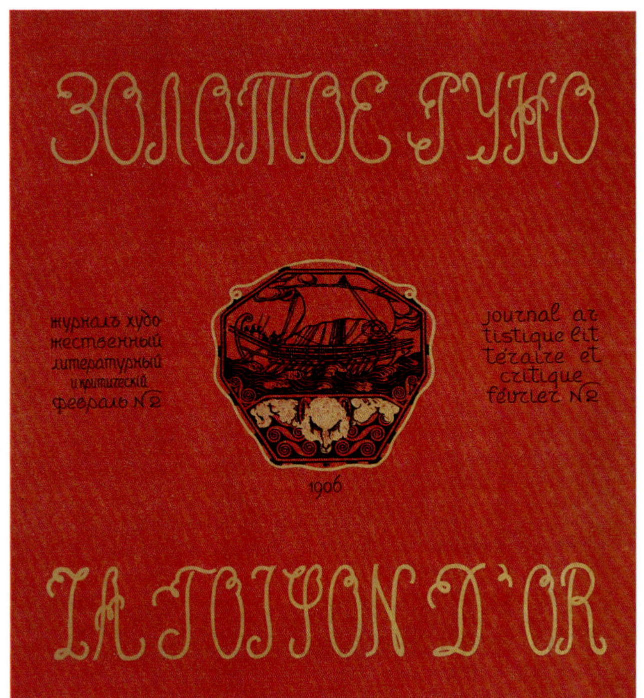

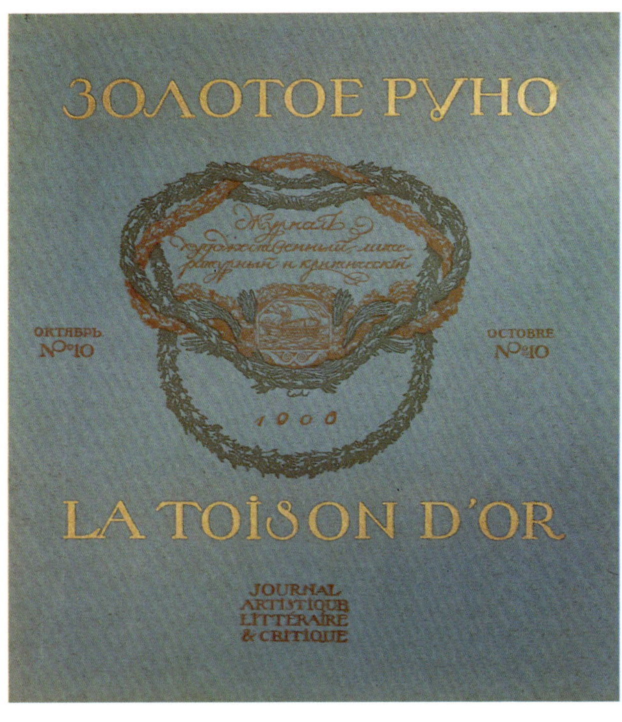

Top: **Nikolai Feofilaktov**
108. Cover of *Northern Assyrian Flowers:
"Skorpion's" Fourth Literary Miscellany*,
Moscow, 1905
State Lenin Library

Above: **Konstantin Somov**
397. *The Firebird*
1907
Cover design for Bal'mont's book of poems *The
Firebird: Music to the Slav's Ear*, Moscow,
1907
Mixed media on paper, 25.4 × 21.1
State Tretyakov Gallery

Above: **Evgeny Lanceray**
200, 201. Covers of *Zolotoe Runo*, 1906 no.2
and no.10
(No.2 done in collaboration with an
anonymous artist, "I")
State Lenin Library

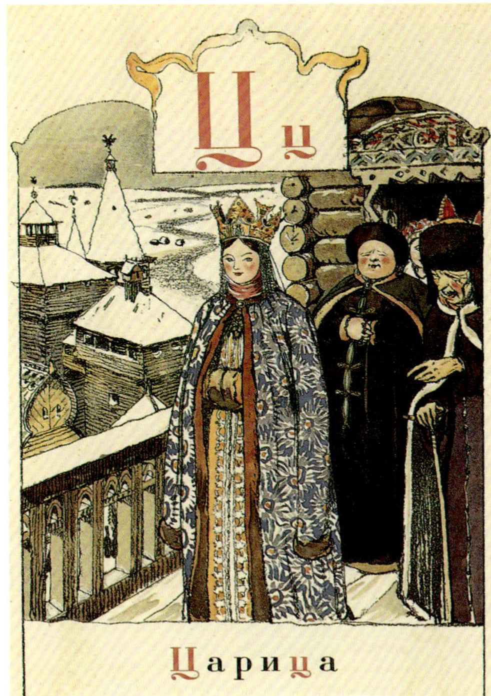

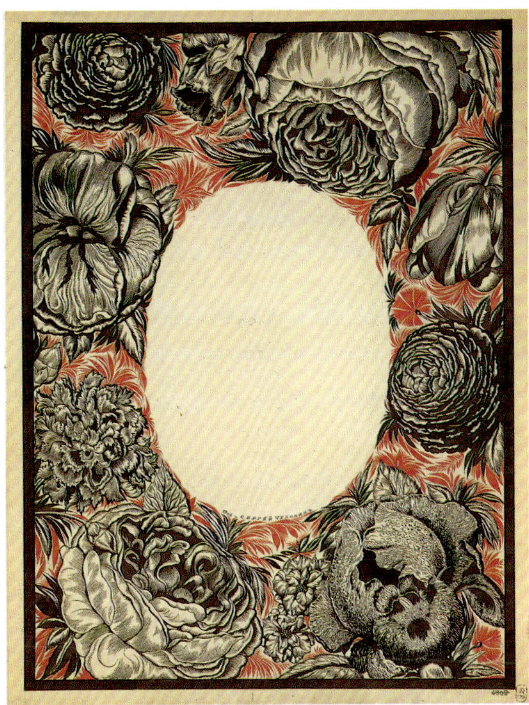

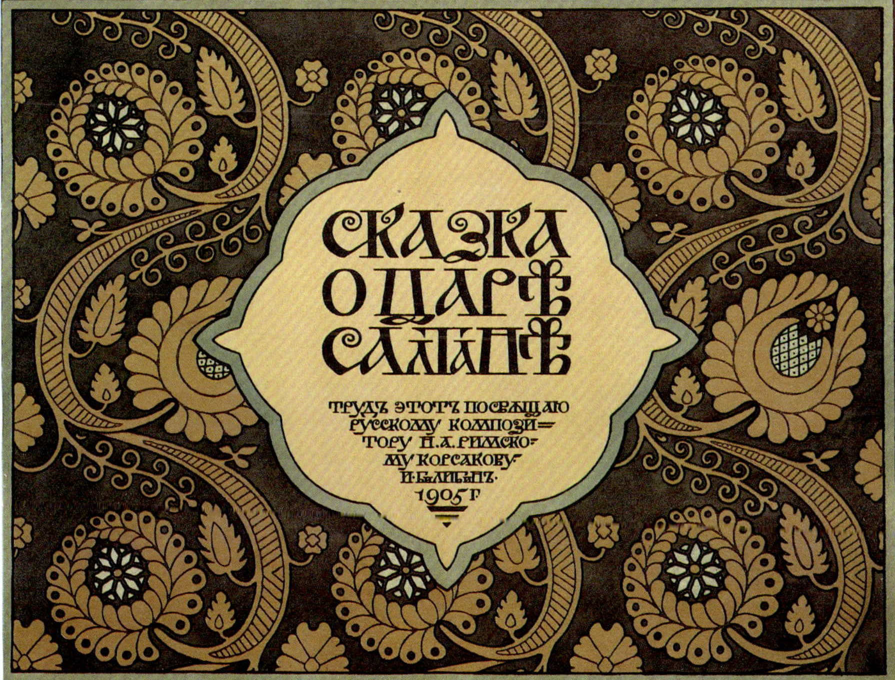

Aleksandr Benois
41. *Queen*, illustration from *Picture Alphabet*, St Petersburg, 1904
State Lenin Library

Sergei Chekhonin
84. Drawing for the frontispiece of the book *Russian Drawing*
1914
Mixed media on yellow paper,
33.5 × 24.9
State Russian Museum

Ivan Bilibin
53. Title-page of Aleksandr Pushkin, *The Tale of Tsar Saltan*, St Petersburg, 1905
State Lenin Library

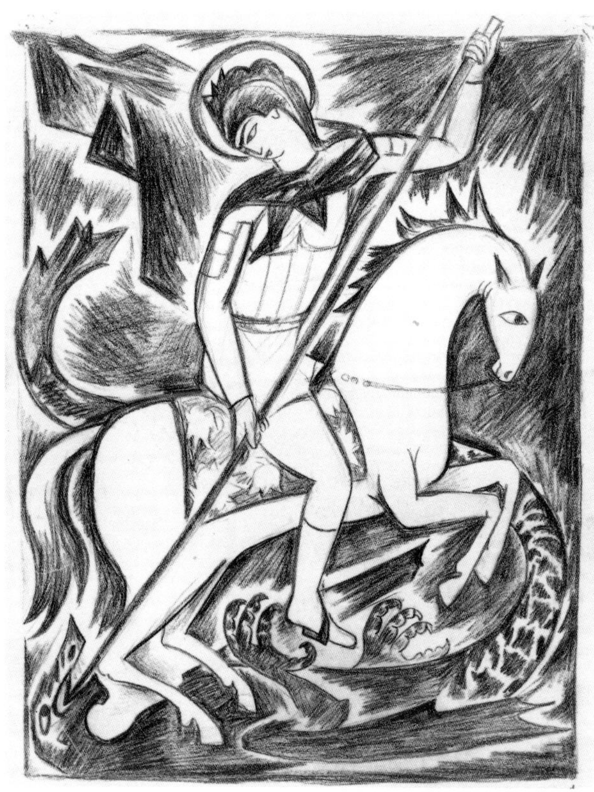

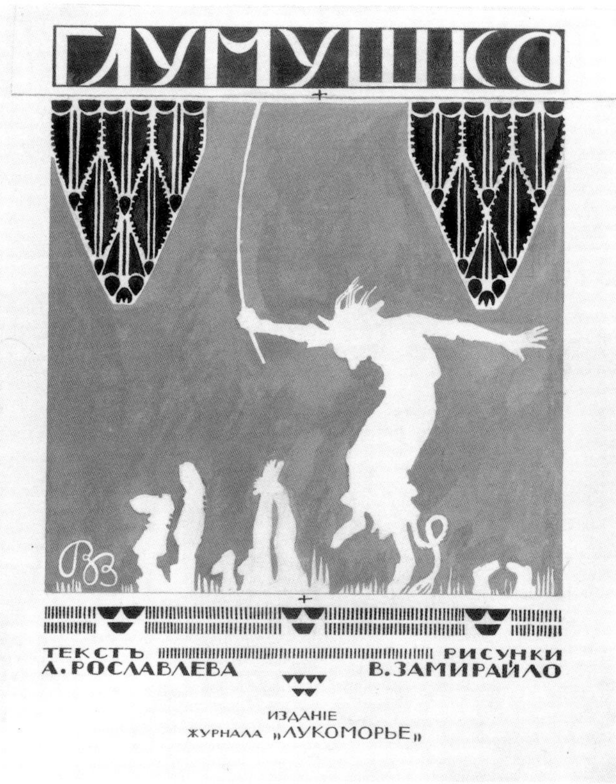

ABOVE LEFT: **Natal'ya Goncharova**
135. *St George and the Dragon*
1914
Drawing for the album *War 1914: Mystical Images of War*
Lead pencil on paper, 31.4 × 23.8
State Russian Museum

ABOVE RIGHT: **Viktor Zamirailo**
487. Cover for A. S. Roslavlev, *Glumushka*,
St Petersburg, 1910s
Mixed media on paper, 30.1 × 23.8
State Russian Museum

BELOW: **Yury Annenkov**
19. Half-title in Aleksandr Blok, *Catiline: A Page from the History of World Revolution*,
Petrograd, 1919
State Lenin Library

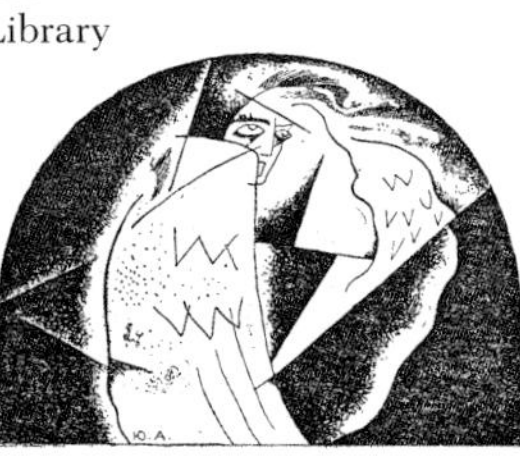

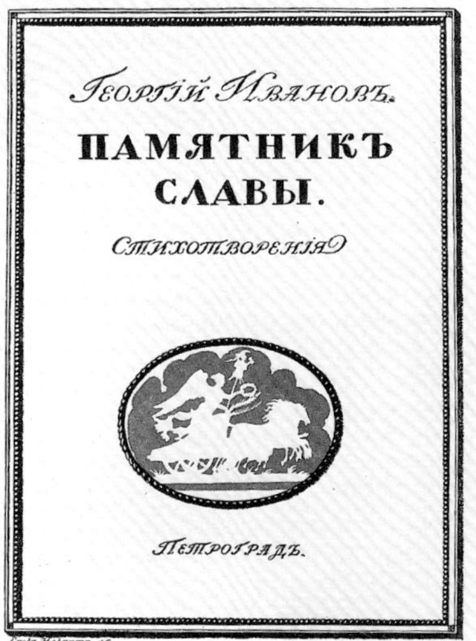

Georgy Narbut
239. Cover for Georgy Ivanov, *In Glorious Memory: Poems*, Petrograd, [1915]
State Lenin Library

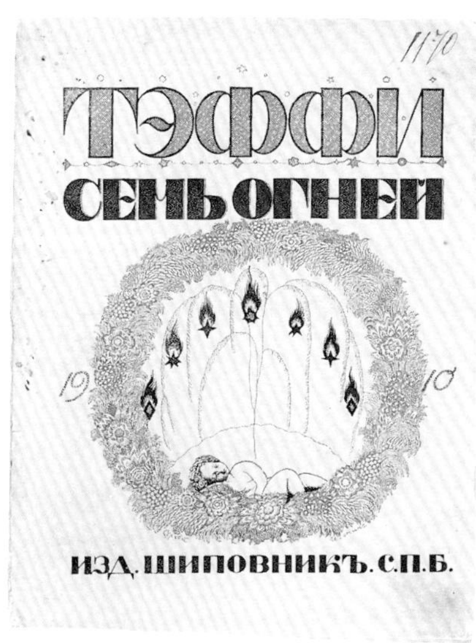

Sergei Chekhonin
82. Cover for N. Teffi, *Seven Fires*,
St Petersburg, 1910
State Lenin Library

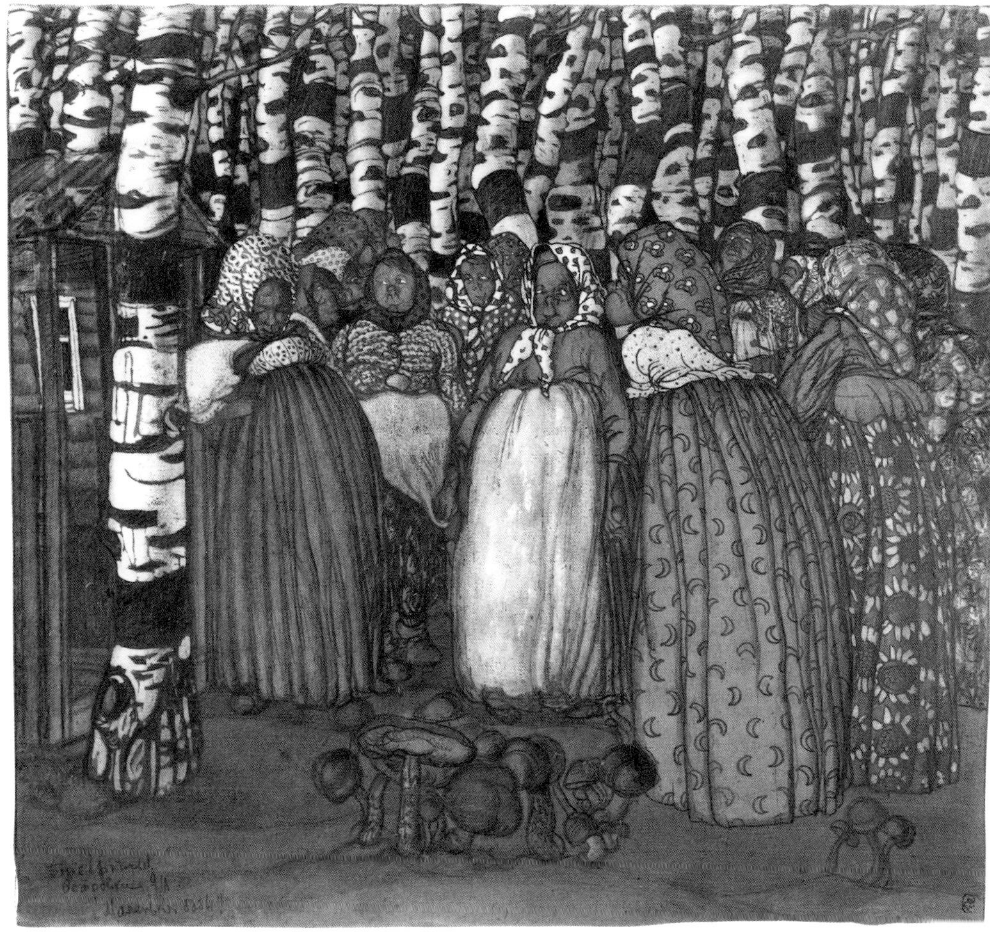

LEFT: **Boris Grigor'ev**
140. *Little Peasant Woman*
1911
Lead pencil and white on grey paper, 41.5 × 43
State Russian Museum

BELOW: **Evgeny Lanceray**
208. Design for the frontispiece
for a book of poems by
Cherubina de Gabriac
1914
Mixed media on cardboard,
37.1 × 28.2
State Russian Museum

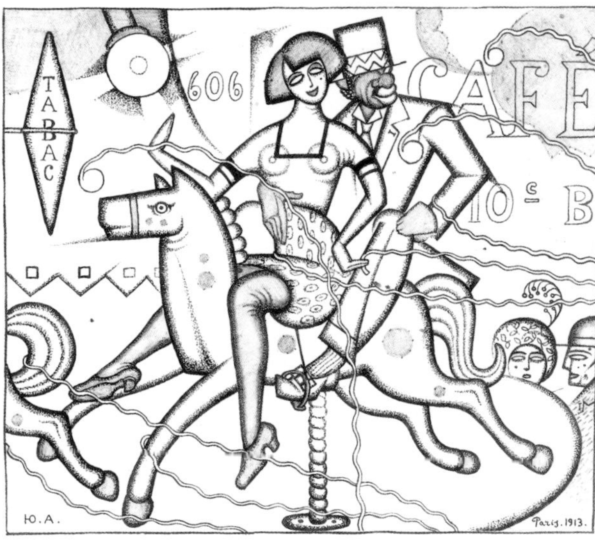

Yury Annenkov
16. *Man and Woman on a
Merry-Go-Round*
Paris, 1913
Mixed media on paper,
19.2 × 21.2
State Russian Museum

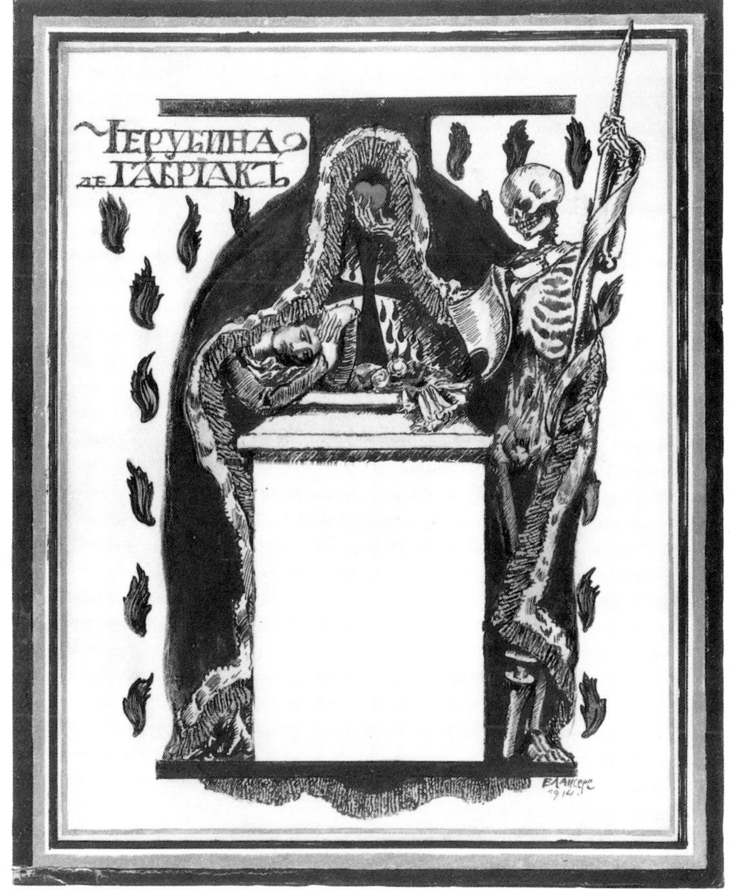

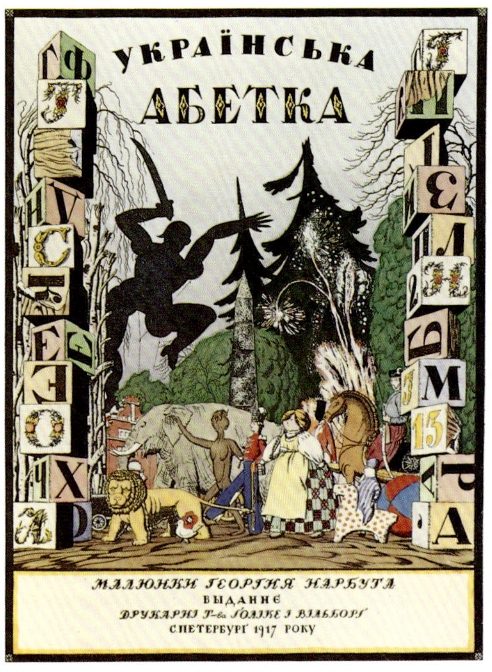

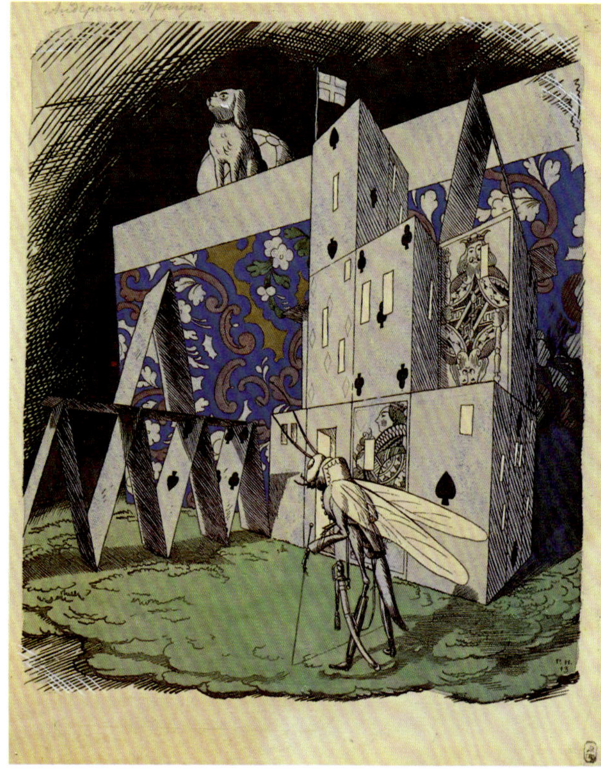

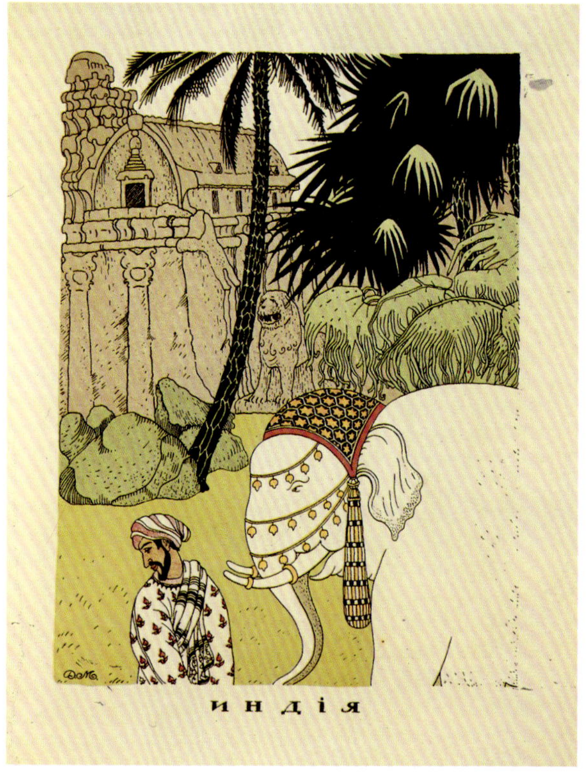

Bottom left: **Georgy Narbut**
237. *Grasshopper in front of the House of Cards*
1913
Drawing to illustrate Hans Christian Andersen's fairy-tale *The High Jumpers*
Mixed media on paper, 32.4 × 25.2
State Russian Museum

Top: **Georgy Narbut**
242. Cover of *Ukrainian Alphabet*, St Petersburg, 1917
State Lenin Library

Bottom right: **Dmitry Mitrokhin**
232. Illustration for Richard Gustafsson, *The Barge: a Fairy Tale*, Moscow, [1913]
State Lenin Library

Opposite: **Boris Zvorykin**
495. Programme for the Imperial Bolshoi Theatre, Moscow, 20 January 1912
Colour lithograph, 34 × 24
State Lenin Library

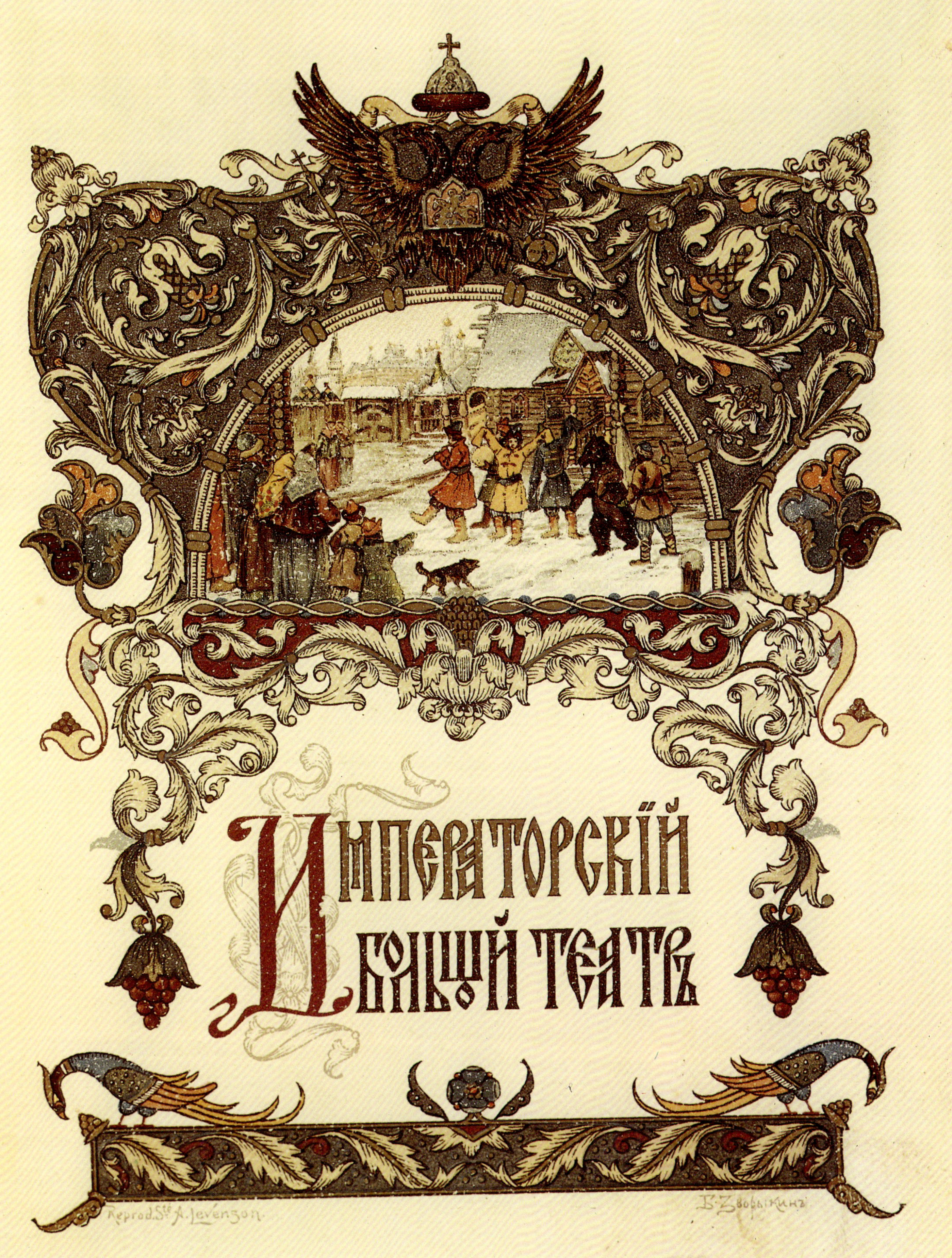
Императорскій Большой Театръ
Reprod. Ste A. Jevenzon
В. Зворыкинъ

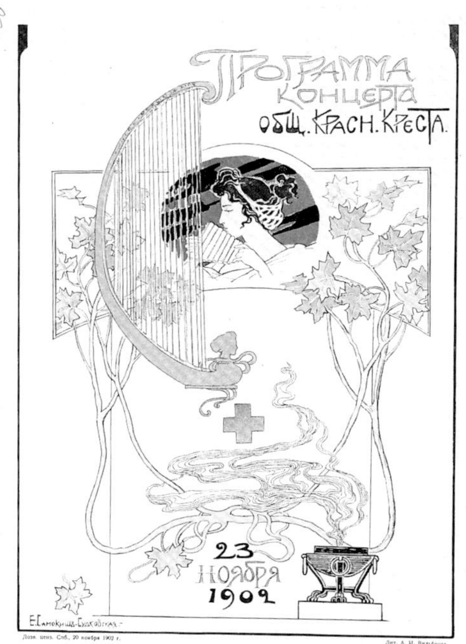

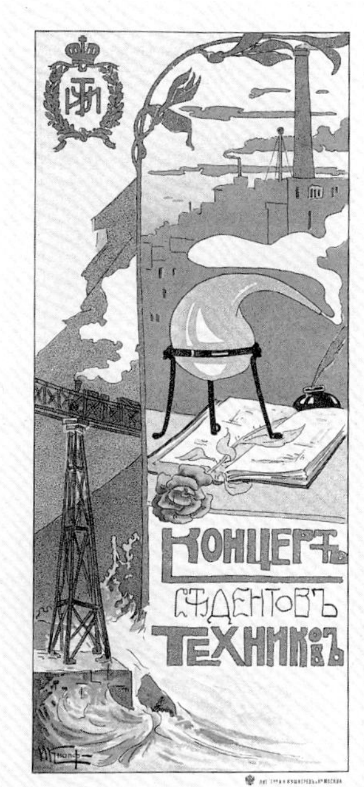

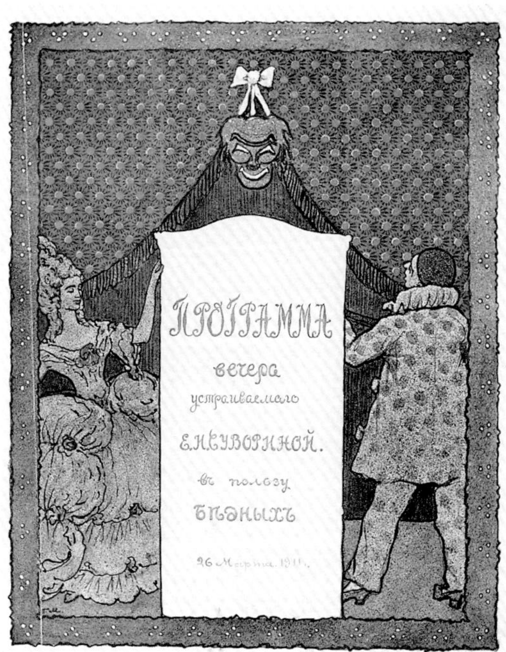

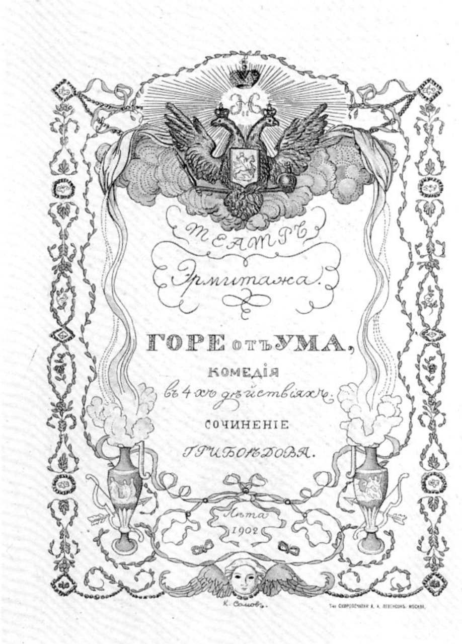

TOP LEFT: **Elena Samokish-Sudovskaya**
302. Programme for Red Cross Society concert
in St Petersburg, 23 November 1902
Colour lithograph, 30 × 24
State Lenin Library

TOP CENTRE: **I. Knopf**
169. Programme cover: Concert of Science and
Engineering Students, Moscow, n.d.
Colour lithograph with gilding, 31.5 × 15
State Lenin Library

TOP RIGHT: **Unknown artist (G. M.)**
550. Programme for Soirée in aid of the Poor
organised by E. N. Suvorina in St Petersburg,
26 March 1911
Colour autotype, 31 × 24
State Lenin Library

OPPOSITE: **Sergei Sudeikin**
420, 422, 421. *England, France* and *Belgium*
1914
Costume designs for A. V. Bobrishchev-
Pushkin's *The Triumph of the Great Powers*,
produced by Vsevolod Meyerhold on
11 October 1914 at the Mariinsky Theatre,
St Petersburg
Mixed media on cardboard, 50 × 30.7;
50 × 33.7; 50 × 33.7
Saratov Museum of Fine Art

Konstantin Somov
393. Programme Cover: Griboedov's *Woe
from Wit* at the Hermitage Theatre, Moscow,
1902
Colour lithograph, gilt, 27.5 × 20
State Lenin Library

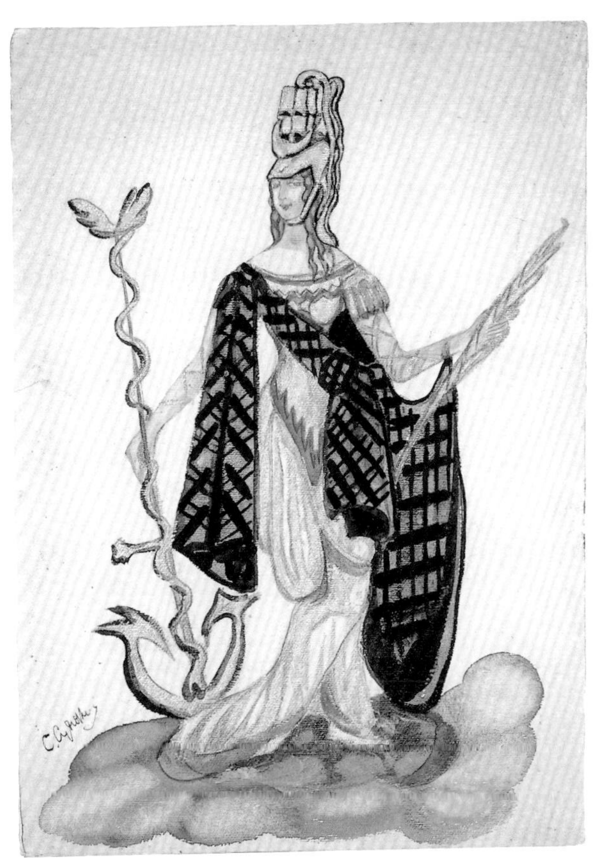

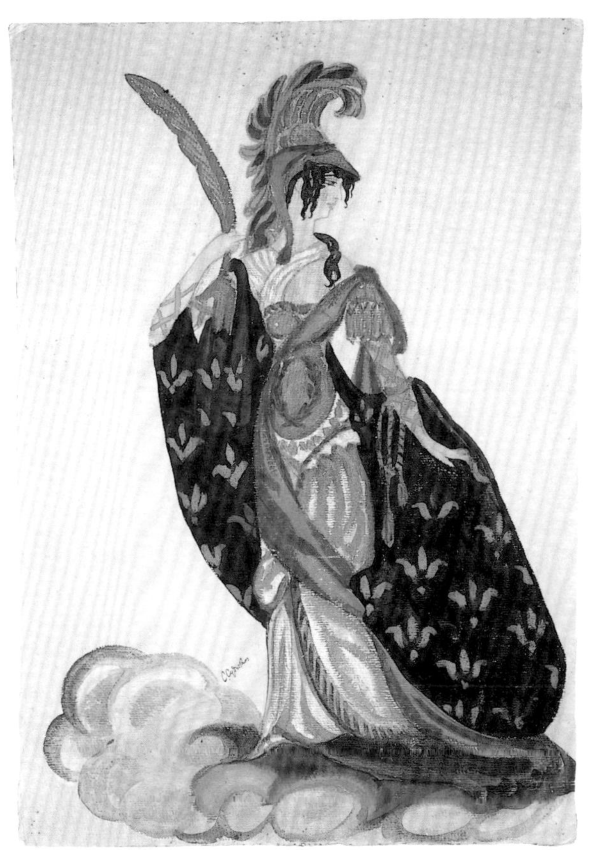

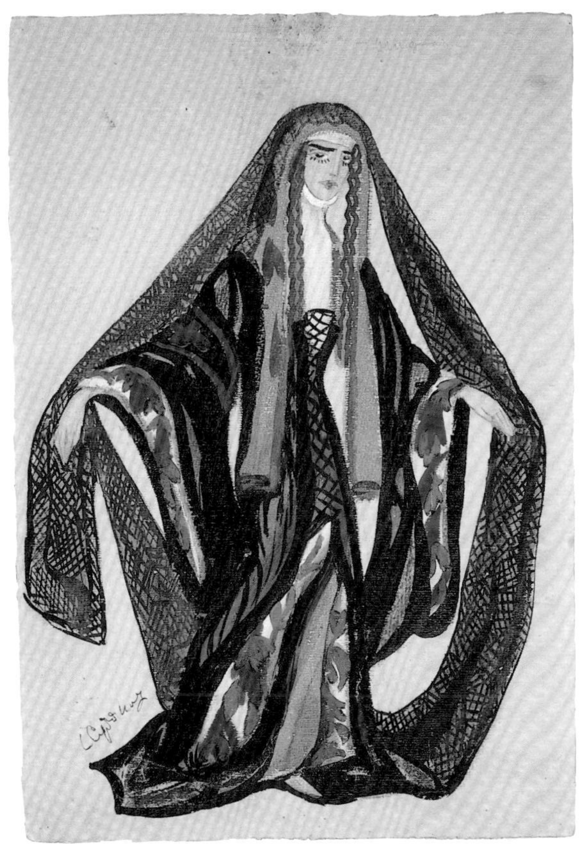

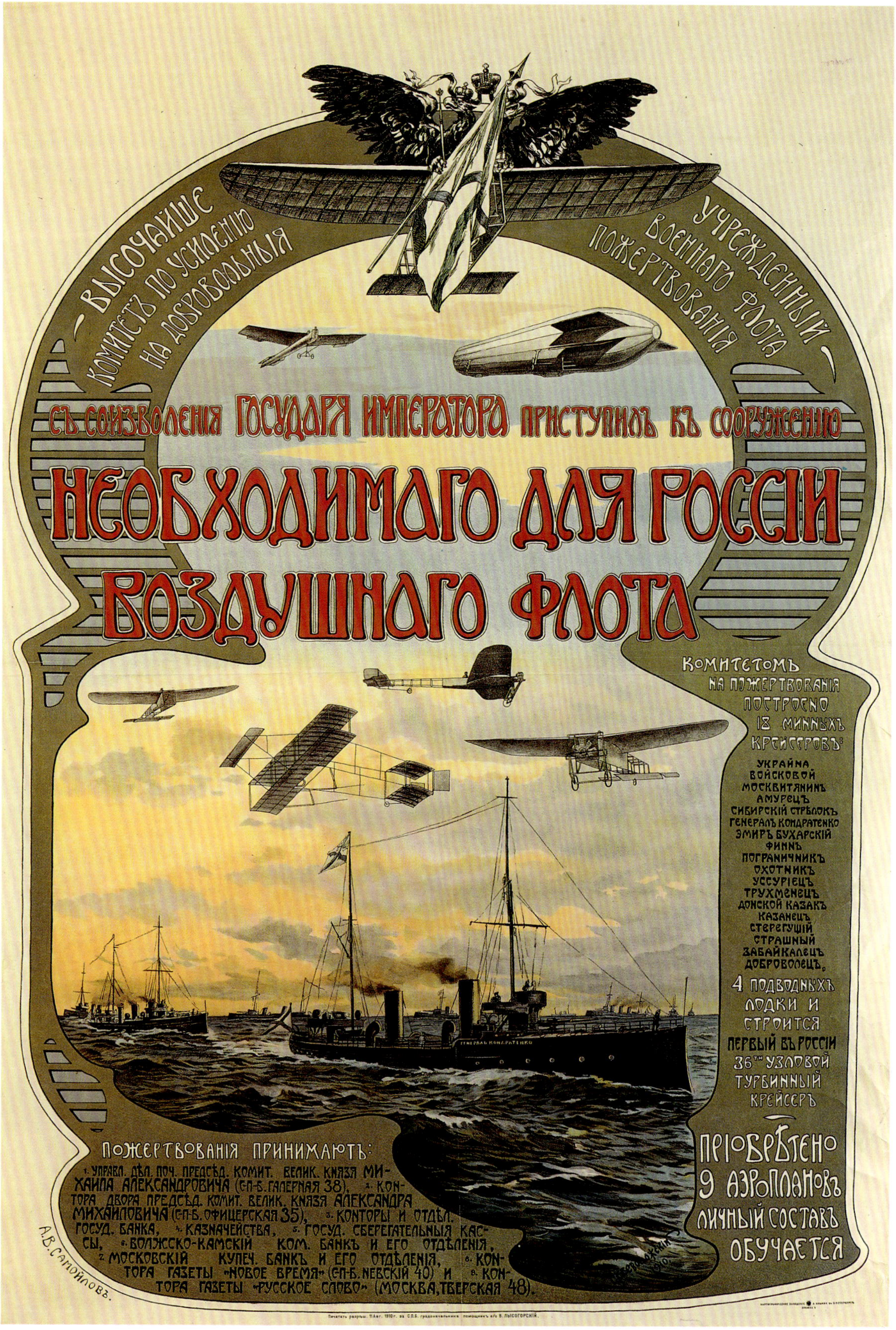

Anatoly Samoilov
298. Poster for Imperial Navy Fund
St Petersburg, 1910
Lithographic poster, 104 × 71
State Lenin Library

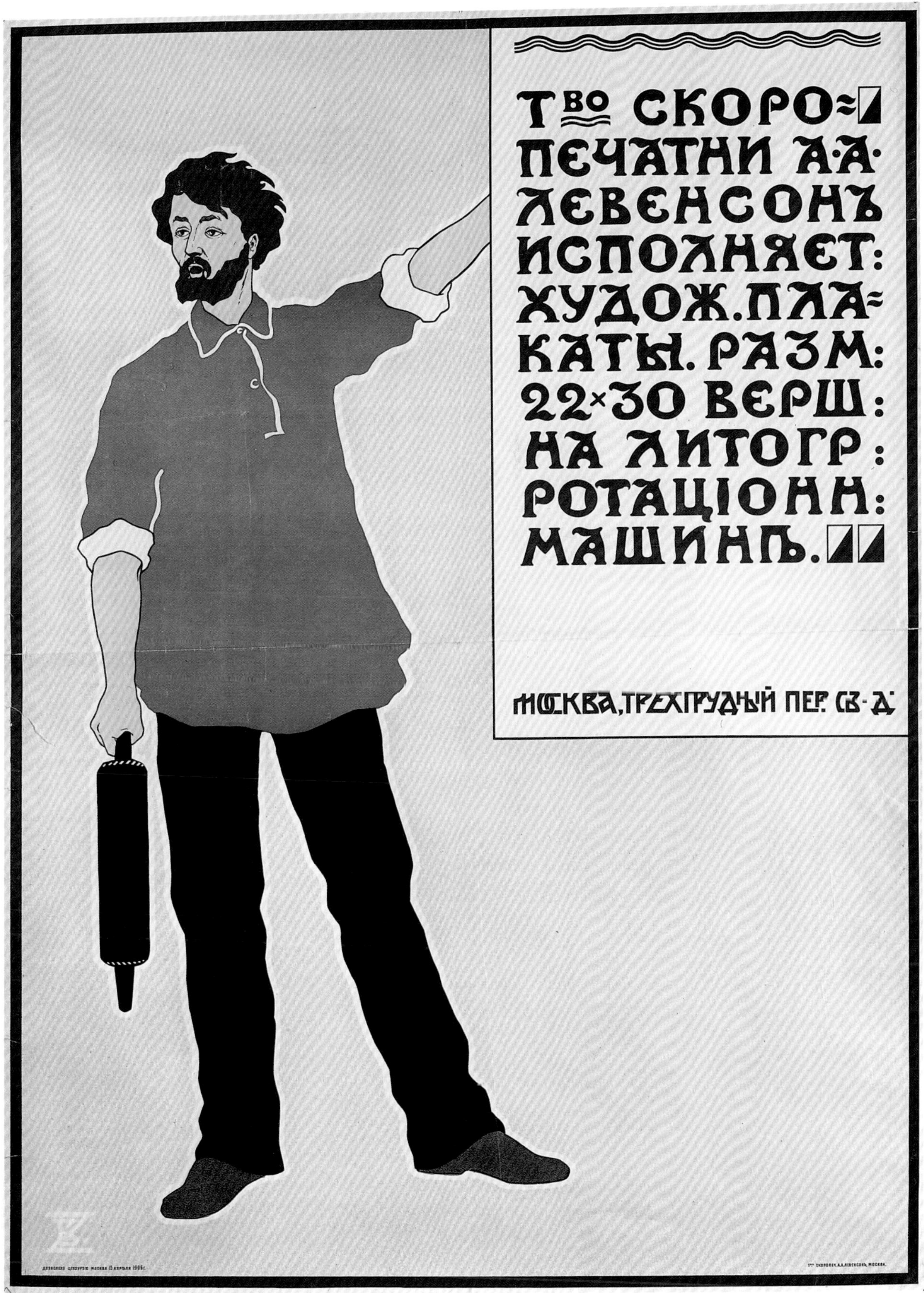

Boris Zvorykin
494. Poster for A. A. Levenson, printers of art
posters
Moscow, 1906
Lithographic poster, 103 × 74
State Lenin Library

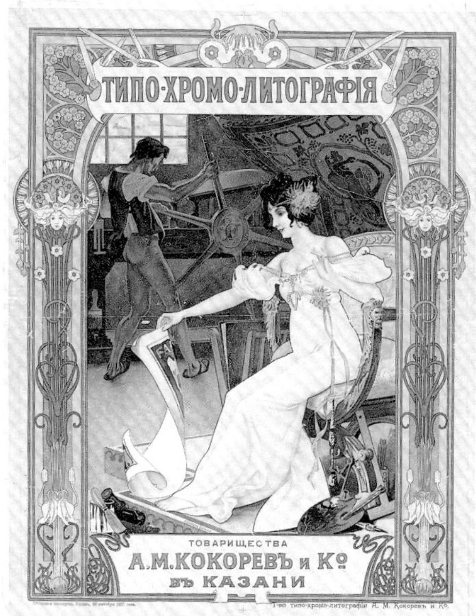
ТИПО-ХРОМО-ЛИТОГРАФІЯ
ТОВАРИЩЕСТВА
А. М. КОКОРЕВЪ и КО
въ КАЗАНИ

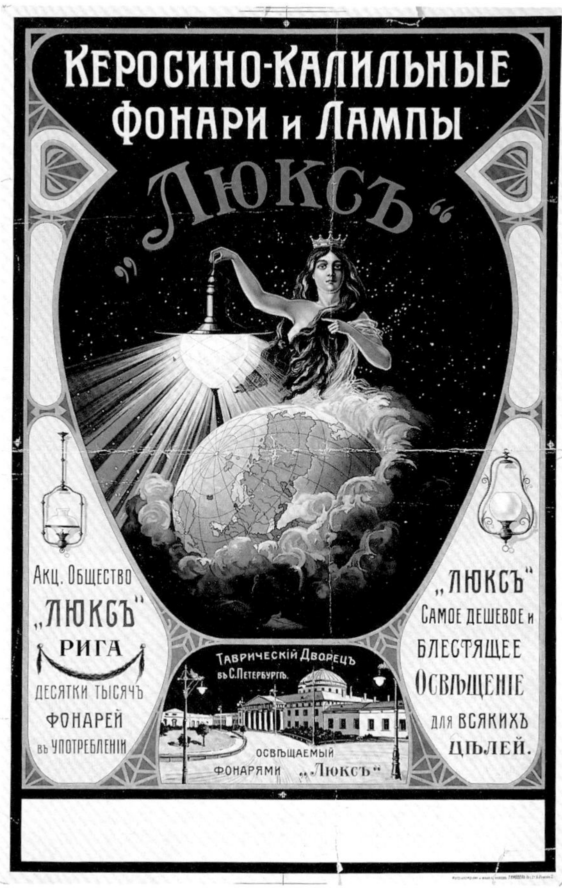
КЕРОСИНО-КАЛИЛЬНЫЕ
ФОНАРИ и ЛАМПЫ
„ЛЮКСЪ"
Акц. Общество
„ЛЮКСЪ"
РИГА
ДЕСЯТКИ ТЫСЯЧЪ
ФОНАРЕЙ
въ УПОТРЕБЛЕНІИ
Таврическій Дворецъ
въ С.Петербургъ.
ОСВѢЩАЕМЫЙ
ФОНАРЯМИ „ЛЮКСЪ"
„ЛЮКСЪ"
САМОЕ ДЕШЕВОЕ и
БЛЕСТЯЩЕЕ
ОСВѢЩЕНІЕ
ДЛЯ ВСЯКИХЪ
ЦѢЛЕЙ.

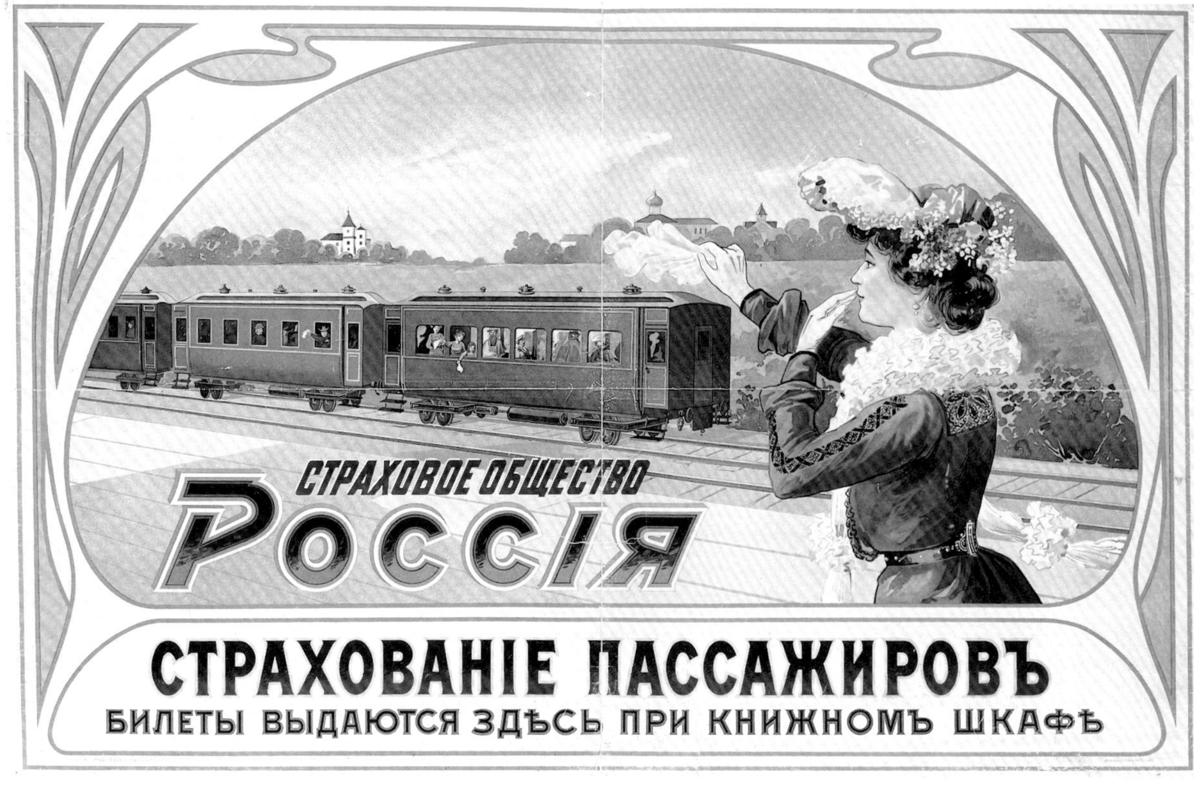
СТРАХОВОЕ ОБЩЕСТВО
РОССІЯ
СТРАХОВАНІЕ ПАССАЖИРОВЪ
БИЛЕТЫ ВЫДАЮТСЯ ЗДѢСЬ ПРИ КНИЖНОМЪ ШКАФѢ

OPPOSITE

ABOVE LEFT:
Unknown artist
497. Poster for A. M. Kokorev & Co.,
typolithographers, Kazan'
Kazan', 1901
Lithographic poster, 51 × 40
State Lenin Library

ABOVE RIGHT: **Unknown artist**
503. Poster for "Lux" Paraffin Lamps
St Petersburg, n.d.
Lithographic poster, 74 × 48
State Lenin Library

BELOW: **Unknown artist**
502. Poster for "Rossiya" Passenger Insurance
St Petersburg, 1903
Lithographic poster, 68.7 × 135
State Lenin Library

RIGHT: **Unknown artist (M. K.)**
516. Poster for Nobel Brothers' Detergent Soap
St Petersburg, n.d.
Lithographic poster, 72 × 55
State Lenin Library

BELOW: **Unknown artist**
505. Poster for Freisinger Brothers' (Riga)
"Russiya" Rubber Tyres
St Petersburg, n.d.
Lithographic poster, 69 × 103
State Lenin Library

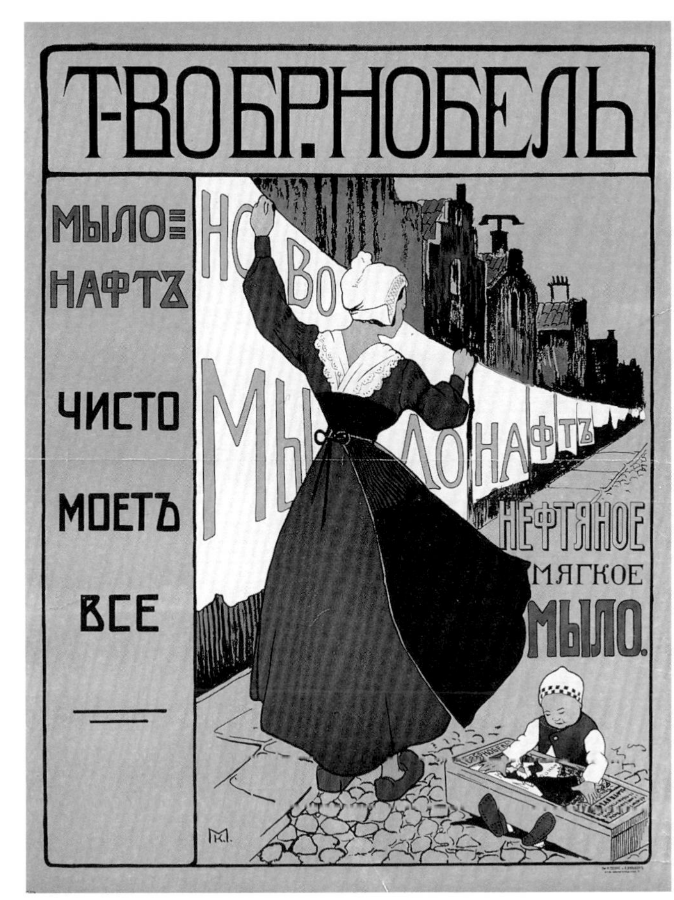

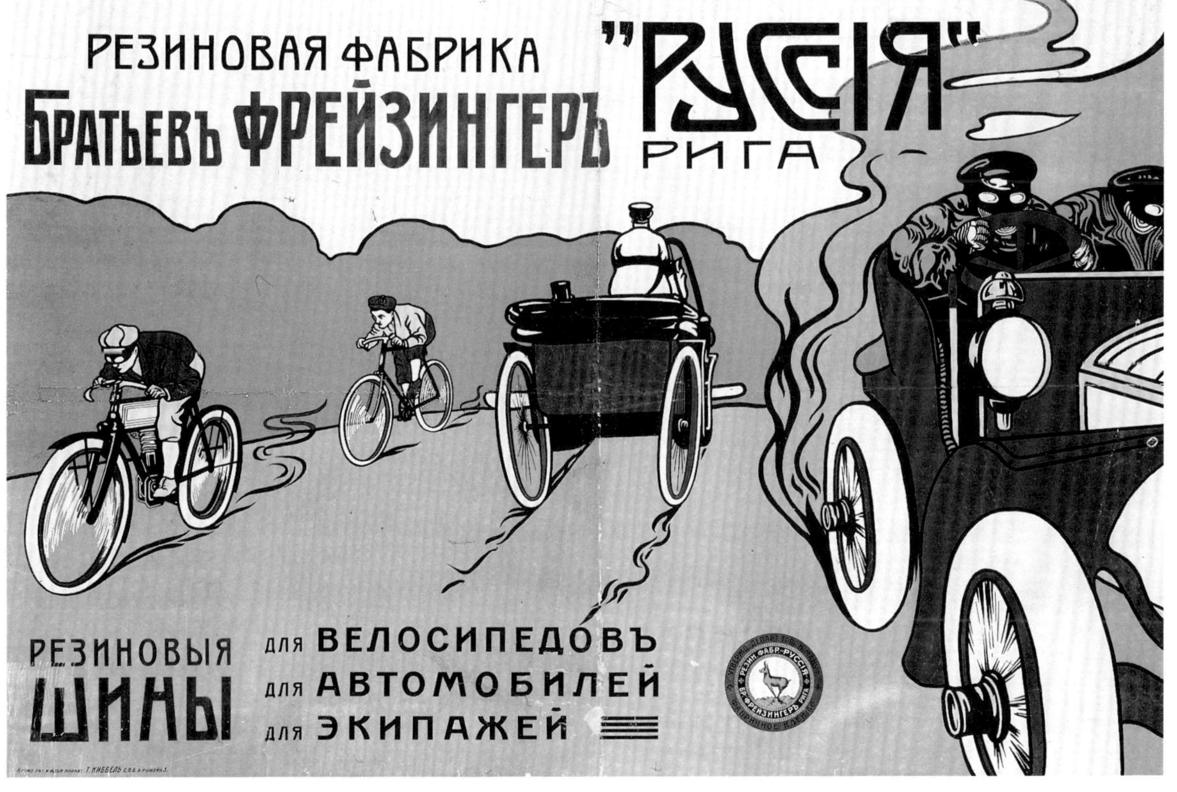

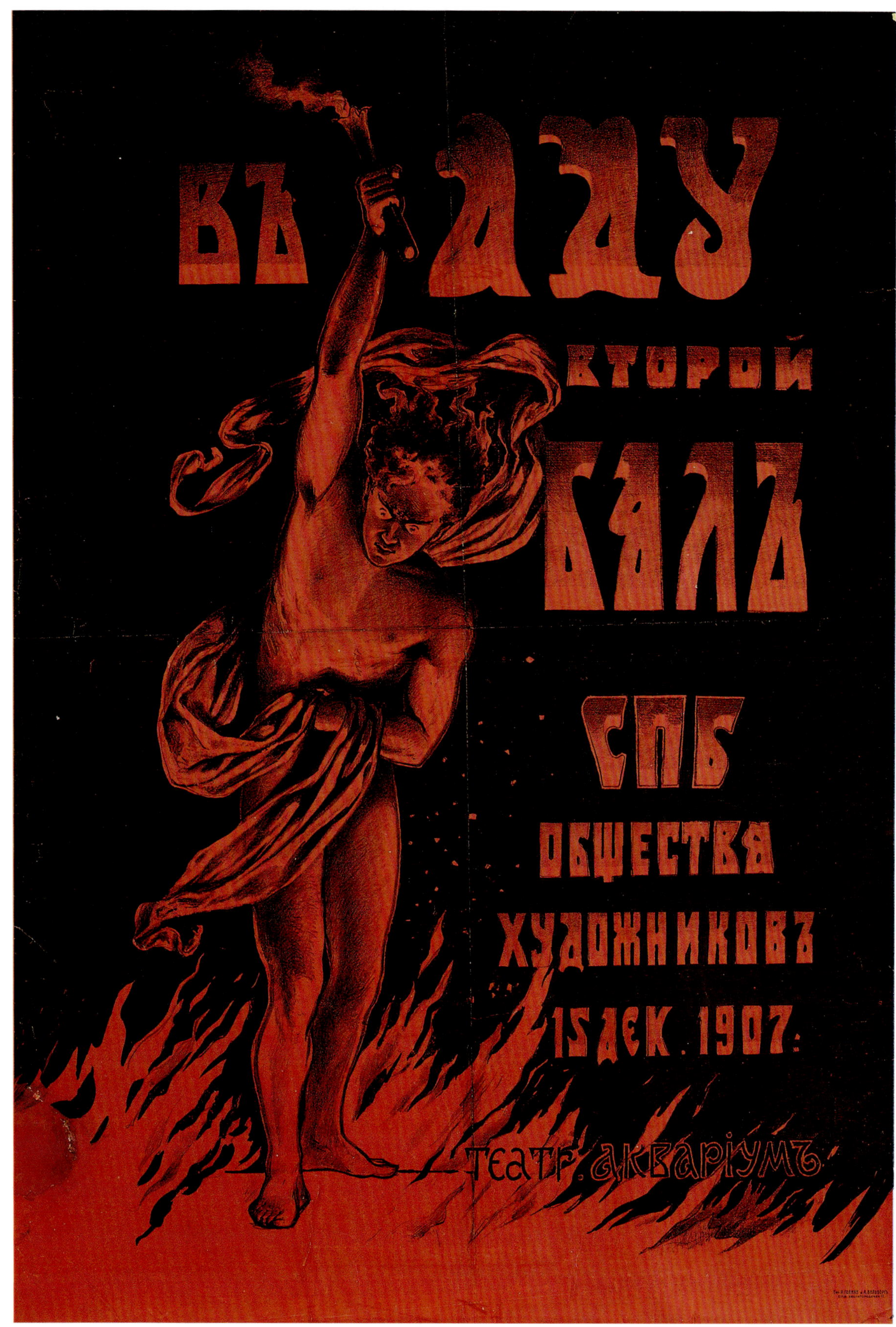

Unknown artist
512. *In Hell*; poster for the Second Ball of the
Society of Artists at the Aquarium Theatre, St
Petersburg, 15 December 1907
Lithographic poster, 92.5 × 61.4
State Lenin Library

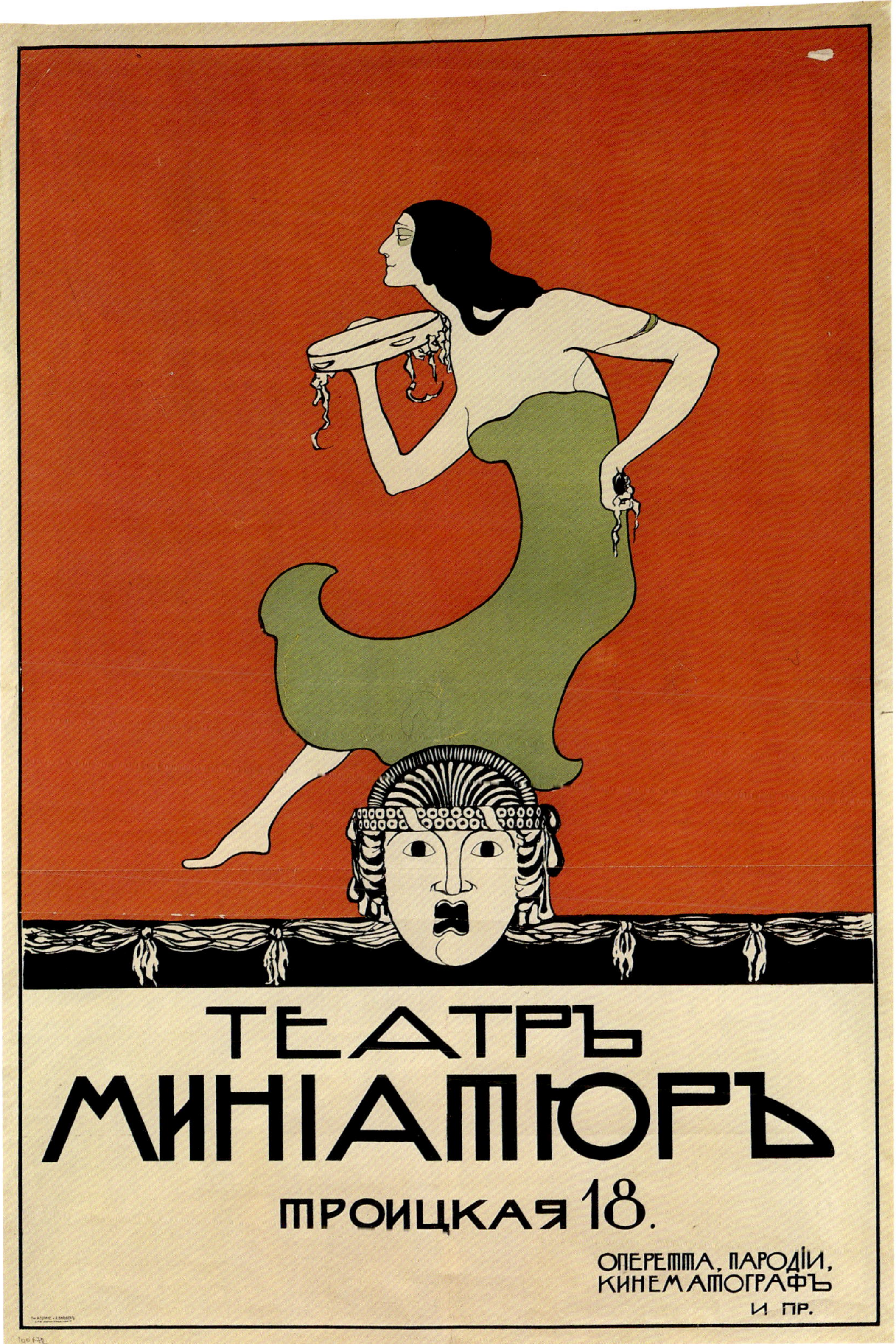

Unknown artist
517. Poster for *Teatr Miniatur*
St Petersburg, n.d.
Lithographic poster, 100 × 71
State Lenin Library

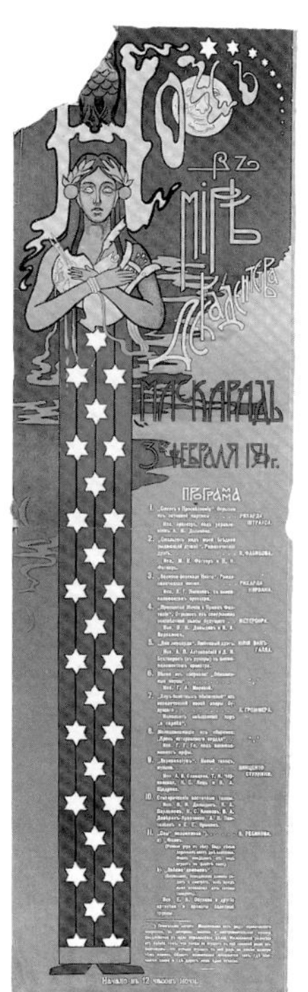

LEFT: **Unknown artist**
498. *Night in the World of Decadence.*
Poster for masked ball, 3 February 1901
St Petersburg, 1901
Lithographic poster, 76 × 22
State Lenin Library

RIGHT: **Luka Zlotnikov**
492. Poster for the journal *Teatr i Iskusstvo*
(*Theatre and Art*)
St Petersburg, 1902
Lithographic poster, 78 × 56
State Lenin Library

BELOW LEFT: **Unknown artist (N. B.)**
513. Poster for *Zhurnal Teatra* (Theatre
Journal of the Literary-Artistic Society)
St Petersburg, [1909]
Lithographic poster, 101 × 68
State Lenin Library

BELOW RIGHT:
Elena Samokish-Sudkovskaya
301. Poster for *First International Costume
Exhibition,* St Petersburg, 1902
Lithographic poster, 86 × 62
State Lenin Library

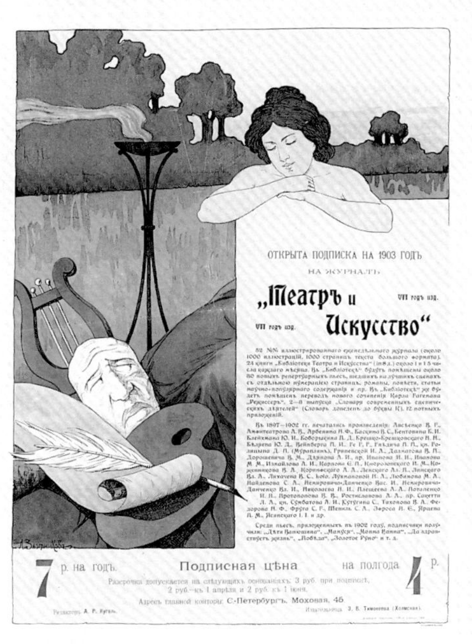

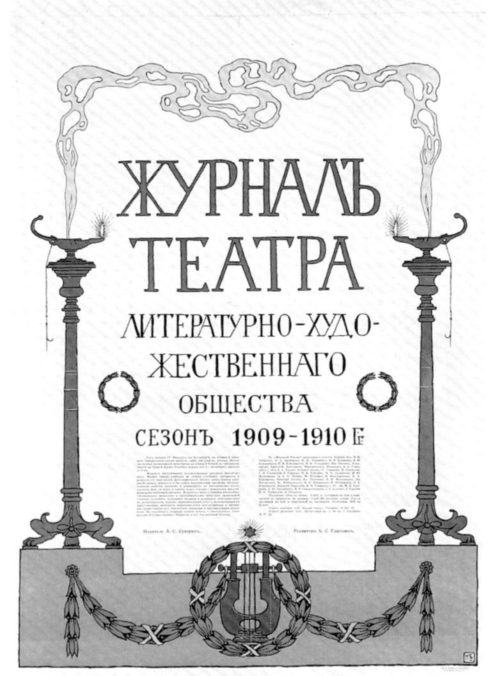

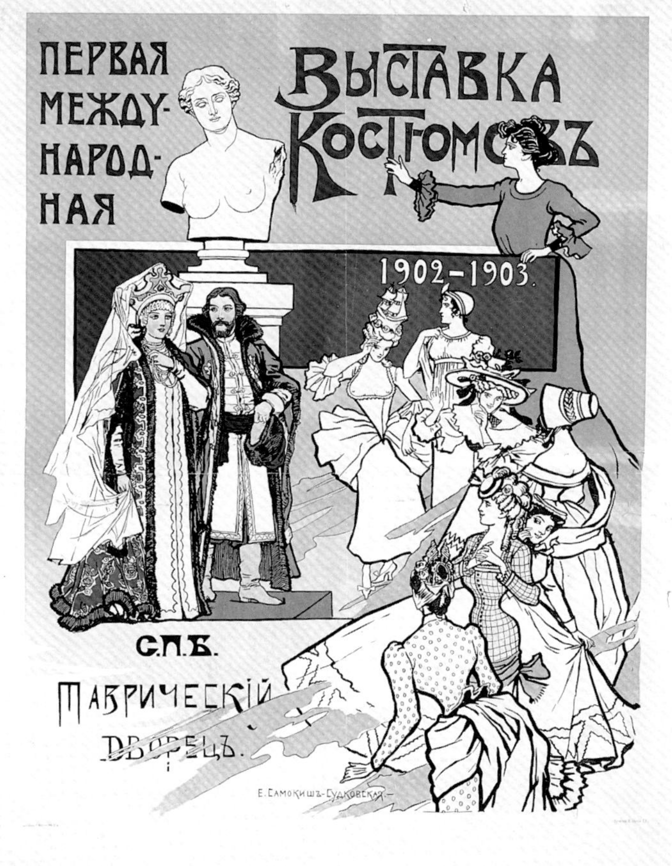

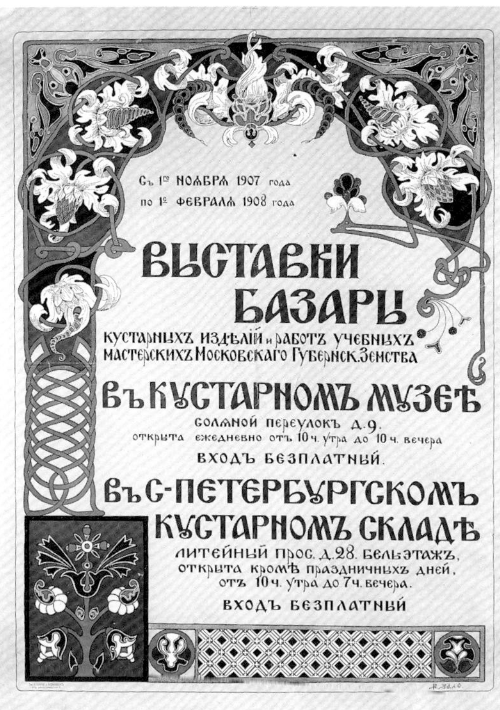

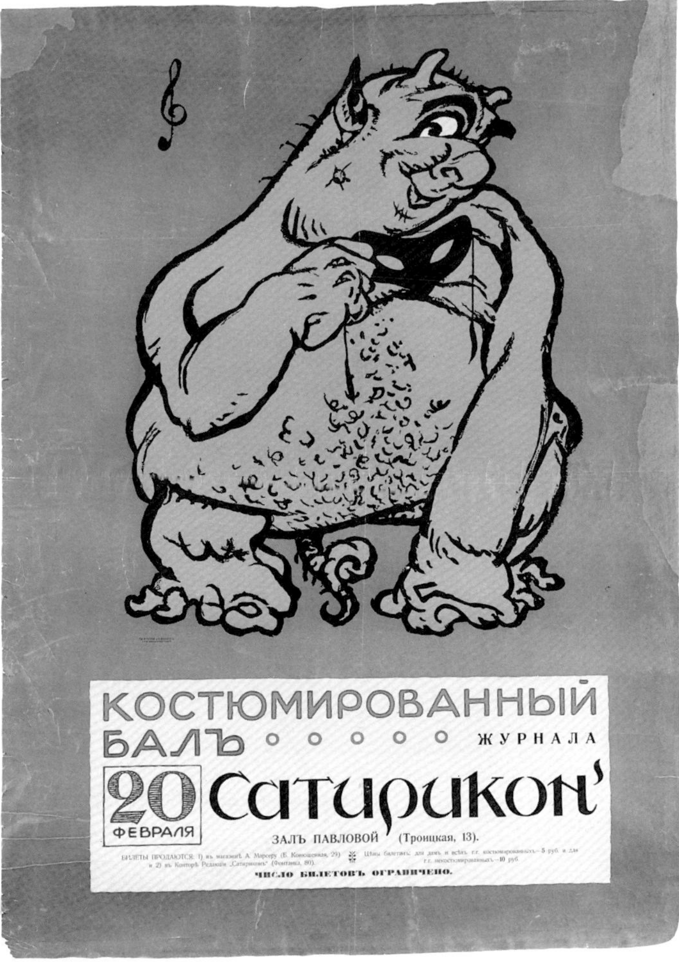

LEFT: **Vasily Zal'**
485. Poster for *Exhibition and Sale of Crafts*
St Petersburg, [1907]
Lithographic poster, 80 × 59
State Lenin Library

BELOW LEFT: **Nikolai Remizov (Re-mi)**
285. Poster for *Satirikon* magazine's costume
ball
St Petersburg, n.d.
Lithographic poster, 114 × 80
State Lenin Library

BELOW: **Unknown artist (E.)**
515. Untitled poster
St Petersburg, n.d.
Lithographic poster, 93.5 × 60
State Lenin Library

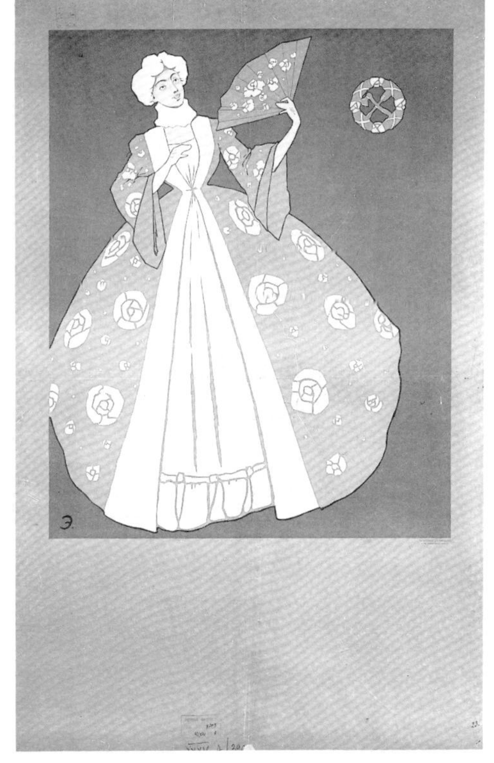

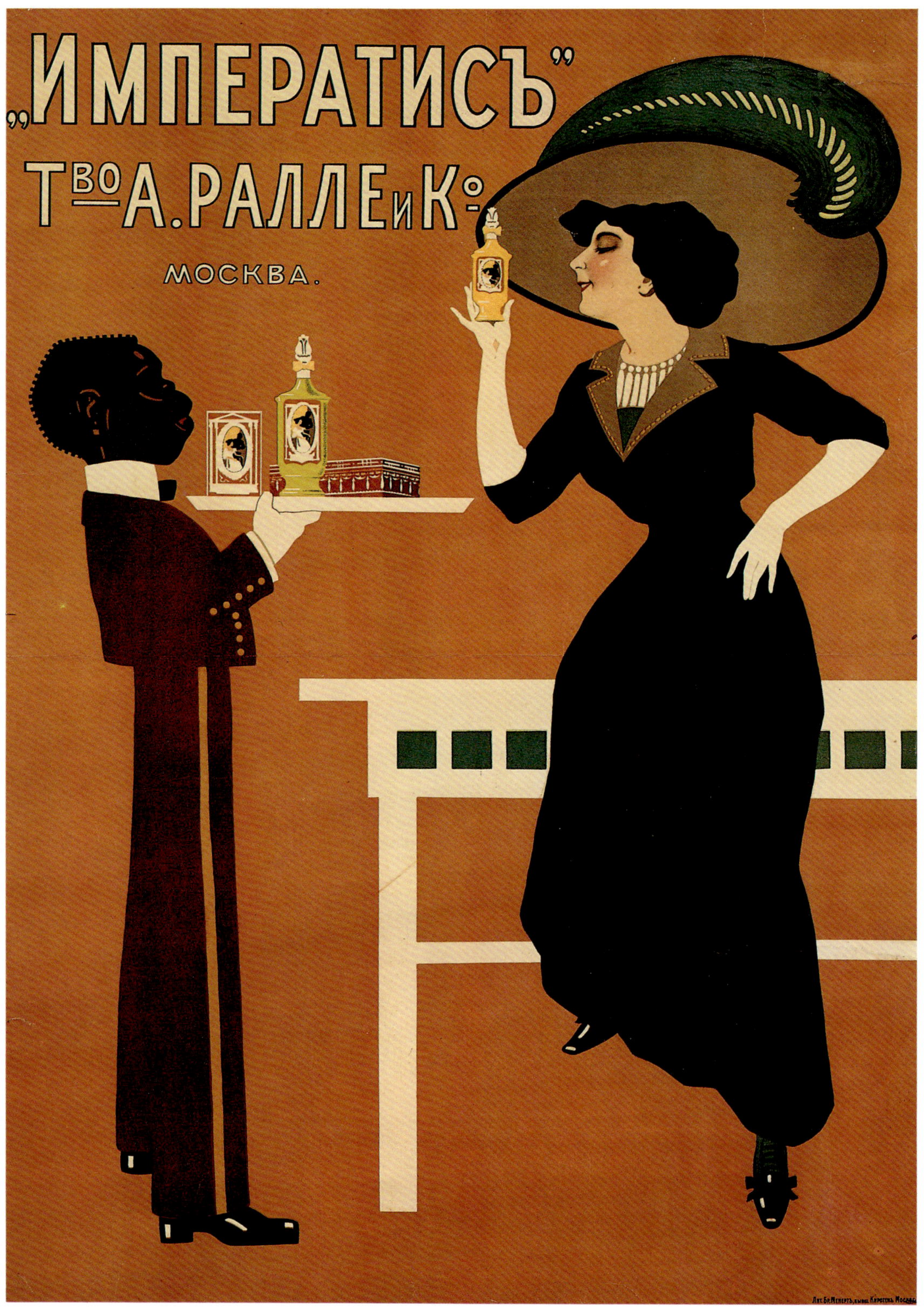

ABOVE: **Unknown artist**
509. Poster for A. Rallet & Co.'s *Imperatis* (Empress) Perfumes
Moscow, n.d.
Lithographic poster, 67 × 47
State Lenin Library

OPPOSITE TOP LEFT: **Unknown artist**
526. Part of cover of price list for A. Rallet & Co., Perfumiers, Moscow
Colour lithographic proof, 29 × 18.5
State Lenin Library

OPPOSITE TOP RIGHT: **Unknown artist**
527. Wrapper for A. Rallet's "Végétal" soap
Colour lithograph, 14 × 19.5
State Lenin Library

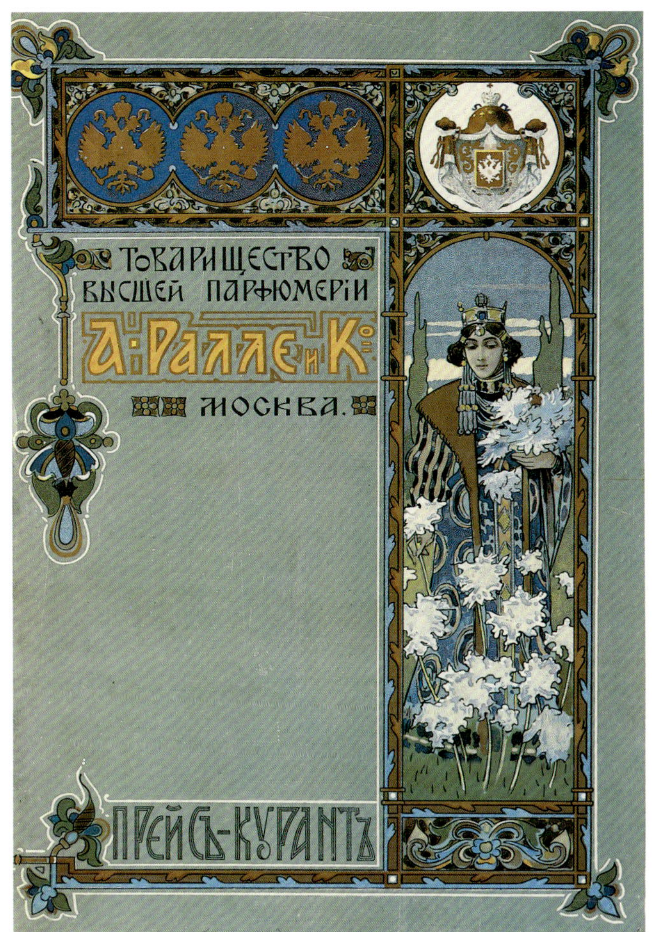

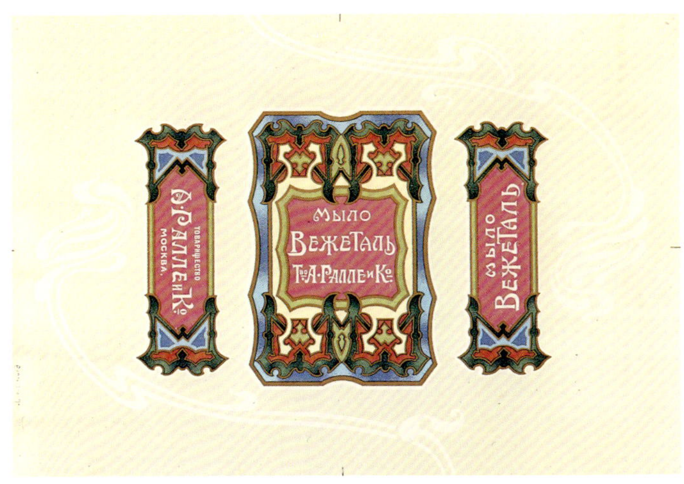

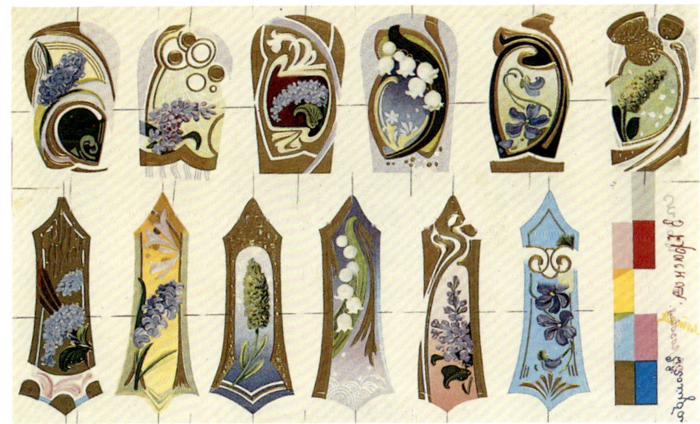

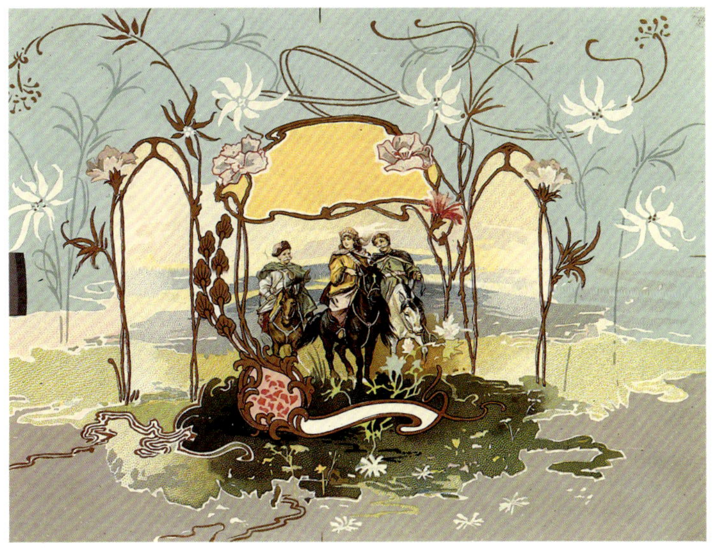

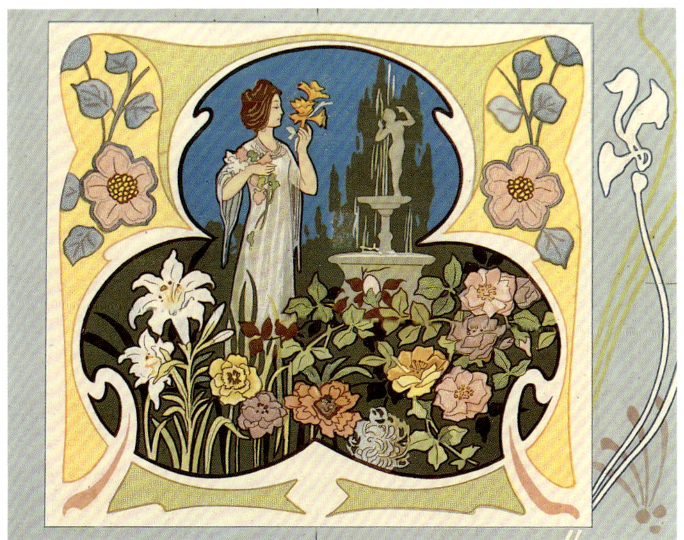

ABOVE: **Unknown artist**
528. Soap wrapper
Colour lithograph, 12.5 × 16
State Lenin Library

CENTRE RIGHT: **Unknown artist**
530. Labels for perfume bottles
Colour lithographic proof, embossed, 12.5 × 20
State Lenin Library

BOTTOM RIGHT: **Unknown artist**
529. Soap wrapper
Colour lithograph, 13 × 17
State Lenin Library

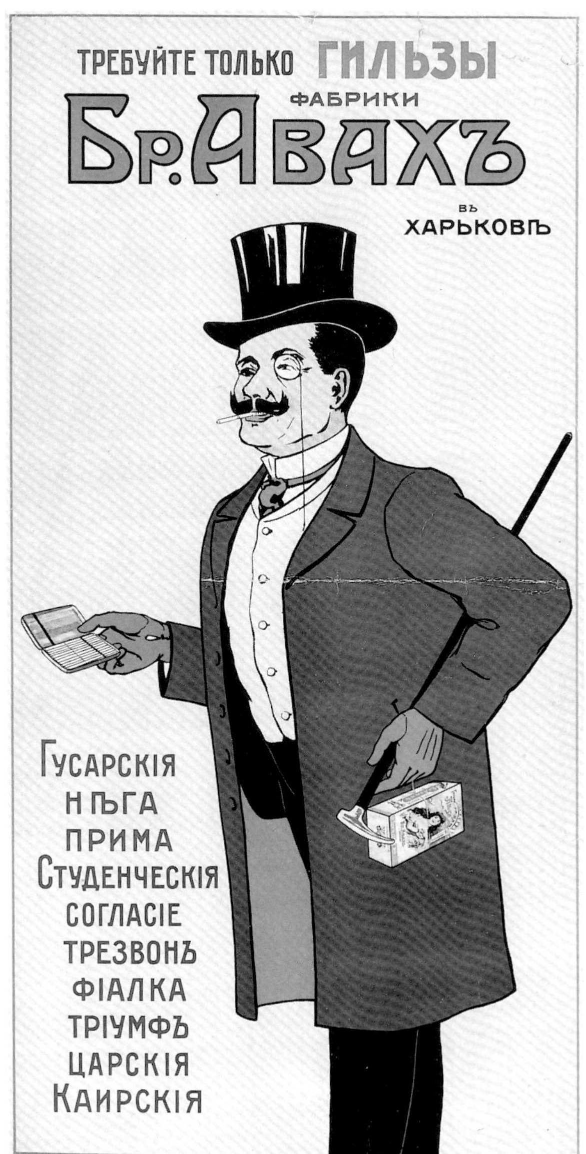

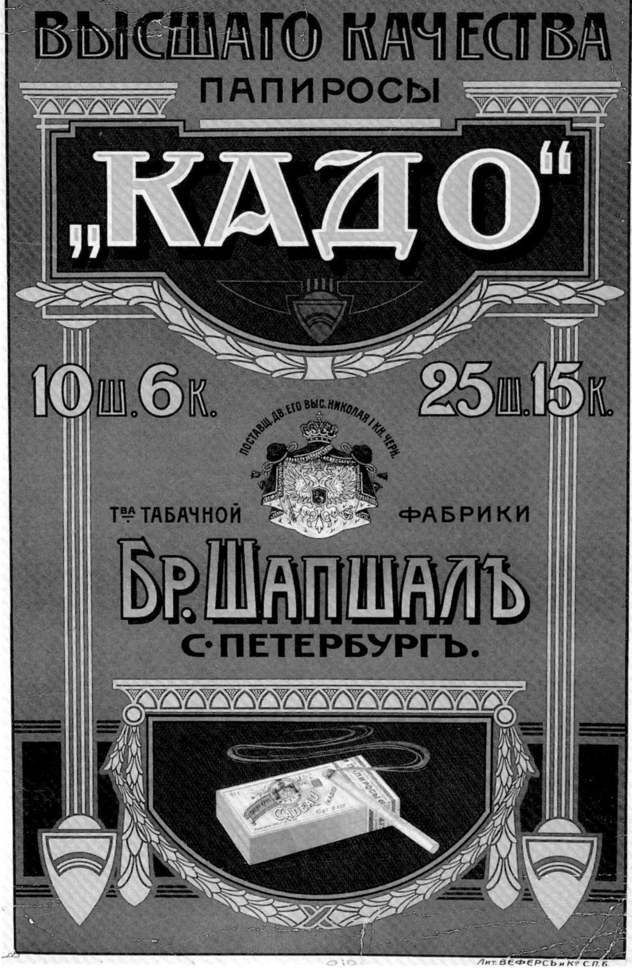

ABOVE LEFT: **Unknown artist**
506. Poster for Avakh Brothers' Cigarette
Papers
St Petersburg, n.d.
Lithographic poster, 70 × 36
State Lenin Library

ABOVE RIGHT: **Unknown artist**
508. Poster for "Kado" (Cadeau) Cigarettes
St Petersburg, n.d.
Lithographic poster, 55 × 36
State Lenin Library

RIGHT: **Unknown artist**
507. Poster for Laferme's "Frou-Frou"
Cigarettes
St Petersburg, 1904
Lithographic poster, 60.7 × 44
State Lenin Library

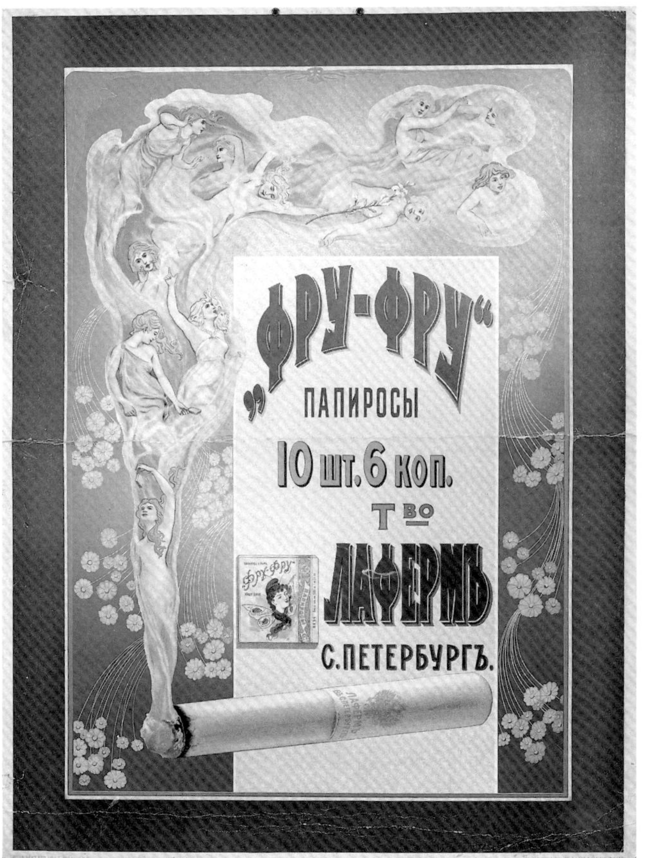

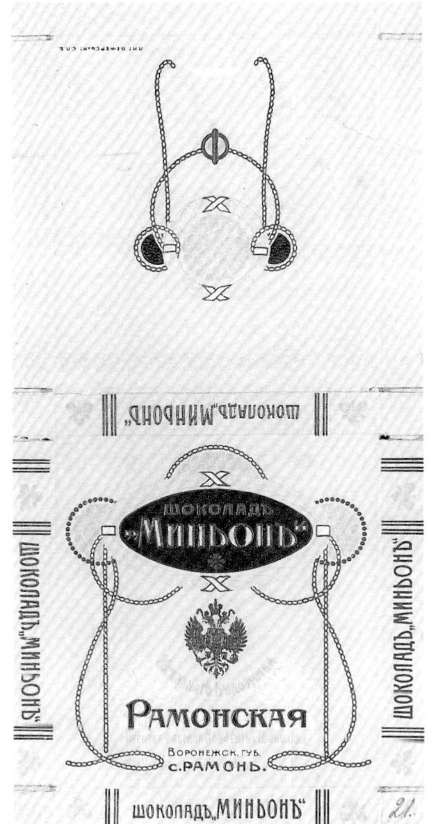

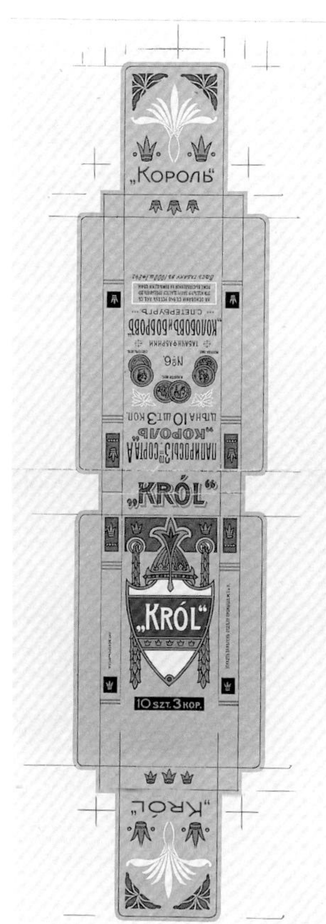

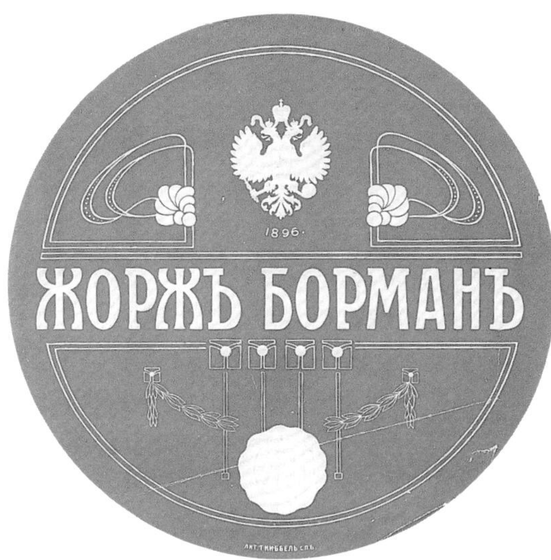

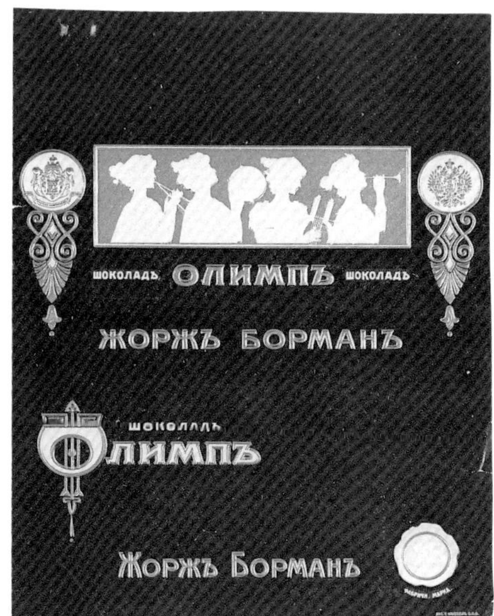

FAR LEFT: **Unknown artist**
540. Wrapper for "Mignon" chocolate, made
by the Ramon Steam Sweet and Chocolate
Factory, Ramon Village, Voronezh Province
St Petersburg, n.d.
Colour lithograph, 30 × 15
State Lenin Library

LEFT: **Unknown artist**
544. Packet for Kolobov & Bobrov's "Król"
(King) no.6 cigarettes
St Petersburg, n.d.
Colour lithograph, 31.5 × 7
State Lenin Library

ABOVE: **Unknown artist**
531. Label for George Borman, sweet
manufacturer
St Petersburg, n.d.
Embossed colour lithograph, diameter: 16
State Lenin Library

BELOW LEFT: **Unknown artist**
532. Wrapper for George Borman's "Olimp"
(Olympus) chocolate
St Petersburg, n.d.
Colour lithograph, gilt and embossed, 17 × 13.5
State Lenin Library

RIGHT: **Unknown artist**
511. Poster for A. Kron' and Co.'s Beer and
Porter
St Petersburg, 1905
Lithographic poster, 61 × 33
State Lenin Library

OPPOSITE: **Unknown artist**
500. Poster for Ustinov's Macaroni
Kazan', 1902
Lithographic poster, 55 × 26
State Lenin Library

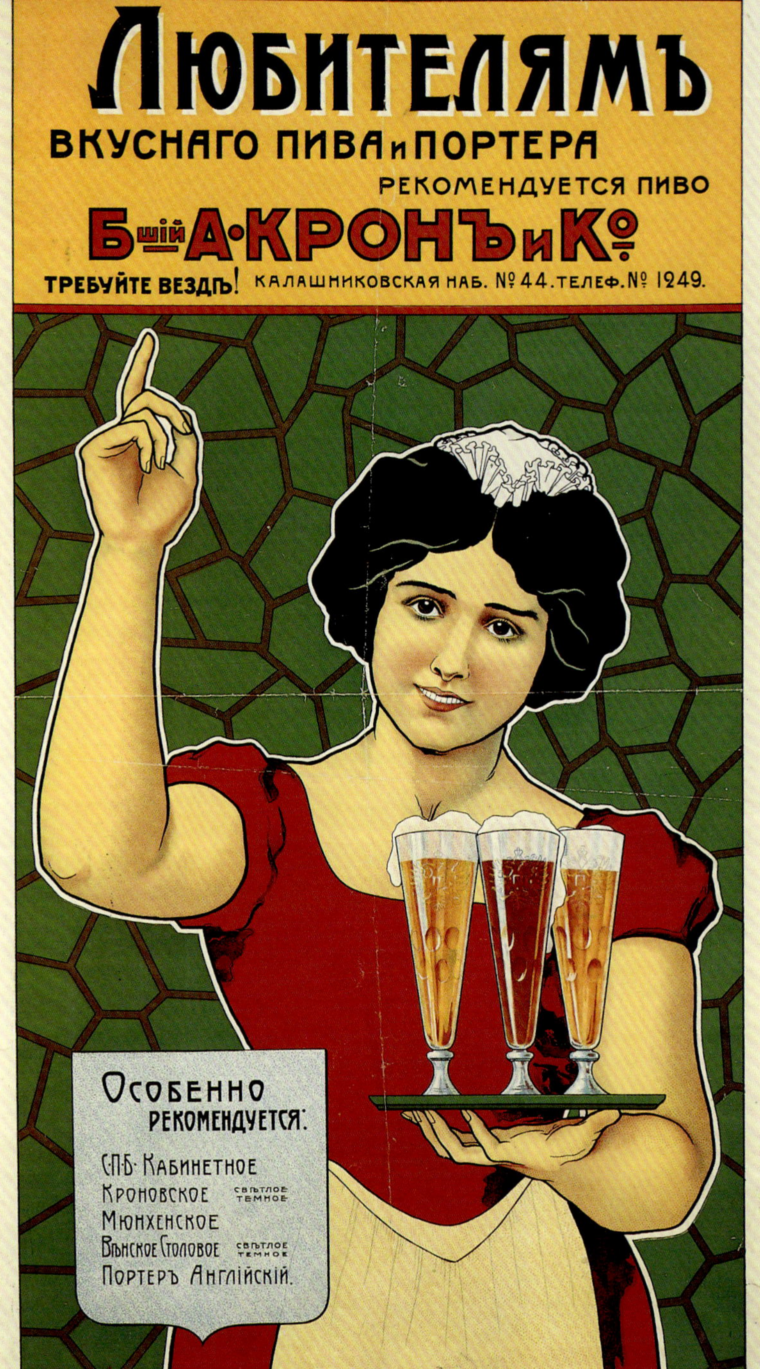

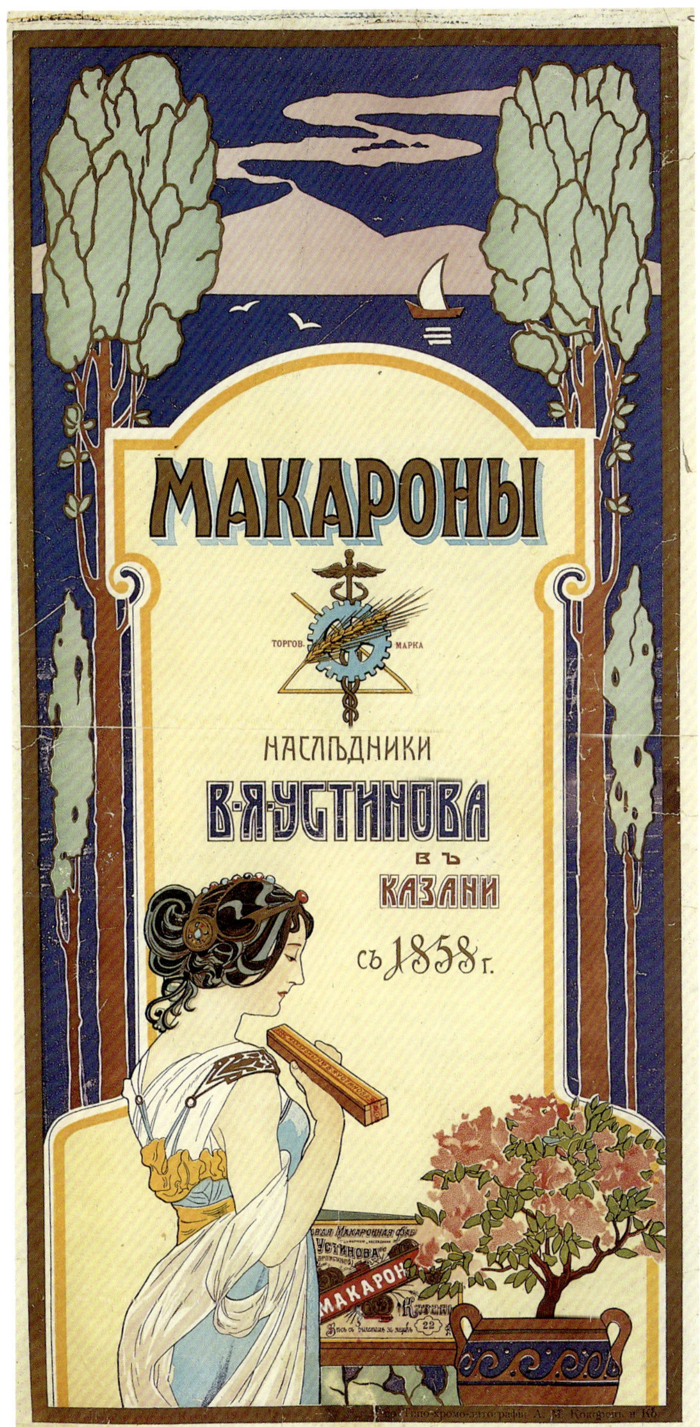

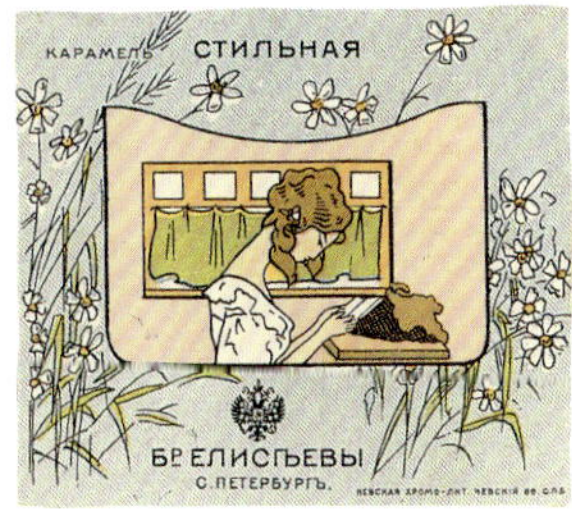

BELOW (LEFT TO RIGHT):
Unknown artists
543, 542. Original designs for sweet wrappers
Gouache on cardboard, 7.5 × 8.5; 8.5 × 8.5
State Lenin Library

541. Original design for sweet wrapper,
"Azra"
Gouache and bronze paint on cardboard, 9 × 8
State Lenin Library

533, 534. Wrappers for Eliseev Brothers'
"Stil'naya" (Stylish) Caramels
St Petersburg, n.d.
Colour lithographs, each 8 × 8.5
State Lenin Library

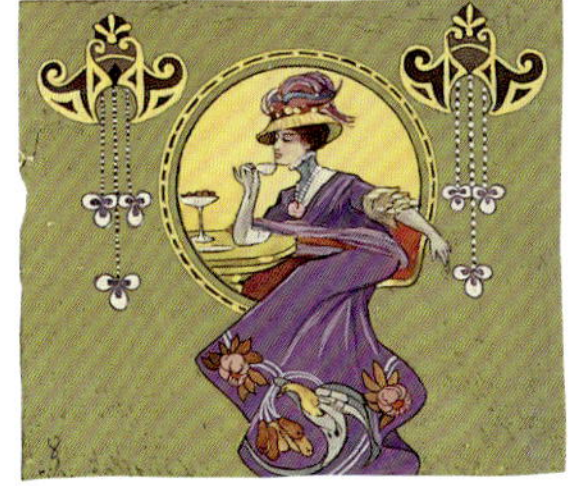

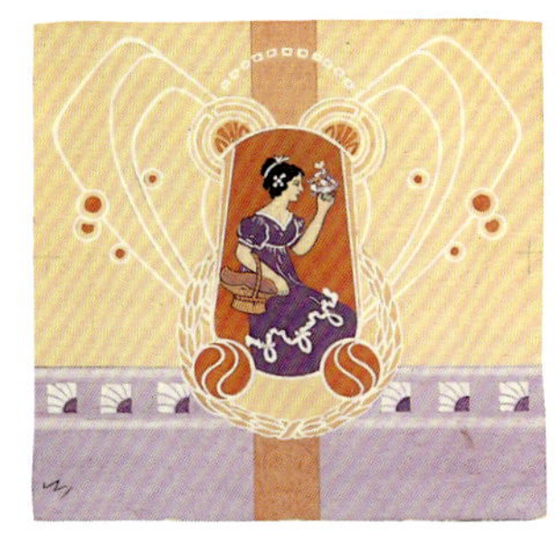

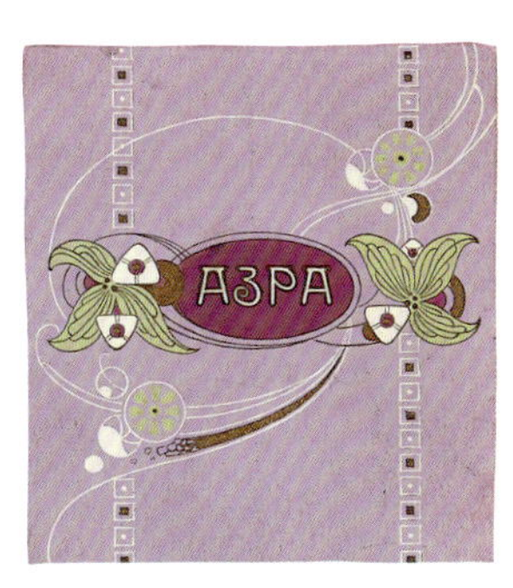

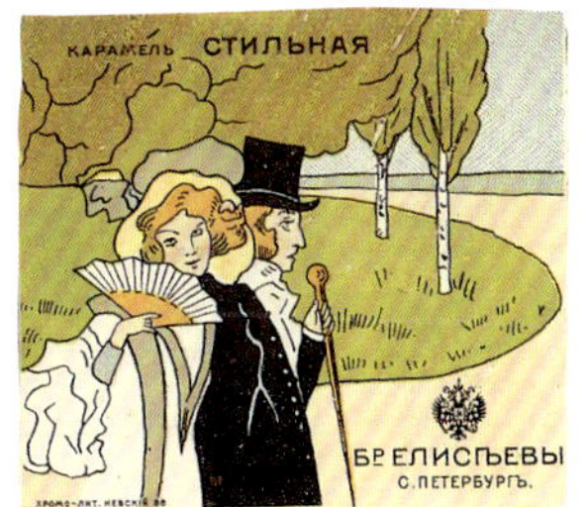

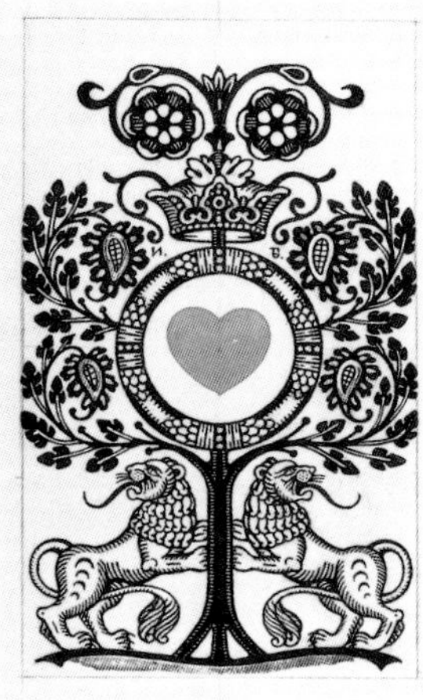 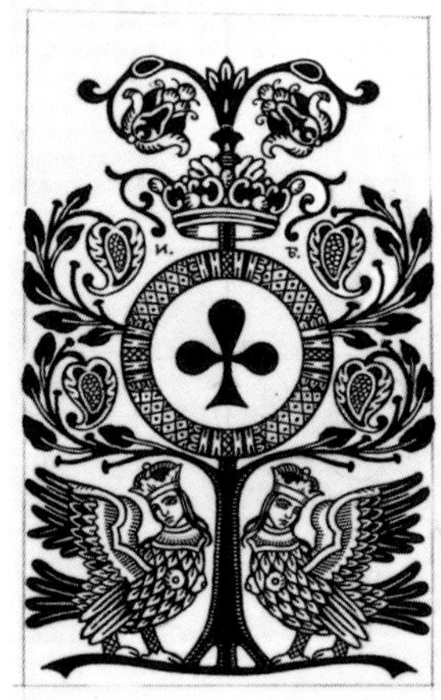

Ivan Bilibin
55, 56. Designs for playing cards: Ace of
Hearts and Ace of Clubs
1911
Mixed media on paper, 24.2 × 13.9; 25.4 × 18.2
State Russian Museum

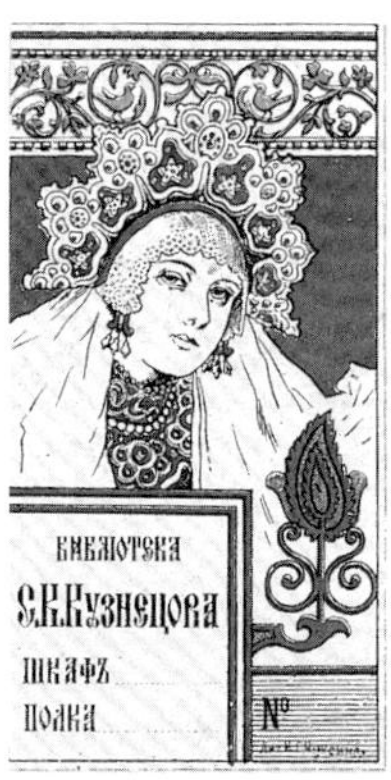 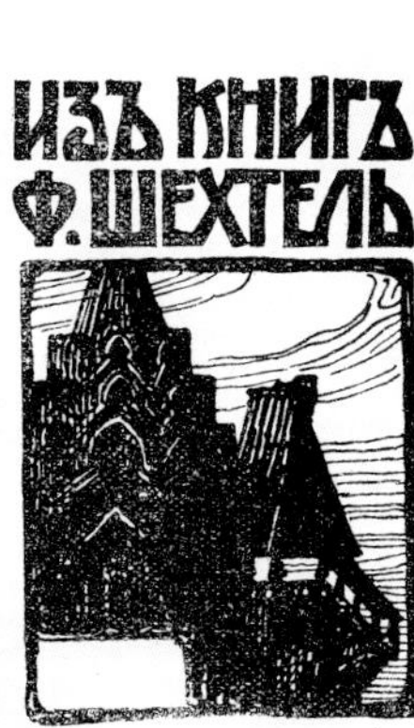 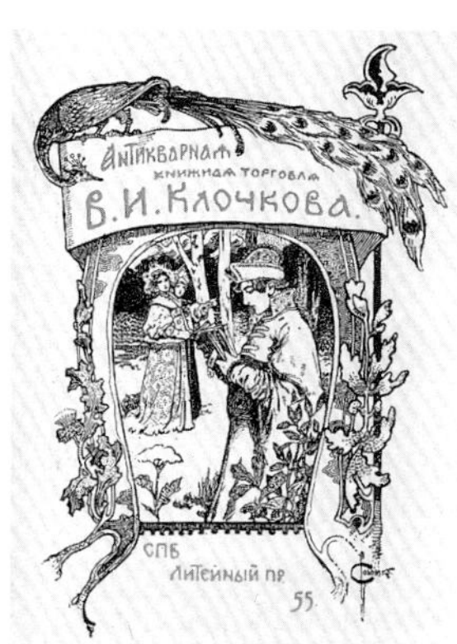

 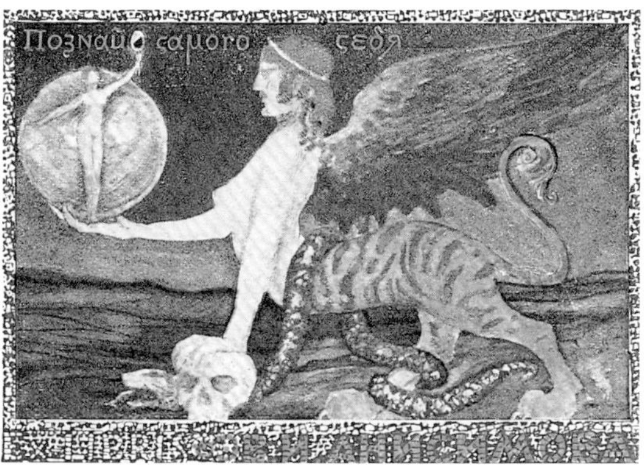

CENTRE ROW

LEFT: **Sergei Solomko**
386. Bookplate for S. K. Kuznetsov
Colour lithograph, 7 × 3.5
State Lenin Library

CENTRE: **Fedor Shekhtel'**
353. The architect's bookplate with illustration
of the Russian Central Pavilion at the Glasgow
International Exhibition, 1901
Line block, 7.7 × 5.1
Private collection

RIGHT: **Sergei Solomko**
385. Bookplate for the antiquarian booksellers
V. I. Klochkov, St Petersburg
Colour lithograph, 9 × 6.5
State Lenin Library

BOTTOM ROW

LEFT: **Ivan Rerberg**
287. Bookplate for ''V. L.''
Colour lithograph, 10 × 14.5
State Lenin Library

RIGHT: **Mikhail Solomonov**
387. Bookplate for V. I. Anisimov: ''Know Thyself''
Autotype, line block, 8 × 10.5
State Lenin Library

GRAPHIC ART

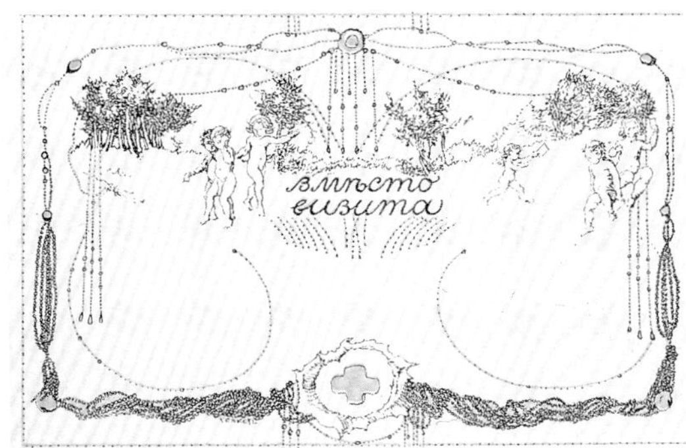

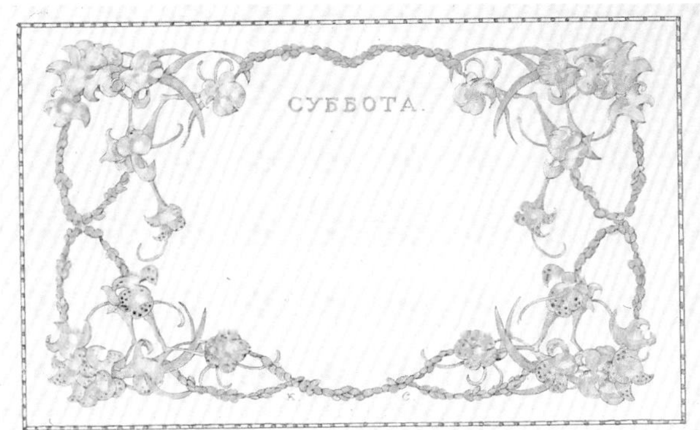

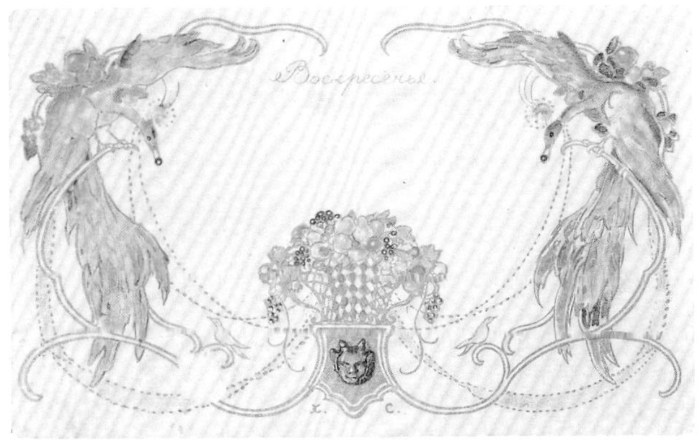

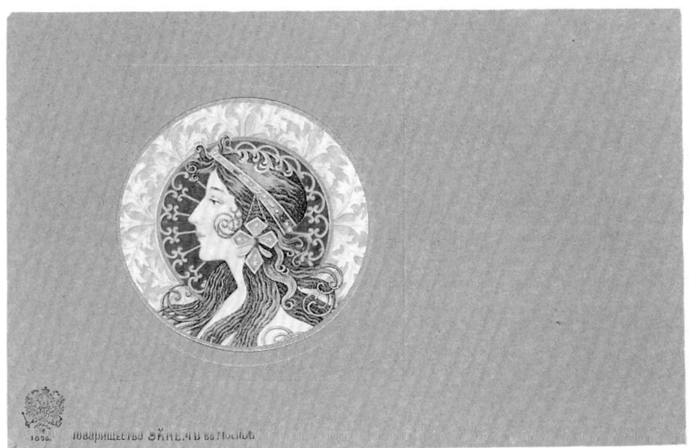

TOP: **Unknown artist**
554. Envelope for the Community of St Evgeny
(Red Cross)
Colour lithograph, 8 × 12
State Lenin Library

CENTRE: **Konstantin Somov**
394, 395. Postcards for the Red Cross:
Saturday and Sunday (from the series *The
Days of the Week*)
St Petersburg, 1904 or 1905
Colour lithographs, 9 × 14
State Lenin Library

BOTTOM: **Unknown artist**
553. Postcard advertising the Einem
Partnership, Moscow
Colour lithograph glued to cardboard, silvered,
9 × 13.5
State Lenin Library

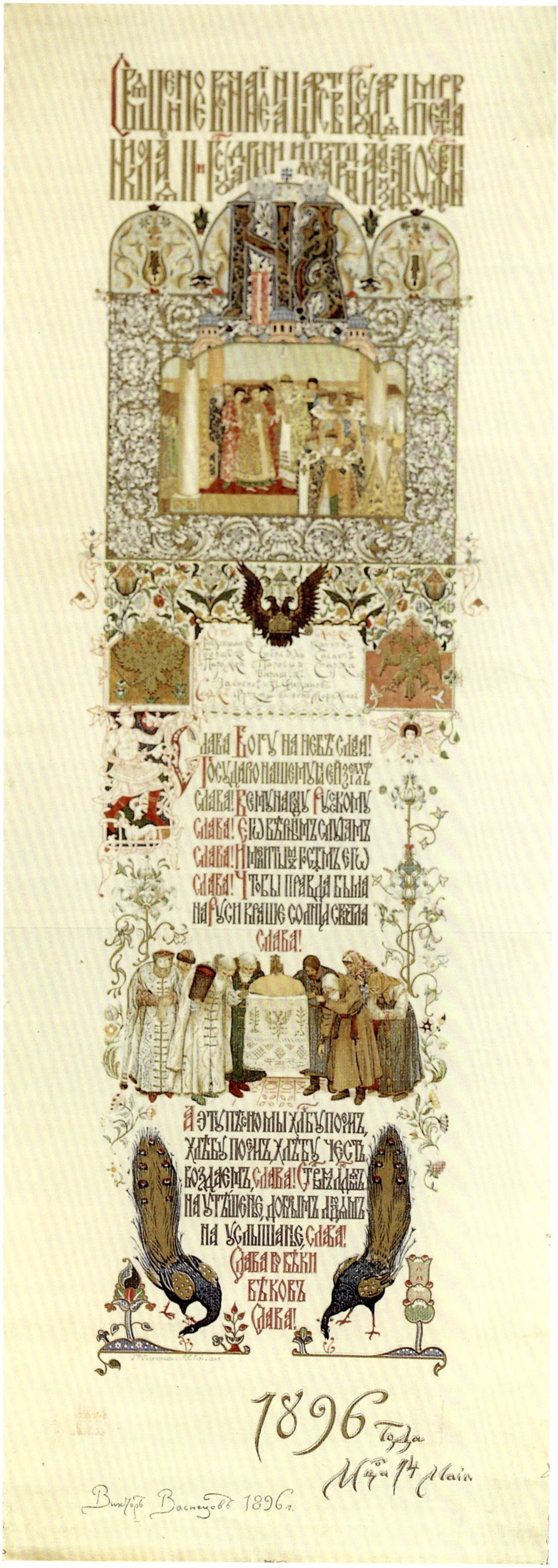

LEFT: **Viktor Vasnetsov**
448. Menu for the coronation banquet of Tsar
Nikolai II and Tsaritsa Aleksandra Fedorovna
Moscow, 14 May 1896
Colour lithograph, 93.5 × 32.5
State Lenin Library

BELOW: **Unknown artist**
548. Menu for the restaurant "Al'piiskaya
Roza" (Alpenrose), Moscow, 30 March 1907
Colour lithograph, 26.5 × 17.5
State Lenin Library

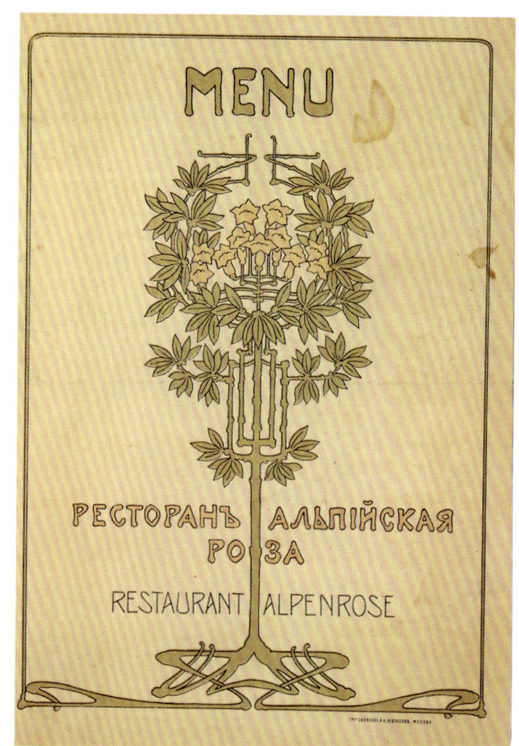
MENU

РЕСТОРАНЪ АЛЬПІЙСКАЯ
РО ЗА

RESTAURANT ALPENROSE

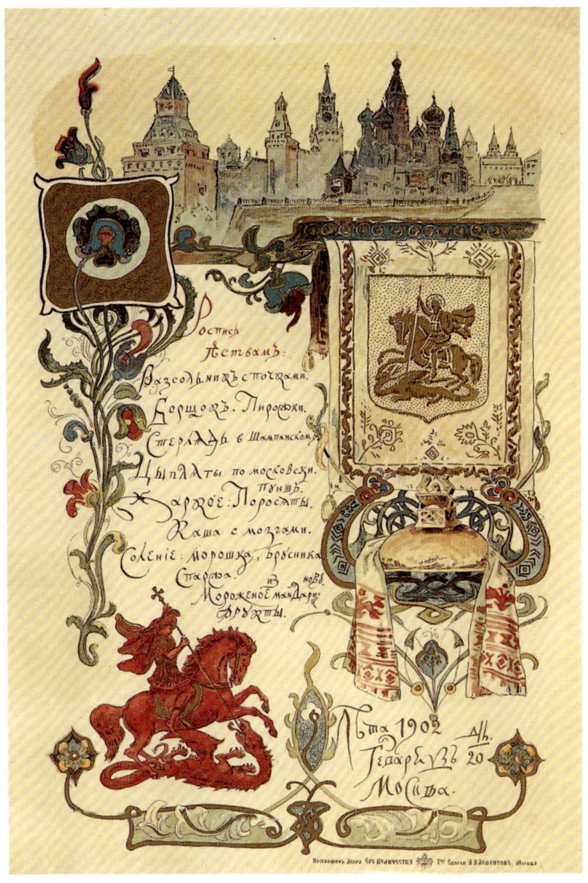

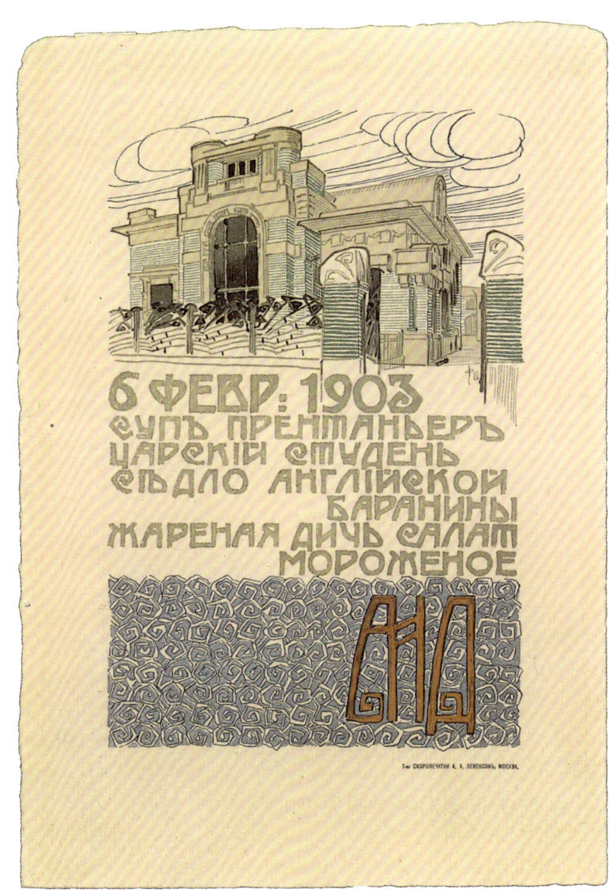

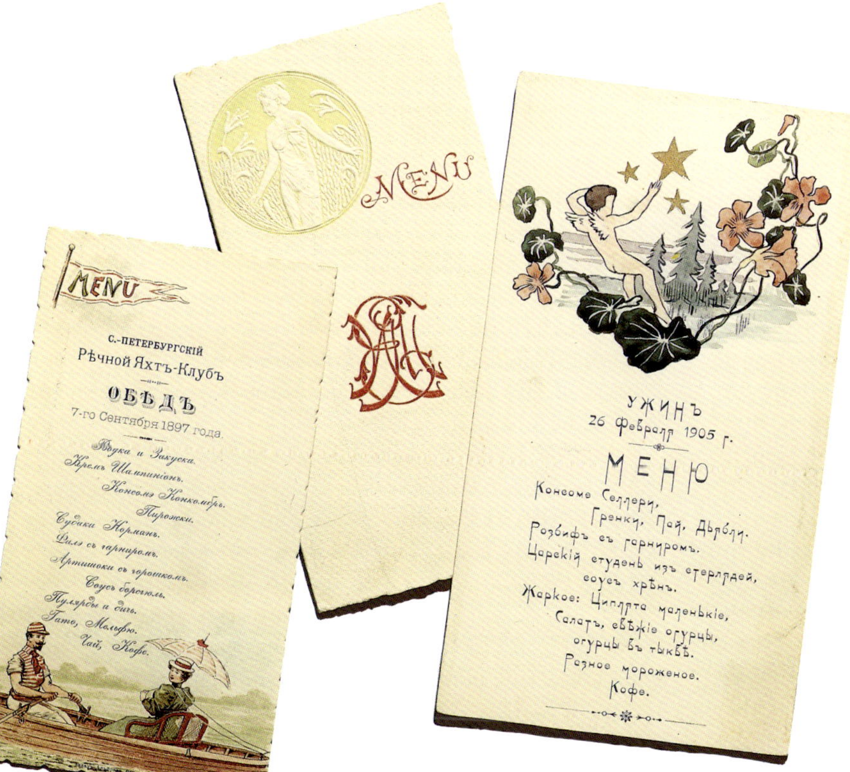

TOP LEFT: **Unknown artist**
546. Menu, Moscow, 20 January 1902
Colour lithograph, 39 × 29
State Lenin Library

TOP RIGHT: **Fedor Shekhtel'**
370. Menu for house-warming party,
6 February 1903, with general view of
the mansion of A. I. Derozhinskaya
Colour lithograph, 39 × 56.2
A. V. Shchusev State Museum of Architecture

BELOW LEFT: **Unknown artist**
545. Dinner menu for St Petersburg River
Yacht Club, 7 September 1897
Colour lithograph, 16.5 × 9
State Lenin Library

BELOW CENTRE:
Unknown artist
549. Dinner Menu, 2 February 1910
Embossing and painting, 17 × 8.5
State Lenin Library

BELOW RIGHT: **Unknown artist**
547. Supper menu, 26 February 1905
Watercolour and gold paint, 20 × 11
State Lenin Library

14

STYLE MODERNE IN RUSSIAN SCULPTURE

OL'GA ZABITSKAYA

tyle Moderne and sculpture – the combination may seem rather unexpected. When speaking of *Art Nouveau* or *Style Moderne* we think first of architecture, including interior decoration, then of refined graphic art, stage design, decorative art, and, finally, of the image of life in this period; least of all do we think of sculpture as an independent art form. The statement of the French scholar and critic Jean Cassou that *Art Nouveau* "certainly did not suit all aspects of art"[1] applies most obviously to sculpture. Indeed, the basic formal and artistic characteristics of the "new style" and the aspirations associated with it would seem to be opposed to the artistic essence and plastic language of sculpture. *Art Nouveau* is decorative, two-dimensional, verbose, grandiose and controlled, while sculpture is monumental, three-dimensional, laconic and spontaneous; it is difficult to find any area of mutual understanding.

In Russia this initial contradiction between the style and the art form was vastly increased by the distinctive history of Russian sculpture, which, unlike Western sculpture, had no long-established tradition. Only at the turn of the century, after accumulating cultural and artistic experience, did it find its own creative potential and embark on a path which led it – after such a long period of stagnation – to an unexpected and rapid rise. It was no accident that patriarchal Moscow, the guardian of the national "soul", became the centre of the renaissance of sculpture. Here a whole school of Moscow sculptors was formed; their work, despite the differences of importance and personality in their talents, formed a single masterly movement in art and determined the course of Russian sculpture in the twentieth century.

The main distinguishing feature of this movement was its new-found creative freedom, which recognised as the only authority the nature of sculpture itself, with its quite distinct artistic character. Having only just escaped from the fetters of the Academy and of the Wanderers, and having freed itself from dependence on literary and philosophical influences and the dictates of painting, sculpture was in no hurry to fall under the sway of the

programmatic rules of the "new style". However, this freedom enabled artists, in pursuit of their own personal artistic goals, to participate in many art movements, including *Style Moderne*. As a rule, the greater the gifts of a sculptor, the more fully and deeply were purely sculptural possibilities exploited, and work could not be allowed to be bound by the framework of a style; conversely, lesser talents would be eager to establish a relationship with a style which was attractive because of the different nature of its artistic problems, preventing any confrontation with the deeper requirements of plastic art. In the latter case, sculpture became one of the various means of expression within the complex language of *Style Moderne*, its purpose being to form an organic part of the particular world of the style. Its value lay in the tactical occupation of an interior space or the surface of a wall of an architectural volume, subordinated to a common idea, and not in the expression of the sculptor's artistic personality. Consequently the greatest convergence with *Style Moderne* was frequently found in the work of gifted but superficial artists and in the sculptural work of painters. The great masters, impelled by their creative quest, went their own way, which might sometimes coincide with or intersect the style, but the success of any alliance that was formed depended on the specific nature of their gifts.

One of the most brilliant figures in Russian sculpture at the turn of the century was Sergei Timofeevich Konenkov, whose creativity flowered at the time when artists were in search of new goals. Of peasant stock, Konenkov was a naturally gifted sculptor who applied his Michelangelesque talent with a truly Russian breadth and assurance. His remarkable ability to use all the resources of sculpture – as a completely independent art form – his natural feeling for materials and his ability to transmit this feeling through the finished pieces, enabled him to create works of unsurpassed artistic power. Konenkov's full-bodied, violent art, a total embodiment of the sculptural principle in the strict sense of the word, was at the opposite pole to the subtlety, the almost morbid refinement of *Style Moderne*. Paradoxically, however, he was responsible for some of the most captivating examples of this style in sculpture. The aesthetic programme of *Style Moderne* with its cult of beauty had affinities with Konenkov's innate feeling for the harmony of form and so coincided with his own creative quest. The diversity of Konenkov's gifts also corresponded to the multi-faceted aspect of the new style, and the convergence both in their areas of interest and in time made some of the works of this sculptor, indeed some groups of his works, harmonious with certain forms of *Style Moderne*. For example, a tendency to antique classicism which appeared in his work following his journey to Greece corresponded to the interest of the new style in ancient art; and the lyric theme of the wooden idols, the well-known *Stribog* (p.185) and *Stari-chok-polevichok*, which expressed the creative transformation of the artist's own relationship with nature, with the forests and with Russia, coincided in formal terms with the Neo-Russian, national-romantic form of *Style Moderne*.

Konenkov's decorative work, orientated towards stylistic unity with architecture and interiors, remained entirely personal. In the wooden relief of the panel *The Feast* (pp.210–11), designed for the dining-room of a Moscow private residence, there is a striking combination of rich plastic carving with a sure feeling for style, and this natural sculptor subordinates the dynamic figures to the overall decorative pattern, compelling them to form part of the ornamental scheme. Konenkov's version of *Style Moderne* was not conscious or programmatic, but rather the result of a creative interchange between the artist and the time; his work preserves all the properties of true sculpture, and he used the decorative motifs of the style almost as coded phrases within the sculptural language.

There was a quite different contact with *Style Moderne* in the case of Anna Semenovna Golubkina, another great artist who contributed to the renaissance of Russian sculpture. In her origins, in the scale of her work and in the creative direction she followed she had much in common with Konenkov – their family backgrounds, their studies at the Moscow College of Painting, Sculpture and Architecture, their vocations as sculptors, their obsessiveness, their talent – but her tone and character were completely different. Golubkina's gifts were contradictory, complex, sometimes unharmonious in artistic terms; she shared with many Russian artists an unceasing agonized searching for truth. Having absorbed well the lessons of Rodin and of Impressionism, Golubkina moved in the direction of more intense internal drama and expression. While Konenkov's connection with *Style Moderne* was the shared perception of the world through the poetry of beauty, Golubkina was attracted by the nervousness and morbid refinement of the style, and her work shows affinities with the Symbolist element in *Style Moderne*. In the few works by her in which the influence of the new style is clearly felt, such as the vase *Mist* (p.20), there is a certain overloading with ideas, a striving for symbols and for multiple meanings; the piece has a particular sombreness characteristic of the artist's

world view, which does not entirely match the rather "salon" nature of the work. It was basically difficult for Golubkina's talent to coexist with *Style Moderne*, as it did not have the same lightness and organic qualities as Konenkov's; Golubkina's art, with its characteristic anguish, disrupted the aestheticism that was one of the principal precepts of the style.

If the artistic response of Konenkov and Golubkina to *Style Moderne* and the new culture around them might perhaps be characterized as subconscious, in the works of two other major sculptors of the same Moscow circle, Vladimir Domogatsky and Nikolai Andreev, it was programmatic and fully conscious. Domogatsky was one of the few artists to combine a mastery of sculpture with an innate understanding of the aesthetic system of the new style. Although his work cannot altogether be categorized as *Moderne*, it is close to the style, as was that of most innovative sculptors of the time, and he himself was undoubtedly a representative of the *Moderne* culture. An aristocrat, a true intellectual, a scholar and researcher of art, he was connected with *Style Moderne* by the spirit of his own life, tastes, and aesthetic outlook. Domogatsky had the ability to introduce sculptural forms into the familiar *Moderne* interior without sacrificing their plastic qualities. The choice of model, the image, the movement of the sculptural masses, the curves of the lines, all embody the tastes and principles of the new style. The works of Domogatsky reflect not a chance enthusiasm for the art currently in fashion, but an anxious relationship with it, based on a deep penetration into its beauty and enchantment.

Nikolai Andreev, sculptor of the well-known monument to Gogol' in Moscow, also had a conscious relationship with *Style Moderne*. A talented person, a professional writer and a fine graphic artist, Andreev became a sculptor by force of circumstances rather than by vocation. His work is characterized by intellect, taste and feeling. A notable stylist, he rapidly accepted and mastered the principles of the new style and used them to create artistic images not just in sculpture but in other fields. His finest works, such as *Bacchante on a Goat* (p.182), are equal to the best productions of Western European *Art Nouveau*. The decorative qualities and the significance he gave to colour, line and silhouette indicate a complete mastery of the stylistic language. Having "passed his examination in style" with honours, Andreev turned to the solution of purely sculptural problems; but there is a certain light-weight quality, a hollowness to the forms of his works which are in conflict with sculptural principles, and it was no accident that the artist was attracted to ceramic art with its decorative and painterly possibilities.

Mikhail Vrubel's sculpture occupies a special place in Russian art. A great artist, a true painter, organically linked to the culture of *Style Moderne*, his approach to sculpture was that of a painter. Indeed it would not be entirely accurate to classify the works he produced in multicoloured majolica as sculptures. This is a special art form which, depending on the creative urge of the artist and taste of the client, can take on the nature of painting, of decorative architectural detailing or of applied art. However, when placed in a *Moderne* interior, all the forms of Vrubel's majolica became subordinate to the architectural unity dictated by the style. Vrubel's ceramics are normally associated with the Neo-Russian strain of *Style Moderne*, because of his participation in the Abramtsevo group, the cradle of the "Russian style", because of his attraction to images of pagan mythology, transformed through the music of Rimsky-Korsakov, and his predilection for Russian folk tales. However, for all the coincidences between the nationalist artistic quest and Vrubel's own interests, his unique, burning talent could not be confined by any strict adherence to a particular programme or by the methodical study of the real features of folk art. The artist lived in his own enchanted world of colour and form, and he would apply his creative genius to any theme that appealed to him, be it the Russian images of *Sadko* or the *Sea King* on decorative dishes (p.229), the stylized mask of a lion – used both on a gatepost and as part of the decoration of a stove (pp.19, 198) – or the bust entitled *Lel'* (p.178). Indeed, it is the colour, a personal painterly fusion of national traditions, that is the strongest aspect of his ceramic sculpture; with their glittering play of jewel-like tints, these works are a gloriously seductive artistic achievement. From the point of view of style, Vrubel's majolica work unquestionably corresponded to the *Moderne* passion for decorativeness

and universality in art, and it provides a clear example of the anti-sculptural nature of the style, since these works made by a painter conform to the system of the new style far more than the works of greater sculptors. It is noteworthy that many painters of this period tried their hand at sculpture; the *Style Moderne* enabled them to create works that met the general requirements of the style without ever penetrating into the essence and principles of this complex art form.

This brief discussion of the relationship of sculptors to *Style Moderne* cannot fully reflect the whole complex problem of "*Style Moderne* and sculpture", nor can it describe the many variations on this relationship which occurred. However, it can serve to demonstrate that the *Moderne* did not, on the whole, determine the main direction for Russian sculpture at the turn of the century, but was merely one small path within the artists' creative quest. Nevertheless, each artist reacted in one way or another to the new style in art, whether by the conscious application of its aesthetic principles or by an unconscious absorption of the "drug" of *Style Moderne* from the cultural environment.

NOTE

1 Jean Cassou, Emile Langui, and Nikolaus Pevsner, *Le Source du XX-me siècle*, Paris, 1961, p.22.

15

SCULPTURE

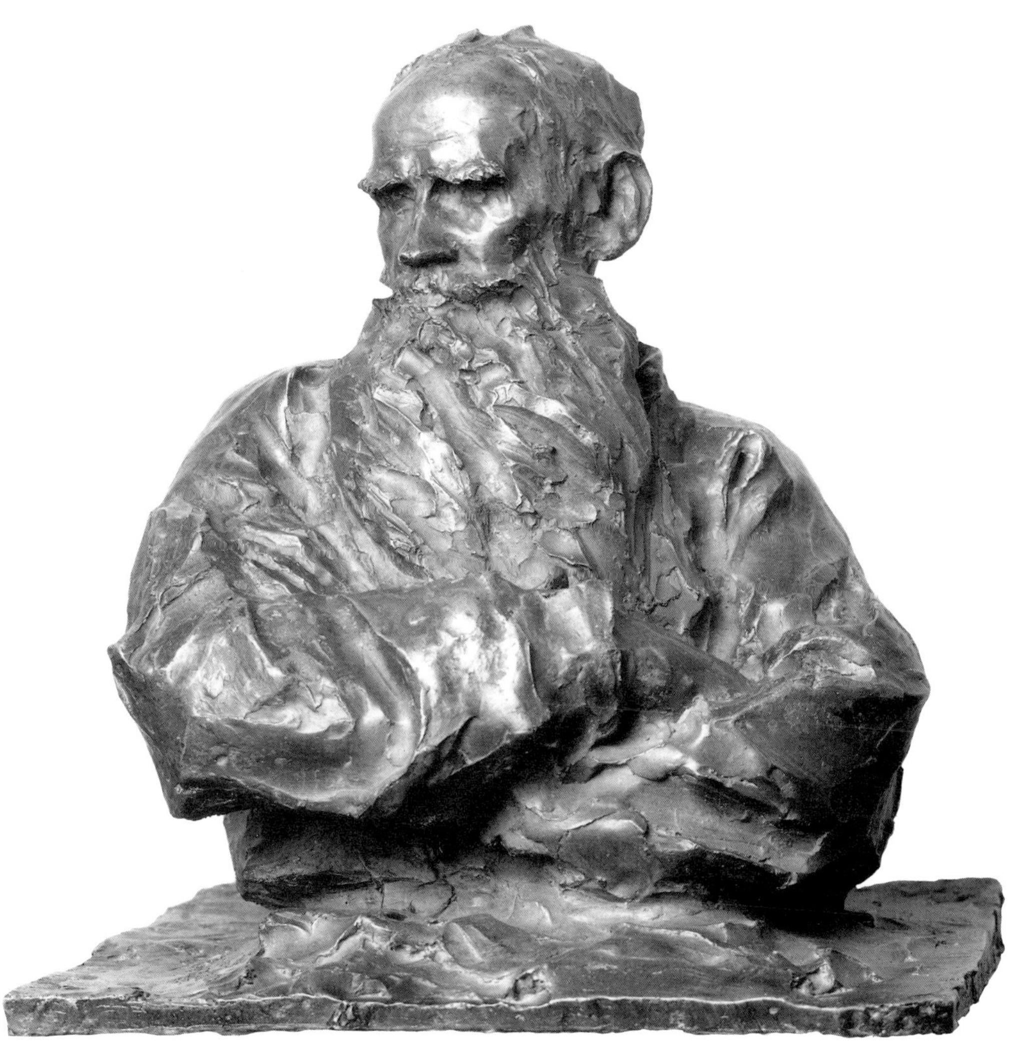

Pavel Trubetskoi
432. Portrait of Lev Tolstoy
1899
Bronze, 34 × 32 × 30
State Russian Museum

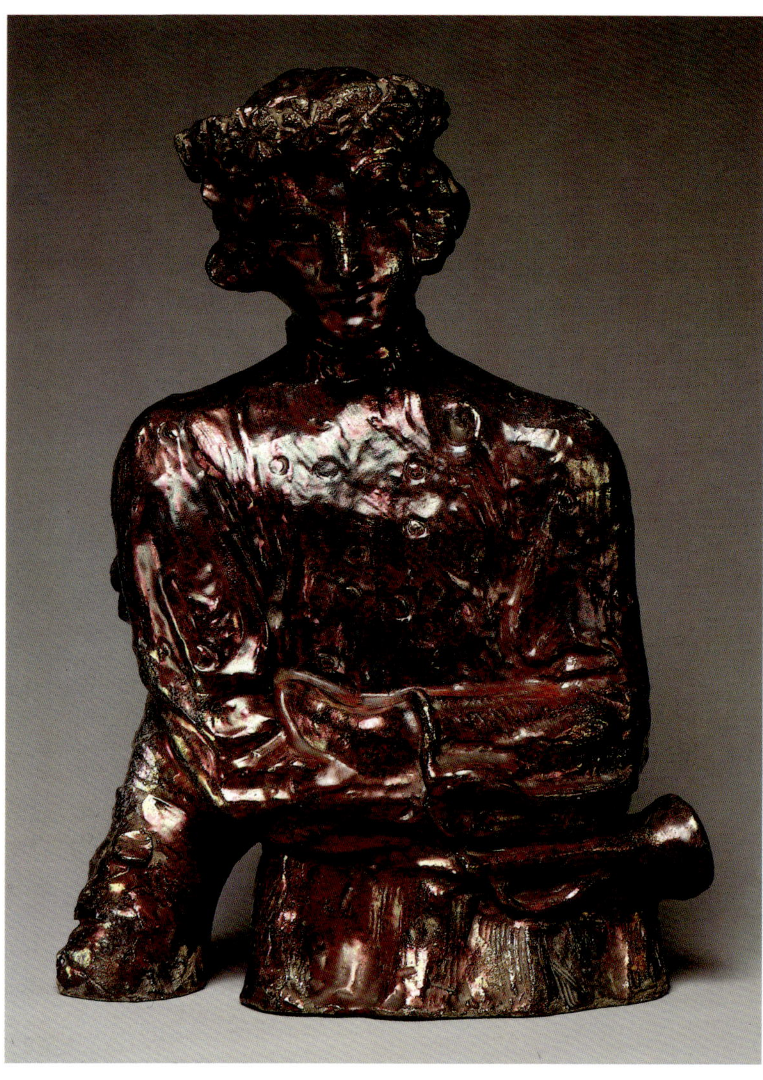

Mikhail Vrubel'
462. *Lel'*
1899
Majolica, 44 × 31 × 17
State Tretyakov Gallery

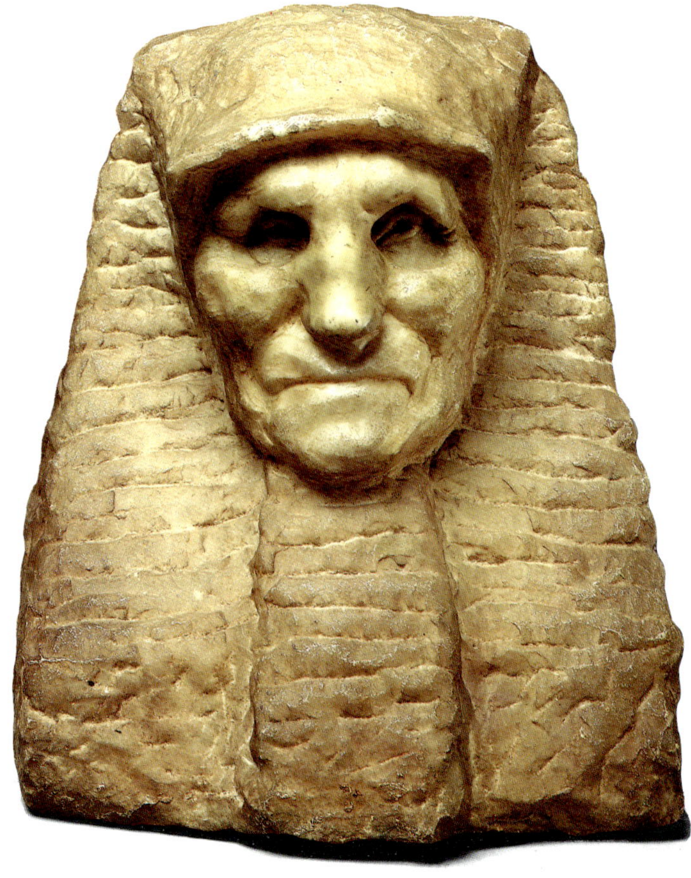

Anna Golubkina
133. *Old Woman*
1908
Tinted marble, 39 × 33.5 × 20.5
Carved signature on right of bust
State Tretyakov Gallery

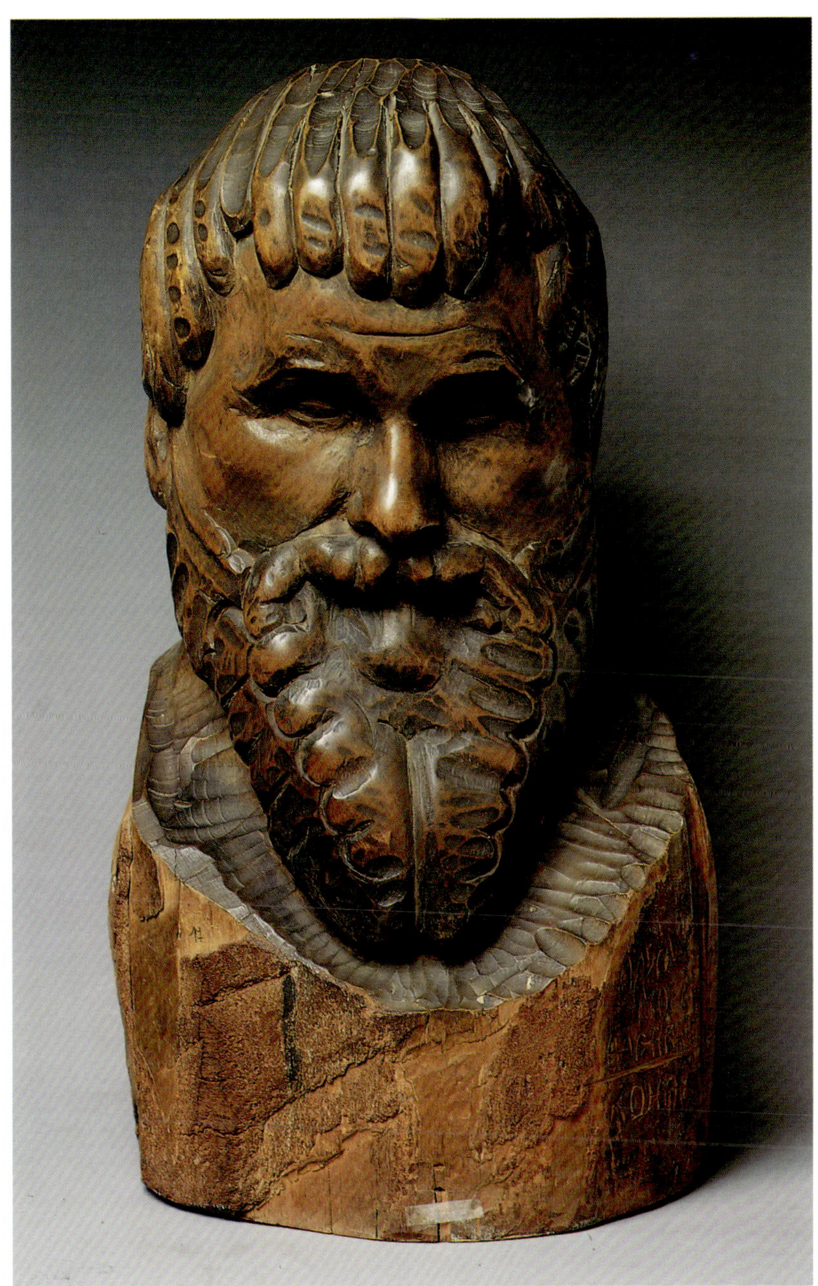

Sergei Konenkov
173. *Portrait of Vasily Denisov*
1909
Wood, 50 × 27.5 × 25
State Tretyakov Gallery

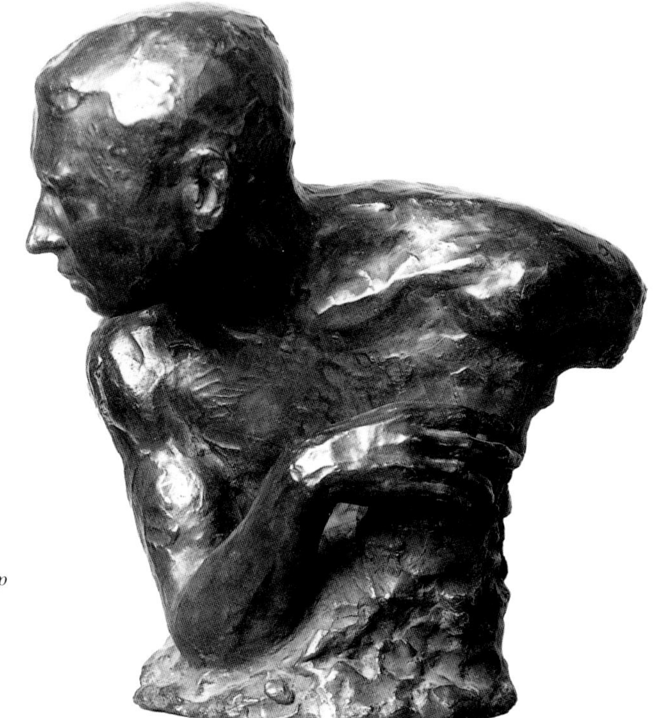

Dmitry Stelletsky
408. *Portrait of Boris Anrep*
Paris, 1909
Bronze, 30.5 × 23 × 15
State Russian Museum

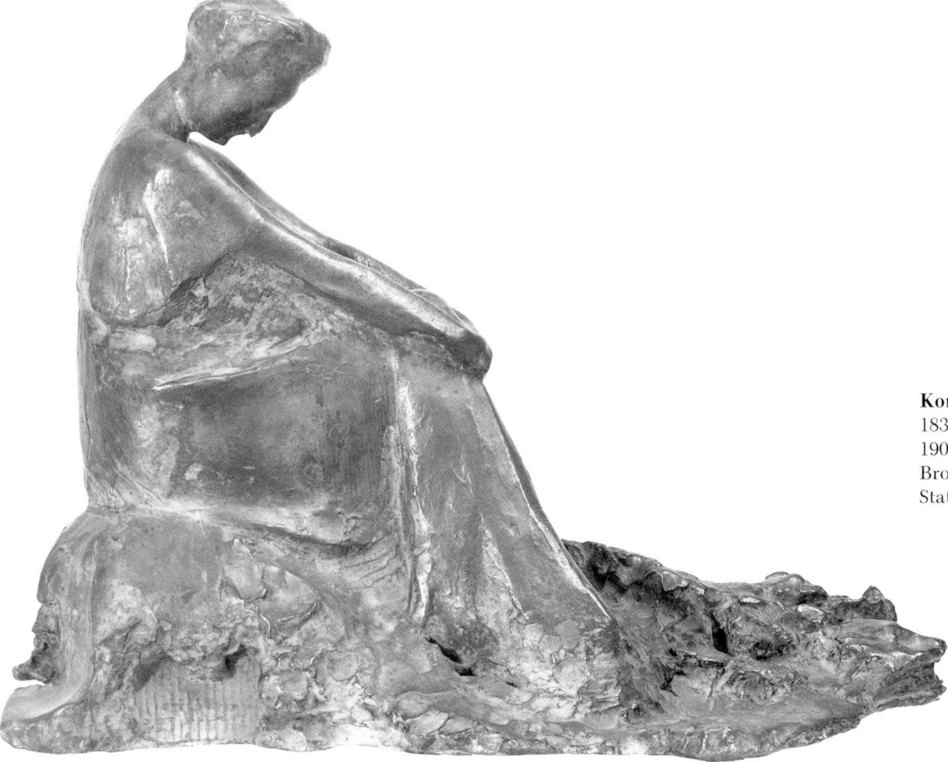

Konstantin Krakht
183. *Portrait of Margarita Morozova*
1905
Bronze, 45 × 58 × 44.5
State Tretyakov Gallery

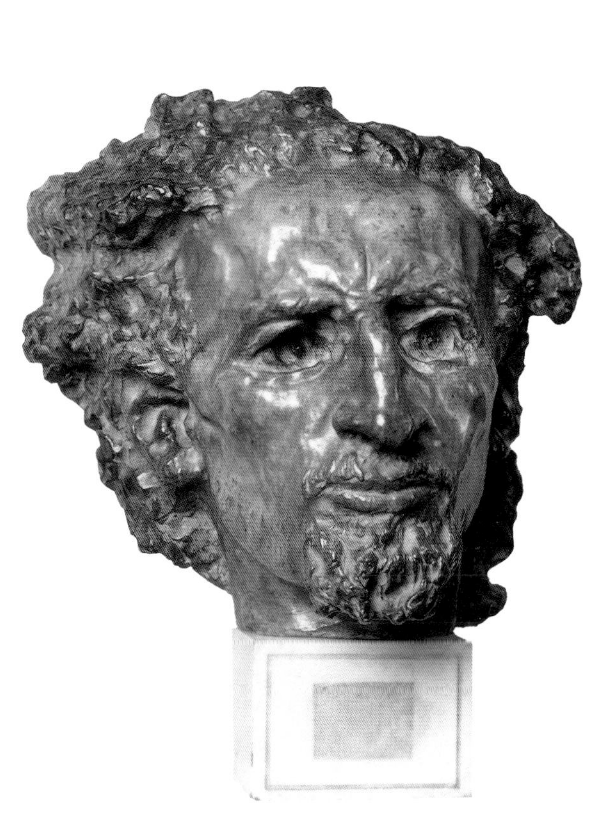

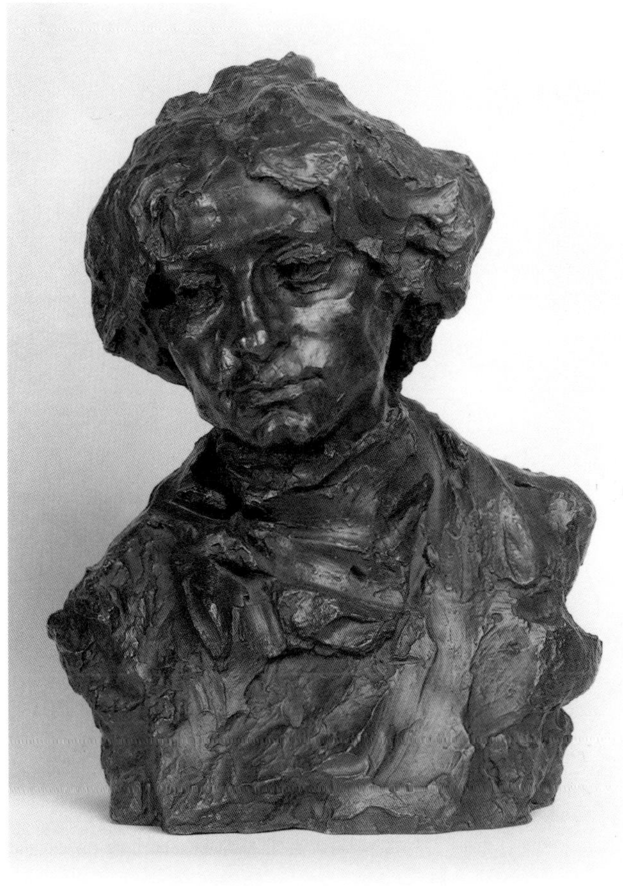

ABOVE LEFT: **Serafim Sud′binin**
410. *Anger*
Paris, 1906
Bronze on marble base, 39 × 40 × 34
State Russian Museum

ABOVE RIGHT: **Anna Golubkina**
131. *Portrait of Mariya Sredina*
1904
Bronze, 48 × 35 × 25
State Tretyakov Gallery

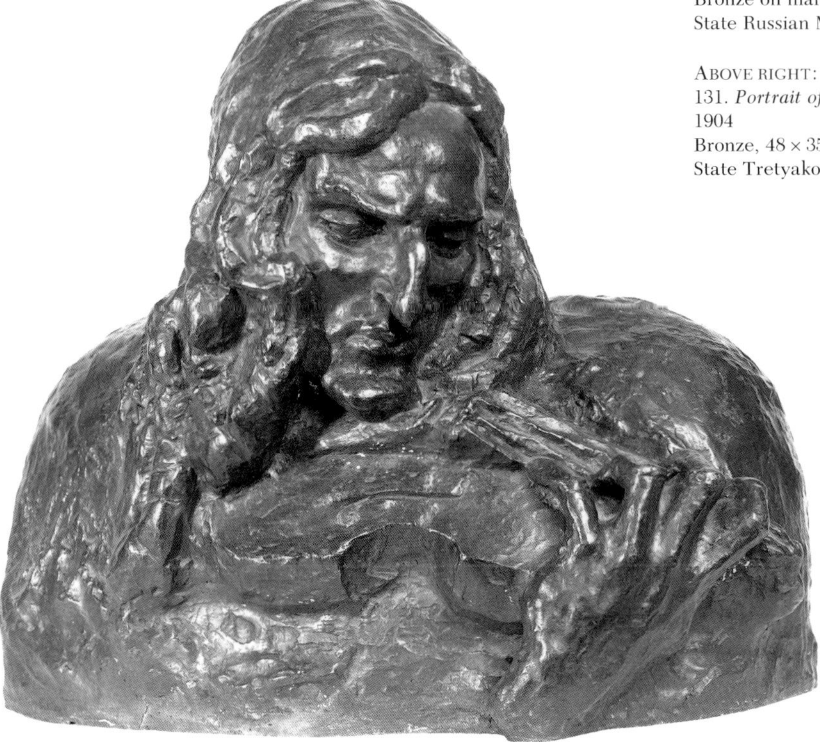

Sergei Konenkov
172. *Paganini*
1906
Bronze, 54 × 68 × 35
State Tretyakov Gallery

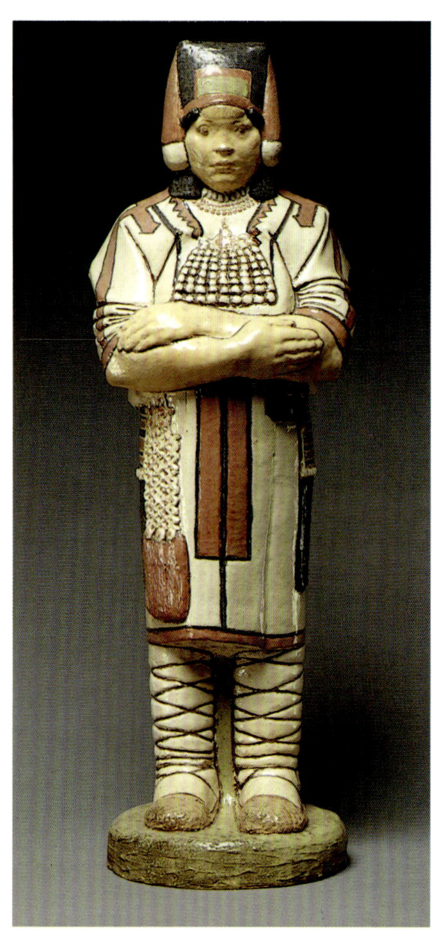

LEFT: **Nikolai Andreev**
8. *Mordvinian Woman with Folded Arms*
1915
Ceramic statuette decorated with painting, slip
and glaze, 53 × 18 × 16
State Tretyakov Gallery

BELOW: **Nikolai Andreev**
6. *Bacchante on a Goat*
1905
Terracotta painted in polychrome,
46.5 × 55 × 21
State Tretyakov Gallery

OPPOSITE: **Nikolai Andreev**
10. *Decorative Mask*
1914–15
Chimneypiece decoration with a portrait of the
Moscow Arts Theatre actress Mariya
Nikolaevna Germanova
Ceramic enamelled in colours, 38.5 × 31 × 18.5
State Tretyakov Gallery

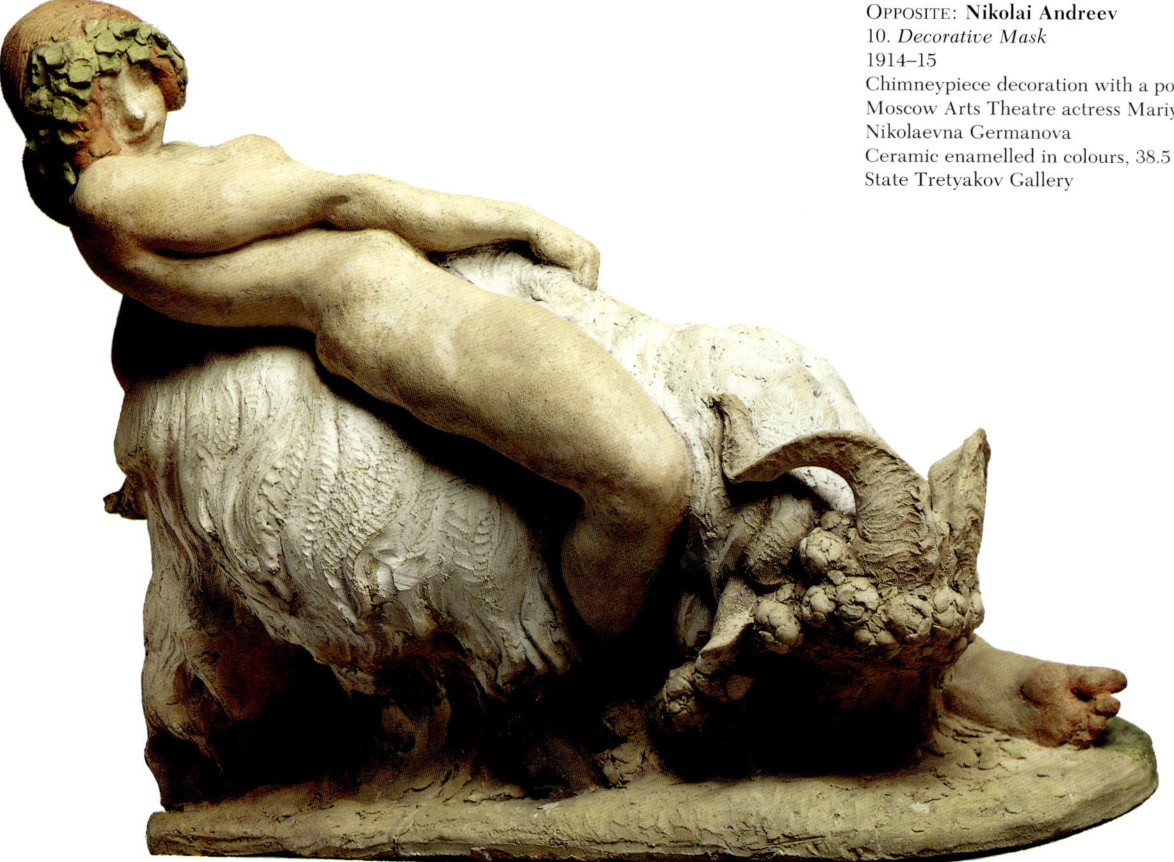

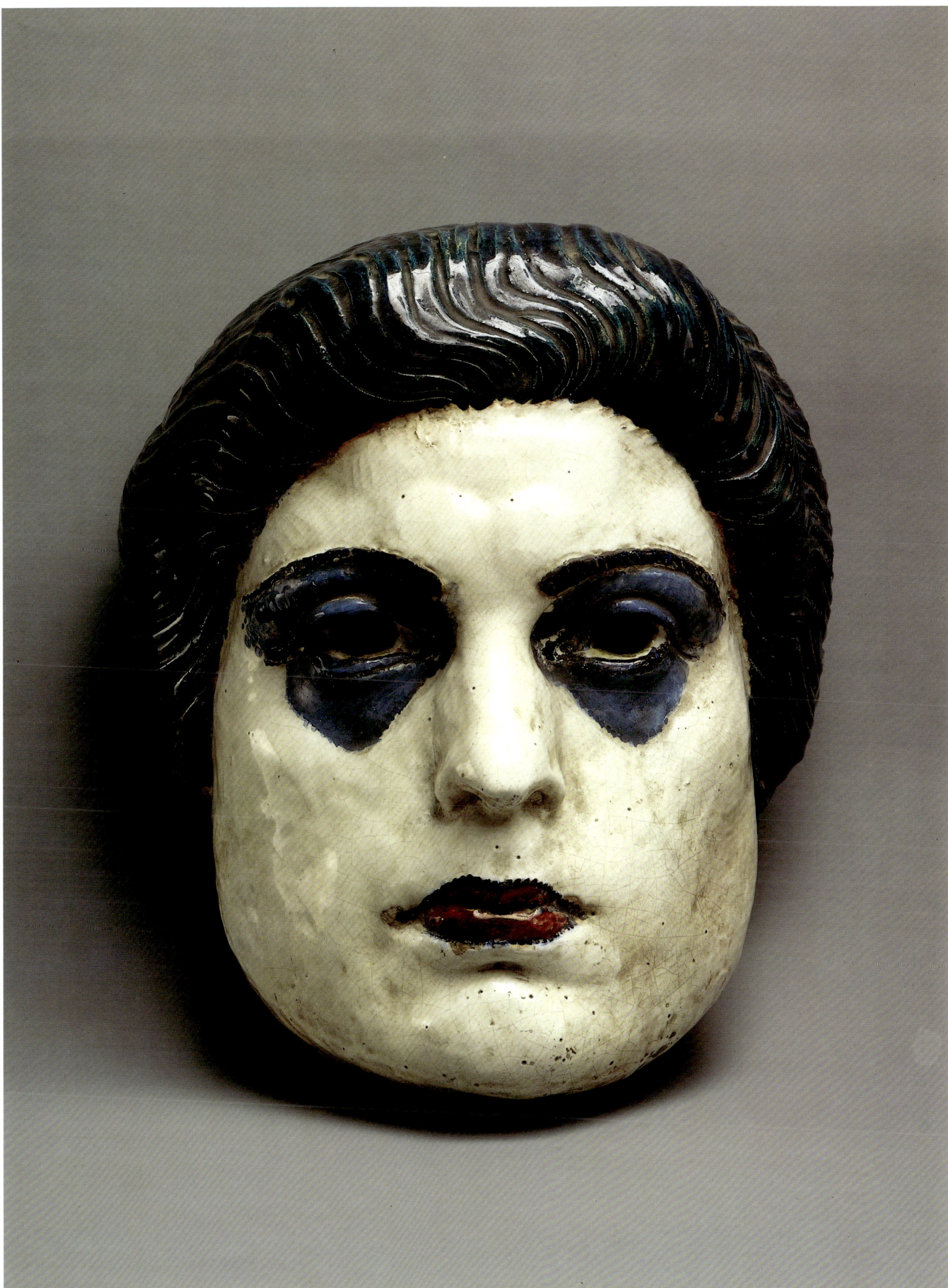

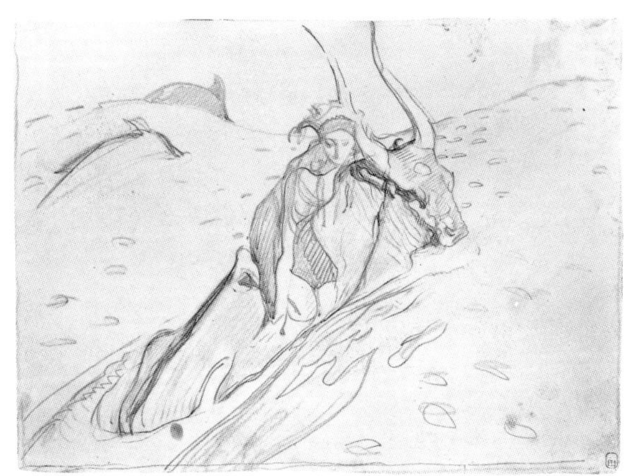

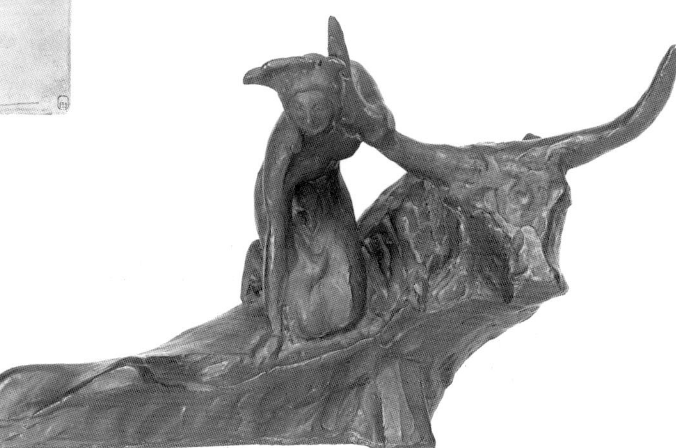

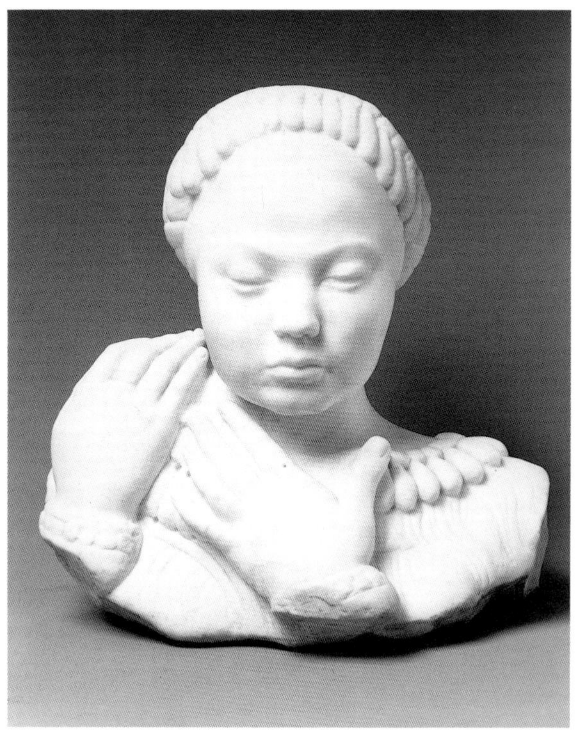

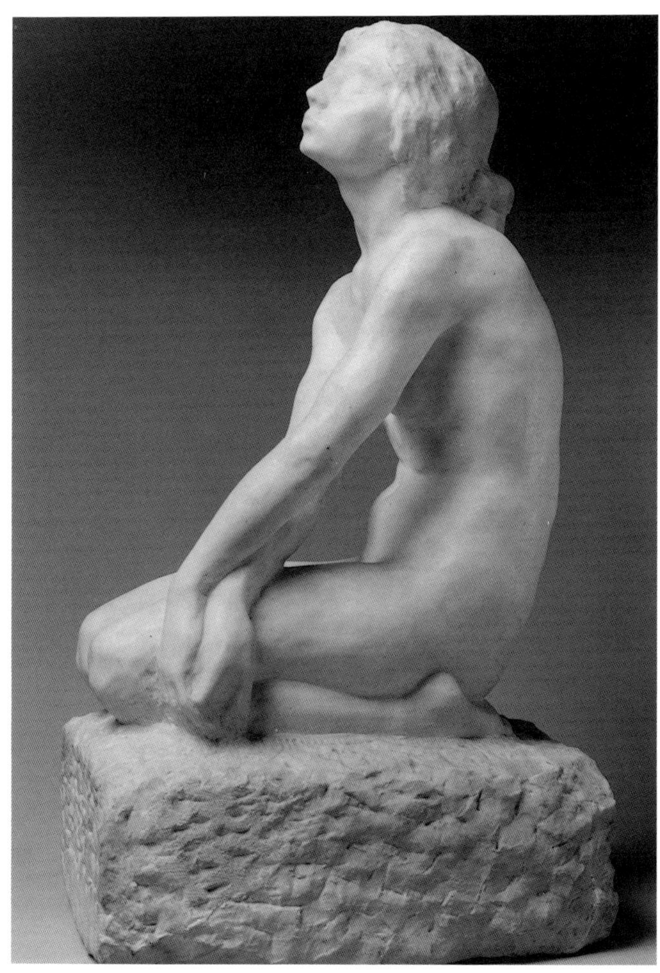

TOP LEFT: **Valentin Serov**
313. *Rape of Europa*
1910
Lead pencil on paper, 23.7 × 31.4
State Russian Museum

TOP RIGHT: **Valentin Serov**
314. *Rape of Europa*
1910
Bronze, 28.5 × 43.5 × 24.5
State Tretyakov Gallery

ABOVE: **Sergei Konenkov**
174. *Beloved*
1909
Marble, 40 × 37.5 × 28
State Tretyakov Gallery

RIGHT: **Vladimir Domogatsky**
100. *Kneeling Female Figure*
1913
Italian marble, 54 × 23.5 × 29
State Tretyakov Gallery

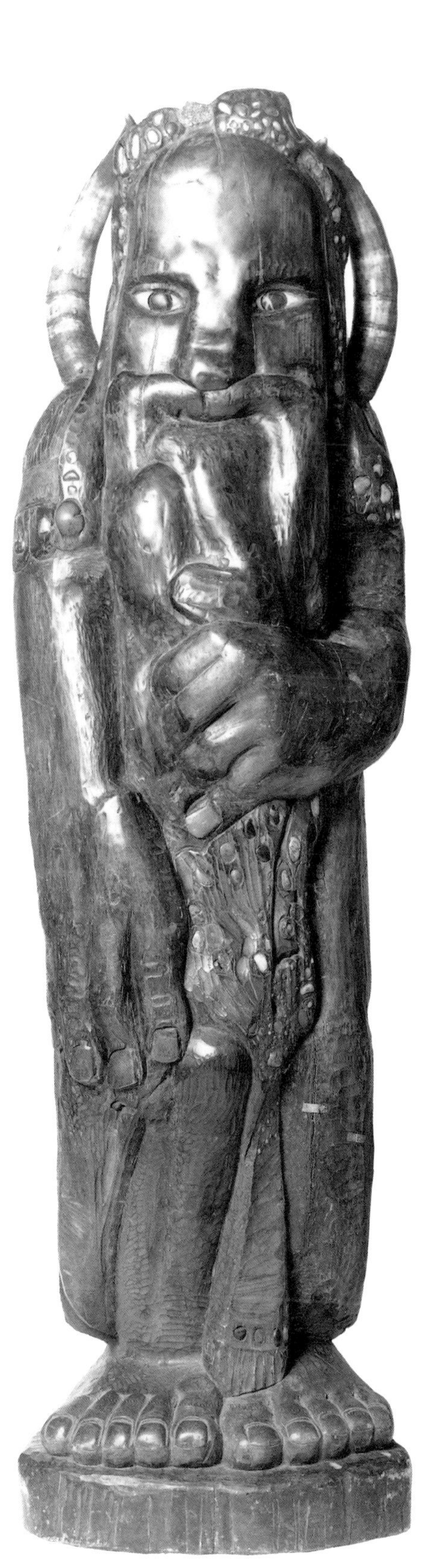

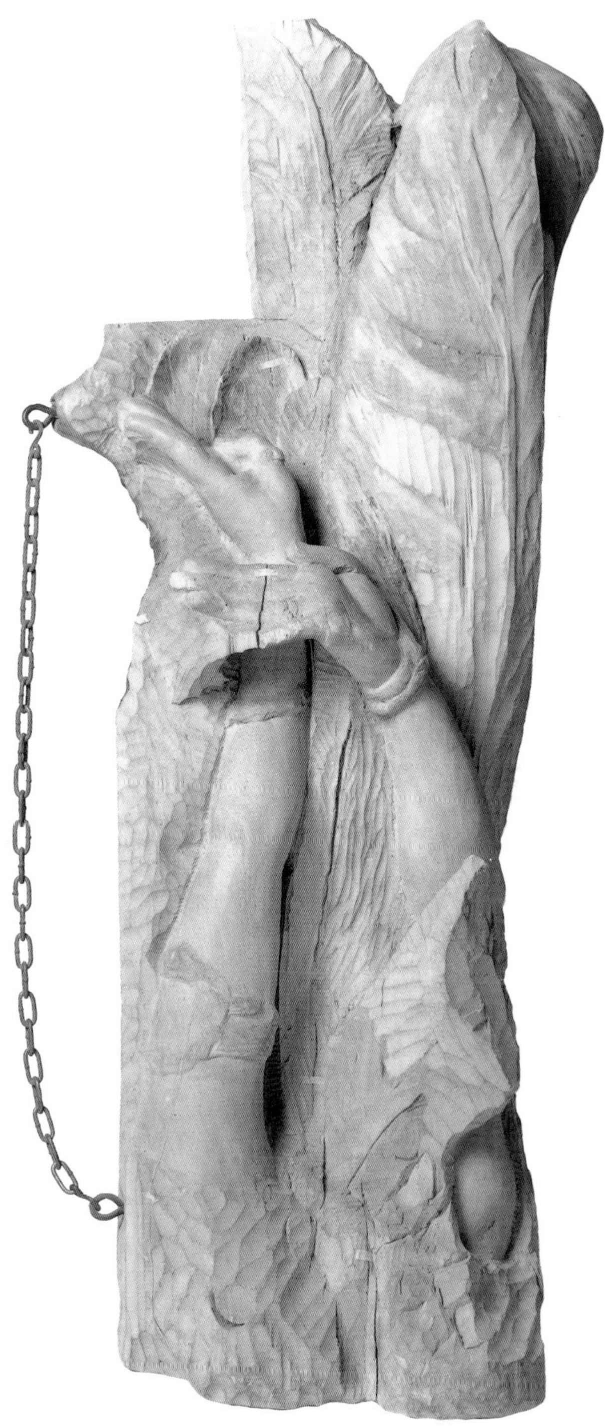

Above: **Sergei Konenkov**
177. *Arms of a Seraph*
1916
Wood, 159 × 66 × 33
State Tretyakov Gallery

Left: **Sergei Konenkov**
176. *Stribog*
1910
Coloured and inlaid wood, 175 × 46 × 43.5
State Tretyakov Gallery

16

MOSCOW *STYLE MODERNE* ARCHITECTURE

LYUDMILA SAIGINA

The work of Moscow architects such as Fedor Shekhtel', Lev Kekushev, William Walcot (Val'kot), Illarion Ivanov-Shits, Adolf Erikhson, Gustav Gel'rikh, Aleksei Shchusev, Il'ya Bondarenko, Ivan Kuznetsov, Vladimir Pokrovsky, Ivan Fomin and Leonid Vesnin reflected the characteristics of the architectural quest of the 1900s, which resulted in the birth and evolution of the *Style Moderne* in Russia.

In Russian architecture at the beginning of the century, *Style Moderne* was the strongest creative trend; it rejected the programmatic historicism of the eclectic architectural system of the second half of the nineteenth century, determined the directions of new research and led to the conception of many new forms and methods. It clearly displayed the life-affirming principle that characterises all Russian culture after it had absorbed the high civilising ideals of nineteenth-century Russian literature and painting. The tendency towards mysticism and the influence of the Decadents were less strongly reflected in Russian *Moderne* architecture, and this fact played a decisive part in the rational aspirations of this style. Because the new style was created at a time when the great social transformation of Russia was beginning, it too played a role in the dramatic struggle which was taking place between different philosophies in every sphere of Russian intellectual and social life.

The increased spiritual needs of the Russian bourgeoisie in the pre-revolutionary period led to the social demand for the creation of their own culture, something that could give a genuinely new expression to the ideals of the third generation of the Russian merchant class, who had played such an active part in social change in Russia. The social demand determined the geography of the *Style Moderne* and its fields of activity. The commercial and industrial centres of Russia – Moscow, St Petersburg, the towns of the Volga, the Urals and Siberia, and also the Ukraine and Central Asia – became the arena for the wide diffusion of the *Style Moderne* into urban building.

The problem of the relations between Russian *Moderne* and Symbolism became central to the process of the establishment of the new style. Symbolism was a universal feature of the artistic consciousness of the period and it was one of the powerful currents of Russian literature. Consequently, the application of the term to architecture is particularly apt in the context of the representational aspects of buildings. The expressive language of *Moderne* architecture developed from the basic system of symbolic images: a specific plastic language, a preferred colour range and the employment of purified forms derived from the plant world. Together these could create unified decorative motifs expressed with the aid of a flowing plastic graphic line, but the actual structure of buildings also changed; the principle of free composition of volumes and spaces, and the adoption of asymmetrical plans made them resemble the creations of the natural world. Furthermore, the use of frame construction and of new building and decorative materials made it possible to reveal the beauty of functional forms, thus confirming the new architectural aesthetic.

In *Style Moderne* the boundaries between the languages of various genres of the visual arts were erased. Easel painting took on the features of monumental painting, sculpture took on those of painting, architectural forms were treated in a plastic way, and graphic art determined the character of the decorative ornamentation of buildings. The peaceful coexistence of fine art with the architectural structure contributed to a new emphasis on the organisation of the environment.

When the types of Russian *Moderne* buildings are examined as structural genres constituting the iconography of the new style, it is possible to identify particular characteristic features and distinctions. In Moscow we may speak of the cult of the individual private house, while blocks of rented apartments were most widespread in St Petersburg. In their use of natural stone as the favoured material for façades, in which symbolic decoration played a significant role, the St Petersburg *Moderne* architects showed affinities with the Scandinavian school. St Petersburg, the representative city of Russian Classicism, also saw the earliest appearance of classical tendencies within *Style*

Moderne, reviving the traditions of Russian artistic culture of the eighteenth and early nineteenth centuries.

The construction of public buildings – railway stations, cinemas, museums, shopping arcades – bore evidence to the preference for openness, publicity and display, while *Moderne* rationalism was clearly manifested in the architecture of commercial buildings, offices, banks and hotels.

Groups of exhibition pavilions formed a distinct genre. In these the features of the new style were more often combined with traditional national forms. This was a result of the function they were assigned as representing Russia at international exhibitions. However, while they manifestly reflected the national-romantic line of development within the *Style Moderne*, the forms of national architecture were subordinated to the prevailing "new style".

Churches, hospitals and almshouses, commissioned by philanthropic members of the merchant class, also tended to be designed in new "national" styles, based on stylisations of forms derived from the monuments of medieval Pskov, Novgorod and Yaroslavl', as distinct from the imitation and copying that had taken place in the preceding period.

THE NEO-RUSSIAN STYLE

The wealth and variety of artistic tendencies within the *Style Moderne* makes it more difficult to say just when it began and ended in Russia. The "classical" period of the style lasted from the mid-1890s to the mid-1900s, in other words the time when similar artistic processes were taking place in the other countries of Europe. However, the origin of the "national-romantic" or "Neo-Russian" version of the style lay in the 1880s in the activities of the artists of the Abramtsevo group who were brought together by the industrialist and art-patron Savva Mamontov. The search for new laws of design and the attempt to develop a new reading of the beauty of medieval monuments led to the creation of a "genuine art" capable of transforming the Russian way of life – an undertaking that is associated with artists such as Viktor Vasnetsov, Vasily and Elena Polenov, Konstantin Korovin, Aleksandr Golovin, Mikhail Vrubel' and others. It was as a result of these stylistic investigations and the artists' interpretations of the images of medieval Russian architecture and folk art that the *Style Moderne* developed in Russia.

The establishment of the style is bound up with the name of Viktor Vasnetsov, whose art became the main source for the development of the Neo-Russian strain. The leading magazines of the time, *Mir Iskusstva* and *Iskusstvo i Khudozhestvennaya Promyshlennost' (Art and Art Industry)* showed considerable interest in his work, and the strength of Vasnetsov's influence was also recognized by Shekhtel'. The first milestone on the road to the creation of the "new style" was the design for the church on the Abramtsevo estate, produced by Vasnetsov in 1881–82 (p.18). The artist employed a new sculptural combination of architectural masses, enlivened by an asymmetrical design and by the contrast between the smoothness of the wall and the restrained decoration. The severe, monumental appearance of this quite small church took on the features of an elusive fairy-tale mystery. The new means of artistic expression in the Abramtsevo church show innate affinities with the coming *Style Moderne*.

The Neo-Russian style was firmly established by Russia's contribution – a pavilion of crafts – to the *Exposition Universelle* of 1900 in Paris (p.19). The architectural form of the pavilion was designed by the well-known theatre artists Konstantin Korovin and Aleksandr Golovin: it was a synthesis of the characteristics of the Neo-Russian style with a significant element of decorative fantasy and a pronounced theatricality. The design concept of the exhibition complex was based on an exploitation of the pictorial qualities of silhouettes of varying heights, which were derived from examples of the wooden architecture of northern Russia. Theatrical planning and the development of effects of colour by means of the play of architectural volumes became an integral part of the national-romantic trend in the *Style Moderne*.

FEDOR SHEKHTEL'

The theatre was also the route by which the major representative of Russian *Style Moderne*, Fedor Shekhtel', came to this style. His work clearly reflected all the contradictory elements that had led to the establishment of the style. Unlike the Abramtsevo artists, who had effected an aesthetic transformation of national architectural forms, Shekhtel' came to the "new style" through the transformation of the spatial structures of Gothic architecture, a tradition which had come to Russia during the Romantic period. The Gothic style was primarily valued by *Moderne* artists for its inner organic nature, by which they understood a unity of architectural form and structure, decoration and function, and a closeness to the organic forms of the natural world. The emotional and spiritual qualities of Gothic architecture, its freedom and the boldness of its spatial structures, were particularly prized.

The turning-point in Shekhtel''s work was the Gothic private house built in 1893 for Z. G. Morozova on the Spiridonovka in Moscow (pp.47–8, 196–7). The composition of the façade was built up from a picturesque balance of masses, rather than a symmetrical arrangement. The design of the building "from the inside out" – based on a new relationship of form to functional requirements – determined the variations in exterior forms, while the freedom of design in the vertical plane and the role of the staircase as the principal axis about which the other rooms were grouped became a distinctive feature of Shekhtel''s subsequent work. This architect was the first to attempt the creation of an integrated and organic living space imbued with the spirit of mediaeval romance. He was also the first architect to commission Mikhail Vrubel', who had a great interest in monumental painting, to undertake the interior design (p.46). The architecture and interiors of this house are filled with fantastic figures, and although its decoration does not show any clear examples of the *Moderne*, the presence of the grotesque is in many ways close to the aesthetic of the style.

The new means of expression discovered by Shekhtel' and Vrubel', and their attempt to blur the boundaries between reality and fantasy, were applied with even greater effect in the interior of the Gothic study (1896) in A. V. Morozov's house in Podsosensky Lane in Moscow (pp.15, 50). The carving of the furniture, the panelled wall and the staircase leading from the study to the library is markedly stylised and organically integrated with the symbolism of Vrubel''s monumental panels on themes from *Faust* (p.198). The unexpected breaks in the vertical dimension of the space, the concentrated spiritual experience created by the symbolism of the paintings, the colour, the light effects, and the variety of decorative forms, enabled the architect to attain an extraordinary dramatic effect in the atmosphere of a small study.

In Shekhtel''s subsequent designs the search for new means of expression in architecture is associated with his work within the national-romantic tendency of *Style Moderne*. The new qualities appeared under the influence of the aesthetic views of the artists of the Abramtsevo group, with whom Shekhtel' had been directly associated since their joint work on the preparation of the All-Russian Exhibition of Art and Industry at Nizhny Novgorod in 1896. The culmination of the development of this Neo-Russian tendency in Shekhtel''s work was the complex of Russian exhibition pavilions he designed for the International Exhibition at Glasgow in 1901 (pp.50–52, 201). A picturesque composition of free-standing pavilions reflected the principles of construction of medieval Russian buildings. Shekhtel' produced a different architectural form in each pavilion, in accordance with the theme it was to represent, and the pictorial qualities of the volumes and forms and the musicality of the rhythmic repetition of details gave clear expression to the emotional content of the architecture of the pavilions. In the composition of their façades he made bold use of colour, contrasting the overall wall colouring with monumental painted panels. In addition to the painting, the combination of a traditional material (wood) with new ones (glass and metal) enabled Shekhtel' to create a refined range of colour for the whole complex. The innovative achievements demonstrated in the Glasgow complex were given permanent embodiment in stone two years later, when Shekhtel' built the Yaroslavl' Railway Station in Moscow (pp.53, 55).

The development of the national-romantic tendency in *Style Moderne* was also reflected in the work of such masters as Aleksei Shchusev, Il'ya Bondarenko, and Vladimir Pokrovsky. The individual styles and the range of interests of these architects, each of whom interpreted

national traditions in his own way, reflected the great latitude of artistic expression possible within the new style. Each could assess and re-evaluate in his own way the achievements and innate qualities of medieval Russian churches, interpreting their designs and structures in ways that corresponded to the *Moderne* aesthetic.

Shchusev's mastery of form enabled him to create a number of excellent buildings in Moscow, a memorial church (1904–08) on Kulikovo Field in the Ukraine (p.193) and the plan of an ecclesiastical complex for the city of Bari in Italy (p.193). Il'ya Bondarenko, like Shekhtel', was associated with the activities of the Abramtsevo workshops in his youth, but in his designs for religious buildings in the 1900s he developed a more generalized pattern for the church: compact, cubic and enriched with extensions and fantastic crowns of bell-towers. The flowing line of *Style Moderne* is felt in the drawings of helmet-shaped cupolas and in the outlines of decorative details.

Pokrovsky's adherence to the tradition of Russian pyramidal architecture is clearly displayed in his church designs. In an unbuilt design for a Historical War Museum (p.222) he developed a complex composition of volumes of different heights, recalling the asymmetrical picturesque planning of medieval Russian buildings. Stylised forms taken from mansions and medieval palaces were used by him in his design of a bank in Nizhny Novgorod (p.223). The powerful bulk of the deliberately exaggerated building contrasts with the historical origin of the structural forms. In this way the architect intensified the dramatic effect of a new building placed in an urban environment with the specific programmatic role of celebrating the rebirth of the traditions of the medieval trading centre. By combining the exposed textures of the timber frame with stylised painting on historical themes and refined decorative compositions Pokrovsky gave a unique colouring to the intense atmosphere of the interiors. The designs for paintings and decorative murals (p.222) are by the distinguished graphic artist Ivan Bilibin.

STYLE MODERNE PRIVATE HOUSES

The continuing search for artistic expression in plastic architectural masses, in new proportions, in the picturesque massing of volumes and in the refinement of decorative details, as well as in the experimental association of painting with architecture, is characteristic of the classical period of *Style Moderne* during the 1900s, and the private houses built by Shekhtel', Kekushev, Walcot and others give abundant evidence of its vigour.

The Moscow *Moderne* private house inherited the charm of its Empire predecessors. Since such houses allowed the style to be developed to the full, because of the architect's greater freedom in the choice of his means of expression, they became the paradigms of *Style Moderne*, its unique aesthetic declaration. Each house was created as a unified artistic organism, an ideally designed environment in which everything was permeated with the aesthetic principle. The unique "museum-piece" quality of the living environment was created with the Utopian desire of eliminating the boundaries dividing the artificially created specimen interiors from their everyday function. The Moscow private houses assimilated the principal features of all the various tendencies of the new style.

These features were most fully displayed in the well-known mansion of S. P. Ryabushinsky (pp.58–61, 206) built by Shekhtel' in 1900–02, the authentic masterpiece of Russian *Style Moderne*. Here the ideas of integrity and organic form are infused with spirituality. The theme of the whole building is the motif of the wave, symbolising a motion that is eternally renewed, unfailing, constantly reborn. Starting in the fence railings of the house, the wave, in the various phases of its existence – from its birth to its crest and its final complete extinction – fills the whole space of the building with its pulsating rhythm. The architecture of the house is characterized by the simplicity of the cubic form, the strict geometry of the planes and the clarity of the whole composition. The design of the façade allows for the interchange of dynamics within the pictorial composition and the duration of their perception in time. The contrast of the strict geometry of the architectural volume and the use of natural motifs in its ornamentation strengthens this sensation. There is an extraordinary intensity in the pictorial design of the façades, while subtle nuances are achieved in the combination of the texture and colour of the principal material with the pictorial qualities of the mosaic frieze. The compositional centre of the symmetrically planned house, the nucleus around which the action revolves, is formed by the hall and the main staircase. The vertical axis of the stairwell, exposed throughout the height of the building, keeps the composition in centripetal motion. The powerful plastic qualities of the staircase, built in stone blocks in the form of the frozen crest of a wave, are repeated in the design of the dining-room fireplace, which is made of the same material. The multiple significance of the symbolism and the polyhedral form of the details, repeated in multiple layers in the infinitely pulsating rhythm of the space, create in this house a fantastic world of images.

The façade of the mansion of A. I. Derozhinskaya (1901–02) in Shtatny Lane (pp.62–3, 202–5) is distinguished by a powerfully plastic design with deliberately enlarged details; the sensation of the real dimensions of the building is lost. The asymmetrical plan reflects the functional organization of the space, the centre of the composition being a vast hall. The interiors of the house have a graphic quality, governed by a refined geometry of form and space, with a predominance of pure linear compositions and a clear preference for simplified decoration. The rationalism is almost physically perceptible. Designs for hall murals on the theme of the "Times of Day" were commissioned from Viktor Borisov-Musatov but were never executed. The harmonious subject compositions with their peaceful rhythms and circular movements, the special luminosity of the images, the presence of a sad melody, and the bright palette used in the tonal arrangement would undoubtedly have softened the severity of the interiors.

In 1902 Shekhtel' designed a new building for the Moscow Arts Theatre, adapting an old building in Kamergersky Lane for this purpose. For a number of reasons, the architect was unable to rebuild the façade of the theatre, although a design for its reconstruction exists (p.57). However, the entrance doorways were redesigned and a high relief by Anna Golubkina, *The Wave*, in which the wave motif so typical of the new style was developed, was mounted above the main entrance. It was similar to an architectural ledge, although there was a real canopy; in other words the work of sculpture could in this case play the part of an architectural member with a specific function, and this became a characteristic feature of the *Style Moderne*. The spiritual inspiration of the playwright Anton Chekhov was the source of the artistic conception of the interiors of the theatre and of its symbol, a seagull flying over the waves. Shekhtel' rejected all the characteristic attributes of theatre auditoria of the period: rich and luxurious details, stucco and gilding. The plan of the auditorium, without any tiers of boxes, proved to be very functional, and the smooth curves of its walls were transformed in the foyer into an expressive plastic element of the decorative scheme.

Decorativeness and spatial exploration characterise the work of the distinguished Moscow architect Lev Kekushev. Like Shekhtel', he found his form of architectural expression by starting from the plastic qualities of exterior masses and the carefully thought-out display of the interiors. The intentional non-harmonization of architectural masses in the composition of the volumes and the abundance of decoration on the completed façades contrast with the emphatically severe design of the interiors. Examples of this are the house of O. List in Glazovsky Lane and the architect's own house on the Ostozhenka.

High quality and artistic expressiveness also distinguish the houses designed by William Walcot (Val'kot) in 1900 for the Northern Housebuilding Association. The expressive outline of his house for Mariya Yakunchikova with its graphically pure volume fits in elegantly with the surrounding buildings and can be seen to great effect from various points-of-view.

A pronounced sculptural quality in the façades, filled with strong projections, bay windows, balconies, and portals, combined with decorative stucco work, characterised not only the architecture of *Moderne* private houses, but also public buildings. A good example of work of this kind is the Hotel Metropol (1898–1903) in Moscow, the design of which was chosen by competition. A design by Kekushev formed the basis of its structural composition, but an additional competition was held for the architecture of the façade of the hotel, and a design by Walcot was chosen for execution (pp.54–5). The composition of this façade uses a whole arsenal of artistic media: the full and expressive plasticity of the architectural elements, the graphic ornamentation of the metal railings, the painterly majolica panels produced from sketches by Vrubel' and Golovin, and the sculptural frieze by Nikolai Andreev. The distinctive innovations in the façade of the Metropol were its composition, which followed the organisational principles of monumental painting, its indissoluble unity, and the way it was linked to the whole artistic conception.

MODERNE CLASSICISM

In the early 1900s, *Moderne* architects mastered the aesthetics of new forms of building construction and began to exploit the special possibilities of artistic expression provided by them, side by side with classic *Style Moderne*. In buildings by Shekhtel' such as the Bank of the Ryabushinsky Brothers (1903), the printing house of the newspaper *Utro Rossii (Morning of Russia)* (1907, p.64) and the premises of the Moscow Trading Society (1909–11, p.64), the artistic possibilities of frame construction were revealed. The design of the frame became the compositional basis of the façade: each rectangular module of the façade carried in itself the features of a distinctive ornamental detail. As always in the works of Shekhtel', the rational structures showed the subtle taste of the architect and his exacting choice of the elements of the restrained decoration, while he softened the severity of the purely geometrical volumes by rounding the corners. Shekhtel' always introduced an expressive decorative element into the geometrical lattice of his façades, emphasising the beauty of the refined volume. In the Ryabushinsky Bank building this was a delicate graphic relief in the form of a gently curving arc, with the visual function of drawing together the verticals of the façade, which moved apart in their upward foreshortening. In the printing house for *Utro Rossii* he displaced the stairwell block in relation to the main volume and introduced an arched motif into the entrance frame. In the composition of the façade of the premises of the Trading Society he included a beautifully designed sculptural arch in the yard entrance and treated each corner of the building in an individual way.

A different approach to the architecture of a commercial building was demonstrated by Roman Klein's design (1906–08) for the Muir and Mirrielees department store (pp.21, 217). He decorated the frame structure, which was clearly revealed in the façade, with elements of Gothic architecture, and the extreme stylisation to which the Gothic decoration was submitted prevented any conflict with its *Moderne* setting. The decoration was concentrated at the angles of the building, as suited its corner site.

Towards the end of the 1900s there were changes in Russian artistic life, and as interest revived in the traditions of national culture the *Style Moderne* fell into disfavour. In these years the final tendency within the new style, *Moderne* classicism, became widespread. Interest in Russian classicism, rejected during the later nineteenth century, had revived at the turn of the century, and the poetic celebration of the heritage of Russian classicism became a distinguishing feature of the artists in the *Mir Iskusstva* group. The Empire style was seen to have many affinities with *Moderne:* the same understanding of the plasticity of the architectural structure and of space, the handling of the plastic qualities of masses, the refinement of detail, and the contrast between flat wall surfaces and decoration. The *Moderne* classical style was characterised by the graphic treatment of forms seen through the prism of *Style Moderne* aesthetics.

The most successful example of this new interpretation of the traditional Empire house is Shekhtel's own house (pp.64, 220), built on the free planning principle of the *Style Moderne*. A four-column portico conceals the stained-glass panels of the central hall, the nucleus of the composition. The classical elements of the façade – the calm smoothness of the wall pierced with windows, the subtle entasis of the columns, the plasticity of the undivided volume, the conventional stucco motifs – are subordinated to the laws of the *Style Moderne* and treated with great refinement.

An example of the convergence of the two stylistic tendencies is the Merchants' Club built by Ivanov-Shits (pp.214–17). The central part of the façade is treated as an Ionic loggia, though without conforming to the strict rules of the order; while the pylons at the sides of the loggia are typical *Moderne* turrets. The design of the details, the window openings and transoms, and the canopy above the entrance are from the *Moderne* vocabulary, but simplified. Severe graphic lines and a certain geometrical dryness to the architecture and to the design of the interiors of this building reflect the personal style of the architect,

The most subtle stylistic experiments during the 1910s are found in the work done by Ivan Fomin within the tradition of classicism. This is distinguished by a free interpretation of Empire forms and a restrained unity of style down to the smallest details. However, these years saw a strengthening of the retrospective tendencies in Russian architecture, which resulted in the Neo-Classical phenomenon. This was radically different from the refined classicism of the *Style Moderne* with its free interpretation of Empire forms. Neo-Classicism strove to recreate as closely as possible the monuments of traditional architecture in contemporary buildings, and this was the movement that was to exert a potent influence on the leading tendencies of Russian architecture in the 1930s and 1940s.

17

ARCHITECTURE AND DECORATION

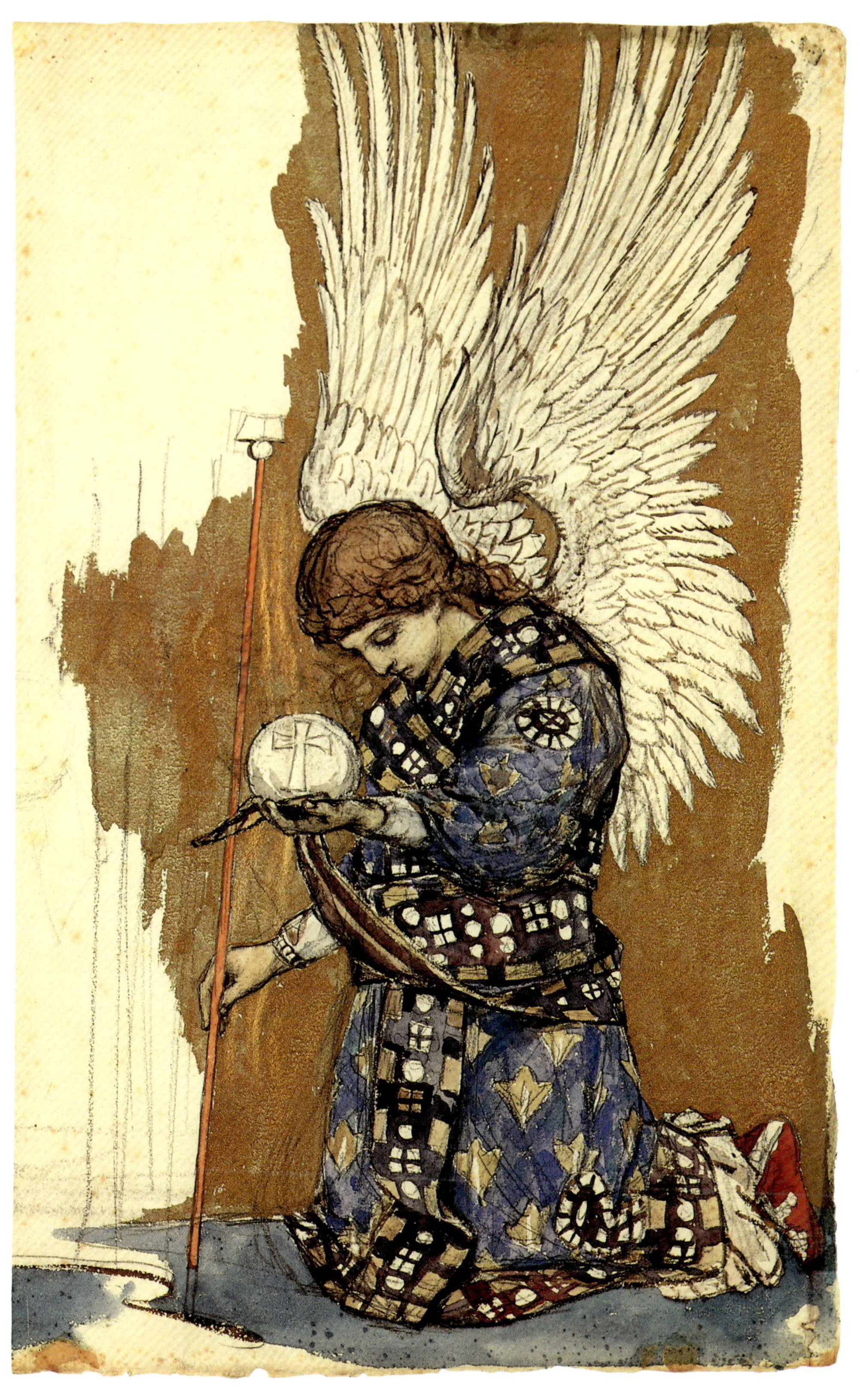

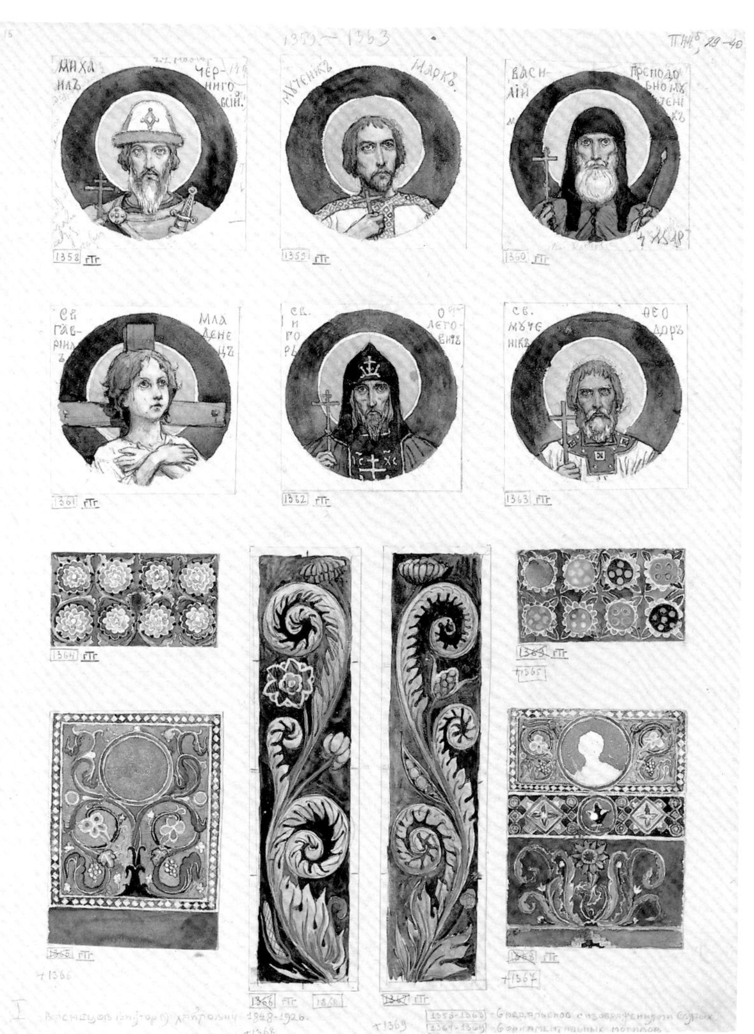

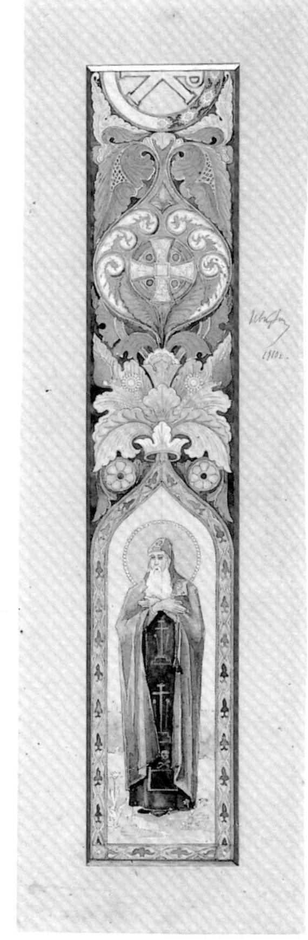

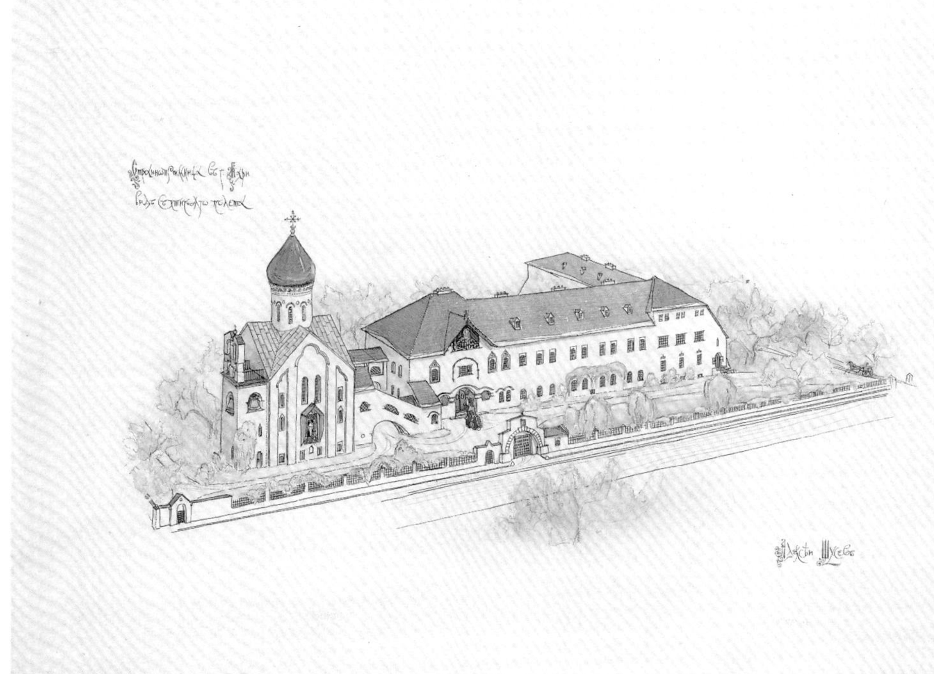

TOP LEFT: **Viktor Vasnetsov**
447. Designs for decoration of the
Cathedral of St Vladimir, Kiev (for full
details see catalogue)
1885–93

TOP CENTRE: **Ivan Kuznetsov**
188, 189. Two designs for
wallpaintings for a church on the
Medvedkovs' estate of Porech'e at
Zvenigorod, near Moscow
1899–1900
Mixed media on paper, 51.4 × 15.8;
36.2 × 16
A. V. Shchusev State Museum of
Architecture

RIGHT: **Aleksei Shchusev**
320. Almshouse and church for Nikolai
Mirlikinsky at Bari, Italy: bird's-eye
view
1912
Mixed media on cardboard, 50.4 × 67.6
A. V. Shchusev State Museum of
Architecture

PREVIOUS PAGE: **Viktor Vasnetsov**
446. *Archangel Michael Kneeling*
1885–93
Unrealized version of design for an
altar in the Cathedral of St Vladimir,
Kiev
Mixed media on paper, 48.7 × 30
State Tretyakov Gallery

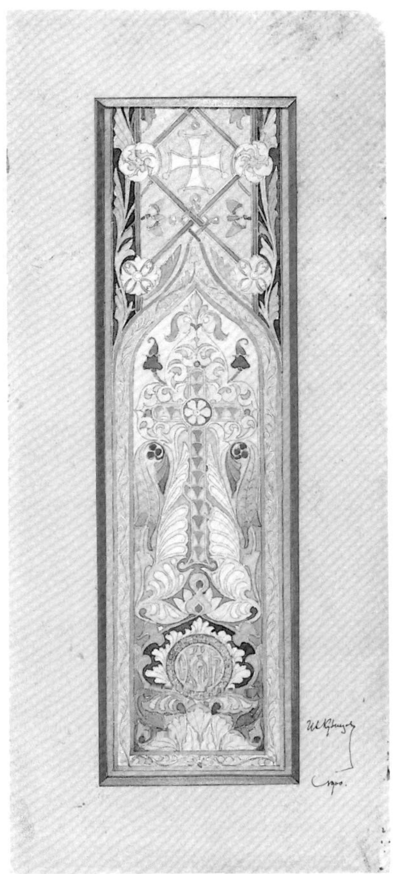

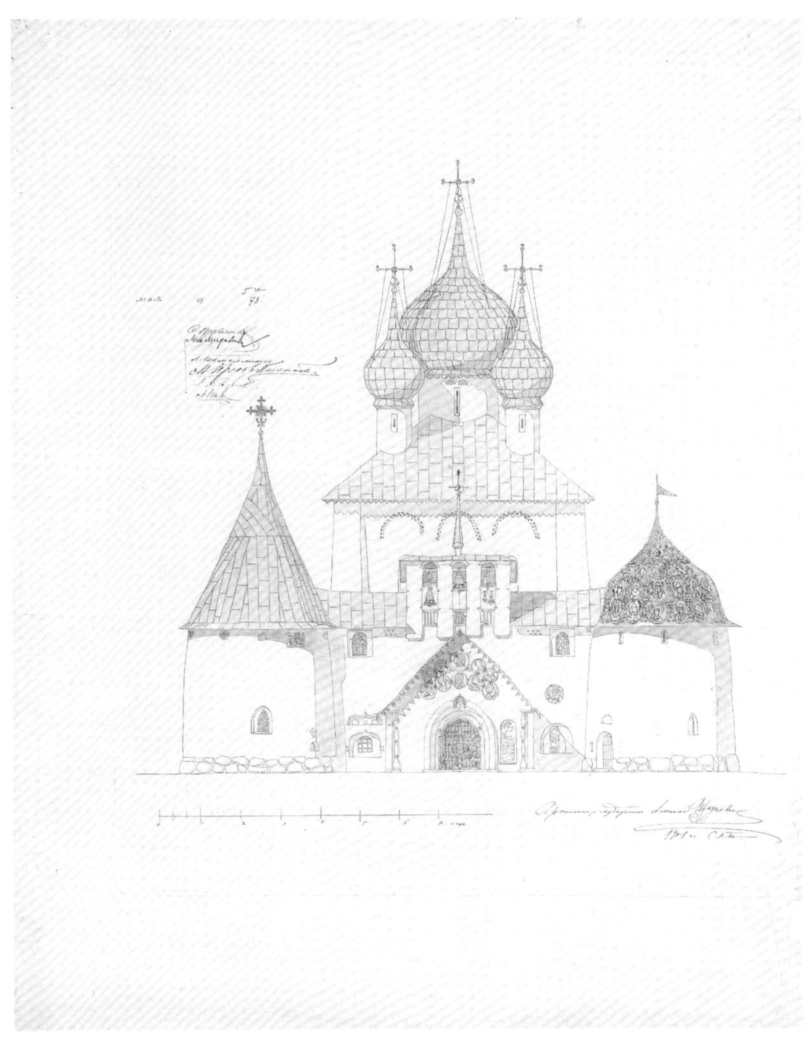

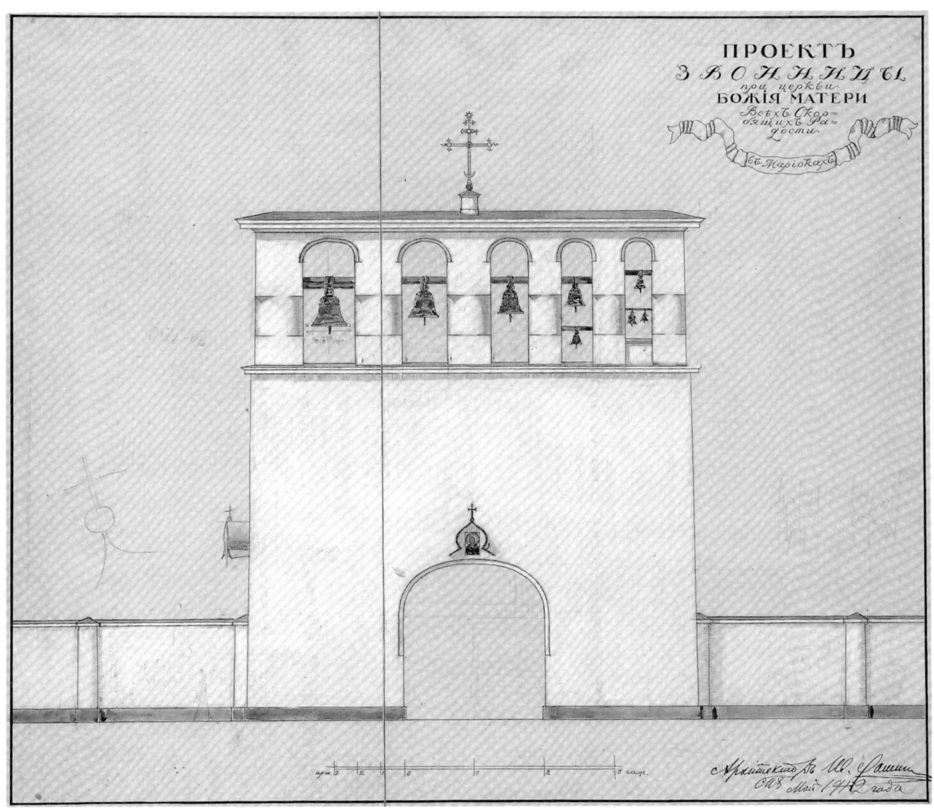
ПРОЕКТЪ
ЗВОНИЦЫ
при церкви
БОЖІЯ МАТЕРИ
Всѣхъ Скорбящихъ Радости
въ Териокахъ

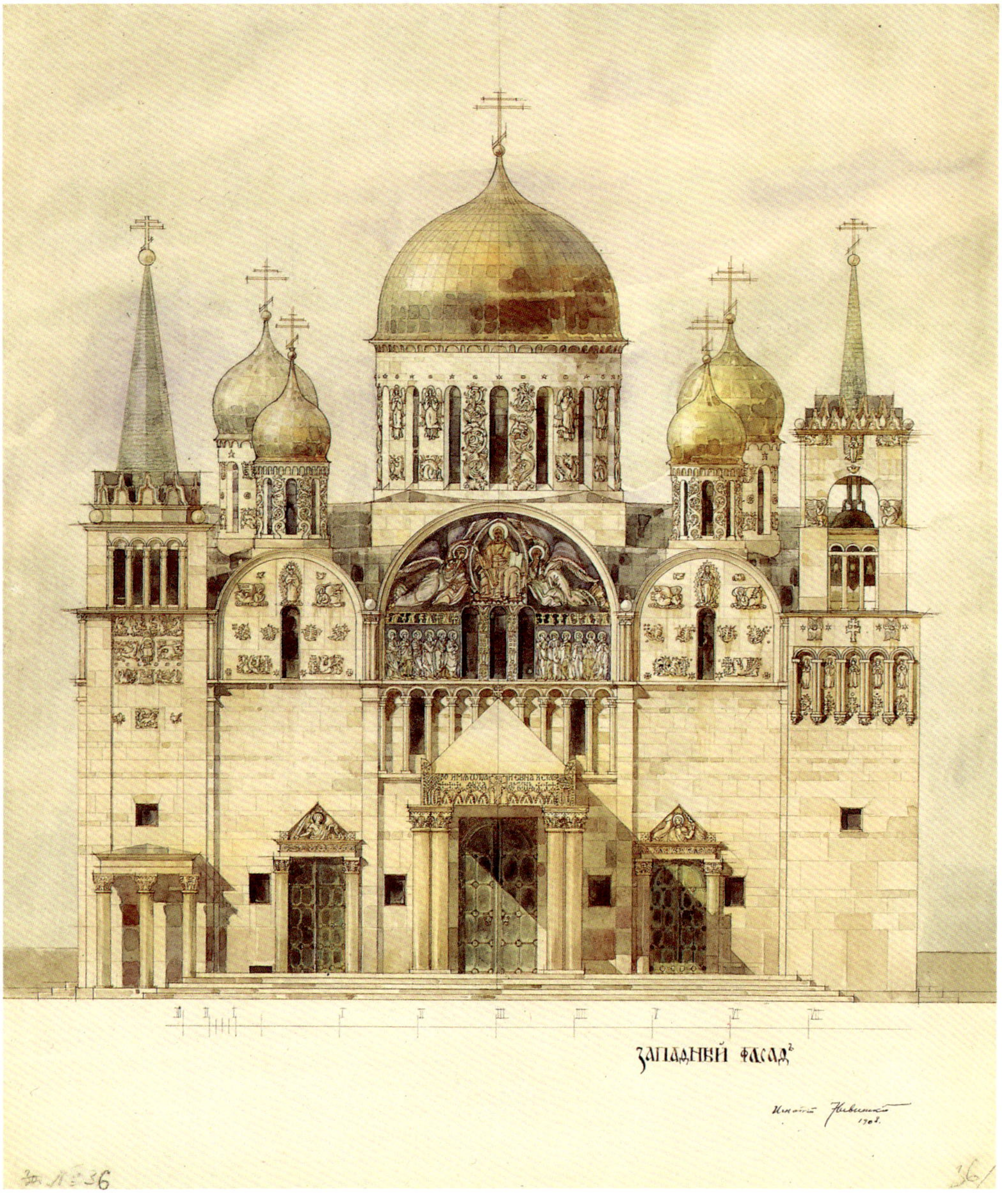

Ignaty Nivinsky
250. Competition project for the church on the
estate of A. M. Mal'tsev at Balakavo, Saratov
province (not executed): western elevation
1908
Ink and watercolour on paper, 58.4 × 48
A. V. Shchusev State Museum of Architecture

Fedor Shekhtel'
Competition project for the church on the
estate of A. M. Mal'tsev at Balakavo, Saratov
province (as executed)
1908–10

BELOW: 375. Western elevation
Mixed media on paper, 84 × 66.8
A. V. Shchusev State Museum of Architecture

OPPOSITE: 376. Longitudinal section
Mixed media on paper, 84 × 66
A. V. Shchusev State Museum of Architecture

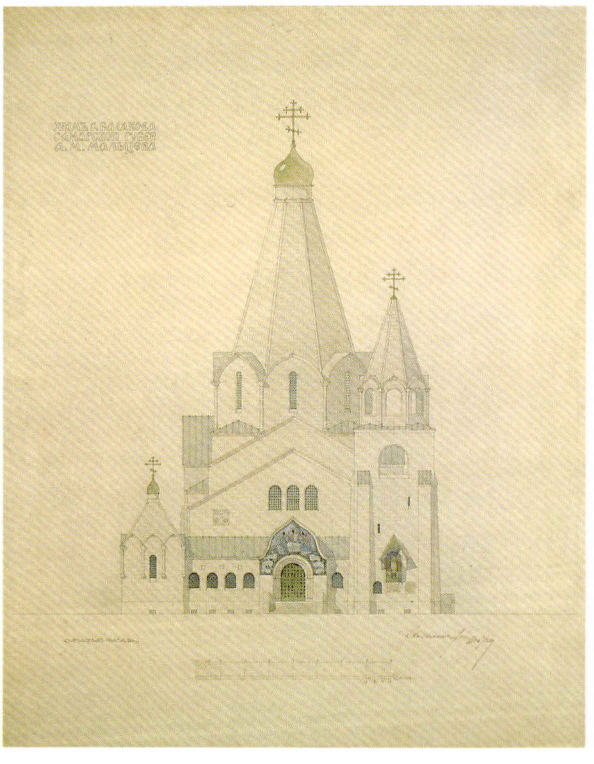

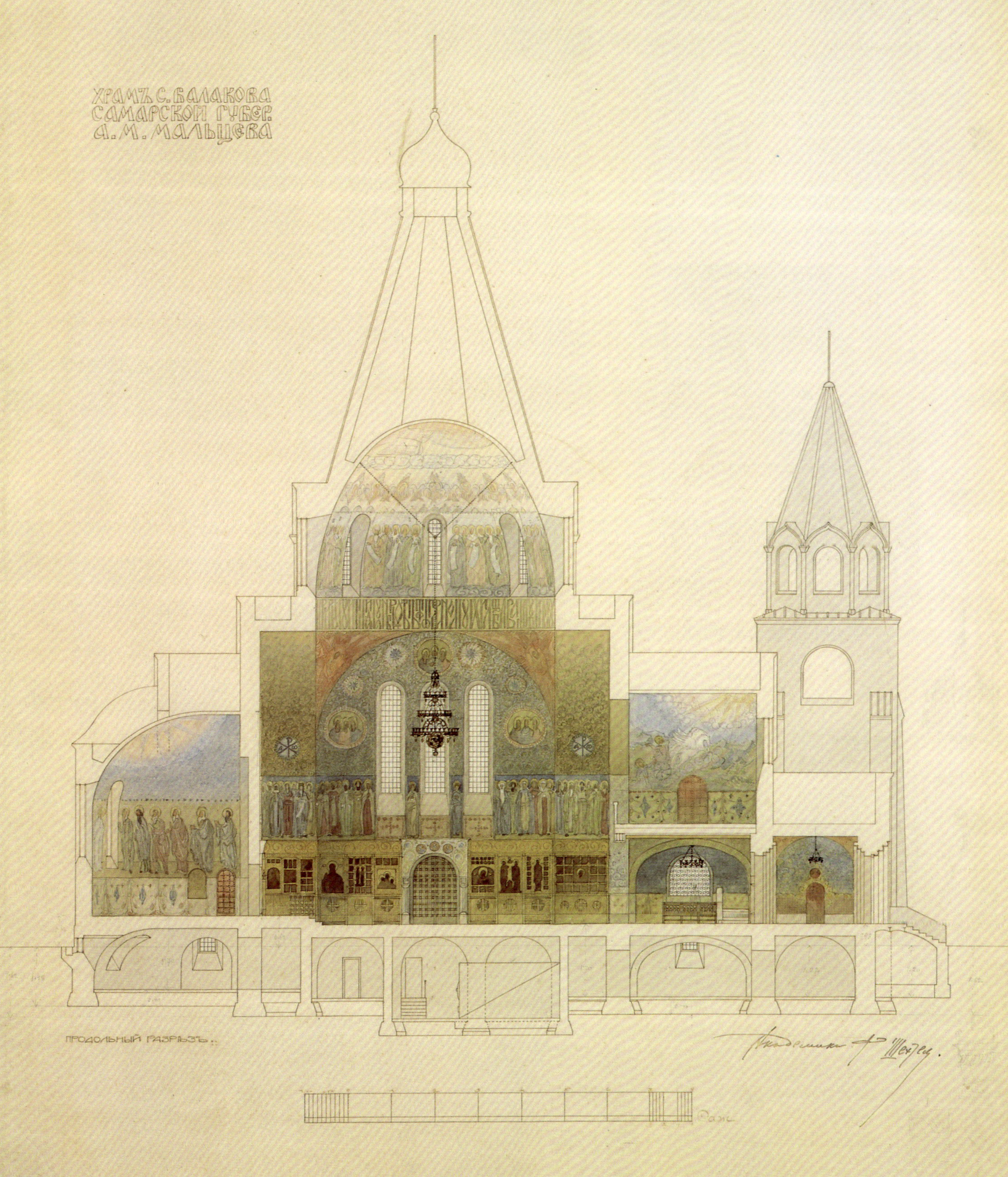

ХРАМЪ С. БАЛАКОВА
САМАРСКОЙ ГУБЕР.
А. М. МАЛЬЦЕВА
ПРОДОЛЬНЫЙ РАЗРѢЗЪ.
Академикъ Ѳ. Шехтель.

Fedor Shekhtel'
Mansion of Z. G. Morozova on Spiridonovka
(Aleksei Tolstoy) Street, Moscow
1893–6

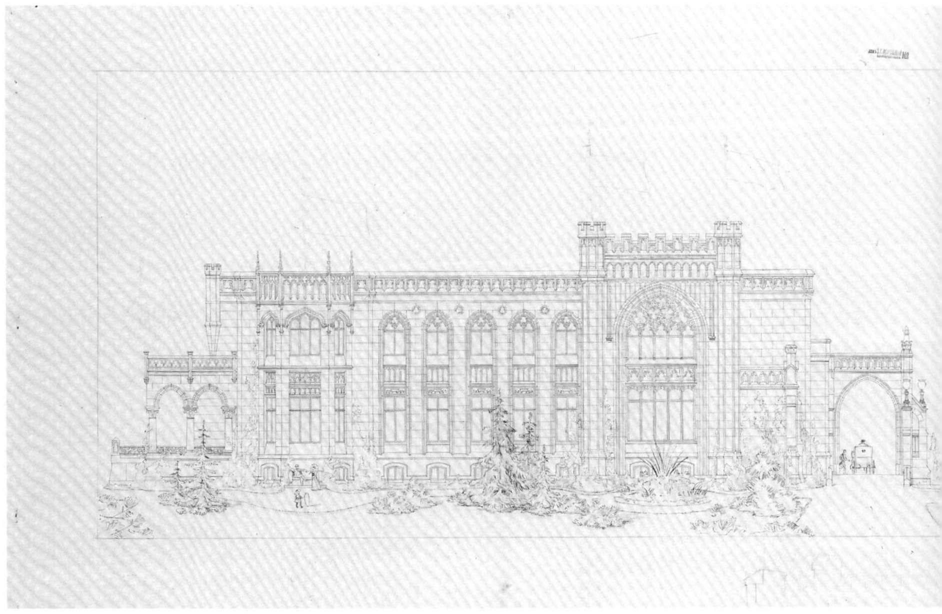

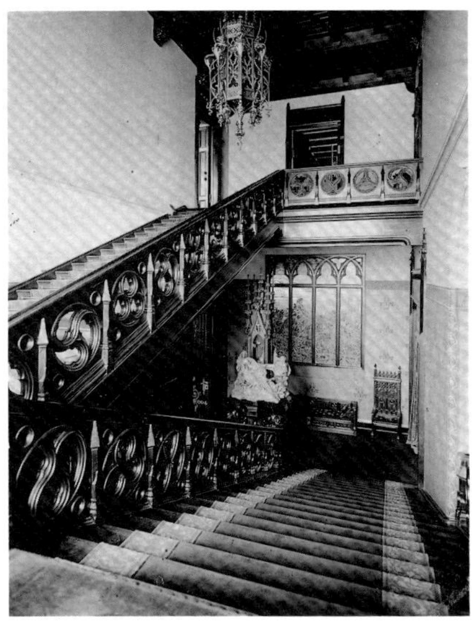

ABOVE: 321. Principal elevation
Indian ink and pencil on paper, 56.2 × 92.4
A. V. Shchusev State Museum of Architecture

LEFT: 330. Main staircase
Photo (1890s)
A. V. Shchusev State Museum of Architecture

BELOW: 329. Main staircase: plan, elevation
and details
Mixed media on paper, 63 × 98.5
A. V. Shchusev State Museum of Architecture

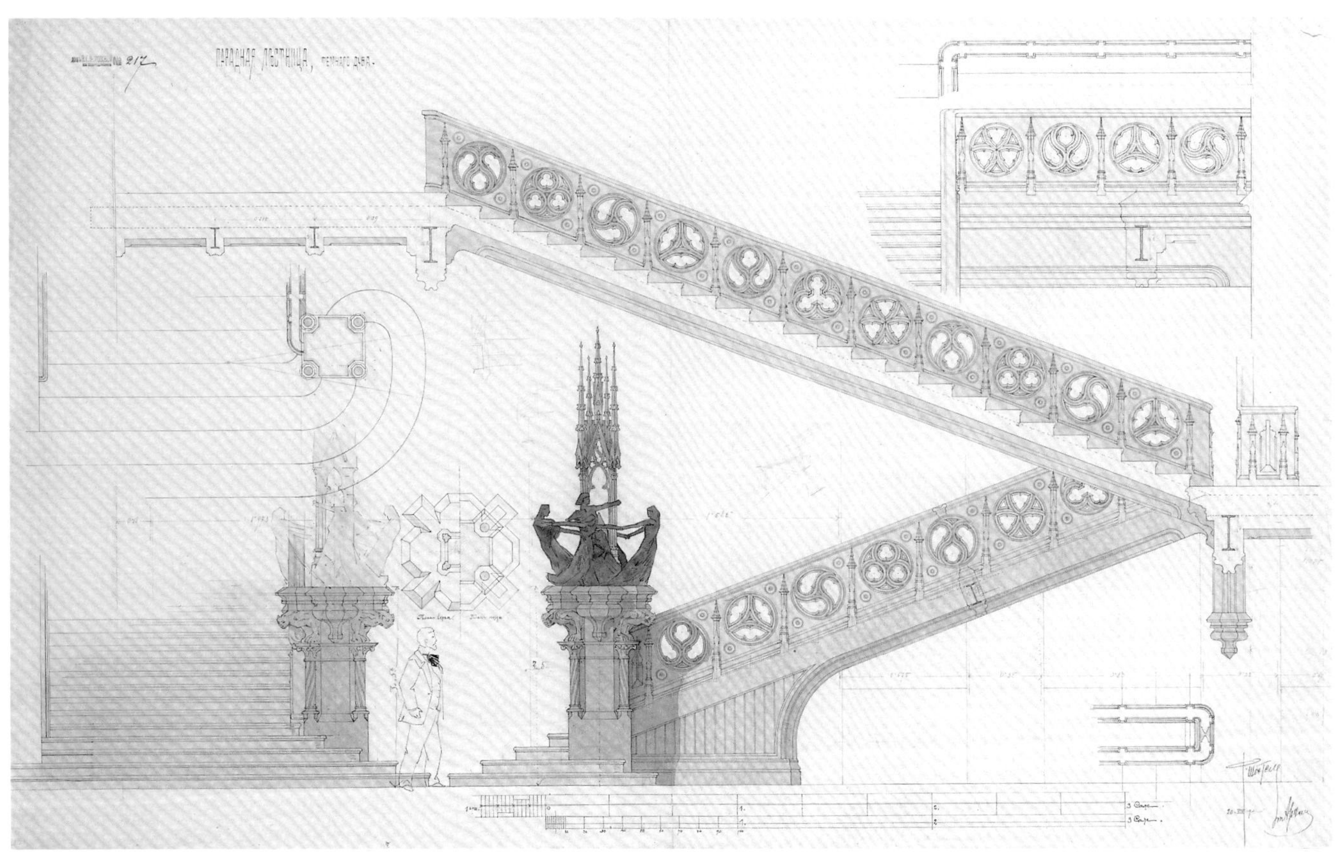

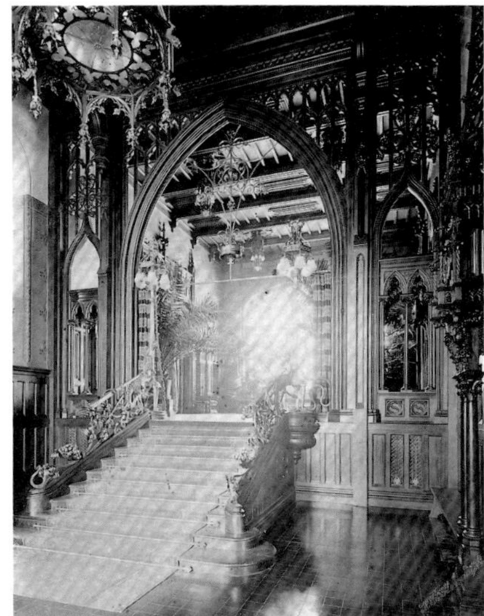

ABOVE: 327. Entrance lobby: stair into
entrance hall
Photo (1890s)
A. V. Shchusev State Museum of Architecture

RIGHT. 324. Entrance lobby: design for
decorative screen facing entrance
Mixed media on paper, 64.6 × 48
A. V. Shchusev State Museum of Architecture

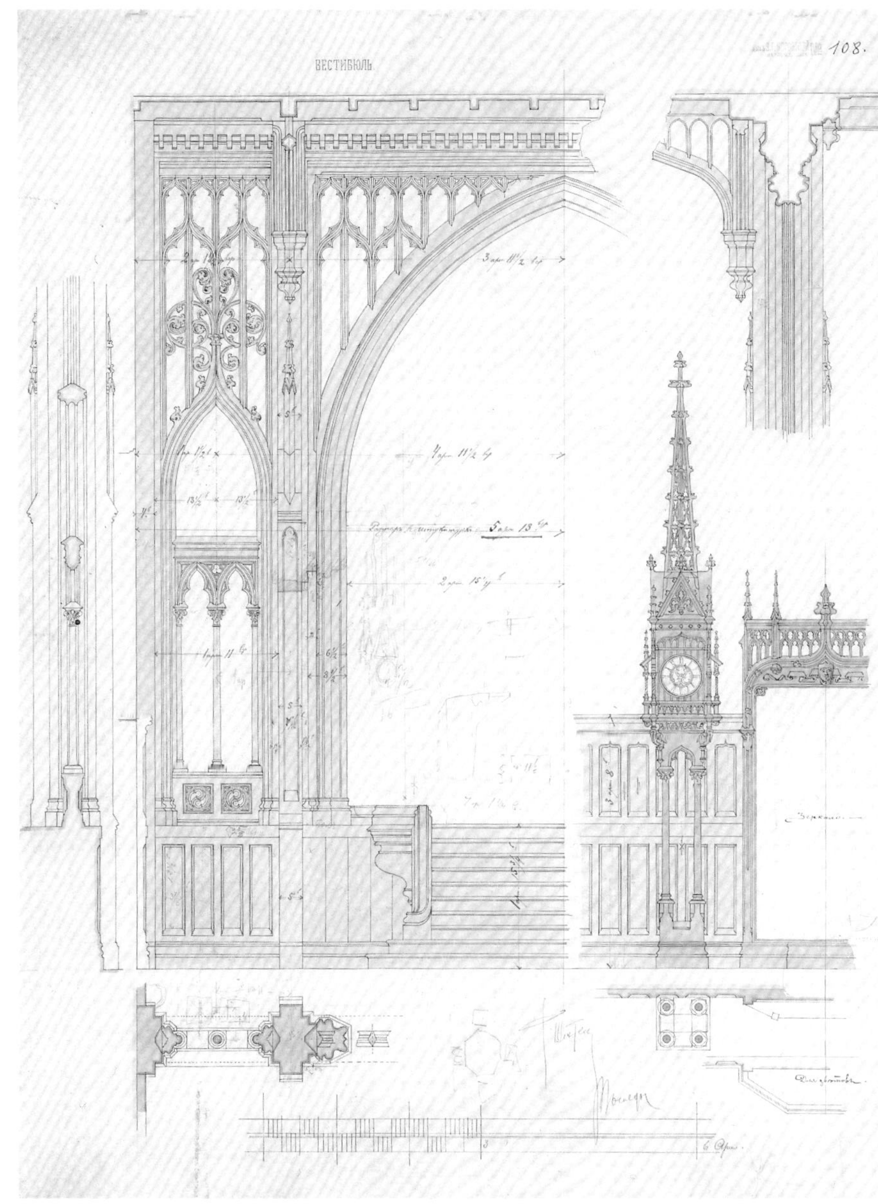

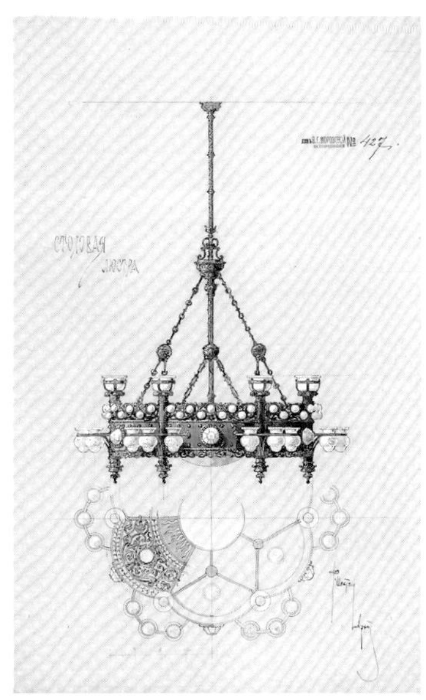

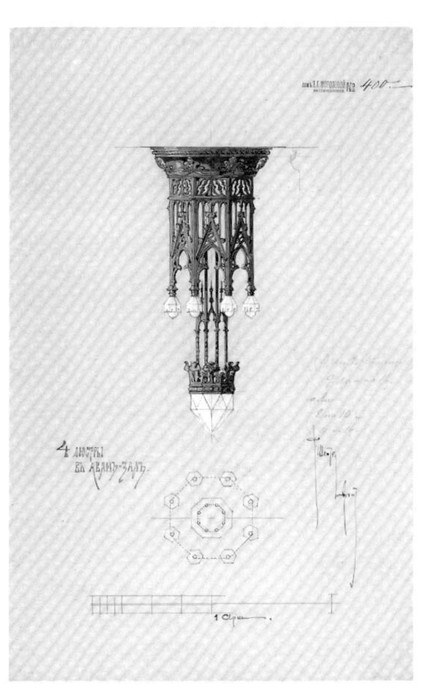

FAR LEFT: 332. Dining-room: design for light
fitting (executed version)
Mixed media on coloured cardboard, 48 × 29.3
A. V. Shchusev State Museum of Architecture

LEFT: 328. Entrance hall: design for light fitting
Mixed media on coloured cardboard,
46.8 × 29.6
A. V. Shchusev State Museum of Architecture

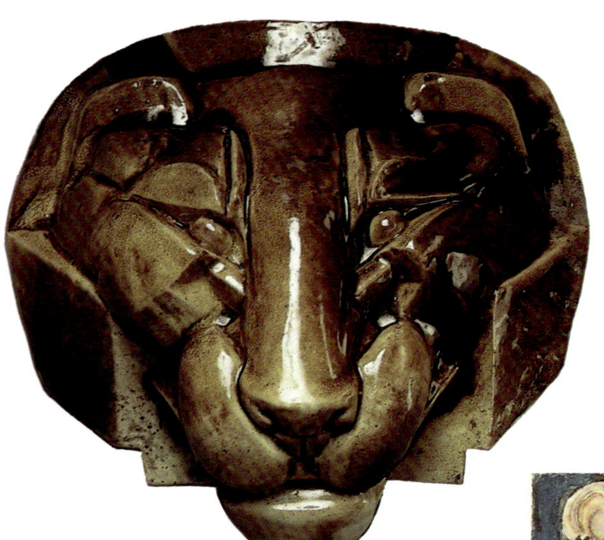

ABOVE: **Mikhail Vrubel'**
457. *Lion's Head*
1891
High relief from the gates of the house of
Savva Mamontov in Moscow
(Sadovoya-Spasskaya no.6)
Majolica, 43.5 × 47.1 × 24
State Tretyakov Gallery

RIGHT: **Mikhail Vrubel'**
461. *Dream on Walpurgis Night: Young Witch;*
Faust, Helen and Euphorion; Witches' Kitchen
1896
Designs for panels in the Gothic Study in the
house of A. V. Morozov in Moscow
Mixed media on paper, 22.4 × 4; 22.2 × 4.8;
22.2 × 4
State Tretyakov Gallery

OPPOSITE LEFT: **Mikhail Vrubel'**
466. *Philosophy*
1898
Design for a panel in the house of
A. V. Morozov in Moscow
Mixed media on paper, 42.5 × 13.7
State Tretyakov Gallery

OPPOSITE RIGHT: **Mikhail Vrubel'**
459. *Venice*
1893
Study for the panel executed in the house of
E. D. Dunker in Moscow
Mixed media on paper, 36.4 × 19.3
State Tretyakov Gallery

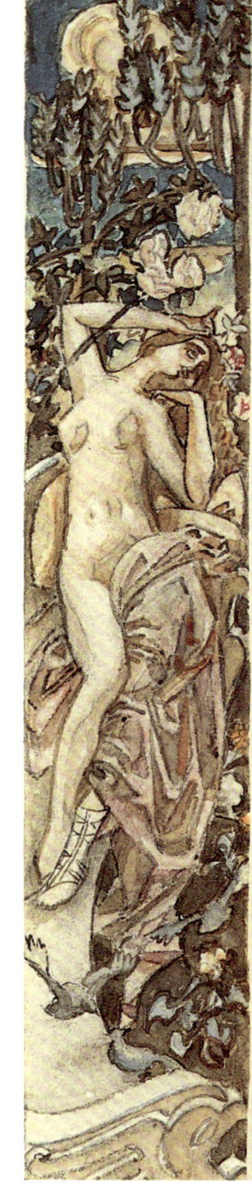
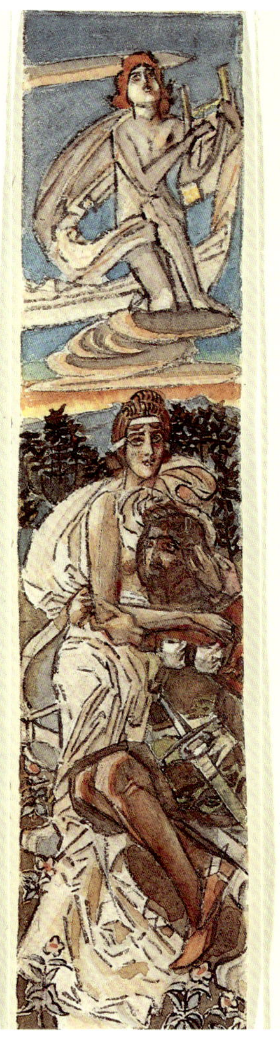
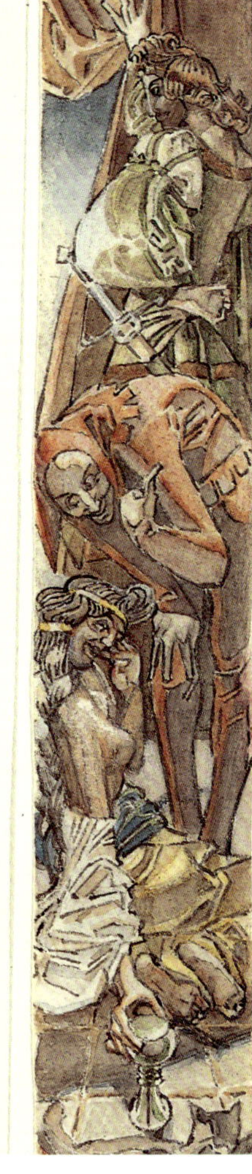

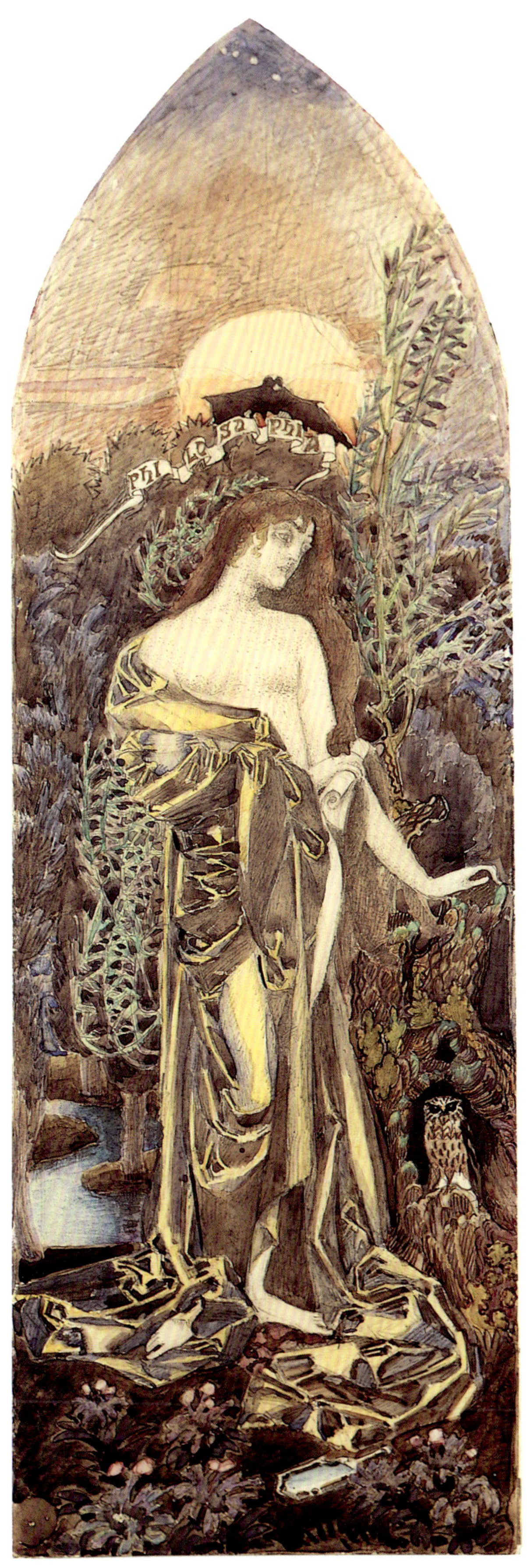

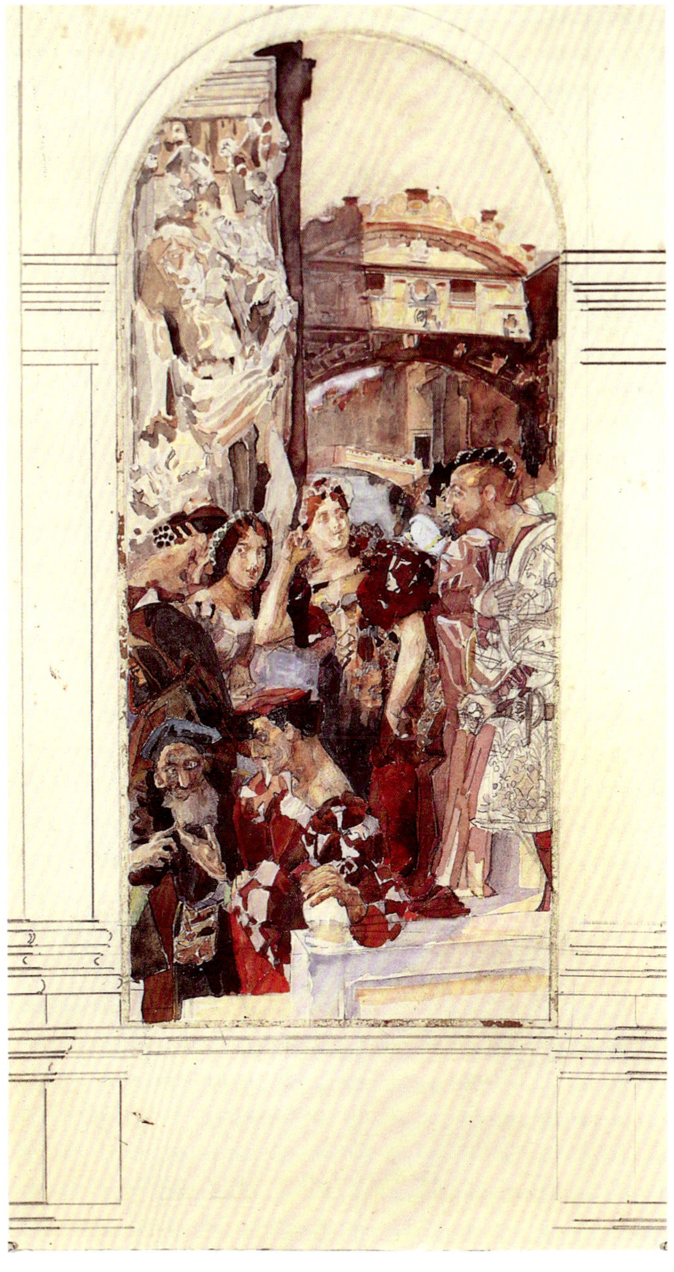

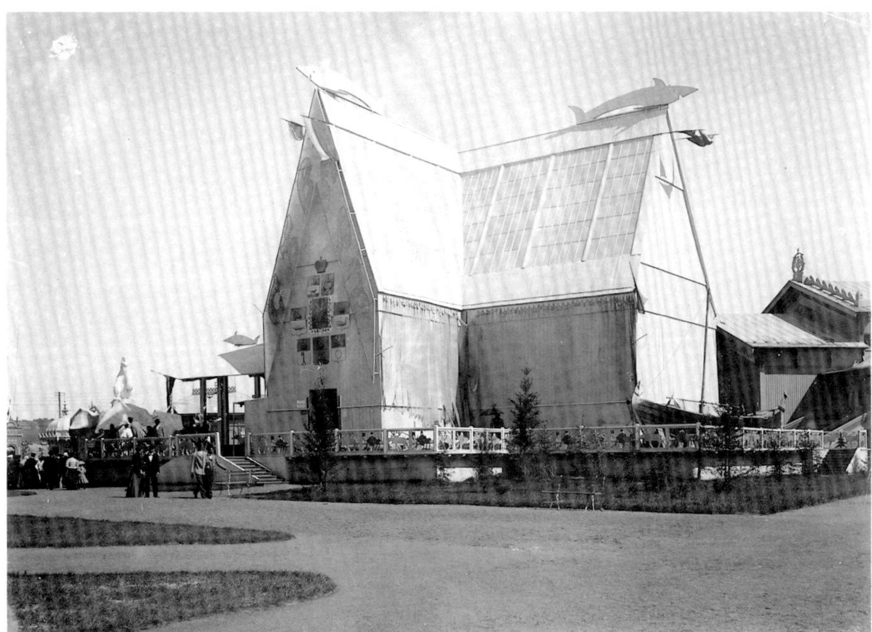

Left: **Konstantin Korovin**
178. Pavilion of the Far North at the Nizhny
Novgorod Exhibition
1896
Photo (1896)
A. V. Shchusev State Museum of Architecture

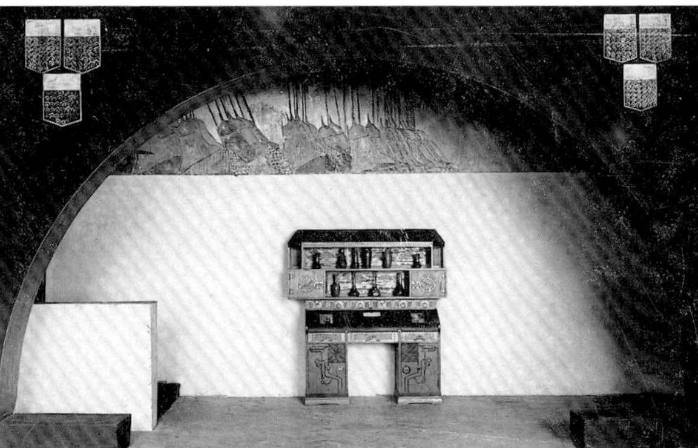

Left: **Ivan Fomin**
117. Detail of installation of Maple Dining-
room at the ''New Style'' Exhibition in
Moscow
1902
Photo (1902)
A. V. Shchusev State Museum of Architecture

Below: **Ivan Fomin**
Project for a private house: perspective
1901
Photo of architect's drawing

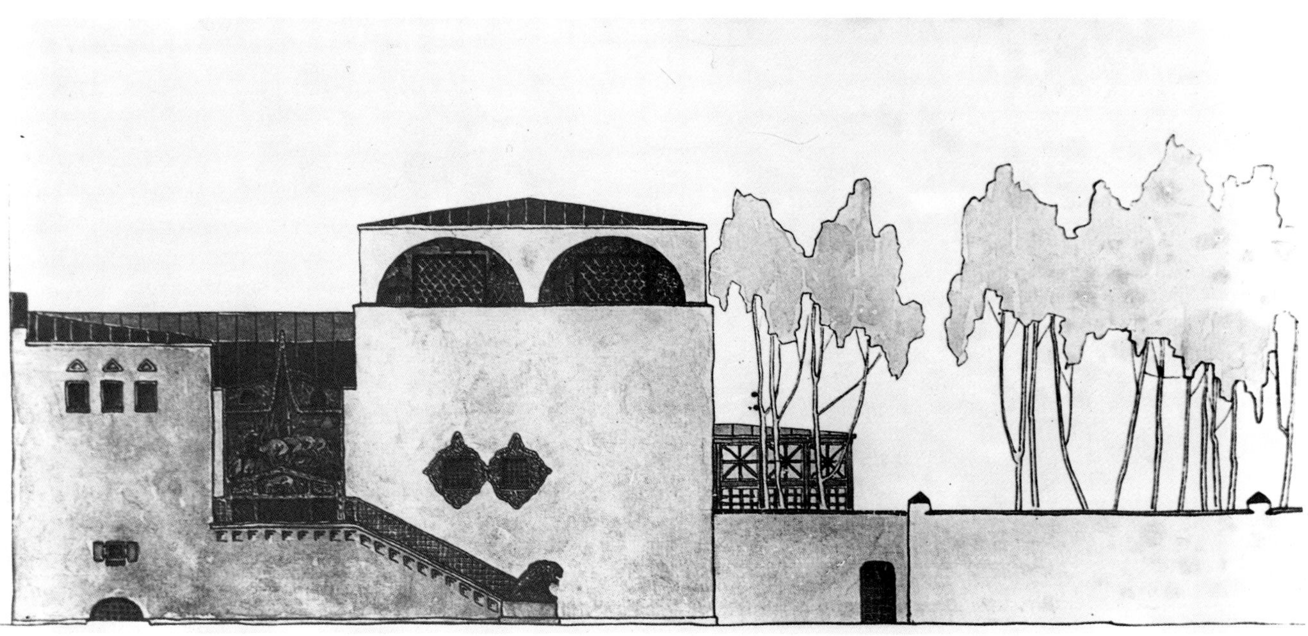

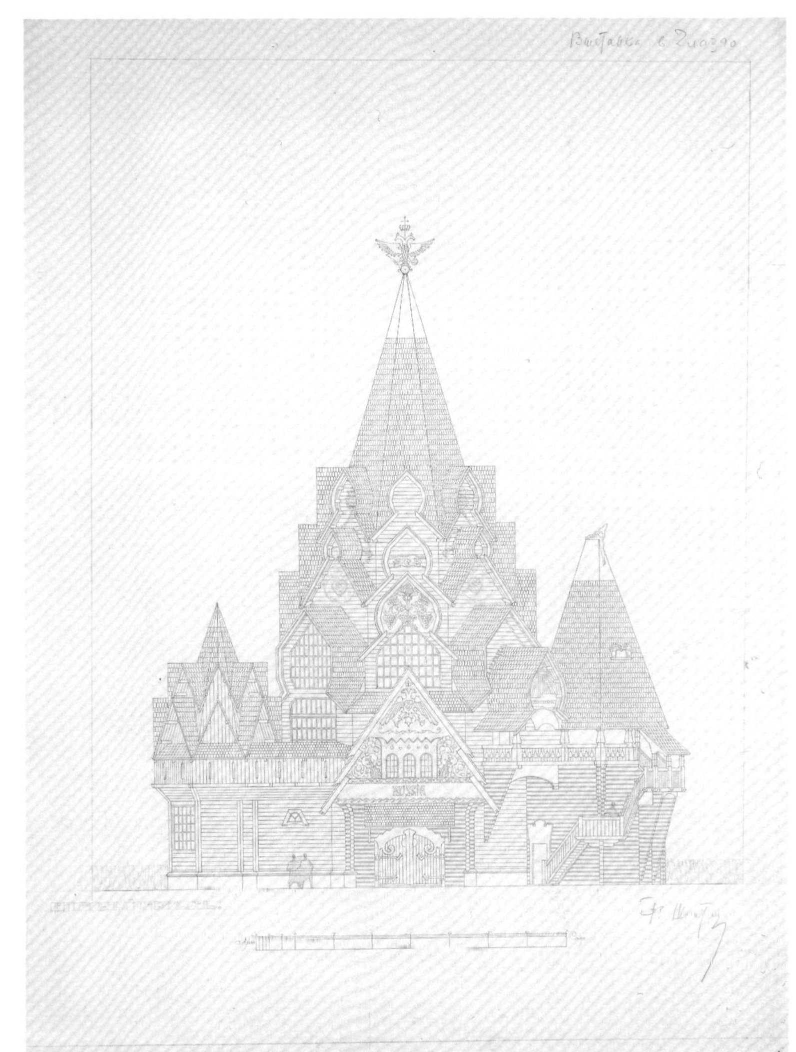

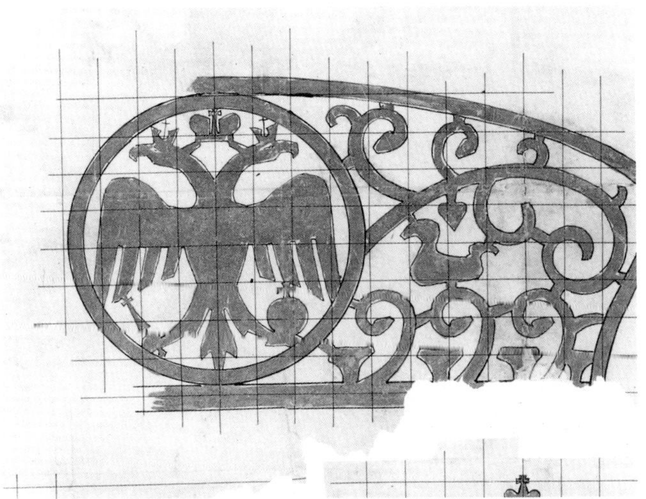

Fedor Shekhteľ
Russian Pavilions at the International
Exhibition, Glasgow
1901

ABOVE LEFT: 345 (detail). Agriculture
Pavilion: detail of finial
Mixed media on tracing-paper, 36.5 × 60.2
A. V. Shchusev State Museum of Architecture

ABOVE RIGHT: 341. Central Pavilion: elevation
Indian ink and pencil on paper, 68.5 × 50
A. V. Shchusev State Museum of Architecture

RIGHT: 352. The four pavilions: (left to right)
Agriculture, Mining, Central, Forestry
Illustration from Glasgow album (no.349)
Phototype from photograph, 20 × 30
A. V. Shchusev State Museum of Architecture

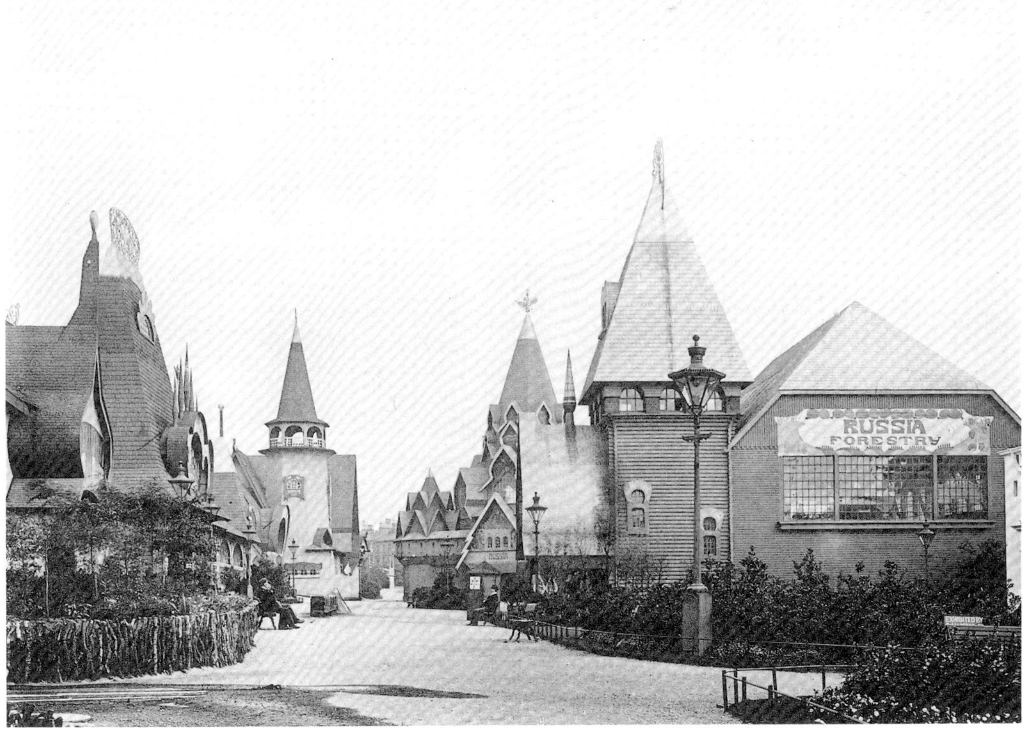

Fedor Shekhtel'
Mansion of A. I. Derozhinskaya on
Shtatny (Kropotkinsky) Lane, Moscow
(now Australian Embassy)
1901–02

RIGHT: 357. Elevation (version not
executed)
Mixed media on paper, 29.3 × 42.6
A. V. Shchusev State Museum of
Architecture

BELOW: 358. Design of railings and
gateway
Pencil and watercolour on tracing paper,
40.2 × 80
A. V. Shchusev State Museum of
Architecture

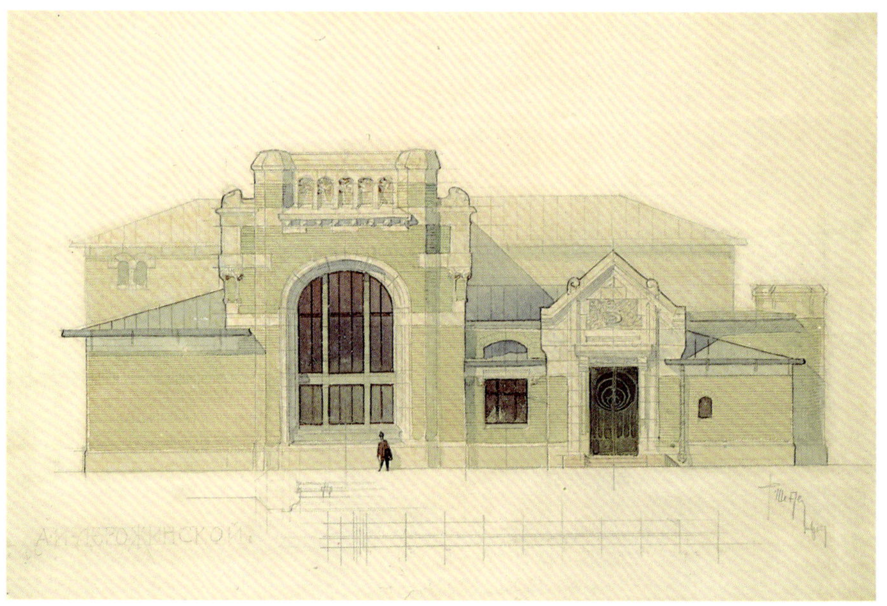

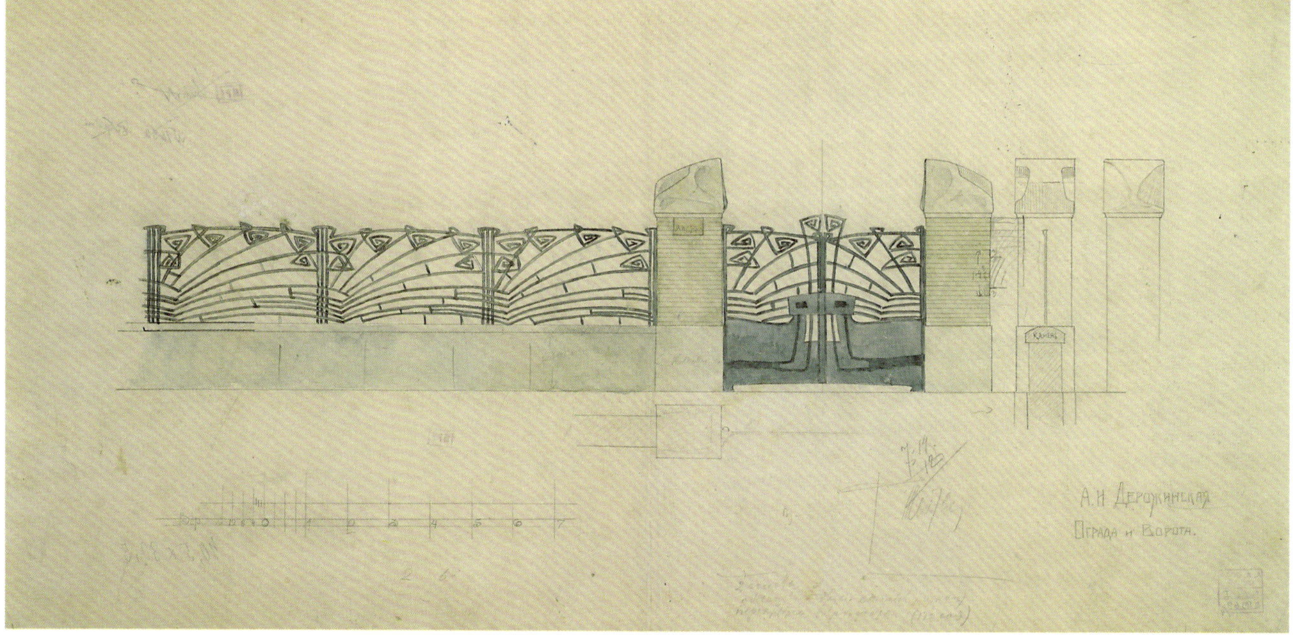

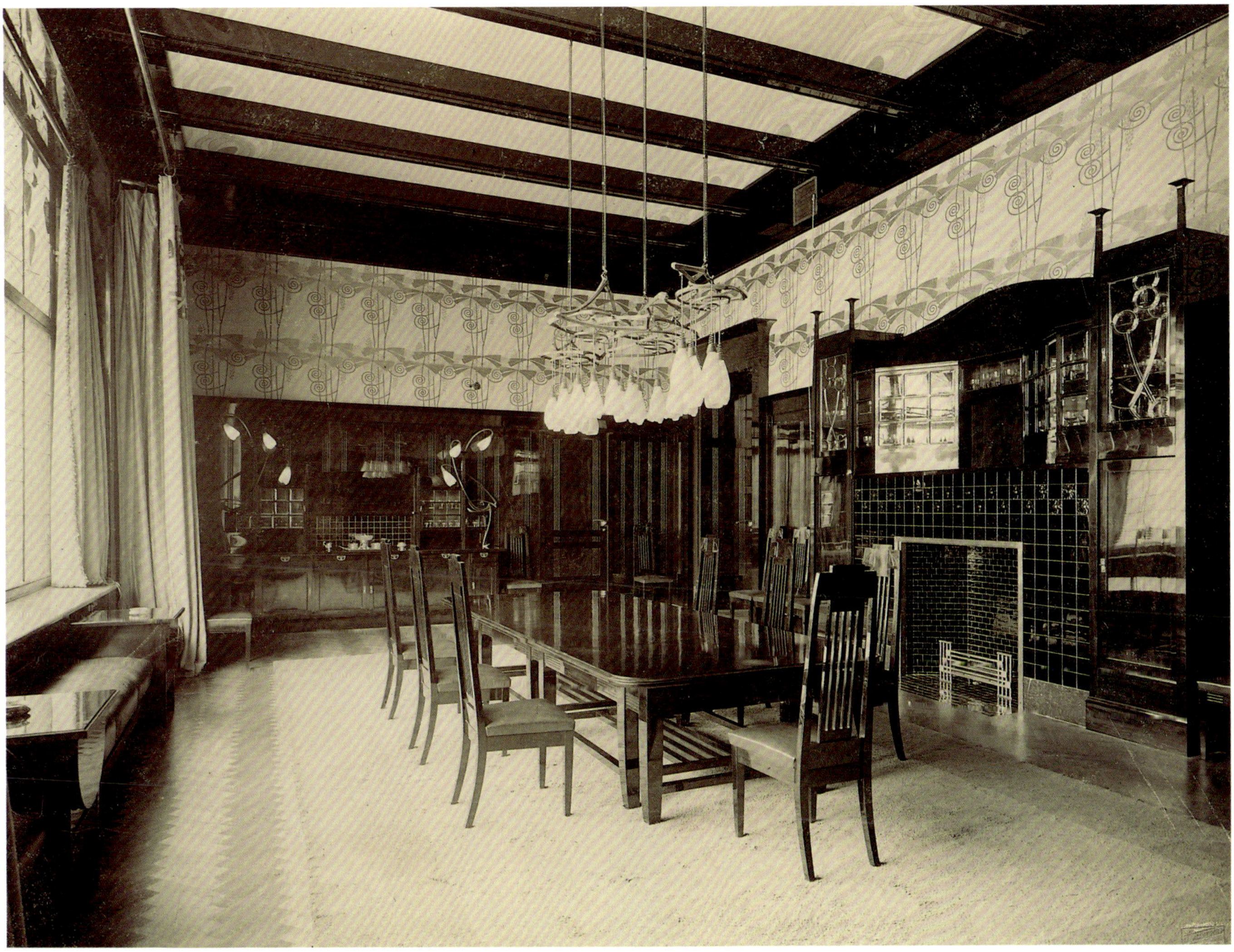

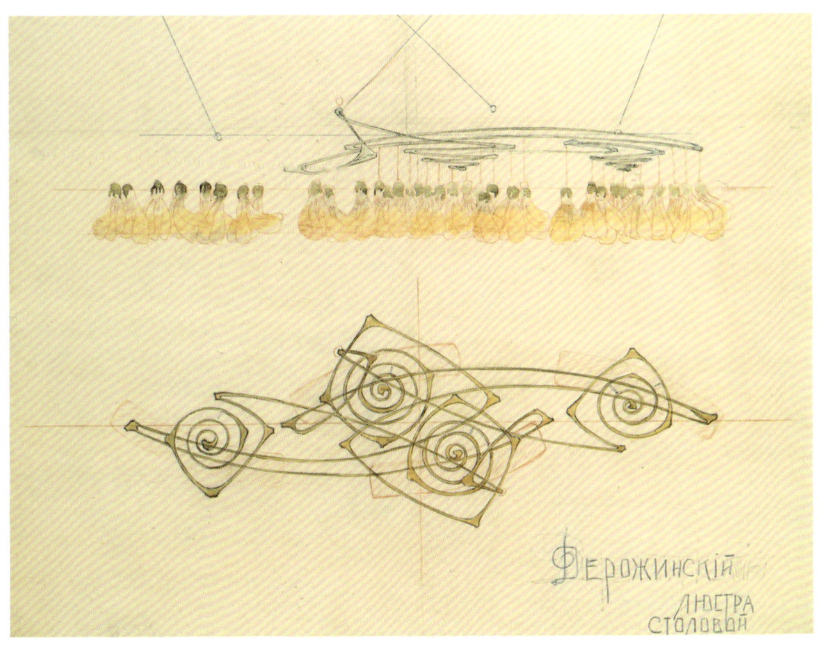

Above: 365. Dining-room: general view
Photo (1900s)
A. V. Shchusev State Museum of Architecture

Left: 364. Design for light fitting in
dining-room
Mixed media on tracing paper, 129.5 × 80.2
A. V. Shchusev State Museum of Architecture

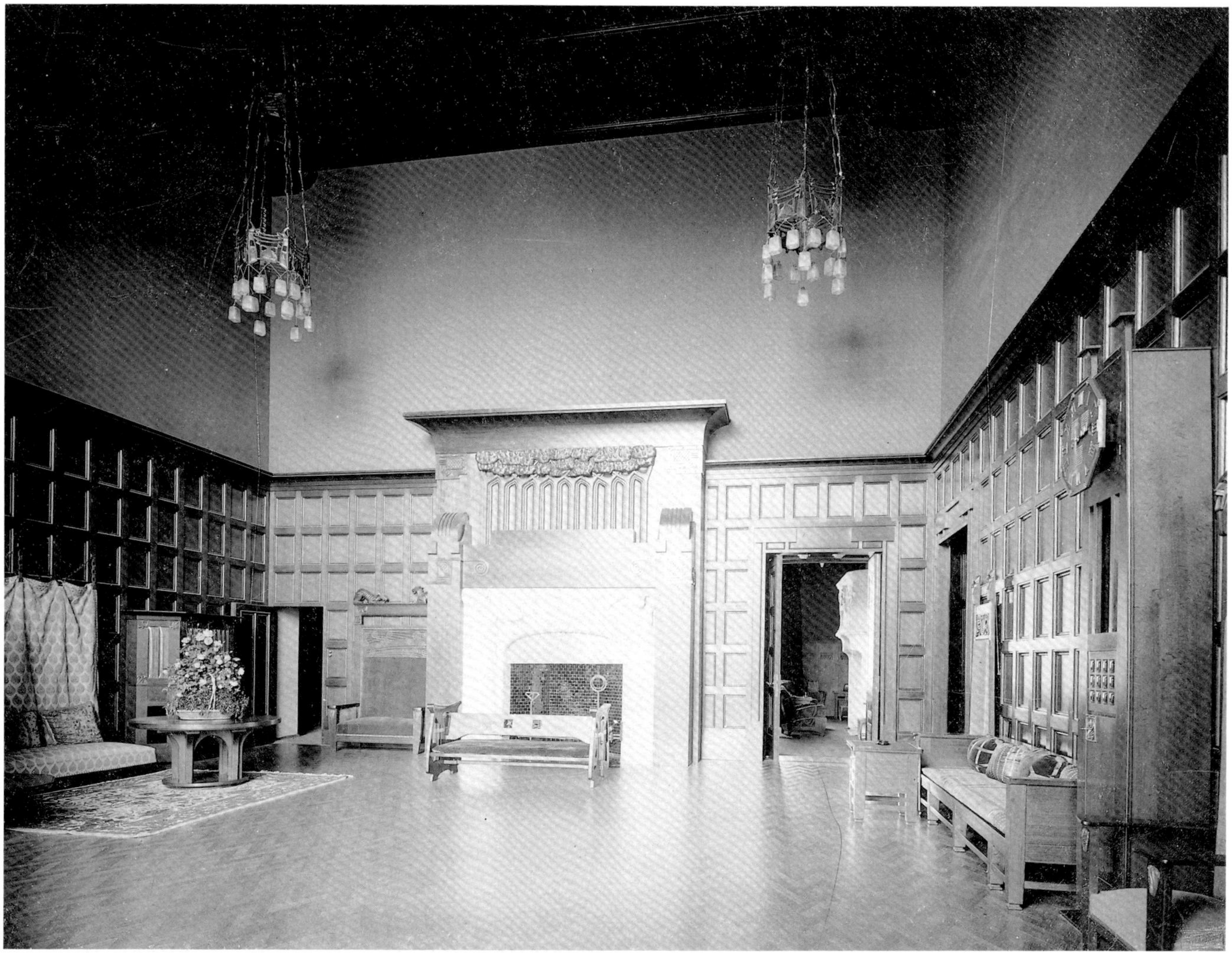

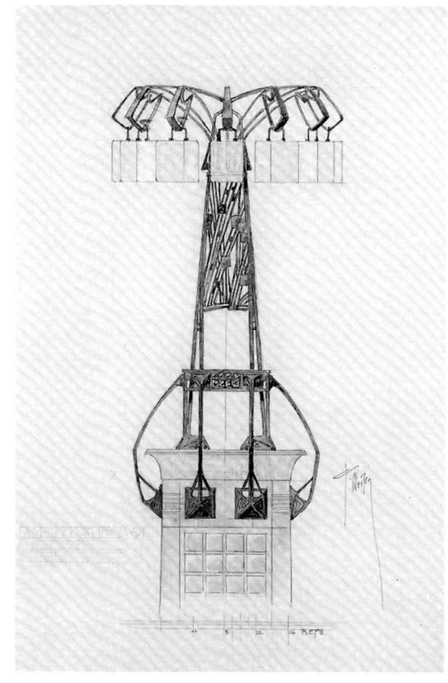

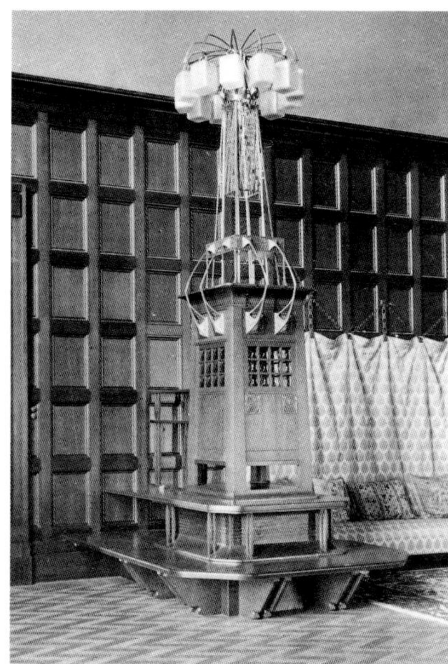

Fedor Shekhtel'
Mansion of A. I. Derozhinskaya
1901–02

ABOVE: 362. Great Hall
Photo (1900s)
A. V. Shchusev State Museum of Architecture

RIGHT: 361. Great Hall: design for light fitting
Mixed media on paper, 28 × 32
A. V. Shchusev State Museum of Architecture

FAR RIGHT: Great Hall (detail of light fitting)

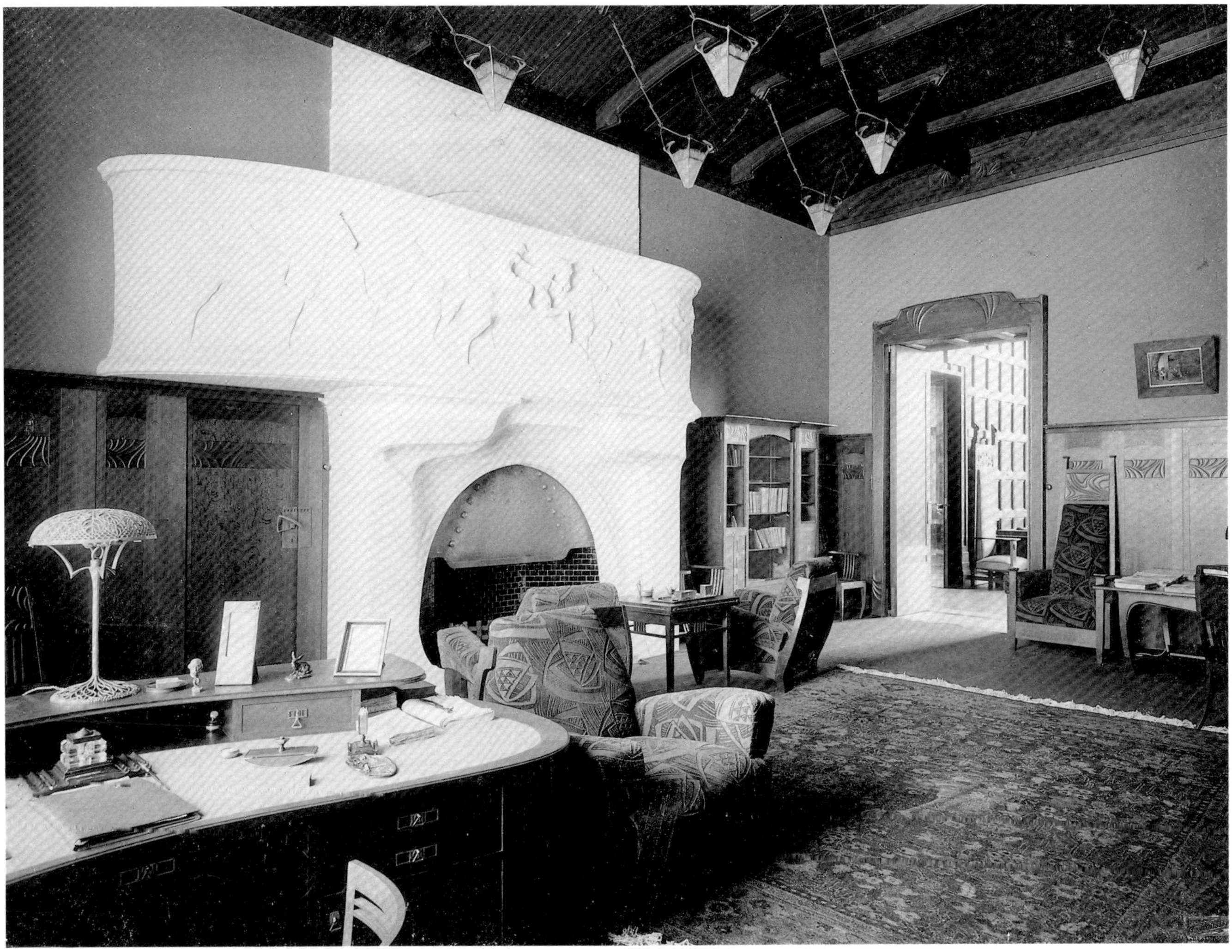

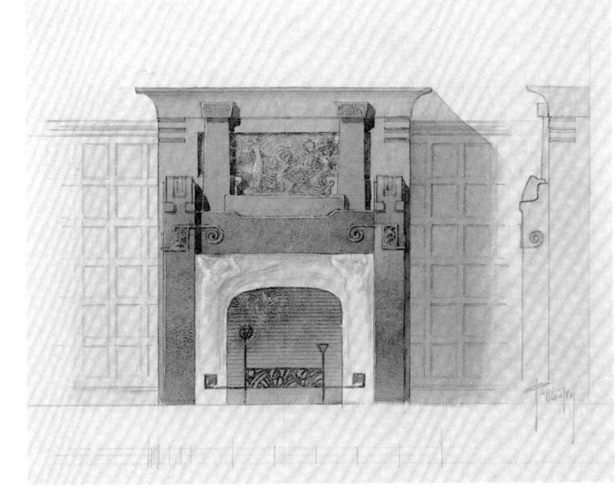

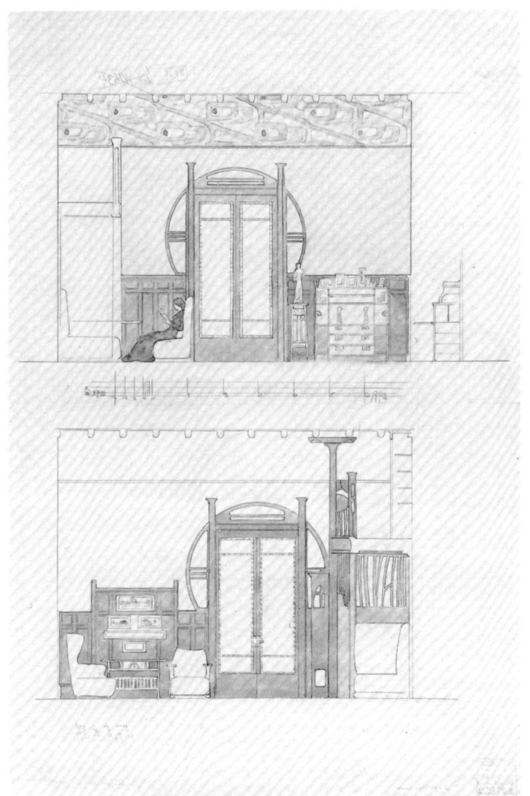

Top: 367. Study: general view
Photo (1900s)
A. V. Shchusev State Museum of Architecture

Left: 368. Ladies' morning room: wall
treatments
Mixed media on tracing paper, 57.5 × 36.7
A. V. Shchusev State Museum of Architecture

Above: 360. Great Hall: design for fireplace
Mixed media on coloured paper, 41.2 × 54.7
A. V. Shchusev State Museum of Architecture

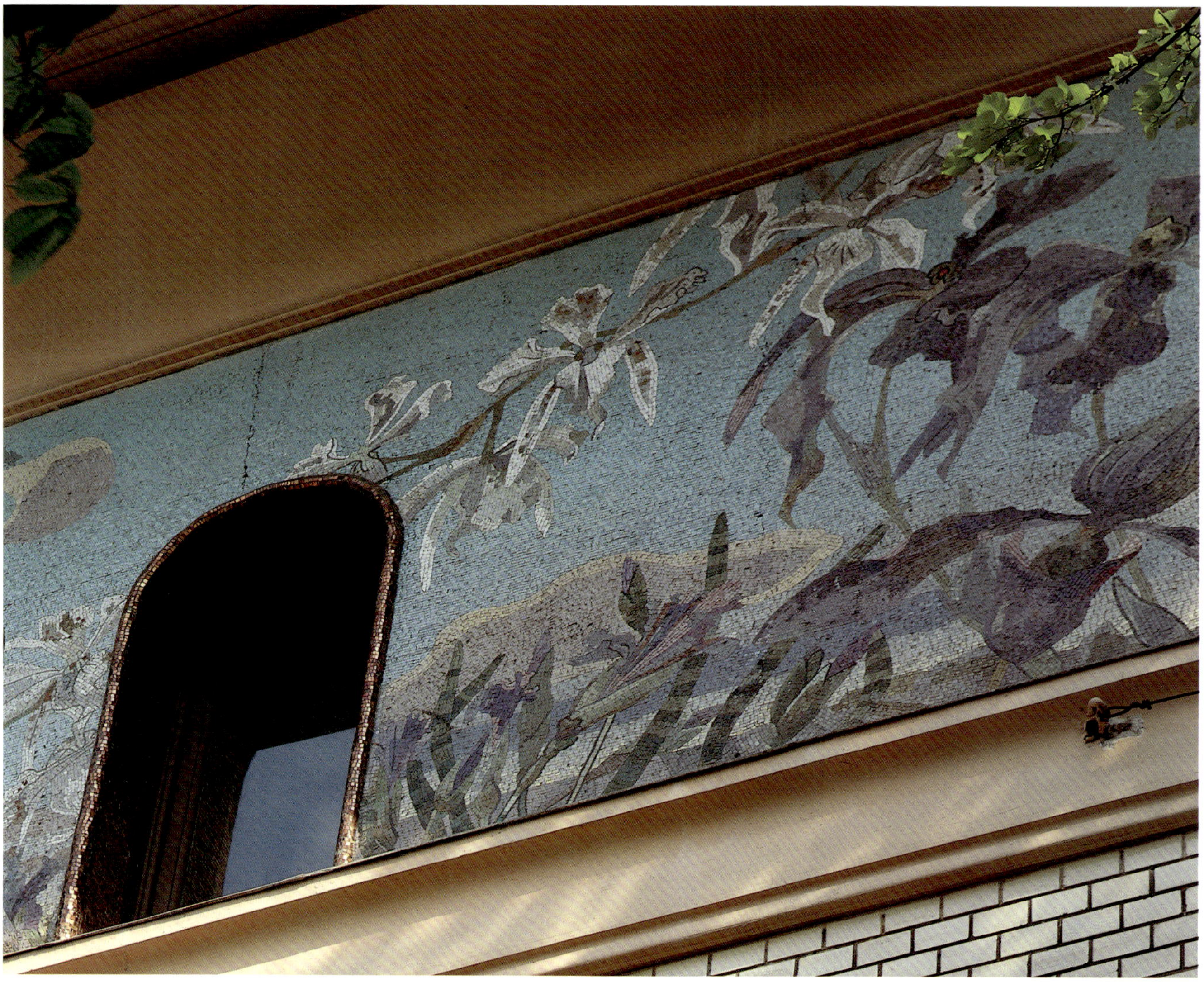

Fedor Shekhtel'
Mansion of S. P. Ryabushinsky on Malaya
Nikitskaya (Kachalov Street), Moscow (now
Gorky Museum)
1900–02

ABOVE: Detail of exterior mosaic frieze

RIGHT: 373. Designs for exterior mosaic frieze
Watercolour on paper, 29 × 42
A. V. Shchusev State Museum of Architecture

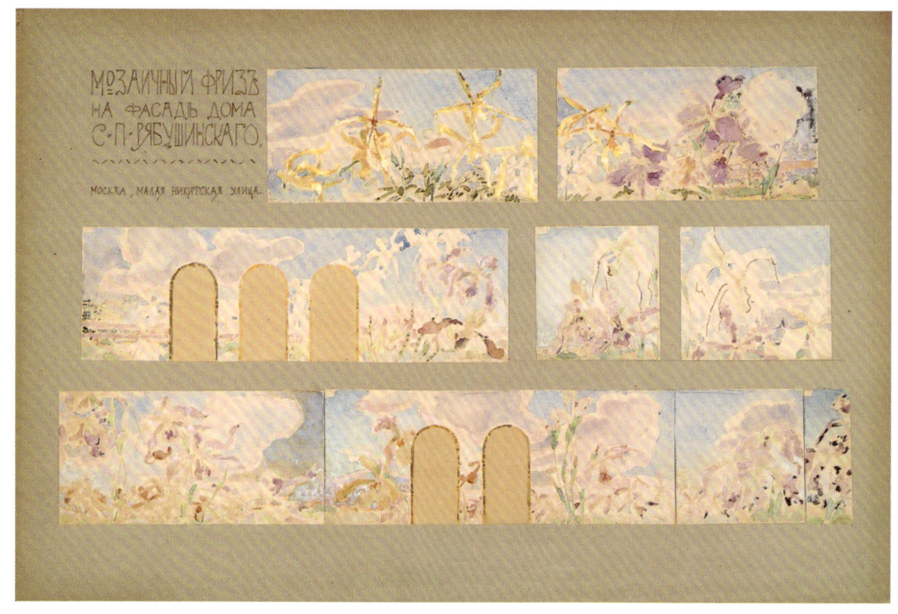

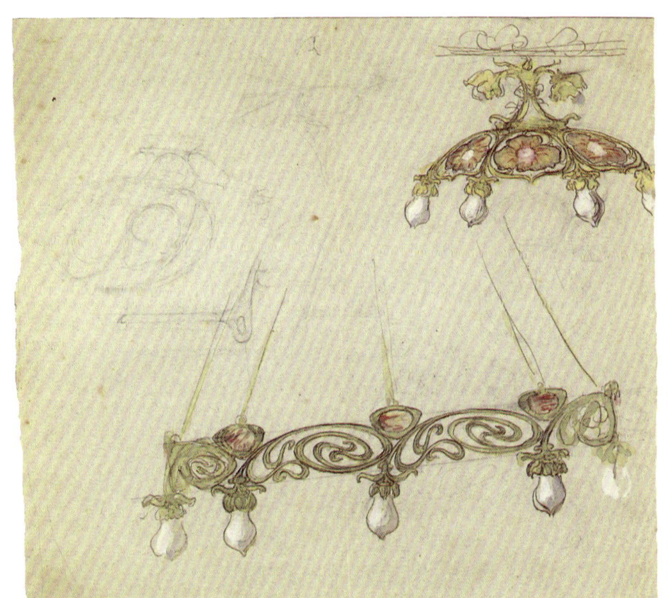

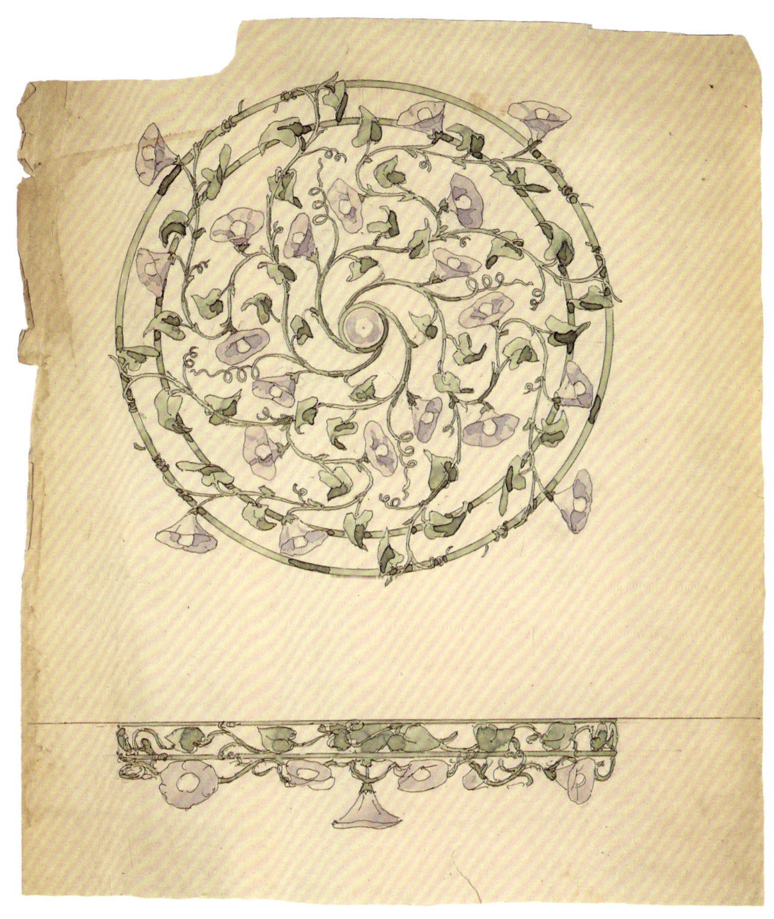

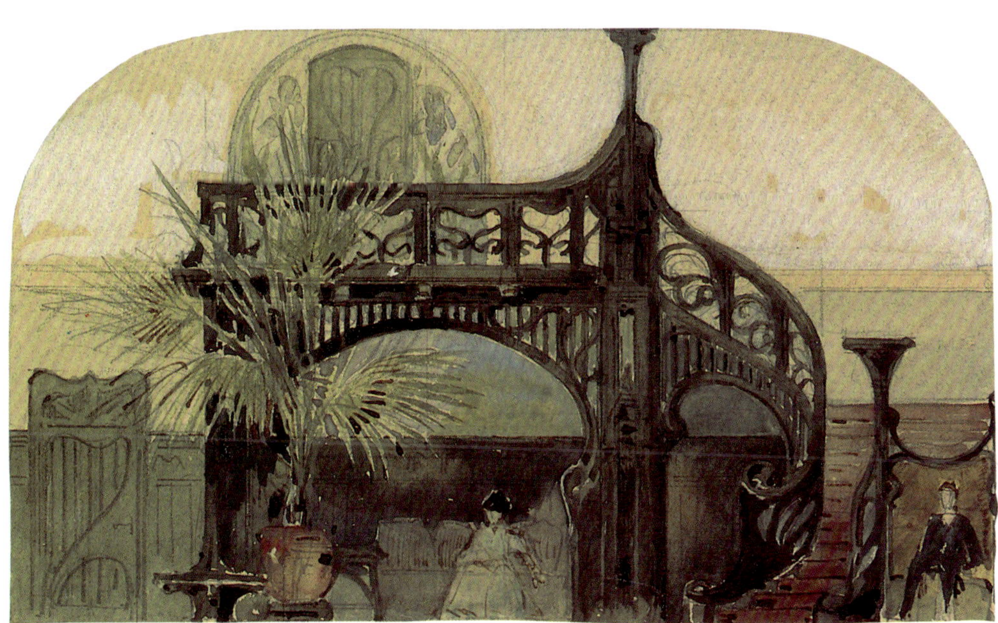

ABOVE: **Ivan Kuznetsov**
190, 191. Baev Mansion, Moscow:
designs for light fittings
1910
Mixed media on paper, 35 × 37.8;
41.5 × 34.3
A. V. Shchusev State Museum of
Architecture

LEFT: **Fedor Shekhtel'**
338 (detail). Estate of Savva
Morozov at Pokrovskoe-Runtsovo,
near Moscow: wall treatment for
Great Hall
1900
Mixed media on cardboard, 27 × 38
A. V. Shchusev State Museum of
Architecture

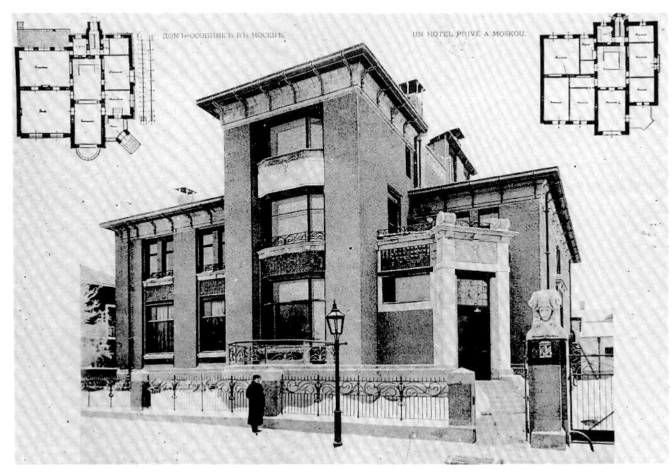

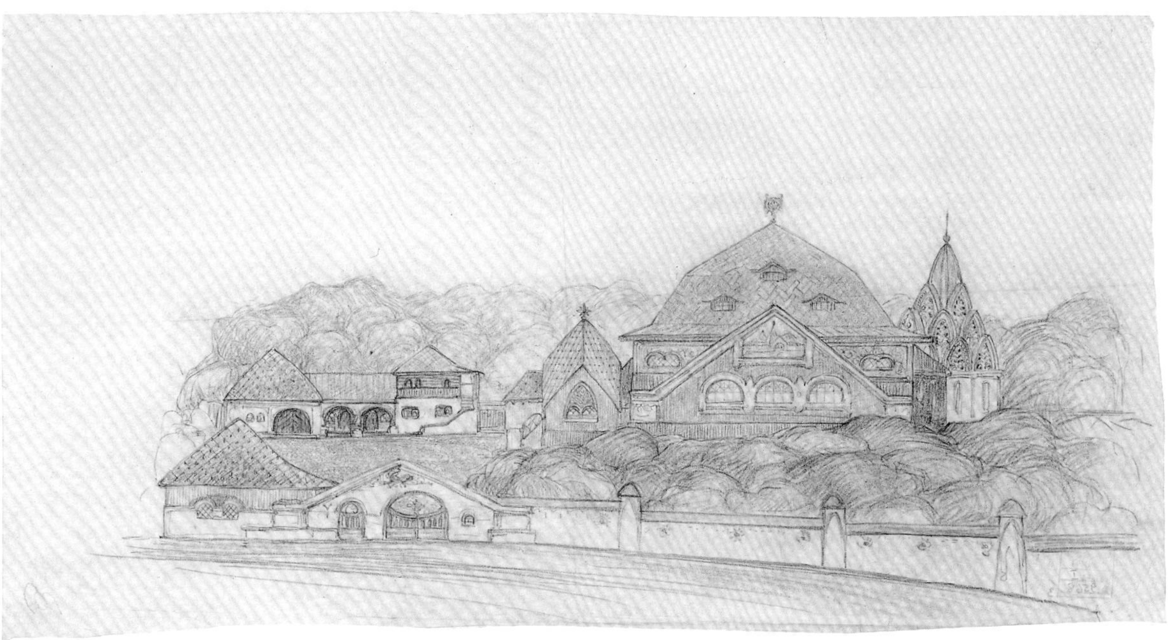

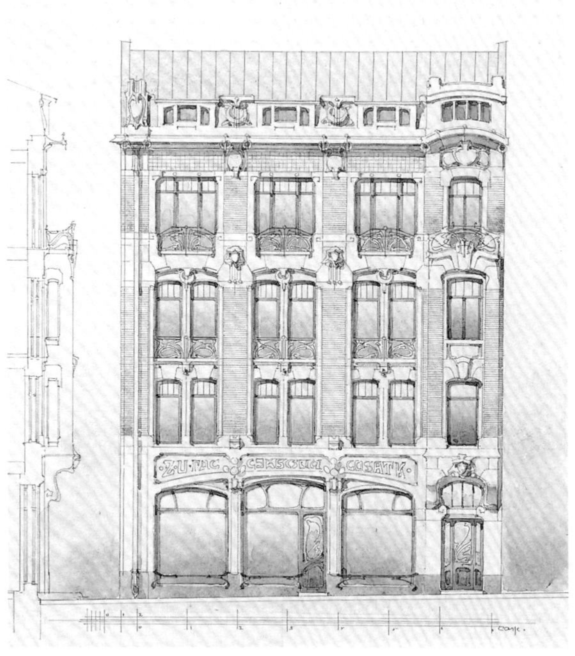

TOP: **William Walcot (Val'kot)**
473. House in Mertvy (N. A. Ostrovsky) Lane, Moscow
1900–02
Photo (1900s)
A. V. Shchusev State Museum of Architecture

ABOVE: **Leonid Vesnin**
454. Project for unidentified dacha: perspective
1900s
Pencils on tracing paper, 32.5 × 61
A. V. Shchusev State Museum of Architecture

LEFT: **Illarion Ivanov-Shits**
159. Elevation of apartment house (with commercial accommodation on ground floor): elevation
1900
Indian ink and watercolour on paper, 34 × 29
A. V. Shchusev State Museum of Architecture

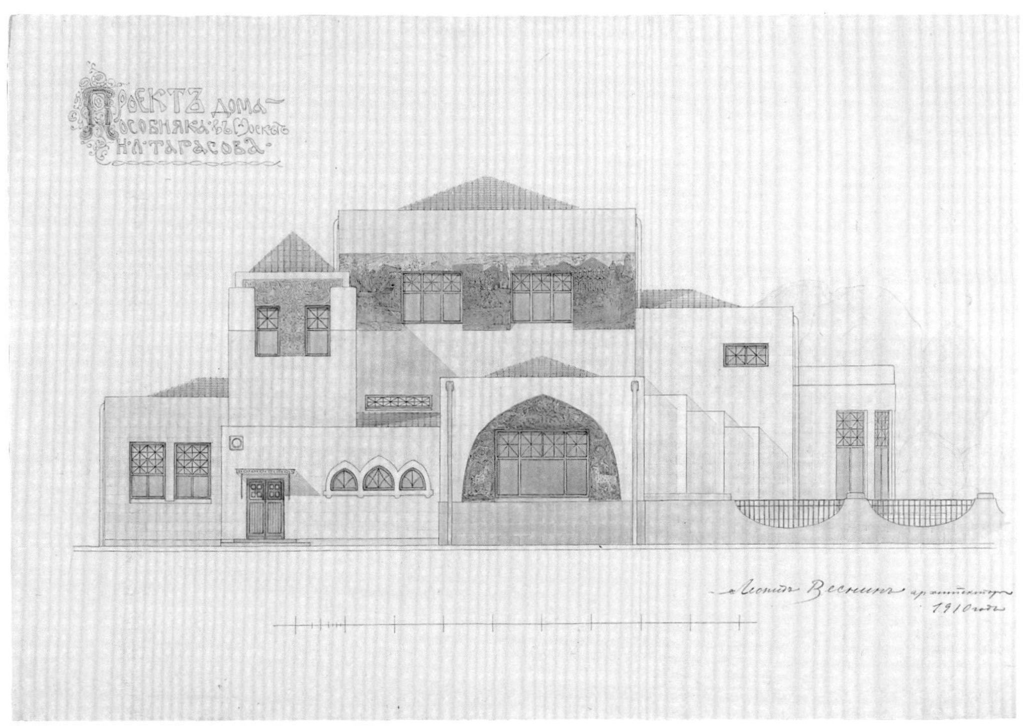

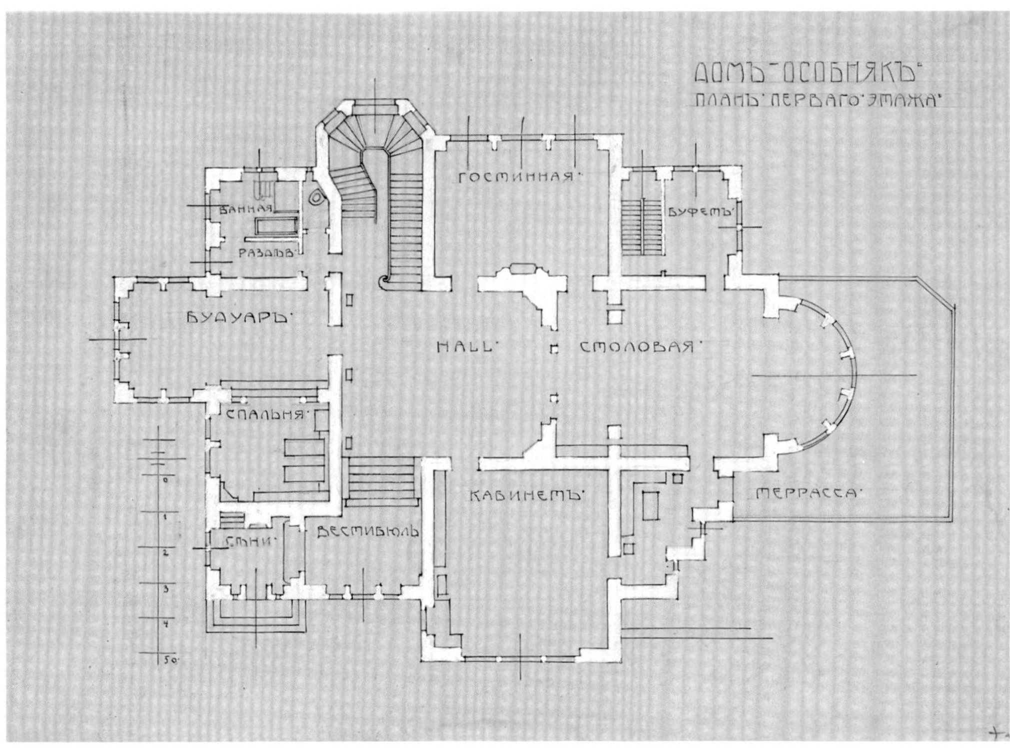

Leonid Vesnin
House of N. L. Tarasov, Moscow
1910

TOP: 451. Elevation
Indian ink and watercolour on paper,
52.3 × 74.2
A. V. Shchusev State Museum of Architecture

ABOVE: 453. Plan of ground floor
Coloured ink and white on coloured
cardboard, 26.6 × 36
A. V. Shchusev State Museum of Architecture

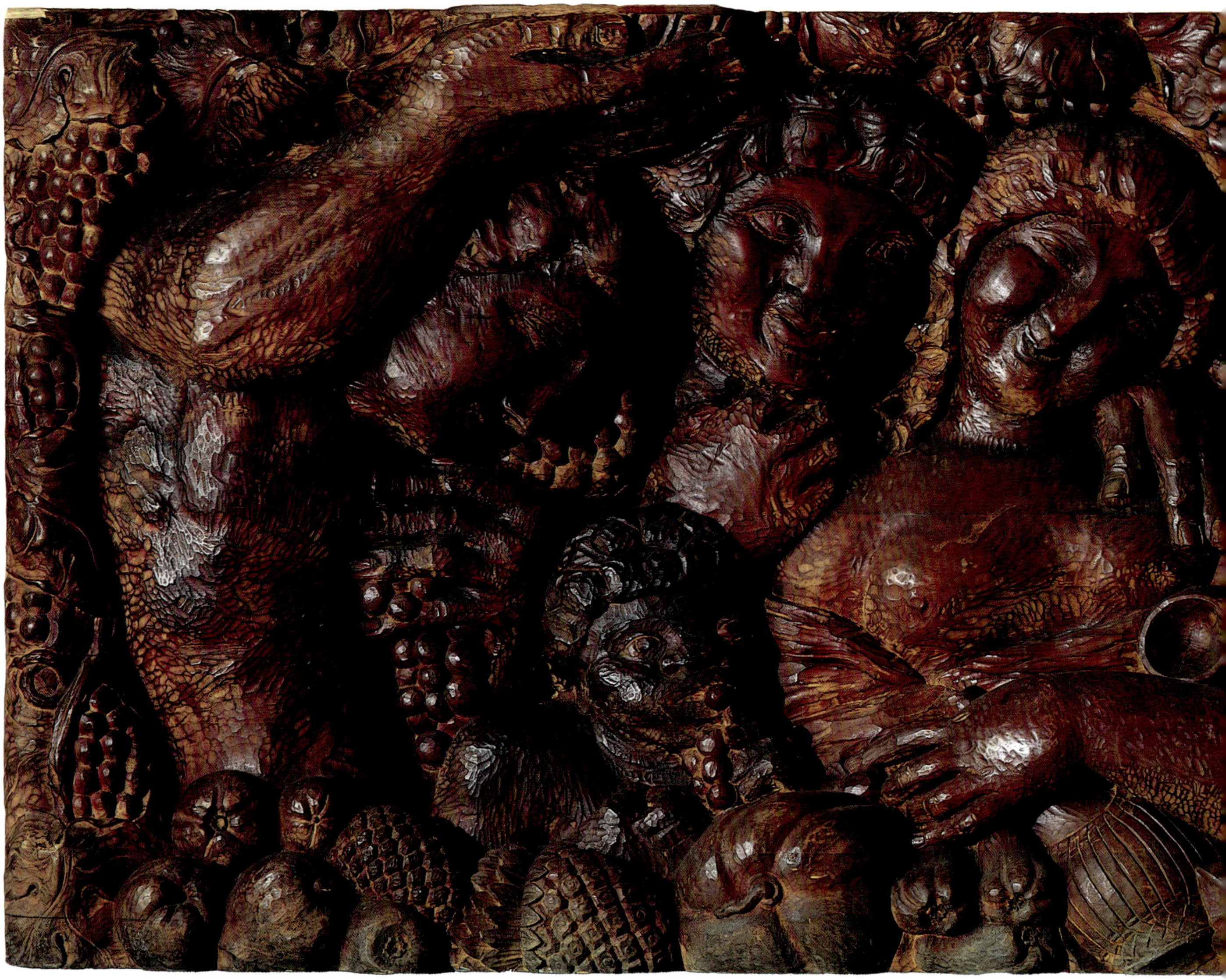

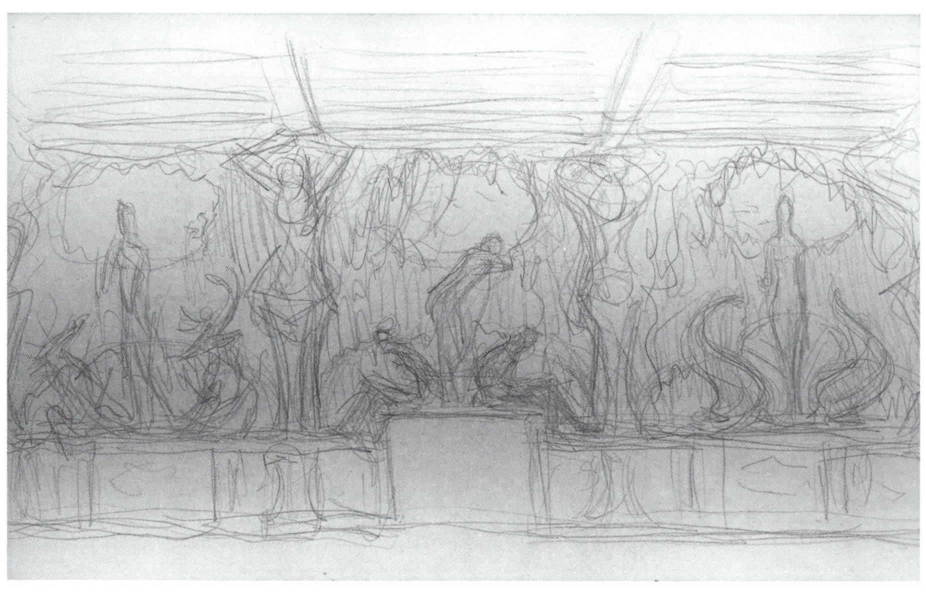

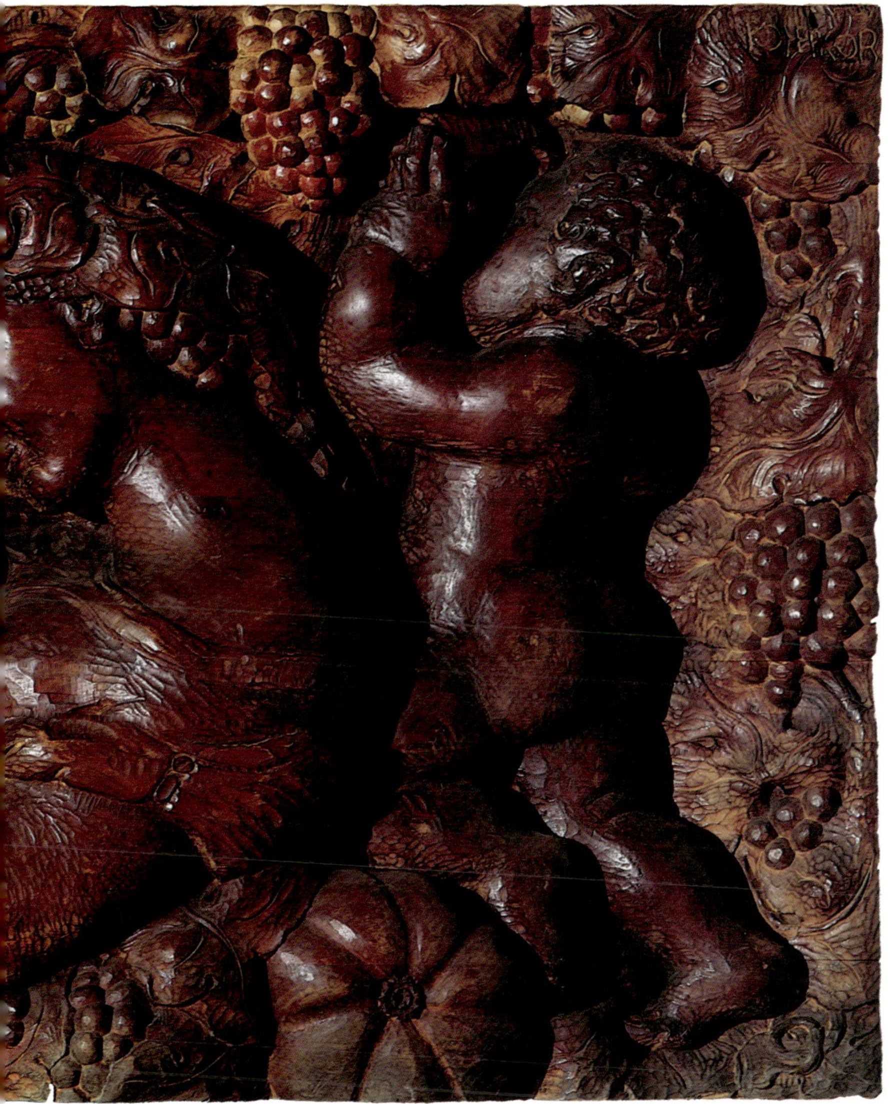

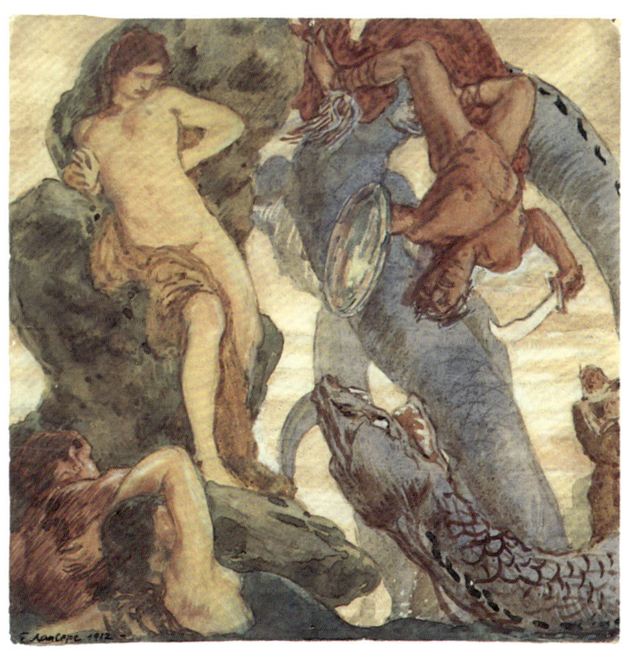

Above: **Sergei Konenkov**
175. *The Feast*
1910
Coloured wood, 86,5 × 186.5 × 31
State Tretyakov Gallery

Above right: **Evgeny Lanceray**
206. *Perseus*
1912
Design for a mural for the house of
G. G. Tarasov in Moscow
Gouache on cardboard, 25.1 × 24.5
State Tretyakov Gallery

Opposite: **Valentin Serov**
316. *Diana; Eros, Apollo and Daphne; Venus*
1911
Design for a mural for the dining-room of the
house of V. V. Nosov in Moscow
Lead pencil on paper, 25.4 × 45.7
State Tretyakov Gallery

Illarion Ivanov-Shits
Mart'yanych Restaurant:
Designs for decoration of
cellars of Upper Trading Rows
(now GUM), Red Square,
Moscow
1905

TOP LEFT: 157. Design for
buffet
Pencil and watercolour on
paper, 29 × 46
A. V. Shchusev State Museum
of Architecture

TOP CENTRE: 156. Design for
booth
Mixed media on paper,
26.7 × 42.3
A. V. Shchusev State Museum
of Architecture

TOP RIGHT: 158. Egyptian
buffet, design for decorative
panel
Mixed media on paper,
30.3 × 52
A. V. Shchusev State Museum
of Architecture

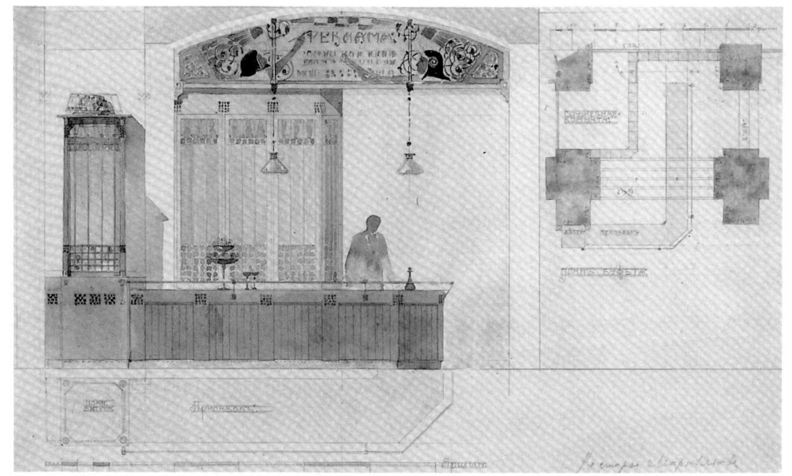
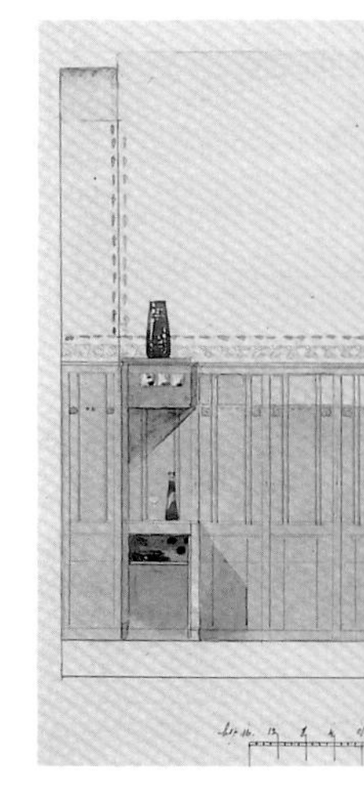

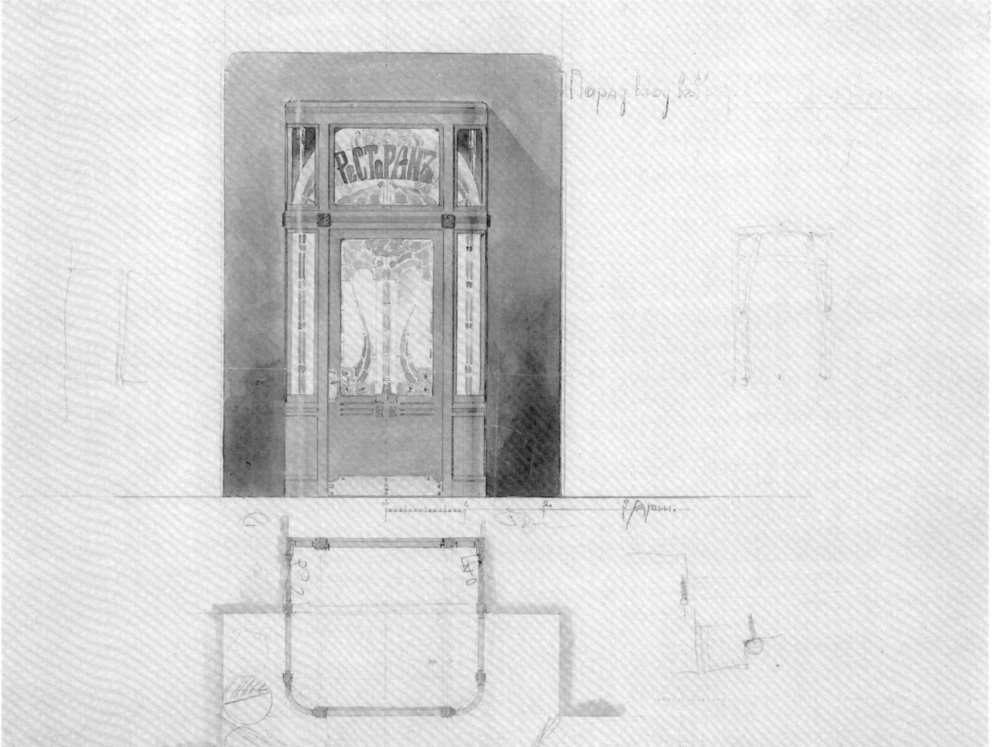

ABOVE: 155. Entrance from Red Square
(variant), plan and elevation
Pencil and watercolour on paper, 44 × 56.8
A. V. Shchusev State Museum of Architecture

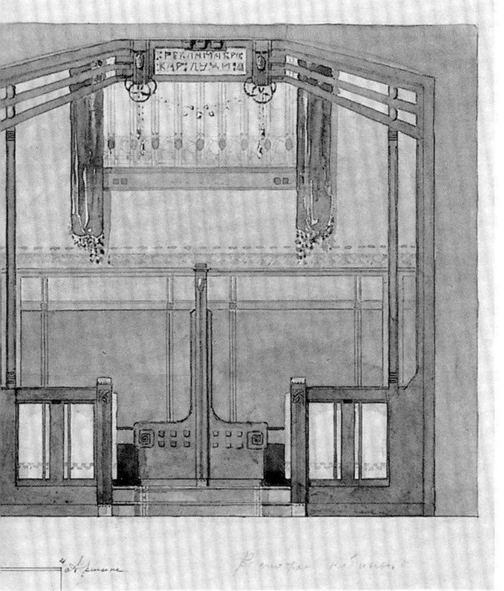

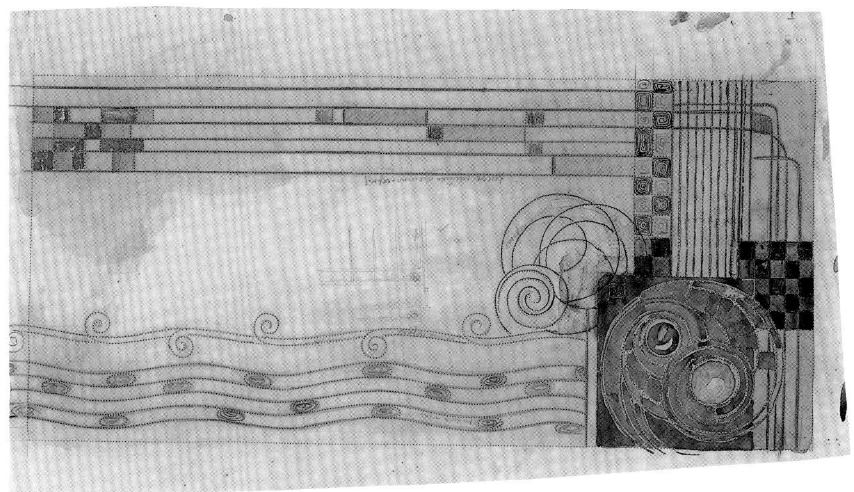

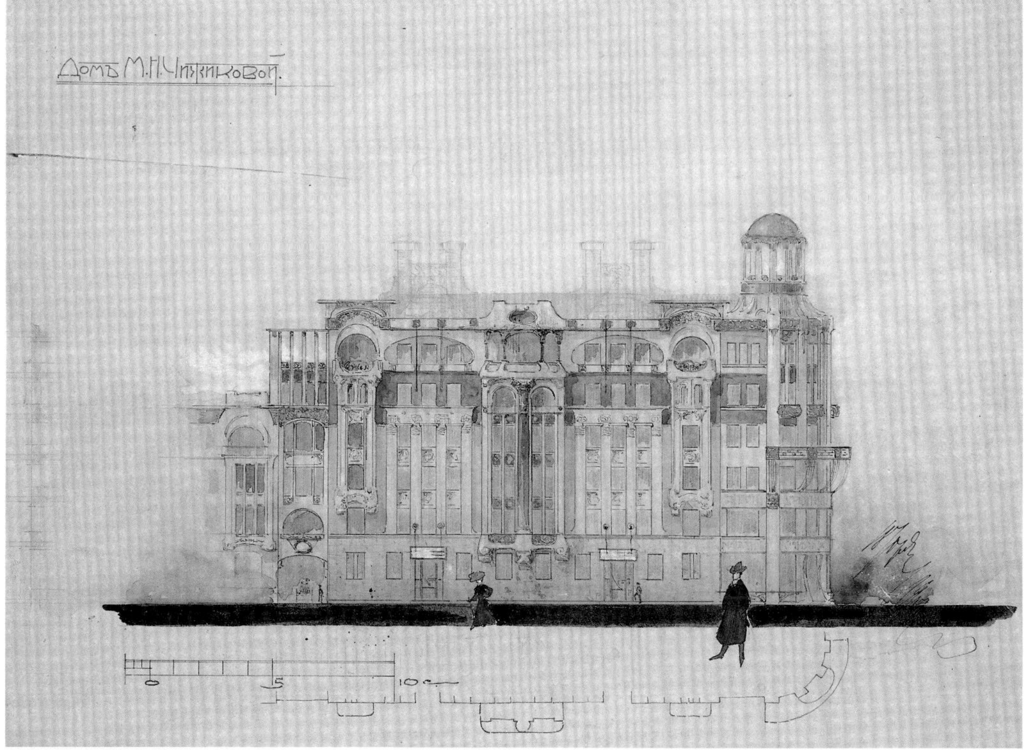

Above: **V. V. Iordan**
145. Design for the Chizhikova apartment
house on the Arbat, Moscow
1907
Mixed media on coloured paper, 49 × 63.5
A. V. Shchusev State Museum of Architecture

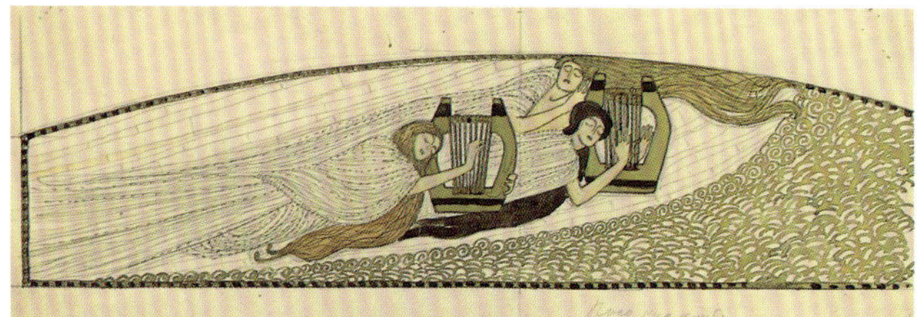

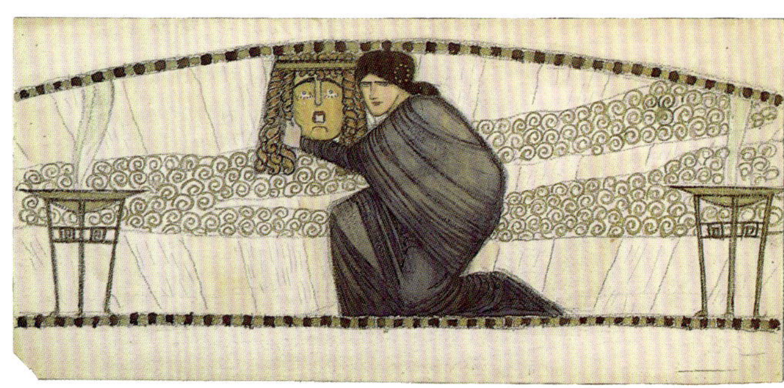

ABOVE: **Illarion Ivanov-Shits**
Merchants' Club on Malaya Dmitrovka
(Chekhov Street), Moscow
1907–08
152, 153, 154. Designs for decorative panels in
entrance hall
Mixed media on paper, 17.2 × 48; 24 × 49.3;
22.8 × 49.4
A. V. Shchusev State Museum of Architecture

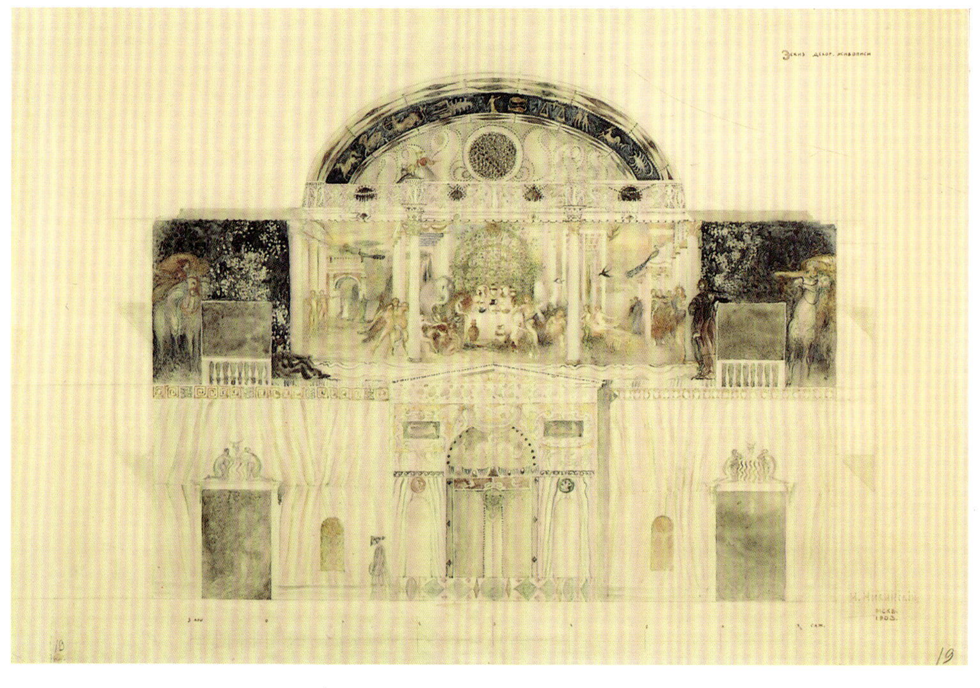

BELOW: **Ignaty Nivinsky**
249. Design for decorative wall paintings in the
café of the Hotel Metropol, Moscow
1903
Mixed media on paper, 44.5 × 65
A. V. Shchusev State Museum of Architecture

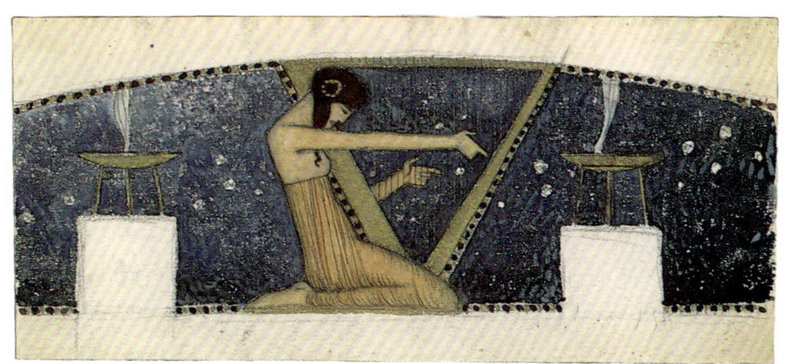

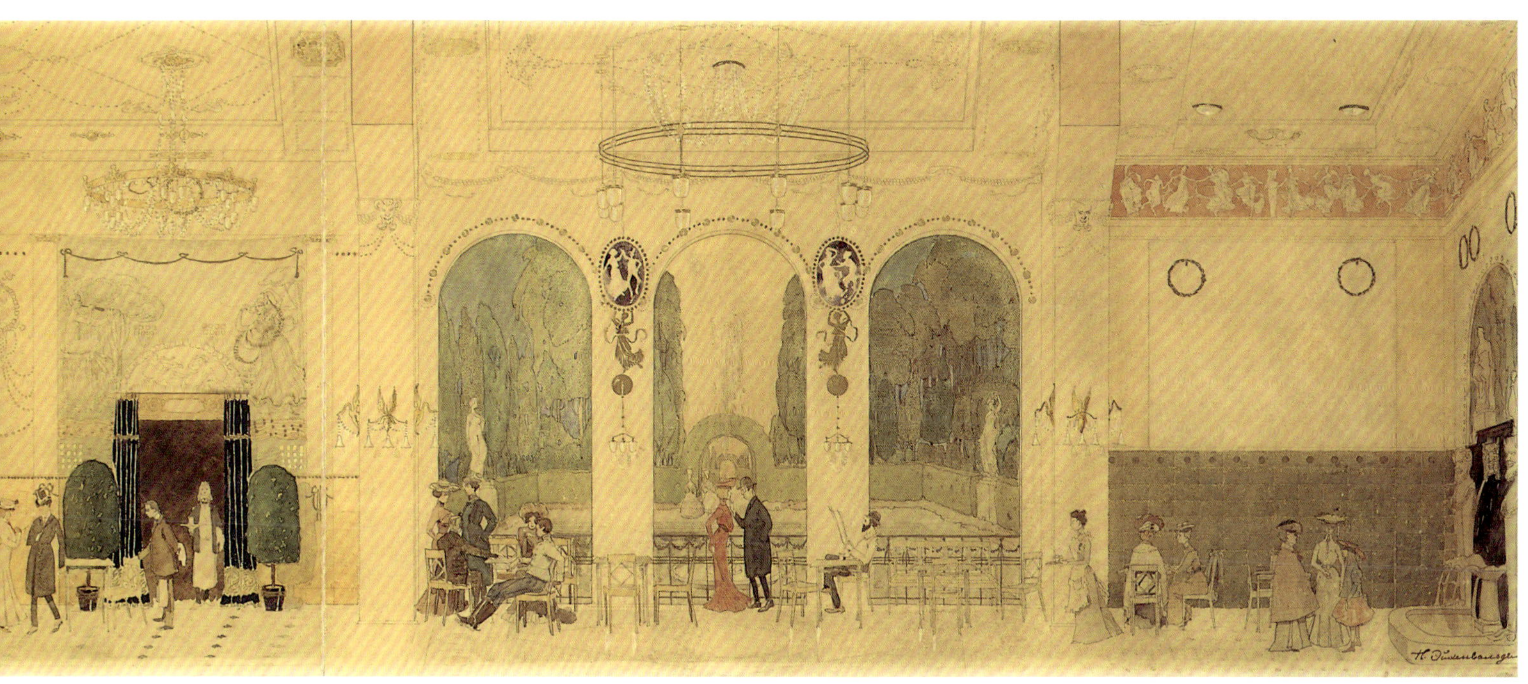

ABOVE: **N. A. Eikhenval'd (Eichenwald)**
104. Filippov apartment house on Tverskaya
Street, Moscow: design for interior of café
1910–12
Mixed media on paper, 36.2 × 128.2
A. V. Shchusev State Museum of Architecture

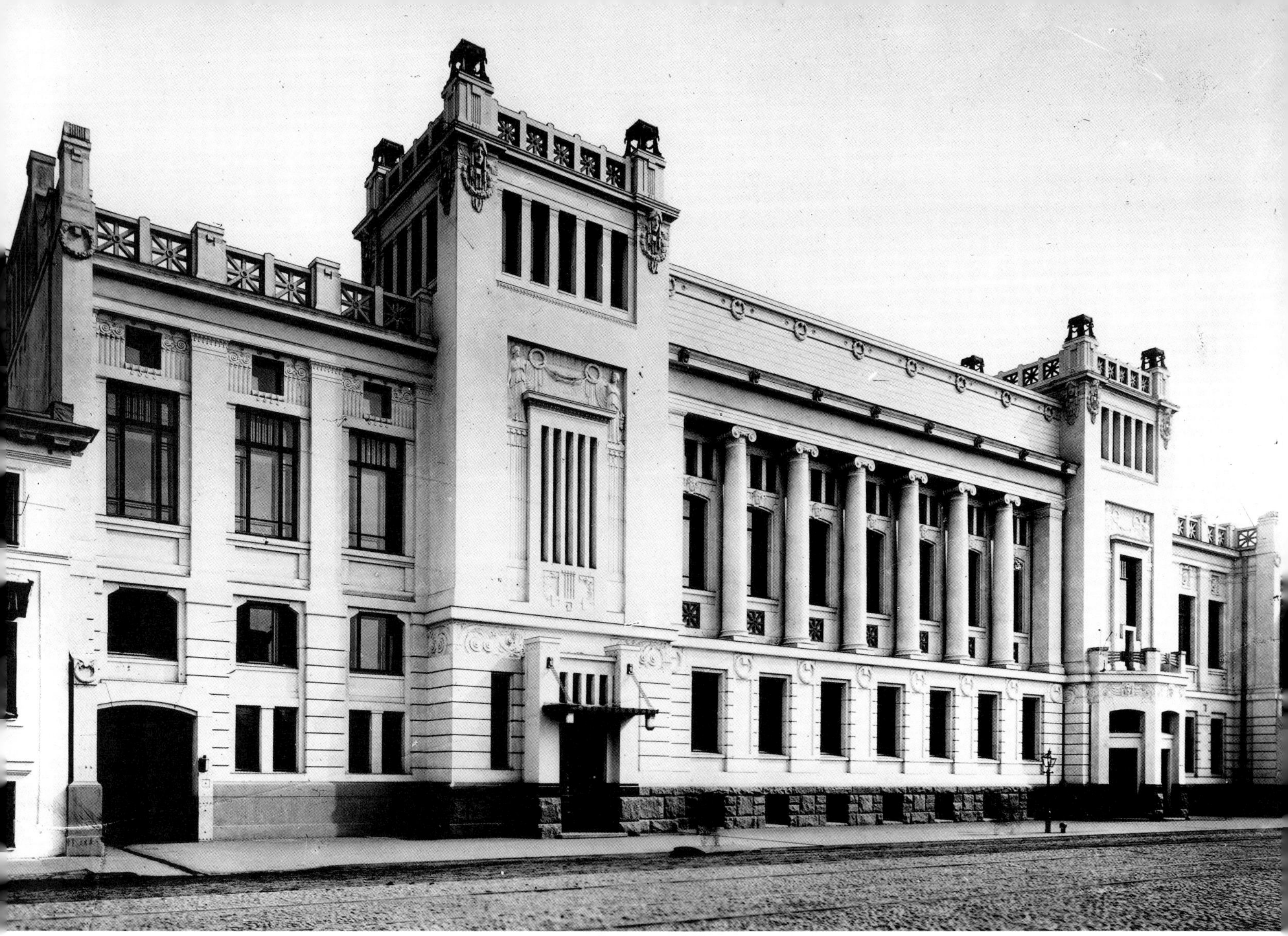

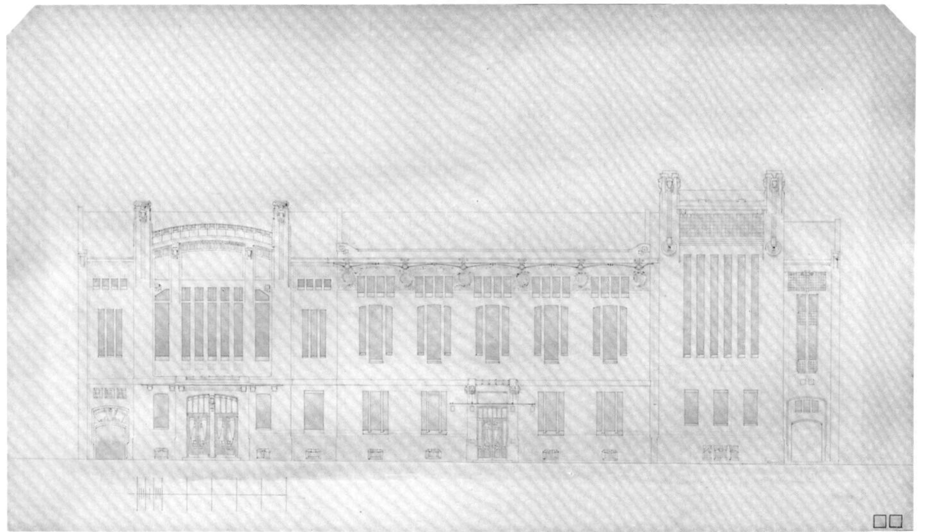

Illarion Ivanov-Shits
Merchants' club on Malaya Dmitrovka
(Chekhov Street), Moscow
1907–08

ABOVE: Street elevation

LEFT: 148. Elevation (variant)
Mixed media, on paper, 54.5 × 93.5
A. V. Shchusev State Museum of Architecture

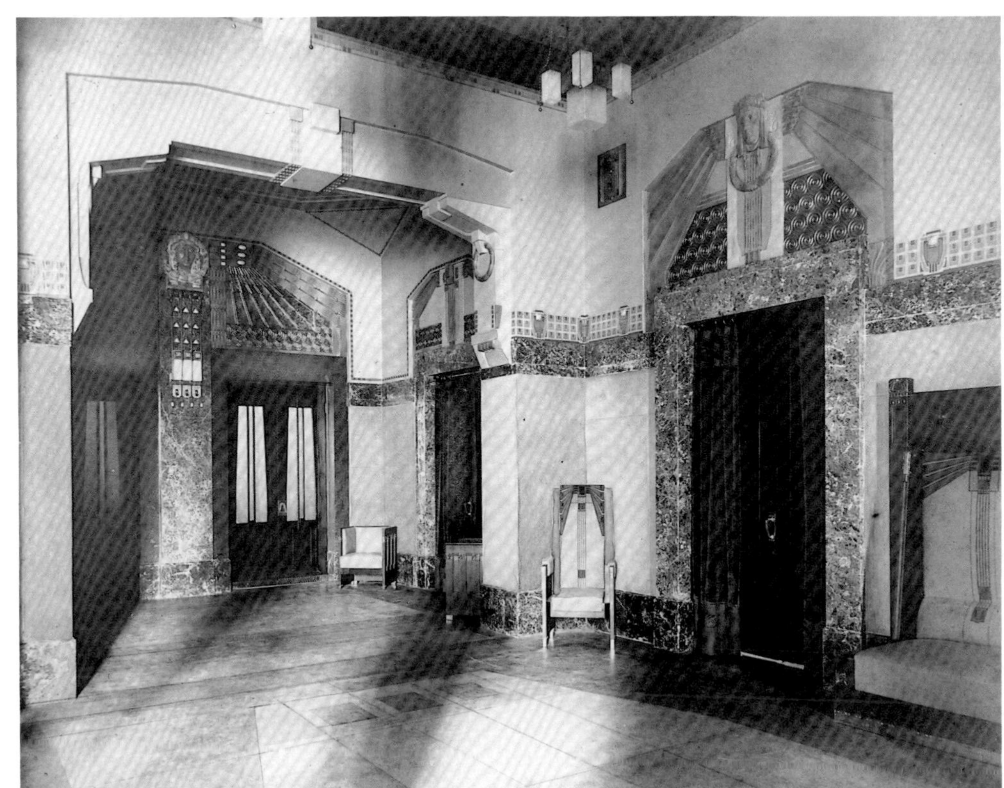

RIGHT AND BELOW LEFT:
Illarion Ivanov-Shits
151, 150. Merchants' Club: Two views of
entrance hall
1907–08
Photos (1900s)
A. V. Shchusev State Museum of Architecture

BELOW RIGHT: **Roman Ivanovich Klein**
168. Muir and Mirrielees Department Store,
Teatralnaya Square, Moscow: longitudinal
section 1907–08
Indian ink and watercolour on paper,
65,5 × 60.5
A. V. Shchusev State Museum of Architecture

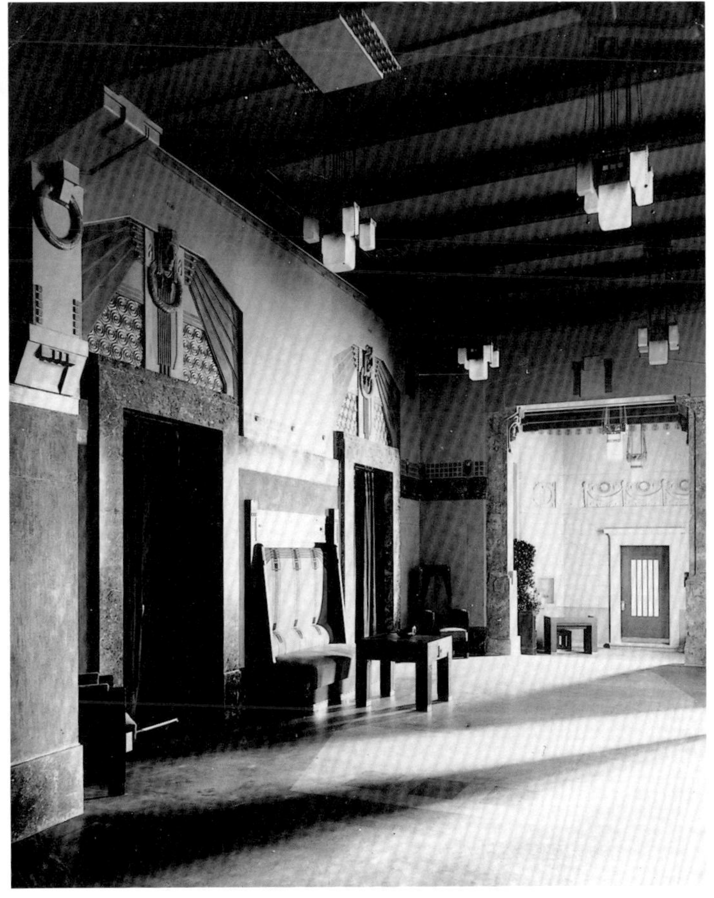

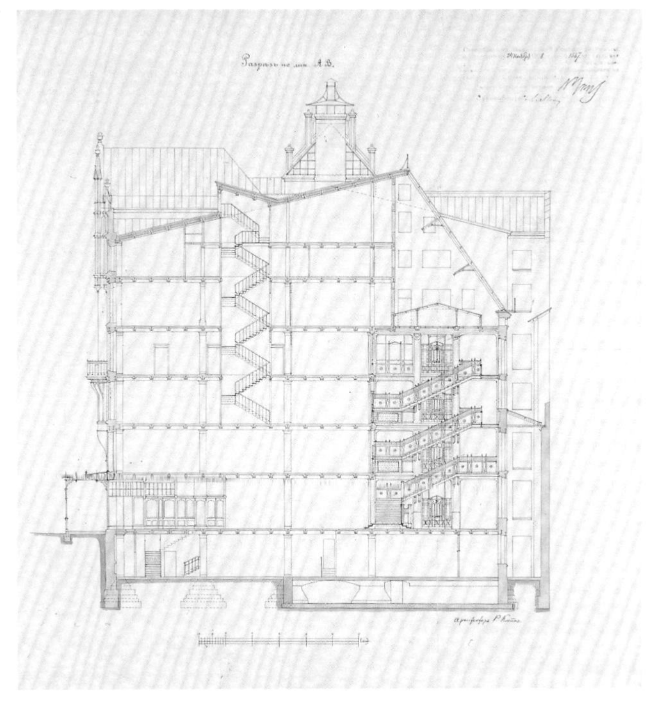

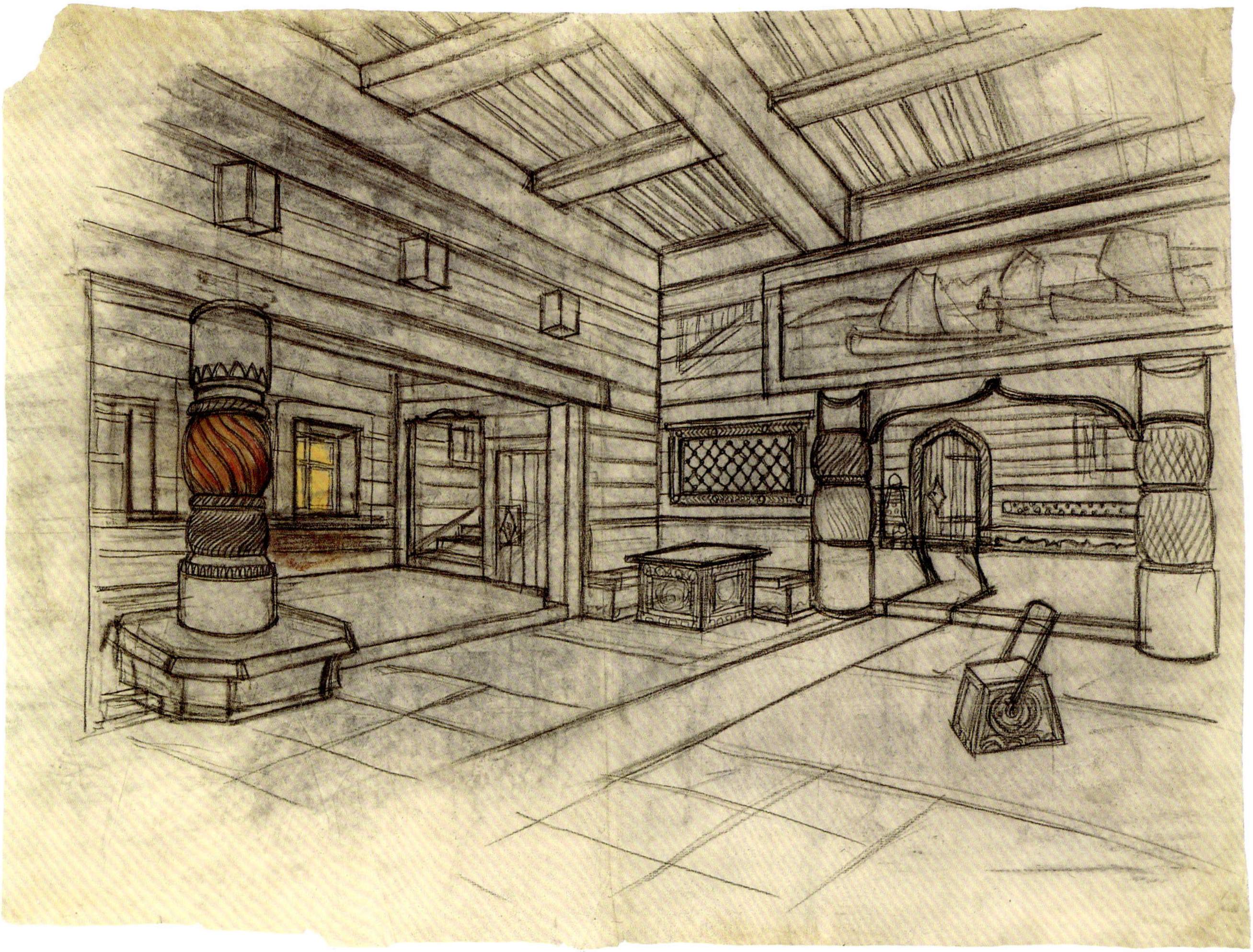

Leonid Vesnin
Nosenkov's dacha at Ivanovo near
Moscow
1908–09

ABOVE: 450. Interior
Mixed media on tracing paper,
54 × 71.5
A. V. Shchusev State Museum of
Architecture

RIGHT: 449. Perspective
Charcoal and pastel on coloured
paper, 30.7 × 48.9
A. V. Shchusev State Museum of
Architecture

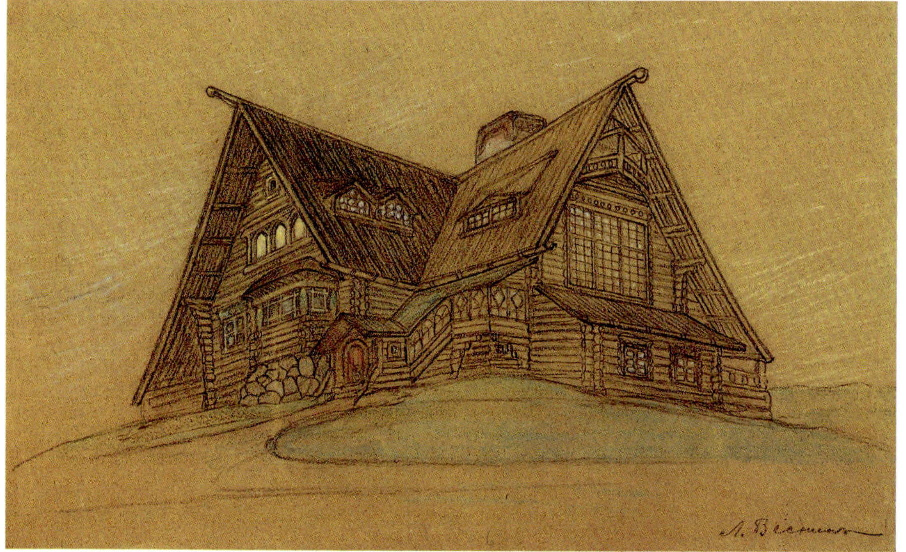

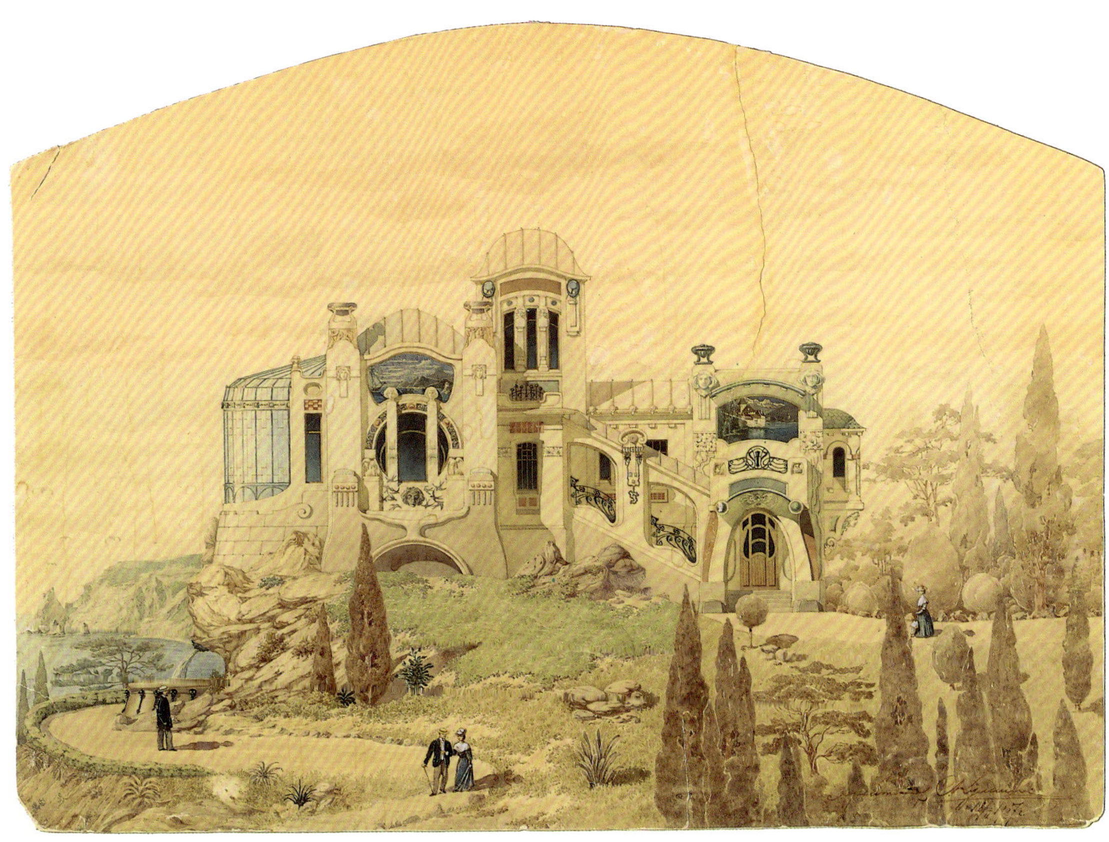

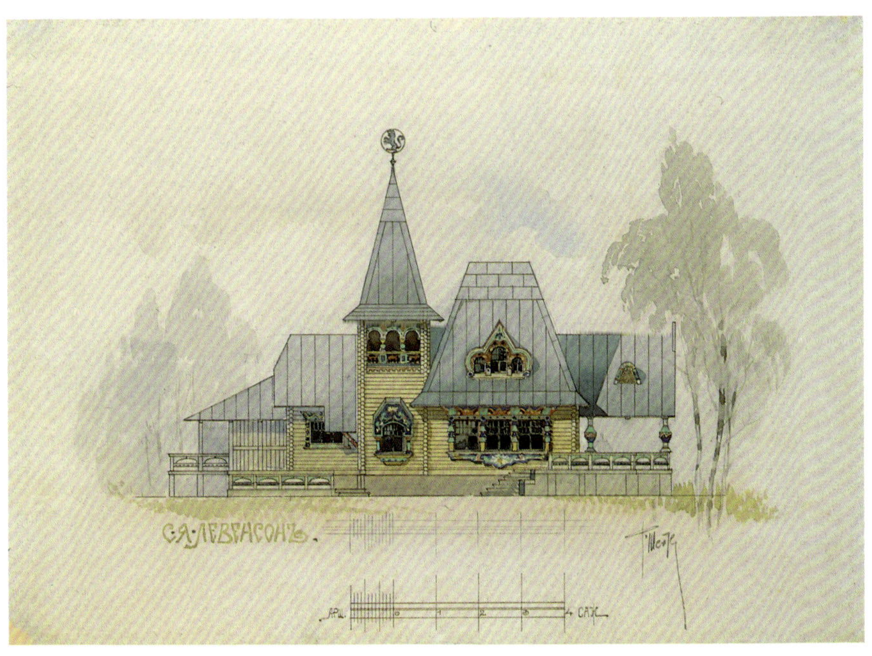

Above: **S. F. Kulagin**
185. Project for a villa in the Crimea
1907
Mixed media on paper, 44 × 58.8
A. V. Shchusev State Museum of Architecture

Left: **Fedor Shekhtel'**
339. Design for dacha of S. Y. Levenson at
Peredelkino, near Moscow
1900
Ink and watercolour on paper, 34.5 × 55
A. V. Shchusev State Museum of Architecture

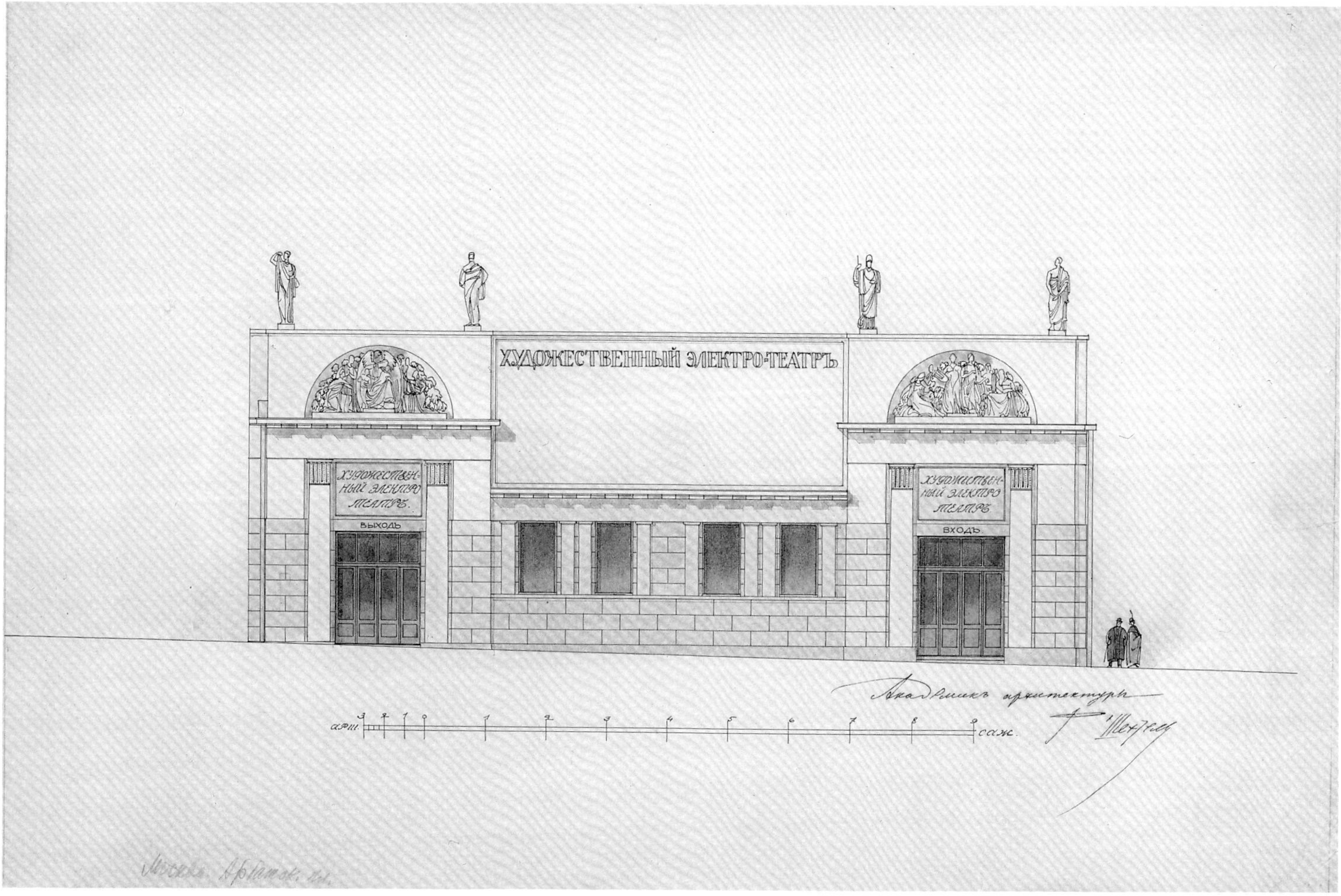

Главный фасадъ.

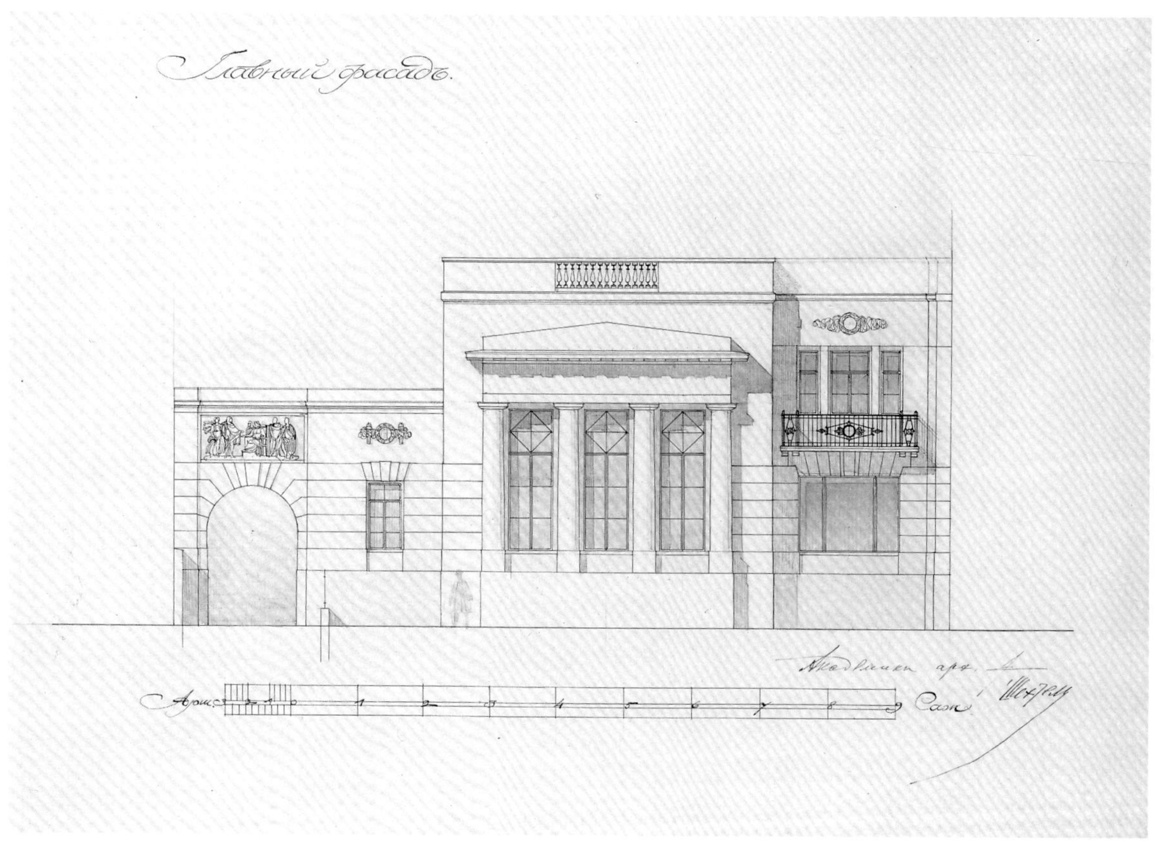

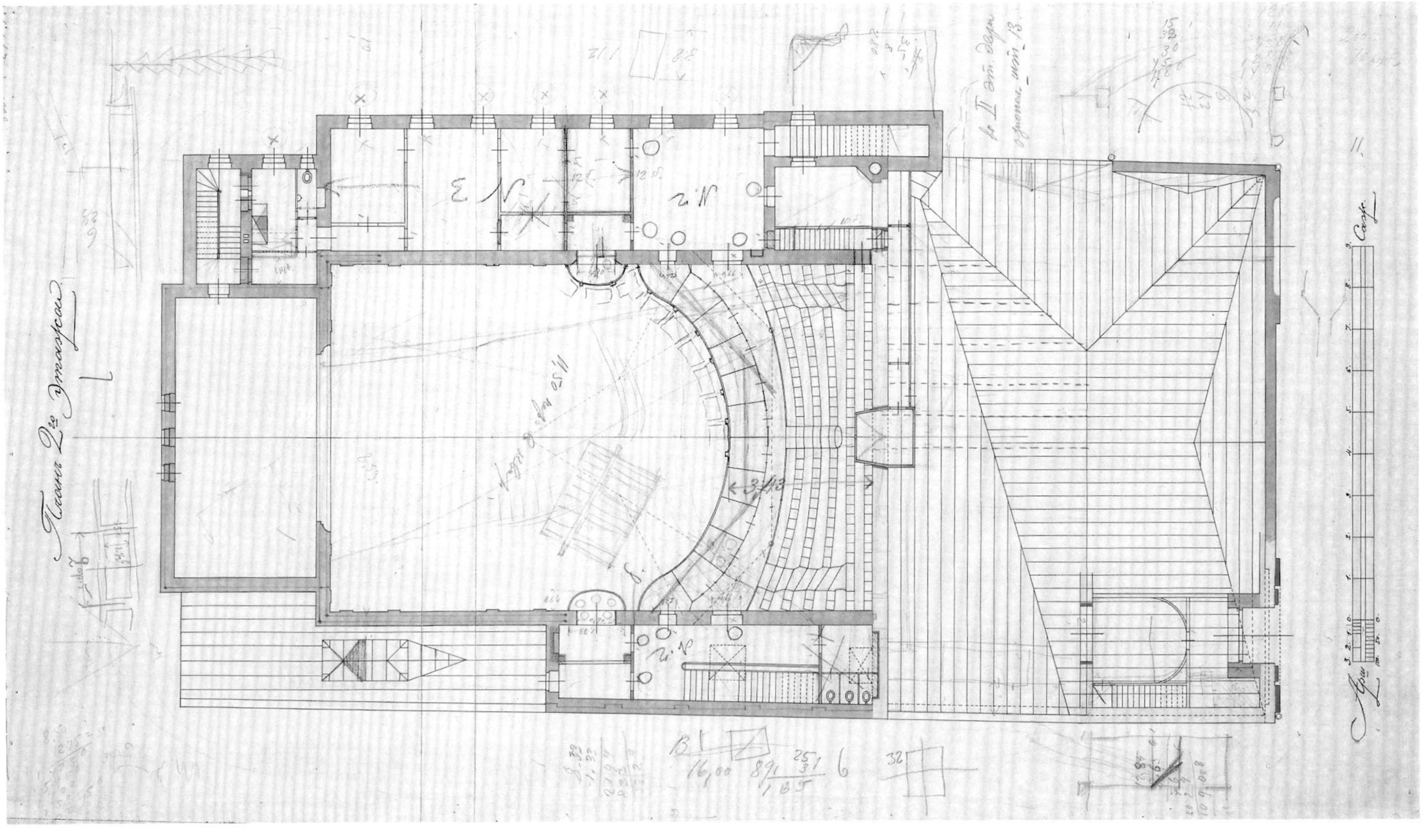

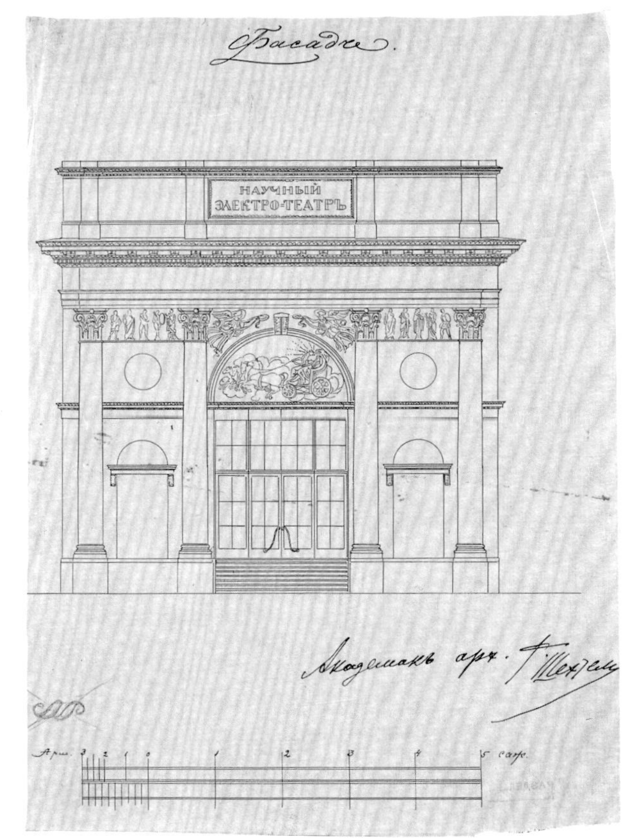

Fedor Shekhtel'
"Arts" Cinema on Arbat Square, Moscow
1912

Opposite above: 379. Elevation
Mixed media on paper, 37.7 × 55.5
A. V. Shchusev State Museum of Architecture

Above: 380. Plan of the first floor
Mixed media on paper, 37.9 × 64.2
A. V. Shchusev State Museum of Architecture

Opposite below:
Fedor Shekhtel'
377. The Architect's own house on Bol'shaya
Sadovaya, Moscow: elevation
1909–10
Indian ink and watercolour on paper,
31.8 × 43.7
A. V. Shchusev State Museum of Architecture

Right: **Fedor Shekhtel'**
382. Exhibition Building in Kamergersky Lane,
Moscow: elevation (version not executed)
1913–15
Indian ink and pencil on tracing paper,
31.5 × 22.8
A. V. Shchusev State Museum of Architecture

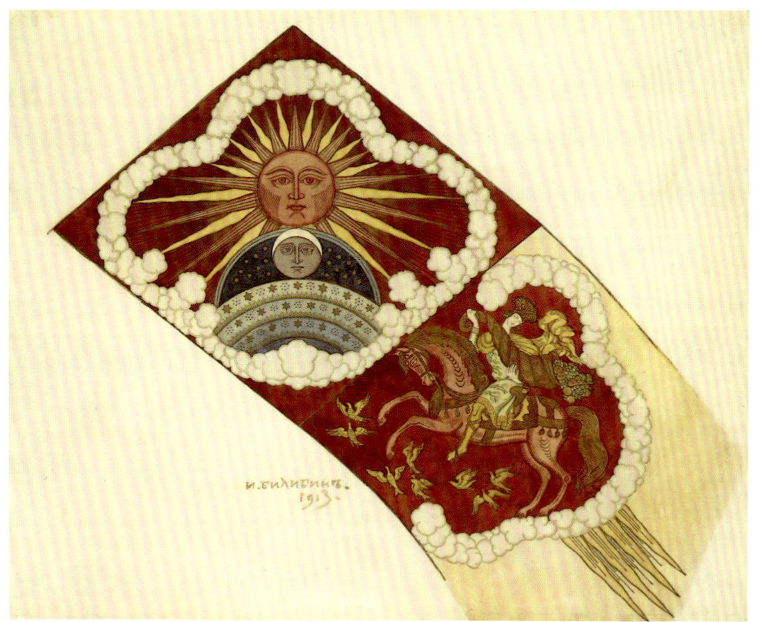

LEFT: **Ivan Bilibin**
58. *Signs of the Zodiac*
Designs for decoration of vaults for a bank in
Nizhny Novgorod (competition project)
1913
Indian ink, pencil, watercolour on paper
mounted on cardboard, 50.7 × 60.3
A. V. Shchusev State Museum of Architecture

BELOW: **Vladimir Pokrovsky**
271. Competition project for the Museum of
Military History in St Petersburg (not
executed)
1908
Mixed media on cardboard, 74.7 × 99.5
A. V. Shchusev State Museum of Architecture

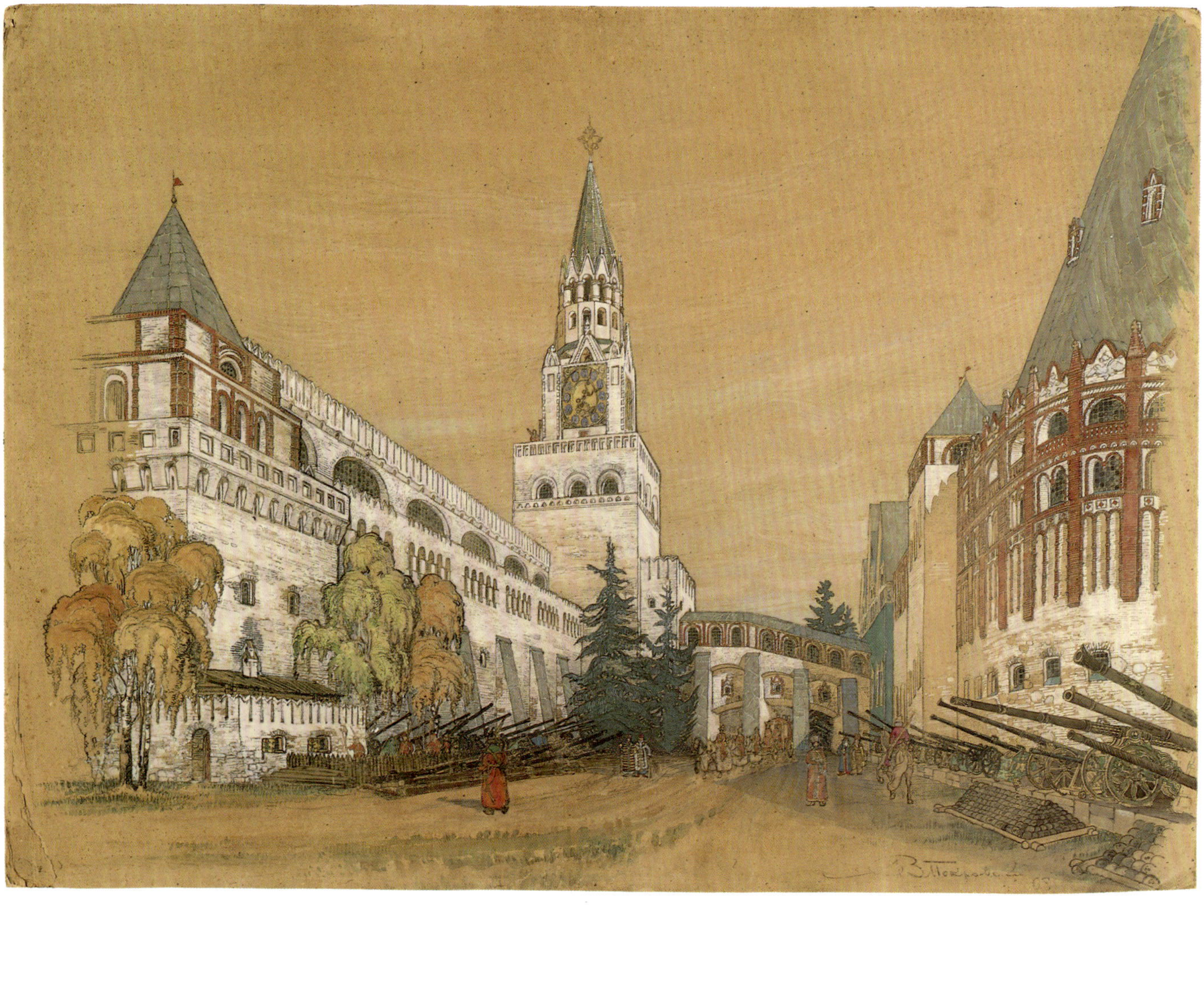

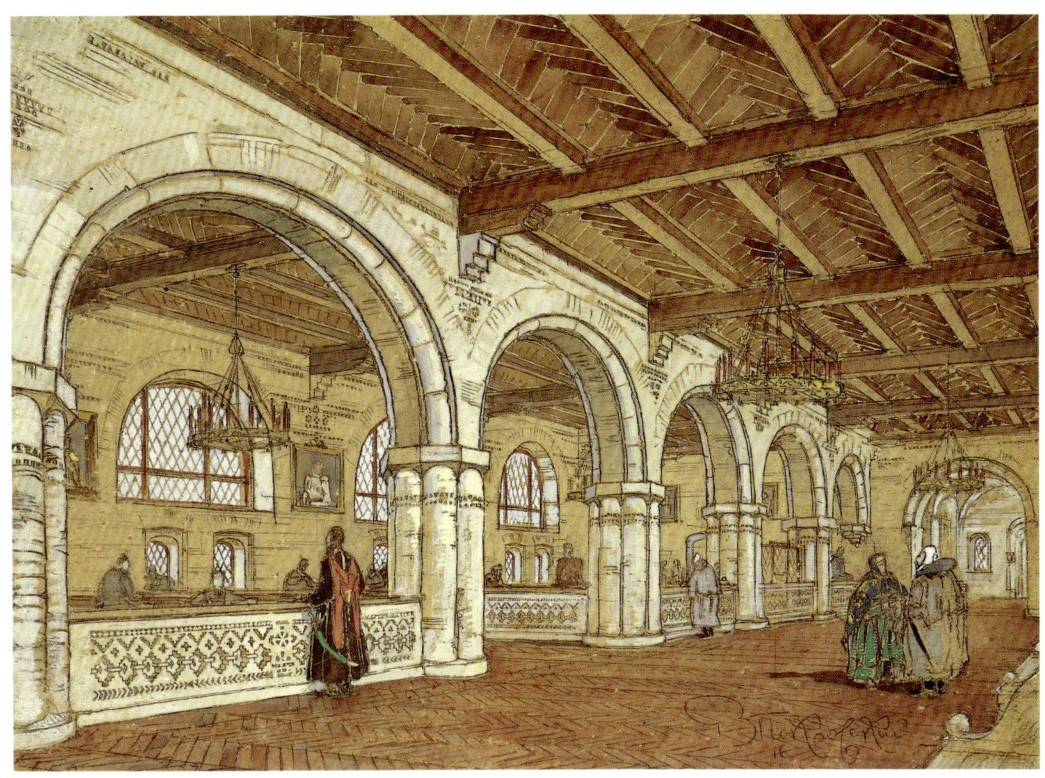

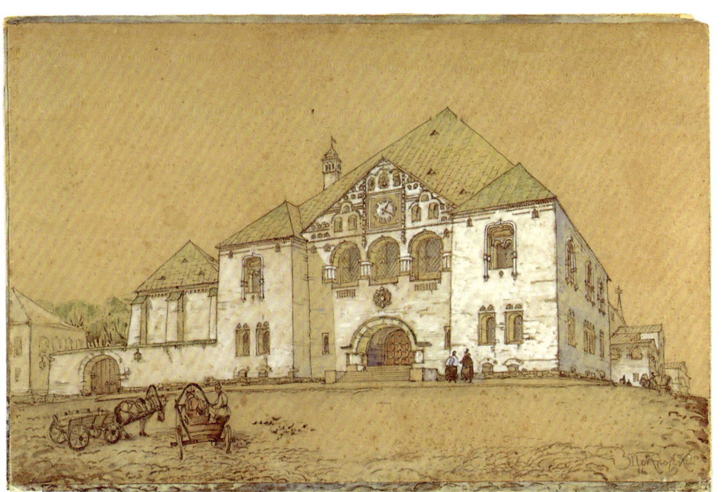

Vladimir Pokrovsky
Competition project for a bank at Nizhny
Novgorod
1916

ABOVE: 273. Interior of banking hall
Mixed media on cardboard, 54 × 71
A. V. Shchusev State Museum of Architecture

LEFT: 272. Perspective
Mixed media on cardboard, 70 × 103
A. V. Shchusev State Museum of Architecture

BELOW: **Aleksandr Benois**
48. *Warrior's Farewell to His Family*
1916
Study for a panel for the Kazan' Station
Oil on canvas, 67 × 107
State Tretyakov Gallery

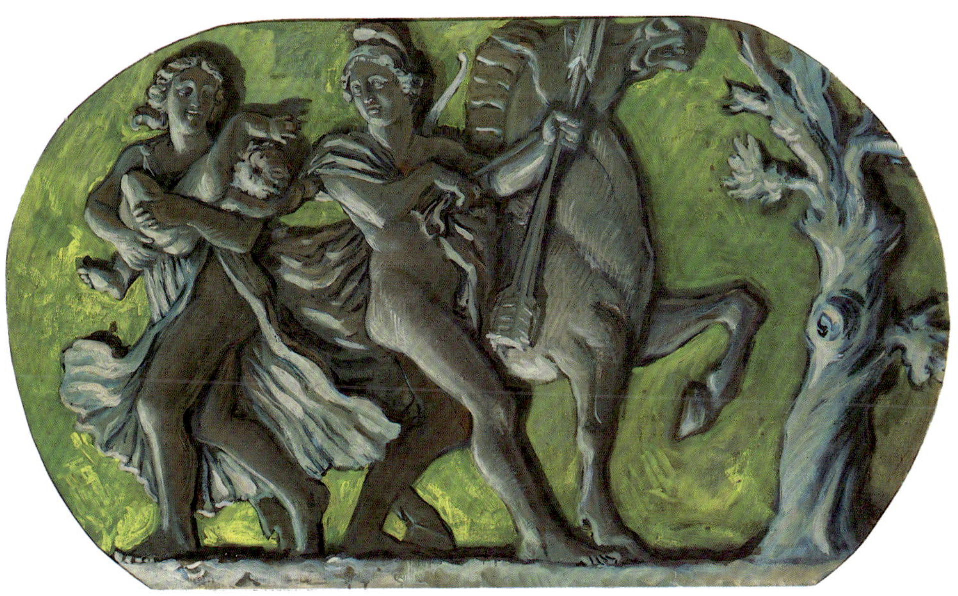

18

THE DECORATIVE ART AND DESIGN
OF RUSSIAN *MODERNE*

OL'GA STRUGOVA

The sources of the new tendencies that developed in Russian decorative and applied art during the 1880s are to be found in the activities of the group of artists working at Abramtsevo, the estate of the patron Savva Mamontov near Moscow. While the members of the group were working jointly on the designs for the façades and interiors of the Abramtsevo church (1882), the basic principles – the essential methods of stylisation – which were to have a decisive effect on the development of the Russian *Style Moderne* were laid down. The inspiration for the new movement was the leading painter Viktor Vasnetsov.

A rediscovery of the national artistic heritage was one of the characteristic features of decorative arts and design throughout Europe in the second half of the nineteenth century, and it also formed one of the main sources of *Art Nouveau* styles. The ideas of John Ruskin and William Morris, who preached a revival of crafts and saw the understanding of medieval culture as a means of renewing art and uniting it with everyday life, were widely disseminated in the countries of Europe. These ideas found fertile ground in Russia too, where the movement towards the traditions of national art became a phenomenon of some importance during the second half of the nineteenth century; but, unlike Western European artists, the Russians began to turn in their work not only to Russian art of the past, but also to contemporary living folk art.

The Abramtsevo artists, including Elena Polenova, who became the manager of the joinery workshop in 1884, were the first to turn towards wood-carving, a very rich tradition in Russian folk culture. The thousand-year-old practices of wood-carving and painting were still alive among the people, and Polenova, together with colleagues from the group, made a number of journeys around Russian villages to collect exhibits for the museum they created at Abramtsevo. The objects they collected often became the sources for her work in furniture design.

The joinery workshop at Abramtsevo was followed by a ceramics workshop, which was transferred to Moscow in 1896. Its manager was Petr Vaulin. Whereas the main characteristic of the joinery workshop was the movement towards national traditions, the quest for the new was more perceptible in the ceramics workshop. This was expressed particularly in the development of new techniques, such as metallic glazing. However, the novelty of Abramtsevo ceramics was far from being a matter of technique alone. Originality of form and a high artistic level marked the fireplaces, sculpture, decorative vessels and architectural ceramics produced in the Abramtsevo workshop. Many of these works received the highest awards at international exhibitions at the turn of the century. The Abramtsevo ceramics workshop exerted a massive influence on the whole art of ceramics in Russia. The articles made at Abramtsevo – furniture, ceramics, fabrics and embroidery – were in great demand, and their high artistic level was due to the participation of many outstanding artists, including Vrubel', Korovin, Viktor Vasnetsov and Serov.

Similar workshops began to appear elsewhere, among which mention should be made of the little-known studio set up in the 1890s by Nikolai Bartram at his estate of Semenovka in the Kursk province. This artist subsequently became one of the outstanding representatives of Russian *Style Moderne* and worked actively for the Moscow Museum of Crafts. Another centre of Russian artistic life, at Talashkino, became a worthy successor to the Abramtsevo traditions. It developed on the estate of Princess Tenisheva near Smolensk, and brought together such outstanding artists as Sergei Malyutin and Nikolai Roerich.

Among the artists working here the most consistent champion of the Abramtsevo traditions was the manager of the joinery workshop, Sergei Malyutin, whose work bore close affinities to Russian folk wood-carving, particularly the carving on houses in the area along the Volga. Sometimes Malyutin used this not simply as a point of departure for stylisation but also for direct copying, and he would occasionally combine details produced from his own drawings with genuine examples of folk carving. The pieces from a dining-room suite made from drawings by Malyutin (p.19) fully reflect the individual nature of this artist's decorative talents. In this case the principal motif of the carving is the sunflower, one of Malyutin's favourite subjects, and the illumination of the projecting parts of the carving intensifies the play of light and shade, emphasising the relief. The carved decoration of these and similar objects is related to the rich brushwork of Malyutin's paintings. The distinctive, often expressive, forms of Malyutin's furniture demonstrate a liberation of creative thought and a freedom from the previously developed stereotypes of the "Russian style".

Aleksei Zinov'ev, who took over the management of the Talashkino workshop after Malyutin's departure, belonged to the next generation of artists. Although he was undoubtedly influenced by Roerich and Malyutin, the great talent of this artist-designer enabled him to develop an individual creative style which was brilliant and personal. He never borrowed motifs directly from Russian medieval or folk art, but the objects he made show an attempt to create an impression of the archaic on the basis of images developed from the artist's imagination. In the chair on wheels (p.230) this is seen in the symmetrically placed fantastic animal heads, which appear to be growing out of the thickness of the wood on the chair back.

One of the outstanding representatives of the national-romantic movement in Russian *Moderne* was the artist Sergei Vashkov, whose creative legacy is rich and varied. For example, he produced a number of architectural designs, and his name is found among those of the teachers at the Stroganov Design School. In 1904, furniture and engraving workshops were set up here, and the nature of their products was largely determined by Vashkov's active participation.

Many objects of decorative and applied art were made from Vashkov's designs by the Moscow firm of P. I. Olovyanishnikov & Sons, established in 1901 and specialising mainly in the production of church plate. Vashkov managed the art department here for a number of years. Among the objects made by this firm, a cross on a carved base depicting Golgotha is of particular interest (p.241); the painted Crucifixion may have been executed by the eminent artist Mikhail Nesterov, since correspondence between Vashkov and Nesterov, kept in the Central State Archive of Literature and Art, reveals that on more than one occasion Nesterov executed commissions for the production of painted icons for Olovyanishnikov.

A number of items of domestic furniture were also made by the firm from Vashkov's designs, including a table on three flat carved supports (no.440). The artist frequently obtained his inspiration from medieval Russian art, and the influence of the architecture of Vladimir and Suzdal' is noticeable in some of his architectural designs. In the design of the table, this influence can be seen expressed in the carved motif of the recumbent lion.

At the beginning of the twentieth century interior design was increasingly affected by rationalistic tendencies, as is well illustrated by the cupboard (p.231) made by the Russian architect Ivan Fomin for the exhibition of *Architecture and Design in the New Style*, held in Moscow in 1902–03. The clear structural outlines of this cupboard and its characteristic trapezoidal shape correspond to the general European trends in furniture design. However, it also displays features characteristic of the Russian national style at the turn of the century, specifically the stability and monumentality of the forms and the use of geometrical carving characteristic of the Russian style of the *Moderne* period. Indeed, national romanticism occupied an important place in Fomin's work at this time.

Fomin was one of the principal organizers of the *New Style* exhibition. This showed the latest achievements of Russian *Moderne* in the field of decorative art and interior design and exerted a great influence on contemporary artists. Leading representatives of *Art Nouveau* from other countries were also attracted to the exhibition, including Charles Rennie Mackintosh as the representative of the Glasgow school, Joseph Maria Olbrich from Darmstadt, and Jan Kotěra from Prague.

Objects in the Russian style decorated with applied ornamentation in stamped brass became quite common at the turn of the century. The decorative motifs on these were similar to those found on carved wooden articles, but their particular colour and texture brought variety to the decorative language of the *Style Moderne*. A huge variety of wooden objects were decorated with this technique, a typical example being the box (no.569) whose form reproduces a twin-layer *teremok* casket. These *teremok* caskets were produced in large quantities at Veliky Ustyug in the north of Russia in the seventeenth century and were used to store money and valuables. Another characteristic article is a bottle holder (no.568) reproducing a *kovsh* or scoop in the form of a water fowl; vessels of this form were common in Russia for several centuries.

A major part in the distribution of objects in the national romantic style was played by the Moscow Museum of Crafts, which was established in the 1870s. In 1910 a Museum of Specimens was set up there, which was to display the most interesting works of decorative and applied art created by many well-known artists. The workshops attached to the Museum of Crafts executed orders for the production of articles modelled on these specimens, and following their successful appearance at the major international exhibitions at the beginning of the twentieth century, their export significantly increased. It is noteworthy that the Western concept of the national characteristics and originality of Russian decorative art and design developed not so much on the basis of genuine works of Russian medieval and folk art, but rather under the influence of such objects, which represent the spirit of the national-romantic tendency in Russian *Moderne*. An example of this is the *matryoshka* toy, consisting of a number of turned dolls fitting inside each other. The first *matryoshka* was made in 1903 from a drawing by Malyutin. Its principle and form were borrowed from Japanese art, but when translated into the Russian national style it took on a completely new resonance and was immediately accepted as a traditional folk toy. Some of the earliest Russian *matryoshky* (pp.234–5) were made in the Sergei Trading Quarter, which is still the major centre for the production of this type of souvenir.

In addition to drawing upon Russian medieval and folk art traditions, artists and architects also turned to the art of Russian classicism of the late eighteenth and first quarter of the nineteenth centuries. This was particularly characteristic of the artists of the *Mir Iskusstva* group. The architect Fomin was one of those who turned to this period of Russian art, retaining his loyalty to classicism for several decades, right up to the 1930s.

Early twentieth-century Neo-Classicism appeared in a number of different forms in Russia. For example, some artists (particularly Evgeny Lanceray, Lev Bakst and others of the *Mir Iskusstva* group) used the traditions of classicism for their own stylisations in the *Moderne* spirit. However, by the 1910s there was an increasingly frequent appearance of a retrospective tendency, a striving to reproduce old forms or, occasionally, to copy them. This was strengthened by the centenary of the war against Napoleon, celebrated in 1912. A good example of this trend is provided by the two chairs (p.237) whose construction draws on the traditions of classicism: the shape of the back in the form of a shield and the use of Karelian birch (a material characteristic of the early nineteenth century) quite clearly demonstrate the source which inspired the unknown designer. However, the proportions of the back, which differ from those characteristic of the early nineteenth century, and the design of the frame ornament and its location on the back indicate an attempt to create something new, in keeping with the *Moderne* period.

Furniture in the spirit of the national-romantic tendency was normally designed for specific interiors, and its manufacture was based on manual work. At the same time, the rational tendency of *Style Moderne* produced forms that were simpler though still expressive. Objects designed in this way became widespread in urban homes, and they were well suited to factory production. However, the simplicity of these objects was by no means always identified with cheapness. As a rule, furniture of this type was characterised by a high quality of manufacture and careful finishing, with particular attention paid to the beauty of the wood during its manufacture, as, for example, the mahogany furniture used in the apartment of the Moscow publisher I. D. Sytin (p.237). In Russian furniture of the rational *Moderne* style it is possible to see the first traces of Constructivism and Functionalism, which were brilliantly represented in the work of Soviet artists and architects in the first post-revolutionary decade.

The most important characteristic of decorative and applied art during the *Moderne* period is its striving for the creation of a unity of design within the interior environment. The furniture, lighting equipment and every object, down to the smallest details of the interior decoration or costume, were designed in a single key. The *Style Moderne* was the creation of painters, and everyday objects became a part of the creative work of many of the most famous members of the national art world. Like their colleagues in other countries, artists such as Viktor Vasnetsov, Vasily Polenov, V. N. Baksheev and Sergei Malyutin designed their own houses, with architecture and decoration that reflected their aesthetic ideals.

The earliest and most distinctive movement in the *Style Moderne* was national romanticism, which turned to the traditions of Russian medieval and folk art. Different artists turned to the most varied sources, including folk woodcarving, medieval Russian architecture of the pre-Mongol period, the rational simplicity and thoughtfulness of the furniture of the traditional peasant house, and the plastic and chromatic richness of objects of the sixteenth and late seventeenth centuries.

At the same time, various tendencies of the new international style were widely encountered in Russia, from the use of whimsical lines in the *Art Nouveau* spirit to various interpretations of rational modernism. The latter style often took on a clearly expressed national colouring.

Thus the distinctive nature of the *Style Moderne* in Russian decorative art design was not only formed by the characteristics of the movement in which the traditions of national art were used. In Russia, as in all other countries, the whole gamut of stylistic tendencies of *Art Nouveau* was represented.

19

RUSSIAN GOLD AND SILVER AT THE TURN OF THE CENTURY

GALINA SMORODINOVA

Russian gold and silver in the late nineteenth and early twentieth centuries was a unique phenomenon. Having absorbed the experience of a thousand years of development, it passed through a period of remarkable national revival. The names of the best jewellery firms – those of Carl Fabergé, Pavel Ovchinnikov, Ivan Khlebnikov – became for the whole world a symbol of the brilliant Silver Age of Russian culture.

The *Art Nouveau* style had its own distinctive characteristics in each country in addition to common stylistic features. In the work of Russian goldsmiths and silversmiths these common features were united with a repertory of national motifs, the taste for which had been growing for some period of time, to form the distinctive Neo-Russian style. This was based on the forms of old Russian jewellery, freely treated and enriched with illustrative elements taken from history, folklore and literature. Subjects used for the decorative design of dishes, albums, blotters and objects for everyday use and personal adornment included the coronation of Mikhail Romanov, the laying of the foundations of St Petersburg and the return of Peter I's troops after the battle of Poltava, while images from fairy tales – the Sirin bird, Princess Volkhova, *bogatyri* (legendary heroes) defending the fatherland, the frog princess, Baba-Yaga and others – were widely used. Scenes from the works of Russian writers and poets such as Aleksandr Pushkin and Mikhail Lermontov were also represented.

The gold and silver of the late nineteenth and early twentieth centuries is striking not only for the variety of the ornamental motifs, but also for the techniques and the rich palette of jewellery materials. In this period, jewellers drew on every technique of decorating precious metal that had been practised during the thousand-year history of their art, including long-forgotten methods such as cloisonné and champlevé enamel. Completely new techniques also appeared, such as those of gloss and matt enamel varnishes.

The style of decoration changed from that of the previous period: the surface of an object was now seen as a distinctive form of decorative panel with its own particular rhythms of colour, texture and line. Strict relationships were replaced with free construction, combining various plant motifs – including both traditional ones and *Moderne* forms – geometrical elements and subjects unmistakably influenced by contemporary painting and graphic art.

In the art of enamelling, the use of colour became more complex and varied, ranging from rich colour harmonies to subdued pastels, while filigree was given a more important role, creating new decorative effects rather than simply forming an auxiliary frame for the enamel design. The traditional filigree ornaments were supplemented with tiny circles of tightly wound spirals, miniature chain-mail, scales, rods, fans with minute balls at their ends, and conventional and almost abstract geometrical forms, all of which considerably enhanced the decorative potential of precious metal objects.

Enamel work was undertaken in practically all the gold and silver factories and workshops, and also in the Jewellers' *Artel's* (co-operatives), of which there were about thirty in Moscow alone. The decorative forms of the new stylistic direction were applied to traditional Russian vessels – the *kovsh* (scoop), *bratina* (loving cup), *solonitsa* (salt cellar) and *gorshochek* (pot) – as well as to the handles of tea-glass holders, sugar-bowls, and vases, which developed lines characteristic of the *Style Moderne*.

The techniques of casting and chasing reached their height at the turn of the century, and there was a new, deeper understanding of the remarkable decorative properties of silver, which gave a magical quality to their portrayals of the splash of waves or a snow storm, the marine and plant kingdoms, or images from fairy tales and history.

The striving for the renewal of artistic forms was most clearly seen in vessels and in objects for everyday use or for personal adornment; it was here that jewellers most successfully adopted the *Moderne* and Neo-Russian styles. In silver vessels – sweet-containers, small vases, tea-glass holders – new forms appeared with characteristic profiles, decorated with stylized cut or engraved ornaments, with smoothly gliding lines, or with surprising three-dimensional naturalistic details, such as handles in the form of sculpted birds, or buds, or the Baba-Yaga of fairy tales, or devils, objects of remarkable extravagance and wit.

The development in decorative and applied art followed a change in interior design which, from the late nineteenth century, affected decorative objects of every kind made to be placed on tables, étagères, cabinets or mantelpieces. Many of these were made of gold or silver: vases, *kovshi*, jardinières, sculpture and frames. Many firms, workshops and co-operatives, including those of Fabergé, Ovchinnikov, Khlebnikov, the Grachev brothers, Bragin and the 4th Jewellery Artel', produced containers, clocks and desk sets, which might include sculptural elements in the form of fairy-tale heroes, impressive dragons, *bogatyri* or allegorical figures.

The fashion for smoking was reflected in the widespread production of cigarette cases. They were made to suit various tastes by the major firms, workshops and co-operatives, and their lids provided opportunities for the widest variety of ornaments: plant forms executed in a whole range of styles, motifs from the marine kingdom – which enjoyed an extraordinary vogue – bathers, portraits of Napoleon or Tolstoy, illustrations to Pushkin's poem *The Snowstorm* and realistic genre scenes of hunting, ploughing, peasant women with children, river crossings, birds, beasts and many others. Legendary themes frequently appeared – images of Il'ya Muromets, the gateway of the *bogatyri*, the frog princess and others.

Particularly interesting in the history of gold and silver are commemorative dishes, albums and blotters, made to record a particular event. Again there is a bewildering richness due to jewellers' wide choice of media, the differences in individual styles of design and the vast range of possibilities in the organic combination of various artistic styles. The variety of motifs was matched by the technical mastery, which exploited the contrast between brilliant and matt textures with very fine chasing or engraving, and gave colour by gilding, patination or enamelling and the use of precious or semi-precious stones. Particularly fine examples were produced by the Khlebnikov and Ovchinnikov firms and also by the Jewellers' Artel's.

Ecclesiastical objects were produced by many firms, the most famous of which was P. I. Olovyanishnikov & Sons, whose history went back as far as 1766 and who had a bell foundry at Yaroslavl' and a church plate factory in Moscow. In the early twentieth century, the firm made extensive use of the drawings of Sergei Vashkov, who made a great contribution to the revival of national forms, and he was largely responsible for the distinctive quality of the firms's products. Striving always to achieve the simplicity of ancient art, Vashkov's subtle stylisations of early Christian symbols and variations on the motifs of medieval Russian art could be harmonised perfectly with contemporary forms.

Among the other artists who worked for P. I. Olovyanishnikov & Sons, P. N. Prokof'ev and P. P. Rykovsky are especially noteworthy; they specialized in copying the church plate in the collections of the Imperial Historical Museum, and also made designs based on N. Martynov's watercolours of historic ecclesiastical objects. The Olovyanishnikov firm also used the ancient technique of cloisonné enamel. A decorated mitre in the State Historical Museum collection (no.258) has compartments with images of the Crucifixion and a Deesis executed in a mixed technique of cloisonné and painted enamelling. The frame of the icon of the *Virgin of Tenderness* (p.26) is interesting in its unusual design of plant ornamentation and the colour range of the enamel, which is close to that of the sixteenth-century Sol'vychegodsk style.

The art of jewellery has a special beauty and subtlety, and fine settings seem almost to crystallize the essence of the most refined and precious artistic styles. The works of this period not only demonstrate its stylistic complexity, based on many historic forms of ornamentation that gave the master jewellers a great freedom in their choice of motifs, but also reveal the astonishing rise in technical mastery of rich and precious materials. Among the jewellery firms of Moscow and St Petersburg who were famous for their decoration were K. Bolin, Carl Fabergé, I. Chichelev, F. Koechli, A. Zengbush, I. Morozov, and the workshop of A. Krumbügel, Makhalov, Y. Rimmer, and Y. Reiman.

The quest of turn-of-the-century artists, their search for the transcendant, is clearly expressed in the inventiveness of the decoration of these jewels. The traditional forms of pendants, necklaces or brooches might include a landscape or a female figure, while the strange enchantment of the insect world also attracted the jewellers: brooches, pendants, and earrings often took the form of butterflies, dragonflies or beetles, studded with precious stones. At the same time, decorative motifs developed the characteristic sinuous lines and textural treatments of the *Moderne*, and the palette was changed: there was now a preference for pastel enamel tones, green and gold chrysolite, coloured pearls, mother-of-pearl and opals. Such jewellery was the perfect expression of the spirit of the age.

The movement for the renewal of the language of art was an essential element in the creation of products of every kind at the turn of the century, and it resulted in the great stylishness and the richness of decorative form which are characteristic of the period. In jewellery, the wide choice of techniques and materials – graphic engraving, the addition of colour through gilding, painted enamel decoration, three-dimensional relief work and the variety of filigree decoration – were formed into an organic whole, a single artistic system that epitomised the *Moderne* tendency towards a synthesis of all the arts.

20
DECORATIVE ARTS

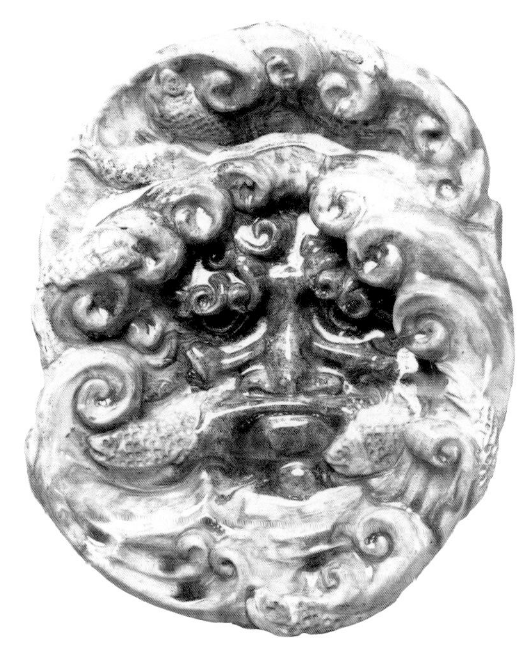

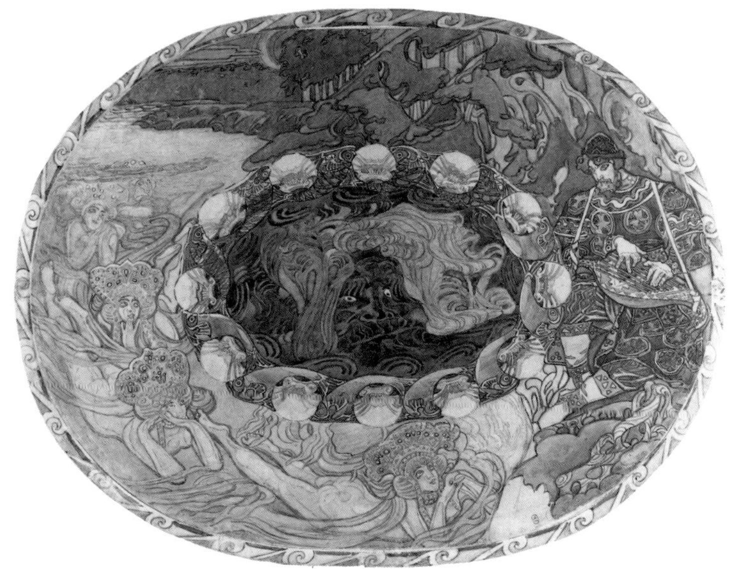

Top: **Mikhail Vrubel'**
458. *Sea King*
Early 1890s
Decorative oval dish
Majolica, 54.8 × 43.3 × 16
State Tretyakov Gallery

Above: **Mikhail Vrubel'**
467. *Sadko*
1899
Design for an earthenware dish
Mixed media on cardboard, 51.8 × 65.9
State Russian Museum

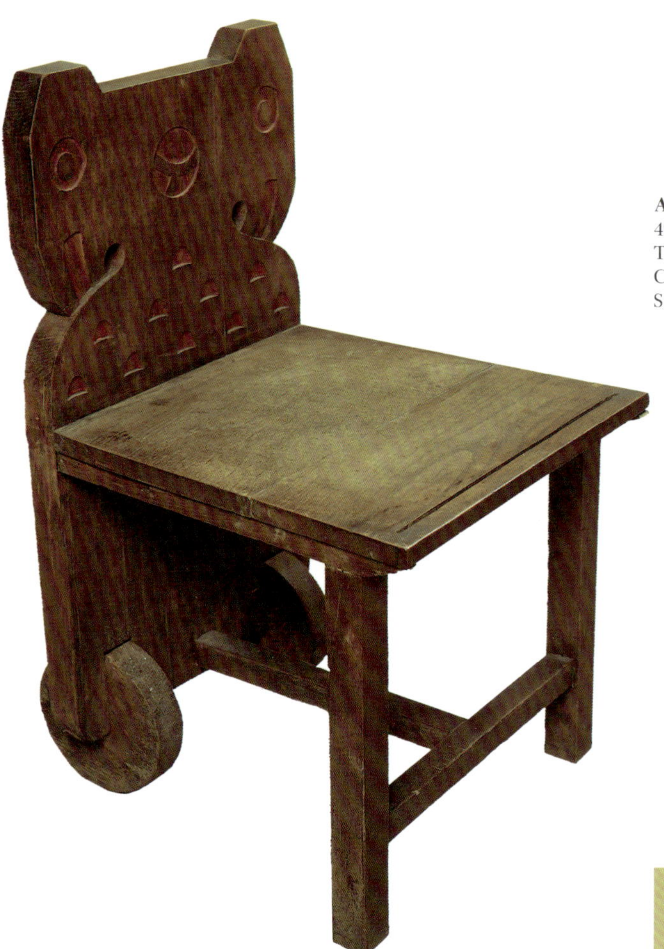

Aleksei Zinov'ev
491. Wheeled chair
Talashkino, 1900s
Carved and painted oak, 73 × 42 × 43
State Historical Museum

Anonymous craftsman
557. Medicine chest
Russia, 1900s
Carved and painted wood with stamped brass,
43 × 27 × 14
State Historical Museum

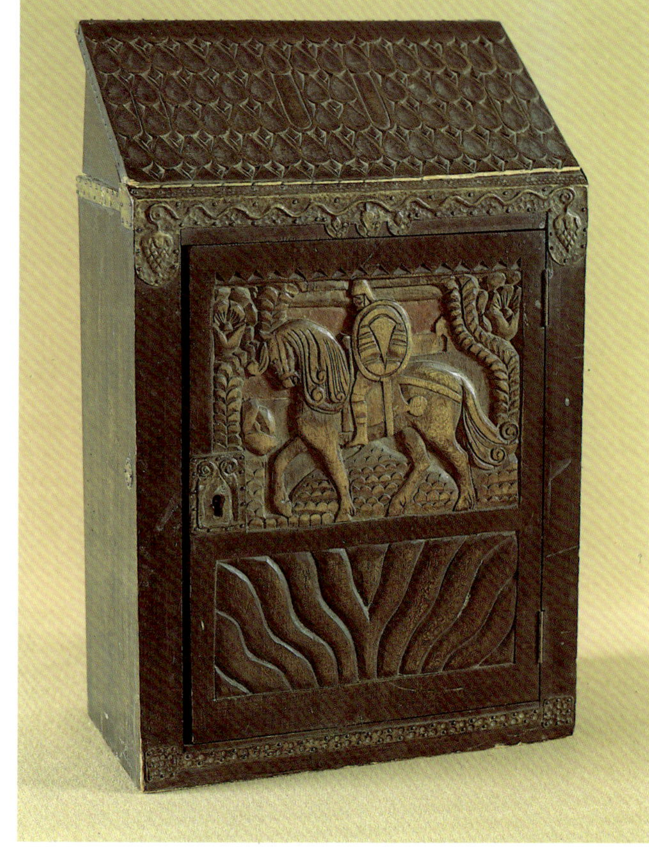

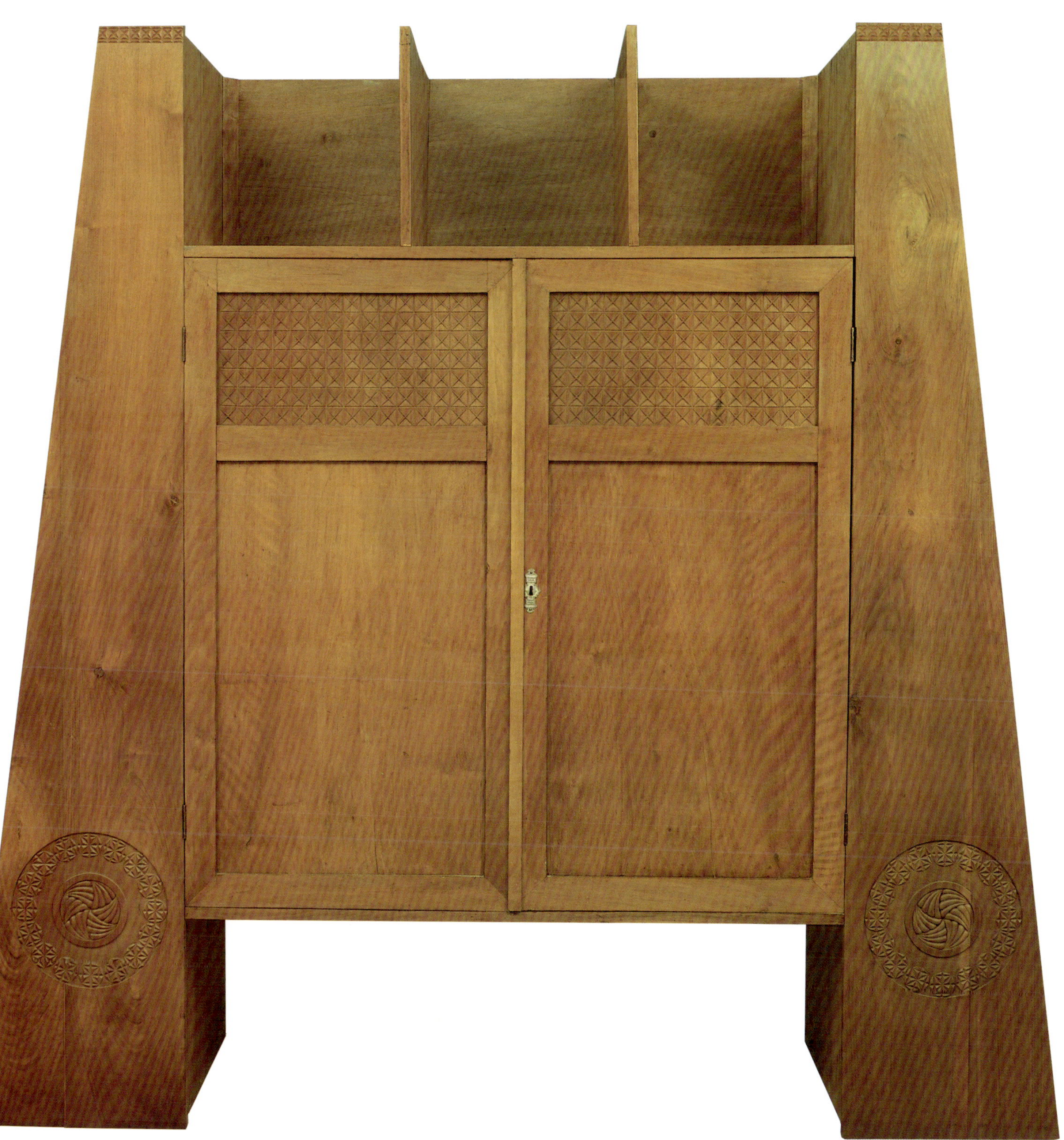

Ivan Fomin
120. Cupboard for a living room, designed for
the "New Style" exhibition
1902
Carved walnut, 180 × 180 × 54
State Historical Museum

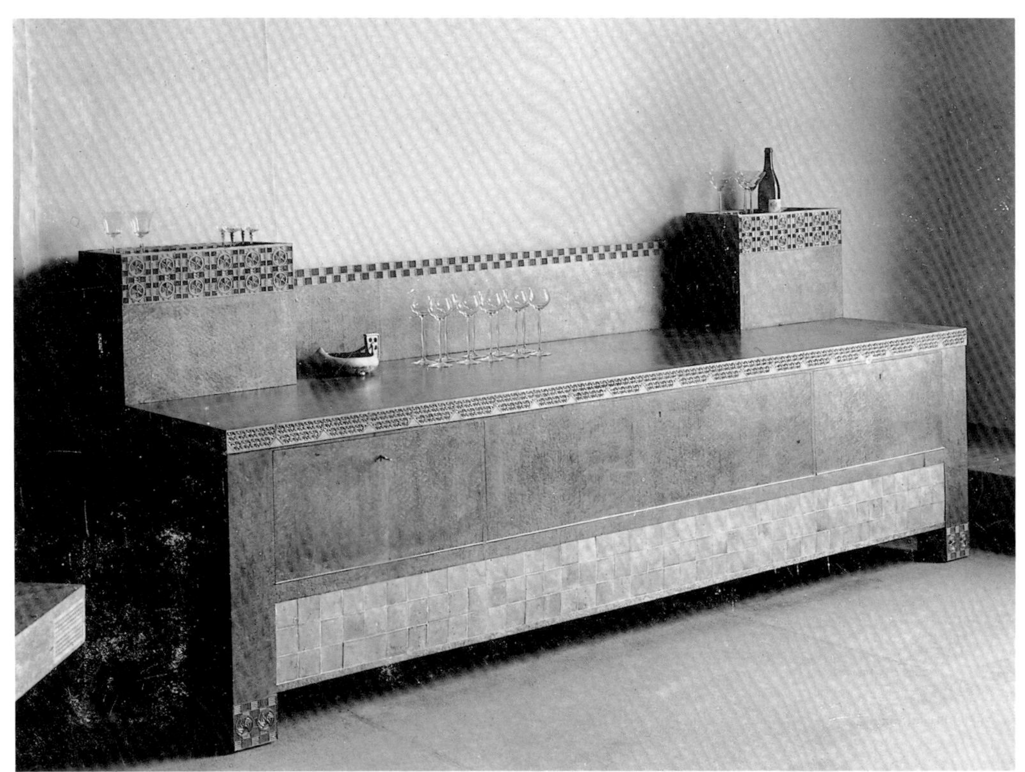

Ivan Fomin
119. Sideboard in grey maple
Photo (1902)
A. V. Shchusev State Museum of Architecture

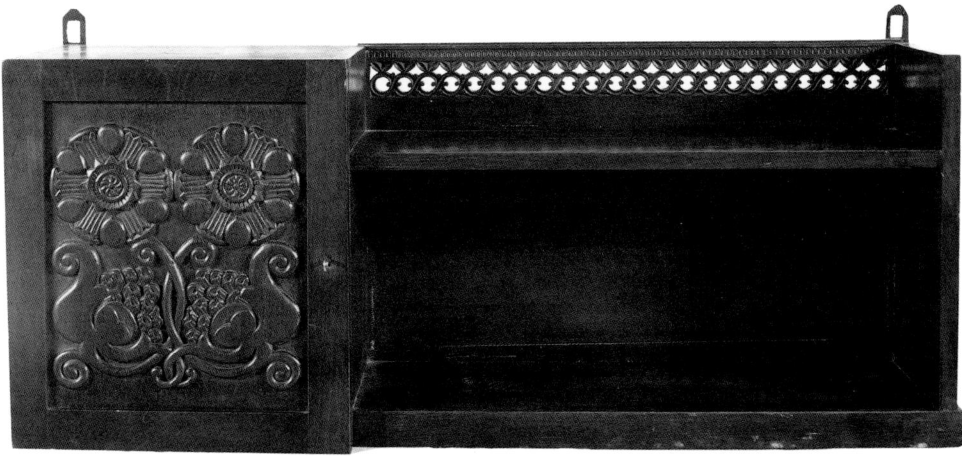

Natal'ya Davydova
86. Shelf with small cupboard
Abramtsevo, between 1905 and 1912
Carved oak, 45 × 113 × 27
State Historical Museum

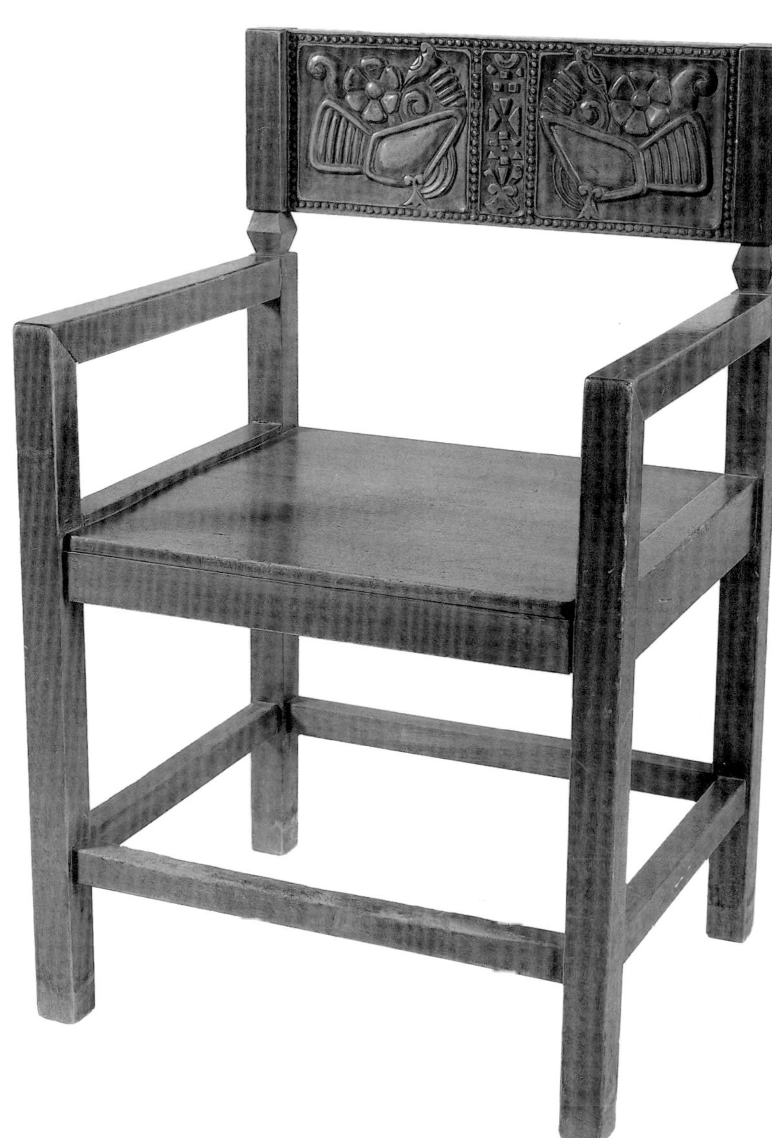

Anonymous craftsman
556. Armchair
Sergiev Trading Quarter, 1910s
Carved oak, 85 × 45 × 54
State Historical Museum

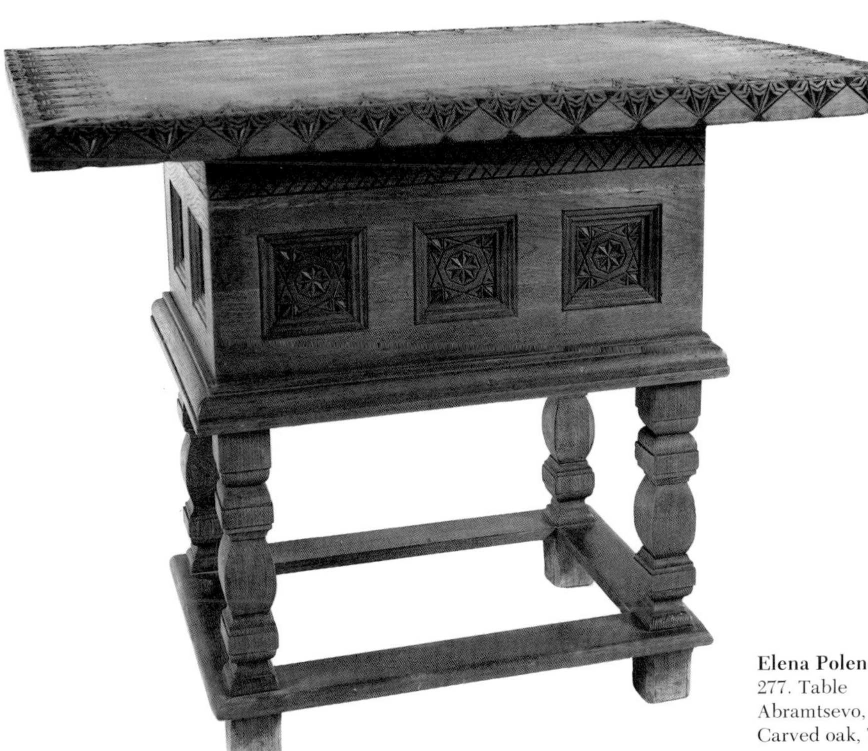

Elena Polenova
277. Table
Abramtsevo, 1880s
Carved oak, 79 × 89 × 65
State Historical Museum

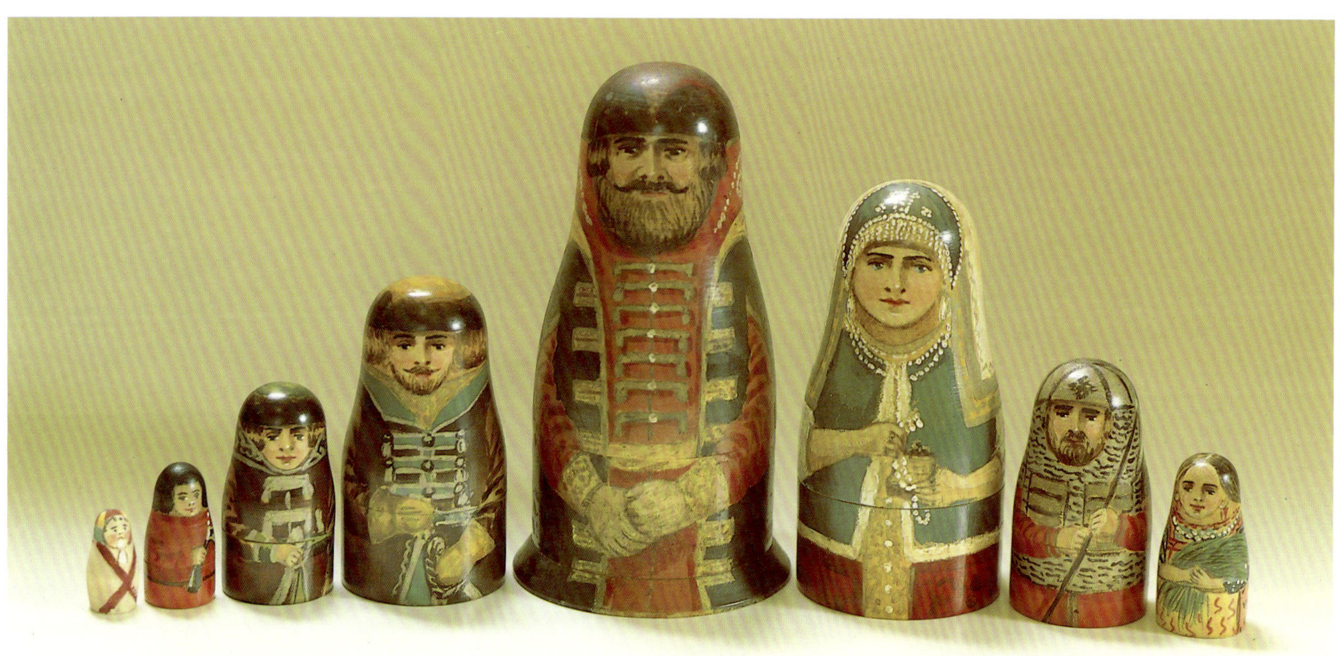

ABOVE: **Anonymous craftsman**
566. *Matryoshka* (8 dolls)
Moscow, workshop of the Crafts Museum,
1910s
Painted turned wood, 15 × 8.2
State Historical Museum

RIGHT: **Lukutin Factory**
212, 213. Two Easter eggs with painted
decoration
1900s
Papier mâché with painted lacquer,
each 14 × 9
State Historical Museum

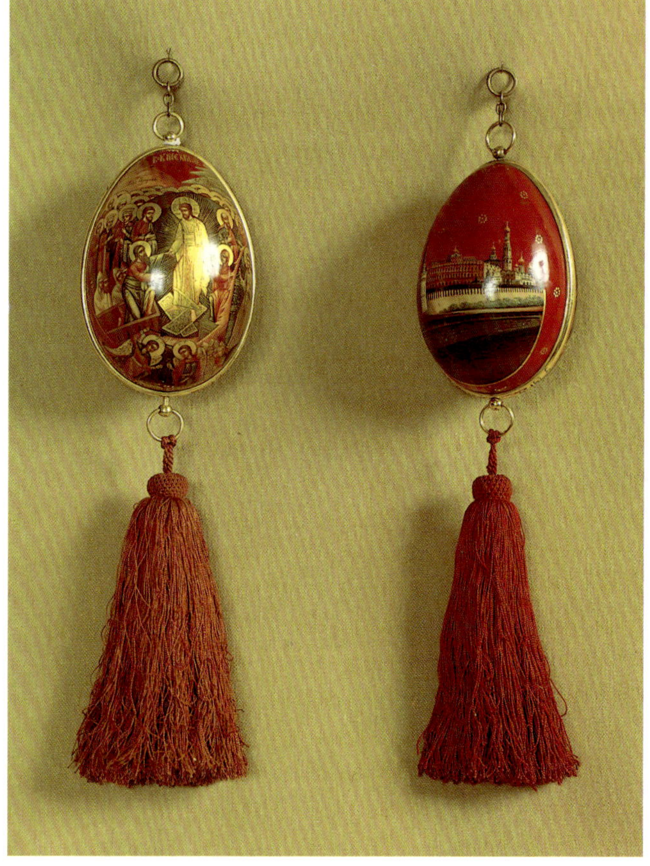

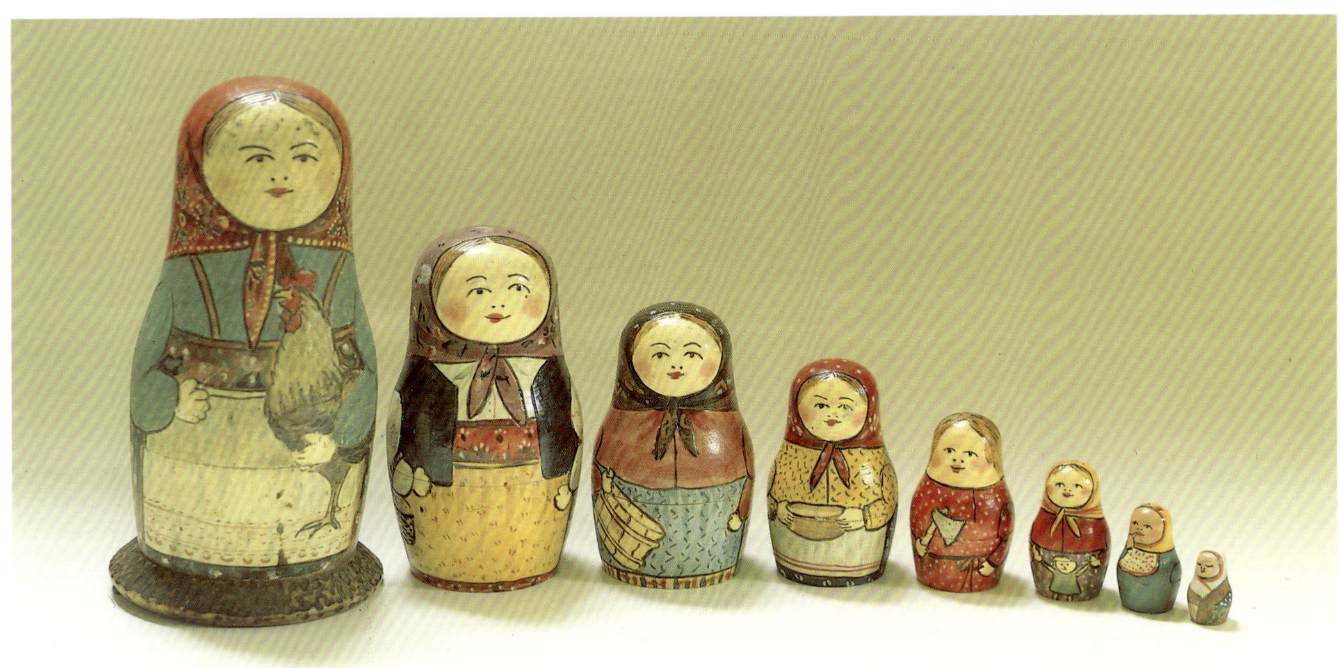

ABOVE: **Ivanov Brothers workshop**
147. *Matryoshka* (8 dolls)
1910s
Turned wood with painting and pokerwork,
15 × 7.5
State Historical Museum

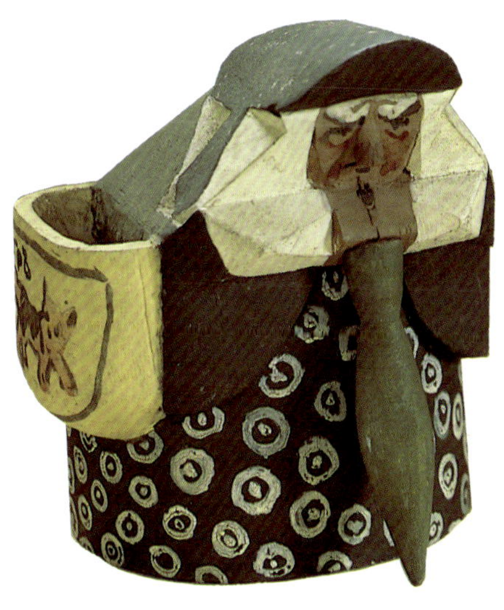

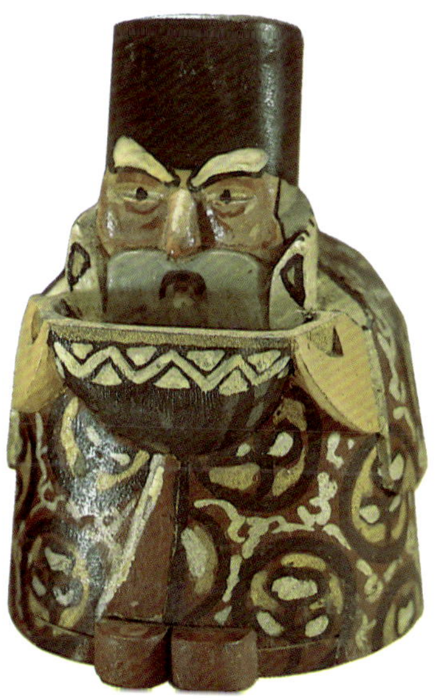

Nikolai Bartram
37, 38. Two money-boxes
Moscow, 1900s
Carved and painted wood, 13 × 9.5; 12.2 × 14.5
State Historical Museum

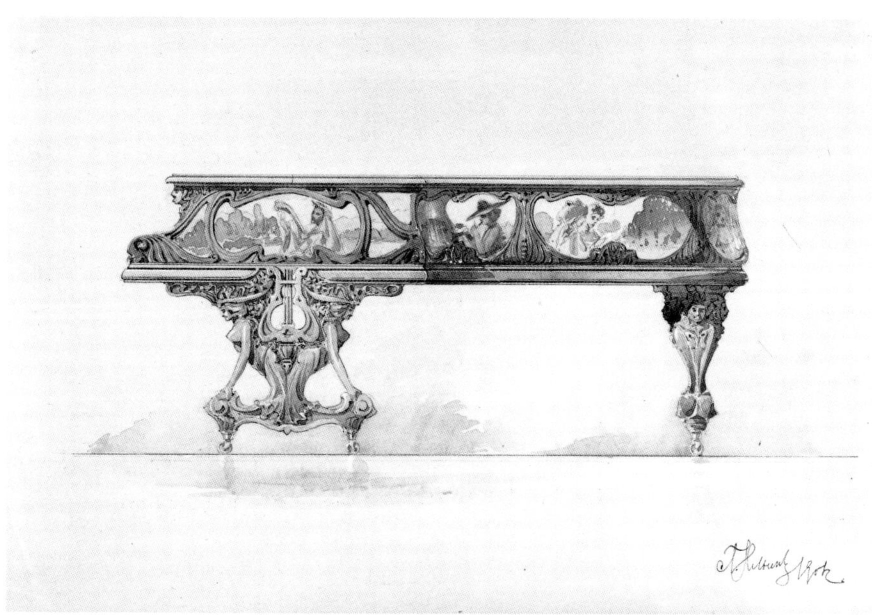

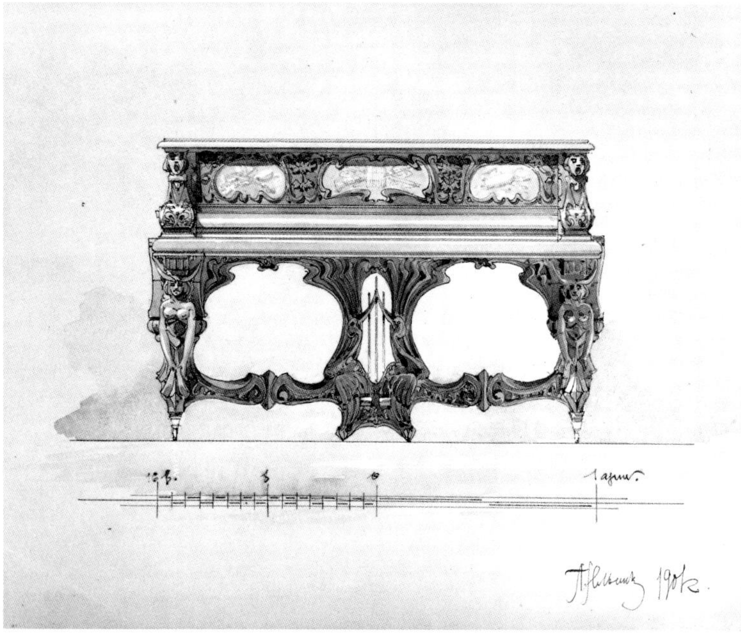

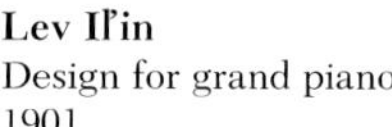

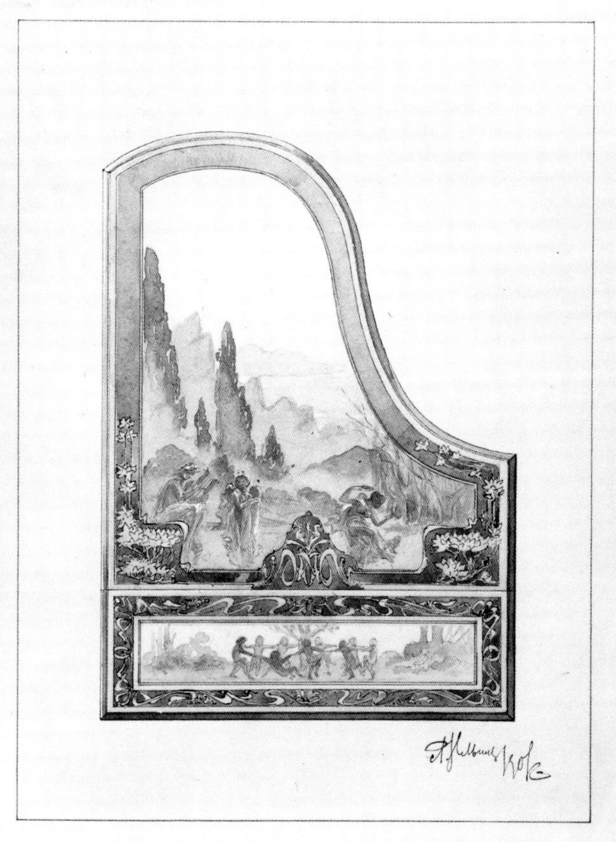

Lev Il'in
Design for grand piano
1901

Top: 143. Side elevation
Ink, watercolour and white on coloured paper,
27.3 × 39.2
A. V. Shchusev State Museum of Architecture

Above left: 144. Front elevation
Ink, watercolour and white on coloured paper,
26.1 × 30.7
A. V. Shchusev State Museum of Architecture

Above right: 142. Design for decoration of lid
Ink and watercolour on coloured paper, 37 × 27
A. V. Shchusev State Museum of Architecture

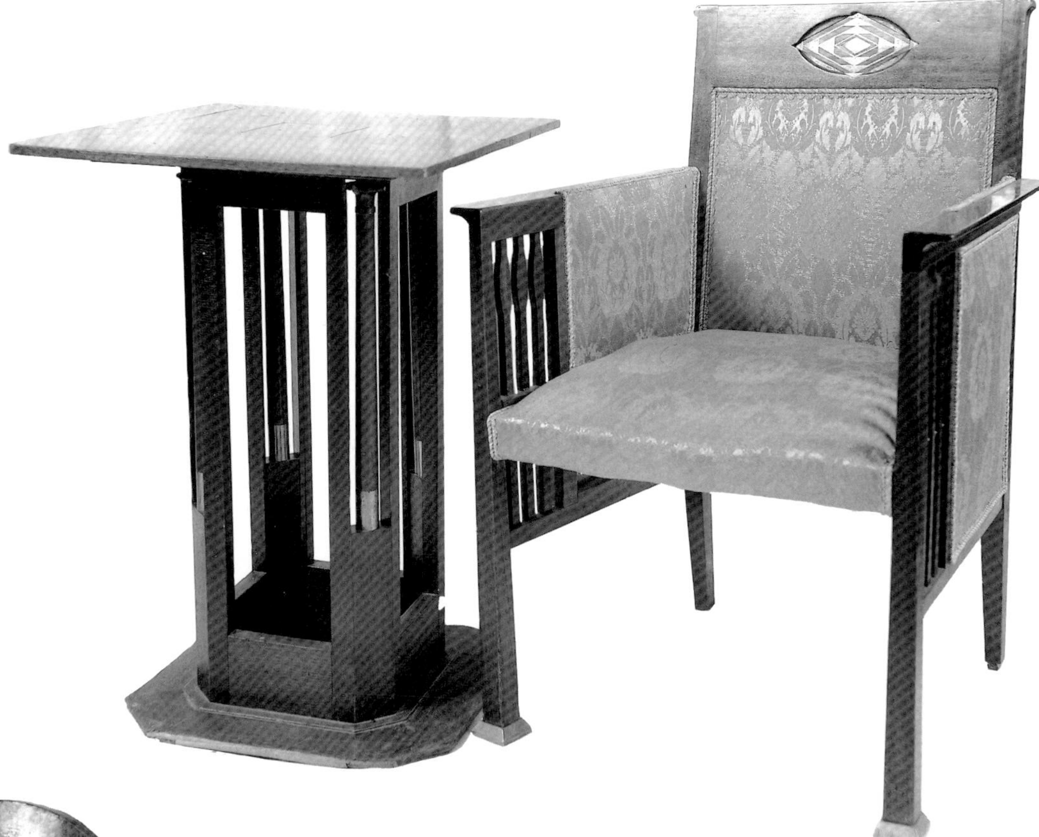

Anonymous craftsman
561. Armchair and side-table, from a suite
belonging to the Moscow publisher I. Sytin
*c.*1903
Mahogany inlaid with metal
State Historical Museum

Anonymous craftsman
559. Chair from the Morozov-Reinbot estate
"Gorki" near Moscow
1900s
Karelian birch inlaid with ebony, 112 × 50 × 50
State Historical Museum

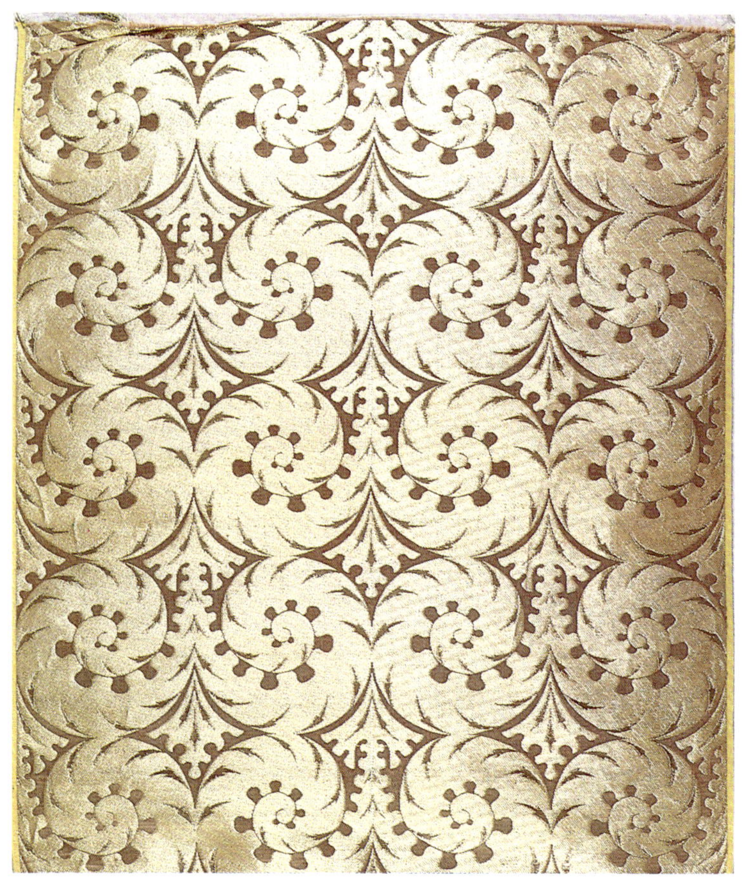

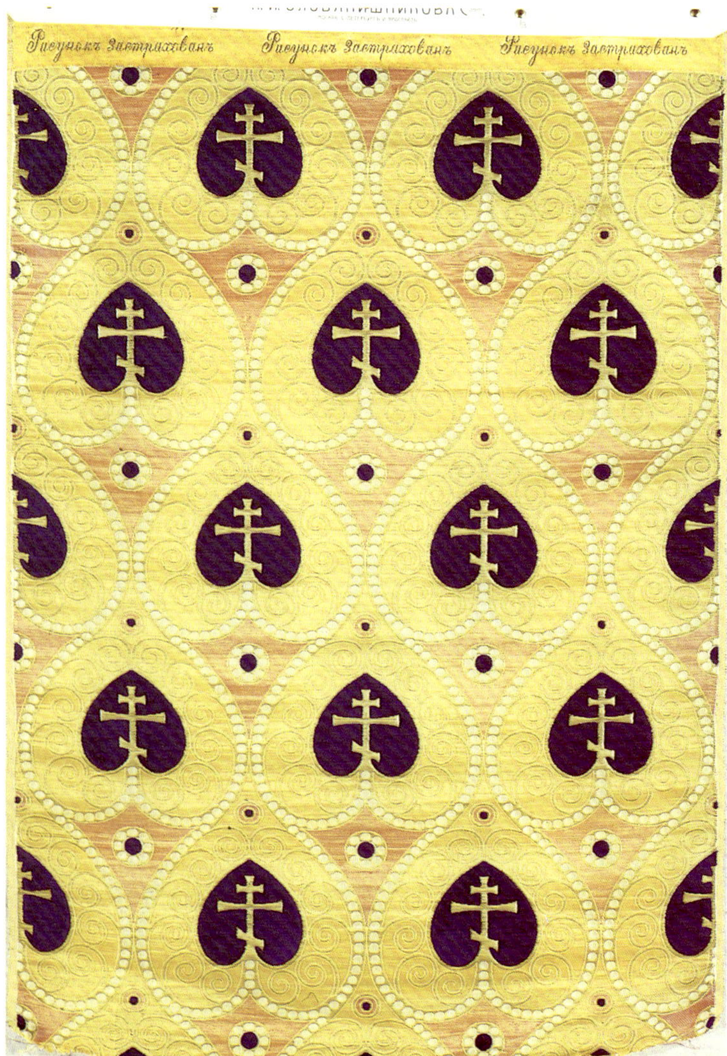
Рисунокъ застрахованъ   Рисунокъ застрахованъ   Рисунокъ застрахованъ

П. И. Словянишникова С-ъ   Т-ва П. И. Словянишникова С
Рисунокъ застрахованъ   Рисунокъ застрахованъ

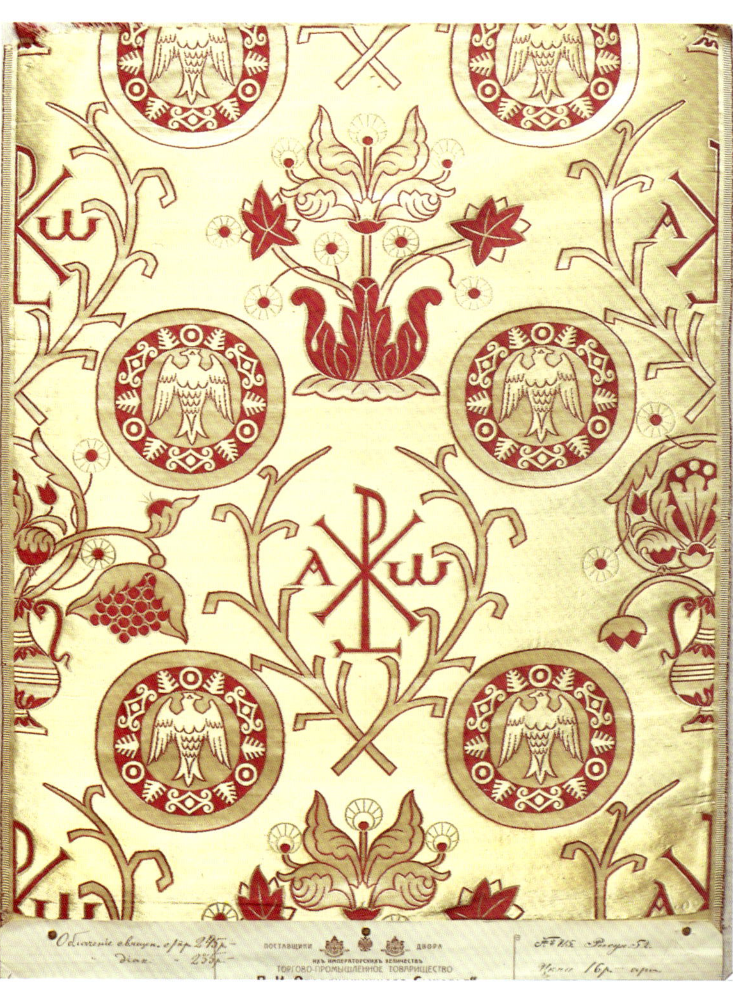
ПОСТАВЩИКИ   ДВОРА
ИЗЪ ИМПЕРАТОРСКИХЪ ВЕЛИЧЕСТВ
ТОРГОВО-ПРОМЫШЛЕННОЕ ТОВАРИЩЕСТВО

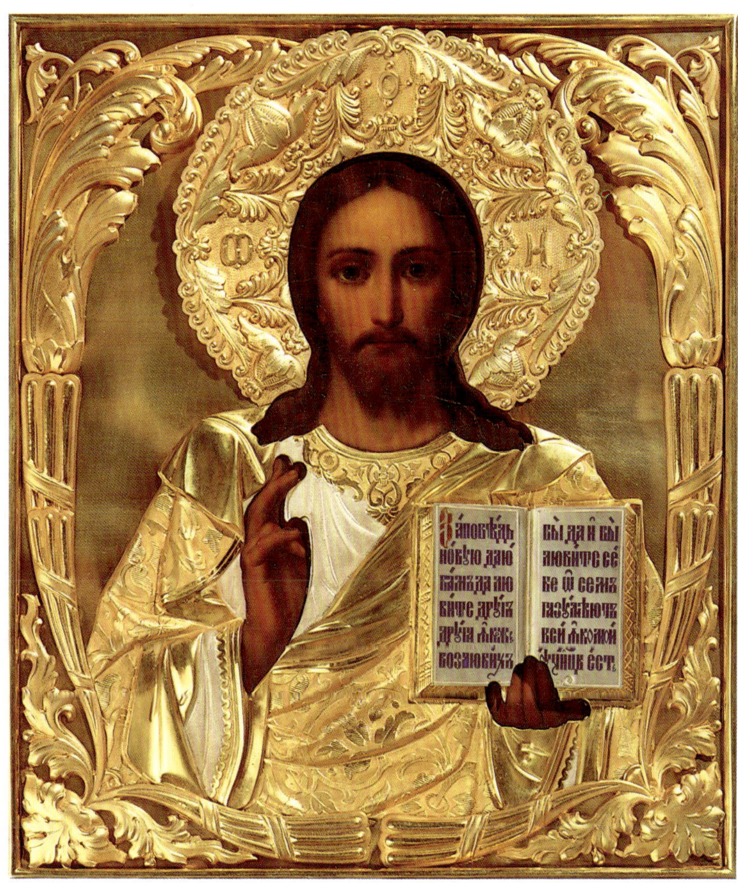

ABOVE: **Ivan Tarabrov**
425. Frame for icon of the Almighty Saviour
Icon: oil on wood
Frame: silver gilt, 22.3 × 27
Moscow, 1908–17
State Historical Museum

OPPOSITE: **P. I. Olovyanishnikov & Sons**
252, 254, 256, 255. Fabric samples
1900s
Brocades and silks with gold thread (for full
details see catalogue)
State Historical Museum

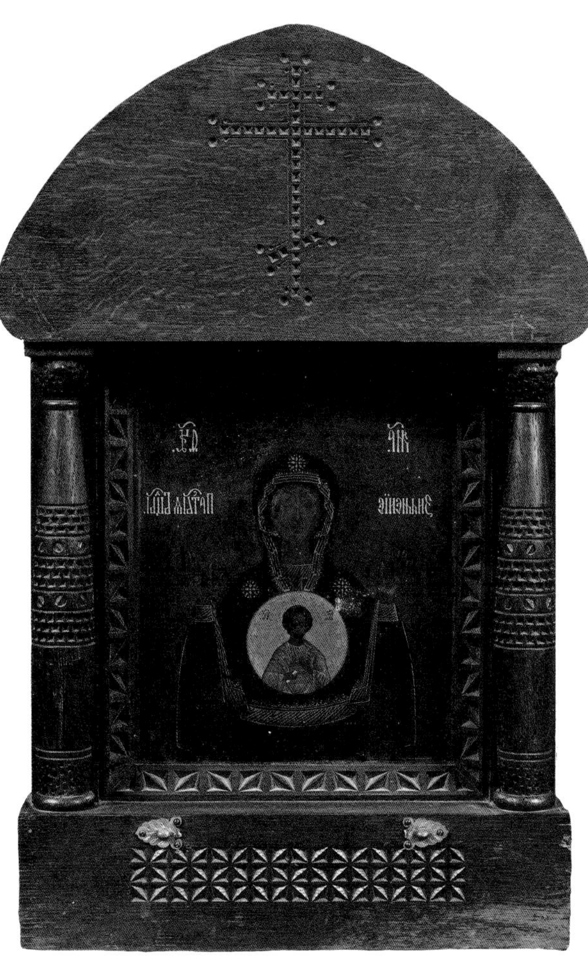

Sergei Vashkov
443. Icon case with icon *Virgin of the Sign*
Moscow (made at P. I. Olovyanishnikov & Sons workshop), 1900s
Carved wood with tempera painting, 60 × 35.5 × 11
State Historical Museum

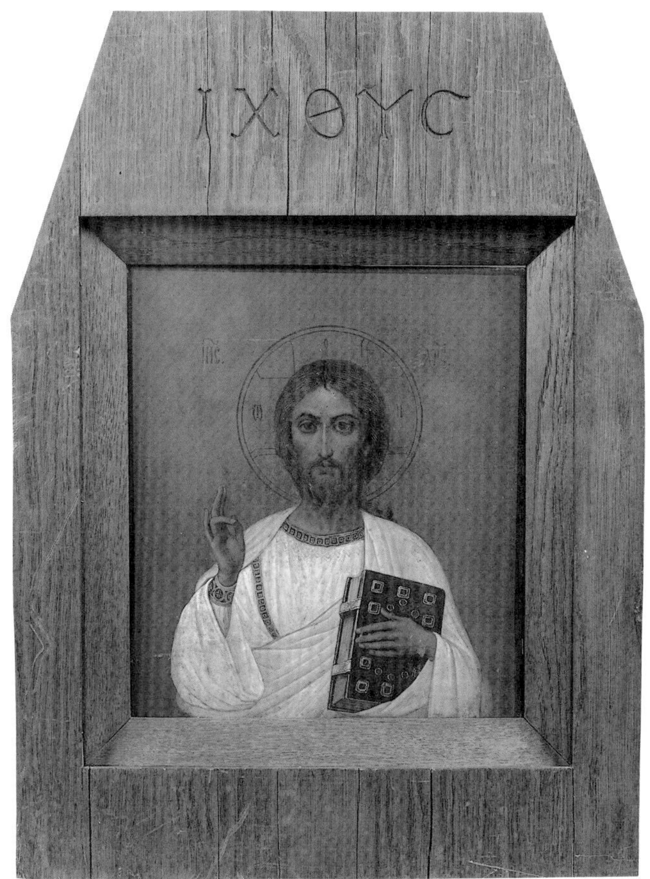

Sergei Vashkov
442. Icon case with icon *Christ Blessing*
Moscow (made at P. I. Olovyanishnikov & Sons workshop), 1900s
Carved wood with tempera painting, 57 × 45 × 6.5
State Historical Museum

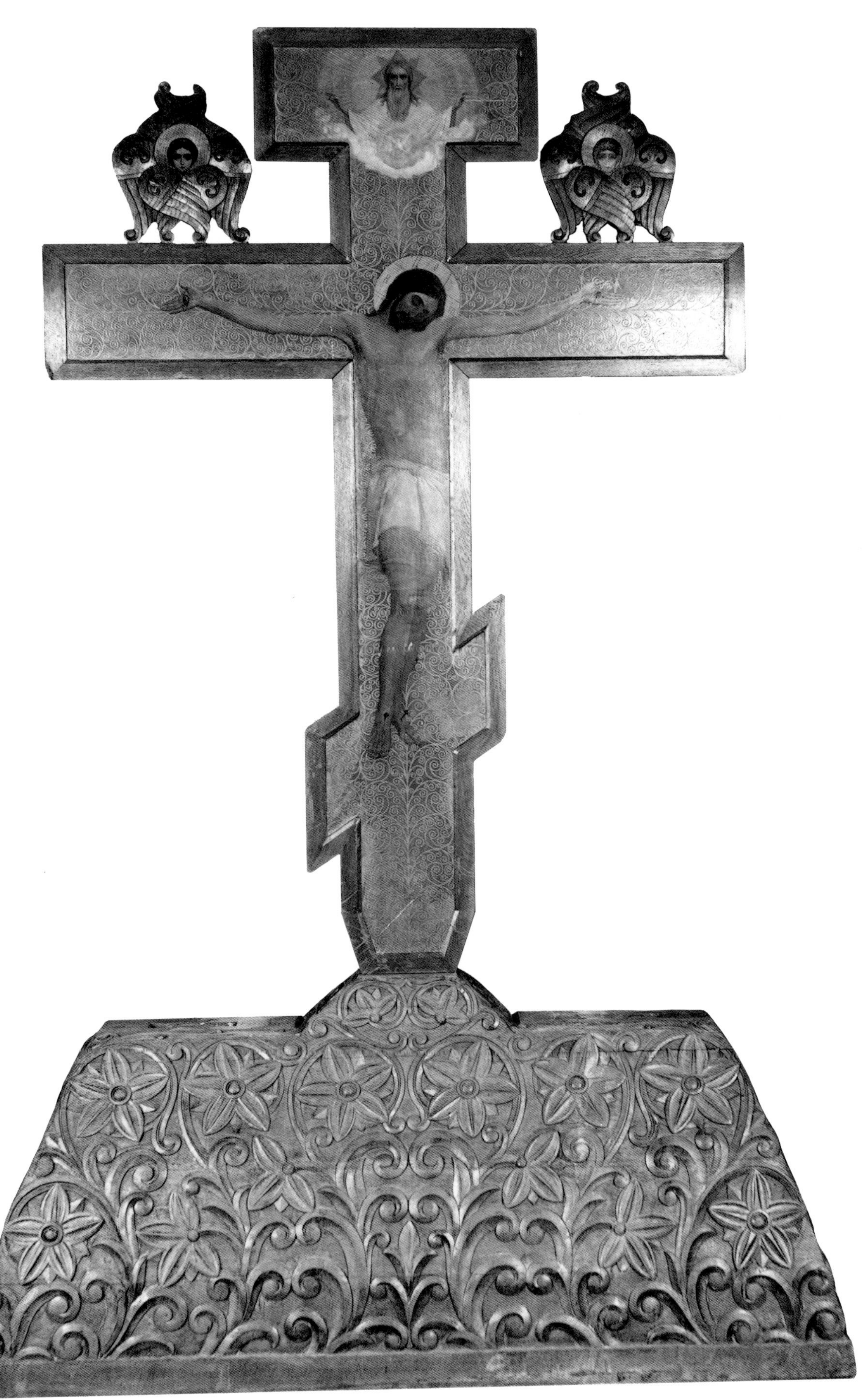

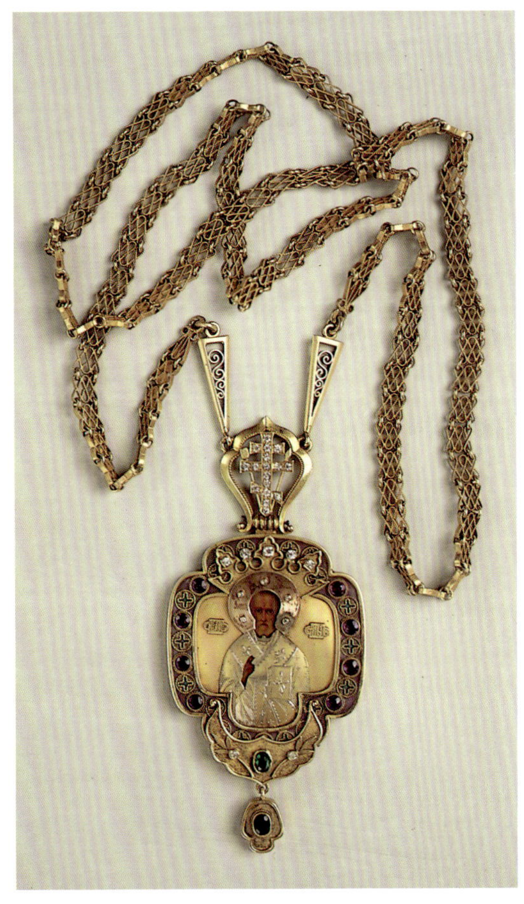

BELOW: **11th Jewellers' Artel'**
23. *Lampada* (icon-lamp)
Moscow, 1908–17
Silver, 17 × 7 × 7
State Historical Museum

ABOVE: **Anonymous silversmith**
584. Panagia
St Petersburg, 1913
Silver gilt with enamel and glass, 15 × 6.7
State Historical Museum

OPPOSITE: **V. Sikagev**
384. Marriage crown
Moscow, 1899–1908
Silver gilt with enamel, Urals stones, glass,
velvet, 19.2 × 18.5
State Historical Museum

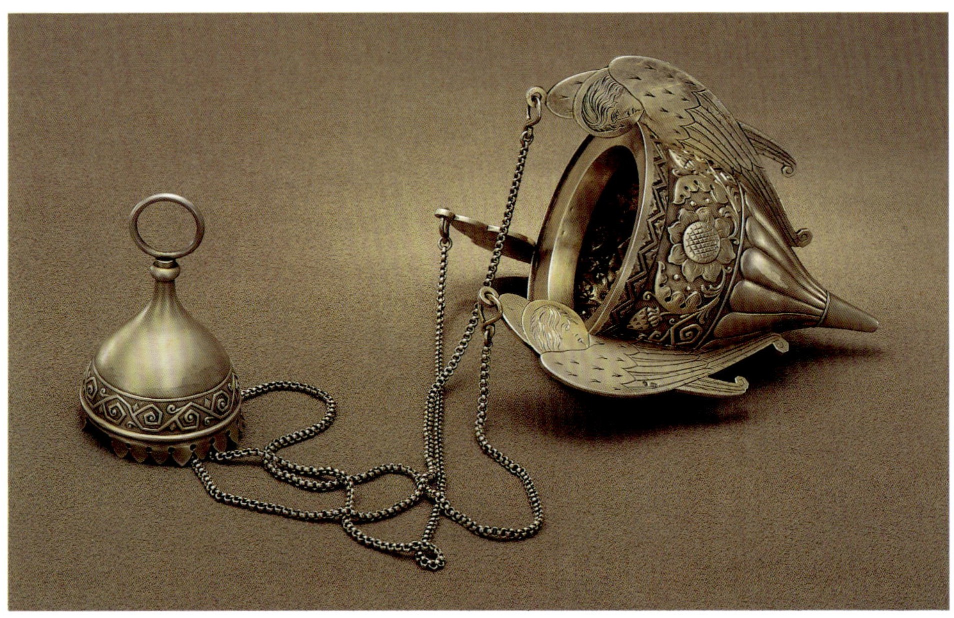

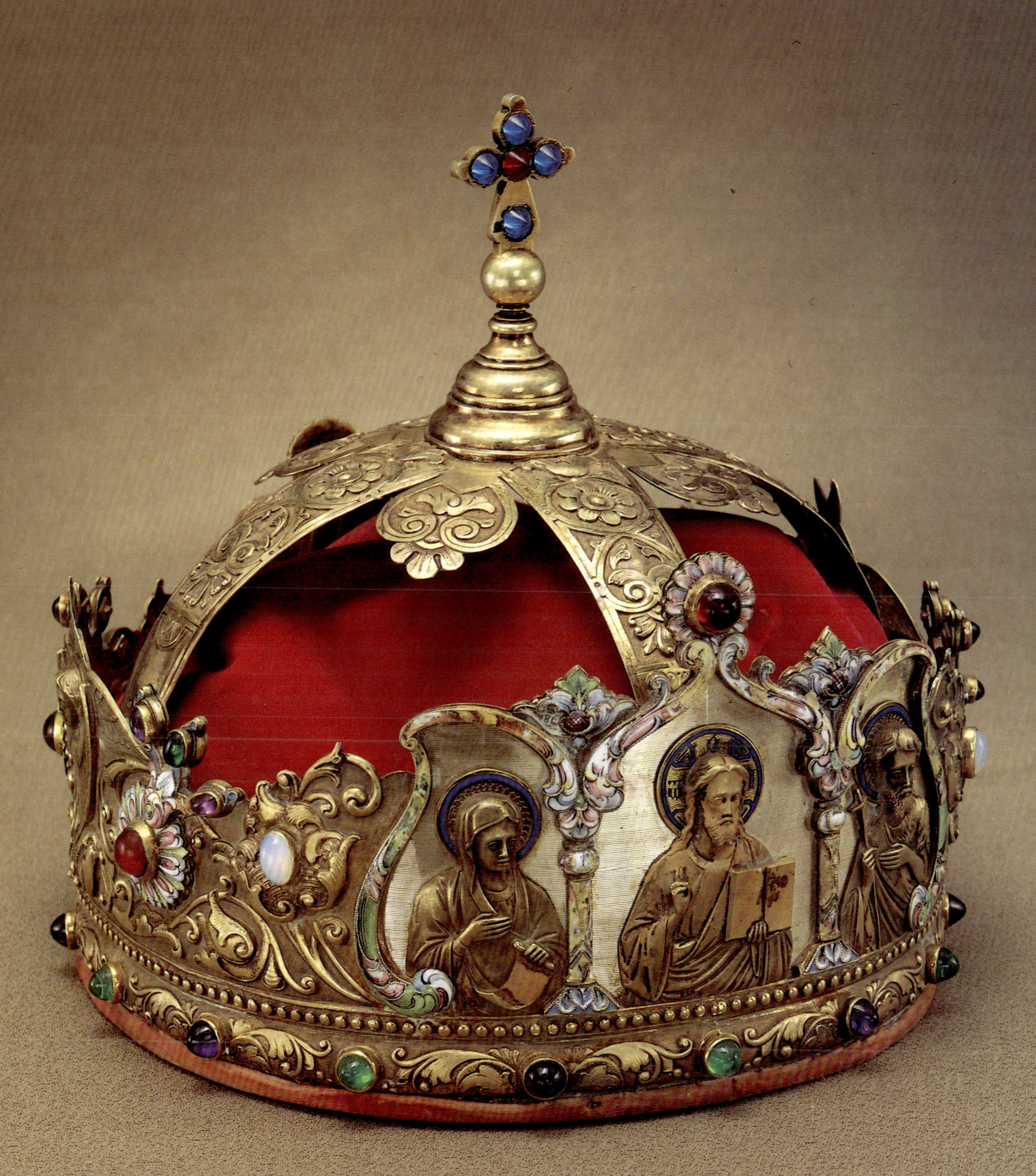

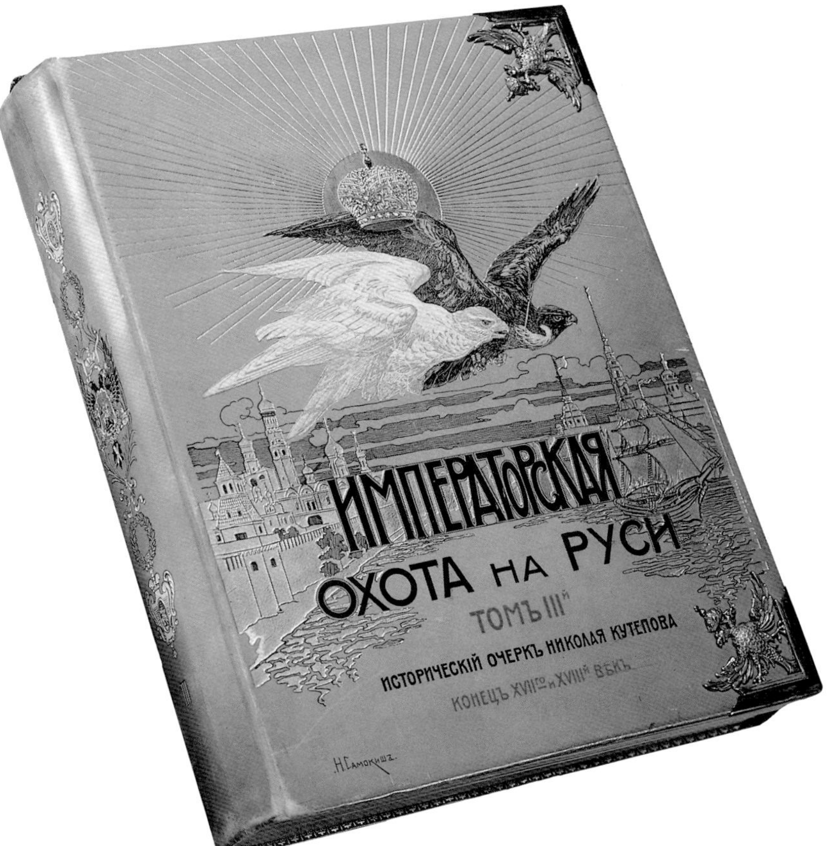

Nikolai Samokish
299. Binding for Nikolai Kutepov, *Tsarist and Imperial Hunting in Russia in the late Seventeenth and Eighteenth Centuries*, vol.3, St Petersburg, 1902
Blue morocco-backed cloth with gold, silver and coloured blocking; metal corners in the form of the Russian imperial double-headed eagle, 37 × 28.5
State Lenin Library

R. Nilsson
248. Binding for Aleksander Pushkin, *Evgeny Onegin*, St Petersburg, 1899
Red leather, gold blocked with appliqué of coloured leather; lined with pale blue morocco gold blocked with border of flowers, 19.7 × 10
State Lenin Library

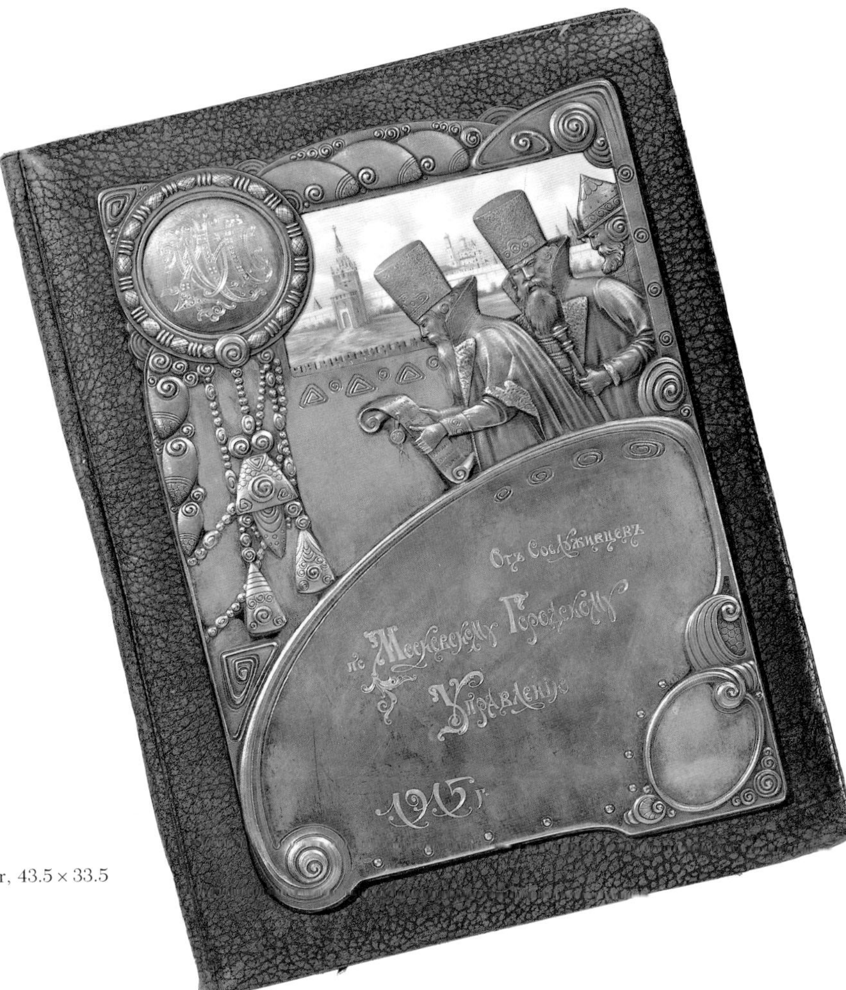

15th Jewellers' Artel'
28. Blotter
Moscow, 1915
Leather, silver, enamel and paper, 43.5 × 33.5
State Historical Museum

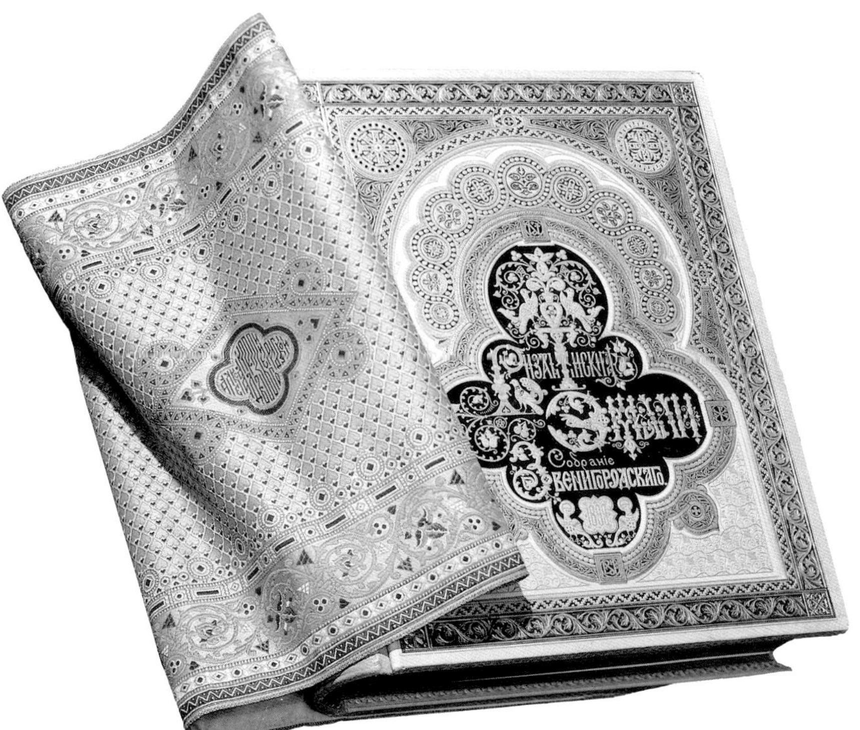

Ivan Ropet
293. Dustcover and binding for Nikodim
Kondakov, *History and Memorials of
Byzantine Enamel*, St Petersburg, 1892, 37 × 30
Dustcover: silk cloth with woven design in gold
and silver (manufactured by the Sapozhnikov
Brothers, Moscow)
State Lenin Library

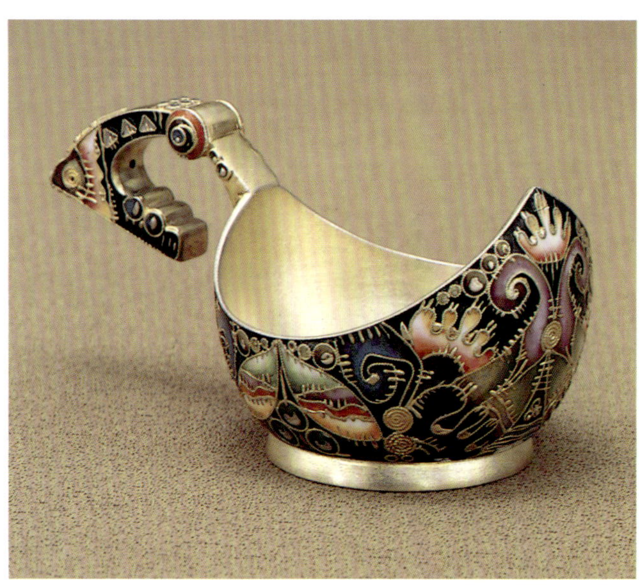

ABOVE: **Fedor Rückert**
295. Small *kovsh* (scoop)
Moscow, 1908–17
Silver gilt and enamel, 4.4 × 9.5 × 5.1
State Historical Museum

RIGHT: **Fabergé Company**
105. Small vase
Moscow, 1893
Silver, 8.5 × 12 × 12
State Historical Museum

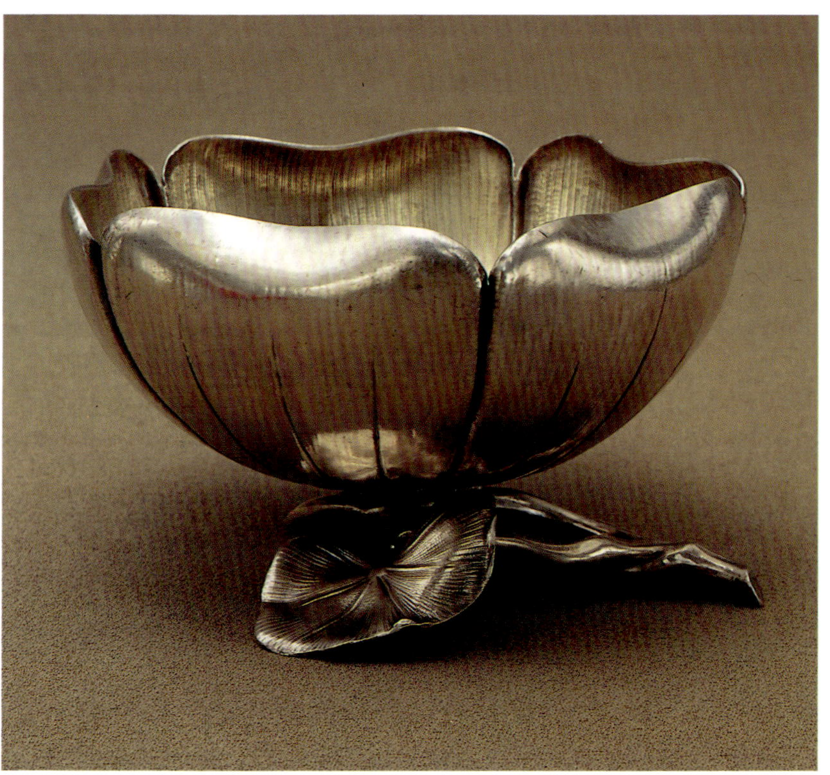

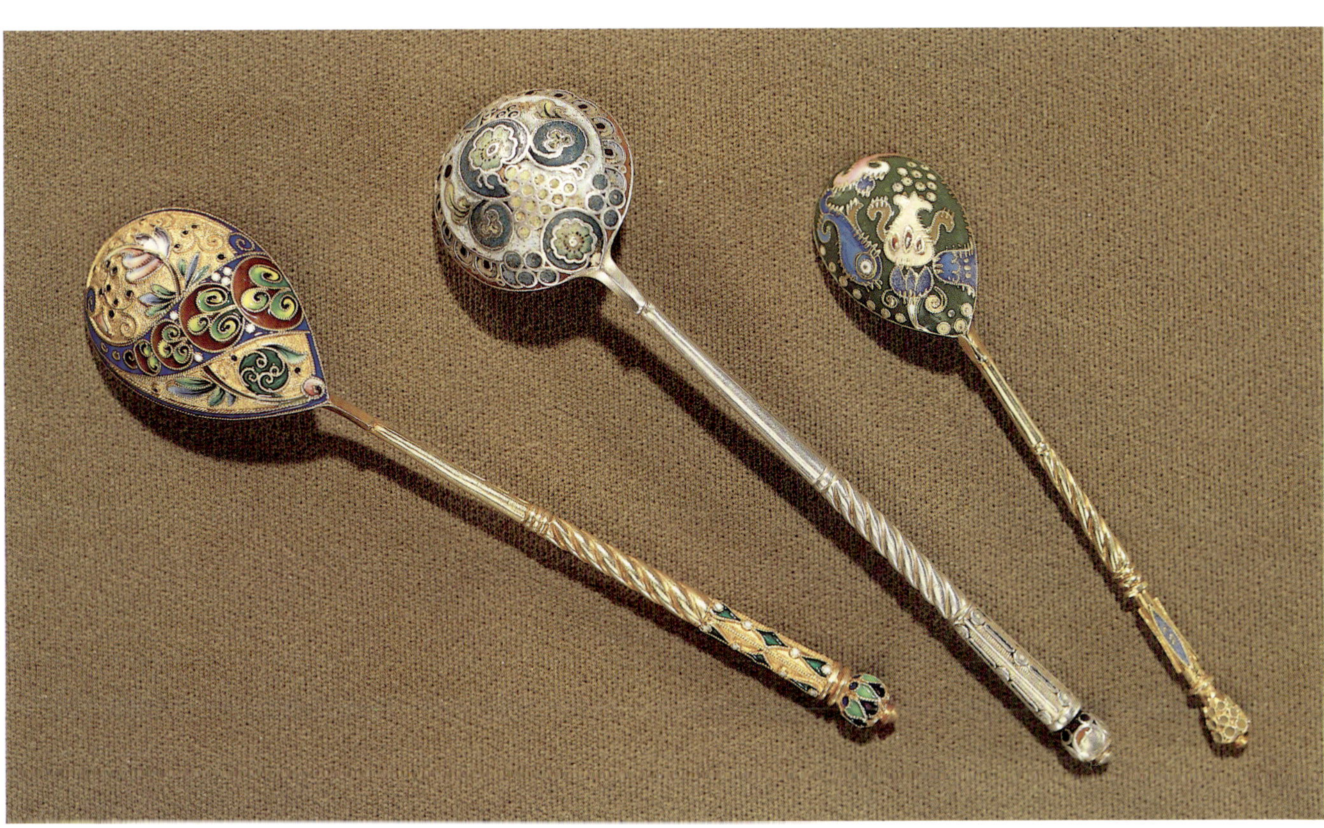

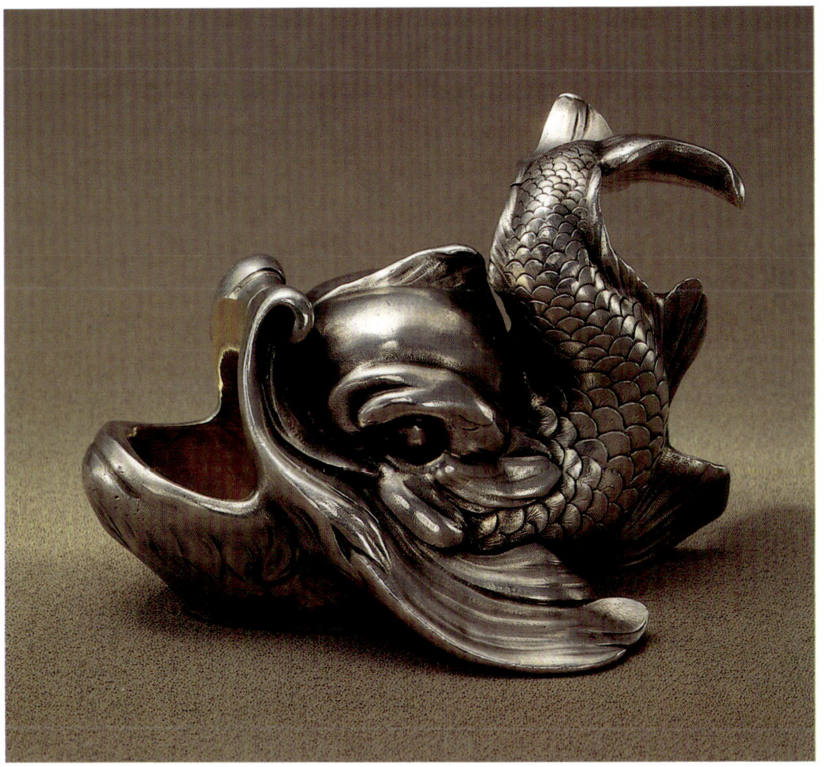

ABOVE (LEFT): **11th Jewellers' Artel'**
24. Tea spoon
Moscow (Fabergé), 1908–17
Silver gilt and enamel, length: 14.3
State Historical Museum

ABOVE (CENTRE): **P. D. Amerikantsev**
5. Tea Spoon
Moscow, 1908–17
Silver gilt and enamel, length: 14
State Historical Museum

ABOVE (RIGHT): **Fedor Rückert**
294. Coffee Spoon
Moscow (Fabergé), 1908–17
Silver gilt and enamel, length: 10.9

LEFT: **Fabergé Company**
106. Ashtray in form of a fish
Moscow, 1908–17
Silver, 8.5 × 10.2 × 12.5
State Historical Museum

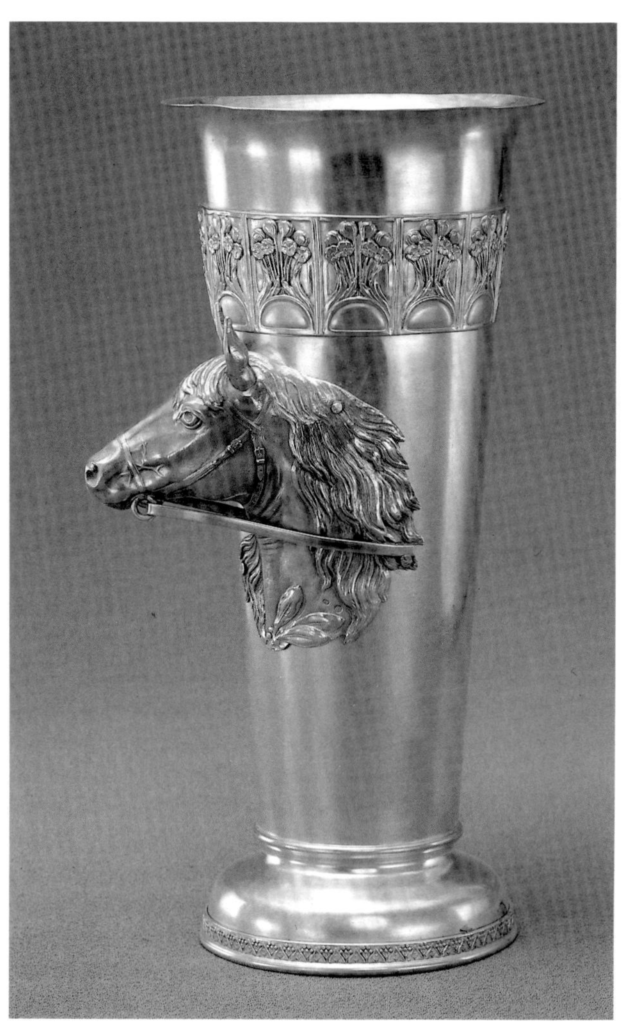

Aleksandr Piskarev
270. Wine beaker
Moscow, 1908–1917
Silver, 21.4 × 9.6 × 9.6
State Historical Museum

Andrei Bragin
75. *Charka* (shallow dish)
St Petersburg, 1899–1908
Silver, 6.6 × 10 × 5.3
State Historical Museum

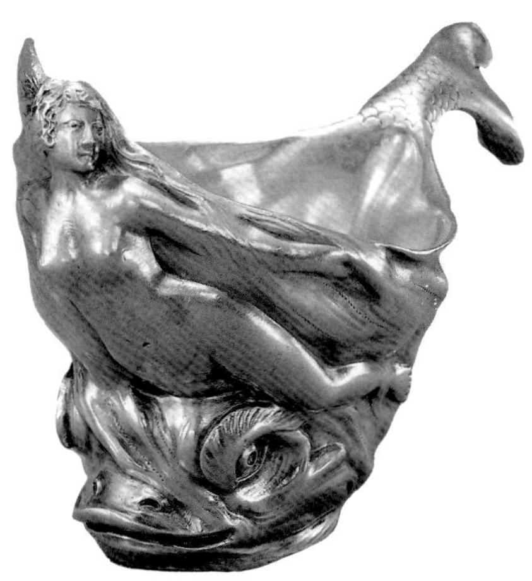

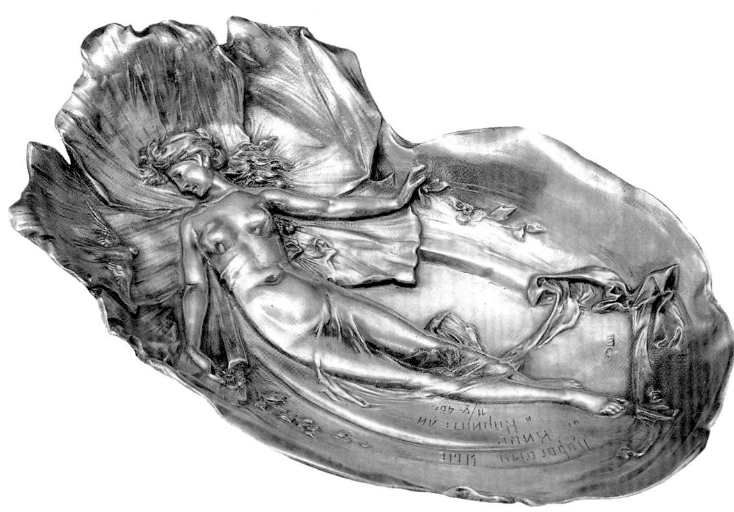

Filipp Terent'ev
429. Dish
Moscow, 1899–1908
Silver, 3.7 × 17.3 × 12
State Historical Museum

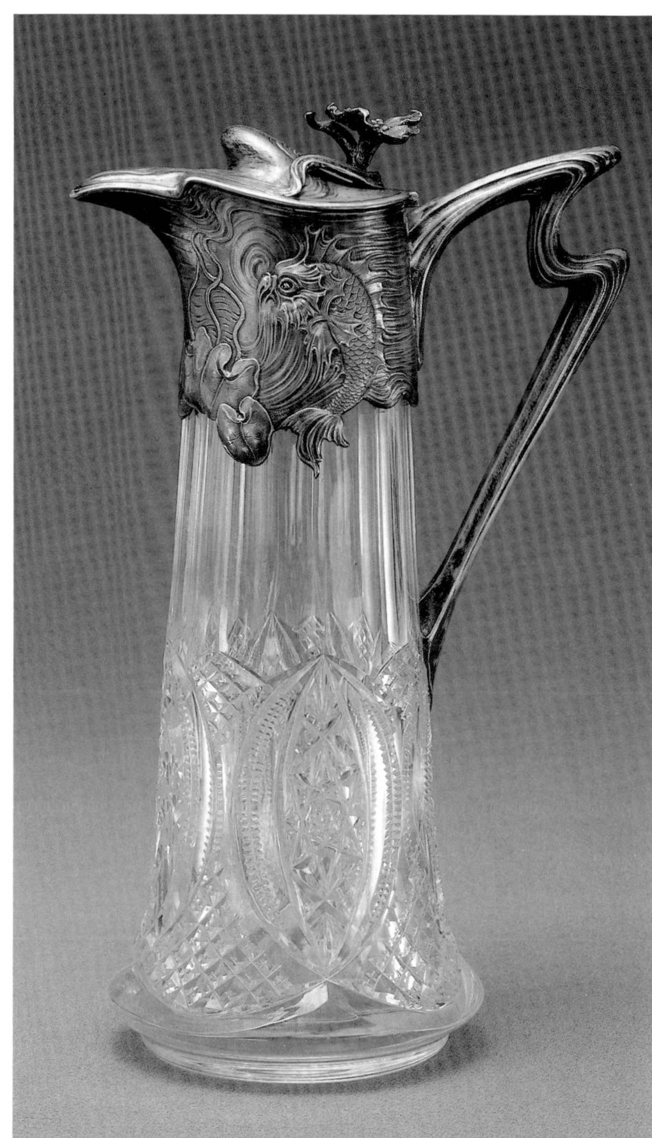

Anonymous silversmith (C. Y.)
577. Jug
St Petersburg, 1899–1908
Cut glass with silver mountings, ht: 28
State Historical Museum

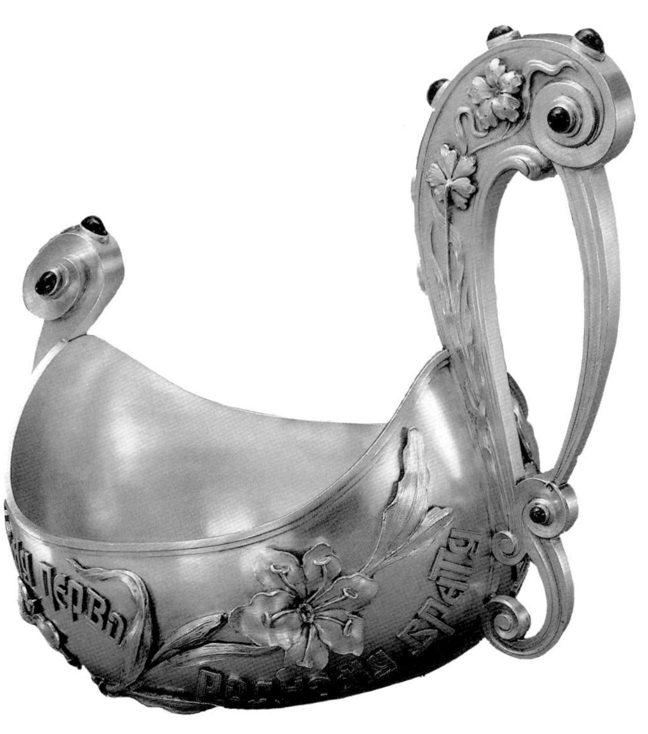

M. V. Folomin
116. *Kovsh* (scoop)
Kiev, 1899–1908
Silver, gilt on the inside, inset with coloured
glass, 25.5 × 30 × 18.5
State Historical Museum

Firm of Ivan Khlebnikov
165. Napkin ring
Moscow, 1899–1908
Silver with gilding and enamel, 4 × 6.1 × 4.3
State Historical Museum

11th Jewellers' Artel'
25. Napkin ring
Moscow, 1908–17
Silver gilt and enamel, 3.8 × 5 × 5
State Historical Museum

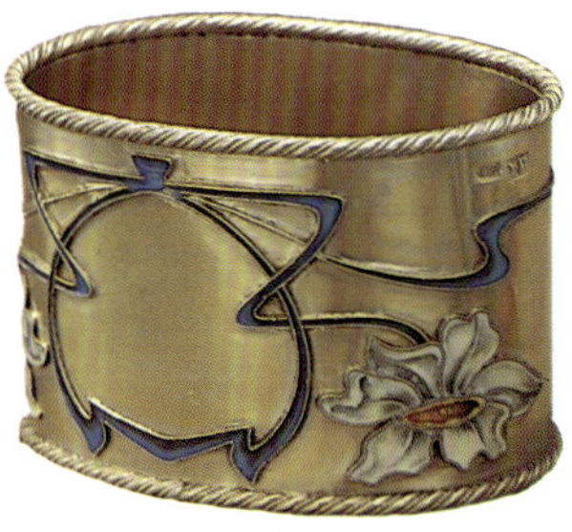

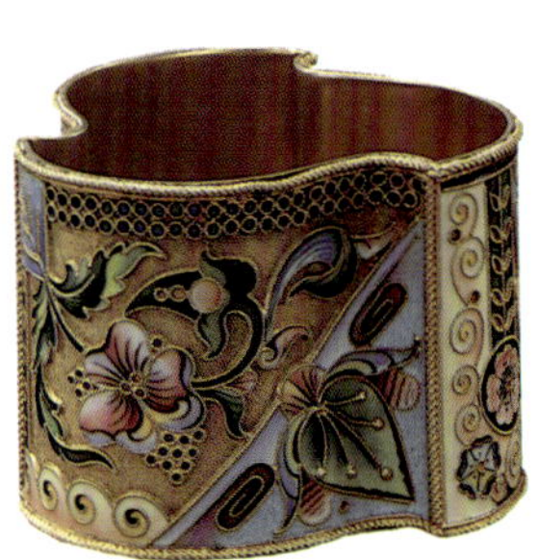

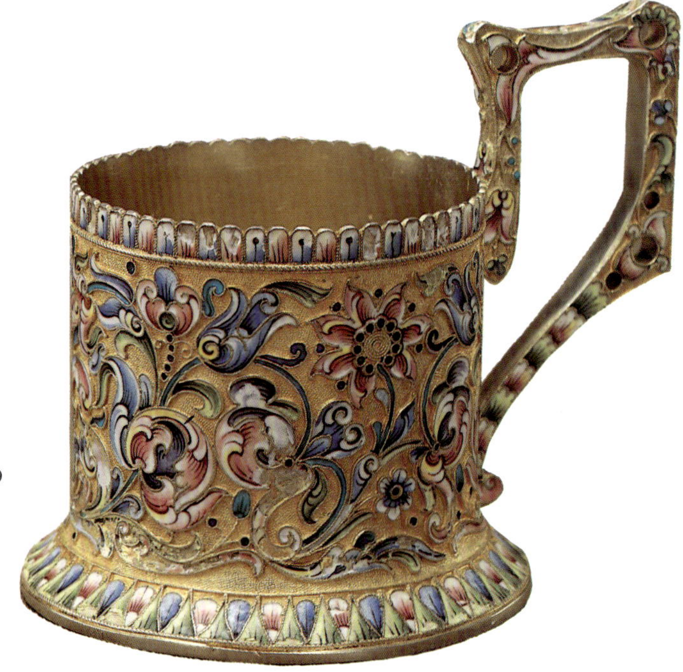

Nikolai Zverev
493. Tea-glass holder
Moscow, 1908–17
Silver gilt and enamel, 9.2 × 11.4 × 9
State Historical Museum

11th Jewellers' Artel'
26, 27. Sugar basin and milk jug
Moscow, 1908–17
Silver gilt and enamel, ht: 5; 6.5
State Historical Museum

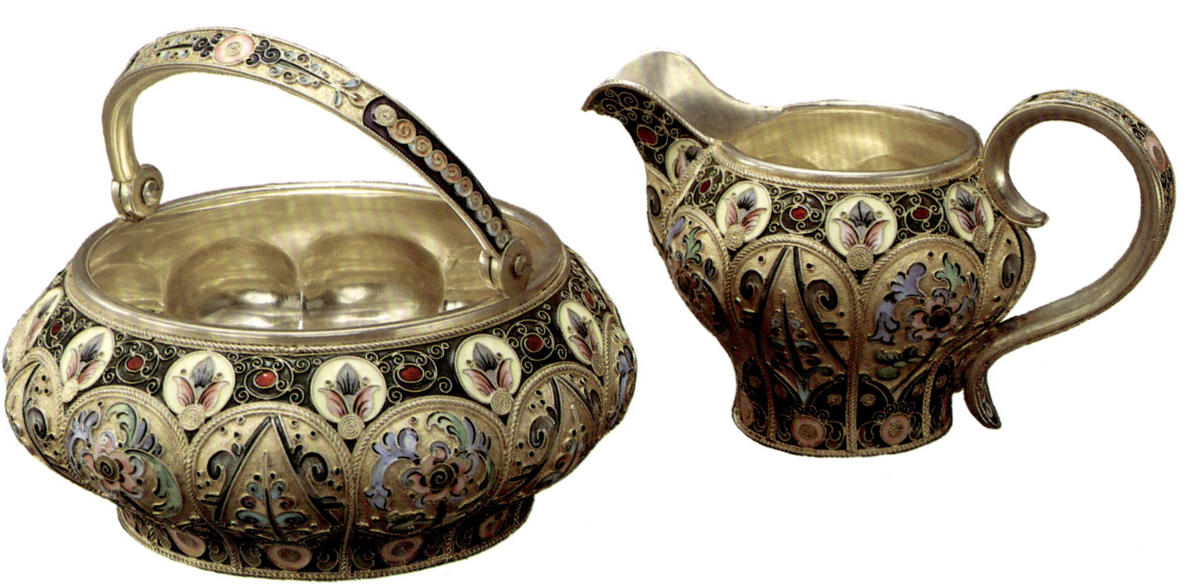

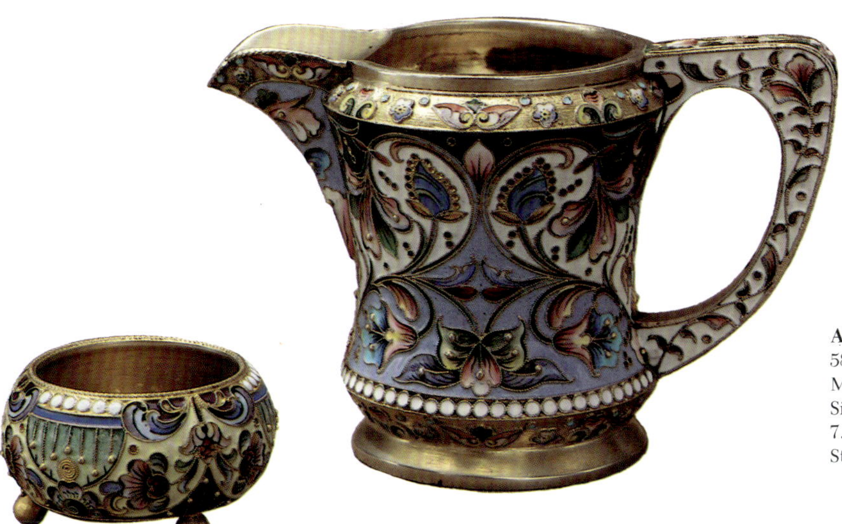

Anonymous silversmith
581, 582. Salt cellar and cream jug
Moscow, 1908–17
Silver gilt and enamel, 3.4 × 3.5 × 3.5;
7.4 × 10.6 × 6.3
State Historical Museum

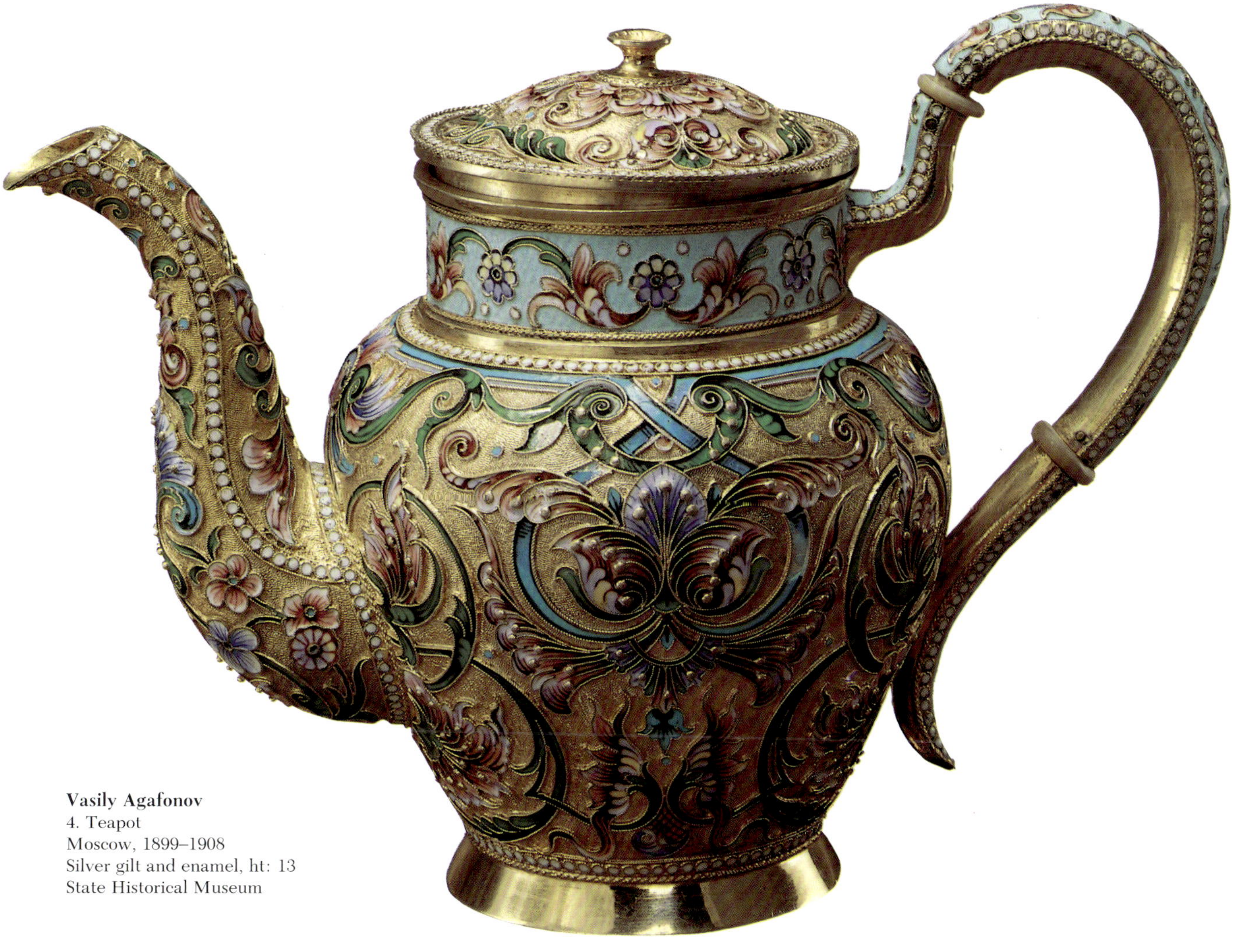

Vasily Agafonov
4. Teapot
Moscow, 1899–1908
Silver gilt and enamel, ht: 13
State Historical Museum

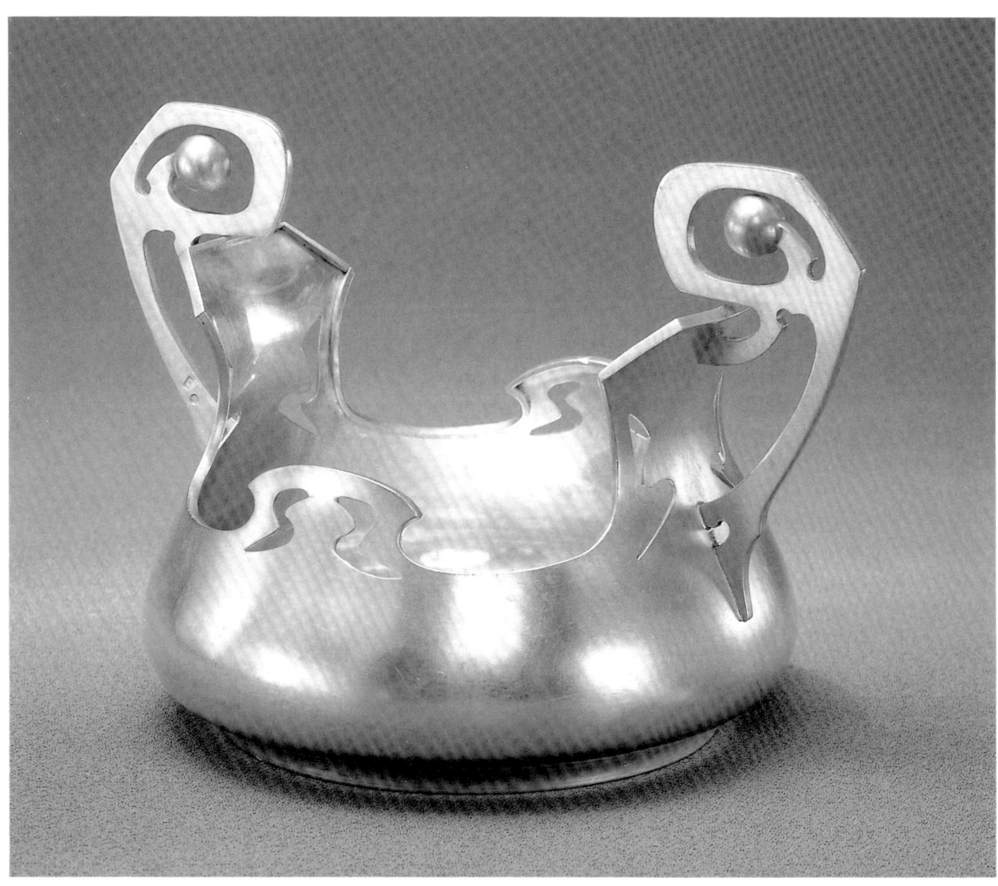

Vasily Andreev
12. Small vase
Moscow, 1908–17
Silver, 12.5 × 17.5 × 10.3
State Historical Museum

Mikhail Tarasov
427. Tea-glass holder
Moscow, 1899–1908
Silver, 9.5 × 12 × 7.2
State Historical Museum

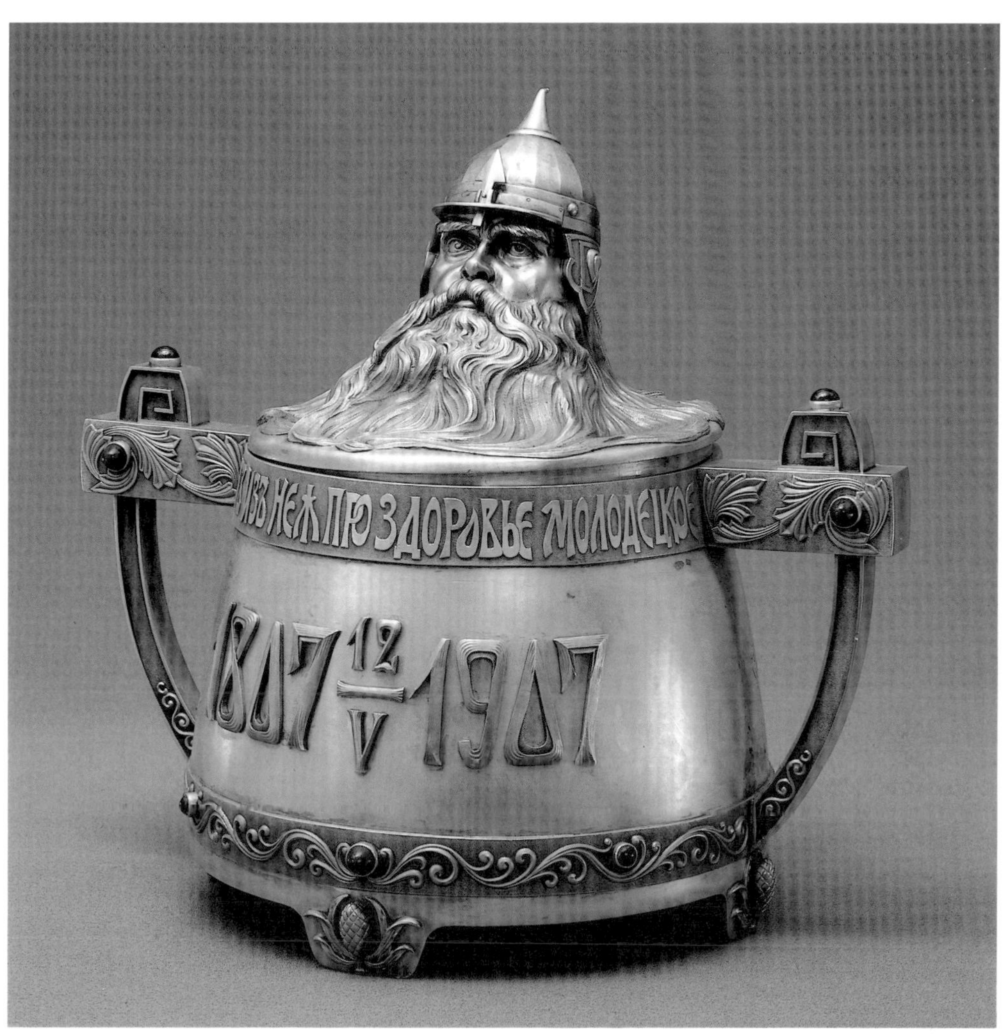

Anonymous silversmith (G. T.)
578. Wine vessel
Kiev, 1907
Silver, 29 × 30.5 × 16.8
State Historical Museum

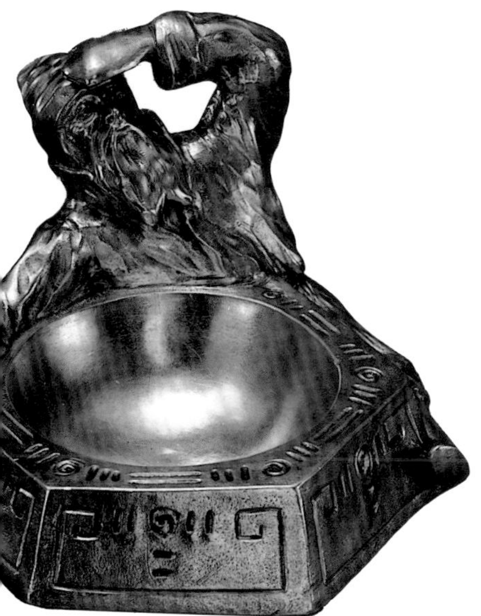

4th Jeweller's Artel'
22. Salt cellar
Moscow, 1908–1917
Silver, 6.1 × 9.1 × 8.5
State Historical Museum

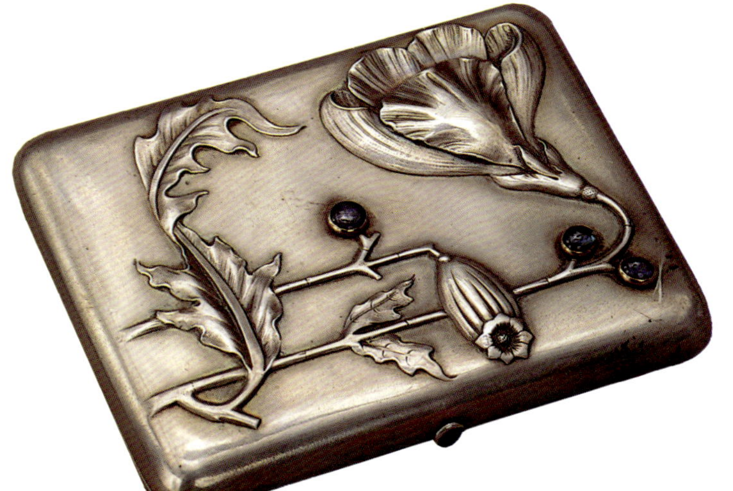

LEFT: **Ivan Tarabrov**
426. Cigarette case
Moscow, 1899–1908
Silver, gold and sapphires, $1 \times 10.3 \times 8.2$
State Historical Museum

BELOW: **Anonymous silversmith**
583. Cigarette case
Moscow, 1908–17
Silver gilt and enamel, $1.2 \times 10.7 \times 8.2$
State Historical Museum

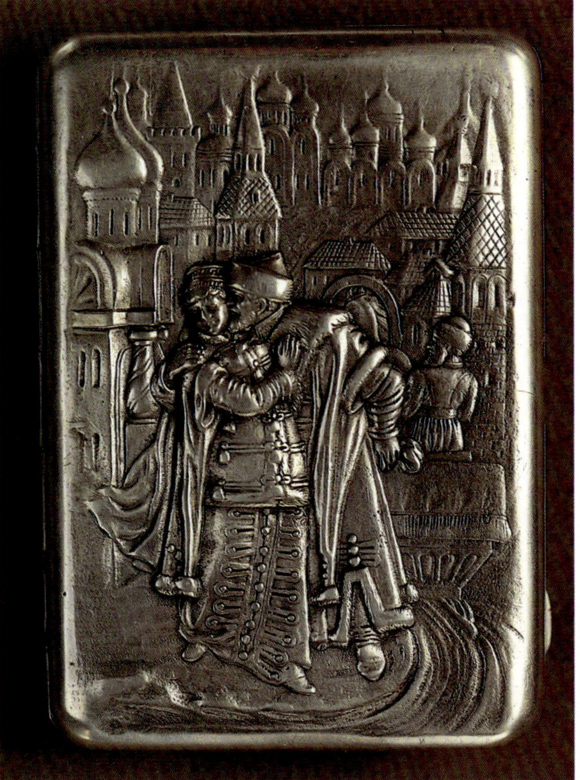

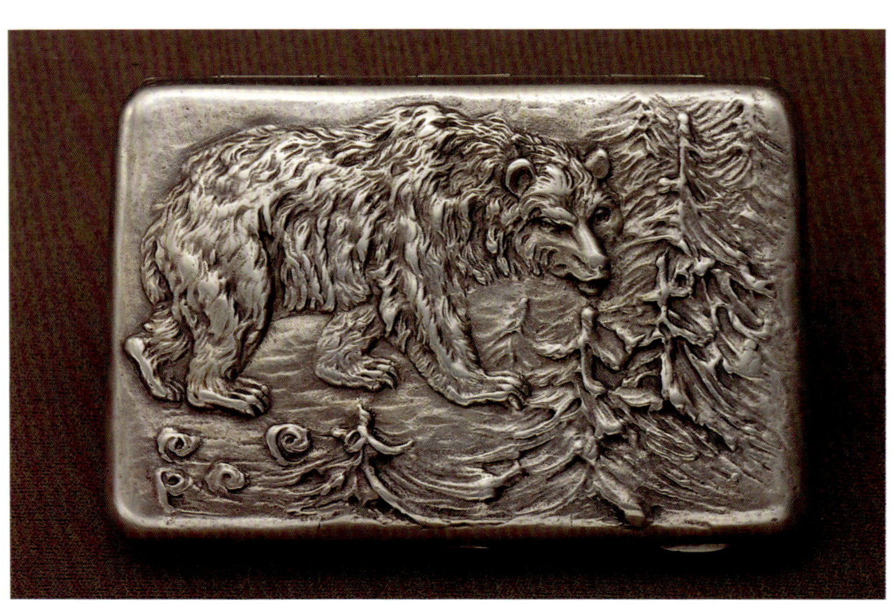

ABOVE AND RIGHT:
Anonymous silversmith (A. R.)
580. Cigarette case (upper and lower sides)
Moscow, 1908–17
Silver, $1.3 \times 11.4 \times 7.7$
State Historical Museum

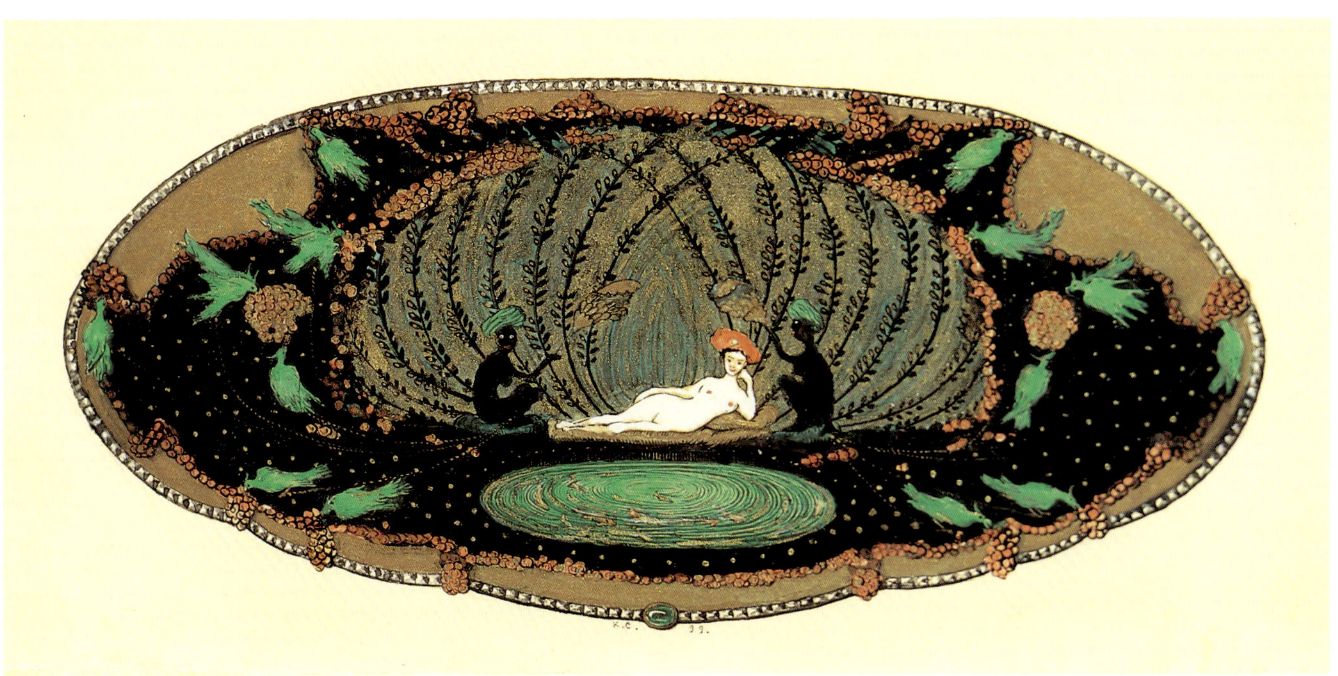

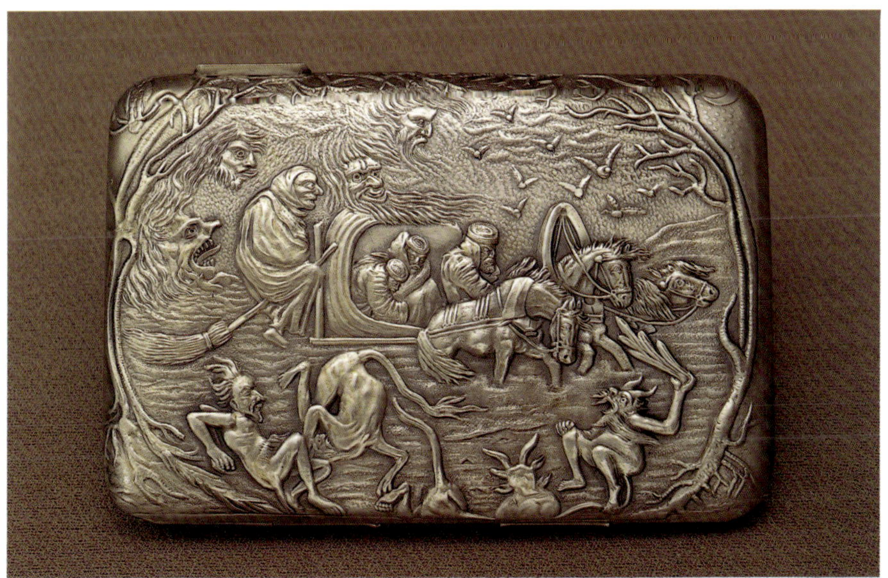

ABOVE: **Konstantin Somov**
390. *Sultana*
1899
Design for a snuff-box executed for the
Lukutin factory
Mixed media on paper, 13.5 × 27.7
State Tretyakov Gallery

LEFT: **Anonymous silversmith (R. D.)**
575. Cigarette case
Moscow (?), early 20th century
Silver, 1.2 × 11 × 7.7
State Historical Museum

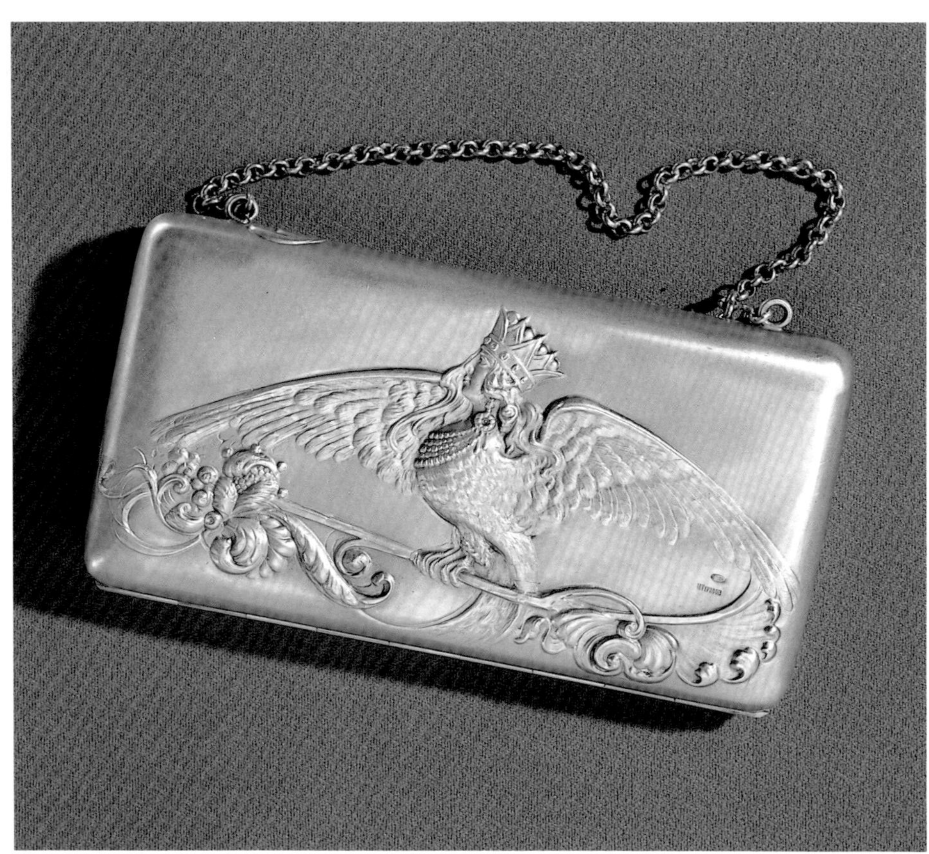

ABOVE: **Mikhail Tarasov**
428. Lady's purse
Moscow, 1908–17
Silver, 20.3 × 10.8 × 3
State Historical Museum

OPPOSITE TOP:
Anonymous silversmith (S. P. I)
579. Lady's purse
Moscow, 1908–17
Silver, 15 × 10.5 × 4
State Historical Museum

OPPOSITE BELOW: **Vasily Naumov**
243. Lady's purse
Moscow, 1899–1908
Silver, 26.5 × 18.5
State Historical Museum

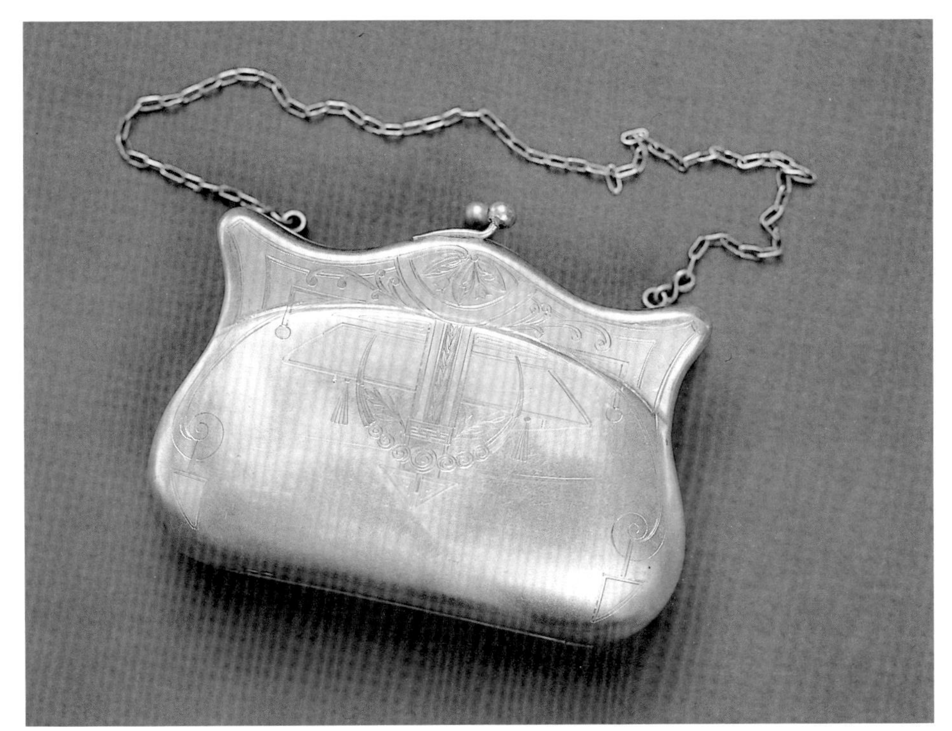

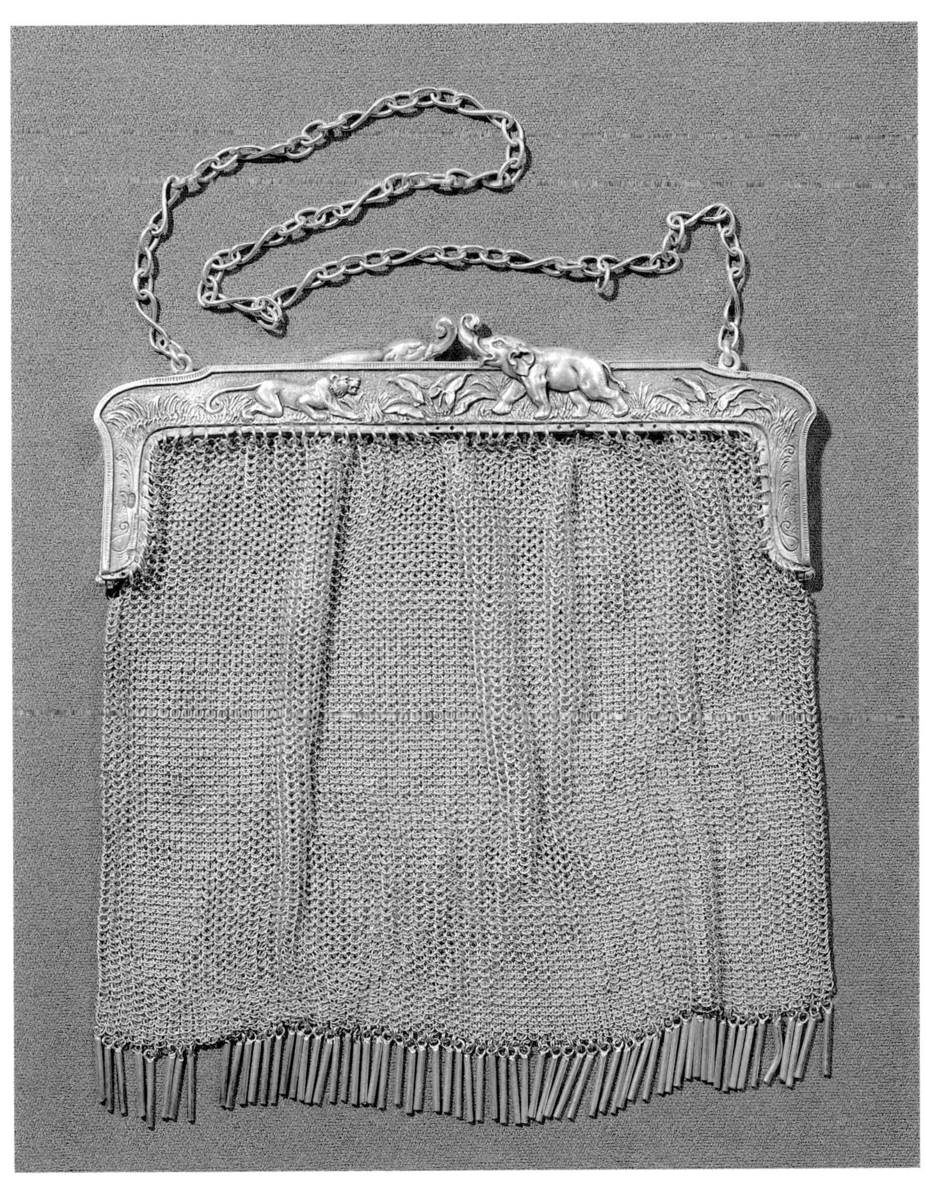

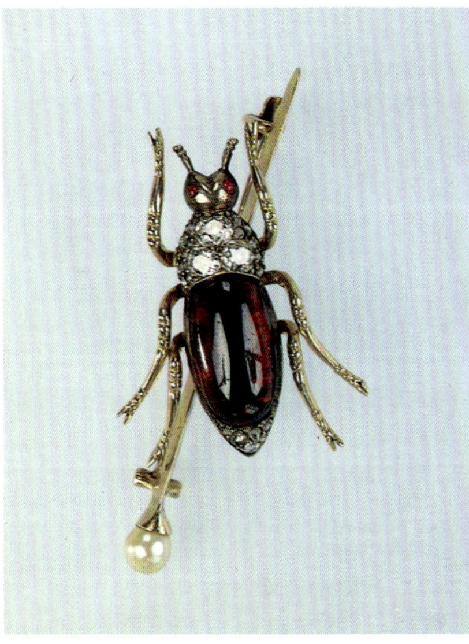

Fredrik Tiander
430. Brooch
St Petersburg, late 19th century
Almandine, two tourmalines for the eyes;
beetle attached to gold pin set with diamonds
and rose-cut diamonds and terminating in a
pearl, length: 5.3
State Historical Museum

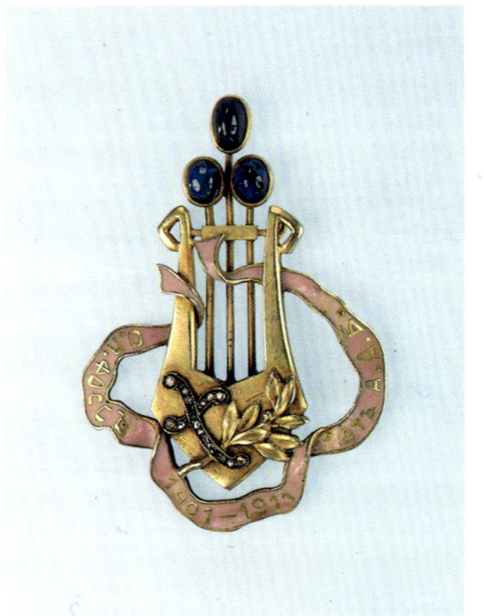

Anonymous Jeweller
574. Pendant
St Petersburg (?), 1911
Gold, enamel, sapphires, diamonds, 4.5 × 3
State Historical Museum

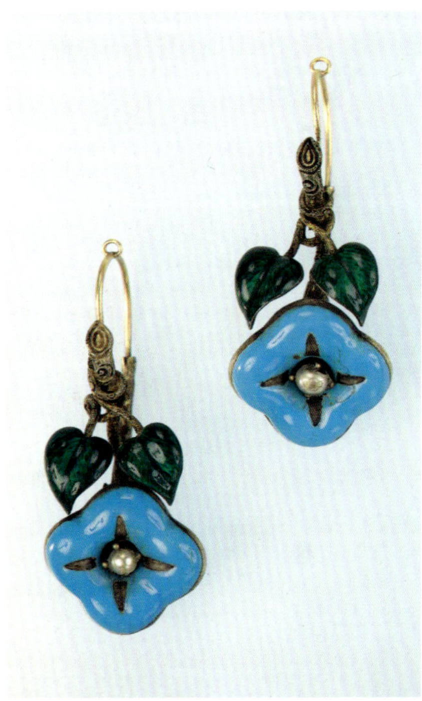

Anonymous Jeweller
571. Earrings
Russia, turn of the century
Gold, silver, enamel and pearls, 5 × 2.4
State Historical Museum

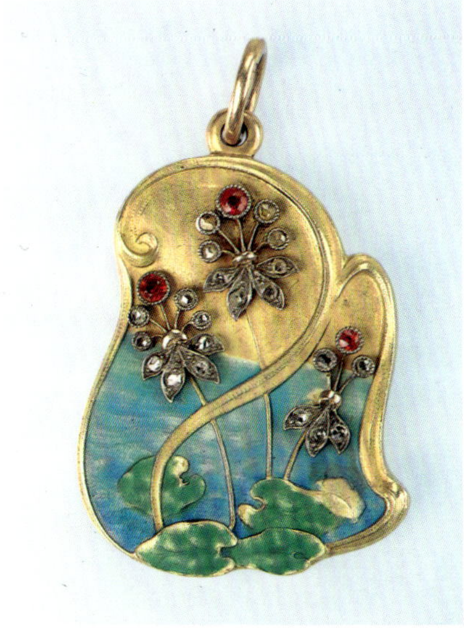

1st Jewellers' Artel'
21. Medallion
Moscow, 1908–17
Gold, diamonds, rubies and enamel, 6 × 4
State Historical Museum

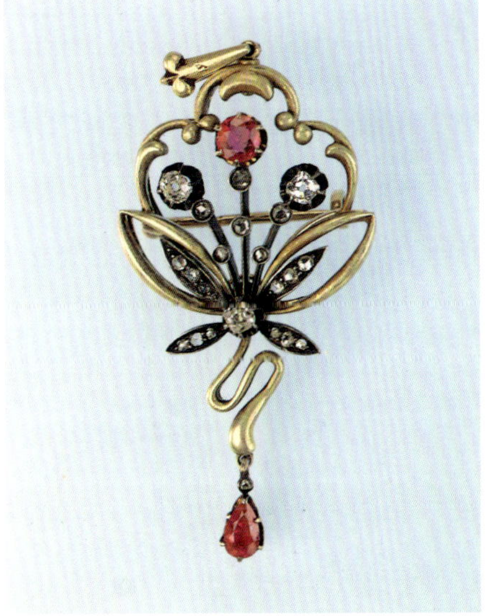

Anonymous Jeweller (N. B.)
572. Pendant brooch
Moscow, 1899–1908
Gold, rubies, brilliants, diamonds, 6 × 2.7
State Historical Museum

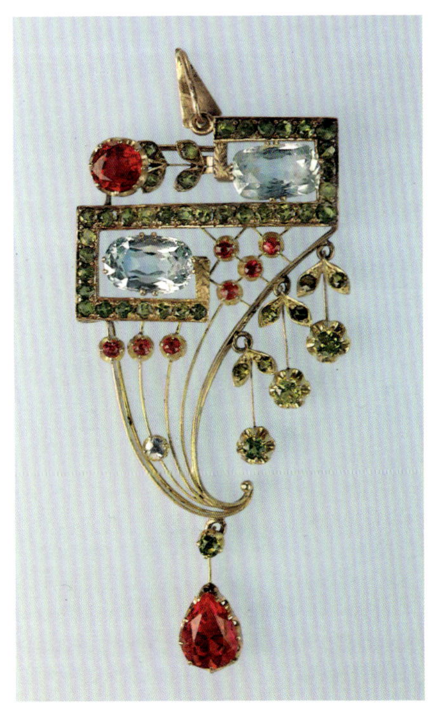

Anonymous Jeweller
573. Pendant
Russia, early 20th century
Gold, chrysoprase, rubies, aquamarines,
7.8 × 3.2
State Historical Museum

21

PHOTOGRAPHY AT THE TURN OF THE CENTURY

TAT'YANA SABUROVA

By the beginning of the twentieth century, photography had become an integral part of the art world in Russia, and its development as an art form was due to the close interaction and interchange of influence with other areas of Russian culture. The traditions of the last decades of the nineteenth century were still maintained, but changes in fashion, and consequently in public taste, compelled artists to seek ways of renewing photographic art, of finding innovative approaches to the essence of the creative process. This they did by adopting new methods of taking and printing pictures, by searching for vivid means of expression, and by transforming the external appearance of the photograph.

Portrait photography continued to be the predominant genre. The appearance at the end of the last century of a large number of photographic studios, which could be visited by members of various social classes, young and old, in St Petersburg, Moscow and the provincial cities of Russia, made portraiture a mass phenomenon. The popular Petersburg magazine *Fotograf (Photographer)* stated: "Photographic portraits . . . have become an essential feature of society, a requirement of every family, every group of friends, comrades, acquaintances, co-workers; the best record of the events and relations of families, friends and society."

The products of most commercial studios in Russia were sober business-like portraits. Having captured the external likeness – doing their best to place their customers in the most favourable light – the photographers created what were essentially society portraits, limiting themselves to the superficial characteristics of the sitters. However, there were at the same time artists who had a different creative outlook: they strove not only to reproduce the external appearance of the person portrayed, but also to embody an artistic image, to reveal the inner world and psychology of the person before the camera, and to reflect social characteristics and individual personality.

The arbiters of fashion in the sphere of professional commercial portrait photography were Boissonnas and Eggler (pp.15, 262–3), the St Petersburg branch of a French company; the court photographer von Hahn; and the major Moscow studios of K. Fischer, P. P. Pavlov (pp.262–3) and I. Brodovsky. New creative approaches to the photographic portrait were demonstrated by N. Krotkov ("Paola") (p.40), Nikolai Petrov, M. A. Scherling and B. Pashkevich among others.

At the end of the nineteenth century, genre was at the forefront of Russian photographic art. "Views", "Types", and "Scenes" were traditional themes in Russia, from the first decades of photographic history. By the 1890s, the considerable progress of photographic technology had opened up unlimited possibilities for genre photographers. Here there was an identity of interest between documentary and artistic photographers, since both were attempting to give a representational significance to their pictures. Genre photography also had a particular appeal to amateur photographers, some of whom, such as the Moscow merchant Aleksei Mazurin (pp.266–8), achieved brilliant results, sometimes even surpassing the professionals in their technique.

Documentary photography required a precise choice of subject to be successful, as well as the ability to record it in an expressive way, reflecting the artist's relationship to the subject represented. At the same time, the photographic creation of works of art – "pictures from nature", imitating the truth of life – required from the photographer a special degree of taste, tact and sense of artistic balance. The work of painters influenced the practice of creating photographic "dramatisations", characterised by a certain refined sentimentality.

From its earliest days, Russian photographers strove to make photography a form of artistic creation, with an orientation towards fine art. The accurate and dispassionate imitation of the surrounding world by means of the camera did not satisfy them. They wanted to demonstrate that works of art could be created with photographic methods. This outlook was also reflected in the way in which both portraitists and genre photographers in Russia consistently described themselves as "artist-photographers", imparting a special meaning to these words.

This creative stance was particularly strong in the period under discussion, and it led naturally to the appearance of artistic associations in many Russian cities. The largest of these groups was the Russian Photographic Society in Moscow. Founded in 1894, it united professionals and amateurs, including photographers who celebrated Russian culture, such as Maksim Dmitriev, Sergei Lobovikov, Nikolai Petrov, Nikolai Svishchov, N. Krotkov, K. Fisher, Aleksei Mazurin and many others. The basic creative task of this organisation was the development of Russian artistic photography as an art form.

The complex and contradictory period from 1890 to 1917 in Russia was reflected in the content of photographs, which recorded the dramatic events of Russian history and the social aspects of life. But, at the same time, the atmosphere of tragedy and the sensation of impending doom drove Russian society towards an escape from harsh reality into a world of beauty and harmony. This may well explain the attempts of many photographers to create beautiful and poetic works, to celebrate the brighter aspects of life, and sometimes to idealise it. The general attraction to the fashionable "Russian theme" also affected photographic art. Photographers frequently portrayed lyrical scenes and folk festivals, recorded Russian architecture with love and knowledge, and reproduced in their works the irresistible beauty of nature.

By contrast with the previous decades, in the years after 1900 photographers used a variety of means to express their creative ideas. According to which movement in fine art they adhered to, Realism or Impressionism, they either welcomed new technical developments as a means of representing reality more accurately or rejected them in an attempt to express, above all else, their personal impressions of the world about them. Different forms of the positive process such as the pigment, gum arabic and bromide-oil methods were widely used.

In the 1900s there was a noticeable change in the external appearance of the photographic print. It became severe and elegant in the spirit of the fashionable *Style Moderne:* positive prints took on characteristic shades, their shape was transformed, their dimensions began to depart from the strict standard, and the style and decoration of the mount changed. This was seen primarily in the products of commercial photographic studios frequented by representatives of the higher Russian aristocracy. The new photographic prints became part of the beautiful world of objects which surrounded a person of refinement at the beginning of the century.

The photographs displayed in the exhibition form a very small part of the collection of the State Historical Museum, which is the largest in the Soviet Union. The portraits, views and genre compositions were produced by artists or photographic studios well known in Russia, and many (nos. 591, 610–12, 610–20, 624–5, 630–6) were shown at competitions and exhibitions of the Russian Photographic Society in Moscow from the 1890s to 1914.

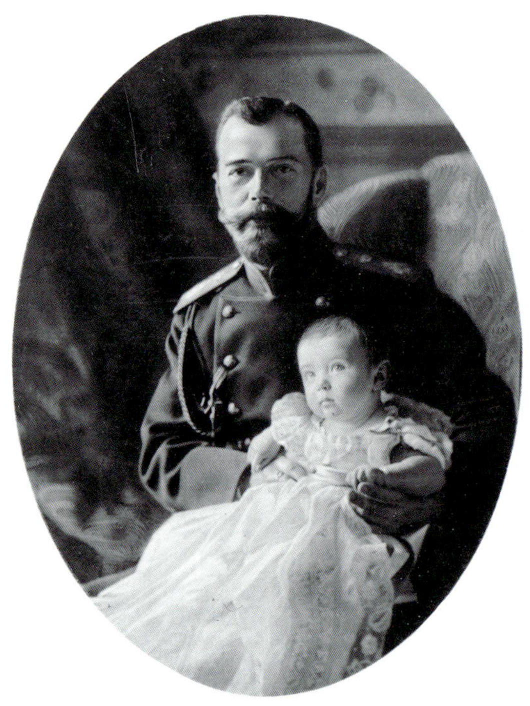

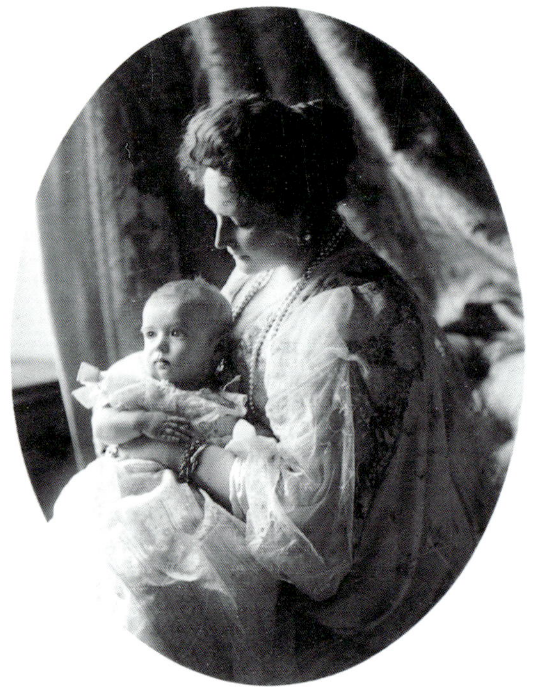

ABOVE LEFT AND RIGHT:
Boissonas & Eggler studio
587, 588. Portraits of Tsar Nikolai II and
Tsaritsa Aleksandra Fedorovna with their son
the Tsarevich Aleksei
1904–5
Photos, each 13.4 × 10
State Historical Museum

BELOW LEFT AND RIGHT: **P. P. Pavlov studio**
614, 613. Two portraits of Princess Yusupova,
Countess Z. N. Sumarokova-El'ston
1900
Photos, each 32 × 22
State Historical Museum

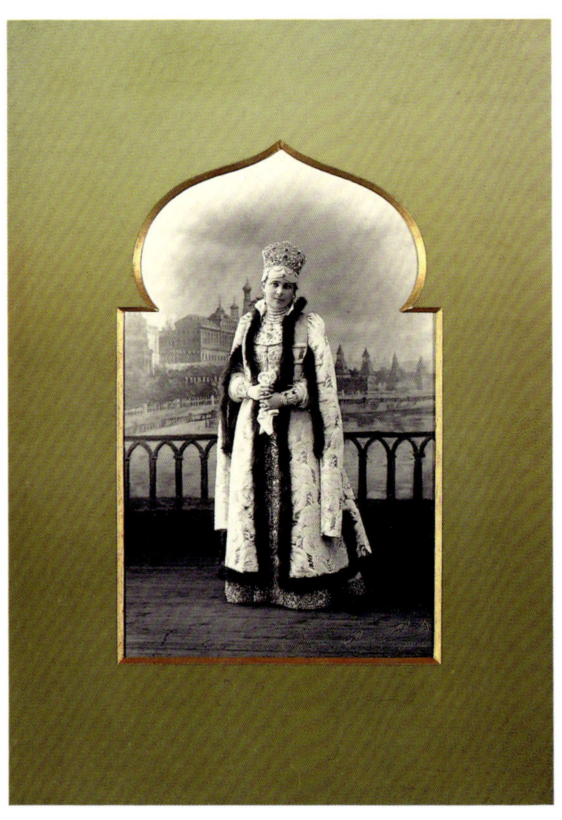

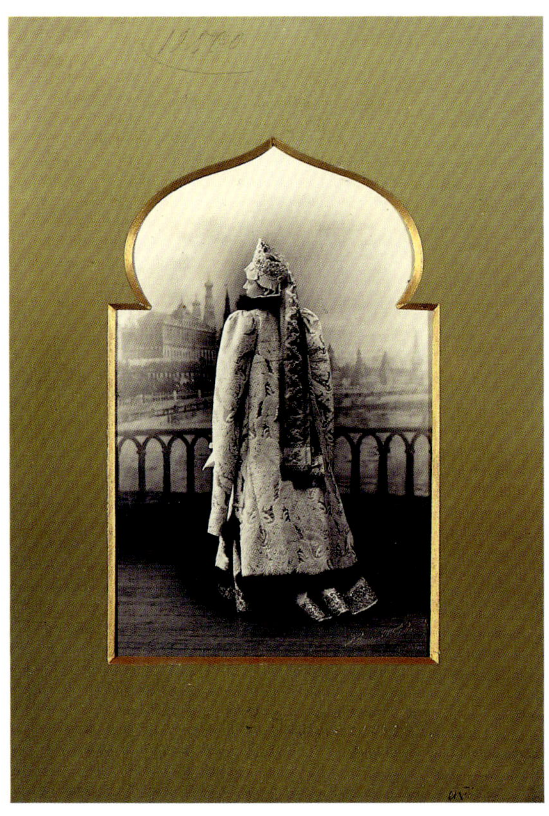

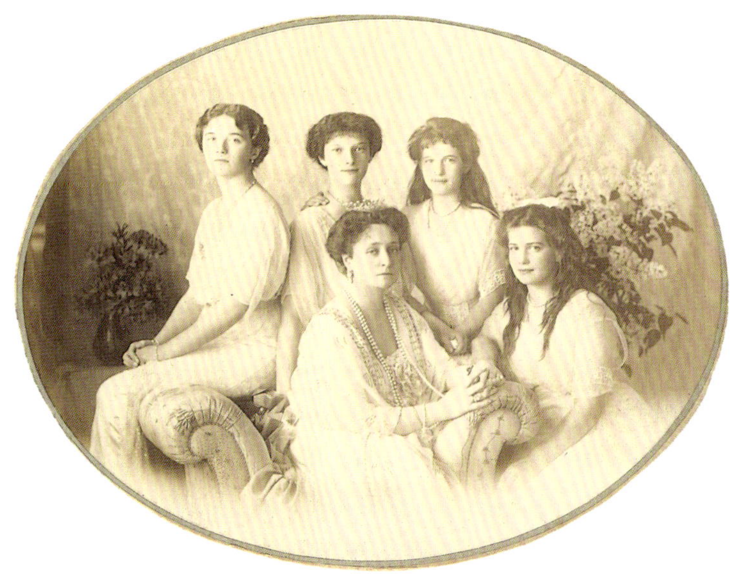

ABOVE: **Boissonas & Eggler studio**
586. Portrait of Tsaritsa Aleksandra Fedorovna
with her daughters Ol'ga, Tat'yana, Mariya
and Anastasiya
1910s
Photo, 15.3 × 19.6
State Historical Museum

BELOW: **P. P. Pavlov studio**
615. Group portrait: A. P. Chekhov with the
cast and directors of *The Seagull*, 7 May 1899,
during the playwright's visit to Moscow for a
special performance of the play at the Moscow
Arts Theatre (for full identification, see
catalogue)
Photo, 35.4 × 47
State Historical Museum

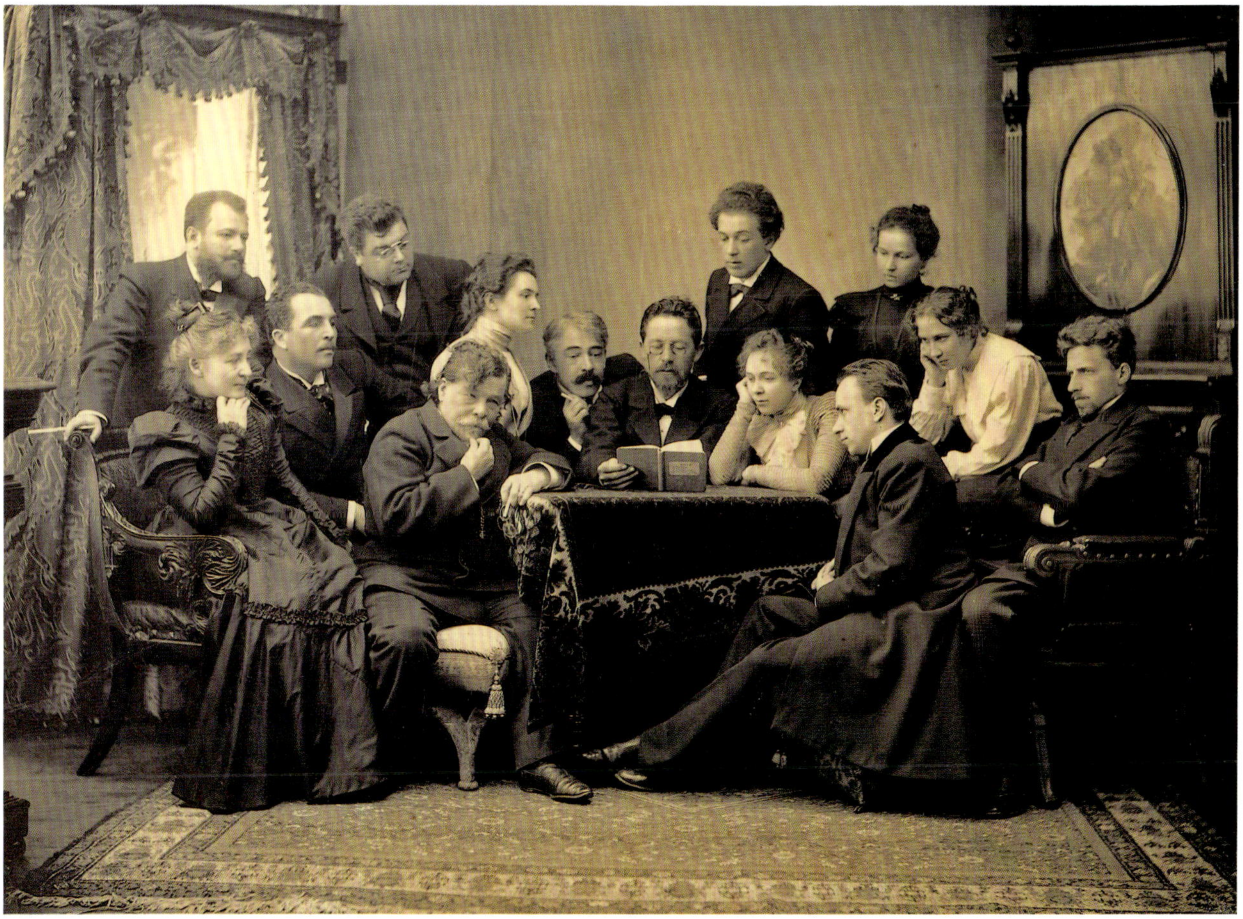

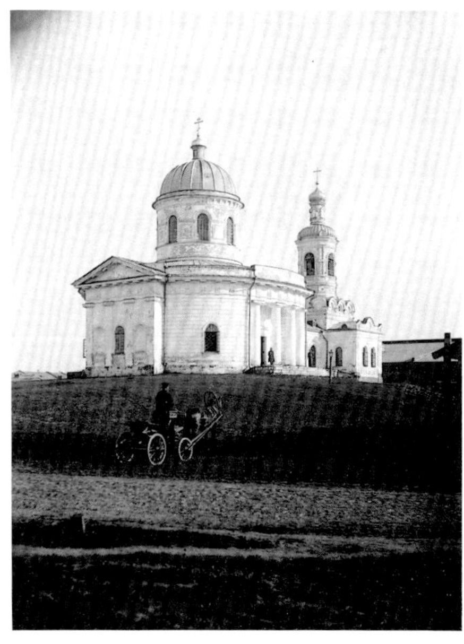

Maksim Dmitriev
596. Armenian church, Nizhny Novgorod
1890s
Photo, 21 × 15.2
State Historical Museum

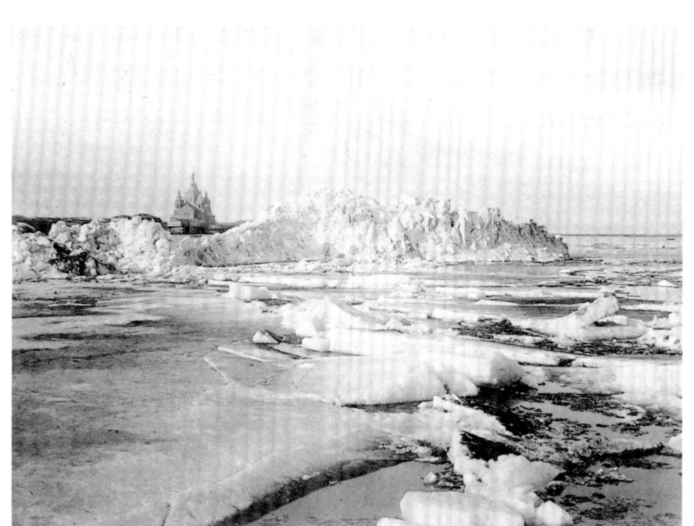

Maksim Dmitriev
594. Cathedral in the New Exhibition Grounds
on the Bank of the Volga at Nizhny Novgorod
1890s
Photo, 16.8 × 22.4
State Historical Museum

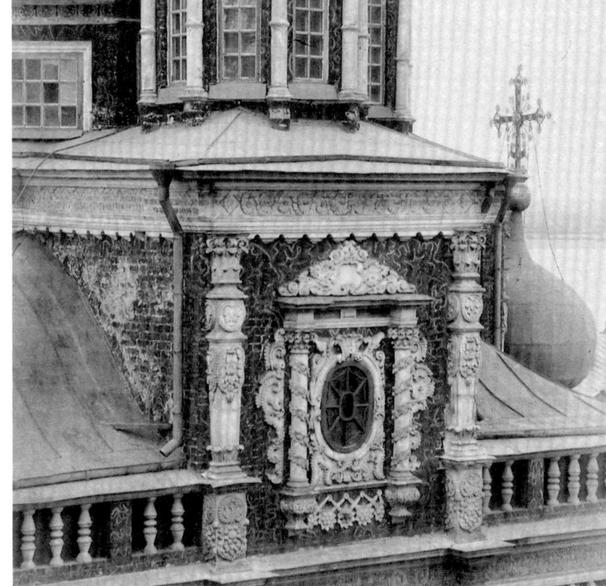

Maksim Dmitriev
593. Church of the Nativity of the Virgin,
Nizhny Novgorod
1890s
Photo, 26.9 × 22.1
State Historical Museum

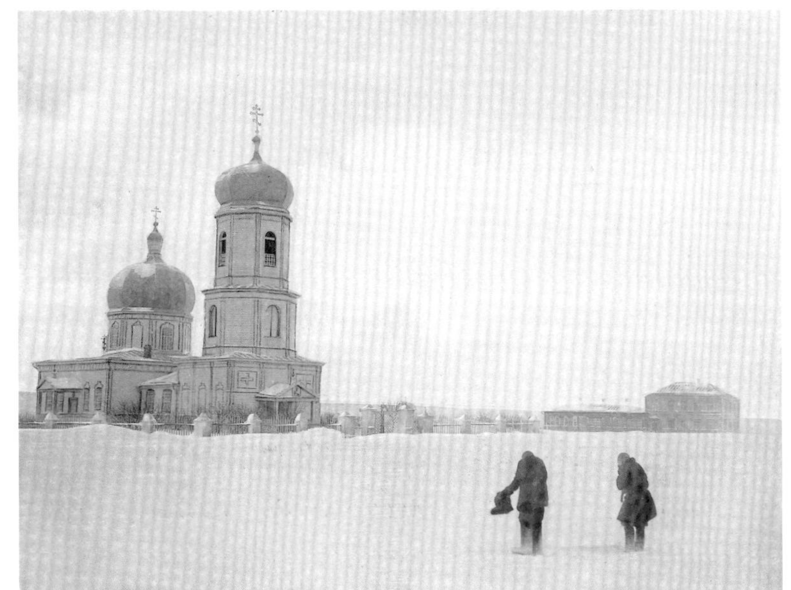

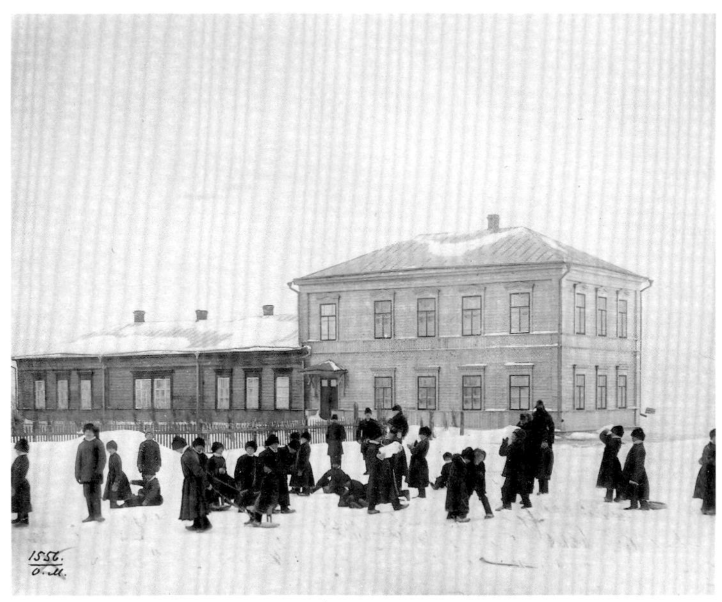

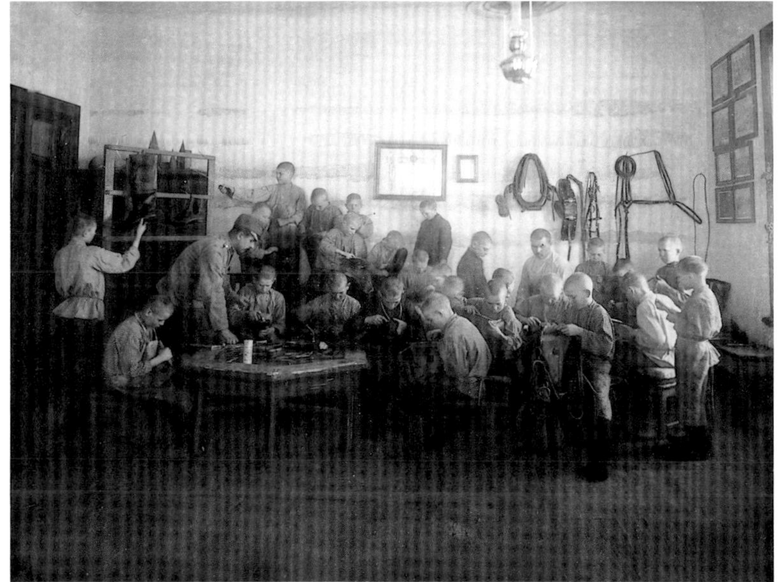

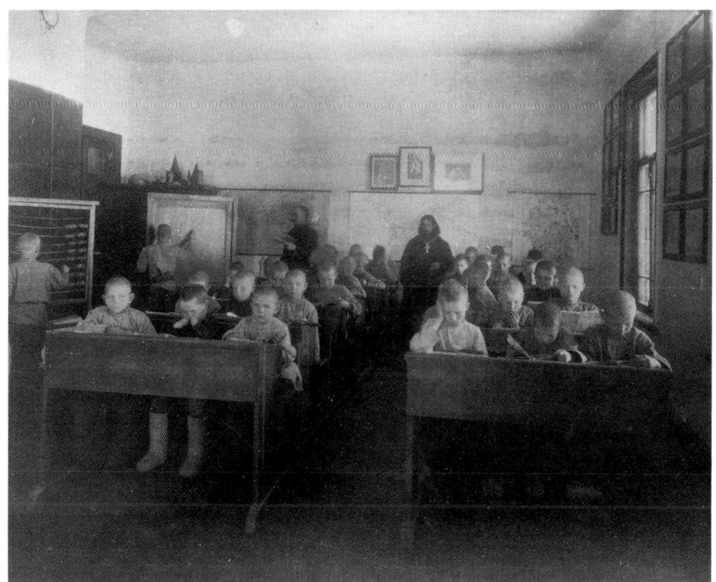

Photographic Album "Agricultural Trades Orphanage for the children of soldiers in the village of Kolokol'tsovko, Samara Province, Nikolaev District", presented to Tsarevich Aleksei Nikolaevich in 1916
State Historical Museum

TOP LEFT: 626. Church by the Orphanage
Photo, 22.4 × 29

TOP RIGHT: 627. Pupils in front of the school and workshops
Photo, 22 × 26

ABOVE LEFT: 629. Classes in the saddlery and shoemaking workshops
Photo, 21.5 × 25.5

ABOVE RIGHT: 628. Pupils in the classroom
Photo, 21.5 × 25.5

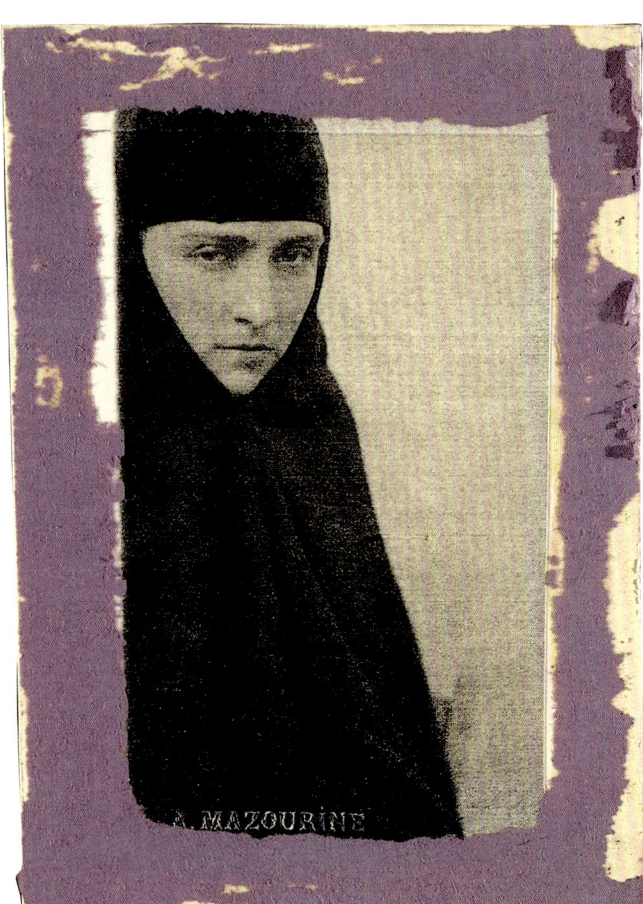

Aleksei Mazurin
600. Nun
1900s
Photo, 15.6 × 11.2
State Historical Museum

Aleksei Mazurin
603. Easter
1900s
Photo, 12.7 × 17
State Historical Museum

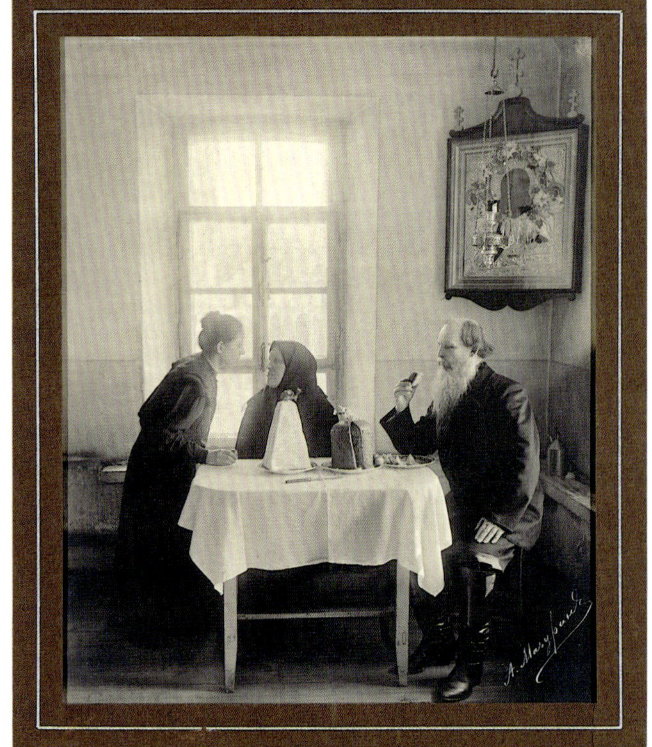

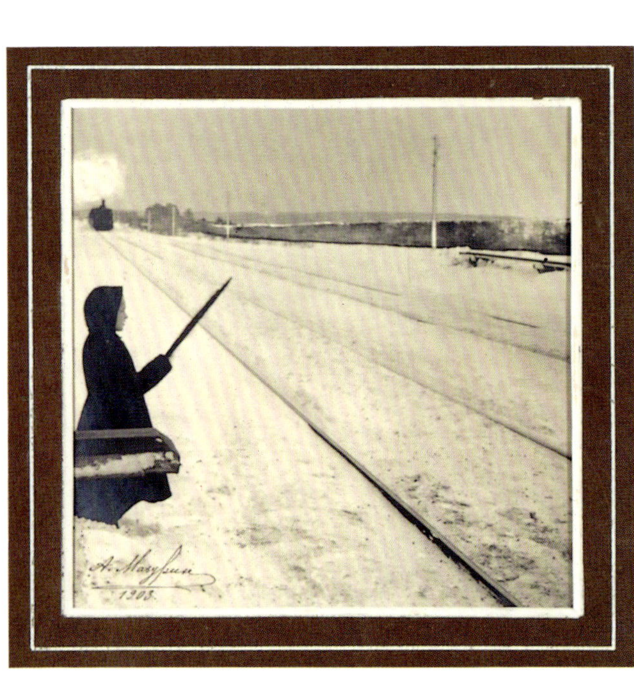

Aleksei Mazurin
604. ''Pointswoman''
1903
Photo, 16 × 16
State Historical Museum

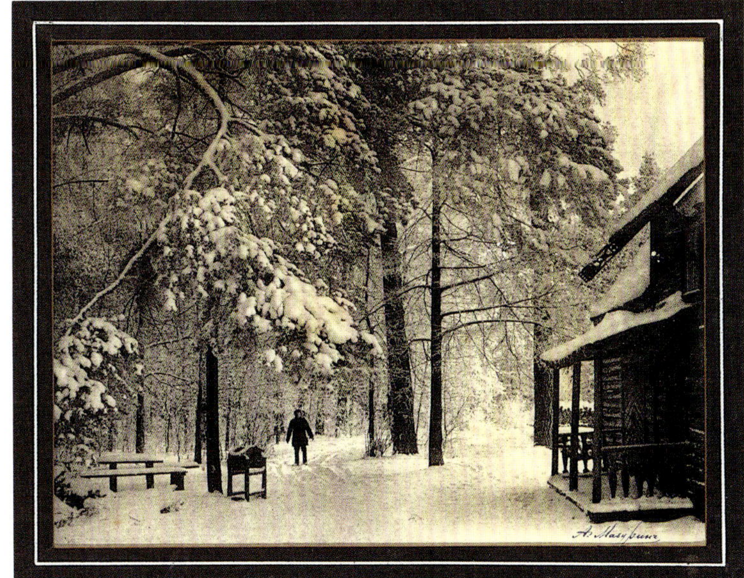

Aleksei Mazurin
608. Winter Landscape
1900s
Photo, 16.7 × 21.5
State Historical Museum

Aleksei Mazurin
606. Winter Landscape
1900s
Photo, 22 × 17.2
State Historical Museum

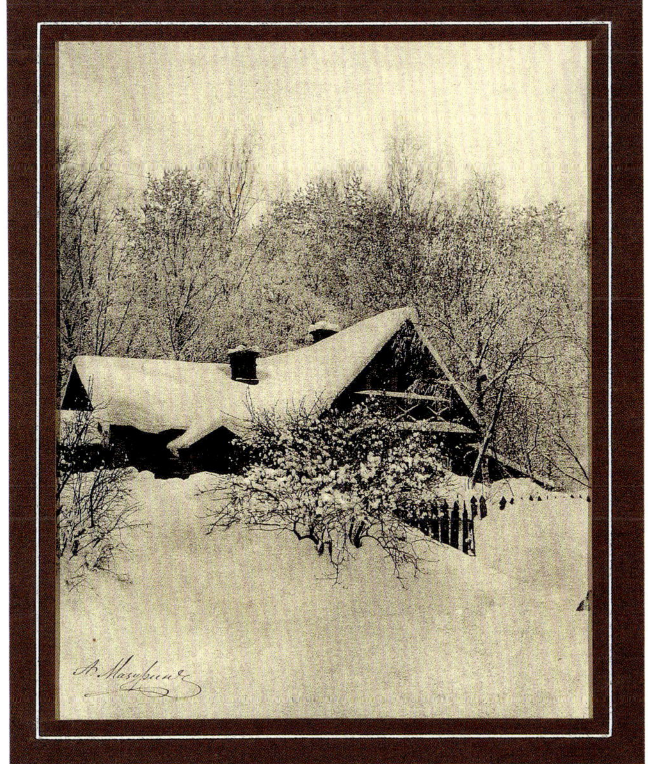

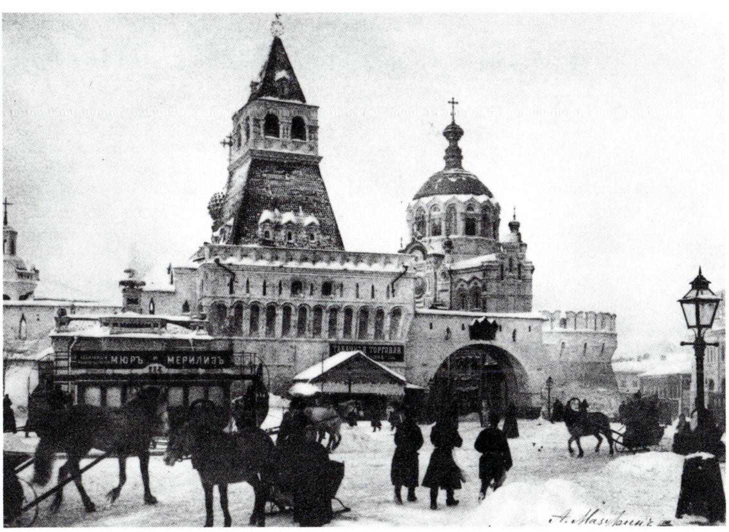

Aleksei Mazurin
609. View of the Nikol'sky Gates of the
Kitaigorod and the chapel of St Panteleimon
on Lubyanskaya (now Dzerzhinsky) Square,
Moscow
1900s
Photo, 17.6 × 22.5
State Historical Museum

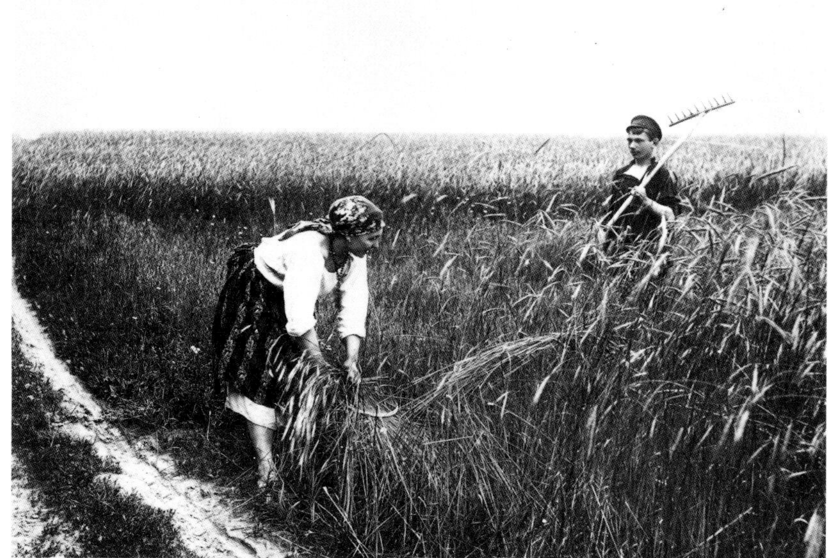

Aleksei Mazurin
601. Harvest
1902
Photo, 22.3 × 16.2
State Historical Museum

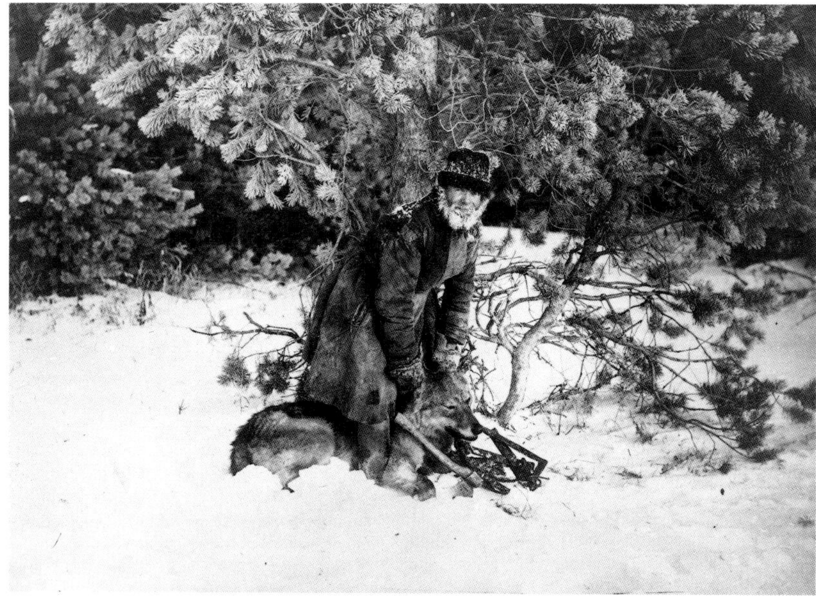

Unknown photographer
636. Huntsman in the Winter Forest
1900s
Photo, 16.5 × 22.5
State Historical Museum

Aleksei Mazurin
602. Birdcatchers
1900s
Photo, 22.5 × 17.1
State Historical Museum

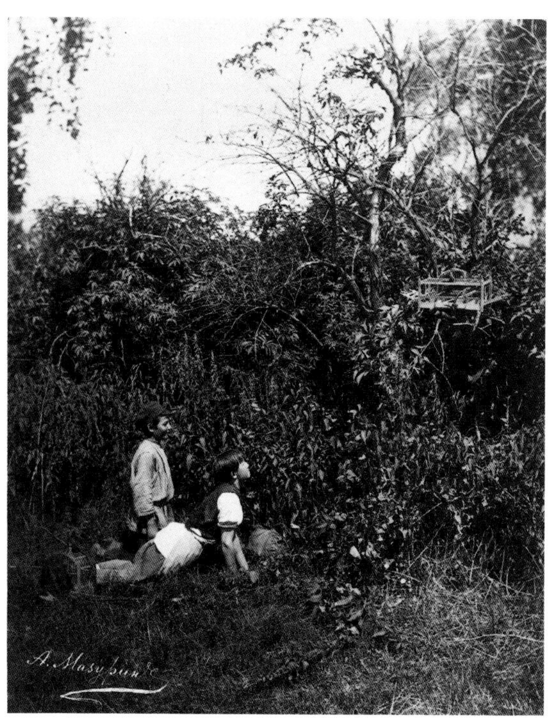

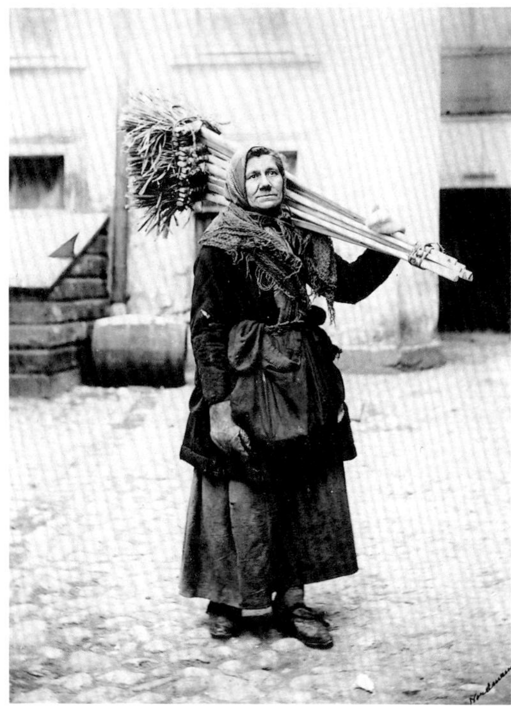

Natal'ya Nordman-Severova
611. Broom seller
1900s
Photo, 16.3 × 11.8
State Historical Museum

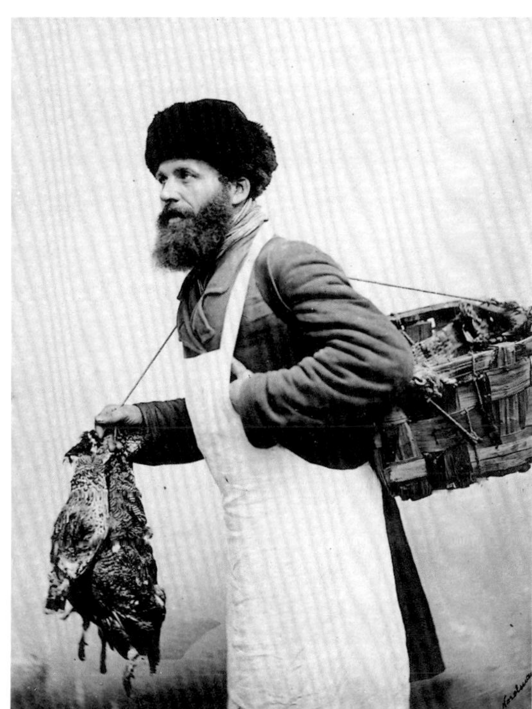

Natal'ya Nordman-Severova
612. "Seller of Game"
1900s
Photo, 15.8 × 11.6
State Historical Museum

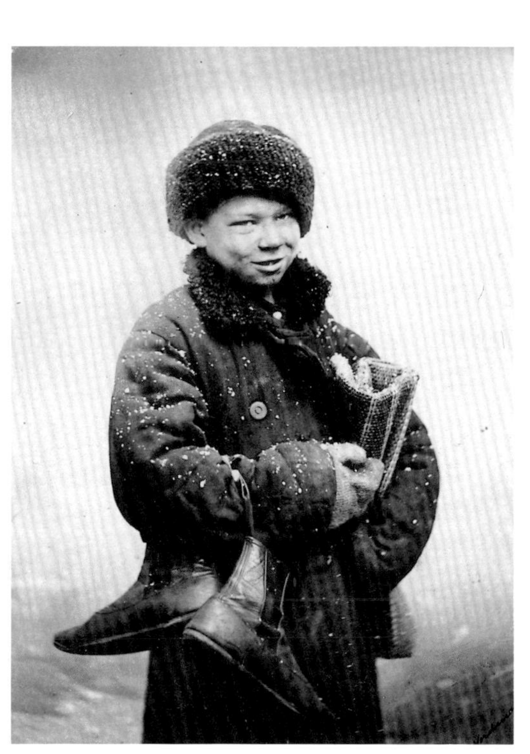

Natal'ya Nordman-Severova
610. "Cobbler"
1900s
Photo, 15.4 × 11.4
State Historical Museum

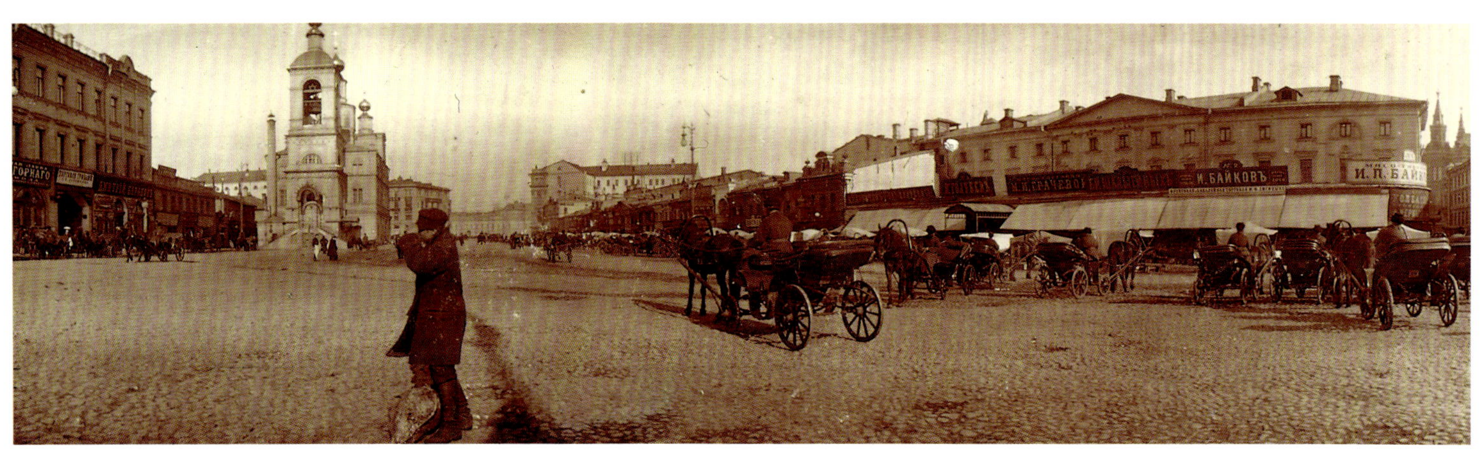

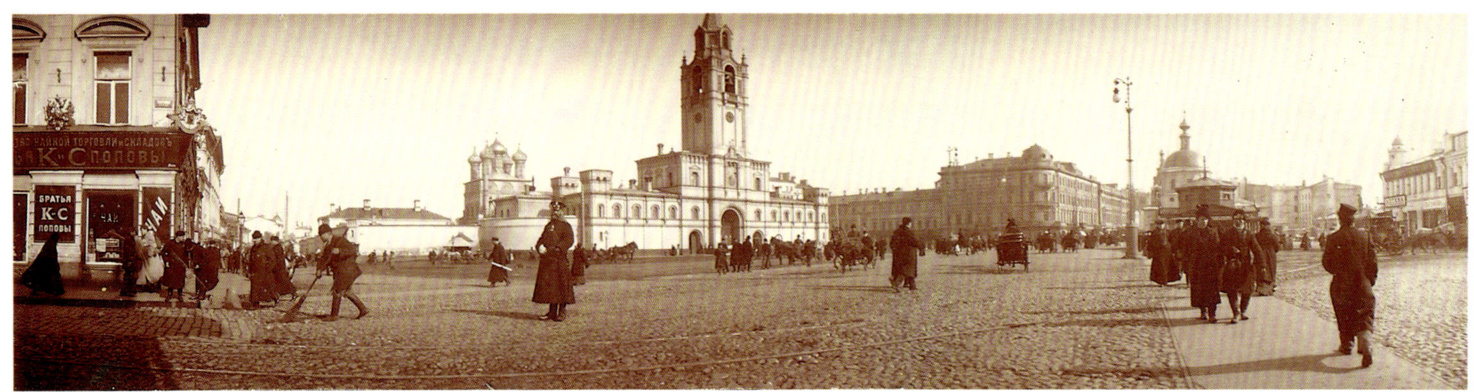

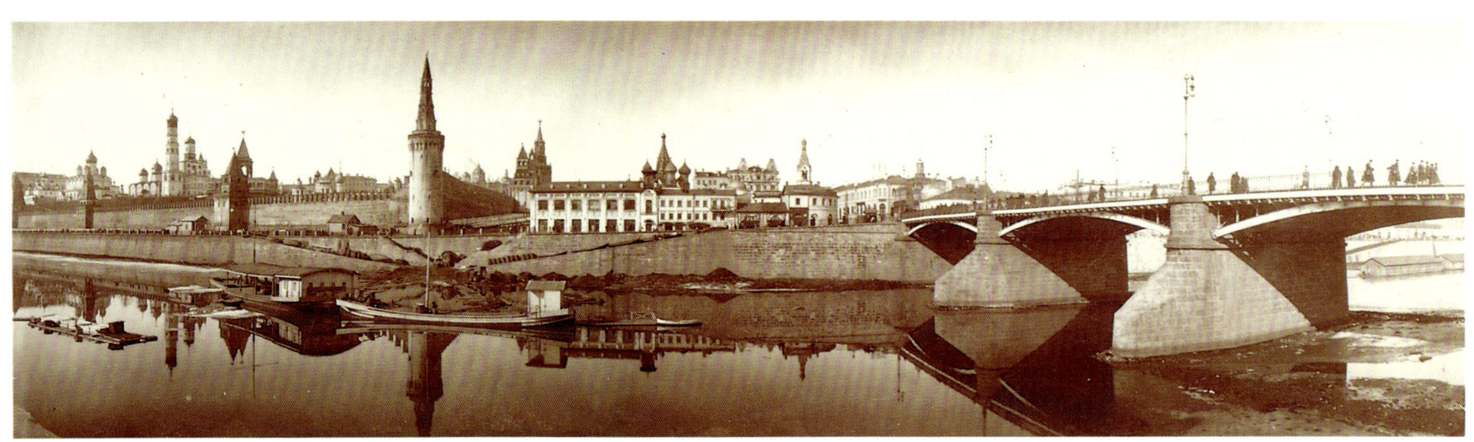

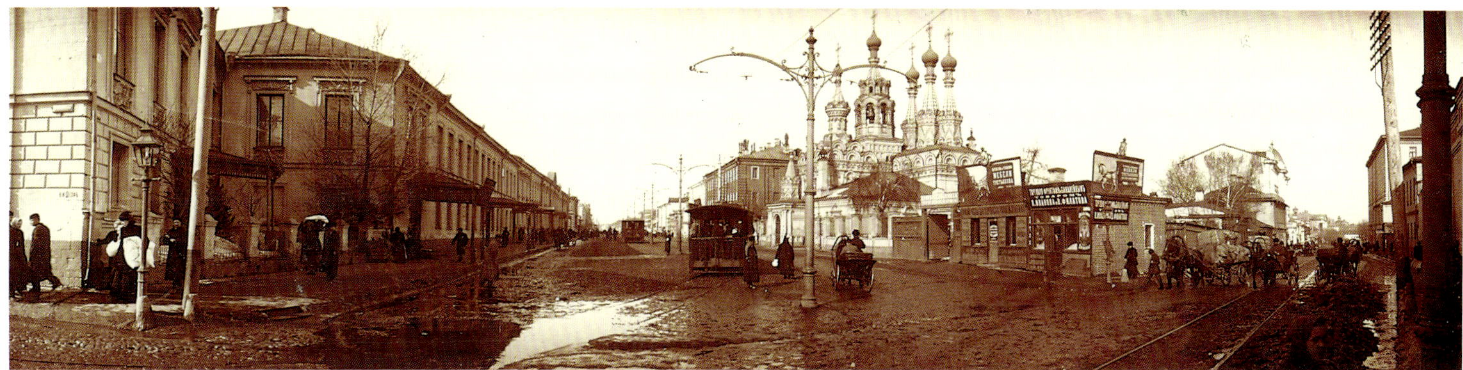

ABOVE: **Unknown photographer**
632. Malaya Dmitrovka (now A. P. Chekhov
Street), Moscow: View of the church of the
Nativity in Putniki
1890s
Photo, 7.7 × 29.5
State Historical Museum

OPPOSITE PAGE

TOP: **Unknown photographer**
635. Okhotny Ryad Street, Moscow: View of
the church of the Paraskeva Pyatnitsa
1890s
Photo, 8.5 × 28.7
State Historical Museum

CENTRE: **Unknown photographer**
631. Strastnaya (Passion) Square (now Pushkin
Square), Moscow: View of the Monastery of
the Passion and Tverskaya Street
1890s
Photo, 7.9 × 29.1
State Historical Museum

BOTTOM: **Unknown photographer**
633. View of the Kremlin and Moskvoretsky
Bridge, Moscow
1890s
Photo, 8.7 × 29.5
State Historical Museum

23

CATALOGUE
OF THE EXHIBITION

NOTE ON THE CATALOGUE

The catalogue of the exhibition falls into four sections: works of art by named artists, listed under artists in alphabetical order; anonymous works of art, listed by categories – Posters, Printed Ephemera, Furniture, Woodwork, Ceramic, Jewellery, Silver and Gold; photographs, listed by named photographers followed by anonymous photographs; films, listed by directors. Dimensions are given in centimetres, height preceding width. Information on titles, dates, media and dimensions have been supplied by the lending institutions.

In the case of film credits, the following abbreviations have been used: Dir – Director; Prod – Producer; Scr – Script; Phot – Photography; Art Dir – Art Direction; Rel – Release date. Length is given in metres, but this does not automatically give duration, since projection speeds vary from 16 to 24 frames per second. Most credits and biographical information are taken from *Silent Witnesses: Russian Films 1908–1919*.

GLOSSARY

A number of Russian titles or words appear in the catalogue, and several of the art schools where the artists trained or taught are referred to by a short name. Translations and some notes on these follow:

Adskaya Pochta. "Hell's Post Office". Satirical journal, first published in 1905.

Alaya Roza. "Crimson Rose". Exhibition group in Saratov (1904).

Apollon. "Apollo". Journal edited by Sergei Makovsky, published in St Petersburg (1909–18).

Artel'. Co-operative; there were some thirty jewellers' Artel's in Moscow during this period.

Ažbè School. Private art school in Munich opened in 1891 by Anton Ažbè (1859–1905), a native of Ljubljana, favoured by Russian students in the city.

charka. Shallow cup, a traditional Russian vessel.

Diaghilev's Salon d'Automne show (1906). Exhibition of Russian art at the Grand Palais, Paris, organised by Diaghilev as part of the 1906 Salon d'Automne.

Golubaya Roza. "Blue Rose": group of Symbolist artists founded in 1906 and exhibiting together from 1907.

Hollósy School. Private art school in Munich run by the Hungarian Simon Hollósy (1857–1918).

kovsh. Water-scoop, a traditional Russian vessel.

Lukomor'e. "Cove": magazine issued by the Petrograd publishing house of the same name.

Mir Iskusstva. "The World of Art": movement formed in 1898 in St Petersburg by Diaghilev, Benois etc., which organised exhibitions and published the magazine of the same name (1898–1904).

Moscow College. Moscow College of Painting, Sculpture and Architecture: the principal art school in Moscow, founded in the 1840s. The most important teachers from the 1890s were Vladimir Makovsky, Illarion Pryanishnikov, Vasily Polenov, Konstantin Korovin and Valentin Serov for painting and S. Volnukhin and Sergei Ivanov for sculpture. In 1918 it was merged with the Stroganov Design School to form Svomas.

Novyi Satirikon. "New Satyricon": satirical magazine, successor to *Satirikon*.

OPKh Drawing School. Drawing School of the Society for the Promotion of the Arts in St Petersburg. Ivan Kramskoi was one of the principal teachers there in the 1860s and later, from 1906, Nikolai Roerich was its director.

Peredvizhniki. "Wanderers": members of the Society for Travelling Art Exhibitions, founded in 1870.

Petersburg Academy. Academy of Arts in St Petersburg, founded in 1757, whose Higher School provided the main official training for artists in the capital. Important teachers during this period included Vasily Vereshchagin, Pavel Chistyakov, Karl Wenig, Arkhip Kuindzhi, D. N. Kardovsky, Il'ya Repin and, for architecture, Leonty Benois.

Satirikon. "Satyricon": satirical magazine published in St Petersburg (1908–13).

Solntse Rossii. "Sun of Russia": magazine.

Stieglitz School. Baron Stieglitz's Central School of Technical Drawing in St Petersburg.

Stroganov Design School. Central Stroganov Institute of Technical Drawing in Moscow, which merged with the Moscow College in 1918 to form Svomas.

Svomas. Free State Art Studios, formed in 1918 through the merging of the Moscow College and the Stroganov Design School. In 1920 it was renamed Vkhutemas.

The 36. Exhibition group of thirty-six, predominantly Moscow, artists formed in 1901 that led in 1903 to the formation of the Union of Russian Artists.

Tenisheva School. Private studio school organised in Moscow by Princess Tenisheva, Il'ya Repin was the most important teacher there at the turn of the century.

Venok. "Wreath": exhibition group organised in Moscow by David Burlyuk (1907–09).

Vesy. "The Scales – Libra". Moscow Symbolist magazine (1904–09).

Vkhutein. Higher State Art-Technical Institute. Replaced Vkhutemas in 1925. It was in turn replaced by the Moscow Institute of Visual Arts in 1930.

Vkhutemas. Higher State Art-Technical Studios. Replaced Svomas in 1920.

Zhupel. "Bugbear": satirical journal first published in 1905.

Zolotoe Runo. "The Golden Fleece". Symbolist magazine (1906–10), which also promoted three "salons" of Russian and French avant-garde art in 1908–09.

Zritel'. "Spectator": the first of the caricature and cartoon journals inspired by the revolutionary events of 1905.

Zvantseva School. Private art school founded by E. N. Zvantseva in St Petersburg.

Abramtsevo Pottery Studio
The ceramic studio at Abramtsevo was founded in 1890, and it was here that Vrubel' and Petr Vaulin carried out their technical experiments. In 1896 the workshop was transferred to Moscow, though retaining the Abramtsevo name, attracting many of the younger generation of sculptors and painters.

1 Faun Mask
Early 20th century
Ceramic, brown glaze, 22×20
State Historical Museum

2 Jug
Early 20th century
Majolica, reduction glaze, ht: 15, diam: 7.8
State Historical Museum

3 Jug
Early 20th century
Ceramic, coloured slip, reduction glaze, ht: 27
State Historical Museum

Vasily Semenovich Agafonov
Master silversmith in Moscow (fl. 1893–1917) who specialised in cloisonné enamel work.

4 Teapot
Moscow, 1899–1908
Silver gilt and enamel, ht: 13
Hallmark with maker's initials
State Historical Museum
[Illustrated p.251]

Anna Andreevna Akhmatova (Gorenko)
1889–1966
Poet.
See nos.87, 207

P. D. Amerikantsev
Master silversmith.

5 Tea Spoon
Moscow, 1908–17
Silver gilt and enamel, length: 14
Hallmark with maker's initials
State Historical Museum
[Illustrated p.247]

Nikolai Andreevich Andreev
1873 MOSCOW – 1932 MOSCOW
Sculptor and graphic artist. Studied at the Stroganov Design School (1885–91) and at the Moscow College (1892–1901) under the sculptor Volnukhin. From 1892 to 1918 he also taught drawing and sculpture at the Stroganov School. He

began to exhibit with Moscow artists' groups in the first years of the 20th century and was active in literary and artistic circles, designing sets for the Moscow Arts Theatre from 1910. As a sculptor, his early work included decorative sculpture in the *Style Moderne* (reliefs for the façade of the Hotel Metropol and the Tretyakov Gallery building, as well as smaller figures from Classical or Russian mythology). In 1903–10 he travelled in the central Russian provinces collecting ethnographical material, which he worked up into a series of ceramic figures based on traditional toys. He was later well-known for his public monuments in Moscow (to Gogol' and others) and for the popular series of sculptures and drawings of Lenin, *Leniniana*.

6 *Bacchante on a Goat*
1905
Terracotta group painted in polychrome, $46.5 \times 55 \times 21$
State Tretyakov Gallery
[Illustrated p.182]

7 *Girl in Mordvinian Costume Shielding Her Face from the Sun*
1912
Ceramic statuette decorated with painting, slip and glaze, $51 \times 14.5 \times 15$
State Tretyakov Gallery

8 *Mordvinian Woman with Folded Arms*
1915
Ceramic statuette decorated with painting, slip and glaze, $53 \times 18 \times 16$
State Tretyakov Gallery
[Illustrated p.182]

9 *Panka*
1915
Ceramic statuette decorated with painting, slip and glaze, $24 \times 32 \times 17.5$
State Tretyakov Gallery

10 *Decorative Mask*
1914–15
Ceramic enamelled in colours, $38.5 \times 31 \times 18.5$
State Tretyakov Gallery
[Illustrated p.183]
   Chimneypiece decoration with a portrait of the Moscow Arts Theatre actress Mariya Nikolaevna Germanova.

11 *Chained Lion*
1916
Terracotta, $42 \times 29 \times 25$
Signed right
State Tretyakov Gallery
   Sculptural sketch for the cover of an album in aid of Russian prisoners of war.

Vasily Ivanovich Andreev
Master silversmith.

12 Small vase
Moscow, 1908–17
Silver, $12.5 \times 17.5 \times 10.3$
Hallmark with maker's initials
State Historical Museum
[Illustrated p.252]

Boris (Ber) Izrailevich Anisfel'd
1879 BEL'TSY – 1973 CHICAGO
Painter, graphic and theatre artist. After graduating from the Odessa Drawing School in 1900, he moved to St Petersburg, where he continued his studies at the Academy School under Kardovsky and Repin. He exhibited with the Union of Russian Artists, was a member of the *Mir Isskustva* group from 1903 and was included in Diaghilev's Salon d'Automne show (1906). He contributed to the satirical magazines *Adskaya Pochta* and *Zhupel* in 1905–06. From 1907 he worked for Komissarzhevsky's theatre, for Diaghilev's companies abroad and for the Mariinsky Theatre in St Petersburg. In 1917 he emigrated to the U.S.A., where he worked for the Metropolitan and Chicago opera companies.

13 *Monsters Striding over Corpses*
1905
Cover design for *Zhupel*
Charcoal pencil, watercolour, gouache, Indian ink, pen and varnish on paper, 30.2×34.8
Signed bottom right
State Russian Museum
[Illustrated p.14]

14 *Mourners*
1905
Drawing for *Zhupel*
Indian ink, pen, brush and white on cardboard, 11.4×26.6
State Russian Museum
[Illustrated p.146]

15 *April*
1906–07
Indian ink, brush, pen and collage on
paper, 28.6 × 22.4
Title inscribed left
State Tretyakov Gallery

Reproduced in V. L. Burtsev (ed.),
Calendar of the Russian Revolution,
Petrograd (Shipovnik), 1917

Yury Pavlovich Annenkov
1889 PETROPAVLOSK-ON-KAMCHATKA – 1974 PARIS
Graphic artist, painter, theatre and
cinema artist. Studied at Petersburg
University and from 1909 at the Stieglitz
School and in the studios of Zaidenberg
and Tsionglinsky. In 1911–12 he was in
Paris, where he studied with Maurice
Denis and Félix Vallotton. From 1913 to
1917 he contributed to the magazines
Satirikon, *Lukomor'e* and *Solntse Rossii*,
and he also worked as a designer for the
theatre and for popular festivals. After
1924 he lived in Germany and France,
working as a theatre and cinema artist.

16 *Man and Woman on a
Merry-Go-Round*
Paris, 1913
Indian ink, pen and lead pencil on
paper, 19.2 × 21.2
Signed with initials bottom left, dated
bottom right
State Russian Museum
[Illustrated p.151]

17 *Jester*
1915
Costume design for Sologub's play *Night
Dances*
Watercolour, bronze paint and lead
pencil on paper, 29.4 × 16.4
Signed with initials bottom and
inscribed
State Russian Museum
[Illustrated p.74]

18 Imprint of Alkonost Publishers
Petrograd, n.d.
Line block, 4 × 5.5.
State Lenin Library

19 Half-title in Aleksandr Blok,
*Catiline: A page from the History of
World Revolution*, Petrograd (Alkonost),
1919
Line block, 4.5 × 6
State Lenin Library
[Illustrated p.150]

Apollon
Magazine published in St Petersburg
1909–17.
See nos.96, 240, 286

Anatoly Afanas'evich Arapov
1876–1949
Painter. Worked in Moscow. He was
included in Diaghilev's Salon
d'Automne show (1906) and was a
member of the *Golubaya Roza* group.

20 *Italian Musicians*
1914
Tempera on cardboard, 58 × 65
Signed and dated bottom right
Saratov State Art Museum
[Illustrated p.123]

1st Jewellers' Artel'

21 Medallion
Moscow, 1908–17
Gold, diamonds, rubies and enamel,
6 × 4
Hallmark with Artel' mark
State Historical Museum
[Illustrated p.259]

4th Jeweller's Artel'

22 Salt cellar
Moscow, 1908–1917
Silver, 6.1 × 9.1 × 8.5
Hallmark with Artel' mark
State Historical Museum
[Illustrated p.253]

11th Jewellers' Artel'

23 *Lampada* (icon-lamp)
Moscow, 1908–17
Silver, 17 × 7 × 7
Hallmark with Artel' mark
State Historical Museum
[Illustrated p.242]

24 Tea spoon
Moscow (Fabergé), 1908–17
Silver gilt and enamel, length: 14.3
Hallmark with Artel' mark and firm's
mark
State Historical Museum
[Illustrated p.247]

25 Napkin ring
Moscow, 1908–17
Silver gilt and enamel, 3.8 × 5 × 5
Hallmark with Artel' mark
State Historical Museum
[Illustrated p.250]

26, 27 Sugar basin and milk jug
Moscow, 1908–17
Silver gilt and enamel, ht: 5; 6.5
Hallmark with Artel' mark
State Historical Museum
[Illustrated p.250]

15th Jewellers' Artel'

28 Blotter
Moscow, 1915
Leather, silver, enamel and paper,
43.5 × 33.5
Hallmark with Artel' mark
State Historical Museum
[Illustrated p.245]

**Lev (Léon) Samoilovich Bakst
(Rozenberg)**
1866 GRODNO – 1924 PARIS
Painter, illustrator and theatre designer.
After attending the Petersburg
Academy as an external student (1883–
87) under Wenig and Chistyakov, he
continued his studies in Paris (1893–96)
in the studio of J.-L. Gérôme, at the
Académie Julian and under Albert
Edelfelt. From 1898 to 1903 he was one
of the organizers and an active
participant in the *Mir Iskusstva* group,
working with Diaghilev on the
decorations of their exhibitions in St
Petersburg and at the Salon d'Automne
(1906). He exhibited with the Society of
Russian Watercolour Painters (1891–97),
Mir Iskusstva (1898–1903) and the
Union of Russian Artists (1903–10). He
was best known as a portrait-painter, as
a prolific graphic artist and above all as
a stage designer, for theatres in St
Petersburg and for Diaghilev's and
other ballet companies abroad. From
1909 he lived in Paris.

29 *Supper*
1902
Oil on canvas, 150 × 100
Signed top right
State Russian Museum
[Illustrated p.108]

The wife of Bakst's friend Aleksandr
Benois modelled for this painting of a
demi-mondaine eating supper in a
restaurant.

30 Cover of *Mir Iskusstva*, 1902 no.
9–10
Line block, 30.5 × 23.5
State Lenin Library
[Illustrated p.69]

31 Set design for *The Heart of the
Marquise*
1902
Watercolour, Indian ink, brush, pen and
lead pencil on paper mounted on
cardboard, 21.5 x 29
Signed and inscribed bottom right
State Tretyakov Gallery

The pantomime *The Heart of the
Marquise* by F. Febvre was produced by
Petipa at the Hermitage Theatre in 1902.

32 *Antique Vision*
1906
Pen and Indian ink on paper, 16.1 × 17.9
Signed and dated bottom right
State Russian Museum
[Illustrated p.41]

Drawing to illustrate A. K. Kondratsev's novel *Satyress* in the journal *Zolotoe Runo*; it was included in Diaghilev's Salon d'Automne exhibition (1906).

33 *Antique Vision*
1906
Illustration from *Zolotoe Runo*, 1906 no.4 (printed version of no.32)
Line block, 17.5 × 19.1
State Lenin Library

34 *Andrei Bely*
1906
Illustration from *Zolotoe Runo*, 1907 no.1
Colour autotype, 19 × 9
State Lenin Library

35 Frontispiece from Aleksandr Blok, *Snow Mask*, St Petersburg (Ory), 1907
Colour lithograph, 13.8 × 10
State Lenin Library, Moscow
[Illustrated p.146]

36 *Dione*
1912
Colour autotype, 21.5 × 14
State Lenin Library

One of the series *Fantasies on Modern Dress* designed for the couturière Paquin.

See also no.299 (illustrated p.139)

Konstantin Dmitrievich Bal'mont
1867–1942
Symbolist poet.
See nos.102, 114, 202, 312, 397–8

Nikolai Dmitrievich Bartram
1879–1932
Designer and craftsman. Established a joinery workshop on the model of Abramtsevo, which he organised and managed from 1893 to 1903 in the village of Semenovka (Kursk province). Later he became one of the outstanding craftsmen of the *Moderne* movement, making many objects for the Moscow Museum of Crafts.

37 Boyar money-box
Moscow, 1900s
Carved and painted wood, 13 × 9.5
State Historical Museum
[Illustrated p.235]

38 Old Woman money-box
Moscow, 1900s
Carved and painted wood, 12.2 × 14.5
State Historical Museum
[Illustrated p.235]

Aubrey Beardsley
1872 BRIGHTON – 1898 MENTON
English illustrator, whose work exerted a strong influence on Russian *Moderne* graphic design.

39 Title-page of *Selected Drawings*, Moscow (Skorpion), 1912
32 × 21.5
The British Library

Andrei Bely (Boris Nikolaevich Bugaev)
1880–1934
Symbolist poet and critic.
See nos.34, 107, 132, 264, 455

Aleksandr Nikolaevich Benois
1870 ST PETERSBURG – 1960 PARIS
Painter, illustrator, theatre designer, art historian and critic. The youngest son of the court architect Nikolai Benois, he studied painting under his brother Albert and as an external student at the Petersburg Academy (1887–88). In 1894 he graduated from the Law Faculty of Petersburg University, and over the next fifteen years he travelled extensively in Europe, working in Paris in 1896–98 and again in 1905–07. He was one of the founders of the *Mir Iskusstva* group and was its ideological leader during the 1890s. He exhibited with the Society of Russian Watercolour Artists (from 1891), with the *Mir Iskusstva* group (from 1899), *The 36* and the Union of Russian Artists (1903–10). He was included in Diaghilev's Salon d'Automne show in 1906. He began his career as a theatre designer in 1900, working for theatres in St Petersburg and Moscow, for Diaghilev's companies abroad and for Paris, Milan and London. From 1918 to 1926 Benois was a curator of French and English paintings at the Hermitage. He moved permanently to Paris in 1926.

40 *Embankment on the Rhine at Basel in the Rain*
1896
Gouache on cardboard, 57.5 × 47.5
Signed and dated bottom left
Saratov State Art Museum
[Illustrated p.106]

41 Illustrations for *Picture Alphabet*, St Petersburg (State Stationery Office), 1904
Lithographs, 32 × 25.5
State Lenin Library
[Illustrated p.149]

42 *Breton Dances*
Primel (Brittany), 1906
Oil on canvas, 69 × 102
State Russian Museum
[Illustrated p.104]

43 *Warning: Orgy*
1907
Drawing for the album *Death*
Gouache, Indian ink and brush on cardboard, 29.6 × 22.7
Signed with initials and dated bottom right
State Tretyakov Gallery

44 Illustrated edition of Aleksandr Pushkin, *The Queen of Spades*, St Petersburg (R. Golicke and A. Wilborg), 1911
Colour lithographs and autotypes, 30 × 24
State Lenin Library

45 Design for the décor for the Emperor's Bedroom in *Le Rossignol*
1914
Bodycolours on paper, 63 × 97
Signed, dated and inscribed bottom
Visitors of the Ashmolean Museum, Oxford

46 Design for the décor of the Throne Room in *Le Rossignol*
1914
Bodycolours on paper, 101 × 109
Signed and dated bottom
Visitors of the Ashmolean Museum, Oxford

Le Rossignol, based on Hans Andersen's tale, with music by Stravinsky and choreography by Boris Romanov, was produced by Diaghilev at the Paris Opéra in 1914.

47 *Allegory of Science and Work*
1916
Study for a decorative panel for the Kazan' Station
Oil on canvas, 66.5 × 107
State Tretyakov Gallery

48 *Warrior's Farewell to His Family*
1916
Study for a decorative panel for the
Kazan' Station
Oil on canvas, 67 × 107
State Tretyakov Gallery
[Illustrated p.223]

The Kazan' Station, the grandest
building in the Neo-Russian style in
Moscow, was built (1913–26) to designs by
Aleksei Shchusev, and Benois was given
the task of overseeing the interior
decoration. His overall design reflected the
situation of the city of Kazan' on the
border of Europe and Asia and the role of
Russia in linking European and Asian
cultures. To carry this out, Benois
commissioned other artists from the *Mir
Iskusstva* group: Lanceray, Kustodiev,
Dobuzhinsky, Serebryakova, Roerich and
Kuznetsov. The two panels in the
exhibition, which he designed himself,
were intended for the coffered ceiling of
the Board Room but were not executed.

49 Illustrated edition of Aleksandr
Pushkin, *The Bronze Horseman*,
originally published 1905; this edition,
Petrograd (Committee for the
Promotion of Art Publications), 1923
Colour lithographs, line blocks, 35 × 28
State Lenin Library

50 *Military Parade During the Reign of
Pavel I*
1939
Bodycolours on paper, 48 × 62.5
Signed and dated bottom left
Visitors of the Ashmolean Museum,
Oxford

Later version of a picture painted in
1907 (now in the State Russian Museum)
as one of a series commissioned by the
Moscow publisher I. Knebel',
reproductions of which were to be hung in
schools.

See also nos.299, 403

Ivan Yakovlevich Bilibin

1876 TARKHOVA, NR. ST PETERSBURG – 1942
LENINGRAD
Painter, illustrator and theatre artist.
While a student at Petersburg
University (where he graduated in
1900), he also studied at the OPKh
Drawing School (1895–98), at the Ažbè
School in Munich (1898) and under
Repin at the Tenisheva School (1898–
1900); he was an external student at the
Petersburg Academy until 1904. He
became a member of the *Mir Iskusstva*
group in 1899, exhibiting with them, the
Union of Russian Artists and other
groups from 1900. He was included in

Diaghilev's Salon d'Automne show
(1906). During the 1890s and 1900s he
travelled extensively in Russia, visiting
historic cities and studying folk art and
architecture, using his knowledge of
these to create the colourful style that
characterised his book illustrations and
also, from 1907, his theatre designs. He
contributed to the journals *Mir
Iskusstva* (1899–1904), *Adskaya Pochta*
(1905–06), *Zhupel* (1905–06) and
Zolotoe Runo (1907). He designed for
theatres in St Petersburg and Moscow
as well as for Diaghilev's seasons
abroad, and taught at the OPKh
Drawing School (1907–17). He lived
abroad – in Cairo, Alexandria and Paris
– from 1920, returning to Leningrad in
1936 to a post as Professor at the
Institute of Painting, Sculpture and
Architecture.

51 Illustration for a fairy-tale
1902
Watercolour and lead pencil on paper,
34.8 × 24.9
Signed and dated bottom left
State Tretyakov Gallery
[Illustrated on front cover]

52 *Historical Exhibition of Works of Art
in the Rooms of the Museum of Baron
Stieglitz*; poster design
1904
Indian ink, pen, brush, watercolour,
bronze paint and lead pencil on paper,
63.6 × 46
Signed and dated bottom right
State Russian Museum
[Illustrated p.37]

53 Illustrated edition of Aleksandr
Pushkin, *The Tale of Tsar Saltan*, St
Petersburg (State Stationery Office),
1905
Colour lithographs, 33 × 26
State Lenin Library
[Illustrated p.149]

54 *Caucasus and Mercury*; poster for
steamship company
St Petersburg, 1911
Lithographic poster (printed by R.
Golicke and A. Wilborg), 101 × 68
State Lenin Library

55 Design for playing card: Ace of
Hearts
1911
Indian ink, pen, brush and gouache on
paper, 24.2 × 13.9
State Russian Museum
[Illustrated p.170]

56 Design for playing card: Ace of
Clubs
1911
Indian ink, pen, brush and white on
paper, 25.4 × 18.2
State Russian Museum
[Illustrated p.170]

Designs for decoration of vaults for a
bank in Nizhny Novgorod (competition
project) 1913 (see also nos.272–3)

57 *Russian Imperial Coat of Arms*
Indian ink, pencil, watercolour, white
on paper mounted on cardboard,
50.7 × 40.6
Signed and dated bottom
A. V. Shchusev State Museum of
Architecture

58 *Signs of the Zodiac*
Indian ink, pencil, watercolour on paper
mounted on cardboard, 50.7 × 60.3
Signed and dated bottom
A. V. Shchusev State Museum of
Architecture
[Illustrated p.222]

Aleksandr Aleksandrovich Blok
1880–1921
Poet and critic.
See nos.19, 35, 203, 399–401, 456

Grigory Mikhailovich Bobrovsky

1873 VITEBSK – 1942 LENINGRAD
Portrait and landscape painter. Studied
at the Petersburg Academy (1893–1900)
and under Repin. He exhibited with the
Union of Russian Artists (of which he
became a member in 1911) and other
groups, making his career in St
Petersburg, particularly as a painter of
highly accomplished society portraits.

59 *Portrait of Miss Samoilova*
1912
Oil on canvas, 112 × 85
Signed and dated top right
State Russian Museum
[Illustrated p.126]

Konstantin Fedorovich Bogaevsky

1872 FEODOSIA – 1943 FEODOSIA
Landscape painter. He studied in his
home town under A. Fessler and Ivan
Aivazovsky, and returned there after
further studies at the Petersburg
Academy (1891–97) under Kuindzhi. He
exhibited with several artistic groups,
including the New Society of Artists
(1904–10), the Union of Russian Artists
(1908–16) and the Society of South
Russian Artists. He was included in

Diaghilev's Salon d'Automne show (1906). His distinctive heroic-romantic landscapes are set on the eastern shore of the Crimea, the legendary land of Homer's Cimmerians.

60 *Ships: Evening Sun*
1912
Oil on canvas, 133 × 155
Signed and dated bottom right
State Russian Museum
[Illustrated p.122]

61 *Morning*
1910
Tempera on canvas, 121.5 × 142.5
Signed and dated bottom right
State Tretyakov Gallery

Viktor El'pidiforovich Borisov-Musatov
1870 SARATOV – 1905 TARUSA
Painter. He studied in Saratov from the age of eleven under V. Konovalov and later at the Moscow College (1890, 1893–95), the Petersburg Academy (1891–93) and in Chistyakov's studio, and in Paris at the Académie Cormon (1895–98). Here he fell under the influence of Puvis de Chavannes. He also visited Munich in 1897 and 1898, returning to Germany in 1904 for a one-man show in Berlin organised by Paul Cassirer. He was a leading member of the Moscow Society of Artists from 1899 until his early death and also of the Union of Russian Artists from 1904, and he participated in the Paris Salon d'Automne of 1905. In 1902 he made designs for murals for the house Shekhtel' was building for A. I. Derozhinskaya, but these were not executed. His work is characterised by elegiac evocations of a transparent dream-world: "When life frightens me, I find repose in art. . . . I sometimes seem to be living on an uninhabited island. And it is as though reality does not exist."

62 *Tree in Sunlight*
1897
Oil on canvas, 63.5 × 50.6
Saratov State Art Museum
[Illustrated p.102]

63 *Harmony*
1900
Tempera on canvas, 162 × 90.5
Signed and dated bottom right
State Tretyakov Gallery
[Illustrated p.34]

64 *Spring*
1898
Oil on canvas, 71 × 98
Signed and dated bottom left
State Russian Museum
[Illustrated p.100]

65 *Zubrilovka*
1901
Watercolour, white, brush, pen and lead pencil on cardboard, 46.2 × 36.9
Signed, dated and inscribed with title bottom right
State Tretyakov Gallery
[Illustrated p.38]

66 *Pond*
Early 1900s
Watercolour, gouache and lead pencil on paper, 22.5 × 22.5
Signed bottom left
State Russian Museum
[Illustrated p.102]

67 *Meeting by the Column*
1901–03
Watercolour, pen and Indian ink on paper, 17.8 × 12.2
Signed bottom right
State Russian Museum
[Illustrated p.21]

68 Unidentified illustration
Line block, 10 × 17.5
State Lenin Library

69 Unidentified illustration
Line block, 14 × 13
State Lenin Library

70 Cover for literary anthology
Severnye Tsvety (Northern Flowers), Moscow (Skorpion), 1901–03
Coloured autotype, 23 × 15
State Lenin Library, Moscow

71 *At the Summer House*
1904–05
Pen and Indian ink on paper, 19.1 × 14
Signed bottom right
State Tretyakov Gallery
[Illustrated p.102]

72 Cover design for *Mir Iskusstva*, 1905 no.1
1904
Watercolour, Indian ink, pen and brush on tinted paper, 33.5 × 26.6
Signed bottom with monogram
State Tretyakov Gallery
[Illustrated p.70]

Fedor Vladimirovich Botkin
1861–1905
Painter. He graduated from the Law Faculty of Moscow University, then studied at the Accademia in Milan, in Florence and in Paris under Alfred-Philippe Roll. After 1901 an incurable nervous disease confined Botkin in a clinic near Paris until his death. In 1897 he introduced Sergei Shchukin to the art-dealer Durand-Ruel, through whom the collector discovered the French Impressionists.

73 *Silhouette of a Woman*
1897
Design for a woollen embroidery
Oil on canvas, 76 × 67
Signed bottom right
State Tretyakov Gallery

74 *Portrait of an Unknown Woman*
1900
Oil on canvas, 91 × 63.5
Signed top and bottom right
State Tretyakov Gallery
[Illustrated p.109]

Andrei Stepanovich Bragin
Master silversmith from 1852, known for his gold cigarette-cases.

75 *Charka*
St Petersburg, 1899–1908
Silver, 6.6 × 10 × 5.3
Hallmark with maker's initials
State Historical Museum
[Illustrated p.248]

Iosif Emmanuilovich Braz
1872 ODESSA – 1936 PARIS
Painter. Studied at the Odessa Drawing School under Kiryak Kostandi, at the Petersburg Academy (1895–96) and under Repin, then at the Munich Academy and in private studios in Paris. He worked in St Petersburg and was a member of several artistic groups and participated in their exhibitions: *Mir Iskusstva* (1900–03, 1911–17), *The 36*, Union of Russian Artists (1903–06), Society of South Russian Artists etc. He emigrated in 1928.

76 *Portrait of Elena Tolstoy*
1900
Oil on canvas, 99 × 104
Signed and dated bottom right
State Russian Museum
[Illustrated p.111]

Countess Elena Mikhailovna Tolstoy, née Chetkova (1865–1956), was the wife of Count Dmitry Ivanovich Tolstoy, Director of the Hermitage.

Isaak Izrailevich Brodsky
1884 SOFIEVKA – 1939 LENINGRAD
Painter and graphic artist. He studied at
the Odessa Drawing School under
Kiryak Kostandi (1896–1902), at the
Petersburg Academy (1902–08) and
under Repin. In 1909–11 he visited
Germany, France, Italy, Greece, Spain
and Austria on a travelling scholarship
from the Academy. He exhibited with
the Union of Russian Artists (1907–18)
and with other artists' groups both
before and after the October
Revolution, becoming president of the
Kuindzhi Society in 1930. He was
director of the All-Russian Academy of
Arts in Leningrad from 1934 until his
death.

77 *Grey Day*
1909
Oil on canvas, 45.5 × 69.5
Signed and dated bottom right
State Russian Museum
[Illustrated p.122]

78 *Tavern in a Cave*
1910
Oil on canvas, 94.5 × 99.7
State Tretyakov Gallery

Lev Aleksandrovich Bruni
1894 MALAYA VISHNERA (NOVGOROD PROVINCE) –
1948 MOSCOW
Painter, graphic artist and book
designer. He studied at the Tenisheva
School (1904–09) and the Petersburg
Academy under Roubaud and
Tsionglinsky (1909–11), and in Paris
under J.-P. Laurens at the Académie
Julian. He exhibited with several artists'
groups from 1915, including *Magazin
(The Store)*, Moscow, in 1916. Later he
taught at the Stieglitz School (1920–21),
at Vkhutein, at the Moscow Institute of
Textiles (1930–33) and, from 1935 until
his death, at the Academy of
Architecture of the U.S.S.R.

79 *Nude*
1915
Drawing from the series *Reminiscences
of the Khevsurs*
Indian ink, pen, brush and white on
paper, 36.3 × 29.9
Signed bottom right
State Russian Museum
[Illustrated p.28]

Valery Yakovlevich Bryusov
1873–1924
Poet, essayist, translator and leader of
Russian Symbolism. He managed the
Moscow publishing house Skorpion and
was editor of their magazine *Vesy*.

80 Cover of his own book *Urbi et Orbi:
Poems 1900–1903*, Moscow (Skorpion),
1903
Printed with bronze ink, 22 × 17
State Lenin Library

81 *Erotopaegnia*, Moscow (Al'tsiona),
1912
52 × 30
The British Library

See also nos.224, 229

Sergei Vasil'evich Chekhonin
1878 LYKOSHINO (TVER' PROVINCE) – 1936
LÖRRACH (GERMANY)
Designer and graphic artist. Studied in
St Petersburg at the OPKh Drawing
School (1896–97) and the Tenisheva
School under Repin (1897–1900). He
worked at the Abramtsevo pottery
studio in Moscow (1904–07), ran a
school of enamelling at Rostov-
Yaroslavsky (1913–17) and later was
artistic director of the State Porcelain
Factory in Petrograd-Leningrad
(1918–23, 1925–27). From 1928 he lived
and worked in Paris.

82 Cover for N. Teffi, *Seven Fires*,
St Petersburg (Shipovnik), 1910 (copy
signed by the author)
Line blocks, 21.4 × 16
State Lenin Library
[Illustrated p.150]

83 *Wolf-Cub*
1913
Drawing to illustrate the fairy-tale by
Verkhustinsky
Indian ink, pen, brush and gouache on
cardboard, 23.1 × 26.4
Signed and dated bottom left
State Russian Museum

84 Drawing for the frontispiece of the
book *Russian Drawing*
1914
Indian ink, pen, brush, gouache and
lead pencil on yellow paper, 33.5 × 24.9
Signed and dated bottom
State Russian Museum
[Illustrated p.149]

85 Cover for Innokenty Annensky,
Posthumous Verses, Petrograd
(Kartonnyi Domik), 1923
Line block, 19 × 13.3
State Lenin Library, Moscow

Natal'ya Yakovlevna Davydova
1873–1926
Designer. Studied at the Moscow
College. She was a leader of the first
wave of the National Style in design, in
1891 taking over the embroidery
workshops of peasant women at the
Solomenko art colony. She was a
designer at Abramtsevo, principally of
textiles and embroidery, from the mid-
1890s, later becoming head of the
furniture section of the Moscow
Museum of Crafts.

86 Shelf with small cupboard
Abramtsevo, between 1905 and 1912
Carved oak, 45 × 113 × 27
State Historical Museum
[Illustrated p.232]

**Ol'ga Lyudvigovna
Della-Vos-Kardovskaya**
1875 ST PETERSBURG – 1952 LENINGRAD
Painter and graphic artist. Studied at
the Schreider School in Khar'kov (1891–
94), at the Petersburg Academy School
(1894–99) and in Munich at the Ažbè
School (1899–1900). She exhibited with
the New Society of Artists (1903–17),
the Union of Russian Artists (1911–16)
and other groups.

87 *Portrait of Anna Akhmatova*
1914
Oil on canvas, 85 × 82
Signed bottom right
State Tretyakov Gallery
[Illustrated p.125]

Vasily Ivanovich Denisov
1862 ZAMOŚĆ – 1921
Painter, illustrator and theatre artist.
He trained as a musician at the Warsaw
Music Institute, but in 1895 began to
paint, studying for a time under
Konstantin Korovin in Moscow, where
he settled. In 1907 he designed sets for
Komissarzhevsky's theatre in St
Petersburg – for Ibsen's *Love's Comedy*
and Maeterlinck's *Pelléas et Mélisande*
– and subsequently for productions at
the Opera there – Musorgsky's *Boris
Godunov* and Rimsky-Korsakov's *Sadko*.
He was included in Diaghilev's Salon
d'Automne show in 1906 and
participated from that year in
exhibitions of the Moscow Society of Art
Lovers, the Moscow Society of Artists
and *Mir Iskusstva*. In 1912 he
accompanied the sculptor Konenkov on
a journey to Greece. His paintings and
drawings have a marked religious and
mystical tone.

88 *Night*
1901
Oil on canvas, 117.5 × 125.5
Inscribed with title, date and monogram
on canvas verso
State Tretyakov Gallery

89 *Sin*
1902
Black watercolour, black and lead
pencils on paper, 44 × 52.7
State Tretyakov Gallery
[Illustrated p.115]

90 *Sorrow (Giotto)*
1904
Oil on canvas, 143 × 107
State Russian Museum
[Illustrated p.113]

91 *Landscape*
1906
Watercolour, white, aluminium powder
and oil on cream paper, 40.9 × 54.2
Dated on verso
State Tretyakov Gallery

92 *Composition*
1906
Gouache, lead pencil, Indian ink, brush
and pen on blue paper, 40 × 53.2
Inscribed and dated on verso
State Tretyakov Gallery
[Illustrated p.114]

See also no.173

Mstislav Valerianovich Dobuzhinsky
1875 NOVGOROD – 1957 NEW YORK
Painter, graphic and theatre artist. He
studied at the OPKh Drawing School in
St Petersburg (1885–87) but went on to
the Law Faculty of Petersburg
University (1895–99). He resumed his
art studies in Munich (1899–1901), at
the Ažbè and Hollósy Schools, and on
his return he studied etching with Vasily
Mathé. He was one of the leading
artists in the *Mir Iskusstva* group,
joining them in 1902 and participating
in their exhibitions until 1924, and he
exhibited with the Union of Russian
Artists (1904–09) as well as in many
cities outside Russia. He was included
in Diaghilev's Salon d'Automne show
(1906). He worked extensively on books
and magazines and designed theatre
productions for St Petersburg and
Moscow and for Diaghilev's seasons
abroad. After 1924 he lived in Lithuania
and in 1939 moved to the U.S.A.

93 Cover and illustrations for Aleksei
Remizov, *Morshchinka: Fairy Tale*,
St Petersburg (Shipovnik), 1907
Line blocks, 12 × 16
State Lenin Library

94 *The Devil*
1906–07
Illustration from *Zolotoe Runo*, 1907
no.1
Colour autotype, 23.5 × 16.7
State Lenin Library
[Illustrated p.147]

95 Imprint of Ory (The Hours)
Publishers
St Petersburg, 1907
Line block, 5.5 × 3.5
State Lenin Library

96 Cover of *Apollon*, 1911, no.1.
Gold printing, 25.5 × 20
State Lenin Library

97 *Urban Landscape (At Dusk)*
1911
Gouache and lead pencil on blue paper,
21 × 30.5
Signed with initials and dated
(2.11.1911) bottom left
State Tretyakov Gallery

98 *Harbour on the Pryazhka River*
1914
Oil on canvas, 54.5 × 71.7
Signed and dated bottom right
State Tretyakov Gallery
[Illustrated p.130]

99 *Night in St Petersburg*
1924
Gouache on grey paper, 47.5 × 78.6
Signed and dated bottom right
State Tretyakov Gallery

Vladimir Nikolaevich Domogatsky
1876 ODESSA – 1939 MOSCOW
Sculptor. He attended the Law Faculty
of Moscow University (1897–1902)
while also studying sculpture with
Volnukhin (1895–1902), and he
continued these studies with Sergei
Ivanov (1903–04). He also widened his
experience by travelling abroad, paying
four visits to Paris between 1896 and
1912. Through exhibitions from 1904
with a number of artists' groups
(including the Union of Russian Artists
and *Mir Iskusstva*), he established a
reputation as a portrait sculptor,
working principally in stone. He began
teaching in 1908, working during the
1920s at the State Academy of Artistic
Sciences.

100 *Kneeling Female Figure*
1013
Italian marble, 54 × 23.5 × 29
Signed with monogram on base
State Tretyakov Gallery
[Illustrated p.184]

Modest Durnov
1867–1928 MOSCOW
Architect and graphic artist. He studied
painting (under Polenov) and
architecture at the Moscow College
(1881–88) and from 1889 participated in
exhibitions with various artists' groups,
including, later, *Mir Iskusstva* and the
Union of Russian Artists; he was
included in Diaghilev's Salon
d'Automne show (1906). He designed
and illustrated books and was the
architect of a number of buildings in
Moscow and in the provinces.

101 Imprint of Grif (Griffin) Publishers
Moscow, n.d.
Colour lithograph, 3 × 3.5
State Lenin Library

102 Cover of Konstantin Bal'mont, *Only
Love*, Moscow (Grif), 1903
Autotype, 19.7 × 15
State Lenin Library
[Illustrated p.68]

Ivan Semenovich Efimov
1878 MOSCOW – 1959 MOSCOW
Sculptor, painter and designer. He
began his artistic training at the
Zvantseva School (1898–1901) while a
student of Natural Sciences at Moscow
University. He attended the Moscow
College (1906–08, 1911–13), studying
under Serov, Korovin and Volnukhin,
and also studied ceramic techniques at
the Abramtsevo pottery studio; he lived
abroad, mainly in Paris, from 1908 to
1911. He exhibited with various artists'
groups from 1907. As a sculptor, he
specialised in animal subjects, working
in a wide variety of techniques, and also
did monumental decorative work,
including reliefs for the Moscow Metro
stations and interiors of the Yaroslavl'
and Leningrad railway stations in
Moscow. With N. Simonovich-Efimova
he ran a marionette theatre (1920–40),
and he taught at Vkhutemas (1918–30).

103 *Head of a Lioness*
1912
Bronze, 41.5 × 44.5 × 21.5; wooden base,
ht: 6
State Tretyakov Gallery

N. A. Eikhenval'd (Eichenwald)
Architect

104 Filippov apartment house on
Tverskaya Street, Moscow: design for
interior of café
1910–12
Indian ink, pencil and watercolour on
paper, 36.2 × 128.2
Signed bottom right
A. V. Shchusev State Museum of
Architecture
[Illustrated pp.214–5]

Fabergé Company
From 1870 the family concern (founded
in 1842), making jewellery, gold and
silver, was run by Peter Carl Fabergé
(1846–1920). He was joined in 1882 by
his younger brother Agathon and in this
year won his first great success at the
1882 Pan-Russian Exhibition in
Moscow. He began making jewelled
Easter eggs for the Imperial family in
1884. International fame came after the
Paris *Exposition Universelle* of 1900,
and in the years following the firm's
production underwent a huge
expansion. The head workmasters
during this period were Mikhail Perchin
(1886–1903) and Henrik Wigström
(1903–18).

105 Small vase
Moscow, 1893
Silver, 8.5 × 12 × 12
Hallmark with firm's name
State Historical Museum
[Illustrated p.246]

106 Ashtray in form of a fish
Moscow, 1908–17
Silver, 8.5 × 10.2 × 12.5
Hallmark with firm's name
State Historical Museum
[Illustrated p.247]

See also nos.24, 294

Nikolai Feofilaktov
1878–1941
Graphic artist. He worked in Moscow
and was the principal designer for
Bryusov's publishing house Skorpion
and its magazine *Vesy*. His work was
included in Diaghilev's Salon
d'Automne show (1906).

107 Cover from Andrei Bely, *Gold in
Azure*, Moscow (Skorpion), 1904
Line blocks, 20.5 × 15.6
State Lenin Library
[Illustrated p.71]

108 Cover and vignettes in *Northern
Assyrian Flowers: "Skorpion's" Fourth
Literary Miscellany*, Moscow
(Skorpion), 1905
Line blocks, 24 × 19
State Lenin Library
[Illustrated p.148]

109 Decorative heading, "Contents",
from *Northern Assyrian Flowers*,
Moscow (Skorpion), 1905
Line blocks, 9.5 × 12
State Lenin Library

110 *Homage to Beardsley*
1905
Illustration in *Vesy*, 1905 no.5
Line block, 24.5 × 18.7
State Lenin Library

111 Imprint from *Zolotoe Runo*
1906
Line blocks, 8 × 7.5
State Lenin Library

112 Cover from *Vesy*, 1906 no.5
Line blocks, 22.2 × 17.5
State Lenin Library
[Illustrated p.66]

113 *Autumn*
1910
Illustration in Mikhail Kuzmin, *The
Chimes of Love*, Moscow (Skorpion),
1910
Phototype, 28 × 24.3
State Lenin Library

See also no.481

Fidus (Hugo Höppener)
1868 LÜBECK – 1948 SCHONBLINK, NR. BERLIN
German painter and graphic artist.
Attended Lübeck Art School and
became the sole pupil of the nature
prophet Karl Wilhelm Diefenbach, who
named him "Fidus". After further
studies at the Munich Academy (1889–
92) he settled in Berlin.

114 Cover of Konstantin Bal'mont, *We
Will Be as the Sun: Book of Symbols*,
Moscow (Skorpion), 1903 (copy signed
by the author)
Lithograph, 19.6 × 15.7
State Lenin Library
[Illustrated p.70]

Pavel Nikolaevich Filonov
1883 MOSCOW – 1941 LENINGRAD
Painter. He studied at Lev Dmitriev-
Kavkazsky's school of painting and
drawing in St Petersburg (1903–08) and

at the Academy as an external student
(1908–10). In 1911–12 he travelled in
France and Italy. He was a founding
member of *Soyuz Molodezhi* (The
Union of Youth) and participated in
their exhibitions (1910–14, 1917–19) and
in that of *Oslinyi Khvost (Donkey's Tail)*
in 1913. He formulated the theory of
Analytic Art, later (1925–32) organising
the Masters of Analytic Art (Filonov
School) in Leningrad.

115 *Feast of Kings*
1913
Oil on canvas, 175 × 215
State Russian Museum
[Illustrated pp.132–3]

M. V. Folomin
Master silversmith.

116 *Kovsh*
Kiev, 1899–1908
Silver, gilt on the inside, inset with
coloured glass, 25.5 × 30 × 18.5
Hallmark with maker's mark
State Historical Museum
[Illustrated p.249]

Ivan Aleksandrovich Fomin
1872 OREL – 1936 MOSCOW
Architect. Studied at the Petersburg
Academy (1894–97, 1905–09) and in
Leonty Benois's studio. From 1897 to
1905 he worked in Moscow as assistant
first to the architect Lev Kekushev and
then to Shekhtel', during which time he
made an important contribution to the
"New Style" exhibition (1902). Among
his works are the Poletsev house (1911–
13) and Abamelek-Lazarev houses in St
Petersburg, the Chemical Institute at
Ivanovo (1929) and the Mossovet
Building in Moscow (1929–30). He
contributed to the History of Russian
Art (1911), edited by Igor' Grabar'.

....
Maple Dining-room at the Exhibition of
Architecture and Design of the New
Style in Moscow
1902

117 Detail of installation
Photo (1902), 19.7 × 27.7
A. V. Shchusev State Museum of
Architecture
[Illustrated p.200]

118 Corner with stove
Photo (1902), 29 × 20.2
A. V. Shchusev State Museum of
Architecture
[Illustrated p.57]

119 Sideboard in grey maple
Photo (1902), 33.7 × 23.8
A. V. Shchusev State Museum of
Architecture
[Illustrated p.232]

120 Cupboard for a living room,
designed for the "New Style" exhibition
1902
Carved walnut, 180 × 180 × 54
State Historical Museum
[Illustrated p.231]

121 Project for priests' building,
refectory and cells at the Ferapontov
Monastery in Vologda Province:
elevation
1904
Coloured ink and watercolour on paper,
57.8 × 69.5
Signed and dated bottom right
A. V. Shchusev State Museum of
Architecture

122 Design for church of the Mother of
God, Joy of all Who Sorrow, on the
Kartavtsov estate at Merijoki, Finland
1912
Indian ink, watercolour and white on
paper mounted on cardboard,
60.7 × 69.5
Signed and dated bottom right
A. V. Shchusev State Museum of
Architecture
[Illustrated p.192]

Aleksandr Fedorovich Gaush

1873 ST PETERSBURG – 1947 SIMFEROPOL'
Landscape and still-life painter. Studied
under Chistyakov and at the Petersburg
Academy (1893–99). He was one of the
founders of the New Society of Artists,
with whom he exhibited (1904–07), and
he also participated in exhibitions of
other Russian artists' groups, including
Golubaya Roza, and in exhibitions
abroad. His easel paintings were
intended as harmonious and colourful
decorations for the rooms of private
houses. He was curator of the Museum
of Old St Petersburg (1907–20) and was
one of the founders of the *Petrushka*
theatre in Leningrad (1924). In 1924 he
moved to Odessa, and in 1935 to the
Crimea.

123 *Peacocks by a Fountain*
1911–15
Oil on canvas, 71.5 × 107
Signed bottom right
State Russian Museum
[Illustrated p.119]

Aleksandr Yakovlevich Golovin

1863 MOSCOW – 1930 DETSKOE SELO, NR.
LENINGRAD
Theatre designer, painter, designer and
graphic artist. Studied at the Moscow
College (1881–89), under Makovsky,
Polenov and Pryanishnikov, and in Paris
with Colarossi and Jacques-Emile
Blanche (1889) and later at Witte's
studio with R. Collin and O. Merson
(1897). He first exhibited in 1893 with
the *Peredvizhniki* and subsequently
with various Moscow groups, with *Mir
Iskusstva*, *The 36*, the Union of Russian
Artists etc. During the 1890s he made
designs for the Abramtsevo workshops,
and at the end of the decade travelled
in Spain and Italy. Together with
Korovin he designed the crafts section
of the Russian Pavilion at the Paris
Exposition Universelle of 1900. His
work in the theatre began in 1898, and
from 1902 to 1917 he worked for the
Imperial Theatres in St Petersburg,
becoming chief artist there in 1908; he
also collaborated with Vsevolod
Meyerhold and designed productions
for Diaghilev's seasons in Paris in 1908
(Musorgsky's *Boris Godunov*) and 1910
(Stravinsky's *Firebird*). From 1927 he
worked with Stanislavsky. His theatre
designs were included in Diaghilev's
Salon d'Automne show (1906).

124 *Pond in a Forest*
1909
Tempera on canvas, 124 × 106
State Russian Museum
[Illustrated p.116]

125 Programme: Théâtre de l'Ermitage
Moscow (printed by A. A. Levenson),
25 January 1909
Lithograph with gilding, 29 × 25.5
State Lenin Library

126 *Portrait of a Woman*
1910s
Gouache and tempera on canvas,
130 × 95
State Tretyakov Gallery
[Illustrated p.127]

127 Imprint of Kartonnyi Domik (House
of Cards) Publishers
Petrograd, n.d.
Line block, 3.5 × 2.5
State Lenin Library

128 *The Grave of the Commendatore*
Tempera on plywood, 79 × 115
signed bottom left
State Russian Museum

Set design for the production of
Dargomyzhsky's *Stone Guest* (Act III) at
the Mariinsky Theatre, Petrograd, in 1917.

129 Cover of *Zapiski Mechtatelei* (*Notes
of Dreamers*), no.1. Petrograd
(Alkonost), 1919
Line block, 26.4 × 20
State Lenin Library

See also no.181

Anna Semenovna Golubkina

1864 ZARAISK (RYAZAN' PROVINCE) – 1927 ZARAISK
Sculptor and painter. She studied with
Volnukhin at the architect Gunst's art
classes in Moscow (1889–90), then at
the Moscow College under Sergei
Ivanov and at the Petersburg Academy
School (1894) under Beklemishev. In
Paris she studied at the Académie
Colarossi (1895, 1897) and also worked
under Rodin (1897, 1899, 1903),
studying the technique of sculpting in
marble. She visited London in 1903. She
exhibited with many Russian artists'
groups, including *Mir Iskusstva*, *The 36*
and the Union of Russian Artists, and
her work was included in exhibitions in
Paris, Rome and New York. The
exhibition of her work in Moscow in
1914–15 in aid of war wounded was her
first individual show in Russia.
Golubkina's first Symbolist compositions
date from the years 1899–1902 and
include the vase *Mist* and the relief *The
Wave* that she executed above the
entrance of the Moscow Arts Theatre
for Savva Mamontov. She was also
active as a teacher, at the Prechisten
workers' courses (1913–16) and at
Vkhutemas (1918–22).

130 Vase: *Mist*
1899
Marble, 52.5 × 32.5 × 31
Signed with initials on base
State Tretyakov Gallery
[Illustrated p.20]

131 *Portrait of Mariya Sredina*
1904
Bronze, 48 × 35 × 25; cast stamped:
Foundry Emilio Robecchi, Moscow
State Tretyakov Gallery
[Illustrated p.181]

Mariya Grigor'evna Sredina (c.1875–
before 1934) was the wife of the artist
A. V. Sredin. She subsequently married
the composer A. Y. Grechaninov.

132 *Portrait of Andrei Bely*
1907
Bronze, $42 \times 43 \times 34$
State Russian Museum
[Illustrated p.69]

133 *Old Woman*
1908
Tinted marble, $39 \times 33.5 \times 20.5$
Carved signature on right of bust
State Tretyakov Gallery
[Illustrated p.178]

134 *"Oh, yes! . . ."*
1913
Tinted wood, $47 \times 35 \times 30$
Carved initials on right of bust
State Tretyakov Gallery
[Illustrated p.35]

Natal'ya Sergeevna Goncharova
1881 NAGAEVO (NR. TULA) – 1962 PARIS
Painter, graphic and theatre artist. She
studied sculpture and then painting at
the Moscow College (1901–09) under
Trubetskoi and Korovin, and it was here
that she met her life-long companion
Mikhail Larionov. She was included in
Diaghilev's Salon d'Automne show in
1906 and exhibited frequently from that
year: in the *Venok (Wreath)* show
(1907–08), the *Zveno (Link)* show in
Kiev (1908) and the three salons of
Zolotoe Runo (1908–9), the last of which
she and Larionov dominated. She was
one of the organisers of the exhibition
societies *Bubnovyi Valet (Jack of
Diamonds)* (1910–11), *Oslinyi Khvost
(Donkey's Tail)* (1912), *Mishen' (Target)*
(1913) and others. In 1912–14, together
with Larionov, she evolved the theory
of Rayonism. In 1915 she moved to
Paris, where she was associated with
Diaghilev's *Ballets Russes* until 1929.

135 *St George and the Dragon*
1914
Drawing for the lithograph in the album
War 1914: Mystical Images of War
Lead pencil on paper, 31.4×23.8
Monogram and title inscribed on verso
State Russian Museum
[Illustrated p.150]

136 *The Pale Horse*
1914
Drawing for the lithograph in the album
War 1914: Mystical Images of War
Lead pencil on paper, 31.8×24.3
Monogram and title inscribed on verso
State Russian Museum
[Illustrated p.12]

The pale horse carried an apocalyptic
rider, symbolic of death.

137 *Russian Woman with Purple Blouse*
1914
Costume design for *Zolotoi Petushok
(The Golden Cockerel)*
Watercolour and bodycolours on paper,
38×26.5
Trustees of the Victoria and Albert
Museum

138 *Russian Peasant in Red Shirt with
Yellow Sleeves*
1914
Costume design for *Zolotoi Petushok
(The Golden Cockerel)*
Watercolour and bodycolours on paper,
38×27
Trustees of the Victoria and Albert
Museum

Rimsky-Korsakov's ballet-opera *Zolotoi
Petushok* (1908) was produced by
Diaghilev in 1914 at the Paris Opéra with
choreography by Fokine and sets and
costumes by Goncharova.

See also no.210

Igor' Emmanuilovich Grabar'
1871 BUDAPEST – 1960 MOSCOW
Painter, art historian and critic. Having
graduated from the Law Faculty of
Petersburg University in 1893, he
studied at the Petersburg Academy
(1894–96), in Repin's studio and then at
the Ažbè School in Munich (1896–99).
He first exhibited in 1898 and later
participated in the exhibitions of the
Mir Iskusstva group (from 1902) and of
the Union of Russian Artists (1903–10);
he was included in Diaghilev's Salon
d'Automne show (1906). In 1903 he
moved to Moscow, and he travelled
extensively in 1914 (Egypt, U.S.A.) and
the early 1920s (Western Europe). In
1910 he published his monumental
History of Russian Art, and he was
director of the Tretyakov Gallery in
1913–25. He organised the State Art
Restoration Workshops (1918–30) and
later taught at and directed the Moscow
Institute of Fine Arts (1937–43) and
headed the All-Russian Academy of
Arts (1942–47).

139 *Lady with a Dog*
1899
Oil on canvas, 150×114.5
State Tretyakov Gallery
[Illustrated p.110]

Boris Dmitrievich Grigor'ev
1886 MOSCOW – 1939 CANNES
Painter, graphic and theatre artist. He
studied at the Stroganov Design School
in Moscow (1903–07) under

Shcherbinovsky and then under Kiselev
and Kardovsky at the Petersburg
Academy School (1907–12). Whilst
living in Paris (1912–14) he started to do
drawings for the St Petersburg
magazines *Satirikon* (1912–13), *Novyi
Satirikon* (1914) and *Lukomor'e* (1913–
16). He returned to St Petersburg, but
settled in France in 1919.

140 *Little Peasant Woman*
1911
Lead pencil and white on grey paper,
41.5×43
Signed, dated and inscribed with title
bottom left
State Russian Museum
[Illustrated p.151]

141 *In Winter: Huntsmen in the
Country*
1911
Pen, Indian ink and white on grey-
brown cardboard, 24.5×24.4
Signed bottom right
State Russian Museum

Lev Aleksandrovich Il'in
1880–1942
Architect. Graduated from the
Petersburg Institute of Civil Engineers
in 1902, and his practice was based in
that city. He designed apartment
houses, private houses and public
buildings.

Design for grand piano
1901

142 Design for decoration of lid
Coloured ink and watercolour on
coloured paper, 37×27
Signed and dated bottom right
A. V. Shchusev State Museum of
Architecture
[Illustrated p.236]

143 Side elevation
Coloured ink, watercolour and white on
coloured paper, 27.3×39.2
Signed and dated bottom right
A. V. Shchusev State Museum of
Architecture
[Illustrated p.236]

144 Front elevation
Coloured ink, watercolour and white on
coloured paper, 26.1×30.7
Signed and dated bottom right
A. V. Shchusev State Museum of
Architecture
[Illustrated p.236]

V. V. Iordan
Architect. Worked in Moscow, where, from the 1890s, he designed apartment houses, public buildings and offices.

145 Design for the Chizhikova apartment house on the Arbat, Moscow
1907
Coloured ink, pencil, watercolour and white on coloured paper mounted on cardboard, 49 × 63.5
Signed and dated
A. V. Shchusev State Museum of Architecture
[Illustrated p.213]

Ivanov Brothers workshop
One of the principal workshops in the Sergei Trading Quarter, specializing in the manufacture of folk toys.

146 *Matryoshka* (12 dolls)
1910s
Turned painted wood, 22 × 10.5
State Historical Museum

147 *Matryoshka* (8 dolls)
1910s
Turned wood with painting and pokerwork, 15 × 7.5
State Historical Museum
[Illustrated p.235]

Vyacheslav Ivanov
1866–1949
Symbolist poet and writer.

See no.404

Illarion Aleksandrovich Ivanov-Shits
1865–1937
Architect. Studied at the Petersburg Institute of Civil Engineers (1883–88) and by the early 1890s had become one of the leading architects in Moscow, where he later taught at the Moscow College. His buildings in the city include: Morozov Children's Clinic (1903–05), Merchants' Club (1907–08), Soldatenkovskaya (now S. P. Botkin) Hospital (1908–13), Shanyavsky Peoples' University (1910–13).

Merchants' Club on Malaya Dmitrovka (Chekhov Street), Moscow
1907–08

148 Elevation (variant)
Indian ink, pencil, watercolour on paper, 54.5 × 93.5
A. V. Shchusev State Museum of Architecture
[Illustrated p.216]

149 Entrance hall, wall treatment
Indian ink, pencil, watercolour and bronze powder on cardboard, 26.8 × 72.5
A. V. Shchusev State Museum of Architecture

150 Entrance hall, general view
Photo (1900s), 27.5 × 22
A. V. Shchusev State Museum of Architecture
[Illustrated p.217]

151 Entrance hall, general view
Photo (1900s), 24 × 30
A. V. Shchusev State Museum of Architecture
[Illustrated p.217]

152 Design for decorative panel in entrance hall
Indian ink, pencil, watercolour and bronze powder on paper, 17.2 × 48
A. V. Shchusev State Museum of Architecture
[Illustrated p.214]

153 Design for decorative panel in entrance hall
Pencil, watercolour and bronze powder on paper, 24 × 49.3
A. V. Shchusev State Museum of Architecture
[Illustrated p.214]

154 Design for decorative panel in entrance hall
Indian ink, watercolour and bronze powder on paper, 22.8 × 49.4
A. V. Shchusev State Museum of Architecture
[Illustrated p.215]

Mart'yanych Restaurant: Designs for decoration of cellars of Upper Trading Rows (now GUM), Red Square, Moscow
1905

155 Entrance from Red Square (variant), plan and elevation
Pencil and watercolour on paper, 44 × 56.8
A. V. Shchusev State Museum of Architecture
[Illustrated p.212]

156 Design for booth
Coloured ink, pencil, watercolour and white on paper mounted on cardboard, 26.7 × 42.3
A. V. Shchusev State Museum of Architecture
[Illustrated pp.212–3]

157 Design for buffet
Pencil and watercolour on paper mounted on cardboard, 29 × 46
A. V. Shchusev State Museum of Architecture
[Illustrated p.212]

158 Egyptian buffet, design for decorative panel
Indian ink, pencil and watercolour on paper, 30.3 × 52
A. V. Shchusev State Museum of Architecture
[Illustrated p.213]

159 Elevation of apartment house (with commercial accommodation on ground floor): elevation
1900
Indian ink and watercolour on paper, 34 × 29
A. V. Shchusev State Museum of Architecture
[Illustrated p.208]

Nikolai Konstantinovich Kalmakov
1873 NERVI (ITALY) – 1955 PARIS
Painter and theatre artist. Received no formal artistic education. He participated in group exhibitions from 1906 and had an individual exhibition in St Petersburg in 1913. He designed sets for theatres in both St Petersburg and Moscow. He lived abroad (in Estonia, Brussels and Paris) from the early 1920s.

160 *Chinese Woman*
1913
Watercolour, gouache, silver paint, lead pencil, pen and Indian ink on cardboard, 56 × 38.5
Signed with initial and dated bottom left
State Russian Museum
[Illustrated p.130]

161 *Diana and Endymion*
1917
Oil, silver and bronze on canvas, 90 × 90
Signed with initial and dated centre left
State Russian Museum
[Illustrated p.131]

   Version of the painting *Endymion* (*c.*1913, whereabouts unknown), shown at the artist's one-man exhibition in St Petersburg in 1913.

162 Bookplate for N. Teffi
1913
Colour lithograph, 5.5 × 6
State Lenin Library

Vasily Vasil'evich Kandinsky

1866 MOSCOW – 1944 NEUILLY-SUR-SEINE

Painter and graphic artist; pioneer of abstraction. After a childhood and youth in Odessa he returned to Moscow, attending the Law Faculty of the University (1886–92). In 1896 he went to Munich, where he studied at the Ažbè School (1896–98) and at the Academy under Franz von Stuck (1900). He remained in Germany until 1914, where he was a founder of *Phalanx* (1901), the *New Artists' Association of Munich* (1909) and the *Blaue Reiter* (1911). He travelled frequently to Russia during these years and participated in many group exhibitions: New Society of Artists, St Petersburg (1904–06), *Bubnovyi Valet (Jack of Diamonds)* (1910, 1912) and the exhibitions organised by Vladimir Izdebsky in Odessa, St Petersburg and Riga (1909–14). In 1919 he worked on the reorganisation of museums in Russia, and he was Director of the Museum of Artistic Culture and Professor at Svomas from 1918 to 1921, when he returned to Germany. He was Professor at the Bauhaus in Weimar and Dessau until 1933, when he settled in France.

163 *Album: Poems Without Words.*
Moscow (Stroganov Design School), [1903]
Woodcuts, 33 × 25.5
State Lenin Library
[Illustrated p.146]

164 *St George and the Dragon*
1914–15
Oil on cardboard, 61.4 × 91
State Tretyakov Gallery
[Illustrated p.129]

Firm of Ivan Khlebnikov

Founded by Ivan Petrovich Khlebnikov in St Petersburg in 1867, by the late 19th century the firm had become one of the leading jewellers in Russia, employing some two hundred craftsmen. In 1917 the business was transferred to Moscow.

165 Napkin ring
Moscow, 1899–1908
Silver with gilding and enamel,
4 × 6.1 × 4.3
Hallmark with firm's initials
State Historical Museum
[Illustrated p.250]

Roman Ivanovich Klein

1858 – 1924 MOSCOW

Architect. Studied at the Petersburg Academy (1877–82) and then in Paris with Charles Garnier until 1884. He was principally active in Moscow, where his buildings include the Middle Trading Rows on Red Square (1892), the Pushkin Museum of Fine Arts (1898–1912), the Muir and Mirrielees Department Store (1907–08) and the Borodino Bridge (1912). He taught at the Polytechnic Institute (1916–18) and the Moscow Higher Technical College (1918–23).

Muir and Mirrielees Department Store,
Teatralnaya Square, Moscow
1907–08

166 Elevation on Teatralnaya Square
Indian ink and pencil on paper,
65.5 × 60.1
Signed bottom
A. V. Shchusev State Museum of Architecture
[Illustrated p.21]

167 Plan of ground floor
Indian ink and watercolour on paper,
33 × 40.5
Signed bottom right
A. V. Shchusev State Museum of Architecture

168 Longitudinal section
Indian ink and watercolour on paper,
65.5 × 60.5
Signed bottom right
A. V. Shchusev State Museum of Architecture
[Illustrated p.217]

I. Knopf

Graphic artist.

169 Programme cover: Concert of Science and Engineering Students
Moscow (printed by N. N. Kushnerev & Co.), n.d.
Colour lithograph with gilding, 31.5 × 15
State Lenin Library
[Illustrated p.154]

Friedrich Christian Koechli

Master jeweller. A member of a family of goldsmiths and jewellers, he was active in the period 1870–1908.

170 Brooch
St Petersburg, late 19th century
Gold, brilliants, sapphires and rubies,
2.8 × 2.2
State Historical Museum

Sergei Timofeevich Konenkov

1874 KARAKOVICHI (SMOLENSK PROVINCE) – 1971 MOSCOW

Sculptor. Studied at the Moscow College under Sergei Ivanov and Volnukhin (1892–96) and in 1897 won the school's S. Tretyakov prize, which enabled him to travel in Germany, France, Switzerland and Italy. He continued his studies at the Petersburg Academy School under Beklemishev (1899–1902) and at the same time in the studio of Pavel Trubetskoi. He was a member of the New Society of Artists (from 1908) and the Union of Russian Artists (from 1909) and exhibited widely both in Russia and abroad. In 1912 he travelled to Greece and Egypt. From 1902 to 1923 he lived and worked in Moscow, then in New York until 1945, when he returned to Moscow. His memoirs (extracts from which are quoted in the entries below) were published in 1984.

171 *Whistler*
1905
Majolica, 47 × 34 × 15
State Tretyakov Gallery

Detail from a fountain which formed part of the decorations Konenkov executed, in collaboration with the painter Konchalovsky, for the Filippov Café on Tverskaya Street in central Moscow (now the restaurant of the Tsentral'naya Hotel).

172 *Paganini*
1906
Bronze, 54 × 68 × 35
At back of cast: V. Luk'yanov 1954
State Tretyakov Gallery
[Illustrated p.181]

The first of several images of Paganini made by the sculptor over a period of fifty years in marble and wood: "The name of Paganini is a symbol of a passionate and free spirit. His music conquers darkness. I attempted to express this conviction of mine in sculpture." (*Memoirs* I, p.126)

173 *Portrait of Vasily Denisov*
1909
Wood, 50 × 27.5 × 25
Signed and inscribed on right of base
State Tretyakov Gallery
[Illustrated p.179]

174 *Beloved*
1909
Marble, 40 × 37.5 × 28
Carved signature on right arm
State Tretyakov Gallery
[Illustrated p.184]

Tat'yana Yakovlevna Konyaeva (1888–1935), first wife of the artist.

175 *The Feast*
1910
Coloured wood, 86.5 × 186.5 × 31
Signed top right
State Tretyakov Gallery
[Illustrated pp.210–1]

Executed as part of the decorations
planned by Aleksei Shchusev for the
dining room in the house of M. D.
Karpova in Zamoskvorech'e, in Moscow.
Shchusev asked Konenkov to make a bas-
relief in which "the joy of existence, a
Bacchic mood, should be sensed. . . . I
called it *Pirshestvo (Feast)* in the Russian
manner." (*Memoirs* I, p.139)

176 *Stribog*
1910
Coloured and inlaid wood,
175 × 46 × 43.5
Signed on the right of the base
State Tretyakov Gallery
[Illustrated p.185]

"The stumps and powerful blocks which
I had stored up in the Moscow suburbs (I
took dry stumps of dead trees – I could not
agree to killing a living tree, however
tempting it was) were awaiting their time.
And now it arrived: the forest kingdom, in
the midst of which my childhood and
youth had been spent, beckoned me, and I
followed this summons of nature. I saw
the fantastic heroes of folk tales and
superstitions more clearly than you can see
nearby objects on a sunny day. Within a
short time I had carved *Staren'kii
starichok*, *Velikosila*, *Stribog* and
Starichok-polevichok in wood." (*Memoirs*
I, p.131)

177 *Arms of a Seraph*
1916
Wood, 159 × 66 × 33
Signed at the front
State Tretyakov Gallery
[Illustrated p.185]

Konstantin Alekseevich Korovin

1861 MOSCOW – 1939 PARIS
Painter, theatre artist and designer.
Studied at the Moscow College under
Savrasov and Polenov (1875–86) and at
the Petersburg Academy (1882). From
1884 he attended the drawing soirées at
the Polenovs and he became a member
of the Abramtsevo group: he worked in
the pottery studio and designed sets for
Mamontov's Private Russian Opera
(1885–1900). He designed the Far North
Pavilion at the Nizhny Novgorod
Exhibition of 1896 and, with Golovin,
the Russian Pavilion at the Paris 1900
Exposition Universelle. He worked for
the Imperial Theatres from 1900,
becoming chief scene-painter for the

Moscow Imperial Theatres in 1910, and
also taught at the Moscow College
(1901–18). He exhibited with the
Peredvizhniki (1889–99), the Moscow
Society of Art Lovers (1889–1911), *Mir
Iskusstva* (from 1899), *The 36*, the
Union of Russian Artists (from 1903)
and other groups; he was included in
Diaghilev's Salon d'Automne show
(1906). He lived in Paris from 1923.

Pavilion of the Far North at the Nizhny
Novgorod Exhibition
1896

178 General view
Photo (1896), 16 × 21
A. V. Shchusev State Museum of
Architecture
[Illustrated p.200]

179 Principal elevation
Photo (1896), 21.8 × 15.9
A. V. Shchusev State Museum of
Architecture

180 Cover for *Mir Iskusstva*, 1899
no.11–12
Colour lithograph, 34.5 × 28
State Lenin Library

181 Russian Pavilion at the Paris
Exposition Universelle (project executed
with the collaboration of A. Y. Golovin)
1900
Stereoscopic photo (1900) by
Underwood & Underwood
A. V. Shchusev State Museum of
Architecture
[Illustrated p.19]

182 *Stream*
1902
Oil on canvas, 63.6 × 45.5
State Tretyakov Gallery
[Illustrated p.105]

Konstantin Fedorovich Krakht

1868 VLADIMIR – 1919 MOSCOW
Sculptor. Graduated from the Law
Faculty of Moscow University (1891)
and practised as a lawyer until illness
forced him to abandon his career in
1901. In that year he travelled to Paris,
pursuing his studies in sculpture there
under N. L. Aronson (1902) and
Constantin Meunier (1904) until 1907.
On his return he settled in Moscow,
working principally as a portrait-
sculptor. He was associated with the
Symbolist writers of the *Musaget* group
(1907–14) and organised an art Sunday
school – *Venok (Wreath)* – for factory-
workers. He exhibited with the Moscow

Society of Artists and took part in the St
Petersburg *Venok* exhibition (1908).

183 *Portrait of Margarita Morozova*
1905
Bronze, 45 × 58 × 44.5
Signed on base
State Tretyakov Gallery
[Illustrated p.180]

Margarita Kirillovna Morozova (1873–
1958), the wife of Mikhail Morozov, a
merchant and collector of the work of
Russian and western painters, was close to
Symbolist circles, counting Solov'ev and
Bely, as well as Sergei Bulgakov, among
her friends.

Nikolai Petrovich Krymov

1884 MOSCOW – 1958 MOSCOW
Painter, theatre artist. Studied at the
Moscow College (1904–11) under Serov,
Korovin and Pasternak. He exhibited
with the Moscow Society of Artists
(from 1905), the Union of Russian
Artists (from 1906), and took part in the
Golubaya Roza (1907), *Venok* (1908)
and *Zolotoe Runo* (1909) exhibitions. He
taught at Vkhutemas (1920–22).

184 *Approaching Spring*
1907
Oil on canvas, 52 × 71
Signed and dated bottom right
State Tretyakov Gallery
[Illustrated p.118]

S. F. Kulagin

Architect. Studied under A. Popov. He
was in Moscow from the 1880s, and his
practice included apartment houses,
public buildings and offices, churches,
country estates and dachas.

185 Project for a villa in the Crimea
1907
Indian ink, watercolour and white on
paper, 44 × 58.8
Signed and dated bottom right
A. V. Shchusev State Museum of
Architecture
[Illustrated p.219]

Boris Mikhailovich Kustodiev

1878 ASTRAKHAN' – 1927 LENINGRAD
Painter, illustrator and theatre artist.
Studied in Astrakhan' under P. Vlasov
and at the Petersburg Academy School
(1896–1903) under Savinsky and Repin.
In 1904 he won an Academy travelling
scholarship to France and Spain. He
was a founder member of the New
Society of Artists (1904–06), was
included in Diaghilev's Salon
d'Automne show (1906) and exhibited

with the Union of Russian Artists (from 1907) and *Mir Iskusstva* (from 1910). He lived in St Petersburg-Petrograd-Leningrad, and designed scenery for theatres both there and in Moscow.

186 *Portrait of Renée Notgaft*
1914
Oil on canvas, 111 × 81
Signed and dated bottom right
State Russian Museum
[Illustrated p.126]
   Renée Ivanovna Notgaft (née Koestlin) was the Swiss wife of the well-known collector and museum administrator Fedor Notgaft, a close friend of the artist. Kustodiev was attracted by the distinctive beauty of her "un-Russian" face.

Mikhail Kuzmin
1872–1936
Poet, critic, translator and musician.

See nos.113, 402

Elizaveta Yur'evna Kuz'mina-Karavaeva (Pilenko)
1891 RIGA – 1945 RAVENSBRÜCK
Painter and poet. Studied at the studio of M. Bernstein and V. Tseidler. Participated in the *Soyuz Molodezhi* (Union of Youth) exhibition in 1912. From 1920 she lived in Paris, where she painted murals for two churches. In 1926 she took the veil. During the Second World War she joined the French Resistance; she died in a German concentration camp.

187 *Visitation*
Not after 1917
Watercolour and wax on paper, 21.5 × 17.4
State Russian Museum
[Illustrated p.131]

Ivan Sergeevich Kuznetsov
1874–1942
Architect. Studied at the Moscow College. In the 1900s he worked in Shekhtel's office. His works include houses and office buildings in Moscow.

Project for a church on the Medvedkovs' estate of Poreche at Zvenigorod, near Moscow 1899–1900

188 Design for a wallpainting
Indian ink, pencil and watercolour on paper, 51.4 × 15.8
Signed and dated right
A. V. Shchusev State Museum of Architecture
[Illustrated p.192]

189 Design for a wallpainting
Coloured ink, pencil and watercolour on paper, 36.2 × 16
Signed lower right
A. V. Shchusev State Museum of Architecture
[Illustrated p.192]

Baev Mansion, Moscow
1910

190 Design for light fitting
Pencil, Indian ink and watercolour on paper, 35 × 37.8
A. V. Shchusev State Museum of Architecture
[Illustrated p.207]

191 Design for light fitting
Indian ink and watercolour on paper, 41.5 × 34.3
A. V. Shchusev State Museum of Architecture
[Illustrated p.207]

M. S. Kuznetsov Partnership
Established as a ceramic factory in the first half of the 19th century, it had become by the 1870s the largest concern for the manufacture of pottery, porcelain and glass in Russia.

192, 193 Two details of a stove in the house of M. S. Kuznetsov in Moscow
Early 20th century
Earthenware reliefs with coloured glazes, each 55.5 × 51 × 8
State Historical Museum

Pavel Varfolomeevich Kuznetsov
1878 SARATOV – 1968 MOSCOW
Painter, graphic and theatre artist. Studied at the painting and drawing studio attached to the Saratov Society of Fine Arts under the Italian painter Baracci (1891–96) and at the Moscow College (1897–1904). In 1906 he visited various studios in Paris, and his work was included in Diaghilev's Salon d'Automne show. He was one of the organisers of the exhibitions *Alaya Roza* (Crimson Rose) in Saratov (1904) and *Golubaya Roza* in Moscow (1907). He exhibited with *Mir Iskusstva* (from 1902), *Venok* (1907–08), the Union of Russian Artists (from 1907) and in the *Zolotoe Runo* salons (1908–09), the second of which featured his work prominently. He taught at the Moscow College and at Vkhutein (1916–37). Kuznetsov's search for beauty and harmony was embodied in his poetic images of nature and of Oriental

peoples, who seem to be transported to a fairy-tale country where they have access to the mysteries of nature and everything is filled with majestic peace.

194 *Flowering Garden in Bakhchisaray*
1907
Tempera on canvas, 63 × 70
State Tretyakov Gallery
[Illustrated p.119]
   Bakhchisaray: town in the Crimea.

195 *On the Steppe: Mirage (Evening on the Steppe)*
1911
Oil on canvas, 87.5 × 94
Signed and dated bottom right
Saratov Museum of Fine Art
[Illustrated p.128]

196 *Steppe Landscape with Nomads' Tents*
1911–12
Watercolour on cardboard, 30.3 × 47
State Russian Museum

197 *Oriental Scene*
1912–13
Oil on canvas, 78 × 87.5
State Russian Museum
[Illustrated p.23]

Evgeny Evgen'evich Lanceray
1875 PAVLOVSK, NR. ST PETERSBURG – 1946 MOSCOW
Painter, graphic and theatre artist. The nephew of Benois, he studied at the OPKh Drawing School (1892–96) under Tsionglinsky and Liphardt and in Paris at the Académie Julian under J.-P. Laurens and J.-J. Benjamin-Constant and at the Académie Colarossi (1896–99). He was a member of *Mir Iskusstva* (from 1899), *The 36* and the Union of Russian Artists. He designed sets for theatrical productions in St Petersburg and contributed to the magazines *Zhupel*, *Adskaya Pochta*, *Zritel'*, *Mir Iskusstva* and *Zolotoe Runo* (1905–08). He was artistic director of the porcelain factories and cut glass workshops in St Petersburg and Ekaterinburg (1912–15), moving to Dagestan in 1917, then in 1920 to Tbilisi, where he taught at the Academy of Arts, and in 1934 to Moscow. He travelled extensively within Russia and abroad.

198 Cover of *Mir Iskusstva*, 1901 no.2–3
Gold printing, 32 × 25.5
State Lenin Library

199 *Hunting Scene*
1902
Drawing for Nikolai Kutepov, *Tsarist
and Imperial Hunting in Russia in the
late Seventeenth and Eighteenth
Centuries*, vol.3, St Petersburg (State
Stationery Office), 1902 (see also no.299)
Black and coloured inks, white, brush,
pen and lead pencil on cardboard,
19.5 × 31
Signed and dated centre bottom
State Tretyakov Gallery
[Illustrated p.143]

200 Cover of *Zolotoe Runo*, 1906 no.2
(Done in collaboration with an
anonymous artist, "I")
Black and gold printing, 34 × 31
State Lenin Library
[Illustrated p.148]

201 Cover of *Zolotoe Runo*, 1906 no.10.
Line block (printed by I. Kushnerev &
Co.), 34 × 31
State Lenin Library
[Illustrated p.148]

202 Cover of Konstantin Bal'mont, *Evil
Spell*, Moscow (*Zolotoe Runo*), 1906
Line blocks (printed I. Kushnerev &
Co.), 24.7 × 16.8
State Lenin Library

203 Cover of Aleksandr Blok, *Earth in
Snow: Third Collection of Poems*,
Moscow (Zolotoe Runo), 1908 (copy
signed by the author)
Line block, 25.1 × 16.9
State Lenin Library
[Illustrated p.72]

204 Cover of *Zolotoe Runo*, 1908 no.3–4
Line block, 31.5 × 22
State Lenin Library
[Illustrated p.71]

205 *Perseus*
1910
Design for a mural for the house of
G. G. Tarasov in Moscow
Gouache and sanguine on cardboard,
25.2 × 24.4
Signed and dated bottom left
State Tretyakov Gallery

206 *Perseus*
1912
Design for a mural for the house of
G. G. Tarasov in Moscow
Gouache on cardboard, 25.1 × 24.5
Signed and dated bottom left
State Tretyakov Gallery
[Illustrated p.211]

207 Frontispiece and illustrations for
Anna Akhmatova, *Evening: Poems*,
St Petersburg (Guild of Poets), 1912
(copy signed by the author)
Line blocks, 21 × 14
State Lenin Library

208 Design for the frontispiece for a
book of poems by Cherubina de Gabriac
1914
Watercolour, Indian ink, pen, gouache
and silver paint on cardboard,
37.1 × 28.2
Signed and dated bottom right
State Russian Museum
[Illustrated p.151]

Cherubina de Gabriac: literary
pseudonym of the poet Elizaveta Ivanovna
Dmitrieva (married name Vasil'eva)
(1887–1928)

Mikhail Fedorovich Larionov

1881 TERESPOL' – 1964 FONTENAY-AUX-ROSES
Painter and theatre artist. Studied
under Levitan and Serov at the Moscow
College (1898–1908), where he met
Natal'ya Goncharova, his life-long
companion. In 1906 he visited Paris and
London with Pavel Kuznetsov and
Diaghilev, who included his work in his
Salon d'Automne show. He took part in
the *Zolotoe Runo* salons (1908–09), the
last of which he and Goncharova
dominated. He was one of the
organisers of the exhibition societies
Bubnovyi Valet (Jack of Diamonds)
(1910–11), *Oslinyi Khvost (Donkey's
Tail)* (1912), *Mishen' (Target)* (1913)
and others. In 1912–14, together with
Goncharova, he evolved the theory of
Rayonism. In 1915 he moved to Paris,
where he was closely associated with
Diaghilev's *Ballets Russes* until 1929.

209 Costume design for the Cat in
Kikimora.
1916
Pencil and bodycolours on paper,
51 × 36
Trustees of the Victoria and Albert
Museum

Kikimora, with choreography by
Massine to music by Lyadov, was first
produced by Diaghilev in San Sebastián in
1916.

210 *Goncharova, Diaghilev, Massine
and Beppo, Diaghilev's Valet, at a Café
Table*
1917
Pencil on yellowed paper, 21.8 × 27.5
Trustees of the Victoria and Albert
Museum

Nadezhda Vladimirovna Lermontova

1885 ST PETERSBURG – 1921 PETROGRAD
Painter. Studied at the Zvantseva School
in St Petersburg (1907–10). She
participated in exhibitions from 1911,
including those of *Soyuz Molodezhi* (the
Union of Youth) in 1912–13. With
Petrov-Vodkin she executed paintings in
the church at Ovruch (Ukraine), and she
also designed sets for theatre
productions in St Petersburg.

211 *On the Sofa: Self-Portrait*
1910s
Oil on canvas, 106.8 × 124.5
State Russian Museum
[Illustrated p.124]

Lukutin Factory

212, 213, 214 Three Easter eggs with
painted decoration
1900s
Papier mâché with painted lacquer,
each 14 × 9
State Historical Museum
[Illustrated p.234]

See also no.390

A. Malinin

215 Two versions of the artist's
bookplate
N.d.
Colour lithographs, each 7.5 × 4.5
State Lenin Library

Filipp Andreevich Malyavin

1869 KAZANKA (SAMARA PROVINCE) – 1940 NICE
Painter. Was a lay-brother in the
Orthodox monastery of St Panteleimon
on Mount Athos, where he worked in
the icon-painting studio. Studied at the
Petersburg Academy (1892–99) and in
Repin's studio (1899). He was an
irregular participant in the exhibitions
of *Mir Iskusstva* (from 1899), *The 36*
and the Union of Russian Artists (from
1903) and also exhibited in Italy.
Diaghilev included him in the Salon
d'Automne show (1906). His best works
(including no.217) were painted in a
village in Ryazan' province, where the
local inhabitants acted as models. He
lived in Paris from 1922.

216 *Woman with Red Umbrella*
N.d.
Oil on canvas, 58 × 75
Signed top left
Saratov Art Museum
[Illustrated p.127]

This has been identified as a portrait of
Mara Konstantinova Oliv (see no.311).

217 *Verka*
1913
Oil on canvas, 106 × 84
Signed and dated top right
State Russian Museum
[Illustrated p.121]

Sergei Vasil'evich Malyutin
1859 MOSCOW – 1937 MOSCOW
Painter, designer and graphic artist.
Studied at the Moscow College (1883–
86) under Pryanishnikov, Makovsky and
Sorokin. He exhibited with the
Peredvizhniki from 1891 and from the
turn of the century directed the joinery
workshops at Talashkino, making
designs for furniture and interior
decoration. In 1900 he did sets for
productions of Mamontov's Private
Russian Opera in Moscow. He was one
of *The 36*, a member of the Union of
Russian Artists (from 1903) and a
participant in the *Mir Iskusstva*
exhibitions; he was included in
Diaghilev's Salon d'Automne show
(1906).

218 Cover and illustrations for
Aleksandr Pushkin, *The Tale of Tsar
Saltan*, Moscow (A. Mamontov), [1898]
Colour lithographs, 17 × 25
State Lenin Library
[Illustrated p.145]

219 Cover and illustrations for *Ai, du-
du!: Russian Folk Tales, Songs, Jests
and Stories*, Moscow (A. Mamontov),
1899
Colour lithographs, 20 × 13.5
State Lenin Library
[Illustrated p.143]

220 Sideboard
Talashkino, *c.* 1900
Carved oak, 219 × 88.5 × 152
State Historical Museum

221, 222 Two Chairs
Talashkino, *c.* 1900
Carved oak, each 110 × 43 × 43
State Historical Museum
[Illustrated p.19]

Savva Ivanovich Mamontov
1841–1918
Industrialist, patron and artist. Bought
the estate of Abramtsevo in 1870 and
there formed the artistic colony and
workshops whose members included the
Vasnetsovs, the Polenovs, Korovin,
Serov, Vrubel' and many others. He was
the backer of the Private Russian Opera
and, initially, of *Mir Iskusstva* until his
financial ruin in 1899.

223 *Head of Orpheus*
Abramtsevo workshops (attributed to
Mamontov), beginning of 20th century
Majolica sculpture, reduction glaze, ht:
25
State Historical Museum

Alberto Martini
1876 ODERZO – 1954 MILAN
Italian painter and graphic artist.
Trained under his father in Treviso. In
1898 visited Munich and worked on
Jugend and *Dekorative Kunst*. He
worked extensively on magazines and
books in the period 1904–15 and was
particularly known for his erotic
illustrations. In the 1920s he was
associated with the Surrealists in Paris.

224 Cover and illustrations for Valery
Bryusov, *Axis of the Equator: Short
Stories and Dramatic Sketches (1901–
1907)*, 2nd revised edition, Moscow
(Skorpion), 1910 (copy signed by the
author)
Line blocks, 24.7 × 16
State Lenin Library
[Illustrated p.73]

Dmitry Sergeevich Merezhkovsky
1865–1941
Poet and critic.

225 Portrait of the author (photo) from
his *Complete Works*, St Petersburg and
Moscow (Vol'f), 1911
28.5 × 22
The British Library

Nikolai Dmitrievich Milioti
1874 MOSCOW – 1962 PARIS
Painter of Greek origin. Studied at the
Moscow College (1890s) and at private
studios in Paris. He was included in
Diaghilev's Salon d'Automne show
(1906) and exhibited with the Union of
Russian Artists (from 1907) and
elsewhere both in Russia and abroad.
He was a member and spokesman for
the *Golubaya Roza* group, participating
in the 1907 exhibition and in the *Zolotoe
Runo* salons (1908–09). He lived abroad
from the early 1920s.

226 *Round Dance*
N.d.
Oil on cardboard, 71 × 75.5
State Russian Museum
[Illustrated p.23]

See also no.304

Vasily Dmitrievich Milioti
1875 MOSCOW – 1943 MOSCOW
Painter, graphic and theatre artist of
Greek origin. Studied law and history at
Moscow University. He became
manager of the art section of *Zolotoe
Runo*, was a collaborator on *Vesy* (from
1905) and was one of the organizers of
the *Golubaya Roza* group. He exhibited
with *Mir Iskusstva*, the Union of
Russian Artists, of which he became
secretary, and other groups; he was
included in Diaghilev's Salon
d'Automne show (1906). From 1909 to
1917 he returned to his law practice,
while continuing to work at painting.

227 *Morning*
1905
Watercolour, gouache, pen and Indian
ink on plywood, 21.8 × 22.2
Signed and dated bottom right
State Russian Museum
[Illustrated p.38]

228 *Kiss*
1906
Drawing for *Vesy*, 1906 no.9
Indian ink, pen and lead pencil on
paper, 32.5 × 24.3
Signed bottom left, dated bottom right
State Tretyakov Gallery
[Illustrated p.33]

229 Vignettes for Valery Bryusov, *Axis
of the Equator: Short Stories and
Dramatic Sketches (1901–1906)*,
Moscow (Skorpion), 1907 [1906]
(copy signed by the author)
Line blocks, 24.2 × 16.1
State Lenin Library
[Illustrated p.73]

Mir Iskusstva
Journal of art, philosophy and criticism
published in St Petersburg from 1898 to
1904 as the organ of the *Mir Iskusstva*
(World of Art) group.

See nos.30, 72, 180, 198, 392, 479, 480

Dmitry Isidorovich Mitrokhin
1883 EISK – 1973 MOSCOW
Graphic artist. Studied at the Moscow
College (1902–03) under Apollinary
Vasnetsov and Stepanov, at the
Stroganov Design School (1904) under
Noakovsky and at the Académie de la
Grande Chaumière in Paris (1905)
under Steinlen and Grasset. He first
exhibited in 1903 and his earliest book
designs date from 1904. He worked at
the *Murava* ceramics co-operative

(1907–08), in the graphics department of the Russian Museum (1918–23) and taught at Vkhutein (1924–30).

230 Drawing to illustrate an oriental fairy-tale
1912
Indian ink, pen, brush and lead pencil on paper, 30.1 × 22.9
Signed and dated bottom right
State Russian Museum

231 Cover and illustrations for Wilhelm Hauff, *The Ghost Ship: a Fairy Story*, Moscow (I. Knebel')/St Petersburg (R. Golicke and A. Wilborg), 1913
Colour lithographs, 30 × 22.7
State Lenin Library

232 Cover and illustrations for Richard Gustafsson, *The Barge: a Fairy Tale*, Moscow (I. Knebel'), [1913]
Colour lithographs (lithography by F. G. Keitel'), 30 × 23
State Lenin Library
[Illustrated p.152]

233 Cover and illustrations for Marina Tsvetaeva, *Tsar-Girl: Fairytale in Verse*, Moscow (GIZ), 1922
Line blocks, 18 × 14
State Lenin Library

Ivan Mozalevsky

234 Imprint for the Publishers Al'tsiona (Kingfisher)
Moscow, n.d.
Line block, 3 × 3.5
State Lenin Library

Georgy Ivanovich Narbut
1886 NARBUTOVKA, UKRAINE – 1920 KIEV
Graphic artist and painter. While studying history and philosophy at Petersburg University, he took lessons from Bilibin and studied at the Zvantseva School under Dobuzhinsky, going on to the Hollósy School in Munich (1909–10). He lived in St Petersburg until 1917, then moving to Kiev, where he became vice-chancellor of the Ukrainian Academy of Arts.

235 Cover and illustrations for *Dance, Matvei, Don't Spare Your Shoes*, Moscow (I. Knebel'), 1910
Colour lithograph, 29.5 × 21.7
State Lenin Library

236 Illustrations for Hans Christian Andersen, *The Nightingale: Andersen's Fairy Tales*, Moscow (I. Knebel')/St Petersburg (R. Golicke and A. Wilborg), [1912]
Line block, 30 × 23
State Lenin Library

237 *Grasshopper in front of the House of Cards*
1913
Drawing to illustrate Hans Christian Andersen's fairy-tale *The High Jumpers*
Watercolour, Indian ink, pen, brush, gouache and lead pencil on paper, 32.4 × 25.2
Signed with initials and dated bottom right
State Russian Museum
[Illustrated p.152]

238 *Bird in a Cage*
1913
Drawing to illustrate the fable by Krylov, *The Kitten and the Starling*
Watercolour, Indian ink, brush and pen on paper, 26 × 24
Signed with initials bottom left, dated bottom right
State Tretyakov Gallery

239 Cover for Georgy Ivanov, *In Glorious Memory: Poems*, Petrograd (Lukomor'e), [1915]
Line blocks and embossing, 17 × 12.2
State Lenin Library
[Illustrated p.150]

240 Cover design for *Apollon*
1916
Indian ink, pen and gouache on paper, 33.2 × 26.5
Signed and dated bottom right
State Russian Museum

241 *Pierrot by Moonlight against a Background of Trees*
1917
Watercolour, Indian ink, pen and gouache on paper, 25.4 × 21.2
Signed with initials and dated bottom right
State Russian Museum

242 *Ukrainian Alphabet*, Petrograd (R. Golicke and A. Wilborg), 1917
Lithographs, watercolours, 41.5 × 30.5
State Lenin Library
[Illustrated p.152]

Vasily Dmitrievich Naumov
Master Jeweller in Moscow, active 1896–1917.

243 Lady's purse
Moscow, 1899–1908
Silver, 26.5 × 18.5
Hallmark with maker's initials
State Historical Museum
[Illustrated p.257]

I. Nazarov

244 "Fish" vase
Imperial Porcelain Factory, 1910
Porcelain, underglaze painting, ht: 17
State Historical Museum

Mikhail Vasil'evich Nesterov
1862 UFA – 1942 MOSCOW
Painter. Studied at the Moscow College (1877–81, 1884–86) under Perov, Savrasov and Pryanishnikov and at the Petersburg Academy (1881–84) under Chistyakov. From 1889 he became close to Mamontov's circle at Abramtsevo, though from 1890 to 1910 he was based in Kiev, where he worked on the icons in St Vladimir's Cathedral (1891–95). He also painted murals in Abastuman (1901) and Moscow (1907–12). He travelled widely in Europe and in Russia. He exhibited with the *Peredvizhniki* (1889–1901), *Mir Iskusstva* (1899–1901), *The 36* (1901) and the Union of Russian Artists, of which he was a founder member.

245 *Vision of the Boy Varfolomei*
1889
Oil on canvas mounted on cardboard, 22.8 × 41.5
Signed and dated bottom right
State Tretyakov Gallery
[Illustrated p.103]
   Study for the painting (1889–90) in the State Tretyakov Gallery. This was the first of the cycle Nesterov dedicated to St Sergei of Radonezh (whose secular name was Varfolomei), a leading statesman in 14th-century Russia. One of the first incidents in the life of the saint was his meeting with a mysterious stranger, who blesses him.

246 *The Murdered Tsarevich Dmitry*
1899
Gouache, bronze powder and lead pencil on paper mounted on cardboard, 32.5 × 26
Signed bottom left
State Tretyakov Gallery
[Illustrated p.111]
   Study for the painting now in the State Russian Museum. The painting is inspired by Pushkin's *Boris Godunov*: the Patriarch relates how the soul of the murdered Tsarevich revisits his home a few days after his death.

247 *Portrait of Ekaterina Nesterova*
1905
Oil on canvas, 142.5 × 107.8
Signed and dated bottom right
State Tretyakov Gallery
[Illustrated p.111]

Ekaterina Petrovna Nesterova, née
Vasil'chinkova (1879–1955), wife of the
artist.

See also no.441

R. Nilsson
Bookbinder

248 Binding for Aleksandr Pushkin,
Evgeny Onegin, St Petersburg
(K. Pentkovsky), 1899
Red leather, gold blocked with appliqué
of coloured leather; lined with pale blue
morocco gold blocked with border of
flowers, 19.7 × 10
State Lenin Library
[Illustrated p.244]

Ignaty Ignat'evich Nivinsky
1880/1 MOSCOW – 1933 MOSCOW
Graphic artist, designer and printmaker.
Studied at the Stroganov Design School
(1893–98), going on to teach there
(1899–1905). He undertook technical
studies in printmaking in 1908–13. He
exhibited from 1913 and after the
October Revolution was in charge of
popular festivals in Moscow, also
working in the theatre during the 1920s.
He taught at Vkhutemas, Vkhutein and
other institutions (1921–30).

249 Design for decorative wallpaintings
in the café of the Hotel Metropol,
Moscow
1903
Indian ink, watercolour and white on
paper mounted on cardboard, 44.5 × 65
Signed and dated bottom right
A. V. Shchusev State Museum of
Architecture
[Illustrated p.214]

250 Competition project for the church
on the estate of A. M. Mal'tsev at
Balakavo, Saratov province: western
elevation
1908
Coloured ink and watercolour on paper,
58.4 × 48
Signed and dated bottom right
A. V. Shchusev State Museum of
Architecture
[Illustrated p.194]

The church was built to the designs of
Shekhtel' (see nos.375–6).

P. I. Olovyanishnikov & Sons
The largest firm of church furnishers in
Russia, established in Moscow in 1901.

251 Fabric sample
1900s
Silver brocade with white silk patterned
with silver thread and purple chenille,
58.5 × 73.5
State Historical Museum

252 Fabric sample
1900s
Pale blue silk patterned with yellow and
grey cotton, 57 × 73
State Historical Museum
[Illustrated p.238]

253 Fabric sample
1900s
Gold brocade with green silk, patterned
with pink silk and gold thread, 57 × 79.5
State Historical Museum

254 Fabric sample
1900s
Gold brocade with olive-green silk,
patterned with gold thread, 57 × 76
State Historical Museum
[Illustrated p.238]

255 Fabric sample
1900s
Gold brocade with gold thread
patterned with dark red and white silk,
58 × 80
State Historical Museum
[Illustrated p.238]

256 Fabric sample
1900s
Gold brocade with pink silk and gold
thread patterned with white silk, gold
thread and purple chenille, 56.5 × 88
State Historical Museum
[Illustrated p.238]

257 Icon of the *Virgin of Tenderness* in
silver frame
Moscow (frame: Olovyanishinkov Co.),
1908–17
Icon: Oil on wood; frame: silver gilt
and enamel, 27 × 31
Frame hallmarked with maker's mark
State Historical Museum
[Illustrated p.26]

258 Mitre
1908–17
Silver gilt with pearl, mother-of-pearl,
Urals stones, velvet and fabric, ht: 19.5
Hallmark with maker's mark
State Historical Museum

See also nos.441–3

Anna Petrovna Ostroumova-Lebedeva
1871 ST PETERSBURG – 1955 LENINGRAD
Engraver and painter. Studied at the
Stieglitz School (1889–91) and at the
Petersburg Academy School
(intermittently, 1892–1900) under
Repin, Chistyakov and Mathé. She
studied with Whistler in Paris (1898–99)
and made several journeys in Europe.
In 1906 she studied under Bakst at the
Zvantseva School. She made her first
wood-engravings in 1898. She was a
founder-member of *Mir Iskusstva* and
also exhibited with *The 36* and the
Union of Russian Artists (from 1903).
Her woodcuts were included in
Diaghilev's Salon d'Automne show
(1906).

259 Postcard: Columns of Kazan'
Cathedral
St Petersburg, not after 1903
Colour lithograph, 14 × 8
State Lenin Library

260 Postcard: Turkish weir at Tsarskoe
Selo
St Petersburg, n.d.
Colour lithograph, 13.5 × 9
State Lenin Library

261 *Tyrol*
1906
Watercolour and lead pencil on paper,
18.4 × 23.8
Signed and dated bottom right
State Tretyakov Gallery

262 *Punkaharju: Young Pines*
1908
Watercolour, lead and coloured pencils
on paper, 17 × 23.8
Dated (20 September 1908) bottom right
State Tretyakov Gallery

263 *Pavlovsk Landscapes: Woodcuts*,
Petrograd (Akvilon), 1923 (copy signed
by the artist)
Woodcuts, 18.5 × 14
State Lenin Library
[Illustrated p.36]

"Pan"
Graphic artist.

264 Cover of Andrei Bely, *Ashes*,
St Petersburg (Shipovnik), 1909
(copy signed by the author)
Line block, 26.5 × 19.6
State Lenin Library

Leonid Osipovich Pasternak
1862 ODESSA – 1945 OXFORD
Painter. Studied at the Odessa Drawing
School (1879–81), at Moscow University
and in Sorokin's studio (1881–84) and at
the Munich Academy (1885, 1886–87).
He exhibited with the *Peredvizhniki*,
The 36, and the Union of Russian
Artists; he was included in Diaghilev's
Salon d'Automne show (1906). From
1894 to 1917 he taught at the Moscow
College. He travelled widely in Europe
during these years and lived abroad
from 1921, in Germany and then in
England.

265 *Portrait of Edward Gordon Craig*
1912
Black chalk on paper, 27.7 × 30.1
Signed, dated and inscribed upper right
Visitors of the Ashmolean Museum,
Oxford

   The portrait was drawn when Craig was
directing a production of *Hamlet* at the
Moscow Arts Theatre jointly with
Stanislavsky and Sulerzhitsky.

Vladimir Pchelin
1869–1941

266 *"Tap" Taxi Service and Car Hire*
Moscow, 1910
Lithographic poster (printed by I. N.
Kushnerev), 36 × 53
State Lenin Library

Kuz'ma Sergeevich Petrov-Vodkin
1878 KHVALYNSK (SARATOV PROVINCE) – 1939
LENINGRAD
Painter, theatre artist and writer.
Studied in Samara, at the Stieglitz
School (1895–97), at the Moscow
College (1897–1905) under Arkhipov
and Serov, at the Ažbè School in
Munich (1901) and at private academies
in Paris (1905–08), where his work
showed the influence of Puvis de
Chavannes. He participated in the
Zolotoe Runo salons (1909) and
exhibited with *Mir Iskusstva* (from
1911) and the Union of Russian Artists.
Much of his work during World War I
was based on the tradition of ancient
Russian religious art. He became a very
influential teacher, first at the
Zvantseva School (1910–15) and later at
the principal Leningrad art schools.

267 *River Bank*
Paris, 1908
Oil on canvas, 128 × 159
Signed and dated bottom left
State Russian Museum
[Illustrated p.117]

268 *The Master: Fantasy on an
Oriental Theme*
1907–08
Watercolour, bistre on paper, 24 × 30.6
State Russian Museum

269 *The Virgin of Tenderness Moving
Evil Hearts*
1914–15
Oil on canvas mounted on board,
100.2 × 100
Signed with initials bottom right
State Russian Museum
[Illustrated p.26]

Aleksandr Ivanovich Piskarev
Master silversmith.

270 Wine beaker
Moscow, 1908–1917
Silver, 21.4 × 9.6 × 9.6
Hallmark with maker's initials
State Historical Museum
[Illustrated p.248]

Vladimir Aleksandrovich Pokrovsky
1871–1931
Architect. Studied at the Petersburg
Academy (1892–98), where he was later
to teach (1912–17) His works include a
memorial church near Leipzig (1912–
13), a bank in Nizhny Novgorod (1913)
and the "Fedorovsky Gorodok" complex
at Tsarskoe Selo.

271 Competition project for the
Museum of Military History in St
Petersburg (not executed)
1908
Pencil, watercolour and white on
cardboard, 74.7 × 99.5
Signed and dated bottom right
A. V. Shchusev State Museum of
Architecture
[Illustrated p.222]

Competition project for a bank at
Nizhny Novgorod (see also nos.57, 58)
1916

272 Perspective
Coloured pencil, gouache and
watercolour on cardboard, 70 × 103
Signed and dated bottom right
A. V. Shchusev State Museum of
Architecture
[Illustrated p.223]

273 Interior of banking hall
Pencil, gouache, watercolour and white
on cardboard, 54 × 71
Signed and dated bottom
A. V. Shchusev State Museum of
Architecture
[Illustrated p.223]

Vasily Dmitrievich Polenov
1844 ST PETERSBURG – 1927 KALUGA PROVINCE
Painter and theatre artist. He began to
study painting with Chistyakov and F.
Iordan from 1859, later attending their
classes at the Petersburg Academy
(1863–71), while also studying law at
Petersburg University. He visited Italy,
France and Germany on a travelling
scholarship from the Academy (1872–
76). He participated as a volunteer in
the Balkan War (1876) and as an artist-
correspondent in the Russo-Turkish War
(1877–78), later travelling extensively in
the Near East. He was a member of the
Peredvizhniki from 1878 and from 1880
was one of the organisers of Savva
Mamontov's Abramtsevo Group, while
also teaching at the Moscow College
(1882–95).

274 *Feast of Vladimir at Krasnoe
Solnyshko*
1883
Design for a menu for a ceremonial
banquet on the coronation day of
Aleksandr III
Watercolour and bronze powder on
paper, 42.2 × 27.6
Signed with monogram and dated (16
February 1883) bottom right
State Tretyakov Gallery
[Illustrated p.140]

   At the foot is a musical quotation from
Glinka's *Ruslan and Lyudmila* and the text
"and the sign of joy, child of rain and
light, the rainbow appears again."

275 *Orpheus in the Kingdom of the
Dead*
1898
Design for a programme for a
production of Gluck's *Orphée* at the
Private Russian Opera, 1897–98 season
Watercolour on paper, 43.8 × 13.9
Signed and dated bottom right and
inscribed "Orpheus" on rock at upper
right
State Tretyakov Gallery
[Illustrated p.142]

276 *Orpheus in the Kingdom of the
Dead*
1898
Design for programme (see no.275)
Watercolour and lead pencil on paper,
31.7 × 11
Signed with initials and dated bottom
right
State Tretyakov Gallery

Elena Dmitrievna Polenova

1850–1898 MOSCOW

Painter, designer and illustrator.
Studied under Chistyakov from 1859
and later under Kramskoi at the OPKh
Drawing School (1863–67) and in
S. Chaplain's studio in Paris (1869–70).
Later (1880–82) she returned to the
OPKh Drawing School, studying
watercolour painting with E. Villiers de
l'Isle Adam and attending classes in
ceramics. She was one of the organisers
of Mamontov's Abramtsevo group,
managing the joinery workshops there.
She exhibited with the *Peredvizhniki*
(from 1889) and the Moscow Society of
Artists (from 1894). She was one of the
first artists to collect and illustrate old
Russian folk tales, a genre which was to
become an increasingly popular
hallmark of the National Style.

277 Table
Abramtsevo, 1880s
Carved oak, 79 × 89 × 65
State Historical Museum
[Illustrated p.233]

278 Stool
Abramtsevo, 1880s
Carved oak, 39 × 39 × 40.5
State Historical Museum

279 Framed wall mirror
Abramtsevo, 1880s
Carved oak, 42 × 25
State Historical Museum

280 *The War of the Mushrooms: Folk
Tale*, Moscow (R. Thiele), 1889
Phototypes, hand-coloured with
watercolours, 18.3 × 27
State Lenin Library
[Illustrated p.145]

281 Design for an ornament for a book
Early 1890s
Gouache, bronze powder and lead
pencil on paper, 23.8 × 11
Signed with monogram bottom right
State Tretyakov Gallery
[Illustrated p.142]

282 Frame for an address to the widow
of Emperor Aleksandr III, Mariya
Fedorovna
1894
Gouache, bronze powder, lead pencil
and varnish on cardboard, 35.7 × 27
Signed with monogram bottom right
State Tretyakov Gallery
[Illustrated p.144]

283 Illustration for the Russian fairy-tale
The Firebird
Late 1890s
Watercolour, Indian ink and brush on
paper mounted on cardboard, 31 × 22.2
Signed with initials bottom right
State Russian Museum
[Illustrated p.142]

284 Illustrations for *Russian Folk Tales
and Stories*, Moscow (I. Knebel'), [1906]
Autotypes, 31 × 22
State Lenin Library
[Illustrated p.19]

Aleksei Mikhailovich Remizov
1877–1957
Novelist.

See no.93

Nikolai Remizov (Re-mi)

1887 ST PETERSBURG – [UNKNOWN]

Graphic artist. Studied at the Petersburg
Academy (1908–17) and in Kardovsky's
studio. Did drawings for the magazines
Strekoza (The Dragonfly), *Satirikon* and
Novyi Satirikon and for various satirical
publications during the period of the
1905–07 revolutions, as well as book
illustrations and posters. He lived
abroad from 1918.

285 *Satirikon* magazine's costume ball
St Petersburg, n.d.
Lithographic poster (printed by
R. Golicke and A. Wilborg), 114 × 80
State Lenin Library
[Illustrated p.163]

286 *Apollon*, monthly review
St Petersburg, 1911
Lithographic poster (printed in studios
of OPKh Design school), 58 × 69
State Lenin Library
[Illustrated p.75]

Ivan Rerberg
1865–1938

287 Bookplate for "V. L."
N.d.
Colour lithograph, 10 × 14.5
State Lenin Library
[Illustrated p.170]

See also no.484

Nikolai Konstantinovich Roerich

1874 ST PETERSBURG – 1947 NAGGAR, PUNJAB

Painter, theatre artist, writer and
ethnographer. Studied at the Petersburg

Academy (1893–97) under Kuindzhi
while also studying law at Petersburg
University. In 1901 he attended
Cormon's studio in Paris. He exhibited
with *Mir Iskusstva*, of which he was
chairman from 1910, the Union of
Russian Artists (from 1903) and with
many groups, in addition to one-man
shows both in Russia and abroad; he
was included in Diaghilev's Salon
d'Automne show (1906). He was
secretary of the Society for the
Encouragement of the Arts (OPKh)
from 1901 and became director (1906–
18) of its School in St Petersburg. He
executed designs for Diaghilev's *Ballets
Russes* (1908–14), including those for
The Rite of Spring. He worked on
exhibitions and art education projects in
the U.S.A. (1920–22) before settling in
India (1923), where from 1938 until his
death he was in charge of a research
station in the Himalayas. During the
Second World War he initiated the
international "Roerich Pact" for the
defence of cultural monuments.

288 *Guests from Overseas*
1901
Oil on canvas, 85 × 112.5
State Tretyakov Gallery

289 *Landscape*
1900s
Pastel on cardboard, 46 × 46
Saratov Museum of Fine Art

290 *Stone Age Dance in the North*
1904
Design for a pottery frieze
Gouache on paper mounted on
cardboard, 13.4 × 60.8
State Tretyakov Gallery
[Illustrated p.25]

291 *Patrol*
1905
Oil on canvas, 148 × 148
State Russian Museum
[Illustrated p.112]

292 Design for the décor for *The
Polovtsian Dances*
1909
Tempera and bodycolours on canvas,
58.5 × 84.5
Trustees of the Victoria and Albert
Museum

The Polovtsian Dances are the
centrepiece of Act II of Borodin's *Prince
Igor*, which was given as part of a mixed
programme on the opening night of
Diaghilev's first ballet season in Paris in
1909. The choreography was by Fokine.

Ivan Nikolaevich Ropet (Petrov)
1845–1908
Architect. Studied at the Petersburg Academy (1861–71). A leading exponent of the Neo-Russian style, derived from sevetcenth-century Russian architecture and folk art, he designed the bath-house and museum at Abramtsevo.

293 Dustcover, binding and illustrations for Nikodim Kondakov, *History and Memorials of Byzantine Enamel*, St Petersburg (A. Zvenigorodsky), 1892
37 × 30
Dustcover: silk cloth with woven design in gold and silver (manufactured by the Sapozhnikov Brothers, Moscow)
Book (colour lithographs with gold and silver blocking): printed by M. Stasyulevich, St Petersburg and A. Osterrit, Frankfurt-am-Main
State Lenin Library
[Illustrated pp.141, 143, 245]

Fedor Ivanovich Rückert
Master silversmith, active from 1890 until the 1917 Revolution, known for his cloisonné enamels.

294 Coffee Spoon
Moscow (Fabergé), 1908–17
Silver gilt and enamel, length: 10.8
Hallmark with maker's initials and firm's mark
State Historical Museum
[Illustrated p.247]

295 Small *kovsh*
Moscow, 1908–17
Silver gilt and enamel, 4.4 × 9.5 × 5.1
Hallmark with maker's initials
State Historical Museum
[Illustrated p.246]

Margarita Sabashnikova
1882–1973
Painter and graphic artist. First wife of the poet Maksimilian Voloshin. Her work was included in Diaghilev's Salon d'Automne show (1906).

296 Cover for Konstantin Bal'mont, *Liturgy of Beauty*, Moscow (Grif), 1905
Lithograph, gold blocking, 18.7 × 15.2
State Lenin Library
[Illustrated p.71]

Anatoly V. Samoilov

297 Untitled
St Petersburg, 1901
Lithographic poster (printed by R. Golicke), 77 × 51
State Lenin Library

298 *Imperial Navy Fund*
St Petersburg, 1910
Lithographic poster (printed by A. Il'in), 104 × 71
State Lenin Library
[Illustrated p.156]

Nikolai Semenovich Samokish
1860–1944
Painter. Studied at the Petersburg Academy (1879–85). Specialist in military subjects.

299 Binding and endpapers for Nikolai Kutepov, *Tsarist and Imperial Hunting in Russia in the late Seventeenth and Eighteenth Centuries*, vol.3, St Petersburg (State Stationery Office), 1902 (see also no.199)
Binding: blue morocco-backed cloth with gold, silver and coloured blocking; metal corners in the form of the Russian imperial double-headed eagle
Illustrations: autotypes, colour lithographs, lithographs, line blocks, by Surikov, Serov, Bakst, Lanceray, Benois et al., 37 × 28.5
State Lenin Library
[Illustrated pp.139, 142, 211]

Elena Samokish-Sudkovskaya
1863–1924
Graphic artist. Studied at the Helsingfors Art School under Vereshchagin and later lived and worked for a time in Paris. Exhibited from 1889. Worked in St Petersburg on posters, illustrations for books and journals (*Niva* and others) and postcards.

300 Poster for the journal *Niva* for 1899, offering subscribers a free set of Goncharov's *Complete Works*
St Petersburg, 1898
Lithographic poster (printed by A. F. Marx), 103 × 70
State Lenin Library
[Illustrated p.33]

301 *First International Costume Exhibition*
St Petersburg, 1902
Lithographic poster (printed by R. Golicke), 86 × 62
State Lenin Library
[Illustrated p.162]

302 Programme for Red Cross Society concert, 23 November 1902
St Petersburg (printed by A. I. Wilborg)
Colour lithograph, 30 × 24
State Lenin Library
[Illustrated p.154]

303 Design of Anton Chekhov, *Complete Works*, vols.1–3, St Petersburg (A. F. Marx), 1903, 20 × 13.5
State Lenin Library

Nikolai Nikolaevich Sapunov
1880 MOSCOW – 1912 TERIOKI
Painter and theatre artist. Studied at the Moscow College (1896–1901). Exhibited with the *Peredvizhniki* (1900), *Mir Iskusstva* (from 1902), *Golubaya Roza* (1907), the *Zolotoe Runo* salons (1908–09) and the Union of Russian Artists (1907–10).

304 *Portrait of the Artist Nikolai Milioti*
1908
Oil on cardboard, 77 × 66.7
State Tretyakov Gallery
[Illustrated p.120]
    Another version of this 1908 portrait is in the State Russian Museum, Leningrad.

305 *Mystic Tea-drinking*
1912
Oil on canvas, 93.5 × 128
State Tretyakov Gallery
[Illustrated p.39]

Martiros Sergeevich Sar'yan
1880 NAKHICHEVAN-NA-DONU (ROSTOV) – 1972 YEREVAN
Painter, graphic and theatre artist. Studied at the Moscow College (1897–1904) under Serov and Korovin, returning frequently to his native Armenia. He travelled in the Near East in 1910, 1911 and 1913. He participated in the *Golubaya Roza* exhibition (1907) and in the *Zolotoe Runo* salons (1908–09), in the second of which his work was very prominent.

306 *By the Pomegranate Tree*
1907
Tempera on cardboard, 34.6 × 52.5
Signed and dated bottom left
State Tretyakov Gallery
[Illustrated p.118]

307 *Flowers at Sambek*
1914
Tempera on canvas, 60 × 71
Signed and dated bottom right
State Tretyakov Gallery
[Illustrated p.120]

Aleksandr Ivanovich Savinov
1881–1942
Painter. Studied at the Bogolyubov
Drawing School in Saratov (1897–1900)
under Konovalov and at the Petersburg
Academy School under Tsionglinsky,
Repin and Kardovsky (1901–08),
travelling to Italy on an Academy
scholarship in 1909–11. He taught at
Svomas in Saratov (1918–21) and at the
Academy of Arts in Leningrad (from
1922). He exhibited with the New
Society of Artists (from 1910) and with
other groups both in Russia and abroad.

308 *Old Church at Saratov*
1901
Oil on canvas, 77 × 56.5
Saratov State Art Museum

309 *Dusk*
1902–04
Oil on canvas, 54.5 × 81
Saratov State Art Museum
[Illustrated p.107]

Zinaida Evgen'evna Serebryakova
1884 NESKUCHNOE ESTATE, NR. KHAR'KOV – 1967
PARIS
Painter. The sister of Evgeny Lanceray,
she studied at the Tenisheva School
(1901) under Repin, in Braz's studio
(1903–05) and at the Académie de la
Grande Chaumière in Paris. She
exhibited from 1910. From 1924 she
lived in France.

310 *At the Dressing-Table: Self-Portrait*
1909
Oil on canvas mounted on cardboard,
75 × 65
Signed and dated top right
State Tretyakov Gallery
[Illustrated p.125]

Valentin Aleksandrovich Serov
1865 ST PETERSBURG – 1911 MOSCOW
Painter. As a child he studied under K.
Köpping in Munich (1873–74) and then,
on frequent stays at the Abramtsevo
estate, under Repin (1874–80) and at
the Petersburg Academy (1880–85)
under Chistyakov. He travelled widely
in Europe and was awarded a *grand
prix* at the Paris 1900 *Exposition
Universelle*. He was a member of the
Peredvizhniki (from 1894), *Mir
Iskusstva*, *The 36* and the Union of
Russian Artists; he was included in
Diaghilev's Salon d'Automne show
(1906). Through his friendship with
Savva Mamontov he was closely linked
with the Abramtsevo group. He

designed productions for Mamontov's
Private Russian Opera (1896, 1898) and
later for the Mariinsky Theatre in St
Petersburg. He taught at the Moscow
College (1897–1909).

311 *Portrait of Mara Oliv*
1895
Oil on canvas, 88 × 68.5
State Russian Museum
[Illustrated p.111]

Mara Konstantinova Oliv (1870–1963),
whose first married name was Mamontova
and whose second married name was
Sverbeeva, was a relative of Savva
Mamontov. Serov wrote of his model:
"She is like a little mouse, peering out
with her sharp eyes from a dark corner."

312 *Portrait of Konstantin Bal'mont*
1905
Coloured autotype, 17.5 × 10.5
State Lenin Library

313 *Rape of Europa*
1910
Lead pencil on paper, 23.7 × 31.4
State Russian Museum
[Illustrated p.184]
One of a number of studies made for a
painting of the subject.

314 *Rape of Europa*
1910
Bronze, 28.5 × 43.5 × 24.5
Foundry mark: E. Robecchi, Moscow
State Tretyakov Gallery
[Illustrated p.184]
Sculptural study for the same painting.
Other versions exist in porcelain, and
marble copies were made in 1915.

315 *Departure for the Hunt*
1910
Design for a detail of the curtain for the
ballet *Sheherazade*, to music by
Rimsky-Korsakov
Gouache on paper mounted on
cardboard, 38.5 × 57.5
State Tretyakov Gallery
[Illustrated p.35]

316 *Diana; Eros, Apollo and Daphne;
Venus*
1911
Design for a mural for the dining-room
of the house of V. V. Nosov in Moscow
Lead pencil on paper, 25.4 × 45.7
Inscribed on verso
State Tretyakov Gallery
[Illustrated p.210]

317 *Diana; Eros, Apollo and Daphne*
1911
Design for a mural for the dining-room
of the house of V. V. Nosov
Lead pencil on paper, 26.7 × 43
State Tretyakov Gallery

See also no.299

Aleksei Viktorovich Shchusev
1873 KISHINEV – 1949 MOSCOW
Architect. Studied at the Petersburg
Academy (1891–97) under Leonty
Benois and Repin. In the 1900s he
worked in St Petersburg in the
architectural offices of Benois, Kotov
and Mel'tser, also making independent
designs for ecclesiastical buildings in
Moscow and the Ukraine. He was
involved in the design of Moscow's
Kazan' Station from 1913. He taught at
the Stroganov Design School (1913–18)
and at Vkhutemas (1918–24), and was
director of the State Tretyakov Gallery
(1926–29) and later organiser and
director of the State Architecture
Museum (1946–49). He took part in the
first plan for the reconstruction of
Moscow (1918–25) and built a number
of public and administrative buildings in
the city, including the Lenin
Mausoleum in Red Square.

318 Memorial church on Kulikovo
Field: elevation
1908
Indian ink and watercolour on paper,
65.6 × 50.7
Signed and dated bottom right
A. V. Shchusev State Museum of
Architecture
[Illustrated p.193]

Almshouse and church for Nikolai
Mirlikinsky at Bari, Italy
1912

319 General view of the church
Charcoal, tempera and watercolour on
cardboard, 66.5 × 62.5
Signed bottom right
A. V. Shchusev State Museum of
Architecture

320 Bird's-eye view of whole complex
Indian ink, pencil and watercolour on
cardboard, 50.4 × 67.6
Signed bottom right
A. V. Shchusev State Museum of
Architecture
[Illustrated p.193]

Fedor Osipovich Shekhtel'

1859 ST PETERSBURG – 1926 MOSCOW

Architect, theatre and graphic artist. He studied at the Moscow College (1875–77) and in the 1880s carried out theatrical and graphic work, while working in the offices of the architects K. Tersky and A. Kaminsky. His principal activity as an architect was concentrated in the years from 1893 to 1912. In 1901 he designed the Russian pavilions at the Glasgow International Exhibition. He taught (1898–1925) at the Stroganov Design School, at Vkhutemas and at the Tashkent Polytechnic Institute. From 1908 he was chairman of the Moscow Architectural Society.

....

Mansion of Z. G. Morozova on Spiridonovka (Aleksei Tolstoy) Street, Moscow
1893–6

321 Principal elevation
Indian ink and pencil on paper, 56.2 × 92.4
A. V. Shchusev State Museum of Architecture
[Illustrated p.196]

322 Details of elevations
Indian ink, coloured ink and watercolour on paper, 59.7 × 96.2
Signed and dated (1893) bottom right
A. V. Shchusev State Museum of Architecture
[Illustrated p.48]

323 Details of consoles with corbels
Indian ink, coloured ink, pencil and watercolour on paper, 29.7 × 46.5
Signed right
A. V. Shchusev State Museum of Architecture

324 Entrance lobby: design for decorative screen facing entrance
Indian ink, coloured ink and watercolour on paper, 64.6 × 48
Signed and dated (1894) bottom
A. V. Shchusev State Museum of Architecture
[Illustrated p.197]

325 Entrance lobby: design for balustrade of stair into entrance hall (unexecuted version)
Indian ink, pencil, watercolour and white on coloured cardboard, 47 × 29
Signed right
A. V. Shchusev State Museum of Architecture

326 Entrance lobby: design for balustrade of stair into entrance hall (executed version)
Coloured ink, pencil, watercolour and white on coloured cardboard, 46.3 × 29
Signed right
A. V. Shchusev State Museum of Architecture
[Illustrated p.47]

327 Entrance lobby: stair into entrance hall
Photo (1890s), 28 × 22
A. V. Shchusev State Museum of Architecture
[Illustrated p.197]

328 Entrance hall: design for light fitting
Indian ink, pencil, watercolour and white on coloured cardboard, 46.8 × 29.6
Signed right
A. V. Shchusev State Museum of Architecture

329 Main staircase: plan, elevation and details Indian ink, coloured ink and watercolour on paper, 63 × 98.5
Signed and dated (20 August 1894) bottom right
A. V. Shchusev State Museum of Architecture
[Illustrated p.196]

330 Main staircase
Photo (1890s), 29.2 × 22.2
A. V. Shchusev State Museum of Architecture
[Illustrated p.196]

331 Dining-room: design for fireplace
Indian ink, pencil and watercolour on paper, 63.8 × 46.5
Signed bottom right
A. V. Shchusev State Museum of Architecture

332 Dining-room: design for light fitting (executed version)
Indian ink, pencil, watercolour and white on coloured cardboard, 48 × 29.3
Signed bottom right
A. V. Shchusev State Museum of Architecture
[Illustrated p.197]

333 Dining-room: design for light fitting (version not executed)
Indian ink, pencil, watercolour and white on coloured cardboard, 48 × 29.3
Signed right
A. V. Shchusev State Museum of Architecture

334 Dining-room: general view
Photo (1890s), 33.9 × 41.7
A. V. Shchusev State Museum of Architecture
[Illustrated p.47]

335 Drawing room: decorative treatment of walls and fireplace (version not executed)
Indian ink, pencil, watercolour and white on coloured cardboard, 30 × 40.5
Signed bottom
A. V. Shchusev State Museum of Architecture

....

Mansion of A. V. Morozov, Podsosensky Lane, Moscow (interiors of principal rooms in building designed by D. N. Chikagov in 1869)
1895

336 Gothic Study
Photo (1890s), 42.5 × 34.7
A. V. Shchusev State Museum of Architecture
[Illustrated p.15]

337 Gothic Study
Photo (1890s), 42.6 × 34
A. V. Shchusev State Museum of Architecture
[Illustrated p.50]

....

338 Estate of Savva T. Morozov at Pokrovskoe-Runtsovo, near Moscow: wall treatments for Great Hall
1900
Indian ink, pencil, watercolour and white on cardboard, 27 × 38
Signed bottom right
A. V. Shchusev State Museum of Architecture
[Illustrated p.207]

339 Design for dacha of S. Y. Levenson at Peredelkino, near Moscow
1900
Coloured ink and watercolour on paper, 34.5 × 55
Signed bottom right
A. V. Shchusev State Museum of Architecture
[Illustrated p.219]

....

Russian Pavilions at the International Exhibition, Glasgow
1901

340 Block Plan
Proposed sites of Russian pavilions marked by Shekhtel' in red ink (not corresponding to their final location)
Printed plan, 47.5 × 61.5
A. V. Shchusev State Museum of Architecture

341 Central Pavilion: elevation
Indian ink and pencil on paper,
68.5 × 50
Signed bottom right
A. V. Shchusev State Museum of
Architecture
[Illustrated p.201]

342 Central Pavilion: plan and section
with constructional details
Pencil on coloured paper, 106.5 × 70
Signed
A. V. Shchusev State Museum of
Architecture
[Illustrated p.51]

343 Central Pavilion: details of
elevation, section and plan and of finials
Pencil, Indian ink and watercolour on
coloured paper, 71 × 103.5
A. V. Shchusev State Museum of
Architecture
[Illustrated p.51]

344 Agriculture Pavilion: details of
elevation and of finials
Pencil, Indian ink and watercolour on
coloured paper, 71 × 103.5
A. V. Shchusev State Museum of
Architecture

345 Agriculture Pavilion: details of
finials
Pencil, watercolour and bronze powder
on tracing-paper mounted on paper,
36.5 × 60.2
Signed bottom right
A. V. Shchusev State Museum of
Architecture
[Illustrated p.201]

346 Mining Pavilion: details of plan and
of roof
Pencil and watercolour on coloured
paper, 123.5 × 71.2
A. V. Shchusev State Museum of
Architecture

347 Mining Pavilion: details of plan,
section and entrance
Pencil and watercolour on paper,
117 × 69
A. V. Shchusev State Museum of
Architecture

348 Forestry Pavilion: details of plan,
elevation and section
Pencil on coloured paper, 117 × 69
A. V. Shchusev State Museum of
Architecture

349 Cover, title-page and first sheet of
album *The Buildings of Russian Section
of International Exhibition in Glasgow.
Archit: F. Schechtel in Moscow*,
Moscow (A. A. Levenson), 1901
Printed on green and white paper,
20 × 30
A. V. Shchusev State Museum of
Architecture
[Illustrated p.52]

350 Mining and Central Pavilions
Illustration from Glasgow album
(no.349)
Phototype from photograph, 20 × 30
A. V. Shchusev State Museum of
Architecture
[Illustrated p.51]

351 Agriculture Pavilion
Illustration from Glasgow album
(no.349)
Phototype from photograph, 20 × 30
A. V. Shchusev State Museum of
Architecture
[Illustrated p.50]

352 The four pavilions: (left to right)
Agriculture, Mining, Central, Forestry
Illustration from Glasgow album
(no.349)
Phototype from photograph, 20 × 30
A. V. Shchusev State Museum of
Architecture
[Illustrated p.201]

353 Central Pavilion, illustration on the
architect's bookplate
Line block, 7.7 × 5.1
Private collection
[Illustrated p.170]

....

Yaroslavl' Station, Moscow
1902–03

354 Elevation
Photograph (1900s) of architect's
drawing (signed bottom right), 34 × 47.9
A. V. Shchusev State Museum of
Architecture
[Illustrated p.53]

355 Reproduction of perspective
drawing
Postcard (colour phototype), 9 × 14.1
A. V. Shchusev State Museum of
Architecture

356 General view of station
Tinted photographic postcard (colour
phototype), 9 × 13.7
A. V. Shchusev State Museum of
Architecture
[Illustrated p.55]

....

Mansion of A. I. Derozhinskaya in
Shtatny (Kropotkinsky) Lane, Moscow
(now Australian Embassy)
1901–02

357 Elevation (version not executed)
Indian ink, pencil and watercolour on
paper, 29.3 × 42.6
Signed bottom right
A. V. Shchusev State Museum of
Architecture
[Illustrated p.202]

358 Design of railings and gateway
Pencil and watercolour on tracing paper
mounted on paper, 40.2 × 80
Signed bottom right
A. V. Shchusev State Museum of
Architecture
[Illustrated p.202]

359 View from the street
Photo (1900s), 34 × 48
A. V. Shchusev State Museum of
Architecture
[Illustrated p.62]

360 Great Hall: design for fireplace
Pencil, coloured pencil and watercolour
on coloured paper, 41.2 × 54.7
Signed bottom right
A. V. Shchusev State Museum of
Architecture
[Illustrated p.205]

361 Great Hall: design for light fitting
Indian ink, watercolour and white on
paper, 28 × 32
Signed lower right
A. V. Shchusev State Museum of
Architecture
[Illustrated p.204]

362 Great Hall
Photo (1900s), 34 × 48
A. V. Shchusev State Museum of
Architecture
[Illustrated p.204]

363 Dining-room: design for end wall
with buffet (version not executed)
Coloured ink and watercolour on paper,
44.5 × 64.2
Signed bottom right
A. V. Shchusev State Museum of
Architecture
[Illustrated p.62]

364 Dining-room: design for light fitting
Indian ink, pencil, coloured pencil and
watercolour on tracing paper mounted
on paper, 129.5 × 80.2
A. V. Shchusev State Museum of
Architecture
[Illustrated p.203]

365 Dining-room: general view
Photo (1900s), 34 × 48
A. V. Shchusev State Museum of
Architecture
[Illustrated p.203]

366 Study: design for upholstery fabric
(version in ochre colours)
Pencil and watercolour on tracing
paper, 64 × 73.2
A. V. Shchusev State Museum of
Architecture
[Illustrated p.63]

367 Study: general view
Photo (1900s), 34 × 48
A. V. Shchusev State Museum of
Architecture
[Illustrated p.205]

368 Ladies' morning room: wall
treatments
Indian ink, pencil and watercolour on
tracing paper, 57.5 × 36.7
A. V. Shchusev State Museum of
Architecture
[Illustrated p.205]

369 Bedroom: wall treatment
Indian ink, pencil, watercolour and
white on paper, 39 × 56.2
Signed bottom right
A. V. Shchusev State Museum of
Architecture

370 Menu for house-warming party,
6 February 1903, with general view of
house (signed with initials bottom right)
Colour lithograph (printed by A. A.
Levenson), 39 × 56.2
A. V. Shchusev State Museum of
Architecture
[Illustrated p.173]

Mansion of S. P. Ryabushinsky on
Malaya Nikitskaya (Kachalov Street),
Moscow (now Gorky Museum)
1900–02

371 View from the street
Photo (1900s), 34 × 41
A. V. Shchusev State Museum of
Architecture
[Illustrated p.59]

372 Upper staircase landing
Photo (1900s), 48 × 33.8
A. V. Shchusev State Museum of
Architecture

373 Designs for exterior mosaic frieze
Watercolour on paper mounted on
cardboard, 29 × 42
A. V. Shchusev State Museum of
Architecture
[Illustrated p.206]

374 Dining-room: designs for wall
treatment
Indian ink, coloured ink, watercolour
and bronze powder on paper,
30.2 × 46.8
Signed bottom right
A. V. Shchusev State Museum of
Architecture
[Illustrated p.59]

Competition project for the church on
the estate of A. M. Mal'tsev at
Balakavo, Saratov province
1908–10

375 Western elevation
Coloured ink, pencil, watercolour and
white on paper mounted on cardboard,
84 × 66.8
Signed bottom right
A. V. Shchusev State Museum of
Architecture
[Illustrated p.194]

376 Longitudinal section
Coloured ink, pencil and watercolour on
paper mounted on cardboard, 84 × 66
Signed bottom right
A. V. Shchusev State Museum of
Architecture
[Illustrated p.195]

  These designs were executed; for
another, unexecuted, competition entry,
see no.250.

The Architect's own house on Bol'shaya
Sadovaya, Moscow
1909–10

377 Elevation
Indian ink and watercolour on paper,
31.8 × 43.7
Signed bottom right
A. V. Shchusev State Museum of
Architecture
[Illustrated p.220]

378 Plan of the ground floor
Blueprint on tracing paper, with
annotations in purple ink, 37 × 32.3
A. V. Shchusev State Museum of
Architecture

"Arts" Cinema on Arbat Square,
Moscow
1912

379 Elevation
Indian ink, pencil and watercolour on
paper, 37.7 × 55.5
Signed bottom right
A. V. Shchusev State Museum of
Architecture
[Illustrated p.220]

380 Plan of the first floor
Indian ink, pencil and watercolour on
paper, 37.9 × 64.2
A. V. Shchusev State Museum of
Architecture
[Illustrated p.221]

381 Longitudinal section
Indian ink, pencil and watercolour on
paper, 38.7 × 73.5
A. V. Shchusev State Museum of
Architecture
[Illustrated p.79]

382 Exhibition Building in Kamergersky
Lane, Moscow: elevation (version not
executed)
1913–15
Indian ink and pencil on tracing paper,
31.5 × 22.8
Signed bottom right
A. V. Shchusev State Museum of
Architecture
[Illustrated p.221]

K. Shervashidze
Graphic artist.

383 Cover and illustrations for
Maksimilian Voloshin, *The Deaf Mute
Demons*
Khar'kov (Kamena), 1919
Line blocks, 16 × 12
State Lenin Library

V. Sikagev
Firm of silversmiths.

384 Marriage crown
Moscow, 1899–1908
Silver gilt with enamel, Urals stones,
glass, velvet, 19.2 × 18.5
Hallmark
State Historical Museum
[Illustrated p.243]

Fedor Kuz'mich Sologub
1863 ST PETERSBURG – 1927 LENINGRAD
Poet and prose writer.

See no.17

Sergei Solomko
1859–1928
Graphic artist, illustrator and
watercolourist. He worked for *Jugend*
and illustrated several books for French
publishers.

385 Bookplate for the antiquarian
booksellers V. I. Klochkov, St
Petersburg
N.d.
Colour lithograph, 9 × 6.5
State Lenin Library
[Illustrated p.170]

386 Bookplate for S. K. Kuznetsov
N.d.
Colour lithograph (lithographer:
I. Chuksin), 7 × 3.5
State Lenin Library
[Illustrated p.170]

Mikhail Solomonov
Graphic artist.

387 Bookplate for V. I. Anisimov:
"Know Thyself"
N.d.
Autotype, line block, 8 × 10.5
State Lenin Library
[Illustrated p.170]

388 Binding for V. Korolenko, *Complete
Works*, vol.1. Petrograd (A. F. Marx),
1914
20 × 13.5
State Lenin Library

Konstantin Andreevich Somov
1869 ST PETERSBURG – 1939 PARIS
Painter and graphic artist. Son of the
senior curator at the Hermitage, he
studied at the Petersburg Academy
School under Vereshchagin and
Chistyakov (1888–97), in Repin's studio
from 1894, and at the Académie
Colarossi in Paris (1897–99). He was
one of the organisers of the *Mir
Iskusstva* group in 1899, one of *The 36*
and a member of the Union of Russian
Artists from 1903. He was included in
Diaghilev's Salon d'Automne show
(1906). He lived abroad from 1923. One
of his contemporaries called Somov the
"singer of rainbows and kisses", and he
created his own stylistic world in which
fantasy and reality, naturalism and
theatricality, the 18th and 20th
centuries, are all subtly interwoven.

389 *Lady by a Pond*
1896
Oil on canvas, 89 × 71
Signed and dated bottom left
State Tretyakov Gallery
[Illustrated p.106]
   Done as an assignment for a painting on
a freely chosen subject when Somov was a
pupil of Repin.

390 *Sultana*
1899
Design for a snuff-box executed for the
Lukutin factory
Gouache, Indian ink, bronze powder,
brush and pen on paper, 13.5 × 27.7
Signed with monogram and dated in silver
State Tretyakov Gallery
[Illustrated p.255]

391 *Island of Love*
1900
Oil on canvas, 62.3 × 81.7
Signed and dated top right
State Tretyakov Gallery
[Illustrated p.105]

392 Cover for *Mir Iskusstva*, 1900 no.3–4
Line block, 32 × 25.5
State Lenin Library

393 Programme Cover: Griboedov's *Woe
from Wit* at the Hermitage Theatre
Moscow (printed by A. A. Levenson), 1902
Colour lithograph, gilt, 27.5 × 20
State Lenin Library
[Illustrated p.154]

394 Postcard for the Red Cross: Saturday
(from the series *The Days of the Week*)
St Petersburg (printed by N. Kadushin),
1904 or 1905
Colour lithograph, 9 × 14
State Lenin Library
[Illustrated p.171]

395 Postcard for the Red Cross: Sunday
(from the series *The Days of the Week*)
St Petersburg (printed by N. Kadushin),
1904 or 1905
Colour lithograph, 9 × 14
State Lenin Library
[Illustrated p.171]

396 *Lovers*
Imperial Porcelain Factory, 1905
Porcelain group, overglaze painting,
14 × 18 × 12
State Historical Museum

397 *The Firebird*
1907
Cover design for Bal'mont's book of poems
(no.398)
Gouache, watercolour, bronze powder and
collage on paper mounted on cardboard,
25.4 × 21.1
Dated (February 1907) bottom right
State Tretyakov Gallery
[Illustrated p.148]

398 Cover from Konstantin Bal'mont, *The
Firebird: Music to the Slav's Ear*, Moscow
(Skorpion), 1907
Colour lithograph, 21 × 17
State Lenin Library

399 *Portrait of Aleksandr Blok*
1907
Published in *Zolotoe Runo*, 1908 no.1
Autotype, 31 × 22
State Lenin Library

400 *Teatr*
1907
Cover design for Blok's *Lyric Dramas*
(no.401)
Watercolour, white wash, Indian ink,
brush and pen on paper, 29.3 × 21.7
Signed bottom right, dated (March
1907) bottom left
State Tretyakov Gallery

401 Cover from Aleksandr Blok, *Lyric
Dramas: The Travelling Show; The
King in the Square; An Unknown
Woman*, St Petersburg (Shipovnik), 1908
(copy signed by the author).
Colour lithograph, 17.1 × 12.8
State Lenin Library
[Illustrated p.24]

402 *Portrait of Mikhail Kuzmin*
1909
Colour autotype, 20 × 13
State Lenin Library

403 Title-page for Aleksandr Benois,
*Tsarskoe Selo in the Time of Empress
Elizaveta Petrovna*, St Petersburg
(R. Golicke and A. Wilborg), 1910
Colour lithograph, 32.5 × 25.5
State Lenin Library

404 Cover for Vyacheslav Ivanov, *Cor
ardens*, Moscow (Skorpion), 1911
Colour lithograph (printed by
N. Kadushin), 22.9 × 16.8
State Lenin Library
[Illustrated p.74]

405 *In the Forest*
1914
Oil on canvas, 113 × 142
Signed and dated bottom right
State Russian Museum
[Illustrated p.123]

406 Illustrated book: *Le Livre de la
Marquise: Recueil de Poésie et de
Prose*, St Petersburg (R. Golicke and
A. Wilborg), 1918
Lithographs, 26 × 19
State Lenin Library

407 *Harlequin and Lady*
1921
Oil on canvas, 48 × 37.5
Signed with initials and dated bottom
right
State Russian Museum

Dmitry Semenovich Stelletsky
1875 BREST-LITOVSK – 1947 PARIS
Sculptor, painter, theatre artist and
illustrator. Studied at the Petersburg
Academy (1896–1903) under Zaleman
and Beklemishev and at the Académie
Julian in Paris (1904). He was included
in Diaghilev's Salon d'Automne show
(1906) and exhibited with the Union of
Russian Artists (from 1910), *Mir
Iskusstva* (from 1912), the New Society
of Artists etc. From 1914 he lived in
Cannes and Paris.

408 *Portrait of Boris Anrep*
Paris, 1909
Bronze, 30.5 × 23 × 15
Signed and dated on the back
State Russian Museum
[Illustrated p.180]

   Boris Vasil'evich Anrep (1883–1969),
poet, critic, mosaic artist. After 1917 he
lived in London and Paris.

S. Strenkovsky
Graphic artist.

409 Cinema poster (for I. N. Ermol'ev's
Artistic Films): *Panna Mary (Miss
Mary)*
Moscow, 1916
Lithographic poster (printed by Russian
Partnership), 167 × 70
State Lenin Library
[Illustrated p.83]

Serafim Nikolaevich Sud'binin
1867 NIZHNY NOVGOROD – 1944 PARIS
Painter and sculptor. He moved to Paris
in 1904, where he studied sculpture
under L. Sinaev-Bernstein and J. A.
Ingelbert (1904) and became a pupil
and assistant of Rodin (from 1906). He
was a member of the Union of Russian
Artists (from 1906) and participated in
many exhibitions in Europe and the
U.S.A.

410 *Anger*
Paris, 1906
Bronze on marble base, 39 × 40 × 34
Signed and dated on right
State Russian Museum
[Illustrated p.181]

   Anger belongs to the series "Monsters"
(1906–09), allegorical representations of
the human passions.

Sergei Yur'evich Sudeikin
1882 ST PETERSBURG – 1946 NEW YORK
Painter and theatre artist. Studied at
the Moscow College (intermittently
1897–1909) under Korovin and at the

Petersburg Academy School (1909–10)
under Kardovsky. He took part in the
Alaya Roza (1904) and *Golubaya Roza*
(1907) exhibitions and in the *Zolotoe
Runo* salons (1908–09) and exhibited
with The Union of Russian Artists, *Mir
Iskusstva* (from 1911) etc. He was
included in Diaghilev's Salon
d'Automne show (1906). He did designs
for theatres in Moscow and St
Petersburg, for Diaghilev's company
(executing designs by Bakst and Roerich
as well as his own) and, later, for Paris
(where he lived 1920–22) and New York
(where he settled in 1923). The
reminiscences of refined 18th-century
painting combined with elements of
unpolished folk primitivism reflect the
artist's blending of sentiment and irony.

411 *In the Park*
1907
Oil on cardboard, 53.8 × 66.8
Signed bottom right
State Russian Museum
[Illustrated p.122]

412 Design for frontispiece for *Vesy*,
1907 no.3
1907
Indian ink, white, bronze powder on
paper, 26 × 30.5
Inscribed, signed with monogram and
dated at bottom
State Tretyakov Gallery
[Illustrated p.147]

413 *Russian Venus*
1907
Watercolour, gouache, Indian ink, brush
and pen on cardboard, 29.4 × 37.6
Signed at bottom in silver
State Tretyakov Gallery
[Illustrated p.118]

414 *Oriental Subject*
N.d.
Pen and Indian ink on paper, 12 × 10.5
State Tretyakov Gallery

415 *Ornamental Landscape*
1910
Oil on canvas mounted on cardboard,
62.5 × 70.5
State Tretyakov Gallery

416 *Lovers in the Moonlight*
1910
Set design for O. I. Dymov's play *Spring
Madness*
Gouache, Indian ink, pen, watercolour
and chalk on paper mounted on
cardboard, 19.3 × 26.4
Signed bottom right
State Russian Museum

417 *Park in Front of a Castle*
1911
Oil on canvas, 71 × 90
Signed bottom left
State Russian Museum

   Design for the décor of Tchaikovsky's
Swan Lake for a performance at the Maly
Theatre in St Petersburg in 1911.

418 *Banquet Scene*
Early 1910s
Pen and Indian ink on paper, 11.5 × 18.5
Signed at bottom left and right
State Tretyakov Gallery

419 *Summer*
1910s
Watercolour, wax crayons, lead pencil
and varnish on paper, 40.3 × 31.1
Title inscribed bottom left
State Russian Museum

420, 421, 422 *England, Belgium* and
France
1914
Mixed media on cardboard, 50 × 30.7;
50 × 33.7; 50 × 33.7
Each signed bottom left
Saratov Museum of Fine Art
[Illustrated p.155]

   Costume designs for A. V. Bobrishchev-
Pushkin's *The Triumph of the Great
Powers*, produced by Vsevolod Meyerhold
on 11 October 1914 at the Mariinsky
Theatre, St Petersburg

423 Cover from N. Evreinov, *Pro Scena
Sua*, Petrograd (Prometei), 1915
Colour lithograph, 22 × 16
State Lenin Library

424 *Summer Landscape*
1916
Oil on canvas, 74.5 × 105.5
Signed bottom right; signed, dated and
inscribed with title on canvas verso
State Tretyakov Gallery

Ivan Filippovich Tarabrov
Master silversmith.

425 Frame for icon of the *Almighty
Saviour*
Icon: Oil on wood and silver gilt,
22.3 × 27
Frame: Moscow, 1908–17
Frame hallmarked with maker's initials
State Historical Museum
[Illustrated p.239]

426 Cigarette case
Moscow, 1899–1908
Silver, gold and sapphires, $1 \times 10.3 \times 8.2$
Hallmark with maker's initials
State Historical Museum
[Illustrated p.254]

Mikhail Yakovlevich Tarasov
Master silversmith.

427 Tea-glass holder
Moscow, 1899–1908
Silver, $9.5 \times 12 \times 7.2$
Hallmark with maker's initials
State Historical Museum
[Illustrated p.252]

428 Lady's purse
Moscow, 1908–17
Silver, $20.3 \times 10.8 \times 3$
Hallmark with maker's name
State Historical Museum
[Illustrated p.256]

N. Teffi
1872–1952
Nom-de-plume of Nadezhda
Aleksandrovna Buchinskaya, poet and
prose writer.

See nos.82, 162

Filipp Terent'ev
Master silversmith.

429 Dish
Moscow, 1899–1908
Silver, $3.7 \times 17.3 \times 12$
Hallmark with maker's initials
State Historical Museum
[Illustrated p.248]

Fredrik Tiander
1835 LOVIZA, FINLAND – [UNKNOWN]
Master goldsmith. Trained with his
father and in 1860 came to St
Petersburg as an apprentice. In 1898 he
had his own workshop, selling his goods
through the firm of Morozov.

430 Brooch
St Petersburg, late 19th century
Almandine, two tourmalines for the
eyes; beetle attached to gold pin set
with diamonds and rose-cut diamonds
and terminating in a pearl, length: 5.3
Hallmark with maker's initials
State Historical Museum
[Illustrated p.258]

Pavel Petrovich Trubetskoi
1866 INTRA, LAGO MAGGIORE – 1938
INTRA-PALLANZA
Sculptor. Received no formal art
education and from 1884 worked in
private studios in Milan, and from 1885
in his own studio. He moved from Italy
to live in Moscow (1887–98) and then St
Petersburg (1899–1906). He exhibited
with the *Peredvizhniki* from 1899 and
with *The 36* and was included in
Diaghilev's Salon d'Automne show
(1906). He taught at the Moscow
College (1898–1906). After 1906 he
lived in Paris and the U.S.A., returning
to Italy in 1932.

431 *Portrait of Mariya Tenisheva*
1899
Bronze, $46 \times 45 \times 44$
Signed and dated on left of base
State Russian Museum
[Illustrated p.40]
   Princess Mariya Klavdievna Tenisheva,
née Pyatkovskaya (1867–1928): patroness,
organiser of art schools in St Petersburg
and Smolensk and of the workshops at the
village of Talashkino, where Vrubel',
Golovin and Roerich worked.

432 *Portrait of Lev Tolstoy*
1899
Bronze, $34 \times 32 \times 30$
Signed and dated on base at left
State Russian Museum
[Illustrated p.177]
   Lev Nikolaevich Tolstoy (1828–1910),
writer.

Nikolai Pavlovich Ul'yanov
1875 ELETSK – 1949 MOSCOW
Painter and theatre artist. Studied in
Moscow with V. Mechkov (1888–89)
and at the Moscow College (1889–
1900). He also worked in the studio of
Serov, whose teaching assistant he
became. He was included in Diaghilev's
Salon d'Automne show (1906) and took
part in the *Golubaya Roza* exhibition
(1907) and the *Zolotoe Runo* salons
(1908–09). He travelled in Italy (1907)
and in France and Germany (1909–12).
In 1904 he designed productions for the
Moscow Arts Theatre. He taught at the
Zvantseva School (1900–07), the
Stroganov Design School (1915–18) and
at Vkhutemas (1919–21).

433 *Venetian Shop*
1907
Watercolour and gouache on dark grey
paper, 27.2×38.5
Signed and dated bottom left
State Tretyakov Gallery
[Illustrated p.131]

434 *The Invasion of Pan*
1914
Scene from Ovid's *Metamorphoses*,
from the artist's series *Antichnoe
(Antique Scenes)*
Black watercolour, Indian ink, brush,
pen and lead pencil on cream-coloured
paper, 31.6×43.4
Signed and dated bottom left
State Tretyakov Gallery

435 *The Invasion of Pan*
c. 1914–15
Illustration for Ovid's *Metamorphoses*
Tempera on cardboard, 64×100
Signed bottom right
Saratov Museum of Fine Art
[Illustrated p.27]

Petr Savvich Utkin
1877 TAMBOV – 1934 LENINGRAD
Painter. Studied in Saratov under
Konovalov and Baracci, then at the
Moscow College (1897–1907) under
Levitan, Korovin and Serov. He was
included in Diaghilev's Salon
d'Automne show (1906) and took part in
the *Alaya Roza* (1904) and *Golubaya
Roza* (1907) exhibitions and in the
Zolotoe Runo salons (1908–09), also
exhibiting with other groups.

436 *On the Volga*
1901
Tempera on cardboard, 35×31
Signed bottom left
Saratov Museum of Fine Art

437 *Sleep*
1905
Tempera on canvas, 68×69
Signed and dated bottom right
State Russian Museum
[Illustrated p.22]

438 *Peacocks in a Garden*
1905
Pen and Indian ink on brown paper,
28.1×23
Signed and dated bottom left, signed
with initials bottom right
State Russian Museum
[Illustrated p.118]

439 *Mimosa*
N.d.
Oil on canvas, 45×63
Signed bottom right
State Saratov Art Museum
[Illustrated p.39]

Sergei Ivanovich Vashkov
1879–1914
Designer and architect. Taught at the
Stroganov Design School and in 1904
was instrumental in setting up the
furniture and engraving workshops
there. Worked extensively, principally
in the design of ecclesiastical furnishings
for the Moscow firm of P. I.
Olovyanishnikov & Sons, whose art
department he headed for a number of
years.

440 Lion table
Moscow, 1900s
Carved oak, 78 × 72
State Historical Museum

441 Crucifix (painting attributed to
Mikhail Nesterov)
Moscow (made at P. I. Olovyanishnikov
& Sons workshop), 1900s
Carved wood with tempera painting,
217 × 138 × 36
State Historical Museum
[Illustrated p.241]

442 Icon case with icon *Christ Blessing*
Moscow (made at P. I. Olovyanishnikov
& Sons workshop), 1900s
Carved wood with tempera painting,
57 × 45 × 6.5
State Historical Museum
[Illustrated p.240]

443 Icon case with icon *Virgin of the
Sign*
Moscow (made at P. I. Olovyanishnikov
& Sons workshop), 1900s
Carved wood with tempera painting,
60 × 35.5 × 11
State Historical Museum
[Illustrated p.240]

Apollinary Mikhailovich Vasnetsov
1856 RIABOVO (NR. KIROV) – 1933 MOSCOW
Painter, graphic and theatre artist. Had
no formal artistic training. He exhibited
with the *Peredvizhniki* from 1883 and
with *The 36*, and he was one of the
organisers of the Union of Russian
Artists. He was included in Diaghilev's
Salon d'Automne show (1906). He
taught at the Moscow College
(1901–18).

See no.444

Viktor Mikhailovich Vasnetsov
1848 LOPIAL (KIROV REGION) – 1926 MOSCOW
Painter, designer and architect. Studied
in St Petersburg at the OPKh Drawing

School (1867–68) under Kramskoi and at
the Academy (1868–74) under Basin,
Chistyakov and Vereshchagin. He
exhibited with the *Peredvizhniki* from
1874. In the 1880s he was one of the
organisers of Mamontov's Abramtsevo
group and designed the church there
(1881–2). He executed murals in St
Vladimir's Cathedral in Kiev (1885–96)
and contributed to the design of the
Russian pavilions at the 1900 Paris
Exposition Universelle. He was
extremely active as an illustrator for
books and magazines and in producing
theatre designs.

444 (with Apollinary Mikhailovich
Vasnetsov)
Binding for *Album of Russian Folktales
and Legends* (ed. P. N. Petrov), St
Petersburg (Hermann Hoppe), 1875
End of 19th century
Silver embossed binding decorated with
semi-precious stones, 46.5 × 34.5
State Lenin Library

445 *Archangel Gabriel Kneeling*
1885–93
Unrealised version of design for an altar
in the Cathedral of St Vladimir, Kiev
Gouache, bronze powder and lead
pencil on paper mounted on cardboard,
48.9 × 30
State Tretyakov Gallery

446 *Archangel Michael Kneeling*
1885–93
Unrealised version of design for an altar
in the Cathedral of St Vladimir, Kiev
Gouache, bronze powder and lead
pencil on paper mounted on cardboard,
48.7 × 30
State Tretyakov Gallery
[Illustrated p.191]

447 Designs for decoration of the
Cathedral of St Vladimir, Kiev
1885–93
Watercolour, lead pencil and bronze
powder on paper mounted on
cardboard, 12.2 × 12.3; 12.3 × 11.8;
12 × 11.9; 12 × 11.2; 12.1 × 11.6;
12.1 × 11.7; 6 × 10.6 (× 2); 28.8 × 7
(× 2); 15.4 × 11; 15.5 × 11.5
Artist's inscriptions
State Tretyakov Gallery
[Illustrated p.192]
   The six medallions (top row, left to
right: *Prince Mikhail Chernigovsky*; *St
Mark*; *St Basil*; second row: *The Child
Gabriel*; *Prince Igor*; *St Theodore*) form
part of the decorative scheme for the
central arch; the panels at bottom right
and left form part of the composition *The
Bliss of Paradise* in the choir.

448 Menu for the coronation banquet of
Tsar Nikolai II and Tsaritsa Aleksandra
Fedorovna
Moscow (printed by A. A. Levenson),
14 May 1896
Colour lithograph, 93.5 × 32.5
State Lenin Library
[Illustrated p.172]

Leonid Aleksandrovich Vesnin
1880 NIZHNY NOVGOROD – 1933 MOSCOW
Architect. Studied at the Petersburg
Academy (1901–09) under Leonty
Benois. Working with his brothers
Viktor and Aleksandr, he designed and
built private houses, apartment
buildings, offices and industrial
buildings during the 1900s. After 1923,
when he became a Professor at the
Moscow Higher Technical College
(until 1931), he and his brothers did
collective projects which were in the
forefront of the Constructivist
movement.

Nosenkov's dacha at Ivanovo near
Moscow
1908–09

449 Perspective
Charcoal and pastel on coloured paper,
30.7 × 48.9
Signed bottom right
A. V. Shchusev State Museum of
Architecture
[Illustrated p.218]

450 Interior
Charcoal, coloured pencil and
watercolour on tracing paper mounted
on paper, 54 × 71.5
A. V. Shchusev State Museum of
Architecture
[Illustrated p.218]

House of N. L. Tarasov, Moscow
1910

451 Elevation
Indian ink and watercolour on paper,
52.3 × 74.2
Signed and dated bottom right
A. V. Shchusev State Museum of
Architecture
[Illustrated p.209]

452 Elevation (variant)
Indian ink, watercolour, gouache,
bronze powder on coloured paper,
26 × 55.7
A. V. Shchusev State Museum of
Architecture

453 Plan of ground floor
Coloured ink and white on coloured
cardboard, 26.6 × 36
A. V. Shchusev State Museum of
Architecture
[Illustrated p.209]

454 Project for unidentified dacha:
perspective
1900s
Pencil, coloured pencil on tracing paper,
32.5 × 61
A. V. Shchusev State Museum of
Architecture
[Illustrated p.208]

Vesy
Symbolist magazine published by
Skorpion in Moscow, 1904–09.

See nos.110, 112, 228, 412

Vasily Vladimirov
1880–1931
Painter and graphic artist. Studied in
Moscow (1900–03) and Munich (1904–
06). He was a member of the Moscow
Society of Artists (from 1902) and made
illustrations for magazines and books,
notably those by his friend Andrei Bely.

455 Cover of Andrei Bely, *Return:
Third Symphony*, Moscow (Grif), 1905
(copy signed by the author)
Line block, 21 × 16.5
State Lenin Library
[Illustrated p.147]

456 Cover of Aleksandr Blok, *Verses
about the Beautiful Lady*, Moscow
(Grif), 1905 [1904]
Line block, 20.2 × 16.3
State Lenin Library
[Illustrated p.69]

Maksimilian Voloshin
1877–1932
Painter, poet and art critic.

See no.383

Mikhail Aleksandrovich Vrubel'
1856 OMSK – 1910 ST PETERSBURG
Painter, designer, ceramist and sculptor.
Having studied at the OPKh Drawing
School in St Petersburg (1864, 1868–69)
and at the Drawing School of the
Society of Fine Arts in Odessa (1870–
72), he worked for a law degree at
Petersburg University (1874–79),
continuing his artistic studies with
Chistyakov. He was then an external
student at the Petersburg Academy

(1880–84), studying watercolour
painting with Repin. In 1884 he moved
to Kiev and on his return, in 1889,
joined Mamontov's Abramtsevo circle.
For the next ten years he was closely
involved with the Abramtsevo pottery
workshops and his work done there won
a gold medal at the 1900 Paris
Exposition Universelle. During the same
period he worked with Shekhtel' on the
interior decoration of a number of
private houses, and he travelled in Italy,
Paris, Germany, Switzerland, Athens
and Constantinople. He moved to St
Petersburg in 1904. He exhibited with
Mir Iskusstva (from 1900), the Moscow
Society of Artists (from 1899), *The 36*
(of which he was one of the founders),
the Union of Russian Artists (from 1903)
the New Society of Artists (from 1908),
and in a number of international
exhibitions, including Diaghilev's Salon
d'Automne show (1906).

457 *Lion's Head*
1891
High relief from the gates of the house
of Savva Mamontov in Moscow
(Sadovoya-Spasskaya no.6)
Majolica with enamel and ochre-brown
glaze, 43.5 × 47.1 × 24
State Tretyakov Gallery
[Illustrated p.198]

458 *Sea King*
Early 1890s
Decorative oval dish
Majolica with enamel, dark blue,
turquoise and light-brown glaze,
54.8 × 43.3 × 16
State Tretyakov Gallery
[Illustrated p.229]

459 *Venice*
1893
Study for the panel executed in the
house of E. D. Dunker in Moscow (now
in the State Russian Museum)
Watercolour, bronze powder and lead
pencil on paper, 36.4 × 19.3
State Tretyakov Gallery
[Illustrated p.199]

460 *Flight of Faust and Mephistopheles*
1896
Design for a panel in the Gothic Study
in the house of A. V. Morozov in
Moscow (see nos.336–7)
Watercolour, Indian ink, pen and brush
on paper, 108 × 125
State Tretyakov Gallery
[Illustrated on back cover]

461 *Dream on Walpurgis Night: Young
Witch; Faust, Helen and Euphorion;
Witches' Kitchen*
1896
Design for panels in the Gothic Study in
the house of A. V. Morozov in Moscow
(see nos.336–7)
Watercolour, Indian ink pen and brush
on three sheets of paper, 22.4 × 4,
22.2 × 4.8, 22.2 × 4
State Tretyakov Gallery
[Illustrated p.198]

462 *Lel'*
1899
Majolica, reduction fired with dark
purple glaze and violet lustre,
44 × 31 × 17
State Tretyakov Gallery
[Illustrated p.178]

463 *Elves*
1897
Design for *Morning*, left-hand panel of
the triptych *Times of the Day* in the
house of Z. G. Morozova in Moscow
(see nos.321ff).
Watercolour, white, brush, pen, bronze
powder and lead pencil on grey-green
paper mounted on cardboard,
28.9 × 32.7
State Tretyakov Gallery

464 *The Departing Knight*
1897
Design for *Midday*, central panel of the
triptych *Times of the Day* in the house
of Z. G. Morozova in Moscow (see
nos.321ff).
Watercolour, white, brush, pen, bronze
powder and lead pencil on grey-green
paper mounted on cardboard,
28.8 × 32.7
State Tretyakov Gallery
[Illustrated p.46]

465 *The Prophet*
1898
Oil on canvas, 145 × 131
State Tretyakov Gallery
[Illustrated p.30]

466 *Philosophy*
1898
Design for a panel in the house of A. V.
Morozov in Moscow
Watercolour, bronze powder and lead
pencil on paper, 42.5 × 13.7
State Tretyakov Gallery
[Illustrated p.199]

467 *Sadko*
1899

Design for an earthenware dish
Watercolour, aluminium, lead pencil
and bronze paint on cardboard,
51.8 × 65.9
State Russian Museum
[Illustrated p.229]

468 Design for a fireplace
1899–1900

Gouache, bronze powder, lead pencil
and fixative on paper, 27 × 28.2
State Tretyakov Gallery
[Illustrated p.34]

469 *Exhibition of the Work of 36 Artists*
Moscow, 1901

Lithographic poster, 61 × 47 cm
State Lenin Library
[Illustrated p.23]

470 *N. I. Zabela-Vrubel' by a Piano*
Early 1900s

Oil on canvas, 189 × 60
Signed bottom right corner
State Tretyakov Gallery
[Illustrated p.109]

Nadezhda Ivanovna Zabela-Vrubel'
(1868–1913), the wife of the artist, was a
famous opera singer.

471 *Seraph*
1904

Lead pencil on paper, 29.1 × 18.3
State Russian Museum
[Illustrated p.103]

**William Walcot (Vil'yam Frantsevich
Val'kot)**
1874 ODESSA – 1943 SUSSEX
Architect and perspectivist. Studied at
the Petersburg Academy School under
Leonty Benois (1895–97) and at private
ateliers in Paris. He practised in
Moscow 1898–1904. He moved to
England, working as an etcher and
painter of classical cityscapes. He acted
as an architectural perspectivist in
Rome, London, Paris and New York,
including work for Lutyens on New
Delhi (1912–14) and Sir Patrick
Abercrombie on the County of London
plan (1941–43). He built the house at 61
St James's Street, London, in 1932.

472 Drawing for main elevation of the
Hotel Metropol, Moscow (as executed)
1902

Indian ink and watercolour on paper,
56 × 135.5
A. V. Shchusev State Museum of
Architecture
[Illustrated pp.54–5]

473 House in Mertvy (N. A. Ostrovsky)
Lane, Moscow
1900–02

Photo (1900s), 12.2 × 17.5
A. V. Shchusev State Museum of
Architecture
[Illustrated p.208]

Rudolf F. Wilde von Wildemann (Vil'de)
1868 COURLAND (LATVIA) – 1942
Ceramic artist. Served apprenticeship at
the design workshop of the Prokhorov
printed chintz factory in Moscow, then
studied at the Stieglitz School in St
Petersburg (1894–99), which awarded
him a travelling scholarship to
Germany, France and Italy (1899–
1902). From 1905 he managed the
painting shop at the Imperial Porcelain
Factory (after the Revolution known as
the Lomonosov Porcelain factory).

474, 475 Pair of "Net" vases
Imperial Porcelain Factory, 1910
Porcelain, overglaze painting in enamels
and gold (by M. Shmakov), ht: 18.7
State Historical Museum

Sergei Yaguzhinsky
1862 – after 1937
Graphic artist. Taught at the Stroganov
Design School.

476 Menu for Easter Banquet, 9 April
1903
Moscow (printed by A. A. Levenson)
Colour lithograph, gilt and silvered,
31.5 × 18
State Lenin Library

Mariya Vasil'evna Yakunchikova-Weber
1870 – 1902 SWITZERLAND
Painter, designer and graphic artist.
Studied as an external student at the
Moscow College (1886–88), while also
going to drawing evenings at the
Polenovs' house and working with the
circle for the study of the historical and
archaeological monuments of Moscow
organised by Elena Polenova. She was
also closely associated with the
Abramtsevo group, though living mainly
in Europe from 1888 (where in 1889–90
she studied at the Académie Julian and
in the studios of Bouguereau and
Fleury), returning to Russia in the
summers. She exhibited with *Mir
Iskusstva* (from 1899) and *The 36*.

477 *From the Windows of the Old
House at Vedenskoe*
1897

Oil on canvas, 88.3 × 106.5
State Tretyakov Gallery
[Illustrated p.101]

Vedenskoe was the country estate of the
Yakunchikovs at Zvenigorod near Moscow.
The house was built in the time of Pavel I.

478 *Covers*

Oil on canvas, 73.5 × 56.7
State Tretyakov Gallery
[Illustrated p.107]

The painting depicts a room in the
Yakunchikov house in Moscow.

479 Cover design for *Mir Iskusstva*
1899

Watercolour, gouache and bronze paint
on grey paper mounted on paper,
34.4 × 27.8
Signed with initials top left
State Russian Museum
[Illustrated p.36]

480 Cover of *Mir Iskusstva*, 1899 nos.
13–24
Colour lithograph, 35 × 28
State Lenin Library

Konstantin Fedorovich Yuon
1875 MOSCOW – 1958 MOSCOW
Painter, graphic and theatre artist.
Studied at the Moscow College (1892–
98) under Savitsky, Arkhipov and
Korovin and in Serov's studio (1899–
1900), at which time he also travelled in
Europe. He worked in Moscow and
exhibited with the *Peredvizhniki* (1900),
Mir Iskusstva (from 1903), the Union of
Russian Artists (from 1903) etc. He was
included in Diaghilev's Salon
d'Automne show (1906). He worked in
the theatre from 1911, executing the
designs for the Diaghilev company's
production of Musorgsky's *Boris
Godunov* at the Théâtre des Champs-
Elysées (1913).

481 *Portrait of the Artist Nikolai
Feofilaktov*
1901

Oil on cardboard, 68.3 × 54
Signed and dated bottom left
State Tretyakov Gallery
[Illustrated p.110]

482 *The Vegetable Kingdom*
1908

From the series "The Creation of the
World"
Pen and Indian ink on paper mounted
on cardboard, 50.8 × 67.8
Signed and dated top right
State Tretyakov Gallery
[Illustrated p.115]

483 *The Animal Kingdom*
1908
From the series ''The Creation of the
World''
Pen and Indian ink on paper mounted
on cardboard, 48.8 × 65.5
Signed bottom left
State Tretyakov Gallery
[Illustrated p.114]

Lev Vasil'evich Zak
1892 NIZHNY NOVGOROD – 1978
Painter, graphic and theatre artist, poet
(under the name of Khrisanf) and critic
(as M. Rossiyansky). He left Russia in
1920, eventually settling in Paris.

484 Bookplate for Ivan Rerberg
N.d
Lithograph, 16.5 × 11
State Lenin Library

Vasily Zal'
1871–1919
Graphic artist.

485 *Exhibition and Sale of Crafts*
St Petersburg, [1907]
Lithographic poster (printed by
R. Golicke and A. Wilborg), 80 × 59
State Lenin Library
[Illustrated p.163]

Viktor Dmitrievich Zamirailo
1868 CHERKASSY (KIEV PROVINCE) – 1939
PETERHOF
Graphic artist and painter. Studied at
Kiev Drawing School (1881–86) under
N. Murashko. Worked on murals and
restoration at the Kirillov church, the
Vladimir Cathedral at Kiev etc. Worked
for the magazines *Zhupel*, *Zritel'* (*The
Spectator*), *Lukomor'e* and *Mir
Iskusstva* (1904–16) and exhibited with
the Union of Russian Artists and *Mir
Iskusstva* (from 1904).

486 *The Witch*
1910
Watercolour, Indian ink, pen and lead
pencil on cardboard, 31.4 × 31
Signed and dated (September 1910)
bottom left, title inscribed bottom right
State Russian Museum

487 Cover for A. S. Roslavlev,
Glumushka, St Petersburg (Lukomor'e),
1910s
Watercolour, Indian ink pen and brush
on paper mounted on cardboard,
30.1 × 23.8
Signed with initials bottom left
State Russian Museum
[Illustrated p.150]

Viktor Ivanovich Zarubin
1866 KHAR'KOV – 1928 LENINGRAD
Landscape painter. Studied at the
Schreider School in Khar'kov, at the
Académie Julian in Paris (1893–96) and
at the Petersburg Academy (1894–98)
under Kuindzhi. He lived and worked in
St Petersburg-Petrograd-Leningrad.

488 *Landscape with Fishermen*
1906
Oil on canvas, 102.3 × 142.5
Signed and dated bottom right
State Russian Museum
[Illustrated p.123]

P. Zhitkov

489 Cinema poster: *Leya Lifshits:
Pages of a sad past*
Moscow, n.d.
Lithographic poster (printed by Russian
Partnership), 107 × 73
State Lenin Library
[Illustrated p.83]

Pavel Vasil'evich Zhukovsky
1845 FRANKFURT-AM-MAIN – 1912 WEIMAR
Painter and graphic artist. Son of the
poet V. A. Zhukovsky, he received no
formal art education and lived much of
his life abroad, becoming a friend of
Lenbach, Böcklin and Richard Wagner,
for whom he designed sets and
costumes for the first production of
Parsifal (1882) at Bayreuth.

490 *Woman with a Violin (In Memory
of Böcklin)*
Early 1900s
Gouache, watercolour, bronze paint,
pen and Indian ink on cardboard,
33.8 × 19.7
Signed bottom right; inscribed bottom:
''composition for enamel in gold and
silver''
State Russian Museum
[Illustrated p.103]

Aleksei Prokof'evich Zinov'ev
1880–1942
Designer. Graduated from the
Stroganov Design School in 1903. From
1903 to 1914 he was manager of the
Talashkino workshops in succession to
Malyutin.

491 Wheeled chair
Talashkino, 1900s
Carved and painted oak, 73 × 42 × 43
State Historical Museum
[Illustrated p.230]

Luka Zlotnikov

492 Poster for the journal *Teatr i
Iskusstvo* (*Theatre and Art*)
St Petersburg, 1902
Lithographic poster (printed by
R. Golicke), 78 × 56
State Lenin Library
[Illustrated p.162]

Zolotoe Runo
Art magazine published in Moscow in
1906–09.

See nos.32–4, 94, 111, 200, 201, 204, 399

Nikolai Nikolaevich Zverev
Master silversmith.

493 Tea-glass holder
Moscow, 1908–17
Silver gilt and enamel, 9.2 × 11.4 × 9
Hallmark with maker's initials
State Historical Museum
[Illustrated p.250]

Boris Zvorykin
1872 – [UNKNOWN]
Graphic artist and watercolourist.

494 Poster for A. A. Levenson, printers
of art posters
Moscow, 1906
Lithographic poster (printed by
A. A. Levenson), 103 × 74
State Lenin Library
[Illustrated p.157]

495 Programme (in Russian and
English): Imperial Bolshoi Theatre
Moscow (printed by A. A. Levenson),
20 January 1912
Colour lithograph, 34 × 24
State Lenin Library
[Illustrated p.153]

496 Programme: Imperial Bolshoi
Theatre, *Welcome*
Moscow (printed by A. A. Levenson),
10/23 February 1910
Colour lithograph, 30 × 25
State Lenin Library

ANONYMOUS

Posters

497 A. M. Kokorev & Co.,
typolithographers, Kazan'
Kazan', 1901
Lithographic poster (printed by A. M.
Kokorev & Co., lithography by I. S.
Lapine, Paris), 51 × 40
State Lenin Library
[Illustrated p.158]

498 *Night in the World of Decadence.*
Poster for masked ball, 3 February 1901
St Petersburg, 1901
Lithographic poster (printed by
R. Golicke), 76 × 22
State Lenin Library
[Illustrated p.162]

(A. C.)
499 *Sestroretsk Spa, Summer Season*
St Petersburg, 1902
Lithographic poster (printed by
R. Golicke), 104 × 69
State Lenin Library

500 *Ustinov's Macaroni*
Kazan', 1902
Lithographic poster (printed by A. M.
Kokorev & Co.), 55 × 26
State Lenin Library
[Illustrated p.169]

501 *Night Blini*
Kiev, n.d.
Lithographic poster (printed by
"Progress"), 63 × 71
State Lenin Library

502 "Rossiya" (Russia) Passenger
Insurance
St Petersburg, 1903
Lithographic poster (printed by
T. Kibbel'), 68.7 × 135
State Lenin Library
[Illustrated p.158]

503 *Lux* Paraffin Lamps
St Petersburg, n.d.
Lithographic poster (printed by
T. Kibbel'), 74 × 48
State Lenin Library
[Illustrated p.158]

504 Poster for Helmsing and Grimm,
Principal Agents for the Riga Express
Steam Navigation Company: Riga to
London Line
St Petersburg, n.d.
Lithographic poster (printed by
T. Kibbel'), 102 × 67
State Lenin Library

505 Freisinger Brothers' (Riga)
"Russiya" Rubber Tyres
St Petersburg, n.d.
Lithographic poster (printed by
T. Kibbel'), 69 × 103
State Lenin Library
[Illustrated p.159]

506 Avakh Brothers' Cigarette Papers
St Petersburg, n.d.
Lithographic poster (printed by
T. Kibbel'), 70 × 36
State Lenin Library
[Illustrated p.166]

507 Laferme's "Frou-Frou" Cigarettes
St Petersburg, 1904
Lithographic poster (printed by E. I.
Markus), 60.7 × 44
State Lenin Library
[Illustrated p.166]

508 "Kado" (Cadeau) Cigarettes
St Petersburg, n.d.
Lithographic poster (printed by Vefers
& Co.), 55 × 36
State Lenin Library
[Illustrated p.166]

509 A. Rallet & Co.'s "Imperatis"
(Empress) Perfumes
Moscow, n.d.
Lithographic poster, 67 × 47
State Lenin Library
[Illustrated p.164]

510 N. M. Soldatov's Tea
Moscow, n.d.
Lithographic poster (printed by
Gryzunov & Co.), 46 × 30
State Lenin Library

511 A. Kron' and Co.'s Beer and Porter
St Petersburg, 1905
Lithographic poster (printed by
R. Schwarz), 61 × 33
State Lenin Library
[Illustrated p.168]

512 *In Hell*; poster for the Second Ball
of the Society of Artists at the Aquarium
Theatre, 15 December 1907
St Petersburg, [1907]
Lithographic poster (printed by
R. Golicke and A. Wilborg), 92.5 × 61.4
State Lenin Library
[Illustrated p.160]

(N. B.)
513 Poster for *Zhurnal Teatra* (Theatre
Journal of the Literary-Artistic Society)
St Petersburg, [1909]
Lithographic poster (printed by
R. Golicke and A. Wilborg), 101 × 68
State Lenin Library
[Illustrated p.162]

(A. C.)
514 *Kislovodsk: Summer Season 1911*
St Petersburg, [1911]
Lithograpic poster (printed by
R. Golicke and A. Wilborg), 71 × 101
State Lenin Library

(E.)
515 Untitled
St Petersburg, n.d.
Lithographic poster (printed by
R. Golicke and A. Wilborg), 93.5 × 60
State Lenin Library
[Illustrated p.163]

(M. K.)
516 Nobel Brothers' Detergent Soap
St Petersburg, n.d.
Lithographic poster (printed by
R. Golicke and A. Wilborg), 72 × 55
State Lenin Library
[Illustrated p.159]

517 *Teatr Miniatur*
St Petersburg, n.d.
Lithographic poster (printed by
R. Golicke and A. Wilborg), 100 × 71
State Lenin Library
[Illustrated p.161]

518 Pavlovsk Station: Rollerskating Rink
and Cinematograph
St Petersburg, n.d.
Lithographic poster (printed by
N. Kadushin), 103 × 68
State Lenin Library

519 Cinema poster: *A Woman's
Autumn*, after the novel by Marcel
Prévost
Moscow, [1917]
Lithographic poster (printed by Russian
Partnership), 106 × 72
State Lenin Library

Printed Ephemera

520 Pharmacist's label: Adolf
Marczinzyk, Kiev
Not after 1861
Lithograph and line block, 24 × 8.5
State Lenin Library

521 Pharmacist's label: A. Marczinzyk,
Kiev
N.d.
Embossing, painting, 27.5 × 7.5
State Lenin Library

522 Prescription from F. Gubitsky's
Pharmacy on Tversky Avenue, Moscow
Not after 1861
Embossing, 21.5 × 13.5
State Lenin Library

523 Pharmacist's label: Petr Cherkasov, Ryazan'
Not after 1865
Colour lithograph, 17.5 × 8.5
State Lenin Library

524 Pharmacist's label: A. Seitz, Old Ryazan'
Not after 1865
Embossing, painting, 21.5 × 7.5
State Lenin Library

525 Pharmacist's label: S. Gembchinsky, Tsekhotsinka (Ciechocinka)
Warsaw (printed by B. A. Bukaty), not after 1913
Line block, 20 × 7
State Lenin Library

526 Part of cover of price list for A. Rallet & Co., Perfumiers, Moscow
N.d.
Colour lithographic proof, 29 × 18.5
State Lenin Library
[Illustrated p.165]

527 Wrapper for A. Rallet's "Végétal" soap
N.d.
Colour lithograph, 14 × 19.5
State Lenin Library
[Illustrated p.165]

528 Soap wrapper
N.d.
Colour lithograph, 12.5 × 16
State Lenin Library
[Illustrated p.165]

529 Soap wrapper
N.d.
Colour lithograph 13 × 17
State Lenin Library
[Illustrated p.165]

530 Labels for perfume bottles
N.d.
Colour lithographic proof, embossed, 12.5 × 20
State Lenin Library
[Illustrated p.165]

531 Label for George Borman, sweet manufacturer
St Petersburg (printed by T. Kibbel'), n.d.
Embossed colour lithograph, diameter: 16
State Lenin Library
[Illustrated p.167]

532 Wrapper for George Borman's "Olimp" (Olympus) chocolate
St Petersburg (printed by T. Kibbel'), n.d.
Colour lithograph, gilt and embossed, 17 × 13.5
State Lenin Library
[Illustrated p.167]

533, 534 Wrappers for Eliseev Brothers' "Stil'naya" (Stylish) Caramels
St Petersburg (printed by Nevsky), n.d.
Colour lithographs, each 8 × 8.5
State Lenin Library
[Illustrated p.169]
   The Eliseev Food Emporia in Moscow and St Petersburg were models of opulent *Style Moderne* design. The decor of these shops has survived to the present.

535 Sweet wrapper, Renomé's "Bim-Bom" sweets
Moscow (printed by I. D. Khudyakov), n.d.
Colour lithograph, 9.5 × 9.5
State Lenin Library

536 Wrapper for Renomé's "Grezy" (Daydreams) sweets
Moscow (Y. Kirsten), n.d.
Colour lithograph, 11.5 × 7
State Lenin Library

537 Sweet wrapper, A. S. Kudryavtsev's "Grezy" (Daydreams) sweets
Moscow (printed by Ovorot), n.d.
Colour lithograph, 9.5 × 9.5
State Lenin Library

538 Sweet wrapper, Einem's "Sadko" sweets, Moscow.
N.d.
Colour lithograph, 9 × 8
State Lenin Library

539 Wrapper for I. L. Ding's "Skazka" (Fairytale) sweets
Moscow (printed by A. I. Gil'd), n.d.
Colour lithograph, 8.5 × 8.5
State Lenin Library

540 Wrapper for "Mignon" chocolate, made by the Ramon Steam Sweet and Chocolate Factory, Ramon Village, Voronezh Province
St Petersburg (printed by Vefers & Co.), n.d.
Colour lithograph, 30 × 15
State Lenin Library
[Illustrated p.167]

541 Original design for sweet wrapper, "Azra"
N.d.
Gouache and bronze paint on cardboard, 9 × 8
State Lenin Library
[Illustrated p.169]

542 Original design for sweet wrapper
N.d.
Gouache on cardboard, 8.5 × 8.5
State Lenin Library
[Illustrated p.169]

543 Original design for sweet wrapper
N.d.
Gouache on cardboard, 7.5 × 8.5
State Lenin Library
[Illustrated p.169]

544 Packet for Kolobov & Bobrov's "Król" (King) no.6 cigarettes
St Petersburg (printed by Vefers & Co.), n.d.
Colour lithograph, 31.5 × 7
State Lenin Library
[Illustrated p.167]

545 Dinner menu for St Petersburg River Yacht Club, 7 September 1897
Colour lithograph, 16.5 × 9
State Lenin Library
[Illustrated p.173]

546 Menu, 20 January 1902
Moscow (printed by A. A. Levenson)
Colour lithograph, 39 × 29
State Lenin Library
[Illustrated p.173]

547 Supper menu, 26 February 1905
Watercolour, and gold paint, 20 × 11
State Lenin Library
[Illustrated p.173]

548 Menu for the restaurant "Al'piiskaya Roza" (Alpenrose), 30 March 1907
Moscow (printed by A. A. Levenson)
Colour lithograph, 26.5 × 17.5
State Lenin Library
[Illustrated p.172]

549 Dinner Menu, 2 February 1910
Embossing and painting, 17 × 8.5
State Lenin Library
[Illustrated p.173]

(G. M.)
550 Programme for Soirée in aid of the Poor organised by E. N. Suvorina, 26 March 1911
St Petersburg (printed by A. S. Suvorin)
Colour autotype, 31 × 24
State Lenin Library
[Illustrated p.154]

551 Universal Russian Calendar for 1907
Moscow (I. D. Sytin)
Colour lithograph, 31 × 23.5
State Lenin Library

552 Universal Russian Calendar for 1911
Moscow (I. D. Sytin)
Colour lithograph, 30 × 23.5
State Lenin Library

553 Postcard advertising the Einem Partnership, Moscow
N.d.
Colour lithograph glued to cardboard, silvered, 9 × 13.5
State Lenin Library
[Illustrated p.171]

554 Envelope for the Community of St Evgeny (Red Cross)
N.d.
Colour lithograph, 8 × 12
State Lenin Library
[Illustrated p.171]

555 Imprint of the Publishers Musaget
Moscow, n.d.
Line block, 5 × 3.5
State Lenin Library

Furniture

556 Armchair
Sergiev Trading Quarter, 1910s
Carved oak, 85 × 45 × 54
State Historical Museum
[Illustrated p.233]

557 Medicine chest
Russia, 1900s
Carved and painted wood with stamped brass, 43 × 27 × 14
State Historical Museum
[Illustrated p.230]

558 Lampstand
Russia, 1900s
Wood with stamped brass, 106 × 28 × 28
State Historical Museum

559, 560 Pair of chairs from the Morozov-Reinbot estate "Gorki" near Moscow
1900s
Karelian birch inlaid with ebony, each 112 × 50 × 50
State Historical Museum
[Illustrated p.237]

561, 562, 563 Armchairs and lampstand, from a suite belonging to the Moscow publisher I. Sytin Russia, *c.*1903
Mahogany inlaid with metal, 90 × 62 × 57; mahogany, 77 × 57 × 53; mahogany inlaid with metal, 116 × 49 × 35
State Historical Museum
[Illustrated p.237]

564, 565 Pair of chairs
Russia, 1900s
Mahogany, each 105 × 44 × 47
State Historical Museum

Woodwork

566 *Matryoshka* (8 dolls)
Moscow, workshop of the Crafts Museum, 1910s
Painted turned wood, 15 × 8.2
State Historical Museum
[Illustrated p.234]

567 Toy sledge: gift-packaging for sweets made at the "Einem" factory
Moscow, 1900s
Wood with painting and pokerwork
State Historical Museum

568 Bottle-holder in the form of a swimming swan
Russia, 1900s
Wood, stamped brass, glass insets
72.5 × 59.5 × 26.3
State Historical Museum

569 Twin-layer *teremok* casket
Russia, 1900s
Wood, stamped brass, inset with glass
State Historical Museum

Ceramic

570 Vase decorated with pink flowers
Imperial Porcelain Factory, 1913
Porcelain, underglaze painting, ht: 20.5, diam. at base: 12.3
State Historical Museum

Jewellery

571 Earrings
Russia, turn of the century
Gold, silver, enamel and pearls, 5 × 2.4
No hallmark
State Historical Museum
[Illustrated p.258]

(N. B.)
572 Pendant brooch
Moscow, 1899–1908
Gold, rubies, brilliants, diamonds, 6 × 2.7
Hallmark with maker's initials
State Historical Museum
[Illustrated p.259]

573 Pendant
Russia, early 20th century
Gold, chrysoprase, rubies, aquamarines, 7.8 × 3.2
No hallmark
State Historical Museum
[Illustrated p.259]

574 Pendant
St Petersburg (?), 1911
Gold, enamel, sapphires, diamonds, 4.5 × 3
No hallmark
State Historical Museum
[Illustrated p.258]

Silver and Gold

(R. D.)
575 Cigarette case
Moscow (?), early 20th century
Silver, 1.2 × 11 × 7.7
Hallmark with maker's initials (place mark rubbed)
State Historical Museum
[Illustrated p.255]

(O. I. P.)
576 Tea-glass holder
Moscow, 1899–1908
Silver, 10.2 × 13.5 × 7
Hallmark with maker's initials
State Historical Museum
[Illustrated p.32]

(G. Y.)
577 Jug
St Petersburg, 1899–1908
Cut glass with silver mountings, ht: 28
Hallmark with maker's initials
State Historical Museum
[Illustrated p.249]

(G. T.)
578 Wine vessel
Kiev, 1907
Silver, 29 × 30.5 × 16.8
Hallmark with maker's initials
State Historical Museum
[Illustrated p.253]

(S. P. I.)
579 Lady's purse
Moscow, 1908–17
Silver, 15 × 10.5 × 4
Hallmark with maker's initials
State Historical Museum
[Illustrated p.257]

(A. R.)
580 Cigarette case
Moscow, 1908–17
Silver, 1.3 × 11.4 × 7.7
Hallmark with maker's initials
State Historical Museum
[Illustrated p.254]

581, 582 Salt cellar and cream jug
Moscow, 1908–17
Silver gilt and enamel, 3.4 × 3.5 × 3.5;
7.4 × 10.6 × 6.3
Hallmarks rubbed
State Historical Museum
[Illustrated p.251]

583 Cigarette case
Moscow, 1908–17
Silver gilt and enamel, 1.2 × 10.7 × 8.2
Hallmark rubbed
State Historical Museum
[Illustrated p.254]

584 Panagia
St Petersburg, 1913
Silver gilt with enamel and glass,
15 × 6.7
Hallmark
State Historical Museum
[Illustrated p.242]

PHOTOGRAPHS

**Boissonas & Eggler, photo studio,
St Petersburg**

585 Group photo of the Imperial family
1910s
Photo, 26.7 × 33.8 (15.1 × 18.1)
State Historical Museum
[Illustrated p.15]

Nikolai Aleksandrovich Romanov (1868–1918), Tsar Nikolai II from 1894; Aleksandra Fedorovna Romanova (1872–1918), born Princess Hesse-Darmstadt, married Nikolai II in 1894; children: Tsarevich Aleksei (1904–18), Grand Duchesses Ol'ga (1895–1918), Tat'yana (1897–1918), Mariya (1899–1918), Anastasiya (1901–18).

586 Portrait of Tsaritsa Aleksandra Fedorovna with her daughters Ol'ga, Tat'yana, Mariya and Anastasiya
1910s
Photo, 15.3 × 19.6
State Historical Museum
[Illustrated p.263]

587 Portrait of Tsar Nikolai II with his heir Aleksei
1904–05
Photo, 26.3 × 20.6 (13.4 × 10)
State Historical Museum
[Illustrated p.262]

588 Portrait of Tsaritsa Aleksandra Fedorovna with her son Aleksei
1904–5
Photo, 26.3 × 20.6 (13.4 × 10)
State Historical Museum
[Illustrated p.262]

**Karl Karlovich Bulla photo studio,
St Petersburg**
News photographer and founder of a photographic dynasty. He was assassinated at a performance of the Kiev Opera.

589 Group portrait
Tsar Nikolai II with officers of the Lifeguards of the Izmailov Regiment
1904
Photo, 47.5 × 57.9 (27.3 × 37.2)
State Historical Museum

590 Portrait of P. A. Stolypin
1908
Photo, 25.8 × 18.2 (15.7 × 11.3), signed by Stolypin
State Historical Museum

Petr Arkad'evich Stolypin (1862–1911), Minister of Internal Affairs, Chairman of the Council of Ministers.

Maksim Petrovich Dmitriev
1856–1948
Began to work for Moscow photographer M. P. Nastyukov at the age of fifteen, but his real training was in Karelin's studio in Nizhny Novgorod, where he subsequently opened his own studio. Exhibited in Moscow in 1889.

591 "Fisherman on the Volga" from "The Volga Collection"
1899
Photo, 37.8 × 51.1, signed by the photographer
State Historical Museum

592 Church of the Nativity of the Virgin, Nizhny Novgorod
1890s
Photo, 49 × 33.9 (28.1 × 21.9)
State Historical Museum

593 Church of the Nativity of the Virgin, Nizhny Novgorod
1890s
Photo, 49 × 33.9 (26.9 × 22.1)
State Historical Museum
[Illustrated p.264]

594 Cathedral in the New Exhibition Grounds on the Bank of the Volga
1890s
Photo, 24 × 31.9 (16.8 × 22.4)
State Historical Museum
[Illustrated p.264]

595 Chinese pavilions in the Exhibition Grounds
1890s
Photo, 33.7 × 24.6 (15.8 × 21.5)
State Historical Museum

596 Armenian church, Nizhny Novgorod
1890s
Photo, 34.3 × 24.3 (21 × 15.2)
State Historical Museum
[Illustrated p.264]

597 Bank of the Volga
1890s
Photo, 24.4 × 34.3 (15.8 × 21.9)
State Historical Museum

K. Fischer photo studio, Moscow

598 Group portrait: F. I. Shalyapin with writers and members of the "Wednesday" literary circle
1902
Photo, 33.5 × 44.4 (21.4 × 26.6)
State Historical Museum
[Illustrated p.40]

Left to right: Aleksei Maksimovich Gor'ky (Peshkov) (1868–1936); Leonid Nikolaevich Andreev (1871–1919); Ivan

Alekseevich Bunin (1870–1953); Evgeny Nikolaevich Chirikov (1864–1932); Fedor Ivanovich Shalyapin (1873–1938); Stepan Gavrilovich Skitalets (Petrov) (1868–1941); Nikolai Dmitrievich Teleshov (1867–1957).

N. Krotkov, "Paola" photo studio, Moscow

599 Portrait of Savva Mamontov
1900s
Photo, 28.5 × 20 (14 × 10)
State Historical Museum
[Illustrated p.40]

Aleksei Sergeevich Mazurin
Amateur photographer.

600 Nun
1900s
Photo, 15.6 × 11.2
State Historical Museum
[Illustrated p.266]

601 Harvest
1902
Photo, 31.5 × 36.5 (22.3 × 16.2)
State Historical Museum
[Illustrated p.268]

602 Birdcatchers
1900s
Photo, 34.1 × 24.1 (22.5 × 17.1)
State Historical Museum
[Illustrated p.268]

603 Easter
1900s
Photo, 31.6 × 30.4 (12.7 × 17)
State Historical Museum
[Illustrated p.266]

604 "Pointswoman"
1903
Photo, 33.4 × 27.9 (16 × 16)
State Historical Museum
[Illustrated p.266]

605 On the River
1900
Photo, 27.9 × 32.5 (16.9 × 21.6)
State Historical Museum

606 Winter Landscape
1900s
Photo, 34.7 × 28.6 (22 × 17.2)
State Historical Museum
[Illustrated p.267]

607 Winter Landscape
1900
Photo, 34.2 × 27.6 (22.4 × 15.9)
State Historical Museum

608 Winter Landscape
1900s
Photo, 27.7 × 32.5 (16.7 × 21.5)
State Historical Museum
[Illustrated p.267]

609 View of the Nikol'sky Gates of the Kitaigorod and the chapel of St Panteleimon on Lubyanskaya (now Dzerzhinsky) Square, Moscow
1900s
Photo, 27.5 × 33.5 (17.6 × 22.5)
State Historical Museum
[Illustrated p.267]

Natal'ya B. Nordman-Severova
Amateur photographer. The wife of Il'ya Repin, she was the author of a pamphlet attacking Sergei Shchukin for his patronage of avant-garde foreign art.

610 "Cobbler"
1900s
Photo, 27 × 21 (15.4 × 11.4)
State Historical Museum
[Illustrated p.269]

611 Sweeper
1900s
Photo, 26.9 × 21 (16.3 × 11.8)
State Historical Museum
[Illustrated p.269]

612 "Seller of Game"
1900s
Photo, 26.9 × 21 (15.8 × 11.6)
State Historical Museum
[Illustrated p.269]

P. P. Pavlov photo studio, Moscow

613 Portrait of Princess Yusupova
1900
Photo, 32 × 22
State Historical Museum
[Illustrated p.262]

   Zinaida Nikolaevna (1861–1939), wife of Adjutant-General Prince Yusupov, Count F. F. Sumarokov-El'ston (the elder).

614 Portrait of Princess Yusupova
1900
Photo, 32 × 22
State Historical Museum
[Illustrated p.262]

615 Group portrait: A. P. Chekhov with the cast and directors of *The Seagull*
7 May 1899
Photo, 40 × 53.5 (35.4 × 47)
State Historical Museum
[Illustrated p.263]

The photograph was taken during the playwright's visit to Moscow for a special performance of his play at the Moscow Arts Theatre. Standing: Vladimir Ivanovich Nemirovich-Danchenko (1858–1943), playwright and director, one of the founders and directors of the Arts Theatre; Vasily Vasil'evich Luzhsky (1869–1932), actor; Ol'ga Leonardovna Knipper (1870–1959), actress; Aleksandr Ivanovich Andreev, actor; Mariya Petrovna Nikolaeva (1869–1941), actress; Mariya Lyudomirovna Roksanova (1874–1958), actress. Seated: Evgeniya Mikhailovna Raevskaya (d. 1923), actress; Aleksandr Leonidovich Vishnevsky (1861–1943), actor; Aleksandr Rodionovich Artem (1842–1914), actor; Konstantin Sergeevich Stanislavsky (1862–1938), director and one of the founders and directors of the Arts Theatre; Anton Pavlovich Chekhov (1860–1904), author and playwright; Mariya Petrovna Lilina (1866–1943), actress; Iosif Aleksandrovich Tikhomirov (1872–1908), actor; Vsevolod Emil'evich Meyerhold (1874–1914), actor.

Nikolai Alexandrovich Petrov
Portrait photographer.

616 Portrait of A. N. Severtsov
1900s
Photo, 24.9 × 17.4 (20.5 × 14.9)
State Historical Museum

   Aleksei Nikolaevich Severtsov (1866–1936), Russian biologist.

617 Portrait of the actress
E. M. Karenina
1900s
Photo, 24.9 × 17.4 (20.5 × 14.4)
State Historical Museum

618 Portrait of the actress
M. D. Turchaninova
1900s
Photo, 24.9 × 17.4 (20.3 × 13.6)
State Historical Museum

A. Vasil'ev
Photographer from Samara.

619 "In Expectation!"
1910s
Photo, 17.5 × 24.8 (11.5 × 17.2)
State Historical Museum

620 "Opening Time!!"
1910s
Photo, 17.4 × 24.9 (11.8 × 17.1)
State Historical Museum

E. Wassermann photo studio, Moscow

621 Portrait of Grigory Rasputin
1916
36.8 × 28.4 (22.4 × 17)
State Historical Museum
[Illustrated p.000]

Grigory Efimovich Rasputin (1872–1916), prophet of the Orthodox Church, very influential in court circles. Offspring of Siberian peasants, he lived in St Petersburg from 1907. He fell victim to a palace conspiracy (see Chronology).

Unknown photographers

622 Portrait of Prince Yusupov
1900s
Tinted photo, 21.5 × 19
State Historical Museum

Prince Yusupov, Count Feliks Feliksovich Sumarokov-El'ston (the younger) (1887–1967), member of the Russian high aristocracy, husband of the niece of Nikolai II. He participated in the murder of Rasputin.

623 Portrait of F. I. Shalyapin in the role of Ivan the Terrible in Rimsky-Korsakov's opera *The Maid of Pskov*
1900
Photo, 22.5 × 17.5 (21.1. × 15.3)
State Historical Museum

Fedor Ivanovich Shalyapin (1873–1938), famous Russian bass singer.

624 "Outright!"
1900s
Photo, 26.9 × 22 (16.8 × 12.1)
State Historical Museum

625 "Autumn Mist"
1900s
Photo, 26.9 × 22 (16.8 × 12.1)
State Historical Museum

Photographic Album "Agricultural Trades Orphanage for the children of soldiers in the village of Kolokol'tsovko, Samara Province, Nikolaev District", presented to Tsarevich Aleksei Nikolaevich in 1916

626 Church by the Orphanage
1916
Tinted photograph, 34.2 × 37 (22.4 × 29)
State Historical Museum
[Illustrated p.265]

627 Pupils in front of the school and workshops
1916
Tinted photograph, 34.2 × 37 (22 × 26)
State Historical Museum
[Illustrated p.265]

628 Pupils in the classroom
1916
Tinted photograph, 34.2 × 37 (21.5 × 25.5)
State Historical Museum
[Illustrated p.265]

629 Classes in the saddlery and shoemaking workshops
1916
Tinted photograph, 34.2 × 37 (21.5 × 25.5)
State Historical Museum
[Illustrated p.265]

630 Red Square, Moscow: View of the Kremlin, Historical Museum, Upper and Middle Trading Rows
1890s
Photo, 16 × 37.5 (7.7 × 27.2)
State Historical Museum
[Illustrated pp.2–3]

631 Strastnaya (Passion) Square (now Pushkin Square), Moscow: View of the Monastery of the Passion and Tverskaya Street
1890s
Photo, 16 × 37.5 (7.9 × 29.1)
State Historical Museum
[Illustrated p.270]

632 Malaya Dmitrovka (now A. P. Chekhov Street), Moscow: View of the church of the Nativity in Putniki
1890s
Photo, 16 × 37.5 (7.7 × 29.5)
State Historical Museum
[Illustrated p.271]

633 View of the Kremlin and Moskvoretsky Bridge, Moscow
1890s
Photo, 16 × 37.5 (8.7 × 29.5)
State Historical Museum
[Illustrated p.270]

634 Red Gates Square, Moscow
1890s
Photo, 16 × 37.5 (7.7 × 28)
State Historical Museum

635 Okhotny Ryad Street, Moscow: View of the church of the Paraskeva Pyatnitsa
1890s
Photo, 16 × 37.5 (8.5 × 28.7)
State Historical Museum
[Illustrated p.270]

636 Huntsman in the Winter Forest
1900s
Photo, 24.5 × 32.3 (16.5 × 22.5)
State Historical Museum
[Illustrated p.268]

FILMS

Evgeny Bauer
1865–1917
He came from a musical and theatrical family. He graduated from the Moscow College and worked in the theatre and as an "artistic photographer" before entering cinema as a designer on the Romanov Tercentenary film in 1913. From the end of that year he directed exclusively for Khanzhonkov's company and was soon renowned (and highly paid) for his spaciously designed, slow-paced and subtly lit melodramas, mostly scripted and often photographed by him, which also featured the most popular of Russian stars – Vera Kholodnaya, Vera Karalli and his wife, Lina Bauer. He died while filming *For Luck* in the Crimea. Of some 86 films directed between 1913–17 only 26 are known, but these confirm him as the major artist of pre-Soviet Russian cinema.

637 *Ditya bol'shogo goroda (A Child of the Big City)*
1913
Dir/Art Dir: Bauer. Phot: Boris Zavelev. Cast: Elena Smirnova (Manechka/Mary), Mikhail Salarov (Viktor Kravtsov), Arseny Bibikov (Kramskoi, his friend). Prod: Khanzhonkov. 1135 m. Rel: 5.3.14 [opening scenes and original titles missing].

638 *Nemye svidetely (Silent Witnesses)*
1914
Dir: Bauer. Scr: Aleksandr Voznesensky. Cast: Dora Chitorina (Nastya, a maid), Aleksandr Kheruvimov (a porter, her grandfather), Aleksandr Chargonin (Pavel Kostritsyn), Elsa Kryuger (Ellen, his bride), Andrei Gromov (the neighbours' servant, Nastya's fiancé). Prod: Khanzhonkov. 1245 m. Rel: 29.4.14 [original titles missing].

639 *Tysyacha vtoraya khitrost' (The Thousand and Second Ruse)*
1915
Dir: Bauer. Scr: based on Vladimir Azov's play, *The Thousand and First Ruse*. Cast: Lina Bauer (the cunning wife), S. Rassatov (her husband), Sergei Kvasnitsky (her lover). Prod: Khanzhonkov. 385 m. Rel: 29.5.15 [original titles missing].

640 *Grezy (Daydreams)*
1915
Dir: Bauer. Scr: M. Basov, Valentin Turkin, based on Georges Rodenbach's novel *Bruges la Morte*. Phot: Boris Zavelev. Cast: Aleksandr Vyrubov (Sergei Nedelin), N. Chernobaeva (his wife and Tina Viarskaya, an actress), Viktor Arens (Solsky, an artist). Prod: Khanzhonkov. 1034 m. Rel: 10.10.15 [original titles missing].

641 *Zhizn' za zhizn' (A Life for a Life)*
1916
Dir/Scr: Bauer, based on Georges Ohnet's novel *Serge Panine*. Phot: Boris Zavelev. Cast: Ol'ga Rakhmanova (Khromova, a millionairess), Lilya Koreneva (Musya, her daughter), Vera Kholodnaya (Natya, her adopted daughter), Vitol'd Polonsky (Prince Bartinsky), Ivan Perestiani (Zhurov, a merchant). Prod: Khanzhonkov. 2175 m. Rel: 10.5.16.

642 *Revolyutsioner (The Revolutionary)*
1917
Dir: Bauer. Scr: Ivan Perestiani. Phot: Boris Zavelev. Cast: Ivan Perestiani (Grandad, an old revolutionary), Vladimir Strizhevsky (his son), Zoya Barantsevich (daughter), Mikhail Stal'sky (a dying convict). Prod: Khanzhonkov. 4 reels. Rel: 3.4.17 [first reel and original titles missing].

643 *Za schast'em (For Luck)*
1917
Dir: Bauer. Scr: N. Dennitsyna. Phot: Boris Zavelev. Art Dir: Lev Kuleshov. Cast: Nikolai Radin (Dmitry Gzhasky, a lawyer), Lidiya Koreneva (Zoya Verenskaya, a rich widow), Taisiya Borman (Lee, her daughter), Lev Kuleshov (Enrico, an artist), N. Dennitsyna (Lee's governess). Prod: Khanzhonkov. 4 reels. Rel: 3.9.17 [original titles missing].

Petr Chardynin
1873?–1934
Studied acting under Nemirovich-Danchenko and toured with provincial companies before a meeting with Khanzhonkov in 1908 started him acting in and soon directing films. Slow to adopt cinematic devices, he nonetheless developed the range of Russian screen acting and was a leading director for Khanzhonkov until Bauer's rise prompted a move to Kharitonov in 1916. After 1920, he worked in Latvia and the Ukraine.

644 *Pikovaya dama (The Queen of Spades)*
1910
Dir/Scr: Chardynin, based on Tchaikovsky's opera from Pushkin's story. Phot: Louis Forestier. Art Dir: V. Fester. Cast: Petr Biryukov (German), Aleksandra Goncharova (Liza), A. Pozharskaya (Countess), Andrei Gromov (Eletsky). Prod: Khanzhonkov. 380 m. Rel: 30.11.10 [original titles missing].

645 *Domik v Kolomne (The House in Kolomna)*
1913
Dir: Chardynin, based on Pushkin's verse story. Phot: Wladyslaw Starewicz. Art Dir: Starewicz (?), Boris Mikhin. Cast: Praskov'ya Miksimova (a widow), Sof'ya Goslavskaya (Parasha, her daughter), Ivan Mozzhukhin (a guards officer; Mavrusha). Prod: Khanzhonkov. 610 m. Rel: 19.10.13.

Aleksandr Drankov
1880–[UNKNOWN]
An ambitious photographer with international connections when he turned to cinema in 1907. His attempt to film *Boris Godunov* in that year failed, but he won prestige with the "first" Russian drama, *Sten'ka Razin*. Thereafter he competed fiercely with Khanzhonkov and tried to preempt rivals' films, while gaining notoriety with the lurid *Son'ka* serial (1914–16). He emigrated in 1918 and died in obscurity in the U.S.A.

See no. 657

Iosif Ermol'ev [Ermolieff]
1889–1962
Worked for Pathé before starting a distribution company in Rostov-on-Don in 1912. A producer from 1915, his leading directors were Protazanov and Gardin, with the stars Mozzhukhin and Lisenko, who supplied successes both commercial and cultural up to 1918. Ermol'ev's company provided the nucleus of the later Rus' Collective, while he moved to Paris and established the most enduring of the Russian emigré companies, with Protazanov, Volkov and Tourzhansky. He later emigrated to the U.S.A.

See nos. 655, 663

Vasily Goncharov
1861–1915
A civil servant until 1905, when he tried to enter literary circles, Goncharov was first attracted to literary and art-historical aspects of cinema (see nos. 657, 646). As a director, he moved rapidly from Thiemann to Khanzhonkov, then to Pathé and Gaumont, before returning to Khanzhonkov for the superproductions *The Defence of Sebastopol* (1911), *The Year 1812* and *The Accession of the Romanov Dynasty*.

646 *Russkaya svad'ba XVI stoletiya (A Sixteenth-Century Russian Wedding)*
1909
Dir/Scr: Goncharov, based on P. Sukhotin's play *A Russian Wedding at the End of the 16th Century*. Phot: Vladimir Siversen. Art Dir: V. Fester, based on paintings by Konstantin Makovsky. Cast: Aleksandra Goncharova (bride), F. Fadeeva (her mother), Vasily Stepanov (her father), Andrei Gromov (husband), Petr Chardynin (his father). Prod: Khanzhonkov. 245 m. Rel: 25,4,09

647 *Rusalka (The Mermaid)*
1910
Dir/Scr: Goncharov, based on Pushkin's play. Phot: Vladimir Siversen. Art Dir: V. Fester. Cast: Vasily Stepanov (miller), Aleksandra Goncharova (his daughter), Andrei Gromov (prince). Prod: Khanzhonkov. 280 m. Rel: 30.3.10.

648 *Brat'ya-razboiniki (The Brigand Brothers)*
1912
Dir/Scr: Goncharov, based on Pushkin's poem. Phot: Aleksandr Ryllo. Cast: Arseny Bibikov, Ivan Mozzhukhin (the brothers), Vasily Stepanov (landlord), Dolinina (his daughter), Aleksandra Goncharova (his neice). Prod: Khanzhonkov. Not released [original titles missing].

649 *Krest'yanskaya dolya (The Peasant's Lot)*
1912
Dir: Goncharov. Scr: Arseny Bibikov. Phot: Louis Forestier. Cast: Aleksandra Goncharova (Masha), Ivan Mozzhukhin (Petr), Petr Chardynin (Petr's father), Arseny Bibikov (Maksim). Prod: Khanzhonkov. 875 m. Rel: 13.11.12 [original titles missing].

Kai Hansen

The leading director, with André Maître, of Pathé's Moscow branch from 1909 until at least 1912. Apart from transplanting the parent company's *film d'art* style, he took "local" advice from Goncharov and directed the first Chekhov adaptation, while supporting Khanzhonkov's expansion into superproductions.

650 *Knyazhna Tarakanova (Princess Tarakanova)*
1910

Dir: Kai Hansen, André Maître. Scr: Czeslaw Sabinski, based on Ippolit Shpazhinsky's play. Phot: George Meyer, Tapis. Art Dir: Sabinski, Mikhailov. Cast: V. Mikulina (Princess Tarakanova), N. Aleksandrova (Catherine II), Nikolai Vekov (Orlov), Nikolai Vasil'ev (Prince Potemkin), S. Lazarev (Prince Golitsyn). Prod: Pathé (Moscow)-Film d'Art SAPF. 420 m. Rel: 9.11.10.

651 *Roman s kontrabasom (Romance with Double Bass)*
1911

Dir: Hansen. Scr/Art Dir: Czeslaw Sabinski, based on Anton Chekhov's story. Phot: George Meyer. Cast: V. Gorskaya (Princess Bibulova). Prod: Pathé (Moscow). 240 m. Rel: 24.9.11 [original titles missing].

Aleksandr Khanzhonkov
1877–1945

Russian cinema's foremost producer was a retired cavalry officer who moved from distribution to production in 1908 with a series of classics and folk subjects. His superproductions, prompted by Goncharov, established the company, which also supported Starewicz's puppet animation and a scientific-educational department. With Bauer installed as his leading director from 1914, he promoted cinema among the other arts in a journal called *Pegas*. Abroad from 1918–23, he returned as a consultant to Rus'-film and later suffered persecution before receiving a state pension in 1934.
See nos. 637–649, 658, 660, 661

Nikolai Larin

652 *Doch' Kuptsa Bashkirova (Merchant Bashkirov's Daughter)*
1913

Dir/Scr: Larin. Phot: I. Dored. Cast unknown. Prod: G. Libken's "Volga" Co. (Yaroslavl'). 1610 m. Rel: 19.11.13 [two reels and original titles missing].

The provincial distributor Libken's first production was released (by Pathé) as *Drama on the Volga* after protests from the Bashkirov family.

Pathé Frères

The company established a Moscow equipment and film sales office in 1904, then began to rent films and, prompted by Drankov's success, to produce locally as well. Their *Cossacks of the Don* (1908) and the series *Picturesque Russia*, however, proved no match for Drankov's shrewd appeal, so dramatic production began (see nos. 650, 651) and continued until 1915.

653 *Zavod rybnykh konservov v Astrakhane (Astrakhan' Fish Canning Factory)*
1908

Prod: Pathé Frères (Moscow). 150 m.

One of Pathé's typical non-fiction subjects, before indigenous production forced the company to compete.

Yakov Protazanov
1881–1945

The only Russian director to bridge the pre- and post-1917 periods, enjoying equal success (and controversy) in both. After travels abroad in 1904–07, he began to work in the emerging Russian film companies, first scripting and acting, then directing. He helped make Thiemann and Reinhardt's "Golden Series" an immense box-office success from 1913, then joined Ermol'ev, bringing the legendary Mozzhukhin with him. After directing in France and Germany from 1920–23, he returned to Soviet Russia and became the mainstay of the Mezhrabpom-Rus' studio with a string of popular comedies and dramas.

654 *Ukhod velikogo startsa (The Passing of a Great Old Man)*
1912

Dir: Protazanov, Elizaveta Thiemann. Scr: Isaak Teneromo. Phot: George Meyer, Aleksandr Levitsky (includes documentary material shot at Astapovo). Art Dir: Ivan Kavaleridze. Cast: Vladimir Shaternikov (Lev Tolstoy), O. Petrova (Sof'ya Andreevna), Mikhail Tamarov (Vladimir Chertkov), Elizaveta Thiemann (Aleksandra L'vovna). Prod: Thiemann & Reinhardt. 800m. Not released domestically [original titles missing].

Also known as *The Life of L. N. Tolstoy*, this sensational reconstruction of Tolstoy's last days was banned after legal representation by his widow and by Chertkov, which allowed the producers to flout Russian censorship further in the final "apotheosis" sequence, as they aimed the film at export markets.

655 *Pikovaya dama (The Queen of Spades)*
1916

Dir: Protazanov. Scr: Protazanov, Fedor Otsep, based on Pushkin's story. Phot: Evgeni Slavinsky. Art Dir: Vladimir Ballyuzek, S. Lilienberg, W. Przybytniewski. Cast: Ivan Mozzhukhin (German), Vera Orlova (Liza), Elizaveta Shebueva (the Countess as an old woman), T. Duvan (Countess as a young woman), Nikolai Panov (Count Saint-Germain). Prod: Ermol'ev. 2300 m. Rel: 19.4.16.

Eduard Puchalsky

656 *Antoshu korset pogubil (Antoshu Ruined by a Corset)*
1916

Dir/Scr: Puchalsky. Cast: Anton Fertner (Antoshu). Prod: Lucifer Film Studio (Moscow). 615 m. Rel: 26.1.16. The Czechoslovak comedian Antoni Fertner played successfully in operetta in Poland before creating the film character of Antoshu. He went on to make twenty-four Antoshu shorts for Lucifer between 1915–18, becoming the most popular Russian comic.

V. Romashkov

657 *Sten'ka Razin*
1908

Dir: Romashkov. Scr: Vasily Goncharov, based on the song "From the Island to the Deep Stream". Phot: Aleksandr Drankov, Nikolai Kozlovsky. Music (for performance): Mikhail Ippolitov-Ivanov. Cast: Evgeny Petrov-Kraevsky (Razin). Prod: A. Drankov Studio. 224 m. Rel: 15.10.08.

Vladimir Siversen

658 *Drama v tabore podmoskovnykh tsygan (Drama in a Gypsy Camp near Moscow)*
1908

Dir/Scr/Phot: Siversen. Cast: gypsies. Prod: Aleksandr Khanzhonkov and E. Osh. 140 m. rel: 20.12.08 [original titles missing].

Evgeny Slavinsky
1877–1950
A pioneer Russian cinematographer, whose only extant film as a director is *The Wedding Day*. He later photographed such Soviet classics as *Death Bay* (Room, 1926), *Turksib* (1929) and *The Private Life of Petr Vinogradov* (Macheret, 1935).

659 *Den' venchaniya (The Wedding Day)*
1912
Dir/Phot: Slavinsky. Scr: based on a play by Yakov Gordin. Cast: Jewish travelling players. Prod: S. Mintus (Riga). 1200 m. Rel: unknown [original titles missing].

Wladyslaw Starewicz
1882–1965
Born into a Polish-Lithuanian family, he devised his own remarkable form of puppet animation due to an early interest in photography and entomology. Khanzhonkov backed his insect fables, but Starewicz soon moved into live-action fantasy and topical allegory. He moved via Yalta to Paris, photographing films by other Russian emigrés, before establishing his own studio and resuming animal puppet films

660 *Strekoza i muravei (The Dragonfly and the Ant)*
1913
Dir/Scr/Phot/Art Dir: Starewicz, based on Krylov's fable. Prod: Khanzhonkov. 158 m. Rel: 22.2.13.

661 *Noch' pered rozhdestvom (Christmas Eve)*
1913
Dir:/Scr/Phot/Art Dir: Starewicz, based on Gogol''s story. Cast: Ivan Mozzhukhin (the Devil), Ol'ga Obolenskaya (Oksana), Lidiya Tridenskaya (Solokha). Prod: Khanzhonkov. 1115 m. Rel: 26.12.13 [original titles missing].

662 *Liliya [Bel'gii] (The Lily [of Belgium])*
1915
Dir/Scr/Phot/Art Dir: Starewicz. Poetic text: Boris Martov. Cast: Irina Starewicz. Prod: Skobelev Committee. 360 m. Rel: unknown.

In the winter of 1914, Starewicz left Khanzhonkov and set up his own miniature studio, where he produced this "allegorical tale" about Germany's invasion of Belgium – one of the first of many propaganda and patriotic films which would be widely distributed by the state-funded charitable Skobelev Committee.

See also no.645

Aleksandr Volkov [Alexandre Volkoff]
1885–1942
First an actor, he became a leading director for Thiemann and Reinhardt, then moved, like Protazanov, to Ermol'ev after seeing active service early in the war. He emigrated with Ermol'ev to France in 1920 and became a mainstay of the new company, directing Mozzhukhin in *La Maison du mystère* (1923) and finally *Casanova* (1927).

663 *Kulisy ekrana (Behind the Screen)*
1917
Dir/Scr: Volkov and Georgy Azagarov (?). Phot: Nikolai Toporkov. Cast: Ivan Mozzhukhin (himself), Nataliya Lisenko (herself) Nikolai Panov (the studio director). Prod: Ermol'ev. 2255 m. Rel: 28.11.17 [all but one reel, without titles, missing].

This fragment of a major two-part film (also known as *A Life Destroyed by Pitiless Fate*) offers an intriguing glimpse of the Ermol'ev studios and its major stars "as themselves", which implies a story about the irony of fame, but also suggests a poignant envoi to the Russian cinema about to give way to its Soviet successor.

24

BIBLIOGRAPHY

A short list of works in English relating to the themes of the exhibition and catalogue:

NANCY VAN NORMAN BAER. *The Art of Enchantment: Diaghilev's Ballets Russes*. San Francisco, 1988

YELENA V. BARCHATOVA et al. *A Portrait of Tsarist Russia: Unknown Photographs from the Soviet Archives*. London, 1990

ELENA BORISOVA and GRIGORY STERNIN. *Russian Art Nouveau*. New York, 1988

JOHN E. BOWLT. *The Silver Age: Russian Art of the Early Twentieth Century and the "World of Art" Group*. Newtonville, Mass., 1979, 1982

JOHN E. BOWLT. *Russian Art of the Avant-garde: Theory and Criticism 1902–34*. London, 1988

EDWARD BRAUN. *The Theatre of Meyerhold: Revolution on the Modern Stage*. London, 1979

WILLIAM C. BRUMFIELD. "The Decorative Arts in Russian Architecture 1900–1907", *The Journal of Decorative and Propaganda Arts* (Miami), Russian/Soviet Theme Issue, Summer 1987, pp.12–27

WILLIAM C. BRUMFIELD. "Anti-Modernism and the Neo-Classical Revival in Russian Architecture: 1906–16", *Journal of the Society of Architectural Historians* (Philadelphia), December 1989, pp.371–386

WILLIAM C. BRUMFIELD. "Architectural Design in Moscow, 1890–1917: Innovation and Retrospection" in Brumfield (ed.), *Reshaping Russian Architecture: Western Technology, Utopian Dreams*. Cambridge, 1990, pp.67–110

RICHARD BUCKLE. *Diaghilev*. London, 1979

RICHARD BUCKLE. *Nijinsky*. London, 1971

ELENA CHERNEVICH et al. *Russian Graphic Design 1880–1917*. London, 1990

CATHERINE COOKE. "Map Guide to Moscow Architecture. 1900–1930" in Cooke (ed.), *Russian Avant-Garde Art and Architecture*, AD Profile no.47. London, 1983, pp.81–96

CATHERINE COOKE. "Fedor Osipovich Shekhtel: an architect and his clients in turn-of-the-century Moscow", *Architectural Association Files* (London), January 1984, pp.3–31

CATHERINE COOKE. "Shekhtel in Kelvingrove and Mackintosh in Moscow: two Russo-Scottish exhibitions at the turn of the century", *Scottish Slavonic Review* (Glasgow), Spring 1988, pp.177–205

PAMELA DAVIDSON. *The Poetic Imagination of Vyacheslav Ivanov: A Russian Symbolist's Perception of Dante*. Cambridge, 1989

GEORGETTE DONCHIN. *The Influence of French Symbolism on Russian Poetry*. The Hague, 1958

VALERY DUDAKOV and DAVID ELLIOTT. *One Hundred Years of Russian Art 1889–1989*. London, 1989

DAVID ELLIOTT. *New Worlds: Russian Art and Society 1900–1937*. London, 1986

J. D. ELSWORTH. *Andrei Bely: A Critical Study of the Novels*. Cambridge, 1983

PETER GATRELL. *The Tsarist Economy 1850–1917*. London, 1986

CAMILLA GRAY. *The Russian Experiment in Art: 1862–1922*. London, 1962, 1986

JOAN DELANEY GROSSMAN. *Valery Bryusov and the Riddle of Russian Decadence*. Berkeley, Los Angeles and London, 1985

BEVERLY WHITNEY KEAN. *All the Empty Palaces. The Merchant Patrons of Modern Art in Pre-Revolutionary Russia*. London, 1983

EVGENIIA KIRICHENKO. *Moskva: pamyatniki arkhitektury 1830–1910gg – Moscow: Architectural Monuments 1830–1910s*. Moscow, 1977

EVGENIIA KIRICHENKO. "Theoretical attitudes to architecture in Russia: 1830–1910s". *Architectural Association Quarterly*, Russian Soviet Issue, vol.11, no.2, 1979, pp.9–23

LIONEL KOCHAN. *Russia in Revolution*. London, 1967, 1986

J. LEYDA. *Kino: A History of the Russian and Soviet Film*. London, 1960

MARVIN LYONS. *Russia in Original Photographs 1860–1920*. London, 1977

JOHN MALMSTAD (ed.). *Andrei Bely, Spirit of Symbolism*. Ithaca and London, 1987

RONALD E. PETERSON (ed. and trans.). *The Russian Symbolists: An Anthology of Critical and Theoretical Writings*. Ann Arbor, Michigan, 1986

RICHARD PIPES. *Russia Under the Old Regime*. London, 1974

HARVEY PITCHER. *The Smiths of Moscow: A Story of Britons Abroad*. Cromer, 1984

AVRIL PYMAN. *The Life of Aleksandr Blok*. 2 vols. Oxford, 1970, 1980

WILLIAM RICHARDSON. *Zolotoe Runo and Russian Modernism*. Ann Arbor, Michigan, 1986

JO ANN RUCKMAN. *The Moscow Business Elite: A Social and Cultural Portrait of Two Generations, 1840–1905*. DeKalb, 1984

KONSTANTIN RUDNITSKY. *Russian and Soviet Theatre*. London, 1988

WENDY SALMOND. "The Solomenko Embroidery Workshops", *The Journal of Decorative and Propaganda Arts* (Miami), Russian/Soviet Theme Issue, Summer 1987, pp.126–143

D. V. SARABIANOV. *Russian Art: From Neoclassicism to the Avant-Garde*. London, 1990

HUGH SETON-WATSON. *The Russian Empire, 1801–1917*. Oxford, 1967, 1989

THEOFANOS STAVROU (ed.). *Russia Under the Last Tsar*. Minneapolis, n.d.

ADA STEINBERG. *Word and Music in the Novels of Andrei Bely*. Cambridge, 1982

RICHARD TAYLOR and IAN CHRISTIE (eds.). *The Film Factory: Russian and Soviet Cinema in Documents*. London, 1988

RICHARD TAYLOR and IAN CHRISTIE (eds.). *Inside the Film Factory: New Approaches to Russian and Soviet Cinema*. London, 1991

ROBERT V. THURSTON. *Liberal City, Conservative State: Moscow and Russia's Urban Crisis, 1906–1914*. Oxford, 1987

YURI TSIVIAN et al. (eds.). *Silent Witnesses: Russian Films 1908–1919*. London and Pordenone, 1989

JAMES WEST. *Russian Symbolism: A Study of Vyacheslav Ivanov and the Russian Symbolist Aesthetic*. London, 1970